A Catalogue of English Coins in the British Museum. Anglo-Saxon Series ..

OF

ENGLISH COINS

IN THE

BRITISH MUSEUM.

ANGLO-SAXON SERIES.

Volume II.

(*WESSEX AND ENGLAND TO THE NORMAN CONQUEST.*)

BY

HERBERT A. GRUEBER, F.S.A.,

ASSISTANT KEEPER OF COINS AND MEDALS,

AND

CHARLES FRANCIS KEARY, M.A., F.S.A.

WITH ONE MAP AND THIRTY-TWO PLATES

LONDON.

PRINTED BY ORDER OF THE TRUSTEES

B Quaritch, 15, Piccadilly, W.;

Henry Frowde, Oxford University Press Warehouse, Amen Court, E C ;

C. Rollin & Feuardent, 19, Bloomsbury Street, W C, and 4 Rue Louvois, Paris,

A. Asher & Co , Kegan Paul, Trubner & Co , Longmans, Green & Co

1893.

LONDON

PRINTED BY WILLIAM CLOWES AND SONS LIMITED,

STAMFORD STREET AND CHARING CROSS

PREFACE

BY THE KEEPER OF COINS.

———

This volume of the Catalogue of English Coins in the British Museum contains descriptions of the Coins of Wessex from Ecgbeorht to Eadwig, and of those of All England from Eadgar to the Norman Conquest. Taken in conjunction with the first volume, which dealt with the coinages of Mercia, Kent, East Anglia, and Northumbria, it completes the description of all the Anglo Saxon Coins in the National Collection.

In the lists of moneyers given in the first volume the names of those not represented in the National Collection were inserted. In the present volume this scheme has been further extended by including all known types of Coins, whether or not represented in the Museum series. The names of moneyers and the descriptions of the types of Coins not in the Museum are printed in italics.

As the Coins in the volume are all Silver Pennies (unless otherwise described), the weight only of each piece is given, and not the size or metal.

This volume has been compiled by Mr. H. A. Grueber, F S A., Assistant Keeper of Coins, and by Mr. Charles F. Keary, F.S A , the author of the first volume Mr Keary is responsible for the Introduction, and Mr. Grueber for the description of the Coins, the Indexes, the Illustrations, and for seeing the work through the press

BARCLAY V. HEAD.

CONTENTS.

	PAGE
PREFACE	iii
INTRODUCTION	xi
ARRANGEMENT	xi
Contents of Present Volume	xi
Types and Moneyers not in National Collection included .	xii
Relation of coinage to history . . .	xii
HISTORY	xiii
Ecgbeorht	xiii
Rise of the power of Wessex	xiii
Battles of Camelford and Ellandune . . .	xiv
Extent of power of Ecgbeorht	xv
Institution of a West Saxon coinage . .	xvii
Distinction between Kentish and West Saxon types	xix
Type derived from Frankish coinage . . .	xx
First coming of the Vikings . . .	xxi
Coins carried by Vikings from England to Ireland .	xxii
Æthelwulf	xxiii
Viking attacks on England continued .	xxiii
Æthelbald's rebellion and the partition of the Kingdom	xxv
Æthelbald	xxvii
Extreme rarity of Æthelbald's coins cannot be explained	xxvii
Æthelbearht	xxviii
Æthelred I	xxviii
Viking invasion of England . . .	xxviii
The three great invasions of England during the period covered by the present volume . .	xxix
'Vikings' distinguished from 'Danes' of the tenth and eleventh centuries	xxix
Republican character of the Vikings .	xxx
Invasion of Wessex . .	xxxii
Ælfred	xxxii
First payment of ransom to the Vikings . .	xxxiii
London coinage of Halfdan . . .	xxxiv

PAGE

History—Alfred—continued

Proceedings of Guthorm's army xxxv
Peace of Wedmore xxxv
Increase in the power of English kings . . . xxxvi
Rights of coinage reserved for over-king . . . xxxvii
Last serious attack of the Vikings xxxvii
Chronological arrangement of Alfred's coinage . . xxxviii
Viking coinages, barbarous imitations of Wessex coinage,
&c. xli
Frankish and Scandinavian moneyers . . . xliii
Summary of 'Viking' coinages xlvi
Eadweard the Elder xlviii
Rebellion of Æthelbald xlviii
Extension of West Saxon rule xlix
Building of the burgs l
Submission of Vikings by 'armies' liii
Improvement of coinage under Eadweard the Elder . . lv
Æthelstan lvi
Scandinavian States in Northern Europe . . . lvi
South-Humbrian and Northumbrian Danes . . . lix
Greatness of Æthelstan lxi
Numismatic records of extension of English rule . . lxii
Battle of Brunanburg lxiii
Eadmund lxiii
Eadmund and the Northumbrian Danes . . . lxiii
Submission of the Five Burgs and of Northumbria . . lxv
Eadred lxvi
Revolt of Northumbria lxvi
Northumbrian coinage an evidence of power of Danish
Kings of Northumbria lxvi
Eadwig lxviii
Era of external peace begins with Eadwig . . . lxviii
Religious struggles lxviii
Eadgar lxix
English and Danes in Wales lxix
Homage to Eadgar on Dee lxx
Coinage of Eadgar lxx
Eadweard II lxx
Æthelred II lxx
Causes of the decay of the English nation . . . lxxi
Racial and religious divisions lxxi
Renewal of Northern invasions lxxii
Olaf Tryggvason lxxiii

PAGE

HISTORY—Æthelred II.—*continued.*

Battle of Maldon lxxiii
Olaf and Svend lxxiv
Æthelred's revenge on Danes in England . . . lxxv
Massacre of St Brice lxxvi
Fall of Olaf Tryggvason at Svold lxxvi
Marriage of Æthelred and Emma lxxvii
Invasion of Svend lxxvii
Danegeld lxxviii
Conquest of England by Svend lxxix
Death of Svend lxxix
Invasion of Cnut lxxix
Eadmund Ironside lxxx
Treaty of Olney lxxx
Death of Eadmund Ironside lxxx
Coinage of Æthelred II., its great influence in Scandi-
navia lxxxi
Cnut lxxxii
Scandinavian Empire ruled by Cnut lxxxii
Establishment of standing army of *huscarls* . . lxxxiii
Peace established by Cnut lxxxiv
Cnut's viceroys lxxxvi
Harold I lxxxvii
Murder of Ælfred the Ætheling lxxxvii
Fall of Cnut's Empire lxxxviii
Harthacnut lxxxviii
Coinage of Danish kings lxxxix
Edward the Confessor xcii
The house of Godwine xcii
Norman influence xciii
Harold II xciv
Invasion of Harthacnut and Tostig xciv
Battle of Stamford Bridge xcv
Norman Conquest xcv
Coinage of Edward the Confessor and of Harold II. . xcvi

MONEYERS xcviii
Large number of moneyers' names xcviii
Difficulties in the way of determining exact form intended . xcix
Earlier moneyers' names all Anglo-Saxon forms . . . cii
Appearance of Frankish and Scandinavian names . . ciii
Status of moneyer ciii
Signification of 'Monet,' 'Moneta' cv

	PAGE
Types .	cvi
Their religious character	cvii
Floral designs, buildings, &c , on coins	cvii
Origin of royal bust, crown, helmet, &c .	cvii
Portraiture on coins	cvii
Independent character of types of English coins	cviii
Mints .	cviii
Anglo-Saxon laws relating to mints	cviii
Growth of mints	cix
Difficulties in identifying mints	cx
Changes of dies	cx
Historical notes on doubtful and new mints	cxi–cxxi
Summary of History and Anglo-Saxon coinage	cxxi
Map of England illustrating the Anglo-Saxon Mints	
CATALOGUE—	
Kingdom of Wessex .	1
Ecgbeorht .	1
Moneyers	1
Types	1
Coins .	6
Æthelwulf	9
Moneyers .	9
Types .	9
Coins .	13
Æthelbald .	21
Moneyers	21
Coins	21
Æthelbearht	22
Moneyers	22
Types .	22
Coins	23
Æthelred I	27
Moneyers .	27
Types .	27
Coins	28
Ælfred .	32
Moneyers	32
Types	33
Coins	38

PAGE

KINGDOM OF WESSEX—*continued*

Eadweard the Elder 83
   Moneyers 83
   Types 84
   Coins 87
Æthelstan 101
   Moneyers. 101
   Types 103
   Coins 105
Eadmund 122
   Moneyers 122
   Types 123
   Coins 124
Eadred 142
   Moneyers 142
   Types 143
   Coins . . . 144
Eadwig 156
   Moneyers 156
   Types 156
   Coins 158

KINGDOM OF ENGLAND 163
Eadgar 163
   Moneyers 163
   Types . . 165
   Coins 168
Eadweard II (The Martyr) 191
   Moneyers . 191
   Types 192
   Coins 192
Æthelræd II 197
   Moneyers 197
   Types 202
   Coins 208
Cnut 213
   Moneyers . . . 213
   Types 248
   Coins 255
Harold I. 302
   Moneyers 302
   Types 304
   Coins 307

x   CONTENTS

		PAGE
Kingdom of England— *continued*		
Harthacnut		320
Moneyers		320
Types		321
Coins		325
Edward the Confessor		329
Moneyers		329
Types		334
Coins		339
Harold II		460
Moneyers		460
Types		461
Coins		461
INDEXES		475
General Index		477
Index of Moneyers		495
Index of Types		532
Index of Mints		537
TABLES		541

INTRODUCTION.

THE present volume of the Catalogue of English Coins ARRANGE-
continues and completes the description of the coins which MENT
were struck in this country between the Coming of the
English and the Norman Conquest. As it was impossible to
describe in one volume the whole number of pieces, issued
during this period, which are contained in the National Collection, the arrangement adopted has been to distribute the
coinage into certain classes corresponding to the different
heptarchic kingdoms in which the coins were struck. The
heptarchic kingdoms of which we possess coins are five:
Mercia, Kent, East Anglia, Northumbria, and Wessex. The
coinages of the first four of these districts are described in
Volume I. The coinage of Wessex has been reserved for
the present volume, as it merges into that of All England
These last two series—or say, rather, this single series in
its completeness—is of course more extensive than those
of the other kingdoms put together; and if the first object
kept in view had been the preservation of a uniformity in
the size of the volumes, it would have been better to
describe in Volume I. the coinage of Wessex down, say, to
the reign of Eadgar, and to reserve the coinage of All
England—and Eadgar's coins may fairly be so described—
for the second Volume. But this arrangement would have
involved breaking into a series which is really continuous,
and the compilers of the Catalogue felt that that would be
too great a sacrifice to make for the sake of a merely
superficial uniformity. As it is, we see that the body of
the present volume contains, with indexes, &c., 544 pages
as compared with the 282 pages of Volume I., and the
description of 4106 coins as compared with 2558 previously

described. Thus the whole collection of Anglo-Saxon coins in the British Museum, or, if the expression be preferred, of coins struck by the English previous to the Norman Conquest, numbers at the present moment 6661.

In the last volume the plan was adopted of enlarging the contents of the Catalogue somewhat beyond the limits suggested by its title and its immediate purpose, by inserting, in the lists of moneyers, names which are not represented in the National Collection. Of the present volume the scheme has been further extended to include all types of coins whether or not represented among the Museum coins. The comparative poverty of the National Collection in certain branches—as, for example, in the coins of Æthelred II., of which the Stockholm Museum possesses a much larger number than does the British Museum—rendered this extension of the plan of the Catalogue highly desirable if not absolutely necessary

The period of history covered by the coinage described in this volume extends from the accession of Ecgbeorht of Wessex—the first king of Wessex who struck coins—to the Norman Conquest, or from A D 802 to A D 1066, a period of two centuries and a half To speak, however, with strict accuracy we should date the beginning of the period from the battle of Ellandune. A D 825, for, as will presently be seen, it is not probable that Ecgbeorht struck any money before that event To some extent the present period overlaps that covered by the first volume It is necessary to assume that the reader of the present Introduction has read, or is in a position to read, the Introduction to and the body of the preceding volume, for it would be impossible to repeat at length either the history of the coinage or the description of certain series of coins there given It is, again, not the part of the compilers of the Catalogue to enter into anything like a detailed history of England for the period under consideration The only details to which we need descend are those which immediately affect the issue of the coinage These will not be many As a rule, the point at which the history of the currency touches political history is in the wider social aspects of the latter. It illustrates the peaceful or disturbed state of the country by its excellence or its barbarism ; the wealth of the country at any particular time by its quantity. Some of the coinages with which we have to deal are records of the recovery of England by the English kings, for we find Æthelstan and his successors striking at mint places which a short while before had been in the hands of the Danes. At another time the coinage of England, taken in connection with those of some neighbour countries, is a record of the *rapprochement* which had taken place between England and the Scandinavian countries of Europe. But even in such cases as these we must not look to the coins to give us exact dates or any of the minute details of history.

The reign of Ecgbeorht brings to a close the first great period in the history of the English, that of the long struggles between the heptarchic kingdoms of England. These struggles, as was pointed out in the last volume, were due chiefly, first to the rivalries of Northumbria and Mercia, secondly to the rivalries of Mercia and Wessex. Mercia rose for a second time to pre-eminence under Offa, with whom begins the continuous (penny) coinage of England. and it retained this pre-eminence under Coenwulf, Offa's son. In their reigns the kings of Kent and East Anglia were little better than viceroys to the kings of Mercia. Beorhtric, the king of Wessex, Offa's son-in-law, was in much the same position. Ecgbeorht, the legitimate prince, was driven from Wessex and took refuge at the Court of Charles the Great. It is probable that his exile dates from the marriage of Beorhtric to the daughter of Offa, and was continued till Beorhtric's death, that is for a period of thirteen years (A.D 789–802) *

We need not here stay to discuss the theories which have been enunciated of the imperial ambition which might have been fostered in Ecgbeorht's mind by his friendship with the first emperor of the New Western Empire. For there was in reality nothing essentially new in the policy of

* See *Dic. Nat. Biog* s v Egbert

Wessex under her new king. Ecgbeorht's policy was the
policy of all the heptarchic kings who felt themselves
sufficiently strong to entertain it. The position of Wessex,
however, as an outpost of English conquest, obliged its
king to concern himself much with the subjugation of
his Celtic neighbours, the North Welsh of Wales proper
and the West Welsh of Cornwall This warfare in which
Ecgbeorht was first engaged was the concern of Wessex,
not in any sense a national English warfare. After his
victories over the Celts (First harrying of the West Welsh,
A.D. 815; victory of Camelford A D. 825), the policy of
Wessex required that Ecgbeorht should, if possible, assert
his supremacy over Mercia, or he would once more sink into
insignificance   Ecgbeorht's Welsh wars were so far from
being 'national' wars, that Mercia had taken advantage of
them to invade Wessex. But Mercia was no longer as great
as it had been when Ecgbeorht fled to Francia. Ecgbeorht
was favoured by the failure of the great line of Offa, by the
rise of kings of inferior worth, and, as is probable, by a
disputed succession. (Deposition of Ceolwulf, and accession
of Beornwulf, not of Offa's line, A D. 822 or 4. *See* Vol. I.
p lviii.)

Beornwulf was defeated by Ecgbeorht at the battle of
Ellandune before spoken of. This victory established the
supremacy of Wessex. The *Chronicle* continues, speaking
of Ecgbeorht ' He then sent Æthelwulf his son . . . with
Ealhstân his bishop, and Wulfheard his ealdorman, to Kent
with a large force, and they drove Baldred the king north
over the Thames. And the Kentish people and those of
Surrey, and the South Saxons and the East Saxons turned to
him because they had been unjustly forced from his kinsmen.'[*]

---

[*] *From his magum* *May* may mean only a neighbour But the kinsmen
here meant are probably the former kings of Wessex, such as Ine, of whom
Ecgbeorht was a relation, not a descendant. There is perhaps a difficulty
for this translation in referring the 'him' (*him tocirdon*, 'turned to him') to
Ecgbeorht Mr Earle translates *tocirdon* as 'turned away from,' and refers
the him to Baldred, rendering the whole passage, 'They drove Baldred the
king over the Thames, and the Kentish men threw off their allegiance to
him, as did the men of Surrey, Sussex, and Essex, on the ground that they
had been originally unjustly subdued by his family '

This event heralds the foundation of the West Saxon coinage The addition of Essex to the kingdom of Wessex does not seem to have been maintained

The year following the East Anglians too prayed the protection of Ecgbeorht, and when Beornwulf the king of Mercia sought to punish them, they defeated and slew him. The same fate befell Beornwulf's successor Ludican. Ecgbeorht obtained a sort of supremacy over the East Engle; and in A.D. 829 the Northumbrians even consented to acknowledge his over-lordship

It is now that we first hear of the title of *Bretwalda* about which there has been so much discussion among historians According to the *Chronicle* it is the same as the imperial title which Beda bestows upon some of the early heptarchic kings. Beda ascribes this *imperium* to certain kings, but in a fashion which appears so arbitrary that it is difficult to formulate any tenable theory as to what it could have signified, or what was the bretwalda-dom which the *Chronicle* says is the same thing. But concerning the latter I think we may assume that it was rather a bookish distinction than a real one. A title of pre-eminence which is not bestowed upon the famous and magnificent Offa could not have had any strict relation to the possession of real power Still, an empty title is quite as often an object of ambition as real power, more especially among barbarous or half barbarous peoples; and in reading history we are apt to give too definite a meaning to such words as *submission, tribute, supremacy*. Concerning the real power of Ecgbeorht in England the one thing of which we may be sure is that it did not extend beyond the Humber. The Northumbrians we are told met him at Dore (near Sheffield), or by the stream Dore,* and made submission The formal act, which had no real political significance, was, we may be sure, all that Ecgbeorht required. The Northumbrian kings con-

---

* This Dore continued to be the northern boundary of Mercia See *A S Chron* (Earle) s a 942 The word is simply 'door,' used here for mountain pass We may compare (with a difference) the name Œgisdyr (the River Eyder), 'Œgir's door'

tinued to issue a coinage of their own, uninfluenced by that of southern England

Over Mercia, for some time after the victory of Ellandune, the influence of Wessex, as distinguished from its direct rule, was very great   After their long rivalry, the kings of Mercia remained for some generations the allies of the Wessex kings, allied for the most part both in policy and in blood   It is probable, however, that the ancient rivalries of the two kingdoms would have revived, had not the Viking invasions given a wholly new complexion to English history.

Over Kent, including therewith Surrey and the decayed kingdom of Sussex, the power which the king of Wessex acquired after the battle of Ellandune was much greater ; we have seen that as a result of the battle all this country, that is to say, all the territory south of the Thames, was definitely added to the possessions of the House of Cerdic. Wessex and Kent, however (the latter name henceforward includes Surrey and Sussex) continued to be separate kingdoms, each retaining no doubt its distinctive laws and customs , and generally they were governed by different members of the West Saxon House   When the head of the house was on the throne of Wessex, the eldest son or the heir designate was usually King of Kent.   In one case the King of Kent was especially debarred from accession to the throne of Wessex ; and in another instance we have the relations of the kingdoms reversed, the father reigning as king of Kent and the son as King of Wessex.   But this inversion of the usual arrangement was the result of a rebellion.[*]

The establishment then of the kings of Wessex in the supremacy in Heptarchic England is the first great event in English history covered by the period over which extend the coinages described in this volume.   It is also the last event of importance previous to the Viking invasion of southern England.

The beginning of the West Saxon coinage must not be

---

[*] See below, p xxr

looked upon as brought about by the wide conquests of Ecgbeorht, so much as by the incidental fact that his conquests included Kent. The coinage of this king is in fact really a Kentish rather than a West Saxon coinage. This is shown almost conclusively by the names of moneyers on the coins of Ecgbeorht as compared with the names on the coins of his predecessors, the last kings of Kent, or of the Archbishops of Canterbury, his contemporaries; and again, by the types of Ecgbeorht's coins as compared with those of the same rulers. We must remember, further, that many of the coins of the kings of Mercia were probably likewise struck in Kent, and that when we find, as we do, the same moneyers' names occurring on the coins of a king of Mercia who reigned not long before the battle of Ellandune, and on the coins of Ecgbeorht, the probability is that these moneyers were Kentishmen who struck first for one master of their country, and then for the other.

Applying this test, we find that eight at least of Ecgbeorht's three-and-twenty moneyers, struck either for the kings of Mercia or Kent; in other words, that these men were probably coining in Kent before the battle of Ellandune. This is as many as the average of moneyers who continue in a new reign from the preceding one Thus of Æthelwulf's thirty-eight moneyers a much smaller proportion, only about six, are survivals from the preceding reign. There is therefore a greater air of continuity from the coinage of Ecgbeorht's predecessors in Kent to that of Ecgbeorht himself, than there is from the coinage of Ecgbeorht to that of his son; so that on this ground alone it would be fair to assume that Ecgbeorht began to strike coins only as a king of Kent.

The same conclusion is enforced by a comparison of Ecgbeorht's types with those of his predecessors in Kent, as we shall presently have occasion to see

The reader must be referred to the *Introduction* to the preceding volume for the history of the introduction of a coinage into this country, and of the intimate relations which long subsisted between the currencies issued on the two sides of the English Channel The conclusion to be drawn from the close relationship between the Frankish and English money, is that the coinage was then as much used for purposes of commerce between England and France as for the purposes of internal trade in this country. The close relationship between the English and the Frankish coinages ceases with Ecgbeorht's reign, and, as we shall have occasion to see in the latter part of this sketch, its place is before long taken by a relationship between the coinage of England and those of the Peoples of the North.

Wessex, on her side, we know, had not experienced the want of a currency before the time of Ecgbeorht; yet we cannot suppose that in other elements of civilization Wessex was behind her rival heptarchic kingdoms—with the exception perhaps of Northumbria. It possessed, for example, an admirable code of laws in those of Ine.

If we compare the laws of Ine with the earlier or contemporary Kentish laws (those of Æthelbearht or of Wihtred), we see that while in the latter the fines imposed are evidently reckoned in a current coinage, in the Wessex laws they are reckoned in the *solidus*, the usual money of account. The reckoning by the *solidus* of account is found, it need hardly be said, long before the introduction of an Anglo-Saxon coinage into this country (Vol. I. p. v.). We have, moreover, in the West Saxon laws the value of parts of cattle—parts of the ox, the eye, the horn, &c.—reckoned in the same money of account, and this makes it probable that the custom of cattle payments was still largely in use—though no doubt payment by weight of metal was the usual one.

As, previous to the accession of Ecgbeorht and in the earlier years of his reign, Wessex did not feel the need of a currency, it is quite possible that it continued to do without one till this king's death. Nay, we shall, as will presently appear, find one incident in the numismatic history of the West Saxon kings best explainable on the supposition that, till after the death of Ecgbeorht's grandson, Æthelbald, Kent still provided all the currency of the south. It would not, however, be safe to rely upon this isolated piece of evidence, nor even to assert that Ecgbeorht did not strike money for Wessex.

If we attribute any of Ecgbeorht's coins to Wessex, it seems most reasonable to ascribe to it those with the legends SAX and SAXONIORVM (for SAXONUM),* which we have placed last in the list of Ecgbeorht's types   For at any rate these types are original and owe nothing to the influence of coins struck in Kent before it was acquired by the West Saxons   This attribution is perhaps upon the whole the most reasonable.

If we compare the types of Ecgbeorht's coins with those of the coins of the kings of Mercia and Kent, and the Archbishops of Canterbury, we find that (as has been already said) the large majority of the former are only copies. Thus:

Type ii may be derived from the coins of Ceolwulf I., king of Mercia [A D. 822–823 or 824].   Vol I. p. 40, Pl ix. 4

Type iv. has also a prototype in the coins of Ceolwulf I., king of Mercia.   Ib. p 40, Pl ix. 5.

Type vi. has its prototype in the coins of Coenwulf, king of Mercia [A D 796–822], cf Ib. p 35, Pl. viii 8.

Types vii (reverse) xv (obverse) are copied from coins of Baldred, king of Kent [A D. 806–825]   Ib. p 70, Pl. xi 11 (obv.).   This, as we know, is the king whom Ecgbeorht drove out of Kent.

Types viii and ix. (reverse) are from coins of Cuðred, king of Kent, the predecessor of Baldred [A D. 796–806]   Ib pp 68, 69, Pl. xi. 3, 4 (reverses), 7 (obverse), and 6, 7 (reverses).

The obverses of Types xi. and xii., the reverses of xv., xvi. are all probably only developments of the type of the coins of Baldred   Ib. p 70, Pl. xi. 9 (reverse).

Type i. calls for special notice   Agreeably with the principle, which has been generally adopted in this catalogue, of placing the coins with the indications of a mint-name before those which have none, those pieces

---

* 'Saxoniorum' is a ridiculous form, probably due only to the ignorance of the moneyer or of the clerk who gave him his pattern   Freeman, in his life of Ælfred (*Dic Nat Biog*), says that the title 'Rex Saxonum' was unknown before the time of Ælfred, and was not common afterwards   These coins, of course, show that the former statement is incorrect

which seem to have upon them the monogram of the city of Canterbury are made the first type of the reign. The type is evidently one struck in Kent, and therefore, whatever may be thought of the other types, this one must have been issued subsequent to the battle of Ellandune. And though it is an original type it is far from improbable that it was one of the first coins struck in Ecgbeorht's reign; for this reason, that the monogram on the reverse (C̨B̨C) is without doubt copied from the Karolus-monogram K̨R̨-S on the coinage of Charles the Great. Now Charlemagne died in A.D. 814, and the monogram was not again brought into use on the Frankish coinage until the days of Charlemagne's grandson, Charles the Bald, who came to the throne after the death of Ecgbeorht.* The reverse of this Type i. of Ecgbeorht occurs also on the coins of Ceolnoð, Archbishop of Canterbury (A.D. 833–870), see Vol. i., Pl. xiii. 7. But though the archiepiscopate of Ceolnoð begins before the death of Ecgbeorht, it extends long subsequent to it; so that there is nothing to negative the supposition that the archbishop's coin was copied from that of the West Saxon king. In truth, from the occurrence of this type in the Delgany hoard (see below, p. xxii.), we may feel pretty sure that it was in use before the accession of Ceolnoð. Ecgbeorht's intimate relations with Charlemagne give a certain interest to this example of one of the types of his coins derived from one of those of the western emperor, and to the possibility that this imitation of Frankish coins may have inaugurated

---

* This derivation of Ecgbeorht's C̨B̨C coins from the F̨R̨-S (or K̨R̨-S) coins of Charlemagne has an important bearing upon French numismatics. For it was at one time keenly disputed among French numismatists whether any of the coins which bear this 'Carolus' or 'Karolus' monogram were to be attributed to Charlemagne, or whether all should not rather be ascribed to Charles the Bald, who at the edict of Pitres, A.D. 864 (*Edictum Pistense*, c. 11, Pertz, *Leges* I., p. 190) re-established this type, and made it the sole legal one for his future issues. The fact that the type is found copied on the English coinage before the accession of Charles the Bald, and thirty years or more before the date of the edict of Pitres, is decisive of the controversy. But this argument has, so far as I know, never been employed by French numismatists.

his coinage; though the accidents of commercial relationship have on the whole much more to do with determining
the types of coins than royal alliances or enmities. And this
interest is the greater from the fact above alluded to, that
close relationship between English and Frankish coins ceases
with this or the following reign.

After the introduction of a coinage by Ecgbeorht, which,
it may be assumed we are now agreed, followed upon the
final assertion of the supremacy of Wessex in the battle of
Ellandune, there was no other event of great importance
for the history of southern England or the history of its
coinage until the invasion of the country by the Vikings.
The preparations for this event had already begun. The
first appearance of the Vikings was in the previous
century; and so far as we can ascertain the first attack
made by these northern pirates was upon the English coast.
In the year 787, according to the *Saxon Chronicle*, or 789,
according to the true date, three ships of the pirates landed
upon the southern coast, killed the port-reeve, Beaduheard,
took some trifle of booty and sailed away again. In 793
the pirates appeared in quite a different quarter, on the
Northumbrian coast, where they fell upon the holy island
of Lindisfarne, and slaughtered the greater part of the
monks of Cuthbert's foundation on that island. The saint
revenged himself, the chronicler tells us; for the next year
the pirate fleet was shipwrecked near Monkwearmouth and
the crews were drowned or slain. The attacks next fell
upon South Wales, and the Vikings, driven thence, came for
the first time to Ireland (A.D. 795), which for the next half-
century was to bear the principal brunt of their ravages.[*]

From about this time onwards the pirates began to make
settlements on the Irish coast. It went so far that in A.D.
832 'a great royal fleet'[†] of Vikings came to Ireland, under
the leadership of a certain Turgesius or Thorgisl. This
Thorgisl, after some years of fighting, founded a short-lived

---

[*] *Gwent Chron* s a 795 (Camb Archæol Assoc), *War of the Gaedhil*, &c
(Todd) *R S* pp 4-5, *Ann Ult* s a. 791, *Four Mast* s a 790

[†] *War*, &c. (Todd) *R S* pp 8-9, cf Keary, *Vikings in Western Christen-
dom*, p 174 and note

Scandinavian kingdom in the northern half of Ireland—in
the division called Leth-Cuind or Conn's half. Thorgisl's
kingdom lasted from A.D 812 to A.D. 845 But there
were besides many other settlements of Vikings on the
island.

It is just before the coming of this great fleet of Thorgisl to Ireland that the Viking attacks upon England
begin again, and there seems good reason to believe that
these renewed attacks came, not directly from the Baltic or
the North Sea, but from Ireland The first attack was upon
the island of Sheppey A hoard of English coins—some of
Mercian kings, some of kings of Kent and Archbishops of
Canterbury, with a few of Ecgbeorht's coins—was discovered
in Delgany, near Wicklow, in Ireland, in or about the year
1874. The latest date at which any of these coins could
have been struck was A.D 830; and it seems probable that
all of them, if not actually struck in the county of Kent
(which may very well have been the case with all), were at
any rate current there.   There seems no better explanation
of all the circumstances attending this deposit, the date to
which the latest coin of the hoard belongs, and the place
(the east coast of Ireland) to which it has been carried,
than to suppose that it was carried off to Ireland by the
Vikings who attacked Sheppey in A D. 835.   For who else but
these Vikings were at that period likely to have traversed
the sea between the two countries?   And though it is not
certain, it is highly probable, that the pirates who carried
their hoard over to the sister island, had come thence to
England.*

In A D. 836 the crew of a Viking fleet of thirty-five sail
defeated the English at Charmouth, and in 838 the Vikings
allied themselves with the Celts of Cornwall for an attack
upon the king of the West Saxons. The combined army
was met and defeated by Ecgbeorht at 'Hengestdune'
(Hengstone),† and that event put an end to the Viking

---

* See the paper by Mr (now Sir John) Evans, "A hoard of coins found
at Delgany in Ireland," *Num Chron* 1882, p 61, *sqq*

† *A S Chron s a* 835 [=838?]

attacks in England during the reign of Ecgbeorht, who died either in A.D. 838 or A.D 839.[*]

At the beginning of Æthelwulf's reign the Viking attacks Æll were renewed We find the Vikings in the south of England— defeated at Southampton and victorious at Portsmouth(840)[†] —and in the eastern shires, Lincolnshire, East Anglia, Kent, (841),[‡] and finally plundering both London and Rochester (842)[§]. Then for some years the attacks cease On both sides of England the Northmen were more active than they were in this country In Ireland they had, as we have seen, got so far as to establish a temporary Scandinavian kingdom, and, even after the breaking up of this in 845, their attacks continued to be almost incessant. And it is about the time of the first cessation of the Viking raids on the English coasts that much more serious and determined ones began on the towns and abbeys which lay along the chief rivers of France and Germany, the Loire, the Garonne, the Seine, the Rhine, and the Elbe. The attacks on Ireland probably came from the Norsemen of the west coast of Norway, the attacks on France came from the Baltic countries (Denmark and South Norway) England lay between the two streams

One attack on England, more serious than the preceding ones, has to be noticed. It occurred in A.D. 850 or 851,[‖] and was due to the successes of the Vikings upon the continent The leader of the expedition was a Dane, Rorik by name, who for a time had held a fief of the empire. He had now adopted the life of a Viking, and at the head of his fleet of 350 sail he steered to the English coast, sailed inside the island of Thanet and up the Stour to Canterbury, and from Canterbury he and his fleet came up the Thames to attack

---

* We have a charter of Ecgbeorht and Æthelwulf which seems to give us the exact date of Ecgbeorht's death It is first written in 838, and is confirmed in 839, and at the latter date Æthelwulf says that this year is the first of his reign (Kemble, *Codex Dipl* I, pp 318–321, No 240) Still this last expression is not exact, and we cannot be absolutely certain between the dates 838 and 839

† *A. S Chron* s a 837. ‡ *Ib* 838 § *Ib* 839

‖ *Ann Fuld* 850, *Ann Xant* 850, *Ann Bert* 852, Keary, *Vikings*, &c, p 303, *sqq* It will be seen that the chronology is confused for this period

London, the chief city of the Mercian kingdom.* Beorhtwulf, the king of Mercia, encountered the Vikings in a pitched
battle and was utterly defeated The victors plundered
London and spread north of the Thames. Presently they
again crossed the river and came once more into the territory
of Æthelwulf, king of Wessex, or perhaps, to speak more
accurately, of his son Æthelbald, king of Kent The father
and son collected an army to attack the Danes, and the latter
suffered a defeat at Ockley, which is represented as a signal
one, not in the English chronicles only, but in those of the
Franks.† Howbeit in the same year we find the strangers
wintering for the first time on English ground, namely, in the
island of Thanet. And this event is much more important
than their defeat at Ockley, and much more portentous for
the future than any which had been recorded up to that
time. It seems that the Vikings began about the same
period to take up winter quarters in many of the districts
which had been the scenes of their attacks,‡ and it is
probable that all the different fleets or ' armies' began just
now insensibly to extend their policy, and from being mere
pirates gradually became in some sense an invading
nation. We do not hear of the little army of Vikings ever
being expelled from its settlement upon the edge of Kent,
though we hear once at least of a desperate effort being
made to storm its camp § Still, it is probable that there
were periods in which the Vikings quite disappeared from
English soil ; and though a succession of raids and alternate
defeats and victories of the English are reported in succeeding years (A.D. 853, 855, 860, 865), we have no important
change in the situation to record until the great Viking
invasion of England in the year 866.

The only event in this interval which needs recording
here, for it may have had some influence on the coinage,
is the rebellion of Æthelbald in A.D. 856. In this year

---

* A S Chron s a 851 [A D -F], 853 [B C]

† A S Chron ut sup , Annales Bertian s a 850 (Pertz, vol 1 445)

‡ Steenstrup Normannerne, I p 264, Keary, o c p 306

§ A S Chron s a 853 [A D E], 851 [B C]

Æthelwulf made a pilgrimage to Rome, and on his return through Francia espoused Judith, the daughter of Charles the Bald, king of West Fiancia. This was the second time that an English king had married a Frankish princess, the first occasion being that of the marriage of Æthelbeiht of Kent with Berchta, the daughter of Charibert king of Paris, which brought in its train the evangelization of the English. The marriage of Æthelwulf and Judith was solemnized at Verberie by the famous Hincmar, archbishop of Rheims.* Chailes made it a condition of the marriage that his daughter should be crowned queen and sit beside her consort,† an honour which the English law or custom forbade to the wife of the king.‡ Æthelwulf had several children by his former wife. The succession to the throne rested among the Teutonic people upon no fixed principle of primogeniture, and there aio certainly to be found among them instances in which the superior rank of the mother gave a superior title to the throne—though this was rather among the heathen Teutons, in the case where the king had several contemporaneous wives.§ It is possible, therefore, that this elevation of Judith to the rank of a queen consort was (should she have children) a real menace to the rights of Æthelwulf's eldest son Æthelbald. At any rate it gave offence to a section of the chief men, bishops and caldoimen, of the kingdom; and on his return to his own country Æthelwulf found himself confronted by a rebellion, at the head of which stood his eldest son Æthelbald. Civil war was avoided by the moderation of the king who consented to a partition of the kingdom in a sense the reverse of that which usually obtained between the father and his eldest son To Æthelbald was given the chief kingdom, Wessex, and

---

* *Annales Bert* s. a. 857 (Pertz, vol 1. 450).

† Cf Capit Caroli II , *Coronatio Iudithae* (Pertz, *Leges* I 150)

‡ Assor, *De reb gest Ælfridi* (Wise), pp 10-11, cf Willelmi Malm., *G R A*, II § 113 (*E H S*, pp 168-9)

§ As in the case of Harald *Hárfagr* in Norway Harald's chief wife, wife of highest rank, was Ragnhild, daughter of the king of Jutland, and their son, Erik Blôdox, was, in virtue of his mother's rank, regarded as his father's heir *Haralds Saga hins Hárfagra*, c 21.

his father retained only the (usually) dependent kingdom of Kent *

For convenience of description and reference the plan adopted for the arrangement of the types of the coins of the earlier West Saxon kings has been as follows The types when they display a head or bust are always placed before those which have none , and the coins with the indication of a mint-place precede the coins devoid of any such indication. Thus, in the earlier reigns, the coins with the name of Canterbury head the classes to which they belong This is the arrangement adopted in the first volume, where any attempt to distribute the types into an historical sequence must have proceeded largely on guess-work. From the time of Ælfred an historical arrangement of the types seems possible, and from that period it has been attempted, though the principle of heading the coinage of each reign with the mint-coins has not been abandoned. It is in virtue of this system of arrangement that the coins Pl II. 1–4 appear among the first of Æthelwulf's types. But it does not follow that they were among his earliest issues ; and we might be tempted to explain the juxtaposition of the two names DORIBI and CANT by reading ÆTHELWULF REX CANT[IÆ] and taking DORIBI (for DOROBERNIA) to be the name of the mint This reading would be forced upon us if we had only the types Pl. II 2, 4 But the existence of type Pl II. 1 rather militates against the interpretation suggested Should, however, this reading be the right one, we might suppose that these coins were struck by Æthelwulf subsequent to the repartition of the kingdom in A D 856 The rule over Kent as an under-king did not include the right of striking coins . † of that we may be pretty sure. But when Æthelwulf became once more

---

* Asser, p 9 Asser says only that the eastern part of the kingdom was retained by Æthelwulf, while Æthelbald had the western, the more important division The Chronicle makes no mention of the rebellion of Æthelbald, or the division of the kingdom. Æthelstan, the elder brother of Æthelbald, had previously to his death been king of Kent He struck no coins In fact, it is obvious that these under-kings had not the right of coinage

† See last note

towards the end of his reign king of Kent only, he may very well have continued to issue money for his separate kingdom

Which was the last of Æthelwulf's types we may be reasonably sure It was type xvii. (last type with the bust *) which is retained upon the coinages of Æthelbald and Æthelbearht.

No satisfactory explanation can be offered of the extreme Æthelbald. rarity of Æthelbald's coins, of which only four specimens have ever been described, and only three are now known to exist † An explanation (which has already been hinted at) would indeed be given by the supposition that the so-called West Saxon coinage was still—even at this late date—almost exclusively a Kentish coinage. For it does not seem certain that Æthelbald ever reigned as supreme or independent king in Kent. He was king of Wessex between A.D. 856 and the death of his father in 858 ; and after that date the kingdom of Kent appears to have passed to his brother Æthelbearht ‡ It seems difficult to believe that this explanation is the true one, and that Wessex had not at this date a regular currency of its own, as much as Kent had. And the acceptance of the contrary theory is made a little more difficult by the fact that Æthelbald's solitary type reproduces a type of his father's coinage and is continued in the coinage of his brother and successor

Æthelbald's reign was a scandal to his contemporaries and to the chroniclers of a later time. He not only rebelled against his father, but on his father's death he married his stepmother, that Judith whom we saw married to Æthelwulf two years previously.§ Judith was still only sixteen, and perhaps can hardly be accounted responsible for the incestuous marriage. At Æthelbald's death (A.D. 860), she returned to her father's court, and after some adventures

---

* Pl III. 6

† The genuineness of the existing specimens is much questioned They are all from the same die

‡ We have a charter of Æthelbearht as king of Kent, dated A D 858 Kemble, Codex, no 281 Cf also Will Malm § 117 (E H S, p 171)

§ Asser, p 13, Will Malm l c , Annales Bert (Prudentius) 858

of a more or less scandalous sort, became the wife of Baldwin *Bras-de-fer*, Count of Flanders, and through him the ancestress of Matilda, the wife of William the Conqueror.[*]

Æthelbald No other event of importance for the history of the coinage of Wessex distinguishes Æthelbald's reign (A.D. 858-860), and none of great moment that of his next successor (A D 860-866). During the first the Viking raids cease altogether, in the second they are renewed. In 860 Weland, a leader who had established himself at the Somme, and who was in the act of concluding a treaty with Charles the Bold, finding his hands tied in Francia,[†] took the opportunity of sailing with two hundred ships to the Wessex coast and fell upon and plundered Winchester, the capital of Wessex; he was subsequently defeated by the united fyrds of Hampshire and Berkshire.[‡] In the winter of 865 we read that the Vikings came to Thanet and wintered there:[§] and this appearance of the Danes on the Kentish coast was more ominous than any of the preceding ones, for it was the precursor of a great expedition which took the form of a definite invasion of England, and which before it had come to an end had totally changed the history of this island.

Æthelred I In the spring of 866, the year of the accession of Æthelred, we find the men from Thanet ravaging the whole of Kent, at the moment they were treating with the English on the basis of a bribe to leave the country; and about the same time we find a huge fleet, which had been collected in Francia and Flanders, arriving on the East Anglian coast and establishing itself there, from which time the Viking invasion of England begins.

There are three great invasions by which England was afflicted during the period covered by the present volume. They form the three great epochs in her history during

---

[*] *Annales Bert* (Hincmar), 862-3 She followed Baldwin about dressed as a man (mutato habitu) Charles did not give his consent to the marriage till the year 863

[†] *Annales Bert* 860 (Prudent), 861 (Hincmar), and Keary, o c p 350

[‡] *A S Chron* s a

[§] *A S Chron* s.a Hereafter the references to the Chronicle are not given, as they correspond nearly always to the correct year as given in the narrative

these centuries; and her recovery from the first two, or the assimilation of the new elements which they introduced, constitute the most important part of the history of the intervening periods. The first of these invasions it will be convenient to speak of as the Viking invasion, the second is that of the Danes under Svend (Swegn) and Cnut, and the third is the Norman Conquest which brings our era to a close. All these three invasions were invasions by Scandinavians, but by Scandinavians in such different conditions of civilization and government that they must be reckoned almost as three different nations For this reason, it would be wiser to speak of the first invasion of England, not as the invasion of the Danes but as that of the Vikings. When we examine the lists of moneyers' names for the districts which became subject to these Vikings, we have evidence that there must have been following their banners a very mixed nationality, by no means one of pure Scandinavians. In laws and customs, however, the new-comers were Scandinavians, nay Scandinavians of a very pure type—at any rate, of a type comparitively speaking primitive; and in this respect the Vikings stand contrasted with the Danish nationality, ruled by a single monarch, which was the chief agent in the second invasion of England; and in still more marked contrast to the Normans who were hardly any longer a Scandinavian folk, for they had adopted most of the laws and customs of their neighbours, the Franks In the interval between the attack which we have now to chronicle, which began in A D. 866, and the attacks which began a hundred years later (A.D. 980) and ended in the invasion of Svend and Cnut (A.D 1003–1016), all the Scandinavian nations had undergone a great transformation.

We have some traces of the laws which governed the bodies of Vikings associated at this early period for the sake of plunder or settlement in England. As the ambition of the Vikings grew these bodies increased in size, until from being small armies, they became almost nations. But still the constitution of the larger and of the smaller bodies was the same; and the same likewise was their Constitution in the technical sense, the laws, that is, and the customs by

which their units were held together In the former meaning
of the word we have to note that the smaller and larger
bodies were before everything else, armies, whether actively
engaged in warfare or at rest The invading Vikings of
A.D 860, and the subsequent years, are always spoken of as
the Army (*se here*), occasionally as the Great Army (*se mycla
here*. Sometimes the army divides up into two or more
'Armies,' and long after the first great area of conquest was
over we find mention of a number of lesser armies—the
Army of Northampton, or the Army of Bedford, &c, when
the intention is simply to designate the Vikings settled in
or about Northampton or Bedford The only difference is
that what was 'The Army,' has by this time split up into
several armies. This latter use of the word continues
(chiefly by custom and association) down to the time of the
second era of invasion.

Again, with regard to the Constitution by which these
earlier bodies were governed, we find that they constantly
proclaim themselves Republics. 'We have no king, we
are all equal.'* Yet the title king is sometimes given to
their leaders Of one of these kings a Latin versifier
says.—

'Solo rex verbo socus tamen imperitabat'†

The mere use or disuse of a title, such as the title of
'king,' is of small importance What we may take to be the
essence of the Constitution of these Vikings, that which made
it republican in fact, if not in name, was that their leader
had no rights over the soil, no superiority, or at any rate
no dominant authority except for strictly military purposes.‡

We must bear in mind while we are speaking of the republican character of the Western Vikings (as the Norse
Sagas call the settlers in the British Isles), the changes
which just at this time are taking place in the constitution
of Denmark, Sweden, and Norway. Everybody knows the
story of the taunt of the maiden Gyda to Harald of Norway,

---

* Dudo De Norm Duc i
† Abbo, Bel Par Urbis, i 38, cf Steenstrup, o c 277 sqq
‡ But see the more lengthened treatment of the subject in Steenstrup. le

when he sought to make her his wife, a taunt which was supposed to have been the awakening of the ambition of Harald Fairhair.

'She answered that she would never sacrifice her maiden-hood and take for a husband a king who governed no more of a kingdom than a few *fylkir*.* "And it seems to me wonderful," said she, "that there is no king here who has the will to unite Norway, and become its supreme king, as have done king Gorm in Denmark, and king Eirik at Upsala" '†

Before Harald had realized the policy thus sketched out for him, all of the petty kings of Norway who thought themselves strong enough to resist his encroachment, had entered into a confederacy, and—the feature in the case which more specially concerns us—had obtained the assist-ance of many of the Vikings of the West, i e. of England, Scotland, and Ireland. The settlers in these islands, there-fore, who were of the same class, and perhaps some of them the same individuals who took part in the great expedition of 866,‡ appear in the history of the Scandinavian nations as the representatives, in the countries of their origin, of a bygone or passing order of things, as the opponents of the extended sort of kingship which was the new order of the day in Denmark, Sweden, and Norway.

These considerations are enough to show that in many points beside the mere difference of date, the epoch of the Viking invasion of England in A D. 866-878 must be dis-tinguished from the Danish invasion of the end of the tenth, and the beginning of the eleventh centuries.

During the greater part of the reign of Æthelred I, the doings of the Great Army did not intimately concern the history of Wessex. In A.D. 867 the Army marched north, and as has been already described in the *Introduction* to the

---

* Districts

† *Haralds Saga hins Hárfagra,* c 3. (Heimskringla, ed Unger, p 50)

‡ The battle of Hafirsfjord, in which this confederation was defeated, and the supremacy of Harald assured, is usually dated about A D 870, and if that date be accepted, we cannot suppose that any members of 'the Army' of A D 866 took a part in it But there are reasons for postponing the date of the battle till about thirty years later See *Corpus Poet Boreale,* II 187, &c Cf. also Skene, *Celtic Scotland,* I 3.

previous volume, it took York, killed two rival kings of
Northumbria, and subdued the greater part of that country.
The next year the army marched into Mercia, and this act
affected the West Saxon kingdom in so far as Mercia was
either an acknowledged dependency, or a close ally of that
state   Consequently Burgred the king (whose coins we
observe are of types similar to those of the majority of
Æthelred's coins) sent to seek the aid of his brother-in-
law, the king of Wessex; and a Wessex army commanded
by the two surviving sons of Æthelwulf, Æthelred the
king, and the next in command, the *secundarius* Ælfred,
marched to Burgred's assistance.   The united English army
found the invaders shut up in the stronghold of Nottingham.
After a fruitless siege a compromise was effected, which
brought no honour to any of the leaders of the English
forces; a ransom was paid to induce the ' Army ' to return
again into Northumbria   This was in A D. 868   For the next
two years the doings of the Vikings were confined to the
northern and midland counties, to Northumbria, Mercia,
and East Anglia (Vol I *Introduction*, pp. li. lxi.), and then in
A.D. 871 half of the Army crossed the Thames and began
the invasion of Wessex   The invaders took camp at Reading,
where they were protected by two streams, the Kennet and
the Thames, and the war was for a time confined to attacks
by the English upon foraging parties, and to sorties of the
garrison.   But at length the invaders thought themselves
strong enough to march westward, and they were brought
to an engagement with the English forces under the command of Æthelred and Ælfred, at the famous battle of
Ashdown *   The Danish forces consisted in reality of two
armies, one commanded by two kings, Halfdan and Bægsæg,
and the other by five earls, Asbjorn, Fræne, Harald, and
the elder and the younger Sihtric   The only survivor of
all these leaders was Halfdan, who effected his retreat, and
once more shut himself up in Reading.

d   All these events in the invasion of Wessex passed during
the earlier months of the year 871   Æthelred now died,

---

* Asser (Wise). p 19

and Ælfred the Great, then only twenty-two years old, ascended the throne. Some delay was caused by the ceremonial of accession, which had no doubt to be affirmed by the Witan (Æthelred had left an infant son), and by the funerals of the dead king. The English army was never summoned but for a short period at a time,[*] and was no doubt disbanded during this interval. When Ælfred was again able to collect a force, he was confronted by an utterly changed condition of things in the country. The Danes had received reinforcements and marched westwards. Ælfred was obliged to abandon all the eastern side of his kingdom, and the next important engagement between the English and the Vikings took place at Wilton. This time victory fell to the Danes, but a hard-won victory. After this Ælfred purchased the departure of the invaders from his country.

It is of importance to take note of these money payments to the Danes, in view of the fact which we shall presently see, that many of the coins with the name 'Ælfred' were probably not really made under the auspices of that king, but are barbarous imitations of Ælfred's coins, manufactured either by the Danes themselves, or in districts which their invasions had disorganized. We cannot call these payments a danegeld. For as seems almost certain the danegeld, instead of being, as the earlier historians supposed, a sum gathered together as ransom and paid to the Danes, was in reality a tax (a sort of 'ship-money') imposed to raise money for the arming of a force—essentially a naval force—to protect the country against the Vikings.[†]

Halfdan, the leader of the Vikings, withdrew his forces from Wessex and retired to Mercia. Mercia got rid of the Vikings by paying a ransom, and they returned into Northumbria. Next year (A D 874) the army came back and deposed the Mercian king Burgred, and raised up in his stead a puppet of their own, Ceolwulf, an 'unwise king's thegn.'[‡] 'And he swore oath and gave hostages that it

---

[*] Asser, p. 21 *sqq*

[†] Steenstrup, *Normannerne*, iv p 148 *sqq*

[‡] Asser, p. 26, *A S. Chron* s. a 874. MS **A.** omits the name of the thegn

d

should be ready for them on whatever day they would have it; and that he himself would be ready, and all who would follow him at the army's need.' *

But while Ceolwulf II. remained titular king of Mercia, it is very likely that Halfdan and his Vikings took possession of London. For we have an interesting coin, not in the National Collection, nor published in this catalogue, but described in Mr. Kenyon's edition of Hawkin's *Silver Coins of England*, p. 79, which is without doubt a coin of Halfdan struck at this period in London. The piece is given here.

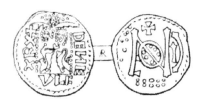

DESCRIPTION.

Obv. VLF (in ex.) DEИE XRX✠
Barbarous imitation of coin of Valentinian I., or of Magnus Maximus as on Ælfred Type iv. (*reverse*), p. 34.

Rev. London monogram as on Ælfred Types vi., vii. (*reverse*), p. 35.

We see that this eccentric coin is in a certain way a link between a very rare piece of Ceolwulf II. of Mercia, and one of Ælfred.

For two years 'the Army' remained in Mercian territory. Then it divided into two sections. One of these, under Halfdan, marched into Northumbria, and began definitely to settle in the country. The northern half of Northumbria was left under the rule of princes of the old English line. But they struck no coins, and probably their power was small. The southern half of Northumbria, the kingdom of York as it is now often called, the Vikings made their own kingdom, and Halfdan was the king of it, so far as they had any king. Thus the ancient kingdoms of Bernicia and Deira reappeared.†

---

* 'Þæs heres þearfe,' the oath of military service.
† *A. S. Chron.* s. a. 876.

But the other half of the Army, whose leader now was Guthorm, or Guðrum, after settling for a short while at Cambridge, sailed out to sea and round to attack once more the kingdom of Wessex, the only one of the four English kingdoms which remained unsubmerged For two years Wessex had to sustain the hardest struggle which it had yet known. Guthorm's army came first to Wareham There it was besieged by Ælfred, and a fleet which came to relieve it was defeated by the fleet which Ælfred had taken advantage of the lull in the Viking attacks to build. (He had already gained one victory with it in A D 875 *) The Viking Army was allowed to depart from Wareham on condition that it would quit the territory of the West Saxons This concession, which appears unadvisable, may have been necessary. Still the result was that it brought to ruin the English defence. The Army went no further than Exeter. There it received reinforcement, and in A D 877 it marched to Chippenham. The resistance of the English seemed to break down on every hand. 'Many they drove over seas, and all the rest submitted to them save Ælfred the king.'† The winter of 877-8 is the winter of Ælfred's entrenchment with a little band of devoted followers on the island of Æthelney (The Princes' Island), at the junction of the Tone and the Parret, about which and his hunted days of wandering, so much picturesque legend has gathered. The spring of 878 saw the revival of his hopes and of the courage of the English. An army secretly assembled under the shade of Selwood forest, and marched upon the Danes encamped in or about Chippenham, who were quite unprepared for its appearance The armies of Ælfred and Guthorm encountered at Æthandune, probably upon the downs close above Westbury. This time the victory of the English was decisive. It was followed by the baptism of Guthorm and his followers at Wedmore, and by a partition of England, which added to the kingdom of Ælfred, roughly speaking, Mercia west of Watling Street and the River Lea, but gave over the rest of England north of the Thames, to

---

* Asser, p 27   † A S Chron s a.

be inhabited and governed by the Viking invaders. It was not however till A.D. 880 that the army of Guthorm fairly settled in its new dominions.

The rest of the reign of Ælfred was devoted chiefly to the fruitful victories of peace.

During the years of peace that followed it is probable that Ælfred extended the shire system into Mercia; that he redacted and amended the laws both of the West Saxons and of the Mercians, above all, that he found the leisure to do more than any king before him, or perhaps any that followed him has done, to spread and encourage knowledge and learning among his people, and to repair as far as might be the ravages which a century of Viking attacks had made in the civilization of England.*

That the new England which rose up out of the anarchy of the war, was different from the England which preceded it we may feel sure. Many of the characteristics of the early Teutonic civilization were unfitted to the changed condition of things. On every hand, not in England alone, the kingly power was becoming more defined. And in all these lands it rested more or less upon a standing army, such as it had been the effect of these wars to create. We may take it that the payments made to the Danes, the creation of a standing army, of a fleet, and the taxes which had to be contributed to these ends, are the main causes of the increase in the coinage which is characteristic of Ælfred's reign.†

One result of the war was that Wessex now finally and completely absorbed the countries south of the Thames. There was never again question of an under-king in Kent. Western Mercia took the place of Kent in this respect. She

---

* The earlier Viking attacks on Northumbria had done not a little to destroy the comparatively high civilization of that country at the end of the eighth century. Compare the letter of Alcuin in Jaffé, *Bibl. Rer. Ger.* Vol. vi p. 22.

† What Ælfred did in the direction of creating a standing army was to divide the Militia into two sections, and keep one half or the other always 'with the colours.' It is probable that in addition to this there was a permanent army for garrison duty. See *A. S. Chron* s. a. 894. For Ælfred's ship-building, see *A. S. Chron* s. a. 897.

became the dependent kingdom, not yet the integral portion of the domains of the House of Cerdic. Æthelred, the leading ealdorman of Mercia, and a man of the old blood royal, was made the lord or the ealdorman (but not, we observe, the king) of the Mercians, and he was married to Æthelflæd, the famous 'Lady of the Mercians,' the daughter of Ælfred and sister of Eadweard the Elder. But of course this under-lordship did not include the right to strike coins; so that if Æthelred issued money at any mint in his dominions, that coinage would bear the name of Ælfred, just as Eadgar's Mercian coinage (struck in the lifetime of Eadwig) would bear Eadwig's name This does away with any external difficulty in the way of accepting the coins which lead ORSNAFORDA as an Oxford coinage, if the internal difficulties in the way of changing an R into a K are not considered too great.*

In the year 884 the Chronicle tells us that the army in East Anglia broke the peace, and at the same time a new Viking army—probably with the connivance of the East Anglians—made a landing in Kent. Ælfred had kept his fleet in good order, and when he had driven away the new comers, he made with his ships an attack on the East Anglian coast, which was only partially successful.† Two years later we find Ælfred rebuilding or refortifying London and giving it over to his son-in-law Æthelred. It may be at this time that the coins with the London monogram were struck. In that case we must consider Halfdan the originator of this important type in the coinage of Ælfred This seems in fact the most reasonable conclusion. Finally, in A D. 892–3, the English sustained the last serious attack from foreign Vikings which she was to know for many years. One Army

---

* All that has been said by J R Green ('Conquest of England,' p 144), and others concerning the evidence afforded by these ORSNAFORDA coins, is founded on a misconception

† Asser gives the impression that Ælfred's attack on East Anglia preceded the breaking of the peace But this cannot have been the case otherwise the expression *opprobriose fregit* would be too unreasonable Even supposing (as Asser also implies) that Ælfred's naval attack was directed more against the English than against the Danes

of continental Vikings came—probably from the Rhine—and another, headed by the famous Hasting, came from France. The Vikings from Northumbria and East Anglia joined their former brothers-in-arms. We described in the last volume the coins probably struck by the Siefred, a Northumbrian leader, who at this time, or the year following, came with a fleet of 110 ships to Hasting's aid, and eventually sailed round to Exeter, whither Ælfred was obliged to carry the English fleet to besiege him; while Æthelred the ealdorman led an army against the invading force, which had marched right across England from the Thames to the Severn These last were encountered and defeated at the battle of Butting-ton, in which Ælfred's son Eadweard, the future king, took part. With intervals this new war lasted till the year 897.[*]

We see that Ælfred took occasion of his latest victories somewhat to extend his empire, and this circumstance is to be noted as the first evidence of a turn of the tide In the succeeding reigns we see the tide running strongly towards a complete recovery of England by the English kings.

Ælfred s long and famous reign ended in A D 901.

₹0 of 1

We may assume that the greater number of Ælfred's coins were struck during the years of comparative tran-quillity which followed the expulsion of the Danes from Wessex. But though this applies to the coins it does not appear to hold true of the *types*

Type i is the type of Æthelred I.'s coins, and was no doubt the type of the first issue of Ælfred

Type ii is that of Æthered, Archbishop of Canterbury, who held his see between A D. 870–889. Vol. I. p 78, Pl. xiii. 9.

Type iii is a variety of Type ii.

Type iv. is the curious and inexplicable type which occurs on the coin of Halfdan (VLFDENE) described above, and on a coin of Ceolwulf II. of Mercia (A D. 874). It resembles certain sceatta types and types of early English gold coins (Vol. I. pp 2. 3, Pl. i 2) and is apparently derived from the solidi of Valentinian I or of Magnus Maximus. Such a case of 'atavism on the part of a coin-type seems almost inexplic-

---

able. The case is clearly an abnormal one, and too much stress must not be laid on it. This type is by the VLFDENE coin closely connected with the London monogram type which almost immediately follows.

Type v., like the previous type, is similar to the coinage of Ceolwulf II. issued in 874 (*See* Vol. I. Pl x. 16).

We come next to the monogram types, Nos. vi.-xii. We have already described a coin with the London monogram, that of Halfdan, struck as it seems in A.D. 874. Probably this coin is the inauguration of the monogram type The monogram upon the reverse of coins had been hitherto essentially a Frankish device. And not only is it *primâ facie* probable that the Vikings would be more familiar than the English with the Frankish currency of this date (so much of which had been paid as ransom into their pockets); but we have evidence in the Cuerdale coins (Vol I. pp. xxix 95, 204 *sqq*) that the Vikings, in the earliest coins which they struck for their own use, were disposed to imitate the coinage of the Franks.* This first London monogram, then, was introduced in A.D. 874. But Halfdan only remained a short time in London. It is highly probable that after his departure the Londoners continued to strike coins with this monogram but placed upon it the head and name of Ælfred. It seems hardly likely that the monogram type should have remained totally in abeyance after its introduction by Halfdan until the year Ælfred was fully and legally lord of London, though it might have done so. For during a part of this time London lay in a deplorable condition. In A.D. 886, as we have seen, Ælfred rebuilt the town and made Æthelred, lord of the Mercians, its governor. From the London monogram are derived the others, Lincoln and Roiseng ? (Castle Rising ?) These types for convenience sake are placed next; though chronologically type x probably precedes some of them. Both the last mentioned places, if the reading of the last monogram be correct, were like London before A.D. 886,

---

* The Frankish king whose coins may be taken to have suggested the London and Lincoln monogram-types is Louis le Bègue (A D 861-879) Compare Gariel, *Monnaies Royales de France sous la Race Carlovingienne*, pl 38

outside the kingdom of Ælfred. Though therefore they bear the name of the king of Wessex they are almost more Viking coins than English ones.

Type xiii. is derived from the St. Eadmund coinage of East Anglia described in Vol I. (see pp. 97–137, Pls xvii.– xix.) the issue of which must have taken place before A.D. 905.

Types xiv and xv. are the types which were copied by Guthorm-Æthelstan when he began to strike coins (Vol. I. pp 95–6, Pl xvi. 12).

Type xvi. with the reverse CNVT, as on the coins of North- umbria described in Vol. I pp. 204–221, Pls. xxiv.-v., is in its obverse similar to Type xiv. Guðred-Cnut of North- umbria reigned from A.D. 877–894.

Type xvii. ('Dorobernia') is the same as that of the coins of Plegmund, Archbishop of Canterbury, who held the see between A D. 890 and 914. In fact, we have now arrived at the types which closely resemble some of those of Ælfred's successor Eadweard I.

Type xviii is the 'Orsnaforda' type, which likewise resembles the earlier types of Eadweard the Elder; and

Type xix. is only a variety of Type xviii, made by intro- ducing a design which is Frankish in origin and is to be found on the coinage of Siefred, king of Northumbria (Vol. I, pp 223, nos 1029–1032, Pl. xxvi. 5–7), who reigned from A D 894 to circ A D 898.

Type xx the Gloucester coin stands rather apart from the other mints, and it may perhaps belong to an earlier part of Ælfred's reign than the other mint-types which follow, viz. —

Types xxi and xxiii. struck at Exeter, Winchester, and Bath; and

Type xxii., the pieds-forts or so-called 'offering pennies,' which read on the reverse ELI MO⁻, but have on the obverse the same legend, AELFRED REX SAXONVM, as have the coins of Type xxi This legend, 'Ælfred rex Saxonum,' connects the last types of Ælfred with Type i. of Eadweard the Elder, which reads EADWEARD REX SAXONVM; and these coins of Eadweard too have on the reverse the three first letters, BAÐ, of the mint Baðan, as on Ælfred's coins of Type

xxiii. This reverse again is similar to that of Type xxi, which, however, has the three first letters of the mints, Exeter and Winchester, arranged in a different manner. Again, the moneyer Eli on the *pieds-forts* connects these coins with Ælfred's piece struck at Bath. It is obvious, therefore, that all these types belong to the latter years of Ælfred's reign.

It may, we think, be taken that all the types from Type xiii.-xxiii. were issued subsequently to what is known as the Peace of Wedmore. And albeit these only include a minority of Ælfred's types, the coins which belong to these types constituted without question a large majority of the issue of this reign. In the Museum Collection the later coins stand to the earlier in the proportion of 384 to 68.

The confusions of this time of invasion and internal warfare, and of a new departure in the history of England, are very well reflected on the coinages of Ælfred's reign; and it results from this that when we have, according to the best lights which we possess, determined the order of Ælfred's issues, we have by no means finished with the classes into which the coins are to be distributed. It seems almost as certain as it can be that all the coins bearing Ælfred's name were not struck under his authority or within his dominions. And we have now to examine again Ælfred's coins with the object of distinguishing two classes: (1) The true Wessex coinage, and (2) The more or less barbarous imitations of the coins of Ælfred.

We must look back for a moment to the previous volume to ascertain the different coinages which we know to have been struck outside the limits of Ælfred's kingdom during his reign. Of these there are three classes, two Christian and one heathen. The first are the coins which commemorate the martyred king Eadmund of East Anglia slain by the Danes in A.D. 870. Most of this coinage must have been struck somewhere between that year, 870, and the year 905. (See Vol. I. pp. xxix. 97-137.) Then there are the coins of Guthorm-Æthelstan (A.D. 878-890), the first Christian Danish king in England (*Ib.* p 95). Finally, there is that curious series the penny coinage of Northumbria, of

which all the known examples formed part of the Cuerdale
Hoard (Ib pp. 201-230). This is the series which more than
any other issued in England deserves the name of a Viking
coinage.

Beside coins of these series, which are what they profess
to be, coins struck outside Ælfred's dominions, we have other
series of more or less barbarous imitations of Ælfred's
coinage, which were probably made in places under the rule
of the Vikings and where society was a good deal disorganized. We have even a series of imitations of the St.
Eadmund coins (Vol. I., Introduction, p. xxix., cf Pl. xvii.,
no. 11; Pl. xviii., no. 10, Pl. xix., nos. 11, 13); then, we have
imitations of the coins of Plegmund, Archbishop of Canterbury (Vol. I., p 79, no 66; p. 80, no. 76), and finally we
have imitations of just the same character of Ælfred's coins
(p. 41) The following numbers of Ælfred's coins may be
designated as probably imitations, and therefore, though
professedly Wessex coins, probably not struck either in
Wessex or under the authority of Ælfred

> p 38, No 2 (St Eadmund)
> pp 41-45, Nos 28-74
> p 46, Nos 81-83 (Lincoln)
> p 48, No 103
> p 49, No 113 (London)
> pp 53, 54, Nos 148-151 (Oxford)
> p 59, No 189 (St Eadmund)
> p 79, Nos 421-427
> p 82, Nos 453, 454

We see that we have a link between the coins of Ælfred
and those of St Eadmund (2), as well as between Ælfred's
coins and those of Northumbria (454) It is in each case most
probable that the coin was made in the district of the least
celebrated type. In other words, the coins of the famous
king of Wessex are likely to have spread farther than those
commemorating St Eadmund, or those struck by Guðred-
Cnut of Northumbria; and therefore imitative coins which
combine Ælfred's types with one or other of these two are
likely to have been made in the country of the St. Eadmund
coinage or in the country of Cnut.

It is just at this point that the confusions and varieties

in the names of the moneyers which appear upon the coins reach their maximum. A large number of the names upon the St. Eadmund series, for example, seem to defy analysis.

Puzzling, however, as these names are, there is one thing that comes out clearly with regard to them, that a large number cannot be English names. Directly we pass outside the region of Ælfred's kingdom these un-English names meet us face to face. But what is strange is that they do not appear to be so much Scandinavian names as Frankish ones.

The majority of the moneyers' names, which we marked as uncertain in the Index to Vol I, belong to this St. Eadmund series. But still among those names about which we need entertain no reasonable doubt by far the greater number are certainly not Old English. We find such names as—

Abboe*	Eldecar ?	Odulbert (Adalbert ?)
Abbonel	Elismus	Odulf
Adalbert	Enodas§	Remigius
Adradus	Ergemond	Risleca (poss Gisleca)
Ainmer	Fredemund	Robert
Albert	Gislefred	Snefreu (Stefan ?)
Alus (Adradus ?)	Grim	Sten
Ansigert†	Gundbert	Stephan
Arus (Adradus ?)	Hludovicus	Walter
Bado ‡	Isiemund	Wandefred
Beringar	Johannes	Wigbald or Widbald
Beslin	Martinus	Wineger
Deinolt	Milo	
Domundan	Odomouer	

Of names which appear to be English we have only Ædinwine or Eadwine, Eadred, Eadwulf, Huscam (= Hussa?), Oswulf, Tedwine, Winedulf, and Wulfold. The remainder are corrupt and obscure. Both in the case of Guthorm's moneyers and of those who struck the St. Eadmund series most appear to have been not Danes but Franks. We have

---

* Cf Pertz, vol 1 p 198, also the well-known Abbo, author of the poem, *Bella Parisiacæ Urbis*

† Anskar or Ansgar, the Saint, Archbishop of Hamburg in the reign of Lewis the Pious, was of Danish origin Cf, however, Forstemann, *Deutsch. Pers*, pp 105–6

‡ Forstemann, o c, p 196

§ A moneyer of Guthorm-Æthelstan

however, the names Grim, Sten (unless this be a contraction of Stefan [*]), which are probably, and Gisleca and Odulf,[†] which are possibly Scandinavian. Among the Frankish moneyers above given we find Abbonel and Enodas striking also for Guthorm-Æthelstan, and another of Guthorm's moneyers, Berter, who has a Frankish name.

It is pretty certain that the St. Eadmund coinage was struck before A.D. 905 It probably belongs to a period when East Anglia, nominally a Danish kingdom, was in a quasi-anarchical condition, at any rate in this sense, that there was no single recognised ruler in the country Such we must believe to have been its state after the death of Guthorm, and very likely before that event For if we take the partition of *Ælfreds and Guðorms Frið* to be the partition of A D 886, we find about fifty years later that a great portion of this kingdom once Guthorm's, has been under the rule of five separate small republics known as the ‘Five Burgs.’[‡] It is quite possible, despite its pious character, and the fact that St Eadmund was martyred by the Danes, that the St Eadmund coinage began in the reign of Guthorm For these Scandinavians were quick to change their creed, and often strangely zealous in their new faith witness the case of Harold Blaatand of Denmark; who, though he was in the first instance a forced convert, had no sooner become so than he set to work at once to imperil and to lose his supremacy over Norway by trying to compel his vassal Earl Hakon to accept baptism.[§]

We can explain the occurrence of Frankish names upon the coins of East Anglia on one of three suppositions : either there were a great many Frankish soldiers in that portion of the Great Army, which, under Guthorm, settled in East Anglia and Mercia , or the army brought over with it a certain

---

[*] *Eng Hist Rev* v , p 134

[†] But cf Pertz, vol 1 , p 93

[‡] The ‘Five Burgs,’ so called, are Lincoln, Nottingham, Derby, Leicester, and Stamford The first was probably never within the kingdom of Guthorm, but the other four were On the character of these miniature republics, see Steenstrup, *Normannerne*, iv 10 *sqq*

[§] *Olafs s Tryggvas* (Heimskringla) c 27 *sq*

number of Frankish captives (thralls), and these having some skill in metal-work were employed to engrave dies and were at the same time authorized to place their names upon them; or finally, that the coins were issued by traders, and the majority of these in East Anglia at this time were men of Frankish descent *

As the English power extends to the north and east we find Frankish and Scandinavian names beginning to appear beside the English moneyers of the West Saxon kings. Thus in the coinage of Eadweard the Elder, we have—

Berngar (Beringar?)	Lanfer	Rinnard (Rinard)
Grimwald	Marbert	Sigot
Gundbert	Pastor	Waltere
Iofermund	Piut	Warimer

We also have the following names, which are probably Scandinavian—

Framwis	Irfara	Sigebrand
Frioðulf	Odo	Sigeferð
Frið	Rægenulf	

In the following reign, Æthelstan (A D 925–940), we have among new names—

Abba	Domences, Dominic	Merten
Baldric	Duriant	Paul
Baldwine	Giongbald	Stefanus
Barbe	Gislemer	
Burdel or Burdel		

of possible or probable Frankish origin, and—

Rægenald	Rægengrim	Þurstan

which may very well be Scandinavian.

And if we continue our inquiry into the succeeding reigns, Eadmund's and Eadred's, we still find a large number both of Frankish and Scandinavian names   In addition to eleven Frankish names from the preceding reign we find on Eadmund's coins—

Abenel	Efrard (Everard,
Agtard	Eberhard)
Bonsom †	Ercimbald,
Dudelet	Hadebald (?)

---

* This is the theory adopted by Mr. York Powell, *English Hist Rev.* v pp 134-5   But see below, p ciii sqq

† This may be a corruption of 'bonus homo,' a pedantry for Godman

And for Danish names we have—

Ærnulf or Arnulf	Regenulf	Ulf
Farman*	Randulf	Deodulf
Ola	Reingrim	Dorulf or Deorulf

Under Eadred only—

| Engilbred | Norbert | OScelric | Walter |

have a Frankish look—

| Godlin | Grim | Unbein |

may be Scandinavian, and so forth. Under Eadwig the Frankish names grow fewer, and by the time we reach the reign of Æthelred II. they have almost disappeared, but the Scandinavian names naturally continue in large numbers.

The various series of coins initiated during Ælfred's reign which we have been recently describing, the coins of Guthorm-Æthelstan, Northumbrian coins from the Cuerdale Hoard, the imitations of the St Eadmund coinage, of the coinages of Ælfred and Plegmund may be grouped together as the Viking coinage of England, and as such they are of considerable interest. It must be remembered that as yet scarcely any English coins had found their way to Scandinavia,† and certainly they had as yet produced no imitative coinage in the Scandinavian countries And though, as we see in the case of the Delgany Find, it is probable that English coins had been carried over into Ireland by the Vikings of that country, they had produced no imitative coinage there either. It is possible, as was noticed in the *Introduction* to Vol. I., that the Swedes possessed a certain currency copied from the coins of Dorstat, which found their way to the north; but that is by no means certain. What is certain is that for the imitation of a lasting Scandinavian currency, Irish, Scandinavian, Norse or Swedish, we must go to a much later date, to the end of the tenth century, that is to say, to the era of the *second* Scandinavian invasion of England, that in which the Danes, now become the

* A York moneyer
† See *Num Chron* 1882 (paper already cited on the Delgany Hoard) p 84

Danish nation, took a leading part. This earlier currency, this mixed collection of original and imitative types, stands apart from any other Scandinavian coinage, and is the only one which represents what we have ventured to speak of as the nationality of the Vikings

If the coinage itself is, as we see that it is, mixed and chaotic, it represents sufficiently well the nation and the governments of that nation which issued it It would not be wise to press the coinage for more information than can reasonably be drawn from it. Numismatists are too apt to make that mistake We cannot tell by what authority these copies of Ælfred's coins were made. The St. Eadmund coins themselves, though they were issued under the auspices of Christians, were coined in a country subject to the Vikings and must have passed current among the latter: the barbarous imitations of the St. Eadmund coins seem to prove that they did so. The Cuerdale-Northumbrian coins again, with their rude workmanship and their imitations of Frankish types, stand quite apart from any other series that we know. Though they bear the names of kings Cnut and Siefred, we can hardly suppose that they were issued under royal authority in the sense in which the contemporary coinage of Ælfred was so.* The only pieces out of all these extra-Wessex series which at all correspond to our ideas of an ordered and regular currency are the coins of Guthorm-Æthelstan. These are the only coins which can be said to imply a state of kingship among the Vikings at all corresponding to the kingship which obtained among the English.†

---

* The genuine coinage of Ælfred, that is

† What is meant by this is that 'king' among these wandering Norsemen is like 'earl,' always a personal and not a territorial title In England it was of course originally the same . but though Ælfred is still nominally 'king of the Angel-cyn,' he is in effect as much King of England, or of the part of England which he rules, as his successors Eadweard or Eadgar It does not seem a too bold conjecture to suppose that Guthorm-Æthelstan, when he adopted Christianity, did so partly with a view to obtaining a more territorial kingdom than had been customary with the Vikings And there can be little doubt that the settlement of Normandy and the vassalage of the Norman dukes is to be explained on the same principle Halfdan in Northumbria probably attempted the same thing He is always spoken of as a tyrant,

It is impossible to do more than hint these various points in which the coinage of Ælfred's time may illustrate the history of the period , in the first place, because it is no part of our purpose to write that history at length, still less to dwell upon all its constitutional aspects; and in the second place, because it is not advisable to overstrain the evidence which can be derived from coins, as numismatists are somewhat apt to do. The history of this period for all the parts outside the kingdom of Ælfred is buried in obscurity, and the confusion of the coinage only reflects the state of confusion of the country.

With the accession of Eadweard the Elder, in A D. 901, we enter upon a simpler period of history and a simpler coinage.

According to the strictest laws of primogeniture, Eadweard was not the heir to the throne. That was Æthelwald,* the son of Æthelred I., who not unnaturally was aggrieved at being passed over by the Witan, and who attempted to raise a rebellion. It is probable that this Æthelwald was a man of no worth or likelihood, whereas Eadweard had already showed his metal in more than one encounter with the Vikings. The course which Æthelwald pursued in his rebellion was an outrage on the patriotism and the religious feelings of his countrymen; and it leaves a taint upon his courage When he found how little support he received at his first rising, he retreated to Wimborne and shut himself up in the city with a nun whom he had ravished from the cloister. He swore that he would die there , but instead secretly left the place and fled north to Northumbria, where he was welcomed by the Northumbrians as a king.† Guðred had probably been dead six or seven years. The people of the north were perhaps

---

but then he had the Christians and the priests (the depositories of the law) against him The story of the 'invention' of Guðred-Cnut (see Vol I. p lxvii), shows the part the Christians played in changing the succession. But the history of Northumbria is buried in too much obscurity for us to say what manner of king Guðred-Cnut was

* 'Æthelbaldus,' Æthelweard

† A. S Chron s a 901, Fl Wig (E II S), pp 117-8

glad to welcome a claimant from a family whose ideas of kingship were more determined than their own. The rival of Eadweard maintained himself for a time; but in A D 905 he and his Northumbrians were defeated by the English at Holme, in Norfolk, far, as we see, beyond the borders of Eadweard's kingdom.* This was the first of a series of engagements which all mark the turn of the tide of victory against the English Vikings.

A like turn of the tide had occurred—it may be as well to note in passing—on the Continent also. The prelude of it is the defeat of the great Viking fleet and army which besieged Paris in A.D 885-7.† And though subsequent and temporary successes followed that defeat, the next great event in the history of the continental Vikings, the settlement of Normandy in A.D. 912, must be looked upon (like the settlement of East Anglia in this country) rather as a register of defeat than a token of victory. In Germany the Vikings sustained a decisive defeat at the hands of Arnulf the Emperor—the successor of Charles the Fat—in A.D. 891 ‡ (It was this defeat abroad which brought about the second Viking invasion of England during Ælfred's reign.) This victory of Arnulf's was a final one as regards the relief of Germany from serious Viking invasions. Let us note that two new elements of warfare became at this time conspicuous by the aid which they gave towards the Vikings' defeats— the increase in the 'cavalry arm'—the development of the heavy-armed man-at-arms of the mediæval type—and the development of military engineering, the building of forts and fortified bridges to hinder the advance of invading armies and invading fleets. In the defence of Paris, above spoken of, it is the fortification that plays the principal part. In Germany, too, at this period the building of forts was being actively carried on. And it is this element in warfare which is the most important one in England for the

---

* According to Florence he had been driven over sea and had returned, p 118 Steenstrup has set right the chronology of this rebellion, o c III 32 sq

† Abbo, Bel Par Urbis (Peitz, vol ii pp 776-805), Annales Vedastini 885-7 (Ib i 522-4); Regionis Chronicon (Ib i 595-6), &c

‡ Annales Fuldenses, s a 891

period on which we are now embarked. This practice of fort-building was the main instrument in the extension of the power of the West Saxon kings over the Scandinavians settled south of the Humber.

After his victory over the Vikings at Holme we find Eadweard renewing his father's compact with the king of the East Engle. This king is not Guthorm-Æthelstan who died in A.D. 890,* but another Guthorm called Eohricson (Eiriksson)

Whenever, upon his coins, Eadweard takes any title in addition to that of 'rex' it is simply 'Rex Saxonum,' as his father and great-grandfather had done before him. But in his charters Eadweard calls himself 'Angul-Saxonum Rex.' Before his death Eadweard had the opportunity of wholly incorporating Mercia with his dominions, and even in the lifetime of Æthelred, the ealdorman of Mercia, and of Eadweard's sister, Æthelflæd, the Lady of the Mercians, Eadweard was the king of this part of England. We may assume, and the types of the coins which bear it favour this assumption, that the rather restricted title 'Rex Saxonum' was only used by Eadweard at the beginning of his reign.†
For Eadweard had very early in his reign the opportunity of extending his immediate rule over some of the Angles north of the Thames, over part of the country of East Mercia, which had previously belonged to Guthorm-Æthelstan. Each step whereby Eadweard gained his extension of territory we cannot trace—not, that is, until we enter upon the succeeding phase, the greatest in the recovery of England from the Vikings—the Building of the Burgs. At the date at which Eadweard begins building these frontier fortresses of his kingdom we find that his power has already extended some way into the old Viking country.

The building of fortresses in England was not inaugurated

---

* A S Chron s a (C 891).

† In Kemble, nos 333, 335 (A D 901 and 903), the title Angol- (or Angul-) Saxonum Rex occurs, in no 337 (A D 904) Eadweard called himself 'Rex Anglorum' These are the only genuine charters given .Ethelred, of Mercia, and his wife Æthelflæd, call themselves in their only genuine charter (K 330, A D 901). 'Monarchiam Merciorum tenentes, &c'

by Eadweard but by his sister, Æthelflæd the Lady of the Mercians. We first read that in A.D. 907 Æthelflæd restored the town of Chester which had lain waste for some time. The town (it is probable) became a mint under Æthelstan But we are not told that Æthelflæd fortified it.* A.D. 911 is the probable date of the beginning of the work of building forts. Æthelflæd's first burg is said, in the Chronicle, to have been at Bremesburg, which Steenstrup places in Hertfordshire Thorpe identifies the place with 'Bramsbury or Bramsby,' in Lincolnshire.† This identification is quite inadmissible, for it is impossible that at this date Æthelflæd's power could have extended into that country. If we accept Steenstrup's allocation we find her beginning near the boundary of her own and her brother's rule. Her second burg, 'Scergeat,' cannot be identified. After that we find her building upon quite the opposite side of her dominions at Bridgnorth, near the Welsh border, and therefore as much against her Welsh neighbours as against the Vikings.

The first burg which Eadweard built was upon the old line of division in the Ælfred-Guthorm peace, that is to say at Hertford on the Lea. But the country north of the Thames had formerly belonged to the Mercian half (Æthelflæd's half) of the West Saxon kingdom, so that it is clear that Eadweard's dominions had extended in this direction. The next burg was built further east, at Witham, half-way towards Colchester and in the country formerly assigned to Guthorm.

From this time forward the work of fortress-building went on apace. In A.D. 914–15 Æthelflæd further built Tamworth, Stafford, and Wedensborough,‡ in Staffordshire, Cherbury in Shropshire, Eddesbury and Runcorn in Cheshire, and Warwick. Then in A.D. 918 (?) Æthelflæd died. Her husband had predeceased her in A.D. 912, and they left only a daughter.§ It was unfitting that Mercia should any

---

* *A S Chron* s a 907 (cf y. 891), Fl Wig p 120
† See *A S Chron* (Rolls Ser) Vol I Index s. v Bremesburh
‡ Wardborough? in Oxfordshire, see *A S Chron* s a 915 and below p cxix
§ Æthelflæd's daughter, Ælfwyn, had been betrothed to Ragnald of York (the Ragnald, son of Ivar, whose biography is given in Vol I p lxix) without

longer be separated from Wessex; and Eadweard the Elder, not without some remonstrance, but without any active opposition, incorporated the Anglian state in his own kingdom.

The following is a table of all the burgs built by Æthelflæd and Eadweard. It is taken from Steenstrup's *Normannerne*, vol. iii., p. 42.

| BUILDER. | BURG. | SHIRE. | YEARS. | |
			ANGLO-SAXON CHRONICLE. [MSS. A–D.]	FLOR. WIGOR.
Æthelflæd	Bremesburg . . .	Hertfordshire	(B. C.) 910 (D.) 909 .	911
,,	Scergeat		(B. C.) 912 .	913
,,	Bridgnorth . . .	Shropshire .	(B. C.) 912 .	913
Eadweard	Hertford (Northern Burg)	Hertfordshire	(A. B. C. D.) 913	913
,,	Witham . . .	Essex . .	(A. B. C. D.) 913	914
,,	Hertford (Southern Burg)	Hertfordshire		
Æthelflæd	Tamworth . . .	Staffordshire.	(B. C. D.) 913	914
,,	Stafford . . .	,,	(B. C. D.) 913	914
,,	Eddesbury . . .	Cheshire .	(B. C.) 914 .	915
,,	Warwick . . .	Warwickshire	(B. C.) 914 (D. 915 .	915
Eadweard	Buckingham . . .	Buckingham-shire .	(A. B. C. D.) 915	915
Æthelflæd	Cherbury . . .	Shropshire .	(B. C.) 915 .	916
,,	Wedensborough . .	Staffordshire	(B. C.) 915 .	916
,,	Runcorn . . .	Cheshire .	(B. C.) 915 .	916
Eadweard	Bedford (Southern Burg)	Bedfordshire	(A.) 919 .	916
,,	Maldon	Essex . .	(A.) 920 .	917
,,	Cledemutha (Gladmouth ?)	South Wales	(C. D.) 921 .	
,,	Towcester . . .	Northamp-tonshire .	(A.) 921 .	918
,,	Waymere . . .	Hertfordshire	(A.) 921 .	918
,,	Huntingdon . . .	Huntingdon-shire .	(A.) 921 .	918
,,	Colchester . . .	Essex . .	(A.) 921 .	918
,,	Stamford (Southern Burg)	Lincolnshire	(A.) 922 .	919
,,	Nottingham (Northern Burg) . . .	Nottingham-shire .	(A.) 922 .	919
,,	Thelwall . . .	Cheshire .	(A.) 923 .	920
,,	Manchester . .	Lancashire .		
,,	Nottingham (Southern Burg) . . .	Nottingham-shire .	(A.) 924 .	921
,,	Bakewell . . .	Peakland .	(A.) 924 .	921

Eadweard's knowledge or consent. Apparently, therefore, there was a party in Mercia opposed to the claims of the West Saxon king, as indeed we should expect there to be.

Whenever a burg is completed we find that submission is made by the dwellers in the immediate neighbourhood. Æthelflæd's first burg was built subsequent to a victory which she had gained over the Danes at Tettenhall or Wednesfield.* This at least appears to have been the case, though the connection between the two events is not clear. It is probable that the West Saxons and Mercians fought together against the Vikings, and that the battle took place in A.D. 911 † Whether therefore it was brought about by Æthelflæd's work, or was the cause thereof, must be left doubtful. When Eadweard had built his burg at Witham, we read that a good deal of the folk submitted to him, which were before subject to the Danes ‡

But it was not to be expected that these works would go on without opposition on the part of the 'Danes' In A D 914 'the Army rode out from Northampton and from Leicester, and broke the peace, and slew many men.' This 'army' was eventually defeated. Except in the early account of the peace between Eadweard and Guthorm Eiriksson, we only now and then hear of kings being concerned in these risings. And we may conclude that a very large part of Danish England or Viking England was at this time under a republican form of government (see what is said above, p. xxx). Possibly we may divide Viking-England into three distinct divisions—East Anglia, where the proportion of Viking, or at any rate of Scandinavian blood was comparatively small, but which had been and probably was still a kingdom ; Northumbria, where the people were anxious to have a king as a counterpoise to the English kingdom ; and the middle region, parts of Cambridgeshire, of Huntingdonshire and Bedfordshire, Northamptonshire, Rutland, Leicestershire, a great part of Derbyshire, Nottinghamshire and Lincolnshire, where the Danes were settled in large

---

* Tettenhall in the Chronicle, Wednesfield in Æthelweard and Florence
† Steenstrup, *Normannerne*, iii 13 *sqq*, shows the identity of the battles of Tettenhall and of Wednesfield The site of the battle is in Staffordshire, but Danes from Hertfordshire may have taken part in it.
‡ *A S Chron* s a 913

numbers (this is the great region of 'bys' and 'thorpes'), but settled under a very loose form of government, divided into different 'armies' under different chiefs. One group of small republics was that known as the 'Five Burgs.'

We have in A.D. 915 an account of a new Viking raid It was directed first against the Welsh. The invaders took prisoner the Bishop of Llandaff, and were eventually defeated by the men of Hereford and Gloucester. Eadweard's severest struggle with Vikings at home took place in A.D. 921. A great army was gathered together from the land of the Mercian Danes, and of the East Anglian Danes These men sought on their side to raise fortifications: they built a fort at Tempsford in Bedfordshire, and from Tempsford they marched on Bedford. But this rising only led to further defeats of the Vikings. Tempsford was taken, and the 'king' [of that body of Vikings] slain. 'Thurferð and the holds, and the Army, which belonged to Northampton, north as far as Welland, the peasantry (landleoda) such as were left, submitted to King Eadweard, and sought his peace and protection; a great number of the folk, both in East Engle and in Essex, who had before been under the power of the Danes, submitted to him; and all the Army in East Engle swore oneness with him, that it would will what he willed.' 'And the army which belonged to Cambridge chose him to be lord and protector as he arede' *

We gather from these quotations, in what form Eadweard extended his power over England. The English folk in many places threw off the lordship of the Danes and became Eadweard's subjects once more: the Danish folk not singly, but in their constitutional bodies commended themselves to him; not thereby wholly abandoning their earlier form of constitution.

No doubt among themselves the Danish communities continued to be small republics within the state These 'armies' rise again to the surface in the troubled years of Æthelred II So do the Five Burgs, only now grown into the Seven Burgs, which notwithstanding seem to have been incorporated

* A S Chron. s a 921

in the English kingdom in Eadweard's reign, or at the latest in that of his son Eadmund. We know too that all Viking England—all Danish England if that expression be preferred—continued to bo governed by its own laws till it once more obtained a Scandinavian sovereign in Cnut. But for larger purposes of administration—for the furnishing of an army, for example, and the manning of a fleet—we may believe that England south of the Humber was now one.

Certain verses quoted in the Chronicle, speaking of Eadmund, Eadweard's son and second successor, assign to this king the especial credit of having subdued the Five Burgs. But that must, one thinks, have only been subsequent to a second revolt. For Æthelstan struck coins at two (or three) of these five towns.* And, as we have said, the Five Burgs are still a sort of political unity long after the days of Eadmund.

In every respect the reign of Eadweard the Elder is one of reviving prosperity for the English, and this character- istic is sufficiently reflected in his coinage. Ælfred's later coinage (the Exeter and Winchester coins for example) are a great improvement upon his earlier ones; and these later types are continued in the earlier coins of Eadweard his son. But, presently Eadweard's coins undergo a further improvement. The busts upon them are sometimes beauti- fully modelled and engraved, and remind us of the best drawings on Anglo-Saxon MSS of the period. The letters in the inscriptions are better made and more clearly cut than heretofore, and, in their reverse types, the coin- engravers launch out, as it were, into a series of elaborate

Coinage of Eadweard the Elder

---

* The attribution of the coins of Æthelstan assigned to Chester was adopted subsequent to the publication of a paper on the mints of Chester and Leicester by Mr Hyman Montagu (*Num Chron*, 3rd Ser, Vol xi p 12 *sqq*). Previously the coins were assigned to Leicester. The reader must be referred to the paper for the arguments by which Mr Montagu sustains the attribution which has been followed in the catalogue. They are of great weight. But at the same time it must be acknowledged that the time when we first find an English king beginning to strike at Nottingham and Derby, is precisely the time when we should look for a Leicester coinage also. It may be, therefore that the supposed Chester coins are Leicester coins after all

ornaments and designs (the hand of Providence,* the representation of buildings, &c), the like of which are not to be found either before or after—unless indeed we go far back to the peaceful and prosperous reign of Offa, king of Mercia, the reign which saw the first faint warnings of that great Viking invasion of which Eadweard in a certain sense saw the end.

It might even be fancied that the types of a building or a wall, such as those of the reverse of Pl. viii. 13 and 14, were commemorative of the building of the burgs, which had done so much to free England from the yoke of the foreigners.†

The Scandinavian populations in the British Islands, or even in the Scandinavian world generally, were at this moment entering upon a transition era which separates what may be called the First Viking Age from the Second Viking Age. When we read in the English Chronicle, as after an interval of forty years we do once more, the accounts of attacks upon England by various bodies of Scandinavians which begin almost directly after the accession of Æthelred II., we might fancy we had gone back two hundred years and were reading the history of the outbreak of the Viking era at the end of the eighth century. The names and expressions which we have been used to in the earlier age, 'the Danes,' 'the Army,' appear again in these accounts. But it would have been impossible for the Scandinavian people to remain stationary during these two hundred years; and, as a matter of fact, we know that they did not do so. Great changes had taken place among all the Scandinavian peoples since the moment at which

---

* This type of the 'hand of Providence' occurs on some imperial coins of the period (Dannenberg, *Deutsche Münzen*, pl 24, 563) This fact is interesting in view of the relations of Eadweard's son (and daughter) to the German Emperor

† Originally they were no doubt derived from the 'temple' type of Lewis the Pious It is possible that this type (like the monogram type) was introduced by the Vikings, and that the coin of Æthelred I which bears this type was struck by Viking invaders in East Anglia (cf Vol I p 94, Vol II p 27) In any case the buildings on Eadweard's coins are only remotely connected with this parent type

they first emerge into the light of history. We may place
the ending of the First Viking Era about the year 912,
which is the date of the treaty of St. Clair-en-Epte.* At
that date the extent of the conquests of the Scandinavians
was practically complete. During the era which preceded
it, out of the three parent Scandinavian countries had
gradually been built up a vast congeries of states, a
Greater Scandinavia. This Greater Scandinavia, with the
older countries, included (counting from the East to the
West) a huge district in the North and West of Russia
extending from Kiev to Lake Ladoga. It included Sweden,
Norway, and Denmark, and a strip of land in North Germany
(Mecklenburg), Northern England, Man, most of the Western
Scottish Islands, the Orkneys and Shetlands. There were,
further, large settlements in Ireland grouping themselves
into what were known as the three kingdoms of Dublin,
Waterford, and Limerick. Then there were the Scandinavian Colonies, the Faroes and Iceland, to complete this
great stretch of territories which were all inhabited by
peoples closely allied in blood, in speech, and in customs.
Here were ready to hand all the materials for forming a
great northern empire; and at one time it was quite within
the bounds of possibility that an empire might have been
formed out of these elements. For not only had the
northern states expanded in the way we have described, but
the constitutions under which they were governed had been
changing likewise. In the three older kingdoms at any rate
monarchies had been established on a tolerably secure basis,
and the establishment of these strong powers in Norway,
Sweden, and Denmark no doubt had an influence on other
Scandinavian settlements. The earls of Orkney (Orkney,
Shetland, and Caithness) were nominally vassals, for a portion
of their territory, of the kings of Norway, for another part, of
the kings of Scotland. But the earls of Orkney who appear
upon the stage of history at this period were men of very
strong character who made themselves into practically

---

* This date has been disputed by Mr Howorth (Archæologia, xlv 211 *sq*)
But not in our judgment on sufficient grounds

independent sovereigns. We know less about the rulers of the Western islands and of Man, or again about the kings in Ireland. But we may feel sure that in these countries also the very nebulous groups of Vikings, which resembled the different 'Armies' which our English Chronicle speaks of as settled, at the beginning of the tenth century, in East Anglia and Mercia, were beginning to group themselves into stronger and better-governed states.

There is another way in which the second era of Scandinavian conquest in England stands contrasted with the first. When the Vikings first came to England, or to any of the other countries of Christian Europe, they came as an army rather than as a navy. In other words, the Viking ships were not originally designed to take part in naval engagements, but were only ships of transport. The earlier Vikings could not fight at sea, for the simple reason that the Christian powers had no fleets to oppose to them. Among the Christian powers the English were the first who set about the building of fleets And in the earlier naval battles between the English under Æthelwulf, or under Ælfred, and their invaders, the former were generally victorious. During the period of the Second Viking Age all the Scandinavian powers had learned to fight at sea, and naval battles were their chief delight *

We have not yet arrived at the outbreak of the Second Viking Age, but so far as England is concerned at a transition era between the two. Among the English, as in other

---

* The era in which the word 'Viking' is found in commonest use, in the Sagas, &c , is during the latter part of the tenth century and the beginning of the eleventh 'Viking' signifies in this use neither more nor less than sea-rover, sea-adventurer But this is not the etymological meaning of the word *vik-ing* Etymologically it is either the man of the *vik* (bay) in the general sense, or else the man of the *Vik* (the Bay *par excellence*) i e the land on the northern side of the Skager-rak This etymological meaning must be the earliest one , so that the change in meaning to the general sense which 'Viking' has in the Sagas, implies a change in the character of the Vikings themselves These changes in meaning may be compared, in the first place (as a mere expansion), with the change in the meaning of the word 'Hellene'; in the second place (as a change from a proper to a general name), with such words as 'myrmidons,' the modern French 'suisse,' and so forth See *Cleasby's Icelandic Dictionary* (Vigfusson), s v 'Viking'

countries, an instinctive tendency towards centralization and stronger government made itself felt. This tendency was strengthened by the vigour of the West Saxon kings who, during the two generations which follow Ælfred, expended all their energy in absorbing into their kingdom the Danes south of the Humber. All the lesser armies or the smaller republics, such as those five burgs, Lincoln, Nottingham, Leicester, Stamford, and Derby, lose their distinct individuality and became levelled away into a larger Dane-Law, a district subject to the English kings though governed according to Danish law and custom. The country north of the Humber, however, remained, and we may surmise became more homogeneous and stronger by the same process which was simplifying and strengthening both the English and the Scandinavian states. So that a good deal of the sense of nationality among the Northumbrians, even among the English of Northumbria, rallied round the Danish kings of that district, and we actually find an Archbishop of York, an Englishman, taking the part of these foreign kings against the kings of Southern England.

The Vikings of Northumberland came very near to submitting to Æthelflæd. But they would not submit to her brother Eadweard. There had been talk, as we saw, of marrying Æthelflæd's daughter to Ragnald, a Norse king of Northumbria. This Ragnald was a ruler whom the Northumbrians had imported from Ireland. And he was only the first of a series of Northumbrian kings who all belonged to the same house, collectively this house is known in the Chronicles as the Sons of Ivar ('Hy-Imhair' in Irish[*]), and Ivar, the founder of the house, has been identified with Ivar, a son of the half mythical or wholly mythical Ragnar Lodbrog[†] The biographies and the coinages of these kings of the house of Ivar were given in the last volume,[‡] and it is not therefore necessary to repeat their history here. But what we have to note is that during the reigns of the

---

[*] Todd, *War of the Gaedhil with the Gaill* (R S), pp 268 *sqq*

[†] The identification is probably mistaken. See Vol I, Introduction, p lxix

[‡] Vol I pp liii, lxviii-lxxii, 231-238

three sons of Eadweard, Æthelstan, Eadmund, and Eadred, these kings do not at once disappear before the power of the West Saxon kings, as did no doubt the petty rulers in Mercia and East Anglia.

Æthelstan, about whose title to succession there was some doubt, was not at the beginning of his reign in a position to attempt the conquest of Northumbria from her new kings; the less so that (as we have said) the English Northumbrians showed that they had enough of the spirit of nationality or separatism left in them to make them ready sometimes to side with their heathen conquerors, rather than allow themselves to be incorporated in the West Saxon kingdom.

One of Æthelstan's first acts was to make peace with the present king of Northumbria, Sihtric Gale, and to give him his sister in marriage. Sihtric Gale died the next year, and Æthelstan was then able to take over the kingdom of York, and add it to his own kingdom He may have done this as heir to King Sihtric, or as protector of his sister. The act was not in all respects a prudent one: for it produced the first great alliance of lesser British princes, directed against the power of the English king. Howel, king of the North Welsh,* Constantine (III.), king of the Scots, and Eadred, king of Bamborough—i.e, Bernicia, the portion of Northumbria which had still been left to the Anglian kings though as under-kings only—were the members of this coalition. But they were, the Chronicle says, subjugated by Æthelstan, and compelled to swear oaths and give hostages to him. Guthfrið [Godfred], king of Dublin, who was a relative of—according to William of Malmesbury he was the son of—Sihtric Gale,† tried to make good his claim to the kingdom of Northumbria. Æthelstan, however, drove him from the kingdom. Guthfrið went first to the king of the Scots; but he did not deem himself safe there from the power of Æthelstan, and so returned to Ireland. A little later another unsuccessful attempt on the Northumbrian kingdom was made by one Turfer. It was probably subsequent to these events that

---

* 'West Welsh' the Chronicle says, by a slip of the pen.

† Wil. Malm G R A (E. II S), p. 212

Æthelstan assumed the title 'Rex totius Britanniæ' which we see on his charters and his coins. (See below p. lxii)

Then followed seven years of peace, the most glorious years which any king of Wessex had yet known. That the titles which Æthelstan assumed were not empty boasts, but that his position was recognised by foreign princes we know. We know that many foreign princes sought the hands of his sisters, the daughters of Eadweard the Elder. The most famous of these marriages was that of the Princess Eadgith (Eaditha), with the Emperor Otto I. Charles the Simple of France married Eadgifu (Eadgiva). This queen and her son Lewis, amidst the troubles which surrounded the late Carlings, sought asylum in England ; it was from England that this Lewis was brought back to be crowned king of the West Franks. Whence he is known in history as *Ludovicus transmarinus*, or Louis d'Outremer. Eadhild (Ethilda) married Hugh the Great, the father of Hugh Capet ; and Ealgifu (Ealgiva) married Louis, king of Provence, son of Boso, and nephew of Charles the Bald's second wife, Richildis Æthelstan had thus intimate relations with nearly all the Christian princes of Western Europe.

Æthelstan's greatness was recognised by the northern powers. Harald of Norway, now nearing the end of his reign, sent an embassy to England.

There are many accounts of the relations of Æthelstan and Harald. The best known story, the one told in *Haralds Saga Hárfagra*, represents the intercourse of the kings as hardly friendly. But we may believe the stories of the practical jokes (for such they really were) which Æthelstan and Harald played upon each other are apocryphal. We must only accept the outcome of the legend that Æthelstan did really become godfather to Harald's son Hakon, who was called Hakon Æthelstans-fostri. Harald Fairhair had no cause to love the Norsemen who were the foes of Æthelstan; for they were the men, or the sons of the men, who had fought under the banner of Kjotvi and his allies at Hafirsfjord. So that friendship between Harald and Æthelstan was as natural as were the friendly relations of Harûn-el-Rashid and Charlemagne. This relationship between England and Scandinavia is of interest; more especially in view of the part which the English coinage played in inaugurating a Scandinavian currency.

In the reign of Æthelstan we have the earliest numismatic record of the conquests of his father in the coins struck by the son at certain mint-places in Mercia, viz. at Chester (?), Derby, Nottingham, and a record of his own conquests in the coins which he struck at York. Another feature of the coinage of Æthelstan is the appearance on it of the title REX TOTIUS BRITANNIÆ [REX TOT. BRIT] of which we have just spoken. We find that this title appears on nearly all the coins with mint names, though in one instance, a coin of Derby, we have a reversion to the antique form Rex Saxonum.* We have already said that the title *rex totius Britanniæ* was probably first assumed after the submission at Eamôt (Emmet) of the Scottish and Welsh kings and of the Northumbrian Guthfrið.†

---

* Which never occurs on the charters of Æthelstan

† On the probably genuine charters of Æthelstan in Kemble we find the king signing or described as follows —

Charter no 345 (date uncertain)			Æðelstanus rex Anglorum, per omnipatrantis dexteram totius Britanniæ regni solio sublimatus
„	347, A D 929	„	regnum totius Albionis deo auctore dispensans
„	348, „ „	„	rex Anglorum
„	353, „ 931	„	rex Anglorum, per omnipatrantis dexteram totius Britanniæ regni solio sublimatus
„	356 (date uncertain)	„	rex Anglorum et æque totius Albionis, . rex totius Brytanniæ
„	357, A D 931	„	totius Britanniæ basileus
„	362, „ 933	„	apice totius Albionis sublimatus, totius Britanniæ rex
„	363, „ „	„	rex et rector totius hujus Britanniæ insulæ, . . . rex totius Britanniæ
„	364, „ 934	„	rex Anglorum per omnipatrantis dexteram totius Britanniæ regni solio sublimatus
„	369, „ 937	„	rex monarchus totius Britanniæ insulæ rex totius Britanniæ

In A.D. 934 Constantine III., king of Scotland, rebelled against Æthelstan ; and the English king sent a fleet and an army to invade his country. It was either just before or just after this event that Constantine married his daughter to Olaf Quaran, a Norse King of Dublin, and likewise, according to one tradition, the brother-in-law of Olaf Tryggvason, subsequently King of Norway.* Three years after this harrying of Æthelstan's in Scotland, Olaf Quaran came back to Scotland bringing with him another Olaf, Olaf Godfredsson from Dublin. A new coalition was formed against Æthelstan. Owen of Cumberland joined it. The fleet of the allies sailed up the Humber and took York Æthelstan must have been taken more or less by surprise. He craftily opened negotiations with the two Olafs But in the interval he and his brother Eadmund hastened the muster of an army. At length the English troops encountered those of the allies at the battle of Brunanburg, and gained that memorable victory the fame of which lives in song

From this time to his death (A D 940) the reign of Æthel- Ead stan was undisturbed On his death he was succeeded by his brother Eadmund, who was then only eighteen years of age. It was natural that when the firm hand of Æthelstan was withdrawn Danish England should think once more of revolt. The Northumbrians chose Olaf Quaran, the son-in-law of Constantine the Third, and one of the two Olafs who had fought at Brunanburg† (Vol. I., pp. lxx., lxxi.) We must remember that the last king of Bernicia had been driven forth, and there was now no ruler to represent the nationality of the Northumbrians. It is likely that since the time (A D 870) when Halfdan first 'gedælde' (divided) the Northumbrian land among his followers, not wholly dispersing the English, a *modus vivendi* had been established

---

* Vol. I p lxx, *Olafs S. Tryggvns* c 33

† 'Anlaf of Ireland' the Chronicle (**D**) calls him But this title is far from distinctive, as almost all the Olafs (Anlafs) who appear in history at this juncture came from Ireland The Chronicle is extremely confusing at this point, and the different MSS (**D E F.**) must be compared with each other and with the corresponding portions of the history of Simeon of Durham

between the two races, and that the English even were not
unwilling to welcome a Norse king from Ireland in default
of a king of the old Bernician stock. For we find that the
Archbishop of York, Wulfstan, allied himself with Olaf. The
Danes of the east too—of East Anglia and of East Mercia—
acknowledged him as king. It was for these republican
'armies' now a choice between Norse kingship or English.

Olaf marched first on Northampton; but this place he
failed to take. At Tamworth he was more successful. The
town was stormed with great slaughter on both sides. Eadmund upon his part had collected an army; he marched
therewith to Leicester and nearly succeeded in capturing
both Wulfstan and Olaf; but they escaped during the
night.* Eventually, through the mediation of the celebrated Odo, himself by descent a Dane,† who had been
lately raised to the Archbishopric of Canterbury,‡ a peace
between the two armies was brought about. The contest
had lasted for at least a year. The effect of the peace was
to make of Northumbria a legally dependent but practically separate Norse kingdom. Olaf accepted baptism; and
Eadmund stood sponsor for him, as Ælfred had done for
Guthorm; or as the Emperor Lewis the Pious had done 116
years earlier for one of the first converted Danes mentioned
in history.§ This event took place in A D. 942. Olaf
Quaran and his cousin Olaf Godfredsson, probably divided
the Northumbrian kingdom between them.‖ But Olaf Godfredsson apparently died in this same year 942; and
Regnald, another son of Godfred, became the second king in
Northumbria.

* *A S Chron* s a. 943

† *Vita S Oswaldi, Arch Ebor* (Raine, Archbishops of York, R S), p 404.

‡ Stubbs, Reg Sac Angl, p 14

§ Einhard, *Annales* (Pertz, i 212), Thegan, *Vita Lud Pii* (Pertz, vol ii
597, sq), Ermoldus Nigellus, *Carmina* l iv (Ibid ii pp 501-516)

‖ See Vol I pp. lxx -lxxi Olaf Quaran is supposed to have been the
brother-in-law of a third Olaf, Olaf Tryggvason, the king of Norway
(see preceding page and cf *Corp Poet Boreale*, ii 84), and the conversion of the Irish king may have been the determining cause of the
conversion of his more distinguished brother-in-law If so, this baptism of
Olaf Quaran was an event of capital importance in the history of Scandinavia.

If, however, Eadmund was compelled to behold a Norse Northumbrian kingdom established upon a more or less legal footing at one end of his dominions, he gained an equivalent by adding to the latter the whole of eastern England. Simeon of Durham, indeed, says that Watling Street was the boundary between the English and Northumbrian kingdoms * But this is certainly a mistake, a reminiscence, perhaps, of the terms of the Ælfred-Guthorm peace. The *Chronicle* specially mentions that the Five Burgs were added by Eadmund to his kingdom † What the exact meaning of this statement is it is not possible to determine. For on the one hand we find Æthelstan striking at at least two of these five towns, and possibly at three; on the other hand, we read of the burning of the seven 'burgs' (and these seven certainly included the earlier five) as much as seventy years later in the reign of Æthelred II.‡

Still, though we cannot define with precision, it does not seem that we have any authority to reject the general sense of the statement that Eadmund made, more completely than his predecessor had done, these Danish republics of East Mercia and East Anglia an integral part of the territory of the West Saxon kings. On the other hand there is no doubt that all Danish England, all the ancient Danelaga, continued to be governed by Danish law and ruled with a certain independence. Before Cnut came and divided all England up into earldoms, we find earls ruling in East Anglia and in Northumbria.

The kingdom of Olaf and Regnald in the north lasted only two years. In A.D. 944 Eadmund drove out both these kings He gave part of their dominions to Malcolm, king of the Scots; no doubt with the object of forestalling any such hostile combination against the English as that which had threatened Æthelstan at Brunanburg. Two years after this Eadmund was murdered by Leofa at Pucklechurch.

---

* Simeon Dunelm , *H R*. ii. p 94 (Rolls Series)
† *A S. Chron* s a 913   ‡ *A S Chron* s a 1015

f

d.   He was succeeded by Eadred the third of the sons of Eadweard the Elder In A D. 947 Eadred received at Tadcaster (in Yorkshire) an oath of allegiance from the Northumbrian Witan with Archbishop Wulfstan at its head. But in A.D. 948 the Northumbrians again revolted. This time they did not look for support to the Irish Norsemen, but elected as their king Erik Blóðöx, the son of Harald Háifagr Erik had been expelled from the throne of Norway by his half-brother Hakon, known as Æthelstan's foster-son. Erik, who had carried with him into exile a large fleet and army, came to York, and was there received as king. Eadred marched an army into Northumbria, and as an act of vengeance, fearfully ravaged the country. Ripon Cathedral was among the buildings burnt by the English army. Eventually the Northumbrians made peace with Eadred, and Erik was driven out But before long the Northumbrians once more took Olaf Quaran for their king, and then Erik for a second time * Eadred died in A.D 955.

Undoubtedly during the last two reigns we find a certain recrudescence of the power of the Norse kings in Northumbria. And in many ways the coins struck by the princes who reigned alongside of Eadmund and Eadred are evidences of this The coins struck by the kings of the House of Ivar are very different from those struck by the mysterious Cnut (Guðred-Cnut) and Siefred of the Northumbrian kingdom during Ælfred's reign. They are not barbarous fabrications such as those earlier Danish-Northumbrian coins ; but are modelled upon the contemporary coins of the Wessex kings, Æthelstan, Eadmund, or Eadred, from which in many instances they are clearly copied (cf. Vol. 1. Pl. xxviii. 4 [Ragnald] xxix. 4 [Olaf Quaran] with Vol. ii. Pl ix. 1, 3, 7–12, 14 [Æthelstan] ; Vol 1. Pl. xxix. 5 [Olaf], with Vol 11. Pl xi 9 [Eadmund] ; and Vol 1. Pl. xxix. 8–11 [Olaf and Eric], with Vol. 11 Pl x 5, 6 [Æthelstan] xi 2–8 [Eadmund], and xii 2–6 [Eadred]).

Again, how much power Eadmund and Eadred possessed in Northumbria during the periods in which they were nomin-

---

* See Vol 1 pp lxxi–ii

ally kings of that country it would not be easy to determine. Against the representations of the historians is to be weighed the fact that Eadmund struck but one coin with the name of the York mint and Eadred none. But then neither of these princes affected very much the placing of mint names upon their coins. Æthelstan's York moneyers are Adelbert, Æðelred, Arnulf, Ecberht (?) Heldalt, Rægenald or Regnald, Rotberht and Sinard (Siward); and of these eight names, four, viz., Arnulf, Ecberht (spelled Ecgbriht), Rægenald or Rægenold, and Rotbert (Rodberht), occur on the coins of Eadmund without mint names, two of the names, Arnulf and Rægenald, are, though not rare, sufficiently so to be fairly characteristic, and Rotbert is somewhat rarer. We may assume therefore that the coins struck by these moneyers, even when the pieces bear no mint-name, were struck at York. Arnulf and Rotbert occur again on the coins of Eadred We have to add Eadmund's known York moneyer Ingelgar, who struck for Eadred also This might in itself be taken as evidence of a continuous currency at the city of York. But on the other hand we have good reason for believing from a comparison of different writers that, as is said in Vol. 1, Olaf Quaran reigned at York from a.d. 941-944, and again from a.d. 949-952, while Erik Blóðox probably reigned from a.d. 948-949, and from a.d. 952-954. These dates are arrived at after a careful comparison of different authorities; for the evidence in regard to dates and periods is very conflicting at this point. It would be difficult to believe that Olaf with an array of eight moneyers and eighteen types, or Erik with his five moneyers and eight types, could have held the kingdom of York for a short period only. Let us further note that Olaf's and Erik's lists of moneyers have several names in common (Ascolu-Aculf, Farman, Ingelgar, Radulf) Eadmund has two of these moneyers, Farman and Ingelgar (the latter his known York moneyer) Of Erik's moneyers Hunred strikes also for Eadred.

It may be noted, by the way, that the occurrence of these names, Ingelgar, Farman, and Hunred, on coins of the Norse and English kings of York alike seems to dispose conclusively of the theory that the moneyers were not local people, but men who travelled in the service of the king

By the expulsion of Erik shortly before the death of Eadred, England gained definite and final possession of the Northumbrian kingdom, and under Eadwig a considerable York coinage is once more found

Put more concisely, the facts with regard to the coinage at York are:—

Under Æthelstan there is a considerable coinage at that town.

Under Eadmund and Eadred it almost disappears.

It reappears under Eadwig.

Then again—

Under Eadmund and Eadred we have a considerable Norse coinage at York.

Under Æthelstan and under Eadwig we have practically none.

If then we are to assume a continued extension of the power of the English kings during the reigns of the sons of Eadweard the Elder, we must suppose that during the reigns of his two younger sons the English rule was extended especially towards eastern England, among the Danes of the Five Burgs, of the rest of Eastern Mercia, and of East Anglia. This is of course more or less in accord with what the chroniclers tell us, for they represent the conquest of the Five Burgs as the principal achievement of Eadmund's reign. Eadred's great achievement was the subjection of the Northumbrian kingdom, though the effects of the achievement were felt not in his reign, but in those of his nephews.

We may consider that England's practical immunity from Viking troubles dates from the accession of Eadwig, not from that of Eadgar the Peaceful This was a sort of anti-cyclone between two storms, and it lasted for twenty-five or twenty-six years.

It was of evil augury for the future that England made this period of calm the occasion for bitter intestine quarrels, which at one time practically went the length of civil war. With the ecclesiastical disputes of this period we have nothing directly to do ; as it is impossible to see any way in which they could have affected the coinage. Their only interest for us is the degree in which they weakened England and prepared the way for the disasters which overtook the next generation. The first effect of the unpopularity of Eadwig was the separation of Mercia from Wessex, which took place in A.D. 957, two years after Eadwig's succession. We may, I think, assume that Eadgar who now obtained the rule of Mercia, ruled as under-king to his brother, just as the former kings of Kent, when they were brothers or sons of the king of Wessex, ruled as under-kings to the king of Wessex; or as Æthelbald, even though king of Wessex, ruled as under-king to his father the king of Kent.* We may assume, for instance, that the five moneyers who struck for Bedford under Eadwig did not all strike between A.D. 955 and 957. For though three of them were moneyers of Eadred (Baldwine, Boiga, Grim), the same three also struck under Eadgar. No doubt the effective rule belonged to the younger brother; and to him belongs the credit if, during Eadwig's reign, the Norsemen made no attempt, even partially successful, to wrest Northumbria from the English kings.

Eadwig died in A.D. 959, and then followed the reign of Eadgar, the fifteen most glorious years in the history of the kings of the house of Cerdic. Eadgar

During this reign the English and the Norsemen found fields for struggle outside the boundaries of the English kingdom. A disputed succession in the kingdom of North Wales invited the interference of English and of Norse troops. Eadgar espoused the side of Howel against his uncle Jago. The latter was assisted by troops sent by Maccus, the king of Man. Howel was successful; he paid allegiance to Eadgar as his over-king, nay, it seems that Maccus was himself compelled to do the same. Cumberland again—a larger country than the modern county—which had been over-run by Norsemen from Ireland and had long before been freed by Eadmund and granted as a fief to

---

* I e, that if he struck coins for Wessex he placed his father's name upon them

Malcolm I. of Scotland (or Alban *), was confirmed to another Malcolm by Eadgar.† These three princes, Howel, Maccus, and Malcolm, were three of the eight under-kings who gave token of their subjection by rowing Eadgar upon the river Dee. The remaining princes were Kenneth, king of Scotland, Dufnall, king of Strathclyde, Juchill, 'king of Westmoreland' (it is difficult to understand a king of Westmoreland by the side of a king of Cumberland and also a king of Strathclyde), and Siefer⁵ or Siefred and Jacob who are also spoken of as kings of Wales. Is it possible that this Jacob is the same as Jago, and that the uncle and nephew had found some sort of *modus vivendi* in North Wales? This celebrated row upon the river Dee—or say universal homage to Eadgar, as 'basileus totius Britanniæ,' took place in A D. 973, two years before Eadgar's death.

Coinage of Eadgar.

Of the coinage of Eadgar we have only to note that in the excellence of design and execution, in the number of the pieces struck, and in the number of the moneyers employed to strike them, it fairly well carries out the impression of magnificence and prosperity which the chroniclers attribute to this reign. We have also to note that there is now a considerable increase in the number of mint-places recorded on the coins. There exist coins of Eadgar struck at Bath, Bedford, Cambridge, Canterbury, Chester (?), Chichester, Derby, Dover, Exeter, Gloucester, Hereford, Hertford (?), Huntington, Ilchester, Ipswich, Leicester, Lewes, Lincoln, London, Lymne, Norwich, Oxford, Rochester, Shaftesbury, Southampton, Stafford, Stamford, Tempsford (?), Thetford, Totness, Wallingford, Wilton, Winchelsea, Winchester, and York.

Eadweard II.

The short reign of Eadweard the Martyr (A.D. 975–979) intervenes, and then we come to the reign of England's

Æthelred II. great disasters, that of Æthelred II. As generally happens in history, Æthelred's character has borne the chief part of the blame for the misfortunes which fell upon England during his long reign Æthelred's *sobriquet* of Unready does

---

* Skene, *Celtic Scotland,* 1 p 362
† Malcolm I, son of Donald, was slain in 954

not of course, as everybody knows, bear its modern signification, but means the Counselless. Freeman gives it rather a
technical meaning of one who acted without advice of the
Witan But it is by no means just to lay the chief blame
for all the misfortunes of England upon its ruler The
truth is, we see, during the whole of this reign, evidences
of a most extraordinary degeneracy in the English people,
for which it is impossible adequately to account; we see
treachery on all sides among the nobility, and very frequently cowardice among the people. It may be conjec-
tured that the English really had very much deteriorated
during the foregoing generations The country was like a
human body which has been overfed on too nourishing or too
stimulating food. It had not yet absorbed the large foreign
element which had settled in the country. It is probable
that the religion of the people had altered very much for
the worse. This is only to be expected when we remember
how very rapid and superficial had been the conversion of the
Vikings. The efforts of Dunstan and Odo to reform the clergy
were rendered necessary by the scandalous condition into
which church discipline had fallen; and no doubt the corruption of the clergy only reflected the corruption of the people.

In trying to understand the history of this new era we
must never lose sight of the fact that there were two lines
of cleavage among the inhabitants of England at this
moment: one a distinction of blood, and the other of
religion The party which represented the secular party of
the previous reigns, the party opposed to Dunstan would be
the people among those of English birth who were, when
the time came, the least bitterly opposed to the half-heathen
Svend in his claim to the throne of England; while of
course among the two nationalities who lived side by side in
England at this moment, the descendants of the Vikings in
the East and North, would be far more favourable to Svend
than the English in the South and West *

---

* Note in this connection an expression used in a verse in the A S
Chronicle (s a 1011) in speaking of Ælfheah the martyr—
    Wæs ða repling, se ðe ær wæs heafod
    Angelkynnes and Cristendomes

Superficially, as we have already said, the points of likeness between the beginning of this second Viking age and
the beginning of the first one, are almost absurdly striking.
It is curious, moreover, that the second age begins almost
exactly two hundred years after the first. We read how
the first age was preceded by a supernatural warning—a rain
of blood which Alcuin saw descending upon the minster at
York. Just before the beginning of the second age, that is
to say on the accession of Æthelred, a bloody cloud was
remarked in the sky. Probably it was only an aurora
borealis; but still it was accepted by the people of the
times as a warning of some coming terror; and the very
next year ravages on the coast began, just like those that
(to read the accounts in the *Chronicle*) began in England
towards the end of the eighth century.

It is probable again that the first invaders in Æthelred's
reign came either from Ireland or from the Western Islands,
and we know that that holds true of the first invaders in
Ecgbeorht's time. Down to Eadgar's time there had been
considerable fighting in the outlying parts of Great Britain
between the English troops and the Vikings of the islands,
and the relations between the English and the Norse
islanders were becoming strained. Maccus, the Norse king
of Man, took, as we saw, one side in the quarrel over the
succession in North Wales, and Eadgar took another.

But these and other points of resemblance in the first and
the second era of Scandinavian invasion are chiefly superficial. We have already pointed out how many points of
difference there were between the two classes of invaders;
this one among the rest, that this second army of Vikings
came in well-armed fleets ready to fight both by sea and land.

In A D. 980 we read that a naval force ravaged Southampton;
another ravaged Chester, and Thanet also was attacked.
The next year there was another fleet on the south coast;
Padstow was harried and the fleet likewise attacked Wales.
In A.D. 982 three ships came to Dorchester; and afterwards
they sailed round to London, which was partially burnt.
There were other attacks in 983 and 986; and in 989 Watchet
was ravaged. This year, too, is memorable for the death of

Dunstan. All these attacks were like the attacks which opened out the first Viking period, merely plundering expeditions, and without any great significance; but the Northern powers in general were, as we have already said, in a far better organized condition for making great conquests than they had been two hundred years before, and it is quite certain that both Denmark and Norway had their eyes upon England, which was already half Danish, and which was much the richest country of any which lay at all near the great belt of Scandinavian States which we described upon an earlier page.

In A D. 991 a fleet came to the east coast and attacked Ipswich; this fleet, it seems, was under the command of three leaders, Olaf, Justin, and Guthmund. The Olaf was the famous Olaf Tryggvason, who four years later was to make himself king of Norway. There is a long and fabulous history relating to this Olaf's birth, and to his early bringing up in Russia; but we really know nothing definite about him before his appearance at this moment upon the stage of history. It is very likely that he came from the Western Vikings, either from Ireland or from the Isles; his first wife, we saw, is said to have been a sister of Olaf, king of Dublin. This year, 991, is memorable not only for the appearance of Olaf, but for the battle of Maldon, in which the English ealdorman Brihtnoth strenuously but vainly endeavoured to resist the invaders, the memory whereof has been preserved in a fine Anglo-Saxon poem. After this defeat, the English paid their first bribe (10,000 pounds of silver) to the Northmen

In A D. 992 Æthelred gathered a great fleet at London intending to revenge the Maldon defeat and to drive the invaders from the Eastern Counties. But he was betrayed by one of his ealdorman, Ælfric, and the enemy had time to escape.

In A D 993, Bamborough, the Bernician capital, was stormed; the army then sailed up the Humber and plundered Lindsay in Lincolnshire This was probably a Danish army, for now a new Scandinavian foe had appeared in the field— the most powerful of all—Svend, king of Denmark

We have said that the troubles of this age are a good deal complicated by being a series of struggles, not merely between the English and Danes, but between heathens or half-heathens and Christians, or again between the high church or monastic party, the party of Dunstan, and the secular party: all these different interests acted and counteracted. Svend may be reckoned the nearest approach to a representative of heathenism. His father, Harald Blaatand, had been converted by force by the Emperor Otto I., but he had apparently taken to his new faith and become a rather zealous Christian; for he did his best to make Hakon, earl of Norway, his vassal, follow him in his change of faith Hakon resisted, and the result was that Norway substantially threw off its vassalage to Denmark and that Hakon became practically an independent king. Svend, Harald's son, who was often in rebellion against his father, apostatized. He had now again become nominally Christian, but his friendship with the earls of the family of Hakon and his subsequent opposition to Olaf Tryggvason, when he became the reformer of Norway, show that his interests were rather with the heathen party than with the Christian. Olaf when he came with Svend to the English coast was still a heathen, but according to the story in Olaf's Saga after he had plundered in England this year, he sailed to the Scilly Isles, where he met a very reverent hermit who converted him by a display of his prophetic powers. It was due to his change of faith that in the year 995 Olaf showed himself willing to come to terms with Æthelred and to receive confirmation at the hands of the English archbishop.

From this time England had two or three years' peace. In A.D. 995 an opening arose to Olaf Tryggvason to secure the crown of Norway Hakon, the old earl and champion of heathenism in that country, had made himself odious by his crimes, and now when Olaf arrived in Norway he found that Hakon had already been hunted into hiding by his bonders, and that everybody was ready to receive him as the representative of Harald's line. From that time to his death (A.D. 1000), Olaf was fully occupied in spreading Christianity by force in Norway and Iceland, and in preparing himself to encounter the growing hostility of his two Scandinavian neighbour states, Sweden and Denmark. The Western Vikings seem during part of the same period (A.D. 995-7) to have been much occupied in Wales, and Svend was probably engaged during these years in an invasion of Saxon and Sclavonic Germany.

Though Æthelred has received the most part of the blame for the feebleness of the English resistance, it was hard for him to find any among his thanes or caldormen who were to be trusted. A sentence of the Saxon chronicler must suffice us to explain the state of affairs, or rather to show that no satisfactory explanation is possible. Whenever a force was gathered against the invaders—

'þonne wearð þær æfre, þurh sum þing, fleam ástiht

there was ever through *some thing* flight determined on '[*]

When the king did take active measures it is difficult to see what purpose they had, unless they were merely dictated by desire for revenge on those who were most open to attack. His idea seems to have been to revenge himself for the incursions of foreign fleets by the massacre of the Norsemen or the Danes settled in his own country. Between A D 995 and 1000, England was left almost at peace. One fleet came in 998 to the Isle of Wight, another in 999 to Kent. They were bribed to withdraw Æthelred took this occasion for a strange display of energy. Though he had failed to meet the fleets that assailed him, he now set to work to attack the Norsemen settled in or hard by his territories. We read that in the year 1000 he ravaged Cumberland and attacked the Isle of Man Cumberland was at that time very largely inhabited by Norsemen who had come over either from Ireland or from the Western Islands, and it is quite possible that the men of Cumberland had furnished some contingents to the invaders of England But that the foreign fleets, least of all those that had come from Norway and Denmark, could be seriously injured by

---

[*] *A S Chron* s. a 998

the harrying of the Norsemen in Cumberland was an absurd notion. One authority states that Æthelred likewise sent a fleet to attack the dominions of the duke of Normandy. Acts such as these quite serve to explain the still more foolish and criminal act of two years later, the celebrated massacre of Saint Brice. The order given was that on Saint Brice's day all the Danish men in England were to be slain.* It is of course impossible to suppose that Æthelred contemplated a massacre of all the people of Danish blood settled in England, many of whom were, as Odo the Archbishop had been, champions, not of Christianity only, but of the high ecclesiastical party Others such as Ulfketil, the earl of East Anglia, were among the most capable defenders of England against the invaders But there can be no doubt that this slaughter of Saint Brice was, as it is always called, a massacre, and perpetrated upon men who were settled peaceably in this country and had no reason to expect attack. They may have been comparatively recent comers, but they had been allowed to settle themselves and become subjects of the English king.

The epoch of these two attacks—the attack upon the Danes in Cumberland, and the massacre of Saint Brice—was a very important one in the history of the Scandinavian nations. The year 1000 was the year of the great coalition made between the three Northern leaders, Svend, king of Denmark, Olaf, king of Sweden, and Erik, the son of Hakon, former earl of Norway. The coalition was directed against Olaf Tryggvason. Sigvald, the leader of the Jomsburg Vikings, a very celebrated little republic of fighting men situated at the mouth of the Oder, was drawn into the alliance and was induced to betray Olaf Tryggvason into the hands of his enemies. The three allied potentates lay in wait for Olaf as the former was returning from a friendly voyage to the Slav king who ruled in the country of the Oder, and as he and Sigvald were sailing in company past the island of Rugen. The battle which ensued—the battle of Svold—is

---

* Hét ofslean calla þa Deniscan men þe on Angelcynne wæron —A S Chron s a 1002, B C D

one of the most celebrated in Scandinavian history In it Olaf Tryggvason fell, and his death was followed by the partition of Norway, the southern part of which went to Svend, the western part to Earl Erik, while a strip was taken from the east and incorporated in the kingdom of Sweden. It was natural that the king of Denmark should have been a good deal occupied with these events and with the settlement of his rule in Norway. But when the news of the massacre of Saint Brice came from England it found the king of Denmark more powerful than he had ever been, and fully prepared to undertake in a more thorough fashion than he had yet done the invasion of England. According to the Northern Sagas he had always intended not merely to ravage the country, but to make himself master of it, and to drive Æthelred from the throne. He is said to have taken an oath to do this at his succession over the Bragi cup; but now for the first time he saw himself in a position to put his purpose in execution, while the Massacre of Saint Brice had given him a sufficient pretext for so doing.

In the year of the massacre, it should be noticed, Æthelred had married Emma (Ælfgifu, the English called her, after Æthelred's first wife), the sister of Richard the Fearless, duke of Normandy; by this act a new influence was imported into English politics. We shall have hereafter to notice the gradual spread in England of the Norman influence, which was, as we shall see, the counterpoise to the spread in this country of Danish influence, or of Scandinavian influence generally. It is curious that in the first year of definite Scandinavian invasion we find these two influences brought into connection in the betrayal of Exeter to Svend's army by a certain Count Hugo, a Norseman, who had been, through the influence of Emma, made the governor of that city.

It was in A D. 1003 that Svend returned to England to avenge the slaughter of his countrymen. He began with the siege of Exeter, which was betrayed to him by the abovementioned Count Hugo. In A.D. 1004 Svend turned his fleet against the eastern counties, burning Norwich and Thetford. This was the country under the rule of an earl or ealdorman of Danish descent, Ulfketil or Ulfkel Snilling, as he is called in the Northern Sagas,* who was son-in-law of Æthelred. Ulfketil was one of the most capable and devoted defenders of the English against the Danes; and this year he succeeded in beating back the enemy from East Anglia. In A.D 1006 a very severe attack was made. The fleet came first to Sandwich. They then settled themselves in Wight and harried everywhere in Hampshire and Berkshire Eventually 36,000 pounds of silver had to be paid to them. If Svend was willing to retire with these bribes, his intention of conquering England for himself could not have been very fixed.

Æthelred once more and for the last time made determined efforts to collect forces to repel the invaders. A law promulgated in A D. 1008 levied a universal land-tax for the support of a fleet. The law is the forerunner of certain taxes instituted by Cnut and Harthacnut for the support of a standing fleet and army which constitute the real danegeld known to English law, a tax which takes an important place in the compilation of 'Domesday.' At the time of the levy of Charles I.'s ship-money these laws were quoted as a precedent. We must take these laws into account as among the concurrent causes of the large coinage of Æthelred's and Cnut's reigns, along with the heavy payments made to the invaders—the danegelds of our history books. We have already said more than once that taxes and tributes more than internal commerce are the origin of large issues of coins at the period about which we write.

All the efforts of the English king were rendered abortive by the mutual jealousies and the acts of treachery of the thanes and caldormen who surrounded him. Fresh Danish attacks followed in the years 1009 and 1010; and in the latter year Æthelred paid a fine of 18,000 pounds of silver, the heaviest ransom that had yet been exacted

The year 1012 saw the martyrdom by the Danes of

---

* *Ólafs Saga hins Helga*, cc 13 & 23 (Unger, *Heimskringla*) In the earlier passage Olaf the Saint is said to have taken the English side in a battle fought by the Danes and English on Hringmara-heath (Hringmaraheiði) in Ulfkel Snilling's land In chapter 23 we are told that Ulfkel was killed by Erik, earl of Norway See p lxxx

Archbishop Ælfheah (Elphegus), which was the typical martyrdom of this second invasion as that of Eadmund was of the first. The two 'passions' were much the same in origin and circumstance; each victim sacrificed himself to save his people or his flock from further sufferings at the hands of the conquerors.

Finally, in A D. 1013, Svend sailed for England with the largest fleet which had yet been seen upon our coasts—and now the definite and decisive conquest of England was undertaken The Danish king received the submission of all England north of Watling Street, and a little later on of all England except London. From London king Æthelred sent his wife, Emma, and her two children, Ælfred and Eadweard, to Normandy to place them under the protection of Emma's brother, Duke Richard the Fearless. In January of the year following (1014) Æthelred himself followed, abandoning his crown to the Dane.

But Svend himself died the next month. It was said that he desecrated the shrine of St. Eadmund, the martyr of the first Viking invasion, in whose honour so many coins were struck; and that the dead saint from his tomb struck king Svend with a mortal illness to which he almost immediately succumbed.

Then Æthelred was recalled by the English party, by the Witan and by the Londoners. He was brought back from Normandy by a Norse fleet belonging to Olaf Haraldsson, or Olaf the Saint, who had already borne arms against Svend; and this fact is interesting, for it is the beginning of the long enmity between Olaf and Cnut On the other side, Svend's son Cnut the Great (Canute) was proclaimed king by the Danish fleet and army. But as a new king there were necessarily difficulties in his way. There was a pretender in Norway as well as in England. For a time therefore Æthelred seemed to carry all before him. He was supported by a stronger personality than his own—that of his heroic son, Eadmund Ironside Cnut returned to England in A D. 1015. He came in an immense fleet, part of which was furnished by his brother-in-law, Olaf, king of Sweden, known in history as Olaf Skotkonung This Olaf had been one of the three powers allied against Olaf Tryggvason at the battle of Svold; another of the allies, Erik, the Norwegian earl—celebrated already as a victor in two of the most famous engagements of the Scandinavian world—joined Cnut with his contingent. 'He,' says the *Ólafs Saga hins Helga*, 'was present at the taking of the castle of London, where he slew Ulfkel Snilling'—Ulfketil the East Anglian earl, Æthelred's most doughty champion.

London was not in fact taken during the lifetime of Æthelred, but he himself scarcely ventured outside of its fortifications, and there he died in A.D. 1016. His son, Eadmund, well called Ironside, was universally chosen as Æthelred's successor by the English party. He did all that it was possible for a man to do to vindicate his rights. He fought against the Dane with doubtful results at Pen Selwood by Gillingham, at Shoiston, and he relieved London which the Danish fleet was investing. But at last he suffered a severe defeat at Assandune (Essington), a defeat brought about by the desertion of one of his thanes, Eadric Striona, who had acted in a similarly treacherous manner on several occasions.

Cnut, says the Chronicle, there won him all the English people (þær ahte Cnut sige & gefeht him ealle Engla þeoda). Still the Danish king thought it wiser to come to a compromise with Eadmund, and at the treaty of Olney, England was divided in much the same way that it had been divided by Ælfred after the peace of Wedmore in A D. 878 Cnut took the whole of the country north of Watling Street and the Lea. Later on in the same year Eadmund was murdered — according to the Norse writers by the aforementioned Eadric Striona ['Henry' Striona].* And Cnut the king took all the English empire.† Eadmund Ironside struck no coins and can hardly be reckoned to have really reigned in England.

In reviewing the coinage of Æthelred II., it must be owned that in appearance it does not by any means tally

---

* 'Heinrekr Strjona,' *Ólafs S hins Helga*, c 24.

† .4 S. Chron (A) s n 1017, Her on þissum geare feng Cnut cyning tó eallon Angelcynnes ryce

with the picture of terror and suffering which the chroniclers draw for us during this reign. It has already been said that a large currency is not at this historical period an evidence of commercial prosperity to the degree that it is with us at the present moment. For coins were used much more for the payment of dues, taxes, or tributes than for the ordinary purpose of currency. It is evident that a large—nay the larger—number of coins coined by Æthelred II. were used for the payment of ransom to the invaders. For at this day larger hoards of his coins have been found in the Scandinavian countries than in our own; and, as we have said above, the National Museum at Stockholm is richer in this series than our own National Collection.* But at the same time it is hardly possible that such an immense number of coins could have been made unless there was a good deal of wealth in the country; and a good many things lead us to believe that in spite of the disorders in which England was plunged during all this reign, the wealth of the country was increasing. Professor Thorold Rogers has noted that the same thing took place during the Wars of the Roses.† It is not only that Æthelred's coins far exceed in number those of any previous reign; that might be an accident of discovery; but that there were in this reign more minting places than there ever were before, and a much greater number of people employed in striking coins.

At any rate there can hardly be a doubt that the wealth of England had grown enormously during the century which followed the death of Ælfred, and still more rapidly during the years subsequent to the accession of Eadgar. The wealth of England made a great impression upon the Scandinavian states of the north.‡ And the effect of the English wealth and the English currencies was more felt during Æthelred's reign than any other.

It is for this reason that in the history of the Numismatics

---

* Compare the catalogue by B L Hildebrand, *Anglo-Sachsiska Mynt i Svenska k. Myntkab*

† *History of Prices*, Introduction to Vol iv

‡ *Ólafs S hins Helga*, c 139 (Heimskringla)

of Northern Europe, Æthelred's reign is the most important of all during the period over which our inquiry extends. Owing to the fact of his heavy payments to the Norse and Danish invaders, Æthelred's coinage became known over the whole Scandinavian world, and evidently constituted a regular currency among the Norsemen in Ireland; to a somewhat less extent among the Norsemen of the Scottish islands and of Man; to a greater extent again in Denmark, Sweden, and Norway. And as in the early years of the eleventh century, the kings of these three last countries began to bethink them of issuing coinages of their own, they one and all modelled them upon the types of Æthelred's coins. Or, to speak with greater accuracy, in almost every instance they modelled their first issues upon one of two types of Æthelred. These types are our nos. iii. and iv. The earliest Scandinavian coins struck in Denmark, Sweden, and Norway respectively were issued by Svend, by Olaf Skotkonung, and by Earl Hakon Eriksson.*

It is curious that in this way we find the coinage of Æthelred II. symbolizing, after a certain fashion, the wide empire which was enjoyed by his successor on the English throne, Cnut the Great. And this fact, the fact of the contrast presented by the wide spread of Æthelred's coins among the Northern people, with the strict limitation of his power of which these very people were the instruments, should be a warning to us as to what conclusions we draw from the study of coins.

The only new types of importance introduced in this reign are those with the Agnus Dei and the Dove.

The accession of Cnut forms a supreme moment in our history We have more than once spoken of the Greater Scandinavia in Europe, that vast chain of Scandinavian states which stretched across the north from Russia to Iceland. England, which was now half Scandinavian in blood, stood almost within that huge arc. And if, out of this congeries of separate states, anything of the nature of a Scandinavian empire were to be created, it was before all things desirable that England should be drawn into it.

---

* Cf. *Num Chron* 3rd Series, Vol vii. p 233

The creation of such an empire Cnut effected. But as soon as he had completed the conquest of England he became an English king much more than a Danish. England became in reality the central state and the seat of government of Cnut's empire, which included this country, Denmark and Norway The kings in Scotland, not the lowland king of Scots only, but two highland kings, likewise acknowledged his supremacy. That he had any power in Ireland seems doubtful. Coins with the name of Cnut were indeed struck in Dublin; but so also were coins with the name of Æthelred The latter certainly could not have been struck by Æthelred himself: they were only imitative coins, the predecessors of a regular Dano-Irish coinage. In the same way we have no reason to assume that Cnut's coins with Dublin mint-marks prove that he had any actual rule in Ireland. Still his power was so great that but for one fatal flaw in the Scandinavian system of government, there seems no reason why his empire should not have been extended over the whole Scandinavian world, with the exception possibly of the Swedish states, *i.e.* Sweden proper and Scandinavian Russia, or Greater Sweden as it was called. For Cnut, as ruler of Norway, possessed Iceland and the lesser colony of the Faroes which were dependencies of Norway.

Cnut began his reign in this country harshly by putting to death several of the chief men in England who had previously opposed him or whose power he feared Among those who were executed was Eadric Striona who, as the Chronicle says, suffered deservedly enough.* Cnut likewise levied an enormous tax of 72,000 pounds of silver for England at large, and 15,000 pounds for London alone; an incidental proof of the high position in the country which the chief city of England had attained, of which there are many other proofs in the history of this time, and to which again the large London coinages of Æthelred and Cnut bear witness.

Taxes of this kind were no doubt heavily felt by the

---

* *A S Chron* s a 1017 The chronicler however only attributes base treachery to Eadric, not the murder of Eadmund

English; but they were necessary to the imperial aspirations
which Cnut cherished. He introduced the traditions of
the Vikings and of the Scandinavian nations into English
politics by constituting for the first time a standing army
and a standing fleet. Neither was very large. The Standing Fleet consisted actually of forty vessels; the standing
army was the crew which manned it.* At other times they
formed a body-guard round the king. These men who were
the far-off descendants of the *Comitatus* of the Prince in the
days of Tacitus's Germani †—went by the name of *huscarls*.
The designation was well understood in the north. No
doubt most of the members of this small standing army
were Scandinavians, and they would serve the secondary
purpose of guarding the king against plots or violence on
the English side. We read of one of the most famous
Earls of Orkney, that he had been commander of Cnut's
huscarls.

In A.D. 1017–18 there was a meeting of the Witenagemot
held at Oxford, which may be taken to mark the cessation
of the severities consequent upon the conquest. At this
assembly it was decreed that the laws of Eadgar should
be observed: we may understand by this expression the
laws which were in force during Eadgar's reign Both
Danes and English united in this decree, which foreshadowed
the principles upon which Cnut intended to govern his newly-
acquired kingdom. The reign of Cnut was as regards

---

* Saxo, p 524 (Muller) says that Cnut's standing army was 6000 strong
(60 ships, 100 armed men on each) If the fleet was of 40 vessels, 4000
would be the number of troops

† Mr William Hunt says (*Dic Nat Biog s r* Canute) 'the *huscarls* have
been frequently compared with the *comitatus* Their strictly stipendiary
character, however, seems to make the comparison invalid' But it must be
remembered that in days before a regular currency existed, the comitatus
could hardly have a strictly stipendiary character, and so far as concerns the
Scandinavian and English people we may believe that the companions of
the king did in very early days receive payment in the precious metals,
i e in the armlets or necklets which constituted a sort of currency The
words *hringbrjotr, baggifa*, &c, which are less epithets than synonyms for
prince, mean, it would seem, essentially the giver of rings (money) to the
household soldiers (*comites*, thegns, or what not), in other words, the enter-
tainer of a large standing force—*cui plurimi comites*, as Tacitus says, *G. c* 13

Britain almost a repetition of the reign of Eadgar. His conduct showed that he did not hold the throne as a conqueror, but as the lawfully elected king of the whole people. It is a marked contrast to the policy adopted by William of Normandy half a century later. The majority of Cnut's troops were sent back to Denmark : and he only reserved forty ships, the crews of which constituted, as has been said, his famous army of huscarls.

The terms of this agreement of Oxford were to a certain extent embodied in a series of statutes identical with or similar to those which bear the name of Cnut in the collection of Anglo-Saxon laws. We may assume that the coins with the legend 'Pax' (PACX) have some reference to the agreement at Oxford, or to the promulgation of Cnut's laws, and to the theory that the peace of Eadgar had been re-established.

We remember that the peace of Eadgar's time was by his descendants first broken through ecclesiastical disputes. In Church matters Cnut was a complete contrast to his father. It is quite possible that the story of St. Eadmund's miraculous vengeance is a contemporary legend. At any rate we find Cnut richly endowing the shrine which his father had desecrated. And on every side the Danish king was a liberal endower of churches and monasteries, not in this country and in his native Denmark only, but even on the Continent. No course could have been wiser from a mere worldly point of view; though we have no reason to suppose that Cnut was actuated chiefly by worldly motives. The founders of the second German Imperial house—or say the first truly German Imperial house—the Brunos and Liudolfs, dukes of Saxony, from whom were sprung Henry the Fowler and the emperors of his line, had been famous for their liberality to the Church. If Cnut desired that his power and wealth should be recognized by the continental princes, and that he should take his due place among the European powers, he could find no better way of bringing himself to their notice than by allying himself as he did by marriage with the German Imperial family, by endowing abbeys in France, and by making a pilgrimage to Rome.

With regard to his own government Cnut adopted a system not unlike that adopted by the emperors in Germany. He divided all his domains into great earldoms. Wessex was one earldom; it was governed by the celebrated Godwine. Mercia was another; its first earl was Eadric Striona, who, we saw, soon met the reward of all his treachery, being put to death at Christmas, A.D. 1017. East Anglia—under Thurkill, a Norseman who had at one time been a comrade of Olaf (the Saint) of Norway—formed a third; Northumbria —under Erik Hakonsson of the House of Hlade, the king's brother-in-law—formed a fourth; Norway, when Olaf had been driven from the throne, was entrusted at first to Hakon the son of Erik, whose house had given so many rulers to the country; but afterwards it was made into a kingdom, and Cnut's son Svend was made king of it. Denmark, when Cnut succeeded to that country, was ruled by Earl Ulf, the brother-in-law of Cnut, and likewise, through his sister Gyda, the brother-in-law of our Earl Godwine. Later on Ulf entered into a sort of conspiracy to make Harthacnut, Cnut's son, king of Denmark; and though Cnut seems to have consented to leave his son in possession of regal powers, his share in this conspiracy cost Earl Ulf his life.

Never therefore, during her history, were the prospects of England brighter than they were during this reign. Though England had been conquered by the Dane she was really the centre of his Danish empire; and if that empire could have been extended to include all the Scandinavian countries, she would still have remained so. The superior wealth of the country, the greater antiquity of its habitation, and the density of its population, its position in the centre of the great arc—say rather great *cusp*—of which we have often spoken, its proximity to the Continent, all tended to secure it a foremost position. But what more than anything else ruined these hopes, as they almost always ruined the hopes of extended Scandinavian rule, were the customs of inheritance which obtained among the northern nations. That which proved fatal to Danish power in this country, was the same cause which weakened the edifice of power which Harald Hárfagr erected in Norway, the custom of inheritance which divided the estate equally among the sons of the deceased. Thus one of Cnut's children succeeded in England, another in Denmark, and a third in Norway.

The result was not in strict accordance with the inten- Harold tions of Cnut. Harthacnut was the son of his wife of highest rank, in fact, his only legitimate son. Besides this, it had been agreed between Emma and Cnut on their marriage, that if she had any son he was to follow his father in England; and Harthacnut was the son of Cnut and Emma. Cnut had two sons by his first wife or mistress Ælfgifu,* Svend (Sveinn) and Harold; Svend he always designed to succeed to the kingdom of Norway, and Harthacnut during his lifetime became, as we saw, king of Denmark; probably he was intended to reign both as king of Denmark and king of England, so as to keep intact the greater portion of Cnut's empire. It does not seem that any place was assigned to Harold.

From what we know of the two brothers, Harold appears to have had the stronger character; they were equally unscrupulous Harold found a party of Danes ready to support his claim to the throne on the death of his father, and, as Harthacnut was absent from the country, all the advantage was on his side. He was however opposed by Earl Godwine and the more English part of the population If Harthacnut had at once come from Denmark to assert his claim, a civil war might have arisen; but as he still stayed away his party became reconciled to Harold.

Harold's principal and most disgraceful act was the measure he took to get rid of one of his rivals, one of the children of Emma and Æthelred II. Ælfred, the Ætheling, was enticed over to England and murdered, many people said by the connivance of Godwine. In the series of events which followed Cnut's death, we see the fatal process of decay which seems among the Scandinavians always to follow a prosperous reign and a period of extended empire. However great they were in other things, these people seem to

---

* Called Alfífa in the Icelandic Sagas, cf *Ólafs saga hins Helga*, c 252 (Heimskringla)

havo lacked some political instinct, the want of which prevented them from taking their proper place in history. Harold and his brother were inferior to their father in character, and Harold was much less popular in England than Cnut, so that the eyes of the English turned towards Eadweard (Edward the Confessor) the son of Æthelred. It was just the same in Norway, where the third brother Svend was unable to retain his hold on the kingdom. Soon after Cnut's death the chief Norse lendermen and the people generally reverted to their loyalty to the old line, and sent to Russia to recall the son of Olaf, Magnus the Good. Svend made but feeble resistance. In the course of a few years we find the tables turned between Norway and Denmark. While Harold was reigning in England, Harthacnut's power had very much decreased in his own kingdom, and Magnus succeeded in recovering a great part of the territory which had been taken from Norway and attached to Denmark. He might have carried his conquests farther, but an agreement was come to between Magnus and Harthacnut, whereby it was decided that the survivor of the two kings should be the inheritor of both.

Harthacnut's two years' reign (A D. 1040–1042) as king of England presents but few events which bear directly on his coinage. The most important was the levy of an extortionate danegeld to provide pay for the crews who manned the ships which accompanied the king from Denmark. The levying of this tax led to serious riots throughout the country, but more especially at Worcester, where a general massacre of the huscarls took place. The city paid heavily for this act of rebellion. The king came in person with his army of Danes, put the inhabitants to the sword, burnt their city, and ravaged the neighbouring country.

By such acts the Danish princes became more and more hateful to this country; and England, as Norway a few years previously, was anxious to revert to her old line of kings. After Harthacnut's death a new claimant to the throne of Denmark, of much greater abilities than the last king, appeared in the person of Svend Estrid's son, a son of Earl Ulf and a nephew of Cnut by his sister Estrid, or Ástríð.

The coinage of the period of Danish rule from Cnut to Harthacnut shows in its general appearance a continuity with that of the previous reign. In especial the likeness of the two series in the formation of the inscriptions and in the reverse types is to be noticed. For in these respects the coinage of Æthelred is distinguished somewhat—not perhaps from that of his brother Eadweard—but certainly from the coinage of Eadgar his father. The double cross on the reverse first becomes common under Æthelred II. (Cf. Pl. xv. 1, 3–5, 7, 10, 11 ; Pl xvi. 2, 7, 11, 12). This type has a certain fiscal significance; for the double cross was made to facilitate the cutting up of the coin into halfpence and farthings. This type of reverse becomes still more usual under Cnut and his immediate successors (cf. Pl. xvii.–xxi. *passim*) It was not afterwards abandoned ; and, as we should see if we continued our inquiries into the later English coinage, it long survived the Norman Conquest.

The whole appearance of the coinage of Æthelred II., as compared with that of the previous reign signifies an increase in fiscality, that is to say, in the use of a circulating medium, consistent with what was said above of the possibly increased wealth and trade of the country, even during the severest days of Danish invasion. Unquestionably the whole history of our Anglo-Saxon coinage points to the fact that if our Northern conquerors were great despoilers, they were likewise great founders of trade and commerce. In all these features the coinage of the kings of the Danish line is but a continuation of that of Æthelred II.

But in minuter points there are some changes. Especially we must note the introduction by Cnut of two varieties of obverse type : (1) the head wearing a pointed helmet, and (2) the head wearing a crown The representation of the pointed helmet is interesting. It is the same helmet which we frequently see upon the Bayeux Tapestry. But historically this type has no special significance. With the crowned head it is different It may have been a purely original device. But it may with equal likelihood have been copied from a similar type to be found on the coinage of the

Emperors in Germany about the same period.* It is to be noted that on the Continent a wider and wider divergence in type and general character between the coinage of France and Germany was at this time declaring itself. Though both series were descended from the earlier Carlovingian denarii, the types of different varieties of this coinage were becoming appropriated to the two divisions of northern Europe, the German-speaking and French-speaking territories. We have seen (long before) one type of Carling coinage—the monogram type—suggesting a type to Ecgbeorht. Another Carling type, the temple, suggested a rare type of Æthelwulf, and perhaps was afterwards copied by some king in East Anglia. But before the period at which we have now arrived the direct influence of the Carling coinage is quite lost sight of in the English currency. Not so, however, its indirect influence through that of Germany If we accept the theory that the crowned bust of Cnut was copied from the crowned bust on some coins of the German emperors, this would be the strongest example of the influence of the German coinage on that of England.

This is in such complete accord with the political history of England at this moment that there does not seem to be any valid reason for doubting that Cnut, who framed his Scandinavian empire so much upon the pattern of the empire of the German emperors, who had his earls of Norway, of Denmark, of Northumbria, of Mercia, of East Anglia, and of Wessex, as the German emperors had their dukes of Saxony, of Lotharingia, of Franconia, of Swabia, and so forth, deliberately adopted the crowned bust upon his coins in imitation of the crowned bust of the German emperors.

Under Cnut the number of mints does not diminish; and most of those cities and burgs which exercised the right of mintage under Æthelred continue to do so in this reign. Of the new mints which appear we shall speak under a

---

* Cf Dannenberg, *Deutsche Munzen der suchs u frank. Kaiserzeit*, Pl. 15, 311. [Otto III , 983–1002]

special heading.* We have referred above to the coins of Cnut which bear the mint name of Dublin.

The exact chronological arrangement of the types of Cnut is rendered not difficult by paying a due regard (1) to the types of the preceding and succeeding reigns, and (2) to what may be called transition types, those which combine a new obverse with an old reverse, or *vice versâ*. Types i.-iii. correspond closely with those which occur on the coins of Æthelred. It may therefore be concluded that these comprise the first issues of Cnut. They could not however have been struck before the death of Eadmund Ironside and Cnut's accession to the western portion of the kingdom. For the mints at which coins of these types were struck are Bath, London, Norwich, Oxford, Shrewsbury, and York. Coins of these types must have been issued in very small numbers, as they are all rare   The National Collection only possesses one specimen of type i ; and that so indistinct as to make the mint place illegible. Of types ii.-vii. it possesses no specimens   Types viii.-x. were evidently coined in large numbers, as numerous specimens of all are known. Of these types nos. v.-x. are all closely allied, and contain the two forms of the royal bust spoken of above, the king wearing a pointed helmet or a crown. While the idea of the crowned bust was, as has been said, probably suggested by the coinage of the emperors, the crown itself is no doubt the exact form of one worn by the king   We find him wearing a similar crown with three fleurs-de-lis in a contemporary MS. in the British Museum. This manuscript records the dedication of the abbey of Hyde, near Winchester, and there Cnut is represented presenting a golden cross to the abbey.† Types xi.-xvi. were probably issued during the second half of the reign, and they are nearly as common as those which immediately precede them; whilst types xvi.-xx., which occur also on coins of Harold I. and Harthacnut, are found in very small numbers, and may reasonably be assigned to quite the end of the reign. We have referred above to the inscription PACX

---

* See below p. cviii *sq*   † B. M. Stowe, 960.

which occurs on the coins of Cnut. Type xvi, on which the king is shown holding the Danebrog or Danish national standard, is perhaps the most interesting of all the types of Cnut. A similar representation is that which occurs on Northumbrian coins of Sihtric and Anlaf [Olaf] (See Vol I, Pl. xxviii. 3 and 5, and Pl xxix 1.)

The types of Harold I. follow in the like order. Nos. i.–iv. are but repetitions of the later types of Cnut; and nos v. and vi. we find again occurring during the reign of Harthacnut. It is a curious fact that of all the types of this last king published by Hildebrand, only nos. i. and ii. are represented in the National Collection, and the dearth of his coins of other types is general They have never been found in this country. That they are English we need not question, as they bear on them the mint names of London, Norwich, and York. The general scarceness of the coins of Harthacnut is of course primarily due to the shortness of his reign, but the fact that his coins are more common in the Scandinavian countries than here, shows that the English treasury was drained to support the army and fleet which Harthacnut had to maintain in Denmark against the ambitious designs of Magnus the Good.

Edward the Confessor.

When Harthacnut died, a portion of the English, or rather of the Danish population of England, desired to keep the Dano-English empire still united by offering the crown to Svend Estrid's son. But it may be doubted if Svend was at that time strong enough to accept it. Magnus of Norway had laid claim to the succession in Denmark, guaranteed by his treaty with Harthacnut, and for some time he continued to assert his claims. Meanwhile the more English party, headed by Earl Godwine, decided to offer the crown to Edward, Æthelred's son, then an exile at the court of the Norman duke. Earl Godwine acts in these negotiations the part of General Monk at the Restoration of Charles II. After Edward's restoration the earl of Wessex retained a position of much greater power than Monk was ever able to attain. The history of England from this time forward is almost more the history of the house of Godwine than of the house of Cerdic.

But at the same time a new element was beginning to enter into English history, namely the introduction of Norman influence; as Freeman says, the Norman Conquest really began in the reign of Edward the Confessor. The reign of Edward the Confessor is of great importance in the history of England on this account alone But it is a curious fact that no trace of the Norman influence is to be detected in the coinage of this reign. The coinage of Normandy, under the contemporaries of Edward—Robert or William—is undistinguishable in its general character from the other French coinages, royal or feudal. The coinage of Edward the Confessor, on the other hand, is continuous with that of the previous reign; and where it does show originality in types these changes are certainly not due to the influence of any French coinage. What is stranger still—though this matter lies outside the subject of the present volume—the Norman coinage in this country has no sharp line of demarcation from the Anglo-Saxon coinage, and it owes nothing whatever to the coinage of the dukes of Normandy. It is probable that for a while William himself continued to strike two distinct classes of coins — for his English subjects and for his Normans in Normandy. After that the coinage of Normandy ceases for a century and more.

It is not necessary therefore to trace at great length the growth of the Norman influence in England before the Conquest. We know that during the earlier years of Edward the Confessor's reign there took place a continuous influx of Normans into this country, and that the new comers gradually absorbed more and more the offices of State. Up to the year 1051 the history of this country is the history of the decline of the power of Godwine and of his house and the rise of the power of the Normans with Robert of Jumièges, who in A.D. 1050 became Archbishop of Canterbury, at their head. In A.D 1051 took place the banishment of Godwine. This was followed, however, in the next year by a counter-revolution; and English influence was once more supreme. This state of things continued not only till the death of Godwine in A.D. 1053, but, under his heir Harold, during all the remainder of the reign of Edward, which was indeed as much the reign of Harold as the reign of Edward the Confessor.

Harold II's reign, which sees the end of this reaction towards the Scandinavian side of English politics, is marked by the same tokens of weakness which sooner or later manifest themselves in the government of other Scandinavian countries. The different earls whom Cnut had appointed to govern under him in England,—the earls of Wessex, of East Anglia, Mercia, and Northumbria, —had during the weaker reigns of Cnut's sons once more split England into a series of smaller States, and the triumph of the Dano-English party meant the revival of the power of these earls. Wherefore as soon as Harold had overcome the rivalry of the Normans he had still to encounter the rivalry of the other earls in England, some of whom were members of his own family.

Let us note how the same sort of thing had been going on in other Scandinavian countries, how that Magnus, who had once all but succeeded in extending his empire over Denmark, had since found a rival in his uncle, St Olaf's half brother, Harold Sigurdsson or Harald Hardrada (Harðráðr). When Harald returned from his long residence in the Greek empire, he claimed half the kingdom of Norway Magnus divided his kingdom with Harald, and they reigned together on comparatively good terms till Magnus' death in A D. 1048, when Harald Hardrada became sole king of Norway. The English Harold did not settle matters so amicably with his kinsmen. The most serious of all the disputes and rivalries which had arisen among Edward's earls was that between Tostig, our Harold's brother, and the earls of Northumbria and Mercia, Morkere and Eadwine. Harold, we know, eventually sided with these earls against his brother, and Tostig was banished.*

There were two external forces threatening England. Magnus had once extended his claim as heir of Harthacnut, not only to Denmark but to England. So far as

---

* A. S Chron s a 1054-5 Wil Malm. G R A § 200   (C II S)

England was concerned he had gone no farther than to make some naval preparations and to send an embassy to Edward the Confessor to assert his rights.[*] Harald Hardrada, who was more adventurous than Magnus, and had probably a larger army of mercenary troops at his command, entertained, from the moment of his accession, the thought of asserting in a more active manner his claims to the throne of England. This was one danger by which the power of Harold Godwineson was threatened. On the other side of this country lay the territory of William, duke of Normandy, who, claiming to be the heir designate of Edward the Confessor, and the favoured of the Pope, was a more serious rival than Hardrada, and had stronger claims than his. When Tostig was driven from this country, he had thus a choice between these two powers, both of which were threatening England. He turned first to William of Normandy and obtained a fleet from him, with which he harried the south coast of England, but was eventually driven off. Then he turned, with far more memorable results, to the other claimant, Harald Hardrada.[†]

It is extraordinary to see how in this brief space the position of England in northern Europe had been entirely changed. Under Cnut, as has been pointed out, though she was a conquered country, England was in reality the greatest of all Scandinavian states, and stood in a position to become the seat of empire over them all; now that she had been shaken, as it were, from her moorings, and the other Scandinavian countries had drifted into separate policies of their own, she lay a prey for two rival claimants, the duke of Normandy in the south, the king of Norway in the north. The results of the prosecution of these two claims is well known. The fact that England was ruled at this time by one of her most capable sovereigns only brings the inherent weakness of her

---

* *A S. Chron* s a. 1046 (**D**). *Magnús S. Góða* (Heimskr ed Unger), cc. 37-39

† *Haralds S. Harðraða*, c 82

position into greater relief. Before the death of Edward the Confessor and the coronation of Harold, Duke William had begun his preparation for an invasion of England; for he knew that he could not acquire the crown by peaceable means only. At the same moment Tostig succeeded in persuading Harald Hardrada to undertake the invasion of the same country from the north. The Norse army arrived in Yorkshire, and sailed up the Humber. Harald Hardrada received hostages from all the northern provinces. He had only just done this, when there appeared upon the field an army which the English Harold commanded. Then followed the battle of Stamford Bridge, in which Tostig and Harald Hardrada were decisively defeated, and both were slain. Meanwhile the Duke of Normandy, having completed his preparations, set sail for England; and by the time that Harold had brought his fatigued army back to the south, William had effected a landing. Then followed the battle of Hastings, which brings our period of history to a close.

Coinage of Edward the Confessor and Harold II.

We have the same criteria for determining the sequence of Edward the Confessor's coinages, viz. the survival of types from the previous reign, the occurrence of transition types, and the survival of one type into the succeeding reign, which were our guides through the coinages of the Danish kings. We may assume that the types with a beardless bust are the earliest of Edward's types. Not probably because the king, who was in his fortieth year when recalled to ascend the throne of his ancestors, and about sixteen years older than the half-brother who preceded him on it, was ever without a beard. We have in the anonymous *Vita Ædwardi Regis*, a contemporary description of Edward: 'Hominis persona erat decentissima, discretæ proceritatis, capillis et barba canitie insignis lactea, facie plena et cute rosea;' * and on the

---

* MSS Harl 526 Publ in *Lives of Edward the Confessor*, ed Luard (Rolls Series), p 396 *Barba* might of course stand for moustache, were Edward ever represented, like Harold Godwine's son, with a moustache only '

Bayeux Tapestry, the king is always represented with a full beard, and is indeed the only figure who wears one Harold and Duke William alike wear their hair after the Norman fashion, that is to say, they shave all but the moustache It seems on the whole reasonable to suppose that the beardless bust of Edward the Confessor is a mere survival of the type of the previous reign.

The majority of the reverse types with the beardless bust occur also in previous reigns; they are the small cross pattée, the short cross voided beneath quadrilateral ornament, and the PACX type (types i.–iv.). The types with beardless bust which are new are the cross with expanding limbs, and the short cross with limbs terminating in three crescents (types v. and vi.). This last type is the connecting link between those with the beardless and with the bearded bust (type vii , &c). The most remarkable of the new types of this reign are (1) types ix. and x., known as the sovereign types, which show the king upon a throne; (2) the types with a facing bust (xiii and xiv.) The obverse of the sovereign type, which represents the king seated facing, holding sceptre and orb, is probably adopted from late Roman coins. The martlets in the angles of the cross, on the reverse of type ix, are commonly called the arms of the Confessor. The facing bust appears now for the first time on coins of the English kings; but it is a type destined to survive all the others. This type likewise may be derived from Byzantine coins; possibly, however, it comes from the German coinage Type xvii. with the reverse type PAX between two lines connects the coinage of Edward with that of Harold II., who adopts this type only. Whether this was mere chance, because it was one of the latest, if not the last type of his predecessor, or whether it was adopted designedly, we need scarcely discuss. Harold knew when he accepted the crown of England that he was beset by enemies on all sides, and his greatest desire therefore might well be for peace—a desire which, unfortunately for him, was not realized. Or we may suppose that he meant by adherence to this type what Cnut meant when he first adopted it, that the ancient laws of the country, the laws of

h

Eadgar, would be maintained in their integrity, and the peace between Englishmen and Norsemen reign as heretofore.

MONEYERS. The names of the moneyers contained in the present volume complete the list of these officials up to the time of the Conquest; and the whole list furnishes us with a larger contribution towards an *Onomasticon Anglo-Saxonicum* than is given by any other series of documents, not even excepting the Charters But there are some special difficulties in the way of making use of these names on the Anglo-Saxon coins which it is necessary to point out here.

In the first place, we are not dealing with the writing of lettered men—men lettered, that is, up to the standard of their age—as we are in the case of the charters. For it must be remembered that the names of the witnesses to the charters were always written by the clerk who drew up the document The duty of the witness was not to sign the instrument, but to attest it by placing his finger on the cross in front of his name; just as we to-day deliver as 'our act and deed' a transfer of land or of shares by placing a finger on the wafer which is attached to the document. The result is that we do not see any great discrepancies in the spelling of the names on the charters: an 'Ælfhere dux' or an 'Æðelwold episcopus,' whose name appears on some half-a-dozen different charters of about the same date, has that name spelt generally in the same way on each. Exactly how the signatures upon the coins were made it is impossible to say We possess no information as to the manner in which the various mints throughout the country were provided with dies for striking coins. In later times, at all events from Henry II. downwards, the supplying of dies appears to have rested with the Exchequer, even in the case of those which were used at the London mint Should this system have been in force before the Norman Conquest, we can then well account for a great similarity of workmanship and minute resemblances which sometimes characterize coins of the same type albeit struck at different mints This strong similarity might also have been brought about by the sending of workmen provided with patterns to the various towns.

But even if the types were supplied in this manner, there can be little doubt that the process by which the names of the moneyers were finally transferred to the dies was in the hands of unlettered people, who were capable of almost any kind of mistake in copying an inscription placed before them It does not affect the question whether these engravers were placing their own names upon the pieces or not; because, even if they were doing so, we must suppose them incapable of signing their own names, and ignorant of the value of the letters which expressed them. If, as is most probable, the great earls and thanes would have been unable to sign their names below a charter, it is not likely that an obscure coin-engraver in Norwich or Exeter would have been able to sign his name upon a coin. It follows therefore that the first class of errors in the proper names would arise from the mistakes which the engravers made in copying the inscriptions, through mere ignorance of the phonetic value of the signs set before them.

A further and subsidiary group of errors would arise in the mechanical process by which the inscriptions were copied and preserved. We have not now to do with men wielding a pen and writing upon parchment; but with engravers making use of one or two tools to punch in letters upon a coin-die. It would seem that they had two implements, or two classes of implements, to work with. One class we might liken to a blunt chisel on a very small scale—or even a screw-driver, the other class was of the nature of a gouge. The one implement makes the straight line in the letters, which is generally wo notice rather wedge-shaped, showing how the cut has broadened out at the end of the stroke; the other implement made the curves. In the formation of each letter the engraver uses one or other of his tools several times. Thus in the commonest form of A for example he uses it four times ($\bar{\text{A}}$); in B he uses it thrice (B). Here, then, we have another and a subsidiary cause of error. It is so easy for a man who understands very little of the use of the signs he is engraving to leave out or to misplace one of the three or four strokes which make up his letter; or to use the wrong implement, the straight one instead of the curved one or *vice versâ;* or even to alter a letter by the mere alteration of the angle at which he holds his tool. Thus B may become P; R may become F, D may become P, which might then be either P or W The slightest stroke will change L into C The faintest shake of the hand may transfer C into F A and H constantly interchange; so in fact do H and M; still more frequently do H and N. In this last instance we have another source of error, the confusion between the Runic H [=N] and the Roman N: it would appear that this confusion long survived the disuse of the body of the Runic alphabet. The smallest stroke gives us C in place of C. (See for examples of the changes of A into H and N, pp. 398 *sqq.* of the coins of Edward the Confessor.)

These errors of the engraver give us by far the largest number of mis-spellings with which we have to deal. Familiarity with the inscriptions gives the numismatist a certain *flair* for these mistakes. But he must always allow a very large margin for errors of this kind.

It has been necessary to dwell at some length on this point, on account of some of the criticisms which were made upon the first volume by writers who are not themselves accustomed to the handling of coins; and of the evidence which these criticisms afforded of how far the considerations which we have detailed above were liable to be overlooked by such writers. These critics supposed that there was no difficulty in deciding what name the moneyer had *intended* to write—as would have been the case had we been dealing with a clerk writing upon parchment—and that therefore the right reading of the name upon the coin was far more a question of philology than of epigraphy. This is by no means the case. The epigraphical considerations must first be weighed; the etymological come after. If, for example, we find a number of coins in one reign, or in a succession of reigns signed by a moneyer 'Earduulf,' and only one or two signed 'Eaduulf,' it is more probable that the engraver has in one or two instances left out the R than

that a new moneyer has appeared who only signs one or
two coins. This epigraphic question is not affected by the
consideration that Eardwulf and Eadwulf are perfectly
distinct names. The same argument would apply to such
names as 'Eadmund' and 'Eadhun'; seeing that H is
throughout these coinages constantly used for M, and that
the last letter of a moneyer's name is very frequently
omitted.

CYTELM would naturally stand for Cytel Monetarius,
and the name Cytel is very common in this coinage. But
if we had a number of pieces in one reign struck by
Lytelman and this form CYTELM only occurred once, it
would be more probable that the engraver of the coin had
made the slight, it might be almost infinitesimal, error of
changing L into C than that a new moneyer Cytel had
appeared in this reign. Any number more of such changes
might be instanced which, slight in themselves, would
convert one moneyer into another. And though both the
names might in themselves be perfectly natural, we should
yet have to consider (after the manner of Hume) where the
fallibility of the human instrument was most likely to
manifest itself. All attempts to decide such questions upon
primâ facie considerations of philology are therefore to be
deprecated.

The reader of this catalogue may here be warned against
a possible source of error which is inseparable from any
printed catalogue of coins. In the present volume about
a hundred different alphabetic forms are used, including as
many as twelve A's, not fewer G's, seven D's, seven or eight Ð's,
seven R's, seven S's—this is of course speaking only of the
single letters; when we include the compound letters the
number of types used in the following pages is increased
very largely. But it is impossible to give all the intermediate forms which actually occur. Take, for example, the
two letters C and F. We have among our types one intermediate form ⊦ which is neither one nor the other. But as
a matter of fact there may be infinite variations in the way
the two horizontal strokes are attached to the perpendicular
stroke. It is extremely hard for the cataloguer to decide

to which of two normal forms he is to relegate any particular intermediate one The same applies to the gradations between H and N. We have one intermediate form H ; but the gradations of the middle stroke are really infinite. M varies indefinitely between that form and Π, and sometimes merges into H, at other times into N P and D have the same number of intermediate forms , and B and D, B and R, V and Y, are very difficult to distinguish.

To set against these difficulties we have the advantage derived from the repetition of the same name a number of times upon the coins. For each variety of coin in the catalogue implies that a different die has been used for the piece, and therefore that the engraver has had a fresh opportunity of correcting his error. And, as has been said before, familiarity with the kind of mistakes that engravers commit allows us to strike an average between many different kinds of spelling and to approximate to the original form which the engraver has probably had before him.

As a matter of fact it is only with regard to quite the minority of names that we are left in any serious doubt. We may get a considerable variety in the spelling of a quite recognizable name, such as Burnwald, Byrnwald, Birnwald, Brynwald, &c. But on the whole the names range themselves into easily recognized forms. During the earlier portion of our history, both in this volume and in the previous one, the moneyers' names are of normal Anglo-Saxon character. That is to say, they are either monosyllabic, such as Brid, Dun(n), Man(n) ; dissyllabic, ending in A, such as Bosa, Buda, Diga, Ella, Hussa, Ifa, Lulla, Oba, Tata, Toega, Tuma, Wina, &c. ; or else ending in one or other of the characteristic old English terminations, such as -beald (bald), -berht (bryht), -broid, -el, -friδ (ferδ), -gar, -geard, -hæd, -heah, -heard (hard), -helm, -here, -hun, -ing, -lac, -laf, -mod, -mund, -noδ, -red, -ric, -sige, -stan, -wald (weald, wold), -weard, -wig, -wine, -wulf (ulf), with a few rarer terminations, -hyse, -uc (Duduc, Lulluc) Precisely the same is the case with the names attached to the charters of the same era No doubt there are some peculiar names, but by comparison very few

We might expect to find here, as in the charters, a certain number of Latin and biblical names   But as a matter of fact we hardly find any among the moneyers of the earlier period. Presumably these names were borne chiefly by ecclesiastics, and the moneyers were all laymen. When we come to Ælfred's reign we have among the moneyers a Samson, a Simon, and a Stefanus. There is nothing in these names to suggest that the bearers of them were not Englishmen.

But as we have already seen it is different when we get to some of the 'Viking' coinages which are contemporary with the coinage of Ælfred. In these we find two varieties of un-English names, some which appear to be Frankish, and others which are certainly Scandinavian. The former are at first the most frequent, but later on the latter become the commonest. It is not easy, amid all the varieties of spelling to which the moneyers' names are subject, to distinguish with certainty between English and Scandinavian names. But we see that certain very characteristic and quite unmistakable prefixes and suffixes are to be found on the coins of the later period: such prefixes as Arn-, Nor-, Od-, Ulf-; such terminals as -cytel, -fara (Irfara), -fugel, -leda. Ulf as a suffix cannot be distinguished from uulf, the proper Anglo-Saxon form—for the two forms are constant throughout the coinage (as on charters likewise).   Dreng again is undoubtedly Scandinavian; so, we may believe, is Winer, which is probably the O. N. *vinr*, slightly Englished.   Oda again is Scandinavian   Some of the Scandinavian names are particularly interesting, such as Sumerleda, Winterleda, Sumerfugel, Winterfugel. Those forms with 'winter' (instead of 'vetr') appear to be hybrids, or forms slightly corrupted by English influence

Fastolf is a good Scandinavian name, which has, further, no small interest for us both historical and literary   It is especially interesting to find Fastolfs at this date striking at Thetford and at Lincoln,—quite in the country, that is, of the well-known Caistor family, the family of the Sir John Fastolf of the Paston letters, the prototype (however really unlike him) of the far more famous Sir John Falstaff.

Concerning the exact status of the moneyers, something

was said in the Introduction to the first volume; though not much more can be said than that we are left without precise information on the subject. As was noticed in the first volume, the extract from the laws of Æthelstan there given seems to point the moneyer out as the actual fabricator of the coin. At any rate he must have been at the smithy to super-intend its fabrication. For if the coin was debased, he was to be punished by having his hand cut off and stuck up 'over the mint-smithy.' The story which Eadmer relates of how Dunstan insisted on the punishment of three false moneyers who were his villeins (*qui in potestate viri erant**) shows that as a class they were men who were more or less in a servile condition. This would not, however, prevent them from being men of some wealth; and it is likely that at the end of our period the right of coining was farmed out to the moneyers. This at least is implied in one or two passages in 'Domesday.'† It appears from all these entries that the moneyers received dies, and it is implied in most that they had to go somewhere (generally to London) to get them. If, therefore, the *monetarius* usually paid a sum down for the right of coining, he was without doubt a person whose position enabled him to put money in circulation He would be in something of the position of the tradesmen who issued copper tokens when a copper coinage was scarce at the beginning of the present century, or still more like the earliest issuers of a token copper coinage in England, such as John, Lord Harrington, in the reign of James I.

The inscriptions on the reverses of the coins throw no light upon the position of the moneyer. These inscriptions

---

* Eadmer, *Vita S Dunstani*, c 27, p 202, Ed Stubbs (Rolls Ser) The punishment inflicted was that decreed in the law of Æthelstan, the loss of a hand

† E g concerning the town of Worcester 'In civitate Wircecestre habebat Rex Edwardus hanc consuetudinem Quando moneta vertebatur quisque monetarius dabat xx solidos ad Lundoniam pro cuneis monetæ accipiendis" And of Hereford in like manner we read 'Septem monetarii erant in civi-tate Unus ex his erat monetarius episcopi Quando moneta renovatur dabat quisque eorum xviii solidos pro cuneis recipiendis et ex eo die quo redibant usque ad unum mensem dabat quisque eorum regi xx solidos, et similiter habebat episcopus de suo monetario xx solidos' The entries for Dorchester, Bridport, and Wareham are similar to that for Worcester

are, it is known, at first the name of the moneyer only, such as DUDD, LULLA, &c. Then a portion of the word 'Monetarius' is added BIORNFREÐ MONETA, &c. Finally the mint place appears, and we have at first ELI BAÐ, BOIGA MONET DEORABI, ᴄENARD MˉON EXE. These forms give place to the universal one with the name of the moneyer followed by ON (in), and then the name of the town.

It has been disputed whether the monetarius was or was not sometimes an itinerary moneyer travelling in the service of the king. There may have been a few moneyers of this kind, but the evidence of the coins is opposed to the belief that there were many.*

We must note that, though the earlier English coins contain a certain number of different contractions such as MON , MONET., &c , almost from the very beginning of the coinage the form MONETA becomes the usual one after the name of the moneyer. Later on it becomes—till the appearance of the mint-names—almost the stereotyped form. In some cases, notably for example in the case of the type introduced by Æthelwulf (no. xvii.), and continued by his successors and on the contemporary coinage of Mercia,† it is obvious that this word 'Moneta' is no necessary contraction, the exact number of the letters in the inscription being carefully arranged beforehand. The question therefore arises whether at this time 'moneta' could really have in the eyes of the coin-engravers stood for 'monetarius.' If it did so, why should they have voluntarily

---

* Mr Ernest Willett gives some statistics with regard to the moneyers of Edward the Confessor, represented in a large hoard found in the City—

'In the account of the City Hoard, Table V (*Num Chron*, vol xvi, p 375) occur 220 different moneyers' names, and an examination of the list will show that 155, or nearly three-fourths, *occur in one town only* Of the remaining 65, 32 occur in only two towns, and 11 in but three, reducing the number of widely distributed names down to 22, or just one-tenth of the whole Of these one, Leofwine, occurs in 19 towns, Godwine in 16, Elfwine in 13, Godric in 12 The rest are distributed as under four occur in 7 towns, four in 6, three in 5, and eleven in 4 '—*Num Chron*, 3rd Series, vol 1, p 33

These facts are certainly opposed to the notion of peripatetic moneyers

† See pp 21, 23 sqq of the present volume, and Vol I, pp 75, 76 Compare also Ælfred, type 1

assisted at this unnatural abbreviation? It is quite possible
that the form 'moneta' at first was a contraction, but that
afterwards it became a substantive word. In the latter use it
could only have signified 'money,' 'coin.' And in that use of
the word a legend such as TORHTVLF MONETA (p. 21) could
only signify Torhtulf's money. It is not necessary to suppose
that the engravers or the users of the coin were sticklers
for grammatical accuracy. It would be enough for either
to understand that 'moneta' meant money, and for them
to see the name of some moneyer before it to interpret
the legend in the sense we are supposing. And the supposition that they did so interpret the word 'moneta,'
receives confirmation by an observable tendency in the later
coinage to put the name of the moneyer in the genitive.
Under Æthelstan we get the form Paules, on which it would
not be wise to insist as it may very well have been intended
for Paulus. But such forms as Amyndes (Amundes),
Durandes, Gotæ, Regðeres, Sigares, Wihtes all under Eadmund; Agtardes, Boigaes, Crimes, Inguces (Ingulfs?),
Oðelrices under Eadred; and Cnapees,* Dunnes, Freðices
under Eadwig, are in the possessive case. It seems impossible to explain the occurrence of even of only these dozen
or so of possessive cases better than on the supposition that
when they were engraved, at all events 'moneta' had come
to stand in popular repute for 'coin,' 'money' only. But
if this were the case, it rather implies that the 'monetarius,'
or person who signs the coin, was the issuer thereof, in the
same sense, that is, that Lord Harrington was the issuer
of the copper token coinage in the reign of James I.

The coins described in the present volume present no
varieties of type to compare in interest with some of the
types described in the previous volume. We have no such
series as the sceattas or as the coins of Offa, king of Mercia.

---

* Boigaes, Cnapees, are of course ungrammatical forms, comparable to the
ungrammatical perfect and past participles (shooted, catched, etc) which
uneducated people use to-day It is possible that the OBAN on p 215
is really ODAN for ODA (see no 77, same page) This is a regular English
possessive case

The majority of the coins present on the obverse a bust, on the reverse some religious symbol. The varieties of these reverse types are moreover not numerous. We have first in frequency some variety of the cross, the cross pattée, the cross crosslet, and the cross moline; then we have A and ω combined, and the Ᵽ or Ᵽ . Very often these symbols appear on both sides of the coin. There are a certain proportion of coins which bear inscriptions in place of types on one or both sides. These are most frequent in the reign of Ælfred The coins of Eadweard the Elder stand out conspicuously by the variety of designs that they show, floral patterns, the hand of Providence, and various forms of buildings—one device seems to be that of a church, possibly the minster church of St. Peter at York.

Until the reign of Edward the Confessor the bust when it appears is always in profile. It is a traceable descendant from the bust on Roman coins, as for example on the *solidi* of Honorius or Arcadius, and at first following its prototypes is always a filleted bust and is beardless. Under Æthelstan we get in one type a crown or the suggestion of one, and this appears once more in the coinage of Eadgar. The coins of Æthelred II. show us for the first time the king wearing a helmet. It is a round helmet, and sometimes seems to have a spiked crown outside it. Under Cnut appears the pointed helmet such as we see on the Bayeux Tapestry, and for the first time a conspicuous crown similar to the crown on the coins of the German emperors. But of the types of the later kings we have already spoken at sufficient length.

During this period the busts on the obverse begin to show often unmistakable signs of attempted portraiture. The busts of Ecgbeorht, Æthelwulf, Æthelbearht, and Æthelred I., are purely conventional. Ælfred's coins show some attempt at portraiture which becomes much more apparent in the coins of Eadweard the Elder, Pl vii. 8 and 9, of Æthelstan, Pl. ix. 13, and Pl x. 2, 3 and 10, of Eadmund, Pl. xi. 10, and of Eadgar, Pl. xiii. 9. The workmanship of many of these coins is highly artistic. The beauty of the work is still more striking when we take into

consideration the extremely low relief of the engraving.
With the accession of Æthelred II. the art of the engraver
conspicuously declines, and we lose all traces of portraiture
for a time, the bust being again quite conventional, but we
find a revival of the latter at any rate on the coins of Edward
the Confessor, whose beard is as conspicuous and as much
of a personal distinction on the coins as it is in the Bayeux
Tapestry.

The whole of the coinage described in the present volume
is distinguished in its general character by its independence of the coinage of the Continent. The dissimilarity is
greatest between the coinages of the two nearest countries,
England and France. We have seen one type of Ecgbeorht
copied from the monogram type of the Carling *denarius*;
another type, the 'temple' type, imitated on a few rare
coins of Æthelred I * We have seen that the crowned bust
of 'Cnut' may have been suggested by the crowned bust
of the German emperors. The crowned bust, facing, of
Edward the Confessor may have come from a like source.
But in almost every other case where we find an approach
between the coinage of England and that of any continental
people, it is an instance of copying from England, and not of
the reverse process.

s

The rapid growth of mint-places, and their importance as
showing the increasing domination of the kings of Wessex,
have already been noticed. Of the laws which regulated the
constitution and the working of the mints, we know little or
nothing. The Anglo-Saxon Chronicle affords us absolutely
no information on these points.† The laws of Æthelstan,
however, are a little more explicit. In the first volume
reference was made to the enactments of the Synod held at
Greatley ‡ in Huntingdonshire, in A.D. 928, when it was
ordered that there should be one kind of money throughout

---

* Pl iv , nos. 5, 6

† The Charter in which Eadgar gives one moneyer of Stamford to the
abbey of Medeshamsted (Peterborough) is of doubtful authenticity (see
.1 S *Chron* s. a 963, and Kemble, 575)

‡ Schmid, *Gesetze der A S* pp 138-9

the whole realm, and that no one should coin save in a
town. Each burg was entitled to have one moneyer: but
certain places, on account of their importance, were to have
two or more moneyers. Thus, Canterbury was to have seven—
four for the king, two for the bishop, and one for the abbot ;
Colchester three—two for the king, and one for the bishop ;
London eight ; Winchester six, Lewes two, Hamtune
[Southampton] two ; Warcham two ; Shaftesbury two ;
Hastings and Chichester, though specially mentioned, were to
have one moneyer each. Many of the burgs availed themselves of this privilege granted by Æthelstan : yet we have
no coins struck during that reign of even some of the places
specially mentioned in the edict of Greatley ; such as
Chichester, Colchester, Hastings, and Lewes. It does not
follow, of course, that these places did not strike coins at
that time : all that we can say is that none are at present
known. A find of Anglo-Saxon and Oriental coins in Skye
in 1891 * has brought to light the new mint of Wardborough, one of the burgs founded by Æthelflæd. This
is of importance, as future finds will very probably increase the number of mints during the reign of Æthelstan,
and thus show that the privilege of coinage was of wider
extent than at present it can be proved to be   During the
successive reigns of Eadmund, Eadred, and Eadwig, the
number of mint places decreases, but with Eadgar they
again increase, till in the reign of Æthelred II. there was no
place of any note which did not exercise the right of coinage.
There is no doubt that the frequent and heavy payments
caused by the Danish invasions was one great cause of the
growth of the mints. The fines and taxes had to be paid in
coin, and this could not have been done had the number of
mints remained restricted   It was the easiest and readiest
way of levying a tax. Religious houses as well as very
small towns and even villages must have had to share in
the burdens, and this would in some way account for many
mints only existing for a very short time. Among such
places may be mentioned Bedwin, Brewton, Darenth,
Otford, Sidbury, Welmesford, Weybridge, Witham, &c.

---

* Proc Soc Ant Scot 1891-92, Vol xxvi p 225

The mint towns mentioned in Domesday form but a very small portion of such as were actually coining money during the reign of Edward the Confessor, and at the time of the making of the Great Survey.

The identification of the various mints is rendered difficult from the fact that as a rule only the three or four initial letters of the names are given in the inscription. London is often written in full, LVNDENE; sometimes LVNDONI, LVNDONIA. Lincoln is sometimes found written LINCOLNE, but we also have the form LINCOLLA. We have DEORBY, GIPESPIC, ĐEOTFORD, and in two instances DEORBII, ĐEOTFORDE. For Salisbury we have the forms SERBY and SERBI, which are enough to show that the whole inscription would have been SEREBYRIG or SEREBIRIG.

These forms are no doubt, properly speaking, those of the oblique case. But it is equally certain that (like the Celtic Kil- in place names, which is also an oblique case) this is the form of the word which survived the longest, and that from this termination 'byrig' in Æglesbyrig, Cadanbyrig, and the rest, the modern forms Aylesbury, Cadbury, &c., are derived. The Latin writers nearly always use this form, and we have in them frequently such phrases as 'quod Glastingabyrig nuncupatur,' 'quod Sceftesbyrig nuncupatur,' 'qui Searesbirig nominatur.'

It is evident from the passages in Domesday cited on a previous page* that the establishment of a large number of local mints was a source of considerable revenue to the king, which was augmented by the frequent changes of the types of the coins. The entry under Worcester which directly mentions the reception of the dies at London is important; it probably shows that the practice of issuing them from the Exchequer existed during the reign of William I. To what extent this custom prevailed we do not know. In later reigns it was general. But in these later reigns the position of the moneyer would be greatly changed. He was no longer the actual maker of the die on which his name occurred, but he became only the officer in

---

* P. cix.

charge of the mint, and as such was responsible for the true standard of weight and fineness of the coins issued by him.

The mints described below are either doubtful or else have been identified for the first time in the course of preparing the present volume of the Catalogue of English Coins.

Ashdown (Æsðedune or Æscedun) in the parish of Blewberry, co Berks, now usually called Aston-Upthorp, is first mentioned in *A. S. Chron.* s a 648, when Coenwealh, king of the West Saxons, gave 3000 hides of land there to his kinsman Cuthred. It was probably the scene of the famous victory of Æthelred and Ælfred over the Danes in A.D. 870. In A.D. 1006 it was occupied for a while by the Danes Why a mint should have been established at this place we have no evidence to show. The only known coins attributed to this mint were struck during the reign of Æthelred II.*

Bedwin (Bedewind or Bedewine) in the union of Hungerford, Wilts, is better known as Great Bedwin, to distinguish it from the smaller place of that name. There is an ancient camp in the immediate neighbourhood In A.D. 675 it was the scene of a battle between Wulfhere, king of Mercia, and Æscwine, king of Wessex. Ælfred gave land there to his elder son, Eadweard.† Edward the Confessor signed a charter there‡; and a grant of land at that place was made to the monks of the church at Abingdon. At the Great Survey ' the king held it, as also did Edward the Confessor: it was never assessed or hided.' The only coins of this mint in the National Collection were issued during the reign of Edward the Confessor §

Brewton or Brutun (Briutune) in the union of Wincanton, Somerset, was distinguished as the site of a monastery founded by Algar, earl of Cornwall, circ. A D. 1005, for monks of the Benedictine order.‖ It was for a time annexed to the abbey of St. Martin of Trouarn in Normandy. The manor was a royal one before the Conquest, and was held by William I, who granted it to William de Mohun, in whose

---

* Hildebrand, *Angl Mynt*, p 37

† Birch, *Cart Sax*, 553 (Alfred's Will)

‡ " Istud factum est ad villam nomine Bedewinde in camera regis," Kemble,

911　　　§ See p 312　　　‖ Collinson, *Hist of Somerset* vol 1 213

possession it was at the time of the Great Survey. The
coins of this place were issued in the reign of Cnut. It
is probable that the mint belonged to the abbot of the
monastery

Bridgnorth (Brydiga, Bricge, or Brigge) in Shropshire,
a burg built by Æthelflæd in A D 912 * There appears
to be no further record of this place till after the Conquest,
when the castle and land there were held by Robert de
Belesme, son and successor of Roger do Montgomery,
Earl of Shrewsbury.

Cadbury (Cadanburh or Cadeberie) in the union of Wincan-
ton, Somerset, was the site of a Roman camp or city, as many
Roman antiquities, coins, &c., have been found there. We
have however no records of this place during the Anglo-
Saxon period At the time of the Survey it was held by
Turstan Fitz Rolf, a Norman, who also resided there.
Alwold held the manor during the reign of Edward the
Confessor, and it was assessed to the geld of twelve hides †
South Cadbury (Sud-Cadeberie), close by, was also held by
Alwold, and later on by Turstan. The coins of this place
belong to the reigns of Æthelred II. and Cnut. (See p. 258,
and Hildebrand, *Ang. Mynt.*, pp. 41 & 207.) Though there
seems no reason why Cadbury should have a mint, there
can be little doubt of this attribution, as on the coins of
Æthelred II. the name of the place is given in full,
'Cadanbyrig.'

Castle Rising (Roiseng or Risinges) in the Lynn division of
the Freebridge Hundred, Norfolk. The evidence of this place
having been a mint during the Anglo-Saxon period has been
discussed by Mr. H. Montagu ‡ It is based on the doubtful
reading of the monogram on the reverse of the coin of
Ælfred (no. 155, p. 54). Mr. Kenyon read the monogram
CROINDEN for Croydon; Mr. Haigh read it ROISENG or
ROISENGER for Castle Rising (?) With this latter reading
we are more inclined to agree, and the coin is ascribed to
Castle Rising in this catalogue. Castle Rising was a place

---

* *A S Chron* s a 912.   † Domesday
‡ *Num Chron*, 3rd Series, IX 335

of considerable importance from a strategical point of view.
It stands on the Wash and in a district frequently attacked
by the Danes.   No other coins which can be assigned to
this place occur till the reign of Stephen, when the mint
appears to have been revived for a short period.

Corbridge (Corabridge) in the union of Hexham, Northumberland, was a Roman settlement, and during the Anglo-
Saxon period the site of a monastery.   There exist however
no records of this place earlier than A.D. 1138.   The only
coin which has been ascribed to this mint reads on the
reverse OIERHD MO COR *   It was struck by Æthelred II.
The attribution is, therefore, very doubtful.

Darenth (Darentune, Dærentan, Derent, or Tarent) in the
union of Dartford in Kent, derives its name from the
river Darent.   In A.D. 934 Æthelstan gave a grant of land
at Darenth to Ælfwald.†   In Domesday it appears as belonging to the Archbishop of Canterbury.   There is only one
coin known which can be attributed to Darenth.   It was
issued during the reign of Æthelstan, and is in the possession of Mr. H. Montagu.   It is of type v., and reads on the
reverse BEORHTVLF DARENT   VRB   In the catalogue it is
erroneously   given   to   Dartmouth (see list of moneyers,
Beorhtulf, p. 101).

Dereham, East (Deorham or Dyrham), in the union of
Mitford and Launditch, Norfolk, was the site of a nunnery
of Benedictines founded by Anna, king of the East Angles,
in A.D. 650 for Withburga, his youngest daughter, whom he
made prioress   The nunnery was subsequently destroyed by
the Danes; but the remains of Withburga were disinterred
and translated circ. A D. 974 to Ely, to which see the manor
of Dereham was given by Edward the Confessor ‡   The
only coins which can be attributed to this mint belong to
the reign of this king.§

Dorchester (Dorceastre or Doreccestre).   There were
two Dorchesters in Anglo-Saxon times, both places of
great importance, and either likely to have possessed a

---

* Hildebrand, *Ang Mynt* p 47   † Kemble, 361
‡ Kemble, 907   § P 356, nos 200-202

mint. It remains to determine whether the DOR on the coins is Dorchester in Oxfordshire or Dorchester in Dorsetshire

Dorchester in the union of Wallingford in Oxfordshire was an ancient British and Roman settlement. In A.D. 654 an episcopal see was established there, and Birinus was its first bishop It ceased to be a see from A.D. 705–870, in which year Leicester having fallen into the hands of the Danes, Dorchester was made the seat of the united bishopric of Dorchester, Leicester, and Lindsey. It continued to be a see until A.D. 1085, when it was transferred to Lincoln.* In ancient charters this place is styled *villa episcopalis*. There is no mention of Dorchester in Oxfordshire having received the right of coinage or of a mint.

Dorchester in Dorsetshire was also a British and Roman settlement. The first mention of it is in a charter of Ecgbeorht, A.D. 833,† containing a grant of lands at Wennland to three sisters, Beornwyn, Alfled, and Unalenburch. The town is there styled *villa regalis*. In Domesday it is again spoken of as a royal demesne. As, moreover, we are expressly informed in Domesday that in this Dorchester there were [in the reign of Edward the Confessor] two mint-masters, each of whom paid to the king one mark in silver and twenty shillings upon a recoinage, it is evident that Dorchester in Dorsetshire was the mint place during the Anglo-Saxon period

Geoðaburh or Joðaburh This place is identified with Jedburgh by Hildebrand.‡ Raine and Dixon identify in like manner Juðanburh with Jedburgh (Archbishops of York, vol. i., p. 116 , cf. A. S. Chron., s. a. 952; also Toller and Bosworth, A. S. Dict , s v Juðanburh). It would seem, however, that the usual names for Jedburgh were Gedword, Geddeweide, Gedewurth, &c It cannot, therefore, be said that this identification is other than doubtful. Jedburgh is not a likely site for the event mentioned in A S. Chron. s. a. 952

---

* Parker, Hist of Dorchester, pp 19–22 † Kemble. 232

‡ Ang Mynt p 497.

Hamtune (Southampton or Northampton). Both places, Southampton and Northampton, are called in the Anglo-Saxon Chronicle and at this period simply ' Hamtune '

Southampton, as the chief port in the west, was a place of considerable importance even in Roman times It was occasionally the residence of the Anglo-Saxon kings; and it suffered much from the incursions of the Danes. Frequent mention is made of this town in the charters of Edward the Confessor, and from Domesday we learn that it possessed two moneyers The Hamtune mentioned in the Edict of Greatley above referred- to* is also undoubtedly Southampton; for all the other towns mentioned in the edict are in the ancient dominions of the kings of Wessex

Northampton was captured by the Danes in A D 917 and served as their head-quarters circ. A.D. 921 In this year, being defeated by Eadweard the Elder, the Danes evacuated Northampton and for nearly a century the town remained undisturbed. The year 1010 witnessed another invasion by the Danes, during which Northampton was burnt to the ground; and in A.D. 1064, during the rising against Tostig, it was plundered and the inhabitants outraged During the reign of Henry II. it received the right of coinage. But the balance of probability is that Southampton alone enjoyed this right in the Anglo-Saxon period. The 'Hamtune' mint was in active operation from the time of Æthelstan to the Conquest, though coins of all the reigns are not represented in the National Collection.

Horndon (Horninduna, Hornyngdone, or Torninduna) in Essex is divided into three parishes, a division which appears to have existed since the time of Edward the Confessor (1) East Horndon was held in the reign of Edward the Confessor by Aluuin, one of the king's thegns. Odo, Bishop of Bayeux, also had twenty acres there (2) West Horndon, otherwise called Little Horndon, was held by two freemen during the same reign At the time of the Survey the manor was held by Edward son of Algot (3) Horndon on the Hill was in the reign of Edward the Confessor

---

* P cxiv

held by Uultic a freeman, probably the same who held East Horndon; but Eustace, Earl of Boulogne, and his under-tenant Garner held it at the time of the Survey.* The only coins of this mint were issued during the reign of Edward the Confessor

Jedburgh, see GeoŠabuih.

Lowik or Luffwick (Luucic, Lufwyk, or Luhwic) in Northamptonshire. Of the early history of this place scarcely anything is known. From Domesday it appears that the manor there was divided between the Bishop of Constance and the crown; as Edwin and Algar held one virgate of the former and Sibold one virgate and a half of the latter. The attribution of the coin reading LVVEIC (no. 20, p 195) to this place is therefore very doubtful.

Lymne (Liman, Limna, or Limene) in Kent. This is the Portus Lemanus of the Romans, one of their most important harbours. The harbour fell into decay at an early period of the Saxon occupation, and Hythe sprang up to take its place In the early part of the eleventh century the lands at Lymne were divided up into several manors. The most important of these was that of Aldington, which became part of the estates of Christ Church, Canterbury, in A.D. 1032. In Domesday it is entered under the general title of *terra militum archiepiscopi*, i e. 'land held of the Archbishop by knight's service.' Coins of this mint range from Eadgar to Edward the Confessor.

Maldon in Essex and Malmesbury in Wiltshire. The similarity in the spelling of the names of these two places makes it, when we have only the initial letters to guide us, almost impossible to distinguish between the coins of the two mints

Maldon is found as Mældune, Mealduna, Mealdune, Meldune, and Meldunum; and Malmesbury as Maildulfesbuih, Malmesbuiensis, Mealmesburh (Mealmesbyrig), Mealdemesbuih, and Meldunum Both places were of considerable importance during the Anglo-Saxon period The first mention of Maldon

---

* Morant, *Hist of Essex*, vol 1 pp 207–216, Wright, *Hist of Essex*, vol ii p 250

is in the *A. S. Chron.* s. a. 913, when Eadweard the Elder came with some of his forces into Essex at Mældune, and encamped there whilst a town was building and fortifying at Wiðam (q v.). Again in A D. 920 the same king came to Mældune and rebuilt and fortified the town. In the next year Maldon was unsuccessfully besieged by a joint army of East Angles or of Vikings from over the sea, and was again besieged and captured in A.D 993. At the Great Survey Maldon formed part of the royal domain, as the king had in it one house, and pasture for 100 sheep, and also 180 houses, which the burgesses held of him.

The first mention of the town of Malmesbury during the Anglo-Saxon period is of the burning of the burg by the Danes, circ A D. 878. The town was afterwards consumed by another fire and rebuilt by Eadweard the Elder. In A.D. 1015 (*A. S. Chron.*) after the murder of the thanes, Sigeferth and Morkere at Oxford, the king ordered that Sigeferth's widow should be taken to Malmesbury. The town owed its origin as well as its name to the celebrated abbey founded in the seventh century by Maildulf, an Irish monk, and is made illustrious by the writings of William of Malmesbury.

Newark (Newarcha or Newerke) in Northamptonshire was an ancient chapelry in the parish of St. John the Baptist, Peterborough. There exists some doubt whether the coin attributed to this town (see no. 13, p. 160) may not have been struck at Newark in Nottinghamshire, in which city a castle is said to have been built by Ecgbeorht. This manor was subsequently held by Leofric, Earl of Mercia, and in Domesday Godiva, his Countess, appears as paying the danegeld for it.

Newport (Niweporte), in the hundred of South Bradfield, Shropshire, is situated near Watling Street. There appear to be no records of its early history. Sir John Evans identifies this mint with Newport in Cornwall, the Celtic name of which was Lanstephadon, or the town of St. Stephen's Church.*

Northampton, see Hamtune.

Otford (Oðnford, Ottanforda, &c.), in the hundred of Cods-
heath, Kent, was the scene of the victory obtained in A D. 773[*]
by Offa of Mercia over Ealhmund of Kent (cf. Vol. I., p. xlv),
and also of the battle in A D. 1016 in which Eadmund Ironside
defeated the Danes. Offa gave the manor of Otford to the
Church of Canterbury, and at the Great Survey it was
assigned to the Archbishop, and continued to form part of
the possessions of the see till long subsequent to the Conquest.[†] There are no coins of this mint in the National
Collection A penny of Æthelred II, reading LEIFÐOÐ
MO . OÐN, is described by Hildebrand, *Ang. Mynt.*, p. 130.
It is of type IV. *var* a

Richborough (Ricyebuih) in Kent is the Portus Rutupiæ
of the Romans. Traces of Roman work are discoverable in
the ruins of the castle There are in fact no evidences
of Saxon occupation. Such occupation, however, might
very well have taken place, and yet have left no durable
traces either in buildings or in walls It is therefore with
considerable doubt that the coins with the legend RIC (see
pp. 289, 422) have been attributed to this place. There is
no mention of Richborough either in the Anglo-Saxon
Chronicle or in Domesday.

Sidbury (Siðestebuih or Sidebuih), a parish near Sidmouth,
Devonshire. This manor was granted to the see of Exeter
by Edward the Confessor during the episcopacy of Leofric,
and it was in the possession of that see at the time of
the Great Survey. The attribution of the coins described
at p. 231 and p. 292 (Æthelred II. and Cnut) is
doubtful.

Sidmouth (Sidmes, Sedemunde, or Sedemude), a seaport in
Devonshire. The most ancient name appears to have been
Sidemen. Numerous Roman antiquities and coins have
been found there At the time of the Conquest, Gyda, mother
of Harold II, was in possession of the manor of Sidmouth ;
but shortly after the Conquest and prior to the Great Survey
it was bestowed by William on the monastery of St. Michael
'in periculo maris,' Mont St Michel in Normandy. The

only coin attributed to this place has the mint name
SIDMES *

Southampton, see Hamtune.

Tempsford (Tæmeseforda or Temesanford), in the union
of Biggleswade, co Bedford, was fortified by the Danes in
A D. 921   Later on in the same year it was taken by
Eadweard the Elder, ' who beset the burg and fought against
it and slew the King, and Earl Toglos and Earl Manna, his
son and his brother, and all those who were there within.'
The city appears to have remained undisturbed till A D. 1010,
when the Danes took it and reduced it to ashes   The coins
attributed to this mint (pp. 173–174) were struck before
the place was burnt by the Danes

Tonbridge (Tonebricg, Tonebrug, &c.) in Kent. Of this
place there are no records before the Conquest. There
was an ancient castle there which is supposed to have been
built before that time. In Domesday the only reference to
Tonbridge is in speaking of Richard de Tonbridge, *alias* Fitz
Gilbert, who held the manor there and was also possessed
of land in various other parts of Kent   The attribution of
the coins of Æthelred II , ascribed to Tonbridge by Hildebrand, is doubtful †

Totleigh or Totley (Totleah or Totele) in the union of
Ecclesall-Bierlow, Derbyshire   Of this place there appear
to be no early records. The coin of Cnut, which is ascribed
to Totleigh, reads TOTEL ‡

Wardborough (Weardburh) in the union of Wallingford,
Oxfordshire. We have scarcely any records of this now
small and unimportant place. In *A S Chron.* s a. 913, we
find that Æthelflæd, lady of the Mercians, built ' in the next
year after midwinter that (burg) at Cyricbyrig (Cherbury)
and that at Weardbyrig,§ and that same year before midwinter
that at Rumcofa (Runcorn) '   Land at Wardborough was
granted by Eadmund to Wulfric A D 944 || Of this

---

* Hildebrand, *Ang Mynt* p 137
† *Ib* p 119, 3828-9   ‡ *Ib* p 304, 3566
§ Steenstrup, *Normannerne*, vol m , p 12, identifies this place with
Wednesborough in Staffordshire (see above p lu)
|| Kemble, 1148

mint only one coin is known. It is of Æthelstan, type v.
p. 103, and bears on the reverse the inscription BYRHTELM
MOT ÞEARDBV. This coin formed part of the Skye hoard
found in 1891, and the presence in the same hoard of coins
struck at Oxford renders its attribution to Wardborough
beyond question

Warmington (Wermington), in the hundred of Polebrook,
Northamptonshire, formed part of the possessions of the see
of Peterborough, during the Anglo-Saxon period; though
the documents which profess to record the grants of it are,
as in the case of Welmesford (q v.), not of the date which
they profess to be.* At the time of the Survey the abbey
of Peterborough still held seven hides and a half at
Warmington. Coins attributed to this mint read ÞORI or
ÞORIME, &c. They were struck during the reigns of
Æthelred II., Cnut, and Harold I.†

Welmesford, Walmesford or Wansford (Welmesforda), in
the union of Stamford, Northamptonshire, was also an ancient
possession of the see of Peterborough. The passage interpo-
lated in *A. S Chron* (E) s a. 657 records the supposed grant
of the manor to the abbey of St. Peter, St Paul, and St.
Andrew, at Medeshamstede, *i e* Peterborough, by Wulfhere,
son of Penda, king of Mercia; and a spurious charter in
Kemble (575) is supposed to confirm the grant. Welmesford is not mentioned in Domesday; but appears to have
been part of the knight's fees which Anketil de St.
Medard held of the abbey. The attribution to Welmesford of the coin of Cnut with mint name ÞELMIAE (no. 556,
p 296) is open to doubt.

Weybridge (Weybricca, Weybrugge, or Wibrieg) is in the
union of Chertsey, Surrey. Two hides of the manor of
Weybridge were granted by Æthelstan to the abbey of
Chertsey, A D. 13 Dec 933.‡ This grant was confirmed by
Edward the Confessor in A D 1062.§ At the Great
Survey the abbey still possessed two hides of land at Wey-

---

* Cf *A S Chron*, s a 963, and Kemble, *Cod Dipl. Sax*, 575
† Hildebrand, *Ang Mynt*, pp 163, 314, 375
‡ Kemble, 363   § *Ib.* 812

bridge, and Alured held them in the time of Edward the Confessor, and after his death. The coins having the mint name ᛈIB or ᛈIBR, struck during the reign of Cnut,[*] can only be doubtfully ascribed to Weybridge.

Winchcombe (Wincelcumb) in Gloucestershire was a place of residence of the Mercian kings. Offa of Mercia founded a nunnery there in A.D. 787. Two years later Coenulf of Mercia laid the foundation of a Benedictine abbey dedicated to St. Mary, which took the place of the nunnery. Coenulf was buried there in A.D. 822. The monastery suffered severely during the Danish ravages and was in a ruinous condition in the reign of Eadgar, when Oswald, bishop of Worcester, rebuilt it, and it was reconsecrated to the Virgin Mary and St. Kenelm.[†] The only coin which can be attributed to this place is that of Cnut, no. 597, p. 299.

Witham (Wiðam) in Essex. This burg was built by Eadweard the Elder in A.D. 913.[‡] There are no further records of it till the compilation of Domesday, from which we learn that it belonged to Earl Harold (Godwine's son) during the reign of Edward the Confessor. At the time of the Great Survey, Peter the Sheriff kept it in the king's hands, and it was some time part of the estate of Eustace, Earl of Bouillon, who married Goda, sister of William I. It subsequently reverted to the crown, and Stephen gave it to the Knights Templars.[§] A coin reading PIÐA, struck during the reign of Harthacnut [||] is attributed to this mint

In completing, as we do in this volume, the description of the whole series of coins struck between the time when the English first began to strike money and the Norman Conquest, it may be well to review in a few words the contents of the two volumes together, and sum up very briefly

---

[*] Hildebrand, *Ang Mynt*, p 307
[†] Rudder, *Hist of Glostershire*, pp 825-26
[‡] *A S Chron* s a 913
[§] Wright, *Hist of Essex*, vol. 1, p 216
[||] Hildebrand, *Ang Mynt.*, p 108

the chief points of historical and artistic interest which the whole series of Early English coinage has to offer.

English coinage began, as we saw, with the series of imitations of the money current among the Franks of the earlier Merovingian dynasty and of their neighbours the Frisians. We saw also reason to conjecture that, at the time at which this first English money was made, some Roman silver and gold coins and a very large number of small Roman copper coins were still current in this country. The first series of English coins consisted of a few gold and a very considerable number of silver pieces (sceattas), which were no doubt chiefly current in the districts nearest to the French coast. But they evidently spread through middle England as far as Northumbria, for we have coins of this series with the name of Mercian and Northumbrian kings. In Northumbria it is probable that the sceattas did not displace the chief currency of the district, which still consisted in the small copper Roman coinage of which we have before spoken, and the result of the introduction of the sceattas was that these coins assimilated themselves in appearance to the small Roman coins   The Northumbrian coinage, called the Styca series, changes from a silver to a copper one, and this Styca series endures until the conquest of Northumbria by the Danes in the year 868.

South of the Humber, the history of the English coinage is affected by the changes which took place in the coinage of Francia. In the latter country the house of Heristal introduced, before the end of the eighth century, a new type of silver coin by the coinage of what was called the *new denarius;* and this money was speedily imitated in England in the penny coinage of Offa (probably struck in Kent) as also in the penny coinages of the kings of Kent, the Archbishops of Canterbury, and a few of the kings of East Anglia. Between the battle of Ellandune in A D. 825, and the death of Burgred in A D. 874, we watch the other South Humbrian coinages disappear and that of Wessex alone survive. As we have pointed out, the early so-called Wessex coins were probably at first struck only in Kent.

The two classes of coins, then, which mark the beginning

of an English coinage—the sceattas of the seventh and eighth centuries and the pennies which succeeded them—were both derived, so far as regards their general appearance and fabric, from similar (Merovingian and Carolingian) coinages on the Continent. But from the very beginning of the English coinage a great originality is shown in the details of the fabrication, such as in the choice of the types, in the forms of the letters in the inscription, &c. In truth the originality is even more conspicuous on the earliest coins,—in the sceattas, for example, and on the first coins issued by Offa, than it is on the later pieces. Still on the whole we may say that in respect of type and general appearance the English currency throughout is markedly independent of influences coming from the Continent. The continental coinage develops into two distinct branches, the French and the German. The English coinage stands apart from both as a distinct series. All these facts argue a very considerable wealth and remarkable commercial activity in this country.

The incursions of the Vikings and the first coins struck by a Scandinavian people during the latter half of the ninth century form the next important feature in the history of the English coinage.

One of these different series of Scandinavian coinages is imitated rather from the Frankish coinage than from the English (See Vol. I pp 204-229, and Pl. xxiv.-xxvii) All the other coins which were struck by or under the influence of Scandinavian conquerors in England, are no more than debased imitations of the current coinage of the country It is at this time that the names of the moneyers upon coins begin to show a curious infusion of foreign elements, and not Scandinavian elements only, among the population of England. In Ælfred's reign we have to note the beginning of the practice of adding the names of mint-places upon the coins, the only mint-places which had before his reign been mentioned on any coins being London Vol. I pp 10-11) and Canterbury (Vol. I. p 41 and Vol. II. pp. 6, 13-14) The chief interest to be found in the mint-names on the coins begins during the reign of Æthelstan.

For in the whole series of coins from this reign down to the reign of Eadgar we have continuous evidence of the recovery by the kings of Wessex of the country from the hands of the Danes. With the exception of three reigns, those of Eadmund, Eadred, and Eadwig, the number of mint-places recorded by the coins goes on continually increasing to the time of Æthelred II.

After the reign of Eadgar we notice a certain change in the appearance of the coins The dies appear to have been made more roughly than heretofore, and we may infer that a greater number of coins than previously were struck from the same die. It is difficult to describe in words this change in the appearance of the English coins; but the general effect of it on the eye and mind is to suggest that after the death of Eadgar, or at any rate after the accession of Æthelred II., the number of pieces issued was considerably greater than at any previous time, and that the more purely commercial character of the coinage was exclusively kept in view, while a striving after art in the manufacture of the dies almost disappeared. Indeed the amount of money coined in the reign of Æthelred II. must have been enormous The payments which are recorded to have been made at various times in this reign and the next—10,000 lbs. of silver, 16,000 lbs., 45,000 lbs., 87,000 lbs.—imply an enormous currency, even though we admit that these large sums could not all have been paid in specie. That such payments in any form should have been possible despite all the misfortunes of England implies that her commercial prosperity had been continually on the increase

In the reign of Æthelred II. we have further that important event in the history of the English coinage, in some respects the most important event of all, the initiative which it gave to the creation of a Scandinavian coinage—currencies initiated by the Danes in Ireland and in Scotland and other currencies for Denmark, for Sweden, and for Norway. As we have already said, the coinage of Æthelred and its imitations symbolize the wide rule of Cnut, who might have built up a lasting Scandinavian Empire if Cnut had had worthy successors, or if the Scandinavian customs of inheritance could have been broken through. Undoubtedly this enormous currency of Æthelred's coinage, and of imitations of it throughout all Scandinavian lands, must have led to an increase in trade between England and other northern countries and paved the way for intercourse of all kinds We know how much the English chronicles are concerned with Norwegian and Danish history at this time, and how much the Icelandic Sagas have to tell us about English history.

Some further tokens of the power and the ambition of Cnut are given by the adoption upon the coinage of a crowned bust, probably copied from the bust on the Imperial German coins, and one or two instances which occur at this time of the copying of German types upon the English money, or the converse, suggest that our relations were (through Denmark and Frisia) rather more with the German Empire than with France The whole state of affairs changed when Edward the Confessor mounted the throne, and Norman influences began to be felt in this country

This history of the spread of English coinages in the North marks the end of the influence of English coinage before the Conquest As we have said, the influence of the new power—the Norman—though it began to be felt during the reign of Edward the Confessor, is not reflected so far as we can gather upon the coinage Perhaps in one case we may see a reflection of it in the so-called 'Sovereign type' of Edward the Confessor, which is the first appearance of what we may call a coat-of-arms upon coins

Thus far as regards the historical interest of the English coinage. Its artistic interest is, of course, very much smaller; but still it is not without artistic interest. In the earliest series of all, the sceatta series, we have a number and variety of designs which in proportion to the extent of the issue is perhaps without precedent in any other coinage of the world. The designs on the sceattas are not themselves for the most part artistically beautiful, but in any history of the development of ornament they ought to take a conspicuous place They present, as was shown in the first volume, some striking examples of the degradation of types, and through degradation of the evolution of fresh types. In the first volume a good deal of space was allotted to tracing the origin, the development, &c, of these designs.

Then, again, the coins of Offa are in a way monuments of artistic excellence, and in the history of Anglo-Saxon art, and of its development out of Celtic art, these coin-types deserve a place alongside of the illuminated manuscripts of the period. After Offa's reign we continue from time to time to have coins which are artistically beautiful Some heads on the money of Eadweard the Elder afford the best examples perhaps of the kind of work of which we are speaking, these, again, could not be neglected in any history of Anglo-Saxon art But after this time, or at any rate after the reign of Eadgar, as we have just stated, the English coinage ceases to have any artistic merit, and an artistic coinage does not again appear in England until the reign of Edward I of the Angevin or Plantagenet line.

In the preparation of this Catalogue the compilers have been under special obligations to Sir John Evans, K C B., Treas R S., who has read the proofs of the Catalogue, and to Mr. H. Montagu, F S A, who has placed at their disposal his manuscript notes on the early coinage of Wessex, and has supplied lists of unpublished moneyers. Their thanks are also due to the Rev. E McClure for his notes on that portion of the Introduction which deals with the mints

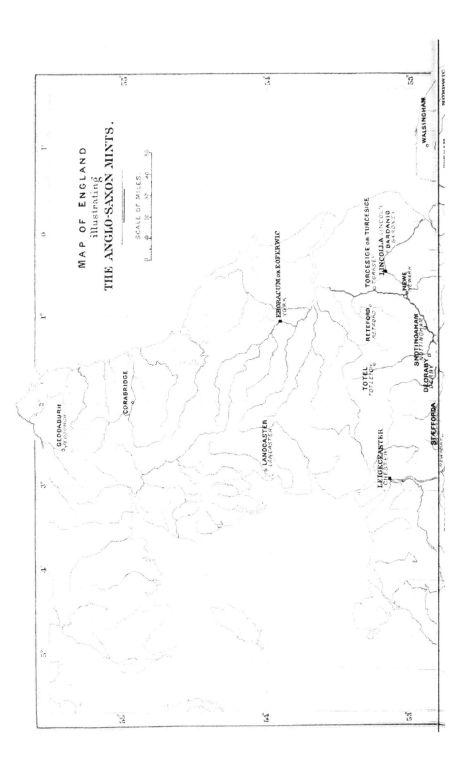

MAP OF ENGLAND
illustrating
THE ANGLO-SAXON MINTS.

SCALE OF MILES.

GEDDABURH
JEDBURGH

CORABRIDGE

LANDCASTER
LANCASTER

EBORACUM or EOFERWIC
YORK

RETEFORD
RETFORD

TORCESIGE or TURCESIGE
TORKSEY

LINCOLIA LINCOLN
BARDANIG
BARDNEY

NEWE
NEWARK

TOTEL
TOTTENGA

SNOTINGAHAM
NOTTINGHAM

DEORABY
DERBY

LEIGECEASTER
CHESTER

STÆFFORDA

WALSINGHAM

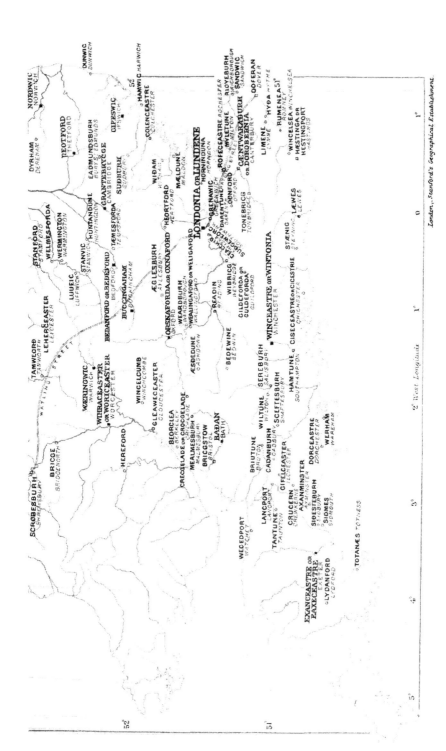

London.—Stanford's Geographical Establishment.

CATALOGUE.

CORRIGENDA

P 1, add name of *Eanwald* to list of moneyers
P 21, l 2, *dele* IN KENT A D 858
P 27 *n*, for Xristiano read Xristiana
P 101, l 51, first col , for *Dartmouth* read *Darenth*.
P 394, l 5, for Oðbern read Oðgrim
P 409, l 6, for „ read ÆÐELPIÐ.

CATALOGUE OF ENGLISH COINS.

ANGLO-SAXON SERIES.

KINGDOM OF WESSEX

ECGBEORHT.

Succ A D 802, DIED A D 838* or 839†

Moneyers.

Aenred
Æðel-, *see* Eðel-
Andred
Beagmund
Beornheard, Beornhart, &c
Beornmod, Biornmod, &c (Canterbury)
Biosel, Bosel [cf Bosa] (Canterbury)
Bosa
Debis
Diormod [cf Biornmod] (Canterbury)
Dynyn [Duning ?]
Eðelmod

Ifa
Oba (Canterbury)
Osmund (Canterbury).
Sigestef
Swefheard, Swefherd (Canterbury)
Swene
Tideman
Tiluune (Canterbury)
Timbearht [cf Tirbearht] (Canterbury)
Tirbearht
Werbeard
Wulqur

DESCRIPTION OF TYPES

Obverse	Reverse
Type 1	
Bust r, diademed Around, inscription between two circles, divided by bust	Monogram for DOROB C°‡ (Dorobernia Civitas) Around, inscription between two circles
[Cf Pl I 1]	

---

* Stubbs   † Theopold See Introduction

‡ This monogram has been likewise read ECBOR, but this reading seems scarcely admissible It is possible that this type is a degradation from the type of Archbishop Wulfred (A D 803-830) See Vol I p 73, Pl XII 7, and the Introduction to the present volume

Obverse.	Reverse.

Type i. var. a.

Similar; inscription not divided by bust. | *Same.*

[Evans Coll.]

Type ii.

Bust r., diademed. Around, inscription between two circles, divided by bust. | Monogram ·Ӿ· (A and ω). Around, inscription between two circles.

[Cf. Pl. I. 2.]

Type iii.

Bust r., diademed. Around, inscription between two circles, divided by bust. | Cross, two limbs moline, two limbs pattés. Around, inscription between two circles.

[Cf. Pl. I. 3.]

Type iv.

Head r., diademed. Around, inscription between two circles. | *Cross crosslet. Around, inscription between two circles.*

[Rud., Pl. 14, 1.]

Type v.

Head r., diademed. Around, inscription between two circles. | *Cross potent. Around, inscription between two circles.*

[Rud., Pl. 27, 1.]

Type vi.

Head r., diademed. Around, inscription between two circles. | Lozenge-shaped pellet, surrounded by four crescents, horns outwards. Around, inscription between two circles.

[Cf. Pl. I. 4.]

Obverse.	Reverse.

Type vii.

| *Head r., diademed. Around, inscription between two circles.* | *Cross pattée. Around, inscription between two circles.* |

[Sainthill, Olla Podrida, Pl. 20, 7.]

Type viii.

| Head r. diademed. Around, inscription between two circles. | Cross pattée, with wedge in each angle (cross pattée over another cross pattée). Around, inscription between two circles. |

[Cf. Pl. I. 5.]

Type ix.

| Head r., diademed. Around, inscription between two circles. | Tribrach moline. Around, inscription between two circles. |

[Cf. Pl. I. 6.]

Type x.

| Cross pattée. Around, inscription between two circles. | Cross crosslet. Around, inscription between two circles. |

[Cf. Pl. I. 7.]

Type xi.

| *Sun?—eight rays pattés issuing from circle enclosing pellet. Around, inscription between two circles.* | *Cross pattée. Around, inscription between two circles.* |

[E. J. G. Piffard Coll.]

Type xii.

| Sun?—nine rays pattés issuing from circle enclosing pellet. Around, inscription between two circles. | Tribrach, limbs fourchés. Around, inscription between two circles. |

[Cf. Pl. I. 8.]

Obverse.	Reverse.

Type xiii.

Cross potent. Around, inscription between two circles.

Cross potent. Around, inscription between two circles.

[Cf. Pl. I. 9.]

Type xiv.

Monogram *.** `Around, inscription between two circles.`

Cross potent. Around, inscription between two circles.

[Num. Chron., N. S., iii. 46.]

Type xv.

Cross pattée. Around, inscription between two circles.

Six rays or limbs pattés, issuing from a common centre. Around, inscription between two circles.

[Rud., Pl. 27, 2.]

Type xvi.

Cross of six limbs pattés. Around, inscription between two circles.

Cross of five limbs pattés. Around, inscription between two circles.

[Evans Coll.]

---

* The monogram here given correctly represents that on the coin. The figure below is taken from the only published representation of the coin. Since the figure was done the compilers have had an opportunity of seeing the original.

Obverse.	Reverse.

Type xvii.

Small cross pattée within four crescents, horns inwards. Across, inscription between two circles. | *Cross pattée. Around, inscription between two circles.*

[Boyne Coll.]

Type xviii.

𝄐𝖠̃𝖮 or 𝄐𝖠̃𝖮 (SAXON) irregularly placed. Around, inscription between two circles. | *Cross pattée. Around, inscription between two circles.*

[Cf. Pl. I. 10.]

Type xix.

Cross potent. Around, inscription between two circles. | *Monogram ΓΛ (for SAX). Around, inscription between two circles.*

[Num. Chron., N.S., iii. 46.]

Type xx.

Inscription ONIO SAX RVM in three lines across field. Around, inscription between two circles. | *Cross pattée. Around, inscription between two circles.*

[Murchison Coll.]

DESCRIPTION OF COINS.*

No.	Obverse.	Reverse.	Moneyer.

SERIES A. WITH NAME OF MINT.

DORÓBERNIA.
[Canterbury.]

Type i.

No.	Obverse.	Reverse.	Moneyer.
1	✠ECCBEΛR NT ΓEX	✠BIORNMOD ᛏONET Wt. 21·0.	Biornmod.
2	✠ECCBEΛR .. REX	BIORHᛏOD ᛏO . . . . (Fragment.)	
3	✠ECCBEΛΓMHT REX	✠BIOSEL ᛏOHETΛ Wt. 22·3.	Biosel, Bosel.
4	†ECCBEΛRH REX	✠BOSEL ᛏOHETΛ Wt. 22·0.	
5	✠ECCBEV ΓNT R	✠BOSEL MONETV Wt. 21·4.	
6	✠ECCBEΛΓ HT REX	✠DIORᛏOD ᛏNEᛏ *Var.* Dots in field of monogram. Wt. 21·8.	Diormod.
7	✠ECCBEΛΓNT ,,	✠OBΛ MONETΛ *Var.* Dot in centre of monogram. Wt. 21·5.	Oba.
8	,, ,,	✠OSMVND MONETΛ Wt. 20·5.	Osmund.
9	✠ECCBEVRNT Γ	✠SᛏEFNᛉRD MON *Var.* Dots in field of monogram. Wt. 21·4.	Swefheard.
	[Pl. I. 1.]		
10	✠ECCBEΛI NT REX	✠TILVVINE MONETΛ Wt. 21·5.	Tiluuine.
11	✠ECCBEΛRIIT EX	✠TIMBEΛRNT ∴ (Broken.)	Timbearht.

* The coins in this volume are all silver Pennies unless it is otherwise stated.

No.	Obverse.	Reverse.	Moneyer.
	SERIES B. WITHOUT NAME OF MINT.		
	Type ii. (ST. ANDREW.)		
12	ECGBEORN RE	✠ ⟩ C ⟩ ANDREA ⟩ Wt. 20·0. [Pl. I. 2.]	No Moneyer.
	Type iii.		
13	ECGBE	ANDRE . . . . . . (Fragment.) [Pl. I. 3.]	Andred.
	Type vi.		
14	✠ECCBEORNT RE	✠DYNYN TONET Wt. 21·0. [Pl. I. 4.]	Dynyn. (Duning ?)
	Type viii.		
15	✠ECCBEORHT REX	✠EDEL✠TOD Wt. 20·0. [Pl. I. 5.]	Eðelmod.
	Type ix.		
16	✠ACGCBQARH REX	✠ÞERNEARD MONET Wt. 20·7. [Pl. I. 6.]	Werheard.
	Type x.		
17	✠HECBEARHT REX	✠DIORTOD THET Wt. 19·2. [Pl. I. 7.]	Diormod.
	Type xii.		
18	✠HECBEARHT REX	✠SVVEFNERD Wt. 17·2. [Pl. I. 8.]	Swefherd

No.	Obverse.	Reverse.	Moneyer.
		Type xiii.	
19	✠ECGBEORHT REX	✠EDELTOD TOHETA Wt. 19·8. [Pl. I. 9.]	Eᵹelmod.
		Type xviii.	
20	✠ECCBEORHT REX	✠BEORNEHART Wt. 22·8.	Beornheard.
21	,, ,,	✠BOZA MONETA Wt. 15·7. [Pl. I. 10.]	Bosa.

AETHELWULF.

Succ. A.D. 838 or 839; died A.D. 858.

(Resigned Wessex to his son Aeðelbald in 856 and reigned in Kent only.)

Moneyers.

Æðel-, *see* Eðel-.
Beagmund.
Biarnmod or *Biarmod.*
Biarnnoð (Canterbury).
Brid (Canterbury).
Degbearht.
Deineah (Canterbury).
Diar (Canterbury).
Duduine.
Dun(n).
Ealgmund [Ealhmund?] (Canterbury).
Fanmund (Canterbury).
Eanwald.
Eardwulf.
Eðelgeard [=*Eðelheard?*]
Eðelheard.
Eðelhere.
Eðelmod [or Eðelnoð?].
Eðelmund (Canterbury).
Eðelnoð.

Eðelred? (Canterbury).
Hebeca? (Canterbury).
Hedebeald [for Herebeald?].
Herebeald (Canterbury).
Herebearht.
Hunbearht [Hunbeant] (Canterbury).
Hunred.
Liaba or Liuba.
Maninc [Manninc] (Canterbury).
Manna, Mann, &c.
Osmund (Canterbury).
Tiruald [Tiduald?].
Torhtulf.
Torhtwald.
Uermund.
Uuealheard, Uuelheard, &c. [=Uelmheard?] (Canterbury).
Uuelmheard [=Uuealheard?]
Uuilheah or Wilheah [cf. Uuelheard] (Canterbury).
Weineah [cf. Deineah.]

DESCRIPTION OF TYPES.

Obverse.	Reverse.
Type i.	
DORIBI or DORIB̄ irregularly written. Around, inscription between two circles.	Monogram CⒶN. Around, inscription between two circles.
[Cf. Pl. II. 1.]	
Type i. var. a.	
Same as reverse of preceding.	Same as obverse of preceding.
[Cf. Pl. II. 2.]	
Type ii.	
DORIBI or DORIB̄ irregularly written. Around, inscription between two circles.	In centre ⚛. Around, inscription between two circles.
[Cf. Pl. II. 3.]	
Type iii.	
Monogram CⒶN. Around, inscription between two circles.	Cross pattée, in angles CYИꞀ (CANT?) Around, inscription between two circles.
[Cf. Pl. II. 4.]	

Obverse.	Reverse.

Type iv.

Monogram ⊕ (SAXONV). Around, inscription between two circles. | Cross pattée over another cross pattée. Around, inscription between two circles.

[Cf. Pl. II. 5.]

Type v.

Cross pattée over another cross pattée. Around, inscription between two circles. | Inscription SAX ONIO in three lines R/M across field. Around, inscription between two circles.

[Cf. Pl. II. 6.]

Type v. var. a.

Same. | Similar, SᴧX ONIO RVM and around, between two circles, OⅭⅭIDENTᴧLIVM, instead of moneyer's name.

[Cf. Pl. II. 7.]

Type vi.

Bust r., diademed. Around, inscription between two circles, divided by bust. | Christian monogram ✳. Around, inscription between two circles.

[Cf. Pl. II. 8.]

Type vii.

Bust r., diademed. Around, inscription between two circles, divided by bust. | In centre ⊼. Around, inscription between two circles.

[Cf. Pl. II. 9.]

Type viii.

Bust r., diademed. Around, inscription between two circles, divided by bust. | In centre ⊼. Around, inscription between two circles.

[Cf. Pl. II. 10.]

Type ix.

Bust r., diademed. Around, inscription between two circles, divided by bust. | Cross pattée, pellet in each angle. Around, inscription between two circles.

[Cf. Pl. II. 11.]

Obverse.	Reverse.

Type ix. var. a.

Head r., diademed. Around, inscription between two circles.	Similar; smaller cross pattée; no pellets in angles.

[Cf. Pl. II. 12.]

Type x.

Head r., diademed. Around, inscription between two circles.	*Cross potent. Around, inscription between two circles.*

[Rud., Pl. 27, 2.]

Type xi.

Bust r., diademed. Around, inscription between two circles, divided by bust.	Cross crosslet. Around, inscription between two circles.

[Cf. Pl. III. 1.]

Type xii.

Bust r., diademed. Around, inscription between two circles, divided by bust.	Star of six rays pattés. Around, inscription between two circles.

[Cf. Pl. III. 2.]

Type xiii.

Bust r., diademed. Around, inscription between two circles, divided by bust.	Cross pattée over another cross pattée. Around, inscription between two circles.

[Cf. Pl. III. 3.]

Type xiv.

Bust r., diademed. Around, inscription between two circles, divided by bust.	Cross pattée over cross pommée. Around, inscription between two circles.

[Cf. Pl. III. 4.]

Type xv.

Bust r., diademed. Around, inscription between two circles, divided by bust.	Cross, two limbs pattés, two moline. Around, inscription between two circles.

[Cf. Pl. III. 5.]

Obverse.	Reverse.

Type xvi.

Bust r., diademed. Around, inscription between two circles, divided by bust. | *Cross, two limbs cross crosslet, two pattés. Around, inscription between two circles.*

[Montagu Coll.]

Type xvii.

Bust r., sometimes diademed. Around, inscription between two circles, divided by bust. | Moneyer's name, &c., upon limbs and between angles of cross formed of beaded lines.

[Cf. Pl. III. 6.]

Type xviii.

Cross pattée over another cross pattée. Around, inscription between two circles. | In centre ⚚. Around, inscription between two circles.

[Cf. Pl. III. 7.]

Type xix.

Cross pattée over another cross pattée. Around, inscription between two circles. | Plain cross, the ends of which touch the inner circle, over cross pommée. Around, inscription between two circles.

[Cf. Pl. III. 8.]

Type xx.

Cross pattée over another cross pattée. Around, inscription between two circles. | Same as obverse type.

[Cf. Pl. III. 9.]

Type xxi.

Cross pattée over another cross pattée. Around, inscription between two circles. | Cross crosslet. Around, inscription between two circles.

[Cf. Pl. III. 10.]

Type xxii.

Cross pattée over another cross pattée. Around, inscription between two circles. | Cross moline. Around, inscription between two circles.

[Cf. Pl. III. 11.]

Obverse.	Reverse.

Type xxiii.

Cross pattée over another cross pattée. Around, inscription between two circles.	Cross, two limbs pattés, two moline. Around, inscription between two circles.

[Cf. Pl. III. 12.]

DESCRIPTION OF COINS.

No.	Obverse.	Reverse.	Moneyer.
	SERIES A. WITH NAME OF MINT.		
	DOROBERNIA. [Canterbury.]		
	Type i.		
1	✠EÐELVVLF REX *Var.* Pellet in centre.	✠BIARNNOÐ MONETA Wt. 18·6.	Biarnnoð.
2	,, ,,	✠BRID MONETA Wt. 18·6.	Brid.
3	✠EDELVVLF REX	✠DEINEAN MONETA Wt. 19·0.	Deineah.
4	,, ,, (Dot L·F)	✠EALMVND MONETA Wt. 19·6.	Ealgmund.
5	,, ,,	✠EALLMVND MONETA Wt. 18·8.	
6	,, ,, (Dots. L·FR·EX·)	,, LI ,, (Fragment.)	
7	✠EÐELVVF REX	✠EANMVND MONET Wt. 19·5.	Eanmund.
8	✠EÐELVVLF REX	✠EÐELERD MONETA Wt. 20·0.	Eðelred ?
9	✠E⊀ELVVL·F REX	✠EDELNYNO NONE Wt. 22·0.	Eðelmund.
10	,, LF ,, ✠	✠HVNBEANT NONET Wt. 18·4.	Hunbearht.
11	✠EÐEL✠VVLF✠ REX *Var.* Pellet in centre.	✠MANINC MONETA Wt. 19·5.	Maninc.

No.	Obverse.	Reverse.	Moneyer.
12	✠EÐELVVLF REX. _Var._ Pellet in centre.	✠MⱭNINᴄ ꞇONEꞆⱭ Wt. 17·8.	
	[Pl. II. 1.]		
13	✠E+ƉELVVL·F REX:	✠OSMVND MONEꞆⱭ Wt. 17·9.	Osmund.
14	✠EÐEL+VVLF+ REX _Var._ Pellet in centre.	✠VVEⱭLHEⱭRD ꞇOEꞆⱭ Wt. 20·0.	Uuealheard, Uuelheard.
15	✠EÐELVVLF REX _Var._ Pellet in centre.	✠VVEⱭLHIEⱭRD Wt. 19·0.	
16	✠EÐELYYLE REX _Var._ Pellet in centre.	✠YYELIHEⱭRD Wt. 18·6.	
17	✠EÐELVVLF REX	✠VVILHEH MONEꞆⱭ Wt. 19·1.	Uuilheah.
	Type i. _var. a._		
18	✠E+ƉELVVLF REᴇᴇ+ _Var._ NⱭ₽ᴄ : pellet in centre.	✠NEREBEYLD MONEꞆⱭ _Var._ Pellet in centre. Wt. 19·1.	Hereb·ald.
19	✠E+ƉELVVLF REX _Var._ Pellets in field.	✠NVNBEⱭNT NONEꞆ Wt. 22·6.	Hunbearht.
20	✠ERFLVVLE ÐE+	✠NVNBEⱭNT MONEꞆ Wt. 20·0.	
	[Pl. II. 2.]		
	Type ii.		
21	✠E+ƉELVVLF REX _Var._ Pellets in type.	+DIⱭR MONEꞆⱭ Wt. 17·5.	Diar.
	[Pl. II. 3.]		
	Type iii.		
22	✠E+ƉELVVLFE RE+ _Var._ Pellet in type.	✠NEBEᴄⱭ MONEꞆⱭ DOꞦ Wt. 19·0.	Hebeca ?
23	,, ,,	,, ,, Wt. 18·5.	
24	,, ,,	·,, ,, ,, _Var._ Order of letters in angles of cross [ᴄNꞆY] Wt. 19·0.	
	[Pl. II. 4.]		

No.	Obverse.	Reverse.	Moneyer.
		Series B. Without Name of Mint.	
		Type iv.	
25	✠ÆEÐELVVCF REX	✠EANÞALD MONETA Wt. 19·6.	Eanwald.
		[Pl. II. 5.]	
		Type v.	
26	✠E✠ÐELVVLF RE: X	✠DIAR I IONETA Wt. 19·4.	Diar.
27	,, REX	✠HEREBEALD MOHET Wt. 20·7.	Herebeald.
28	,, L·F ,,	✠MANNA MONETA Wt. 19·0.	Manna.
29	,, L·F ,,	✠OSMVMD MOMET Wt. 21·2.	Osmund.
30	,, L·F ,,	✠OSMVND MONETA Wt. 20·5.	Osmund.
		[Pl. II. 6.]	
31	,, ,,	✠TORHÐALD MOHET Wt. 18·7.	Torhtwald.
		Type v. *var. a.*	
32	✠ÆEÐELVVLF REX	✠OCCIDENTALIVM Wt. 20·0.	No Moneyer.
		[Pl. II. 7.]	
33	,, ,, *Var.* Pellet opposite each limb of smaller cross.	,, ,, Wt 20·2.	
		Type vi.	
34	✠E✠ÐELVVLF REX	✠DEIHEVH MONETA Wt. 23·3.	Deineah.
		[Pl. II. 8.]	
		Type vii.	
35	✠EÐELVVLF REX	✠OSMVND MCNETA (Broken.)	Osmund.
		[Pl. II. 9.]	

No.	Obverse.	Reverse.	Moneyer.
		Type viii.	
36	EÐELYYLF REX	✠BI𝚲RNNOÐ Wt. 19·7.	Biarnnoð.
		[Pl. II. 10.]	
		Type ix.	
37	EÐELVVLF RE	✠BE𝚲GTYNÐ ꙦO Wt. 19·4.	Beagmund.
		[Pl. II. 11.]	
		Type ix. *rar. a.*	
38	EÐELVVLF REX	✠BE𝚲GTVN Wt. 20·3.	Beagmund.
		[Pl. II. 12.]	
39	,, ,,	✠VVILhE𝚲h· Wt. 18·4.	Uuilheah.
		Type xi.	
40	✠EÐELVVLF REX	✠DEI𝝢E𝚲H MONET𝚲 Wt. 20·6.	Deineah.
41	,, R·EX	✠DEIHE𝚲H MONET·𝚲· *Var.* Pellets in angles of cross. Wt. 20·3.	
42	✠EÐELVVLF RE϶	✠DEI𝝢E·𝚲·H NO𝝢ET Wt. 20·0.	
43	✠EÐELVVLF REX	✠DI𝚲R MONET𝚲 Wt. 18·0.	Diar.
44	,, ,,	✠E¯𝚲NMVMD NONET𝚲 *Var.* Pellets in angles of cross. Wt. 17·4.	Eanmund.
45	,, ,,	✠LI𝚲B𝚲 MONET𝚲 Wt. 20·0.	Liaba.
46	✠EÐELVVLF ERX	✠LIVB𝚲 · MOHET𝚲 · Wt. 19·8.	
47	✠EÐELVVLF REX	✠ΠANN𝚲 ΠONET𝚲 Wt. 20·5.	Manna.
		[Pl. III. 1.]	

No.	Obverse.	Reverse.	Moneyer.
48	✠E✠ELVᒍF REX	✠ΠΛΗ·Η✠MONETΛ Wt. 19·3.	
49	✠Ǝ⅁ƎLVVᒍƎ REX	ᐱT:Ǝ·ИOΠ✠HNᐱΠ✠ Wt. 19·8.	
50	✠EÐELVVLF REX	✠OꙄNVND NONET·Λ· Wt. 20·2.	Osmund.
	Type xii.		
51	✠EFLVVLEÐ EX	✠NEREBEVER MONET Wt. 19·5. [Pl. III. 2.]	Herebearht.
	Type xiii.		
52	✠EFLVVLE✠ E:✠	✠ΙEREBEALD MOИT Wt. 19·5. [Pl. III. 3.]	Herebeald.
53	✠EÐELVVLF RE✠	NYNBEVRHT ΠONEVT (Broken.)	Hunbearht.
54	,, REX	✠LIΛBA ΠOИETΛ Wt. 20·3.	Liaba.
55	,, ,,	OꙄNVND NONETΛ· Wt. 19·8.	Osmund.
56	✠EÐELVV.. REX	. OꙄMVND NONET (Fragment.)	
	Type xiv.		
57	✠EÐELVVLF REX	✠DIΛR ILONITΛ Wt. 17·4.	Diar.
58	✠EÐELVVL·F RE·.·✠	✠NEREBEΛL:D ΠⓄNET Wt. 20·6.	Herebeald.
59	✠EÐELVVLF REX	✠ΠΛHNΛ ΠONETΛ Wt. 20·1. [Pl. III. 4.]	Manna.
60	,, REX	✠OꙄΠVND MOИETΛ Wt. 19·2.	Osmund.
	Type xv.		
61	EÐELVVLF REX	✠EÐELHERE Wt. 20·2. [Pl. III. 5.]	Eðelhere.

No.	Obverse.	Reverse.	Moneyer.
62	EÐELVVLF REX	✠EÐELEHRE (Broken.)	
		Type xvii.	
63	✠ΛEÐELVVLF REX	✠DEĿBEΛ Var. Each letter in angles between three pellets. Wt. 20·5. [Pl. III. 6.]	Degbearht.
64	✠ΛEÐELVVLF REX *Var.* Head diademed.	✠DIΛRM ON ETΛ ꟺOΛO Wt. 20 1.	Diar.
65	,, ,,	✠DVDVI NE MO N E T Λ Wt. 19·2.	Duduine.
66	,, ,,	✠EÐELĿE : ΛRD MO N E T Λ *Var.* Each letter in angles between two pellets. Wt. 22·5.	Eðelgeard.
67	,, ,,	✠EÐELM OD MO N E T Λ Wt. 22·1.	Eðelmod.
68	,, ,,	✠EÐELN OÐ MO N E T Λ Wt. 19·3.	Eðelnoð.
69	✠ΛEÐELVVLF ,,	✠HVNBEΛ RH̅ MO N E T Λ Wt. 19·0.	Hunbearht.
70	✠ΛEÐELVVLF ,,	✠HVNBEΛ RH̅ MO N E T Λ Wt. 19·5.	
71	,, ,,	✠HVNBE ΛR H[T] M O N E T Λ (Broken.)	
72	,, ,,	✠HVNR ED MO N ∴ E ∴ TΛ Wt. 18·2.	Hunred.
73	,, ,,	✠MΛNI NE MO N E T Λ Wt. 20 3.	Manine.

No.	Obverse.	Reverse.	Moneyer.
74	✠ÆÐELVVLF REX *Var.* Head diademed.	✠MAN ·: NN MO N E T A Wt. 20·0.	Manna.
75	,, ,,	✠TIRVA LD MO N E T A Wt. 22·7.	Tiruald.
76	,, ,, *Var.* Head diademed.	✠TORHT VLF MO N E T A Wt. 21·0.	Torhtulf.
77	,, ,,	✠VERMV ND MO N E T A Wt. 20·7.	Uermund.
	Type xviii.		
78	✠ÆÐELVVL REX	✠BRID TONETA Wt. 21·4.	Brid.
79	✠ÆÐELVVLF REX	✠VVILHEAH *Var.* Three pellets around central letter. Wt. 20·6. [Pl. III. 7.]	Unilheah or Wilheah.
80	,, ,,	✠ÞILHEAH TONETA *Var.* Three pellets around central letter. Wt. 18·0.	
	Type xix.		
81	.. EÐELVVLF [REX]	✠TAN [NIN] C T (Fragment.) [Pl. III. 8.]	Mannine.
	Type xx.		
82	✠ÆÐELYYLF REX	✠DVN MONETA Wt. 18·3. [Pl. III. 9.]	Dun.
	Type xxi.		
83	✠EÐELVVLF REX	✠BEALTVND Wt. 19·0. [Pl. III. 10.]	Beagmund.
84	,, ,,	✠BEALTVND Wt. 20·0.	
85	,, ,,	✠BEA[L]TVVND (Broken.)	

No.	Obverse.	Reverse.	Moneyer.
86	EÐELVVLF REX	✠VVELMHEARÞ T Wt. 19·7.	Uuelmheard.
		Type xxii.	
87	✠ÆEÐELYYLF REX	✠DVN ꓔONETÆ Wt. 19·0. [Pl. III. 11.]	Dun.
88	✠ÆEÐELYYLF REX	✠DYYN ꓔONETÆ Wt. 19·2.	
		Type xxiii.	
89	✠EÐELYYLF REX	✠EÐELHERE (Chipped.) [Pl. III. 12.]	Eðelhere.
90	„ „	✠YYELHEARD Wt. 18·2.	Uuelheard or Uuelmheard.

AETHELBALD.

Succ. in Wessex, a.d. 856; in Kent, a.d. 858; died a.d. 860 or 861.

Moneyers.

Beahmund.   *Torhtulf.*

Description of Coins.

No.	Obverse.	Reverse.	Moneyer.
	Bust r. Around, inscription between two circles, divided by bust.	*Inscription upon limbs and between angles of cross formed of beaded lines.*	
1	✠ΛEÐELBΛLD REX	✠TORHT (with letters around cross)	Torhtulf.
		(Montagu Coll.) Wt. 19·7.	
2	,, ,,	,, Wt. 18·0.	
3	,, ,,	,, Wt. 19·8.	

Four specimens of the coinage of this monarch have been met with, three of these are in existence, but the fourth has disappeared. Of the existing specimens one is in the possession of Mr. Hyman Montagu (see No. 1): it came from the collection of Mr. William Brice, who purchased it some twelve years ago of Mr. Webster, the dealer. The second known specimen (see No 2), originally from the Gibbs collection, also formerly belonged to Mr. Montagu, but was disposed of in his sale of Duplicates, 7th May, 1888; whilst the third (see No. 3) is in the possession of Messrs. Spink & Sons, the dealers. As all these three specimens are from the same die, some doubt is entertained of their genuineness. The fourth and missing specimen is figured in Hawkins' *Silver Coins of England,* No. 168, who gave it upon the authority of a plate engraved under the auspices of Mr. John White; but it is further stated by Ruding (vol. i. p. 124) that Mr. Taylor Combe saw this coin in the collection of Mr. Austin and was satisfied as to its authenticity. This coin is of the same type as those above described, but was struck by the moneyer *Beahmund.*

AETHELBEARHT.

Succ in Kent, &c * a d 858, in Wessex a d 861, died a d 866

Moneyers

Æðel-, *see* Eðel-
Budemund
Badenoð
Beagmund or Beahmund
Biarnmod [or Biarnnoð]
Biarnuine
Burnuld
Cealeard [Cealheard ?]
Cenred
Cenueald
Cuuefreð [cf Cynfreð]
Dealla
Degbearht
Deglaf
Denemund
Diurmod
Duduine
Eadulf
Ealdred,
Eðelgeard
Eðelhere
Eðelnoð
Eðelred
Eðelueald
Eðelulf
Eðered [= Eðelred ?]

Healbearht [= Herebearht ?]
Herebeald
Herefreð
Heregeard
Heremund
Hunbearht
Hunred
Liabineg
Lueeman or Lyeeman ?
Manine [Mannine]
Noðulf
Osbearht
Oehere
Setreð or Selfred
Selered [= Selfred ?]
Sigehere
Torhtmund
Torhtulf
Uermund ?
Uihtmund [Uiohtmund]
Uinoð [Uilnoð ?]
Ulanceard
Uulfheard
Uunbearht or Uynbearht [cf Hunbearht]
Wilnoð [= Uinoð ?]

DESCRIPTION OF TYPES

Obverse	Reverse

Type I

Bust r, hair unbound Around, inscription between two circles, divided by bust	Moneyer's name, &c, upon limbs and between angles of cross formed of beaded lines

[Cf Pl IV 1.]

(Similar to Aethelwulf, *Type* xvii)

Type II

Bust r diademed Around, inscription between two circles, divided by bust	Floriated cross with leaf in each angle Around, inscription between two circles

[Cf Pl IV 2]

* In Kent, Essex, Surrey and Sussex

DESCRIPTION OF COINS.

No.	Obverse.		Reverse.	Moneyer.
			Type i.	
1	✠ÆÐELBEΛRH REX		✠BΛDEM (letters arranged around cross) Wt. 20·2.	Bademund.
2	,,	,,	✠BΛDEN OÐ MO N E · T · · Λ · Wt. 18·2.	Badenoð.
3	,,	,,	✠BEΛCM VND MO N E T Λ Wt. 18·8.	Beagmund or Beahmund.
4	,,	,,	✠BEΛHꝞ VND ꝠO N E T Λ Wt. 22·8.	
5	,,	,,	✠BEΛHM VND MO N E T Λ Wt. 19·7.	
6	,,	,,	✠BIΛRNM : OD MO : N E ∴ T Λ Wt. 20·8.	Biarnmod.
7	,,	,,	✠BIΛRNV INE MO N E T Λ Wt. 18·4.	Biarnnine.
8	,,	,,	✠BVRNV ΛLD MO N E T Λ Dot in each angle of cross. (Chipped.)	Burnuald.
9	,,	,,	✠CEΛLE ΛRD MO N E T Λ Wt. 20·0.	Cealeard.
10	,,	,,	✠CENR ED MO N E T Λ Wt. 20·0.	Cenred.
11	,,	,,	✠CENVE ΛLD ꝠO N E T Λ Wt. 23·9.	Cennuald.
12	,,	,,	✠CVNEFR EÐ MO N E T Λ Wt. 18·0.	Cunefreð.
13	,,	,,	✠CVNEFR EÐ MO N E T Λ Wt. 21·0.	
14	,,	,,	✠DEΛL : LΛ MO N E T Λ Wt. 19·6.	Dealla.
15	,,	,,	✠DECBEΛ RH MO N E T Λ Wt. 21·6.	Degbearht.

No.	Obverse.		Reverse.	Moneyer.
16	✠ΛEÐELBEΛRH REX		✠DEGL∴ ΛF MO N E T Λ Wt. 22·2.	Deglaf.
17	,,	,,	✠DENEM VND ꟼO N E T Λ Wt. 21·5.	Denemund.
18	,,	,,	✠DIΛRM OD MO N E · T · Λ Wt. 18·7.	Diarmod.
19	,,	,,	,, ,, ,, ,, Wt. 20·4.	
20	,,	,,	✠DVDVI NE MO N E T Λ Wt. 21·5.	Duduine.
21	✠ΛEÐEBEΛRH REX		✠EΛDV LF MO N E T Λ (Chipped.)	Eadulf.
22	✠ΛEÐELBEΛRH REX		✠EΛLDR ED MO N E T · Λ · (Chipped.)	Ealdred.
23	,,	,,	✠EÐELGE ΛRD MO N E T Λ Wt. 19·4.	Eðelgeard.
24	,,	,,	✠EÐELH ERE MO N E T Λ Wt. 19·8.	Eðelhere.
25	,,	,,	✠EÐELN OÐ MO N E T Λ (Chipped.)	Eðelnoð.
26	,,	,,	✠EÐELR ED MO N E T Λ Wt. 18·0.	Eðelred.
27	,,	,,	✠EÐELRE ED MO N E T Λ Wt. 20·0.	
28	,,	,,	✠EÐER · ED MO N E T Λ Wt. 21·1.	Eðered [= Eðelred?].
29	,,	,,	✠EÐELVE ΛLD ꟼO N E T Λ Wt. 24·5.	Eðelueald.
30	,,	,,	✠EÐELV ⸬LF MO N E T Λ Wt. 19·3.	Eðelulf.
31	,,	,,	✠HEΛBEΛ RH ꟼO N E T Λ Wt. 23·0.	Heabearht [= Herebearht?].
32	✠ΛEÐLBEΛRH REX		✠HEREBE ΛLD MO꞉ N E T∴ Λ∴ Wt. 14·8.	Herebeald.
33	✠ΛEÐELBEΛRH REX		✠HEREFR EÐ ꟼO N E T Λ Wt. 20·8.	Herefreð.
34	,,	,,	✠HEREGEΛ RD MO N E T Λ Wt. 18·8.	Heregeard.

No.	Obverse.		Reverse.	Moneyer.
35	✠ÆÐELBEARH REX		✠HEREMV ND MO NET Ä Wt. 17·6. [Pl. IV. 1.]	Heremund.
36	,,	,,	✠HVNBEÄ RH MO N E T Ä Wt. 18·0.	Hunbearht.
37	,,	,,	✠HVNR ED MO N E T Ä Wt. 18·6.	Hunred.
38	,,	,,	Var. N·.·E·.·T Ä Wt. 19·6.	
39	,,	,,	,, ,, ,, Wt. 21·7.	
40	,,	,,	✠LIÄBI·.· NC MO N E T Ä Wt. 22·6.	Liabineg.
41	,,	,,	✠LIÄBIN CG MO N E T Ä Wt. 18·4.	
42	,,	,,	✠LVCEM ÄN TO N E T Ä Wt. 17·5.	Luceman (Lyceman?).
43	,,	,,	✠MÄNI: NC MO N E T Ä Wt. 21·3.	Maninc.
44	,,	,,	✠NOÐV LF: MO N E T Ä Wt. 20·0.	Noðulf.
45	,,	,,	✠OSBEÄ RH MO N E T Ä Wt. 20·5.	Osbearht.
46	,,	,,	✠OSHE RE TO N E T Ä Wt. 15·7.	Oshere.
47	,,	,,	✠OSHE RE MO N E T Ä Wt. 21·7.	
48	,,	,,	✠SEFR: EÐ MO N E T Ä Wt. 18·6.	Sefreð (or Selfred?).
49	,,	,,	✠SELER: ED MO N E T Ä (Chipped.)	Selered (or Selfred?).
50	,,	,,	✠SIGEHE RE MO N E T Ä Wt. 19·0.	Sigehere.
51	,,	,,	✠TORHM VND TO N E T Ä Wt. 19·4.	Torhtmund.
52	,,	,,	✠TORHT VLF MO N E T Ä Wt. 19·1.	Torhtulf.
53	,,	,,	✠VERMV ND MO N E T Ä (Chipped.)	Uermund.

No.	Obverse.		Reverse.	Moneyer.
54	✠ΛEÐELBEARH REX		✠VIHM VND MONETΛ *Var.* Annulet in centre of cross. Wt. 21·9.	Uihtmund.
55	,,	RE	✠VIIN∴ OÐ MONETΛ *Var.* Pellet in centre of cross. (Broken.)	Uinoð [Uilnoð?].
56	,,	REX	✠VLΛNCEΛ RD TONETΛ Wt. 21·4.	Ulanceard.
57	,,	,,	✠VVLFEΛ RD MONETΛ Wt. 21·3.	Uulfheard.
58	,,	,,	✠VVLFHE ΛR DM O NETΛ Wt. 21·6.	
59	,,	,,	✠VVLFHE ΛRD MONETΛ Wt. 19·6.	
60	,,	,,	✠VVNBEΛ RH MONETΛ Wt. 18·3.	Uunbearht or Uynbearht [cf. Hunbearht].
			Type ii.	
61	✠ΛEÐELBEΛRH REX		✠CENVEΛLD MONETΛ · Wt. 19·0. [Pl. IV. 2.]	Cenueald.
62	,,	,,	✠CVNEFREÐ MONETΛ ∴ (Chipped.)	Cunefreð.
63	,,	,,	✠OSHERE MONETΛ Wt. 19·8.	Oshere.
64	,,	,,	✠TOR[HTMV]ND MONETΛ (Broken.)	Torhtmund.

AETHELRED I.

Succ. in Wessex, a.d. 863; in Kent, a.d. 866; died a.d. 871.

Moneyers.

Æðel-, *see* Eðel-.
Beorneah or Biarneah [Beornhæ].
Beornhæ [cf. Beorneah].
Biarnmod.
Burgnoð.
Cuðhelm.
Dealla.
Deneuald.
Diarulf.
Diga.
Dudda, Dudd.
Dunn.
Elbere.

Ella.
Eðelred.
Heahmod.
Herebeald.
Hereulf.
Hussa.
Liabinc[g].
Lulla.
Mann.
Manninc.
Oshere.
Torhtmund.
Uuine.

Description of Types.

Obverse.	Reverse.
Type i.	
Bust r., diademed. Around, inscription between two circles, divided by bust.	Moneyer's name, &c., in three lines across field; upper and lower portions enclosed in lunettes.
[Cf. Pl. IV. 3.]	
Type i. var. a.	
Same.	*Similar: inscription divided by two lines with curved ends.*
Type ii.	
Bust r., diademed. Around, inscription between two circles, divided by bust.	Moneyer's name, &c., in four lines across field, divided by three straight lines; the upper and lower ones with curved ends.
[Cf. Pl. IV. 4.]	
Type iii.	
Façade of Christian temple. Around, inscription.*	Cross crosslet, pellet in each angle. Around, inscription between two circles.
[Cf. Pl. IV. 5.]	
Type iii. var. a.	
Façade of Christian temple, &c., same as the preceding but of rude work.	Cross pattée, pellet in each angle. Around, inscription between two circles.
[Cf. Pl. IV. 6.]	

* Comp. " Xristiano Religio" coins of Charlemagne, Louis the Pious, &c. The façade on these coins is probably that of St. Peter's at Rome.

DESCRIPTION OF COINS.

No.	Obverse.	Reverse.		Moneyer.

SERIES A. WITH BUST.

Type i.

No.	Obverse.	Reverse.		Moneyer.
1	✠·ÆÐELRED RE✠	HMO BIARNEA NETA	Wt. 15·5.	Biarneah.
2	,, REX	,, *Var.* HMO◇	Wt. 20·8.	
3	✠EÐELRED R EX	DM◇ BIARNM◇ NETA	Wt. 19·5.	Biarnmod.
4	✠·ÆEÐELRED REX	DM◇ BIARNMO NETA	Wt. 19·0.	
5	,,	,, *Var.* DMO	Wt. 20·0.	
6	,,	OD MO BIARNM NETA	Wt. 19·4.	
7	✠EÐELRED R EX	D MON BIARNM◇ ETA ∴	Wt. 18·7.	
8	✠·ÆEÐELRED REX	· Ð MO ∴ BVRENO · NETA ··	Wt. 17·5.	Burgnoð.
9	✠·ÆEÐELRED M REX	. MON . DEALLA · ETA ·	Wt. 19·4.	Dealla.
10	AÐELERED REX	. D MO . DENEVAL . NETA ·	Wt. 18·6.	Deneuald.
11	✠·ÆEÐELRED REX	. F M◇N DIARVL · ETA ·	Wt. 19·0.	Diarulf.

No.	Obverse.	Reverse.	Moneyer.
12	✠EÐLRED REX‾	M✕N +DIGᛏ ∷ · ETᛏ ·　　Wt. 18·6.	Diga.
13	✠ᛏEÐELRED REX	MON DVDDᛏ ETᛏ　　Wt. 17·0.	Dudda.
14	„　　„	· MON · DVDDᛏ · ETᛏ ·　　Wt. 18·3.	
15	„　　„	„　Var. No pellets. Wt. 21·9.	
16	✠ᛏE✠LEDI RE	∴ MON ∴ DVDDᛏ ·.· ETᛏ ·.·　　(Chipped.)	
17	✠ᛏE✠ELRED REX	MON ✠DVNN ETᛏ　　Wt. 19·5.	Dunn.
18	„　　„	·.· MON ·.· ✠DVNN ·.· ETᛏ ·.·　　Wt. 23·9.	
19	„　　„	∴ MON ∴ ✠DVNN: ·.· ETᛏ ·.·　　Wt. 20·0.	
20	„　　„	MON ELBERE ETᛏ　　Wt. 23·4.	Elbere.
21	„　　„	„　Var. M◇N Wt. 20·8.	
22	„　　„	. MON . ELBERE · ETᛏ ·　　Wt. 19·8.	
23	„　　„	: MON : ✠ELLᛏ:·: : ETᛏ :　　Wt. 19·0.	Ella.
24	„　　„	MON EÐELRED ETᛏ　　Wt. 15·5.	Eðelred.

No.	Obverse.		Reverse.		Moneyer.
25	✠Æ✠ELRED REX		MON EÐELRED ETA	Wt. 17·7.	
26	„	„	„	Var. MON Wt. 20·3.	
27	„	„	D MO EÐELRE NETA	Wt 19·8.	
28	„	„	LD MO HEREBEA NETA	Wt. 18·0.	Herebeald.
29	„	„	MON HEREVLF ETA	Wt. 18·5.	Herculf.
30	„	„	MON LIABINE ETA	Wt. 18·3.	Liabine.
31	✠ÆÐELRED	„	·M✠N· LVLLA: ·ETA·	Wt. 18·0.	Lulla.
32	✠ÆÐELRED REX		MON MANN ETA	Wt. 19·7.	Mann.
33	„	„	·MON· MANN ·ETA·	Wt. 19·7.	
			[Pl. IV. 3.]		
34	„	„	„	Var. MON Wt. 18·0.	
35	„	„	„	Var. ·MON· ETA Wt. 18·7.	
36	„	„	„	Var. ·MON· ·ETA· Wt. 17·8.	
37	„	„	MON MANNINE ETA	Wt. 18·4.	Mannine.

No.	Obverse.	Reverse.	Moneyer.
38	✠ ΛEÐELRED REX	MON MΛNINC ETΛ Wt. 20·5.	
39	,, ,,	,, *Var.* MΛNINC Wt. 20·2.	
40	,, ,,	MON OSHERE ETΛ Wt. 16·7.	Oshere.
41	,, ,,	ND MO TORHTMV NETΛ Wt. 17·2.	Torhtmund.
42	,, ,,	ND M TORHTMV ONETΛ Wt. 18·5.	
43	,, ,,	∴MON. VVINE∶ ∴·ETΛ·∴ Wt. 19·8.	Uuine.

Type ii.

| 44 | ✠ ΛEÐELRE D REX | ∴ Λ ∴ CVÐHEL MMONE TΛ   Wt. 20·0. [Pl. IV. 4.] | Cuðhelm. |
| 45 | ✠ ΛEÐELRED REX | ∴ Λ ∴ TORHTM VNDMON ET   Wt. 18·0. | Torhtmund. |

SERIES B. WITHOUT BUST.

Type iii. *

| 46 | Æ·Ð·E·L·RE·D REX | ✗HEΛ·HHOD MT   Wt. 21·5. [Pl. IV. 5.] | Healmod. |

Type iii. *rar. a.*

| 47 | ✠E·ÐEL∶R·E·D· RE | +BEⵔRNⵔΛE   Wt. 21·6. [Pl. IV. 6.] | Beornhac. |

AELFRED

Succ A.D. 871, died A.D. 901

Moneyers.

Abenel
Aduard [Eaduard?]
Ælfstan or Elfstan (London)
Alfwald or Alfwald
Ærelaf [or Æðelulf?] (Ronseng)
Aðelstan or Eðelstan (Canterbury)
Æðered or Eðered (Canterbury)
Æðel-, see also Eðel-
Alumada? [Alumald or Luda?]
Aðelulf [= Æðelulf]
Beagstan
Beornmaer or Beornmer
Beornred or Bernred (Canterbury)
Berehold or Berneald [cf Bernuald, &c]
Berhtere
Bernuald, Bernald, Bernuald, Biarn-uald, Birnuald, Burnuald or Byrn-uald, &c (Canterbury, Oxford)
Biareð [or Biarnred?] (Canterbury?)
Biarnuulf
Biarnred, Biornred (Canterbury)
Birnred [= Bernred for Biarnred, &c]
Birned, see Birnred
Boga
Bosa
Briðard.
Bruned [for Barnred?] (Canterbury)
Buga [= Boga?]
Burqnoð
Burnhere or Byrnhere
Burnelm or Byrnelm
Cenred
Cerman? (Canterbury)
Cialmod or Ciolmod [Ciolnoð?]
Cialulf or Cioluulf
Ciresmen or Herserie?
Cudberht and Cuðberht
Cunculf or Cyneulf
Cuðuult
Dealine or Dealing
Dealla, Dela, &c
Deigmund
Diarald or Diaruald
Diarhelm
Diarmund
Diaruald (Canterbury)
Dudd
Dudreine
Dudig
Duine for Dunne.
Dunna or Dunn

Dunnine or Dunine (Canterbury)
Eadhelm
Eadstan
Eaduald, Eaduald, &c (Canterbury)
Eaduard [cf Aduard]
Eaduulf
Eactan [= Eadstan]
Ealduul
Leberht
Lenulf or Ecwulf
Edeulf [or Edwulf?] (Canterbury)
Edelstan [= Eðelstan]
Elbere
Elda
Elfstan (Canterbury)
Elf-, see also Ælf-
Eli (Bath)
Ericuuald
Eðelheah
Eðelmod
Eðelmund
Eðelred
Eðeluine (Canterbury)
Eðelulf
Eðel-, see also Æðel-
Eðered, see Æðered
Ferlun?
Foleard
Franbald
Garuine?
Geld?
Cioluulf [= Ciolwulf]
Goda
Gu here
Haldhere [= Berehald or Berehold]
Healf?
Heanulf (London)
Hebeca?
Helican?
Herebald.
Herebert or Heribert (Lincoln)
Herefred or Hereferd (Canterbury)
Heremod
Heremund
Hereuult
Hunberht.
Huntreð (Canterbury)
Ida?
Indelbard
Ladine
Latiuald
Luda or Lude [Lyde]

Ludeca or Ludig.
Lulla.
Luning.
Manninc.
Moelf?
Nebeca [Hebeca].
Osgeard.
Oshere.
Osric.
Osuulf.
Regingæd [Regingær].
Resaud? (Canterbury).
Særis?
Samson.
Sefreð.
Sigestef, Siestef, &c.
Sigeuuald.

Simun.
Stefanus.
Tata.
Tidbald.
Tilefcin [Tileuine?].
Tileuuine (London).
Tileuoic [Tileuuine?].
Tiruald or Tirucald (Canterbury).
Torhtmund.
Uigbald or Uuigbald.
Uuine.
Uuiniger, Uuinier, &c.
Uulfard.
Uulfred or Uulfreð.
Uuynberht or Wynberht.
Wiard.

DESCRIPTION OF TYPES.

Obverse.	Reverse.

Type i.

Bust r, diademed. Around, inscription between two circles, divided by bust.	Moneyer's name, &c., in three lines, across field; upper and lower portions enclosed in lunettes.

[Cf. Pl. VI. 1–2.]

Type i. var. a.

Same.	Similar: lunettes broken in centre of curve.

[Cf. Pl. VI. 3.]

Type i. var. b.

Same	Similar: lunettes broken at the angles.

[Cf. Pl. VI. 4.]

Type i. var. c.

Same.	Similar: inscription divided by two lines with curved ends.

[Cf. Pl. VI. 5.]

Type ii.

Bust r., diademed. Around, inscription, divided by bust; inner circle.	Moneyer's name, &c., within and without leaves of quatrefoil; over which, cross pattée with circle in centre and wedges in angles.

[Cf. Pl. VI. 6.]

Obverse.	Reverse.

Type iii.

Inscription arranged to form a cross; in each angle of cross, a compartment containing a trefoil slipped, and in centre, square compartment containing circle. | Open quatrefoil ornament with quatrefoil in centre; leaves (sepals) in cusps; moneyer's name, &c., in compartments of quatrefoil.

[Num. Chron , vol. v. p. 14.]

Type iv.

Bust r., diademed. Around, inscription between two circles, divided by bust. | Two rude figures (Roman Emperors) facing; globe between them; above, rude bust with wings (angel). Around, inscription.

[Montagu Coll.]

Type v.

Bust r., diademed. Around, inscription, divided by bust. | Cross pattée within lozenge, from each angle of which issues a beaded straight line extending to edge of coin and dividing moneyer's name, &c.; crossbar at each angle of lozenge.

[Cf. Pl. VI. 7.]

Type v. var. a.

Same. | Similar: no crossbar at angles of lozenge.

[Cf. Pl. VI. 8.]

Type v. var. b.

Same. | Similar: limb of cross moline ℔ at each side of lozenge.

[Cf. Pl. VI. 9.]

---

* Coins (solidi) of this type were first struck by Valentinian I. A.D. 364-375 (see Vol. I. p. 2, Pl. 1a and 2). The specimen in Mr. Montagu's collection is unique.

Obverse.	Reverse.

Type vi.

Bust r., diademed. Around, inscription.* | Name of mint in monogram (Londonia): ornaments in field.

[Cf. Pl. V. 2–6.]

Type vii.

Very rude bust r. Around, moneyer's name. | Name of mint in monogram (Londonia): ornaments in field.

[Cf. Pl. V. 7.]

Type viii.

Rude bust r., diademed. Around, moneyer's name. | Name of mint in monogram (Lincolla): ornaments in field.

[Cf. Pl. IV. 14.]

Type ix.

Bust r., diademed. Around, inscription. | Name of mint in monogram (Londonia) between moneyer's name, &c., in two lines across field: ornaments in field.

[Cf. Pl. V. 8.]

Type x.

Small cross pattée. Around, inscription in four divisions. | *Name of mint in monogram (Londonia) between moneyer's name, &c., in two lines across field: small cross pattée before and after monogram.*

[Num. Chron., 1870, Pl. iv. 8.]

Type xi.

Small cross pattée. Around, inscription in four divisions between two circles. | Name of moneyer in monogram between name of mint (Lincolla) in two lines across field.

[Cf. Pl. V. 1.]

---

* A Penny of this type, of barbarous fabric, with bust to left, was in the Murchison Collection. It is described in the Sale Catalogue, 1866, No. 189.

Obverse	Reverse

Type XII

Bust r   Around, inscription | Name of mint in monogram ꝑoꝛꟻ (Borɩng?) between moneyer's name, &c, in two lines across field

[Cf Pl V 12]

Type XIII

Small cross pattee   Around, names of king and mint (Dorobernia) between two circles | In centre ꠰.   Around, name of St Eadmund between two circles

[Cf Pl IV 8]

Type XIII *var a*

Similar   name of king only | Same

[Cf Pl VI 10]

Type XIV

Small cross pattee   Around, inscription between two circles, generally in three or four divisions | Moneyer's name, &c, in two lines across field   ornaments

[Cf Pl VI 11-15]

Type XV

Small cross pattée   Around, inscription in three divisions and between two circles | Moneyer's name, &c, in two lines across field, divided by three crosses pattée

[Cf Pl VI 16-17]

Type XVI

Small cross pattee   Around, inscription between two circles | C V   T at extremities of even-limbed N cross   REX in angles

[Cf Pl VI 18]

Type XVII

Small cross pattee   Around, names of king and mint (Dorobernia) between two circles | Moneyer's name, &c, in two lines across field   ornaments

[Cf Pl IV 9-11]

Type XVIII

Names of king and mint (Orsnaforda) in three lines across field   ornaments | Moneyer's name, &c, in two lines across field, divided by three crosses pattee   ornaments

[Cf Pl V 9-10]

Obverse.	Reverse.

Type xix.

| Names of king and mint (Orsnaforda) in three lines across field: ornaments. | Moneyer's name, &c., in two lines across field, divided by long cross on two steps, sideways; pellets in angles of cross: ornaments.* |

[Cf. Pl. V. 11.]

Type xx.

| Bust r., diademed. Around, inscription. | T limbs extended by beaded lines to edge of coin dividing name of mint, &c. (Gleawaccaster). |

[Cf. Pl. IV. 13.]

Type xxi.

| Name of king, &c., in four lines across field. | First three letters of mint (Exanccaster and Winccaster) in pale: ornaments. |

[Cf. Pl. IV. 12 and V. 13.]

Type xxii.

| Name of king, &c., in four lines across field. | Name of moneyer, &c., in two lines across field: in field, pellets. |

[Cf. Pl. V. 14–15.]

Type xxiii.

| Small cross pattée. Around, inscription between two circles and frequently in three divisions. | Moneyer's name and mint (Baϸan) in two lines across field: ornaments. |

[Cf. Pl. IV. 7.]

---

* In the Cuerdale find was a Halfpenny of this type. It is a debased imitation, the cross having no steps, and the legends being blundered. It is figured in the *Num. Chron.* vol. v. p. 162.

No.	Obverse.	Reverse.	Moneyer.
	Series A. With Name of Mint.		
	BAÐAN. [Bath.]		
	Type xxiii.		
	Halfpenny.		
1	✠ER · EDR	ELI (or EIL?) · · · BAÐ [Pl. IV. 7.]	Eli.
		Wt. 8·5.	
	DOROBERNIA. [Canterbury.]		
	Type xiii.		
	(St. Eadmund.)		
2	✠ÆLFRED REX D̅Ö	✠SC EƏDMVIIRE Wt. 18·3. [Pl. IV. 8.]	No Moneyer.
	Type xvii.		
3	✠ELFDER DF✠ ◇RO	· BIƏER ƏM✠ Wt. 20·5.	Biareð (Biarnred?).
4	ƏEIFR✠ RE✠ D̅ÖRO	· BIRIV ƏLDM✠ · Wt. 24·0.	Birnuald or Burnuald.
5	✠ELFRED RF✠ ◇RO	· BIRIV ƏDN✠ · Wt. 20·7.	
6	ƏELFRED REX D̅ÖRO	BVRNV · ƏLDM✠ · Wt. 22·7.	

No.	Obverse.	Reverse.	Moneyer.
7	✠ELFRED REX DORO⌐	BYRNᴠ ᴀLDM✠ Wt. 22·4.	
8	„ „ DORO	BᴀRNᴠ ᴀLDM✠ Wt. 25·3.	
9	✠ELFRED REX DORO	BᴀRNᴠ LDM✠ Wt. 23·5.	
10	„ „ „	DIᴀRV ᴀLDM✠ Wt. 24·6.	Diaruald.
	[Pl. IV. 9.]		
11	✠ELFRED REX DOR⌐O	„ Wt. 21·9.	
12	„ „ DORO⌐	„ Wt. 23·4.	
13	ᴀELFRED⌐ REX D⌐ORO	„ Wt. 23·4.	
14	✠RDIᴠERI✠ EVIORO	DIᴠRV ᴀLDI✠ Wt. 19·6.	
15	✠ELFRED REX DOR⌐O	DIᴀRVᴀ LDM✠ Wt. 22·6.	
16	„ RDX DOR⌐O	DIᴀRᴠ LDM✠ Wt. 24·0.	
17	✠ᴀELFRED REX D⌐O	DIᴀRI ᴀLD✠ Wt. 18·5.	

No.	Obverse.	Reverse.	Moneyer.
18	✠LFRED RE✠ D✠D✠	DLⰗRD ⰜDM✠ Wt. 23·7.	
19	✠ELFRED REX D◇R◇¯	DVNNI NⵡM✠ Wt. 22·2.	Dunnine.
20	,, ,, ,,	DVNNI NⵡM✠ Wt. 20·0.	
21	✠ELFRED RE✠ D◇R◇	EⰗDV ⰗLM✠ Wt. 19·8.	Eaduald.
22	ÆLFRED REX D¯◇R◇	EÐELⵑT ⰗNM✠ Wt. 23·5.	Eðelstan.
23	✠ELFRED REX D◇R◇¯	,, *Var.* orna- ments, ⋰ Wt. 23·3.	
24	✠ELFRED REX D◇R◇¯	EÐELZT ⰗNM✠ ⋰ Wt. 21·8.	
25	,, ,, ,,	ⱵEREF REÐM✠ Wt. 23·0.	Herefreð (Hereferð).
26	,, ,, ,,	HVHFR EÐM✠ Wt. 20·8.	Hunfreð.
27	ⰗELFRED REX D¯◇R◇	TIRVⰗ LDM✠ Wt. 22·7.	Tiruald.

No.	Obverse.	Reverse.		Moneyer.
		BLUNDERED PENNIES.*		
28	NⱯDED✠ ⊏FDORO	BⱯERN EDEM✠	Wt. 23·0.	Biarnred?
29	✠ELEDRHVORO	BⱯRE EÐM✠	Wt. 20·6.	
30	✠ELFRDEVREVORO	BⱯREH EÐEИ✠	Wt. 20·0.	
31	✠ERDELNⱯORO ·	BⱯRE ИDM✠	Wt. 20·6.	
32	✠ELFDERD⊏✠ORO	BIⱯER ƎDM✠	Wt. 22·2.	
33	✠ERDNEⱯREOROB	BRⱯEИ EDИM✠	Wt. 21·7.	
34	✠ELFRDEVNOROⅭ	BRⱯEI EDM✠	Wt. 21·6.	
35	✠ELFDREVDORO	BRⱯII EDM✠	Wt. 19·5.	
36	✠ELFHRVDOROER	BRⱯN EDM✠	Wt. 20·7.	

* The names of the moneyers in this series are nearly always blundered and can only conjecturally be restored.

No.	Obverse.	Reverse.		Moneyer.
37	✠EDRNEÐⱱⲄIΟRΟ	BRⱱN EDM✠	Wt. 18·6.	
38	✠REDΟRΟNDRND	BRⱱ EÐM✠	Wt. 23·2.	
39	✠IREDRⱱDE✠ΟRΟ	BREIE EDM✠	Wt. 18·0.	
40	✠ERDELNⱱΟRΟ·	BREN EDM✠	Wt. 22·4.	
41	✠ELFRDREVΟRΟ	BRNⱯ EDM✠	Wt. 21·0.	
42	✠ELFDRFR DΟRΟ	BDEⱱE IRM✠	Wt. 20·5.	
43	NDRNR✠REÐΟRΟ	RⱱRⱱ EBM✠	Wt. 23·6.	Biarnred or Biarnuald?
44	✠EⲄⱠRÐEVΟRΟE	BⱱRV EDM✠	Wt. 21·4.	
45	✠ELFⱧRVDΟRΟER	BREIL EDM✠	Wt. 20·6.	
46	✠ELⱠRED RE✠ ΟRΟ	BDⱱE CⱱM✠	Wt. 23·2.	

No.	Obverse.	Reverse.	Moneyer.
47	✠ELFRDⱯOROEИ	BEⱯEI EĐM✠ Wt. 23·6.	
48	✠RDIⱯEPI✠EⱯIORO	BERⱯFL EĐM✠ Wt. 20·0.	
49	✠ⱰEᚦⱤDEⱯ · ИORO	BERIⱯ EĐM✠ Wt. 24·6.	
50	ⱯFᚦⱭR✠R · EX D⁻ORO	BIᚻRNI ⱯNDM✠ Wt. 21·7.	
51	✠EⱭⱯNIOROEDR	BIRIN ⱯDII✠ Wt. 18·5.	
52	ⱯELFREⱭX REX D⁻ORO	BIRNⱯ ⱯLDM✠ Wt. 22·3.	Biarnuald or Birnuald.
53	ⱯⱭNDⱯ · Ɑ · ✠RⱭⱭĐORO	,, Wt. 22·0.	
54	ⱯEᚻᚦ✠ REX DO⁻RO	,, Wt. 23·5.	
55	ⱯNⱭDP✠FLⱯDORO	BIRIⱯ ✠MDIⱯ Wt. 21·3.	
56	ORO◊✠ƎD✠IƎIƎⱯ	BIᚱNI IILDW✠ Wt. 19·0.	
57	ⱯⱭEP✠RE✠D⁻ORO	BNRIⱯ ⱯDM✠ Wt. 22·3.	

No.	Obverse.	Reverse.		Moneyer.
58	VϹⱧDΛ · Ϲ · ✚RϹϹꝘ◇R◇	BNRIV ΛDM✚	Wt. 21·1.	
59	ΛϹIЄP✚ PЄ✚ D¨◇R◇ [Pl. IV. 10.]	,,	Wt. 21·4.	
60	ΛϹIЄPF✚ P✚ D¨◇R◇	,,	Wt. 21·9.	
61	ΛϹЄRГ✚ REX D◇R¨◇	,,	Wt. 23·3.	
62	ΛFГϹD✚ R · Є✚ D¨◇R◇	,,	Wt. 19·0.	
63	✚RϹⱯFDDFRIFDIV	BNRIΛ IIDMI✚	Wt. 23·4.	
64	✚✚VVD · DϹV ·	BꓫIΛ ЄRИ	Wt. 20·0.	
65	✚RIINIVRRIIИFRVOD¨	BLIDИI ЄꝹM✚	Wt. 21·5.	
66	NꓣND✚RED◇R◇	ϹЄRMΛ ИM✚	Wt. 22·0.	Cerman ?
67	✚RDIⱯƐPI✚ƐVI◇R◇	DIⱯRⱯ ΛLDI✚	Wt. 20·5.	Diaruald.
68	RELEX✚FR◇ЄD◇	DⱯIRⱯЄ ΛLDM✚	Wt. 22·7.	
69	NDRNDR✚RED◇R◇	ELFZTΛ NM✚	Wt. 25·4.	Elfstan.

No	Obverse	Reverse	Moneyer
70	NND✠RED○R○	EEFꟑꟑΛ NM✠ Wt 22·3	
71	„ „	EIIꟑΛ NM✠ Wt 22·0	
72	✠D✠RFIEΛR○D○E	EĐELV IIEW✠ Wt 20·0	Efeluine
73	ΛⴹIEP✠ RE✠ D⁻○R○	.. EĐERE DM✠ Wt 23·2	Ltered
71	ENRND✠RED✠	REꟑΛ VDM✠ Wt 20·0	Resaud? (cf Desand, Vol I p 79)
		HALFPENNIES	
75	EP✠RE✠E○L○	BNRV ΛDM✠ Wt 9·0 [Pl IV 11]	Birnuald?
76	✠DRN⁻RFV○R○	BRVN EDM✠ Wt 8·6	Biarnred?
77	✠ERNⴹD○R○E	BVE EMN✠ Wt 8·2	Uncertain
78	✠ELFR✠DI✠E	ⴹDⴹV ✠MNꞀ Wt 8·3	I deulf (Edwulf?)

No.	Obverse.	Reverse.	Moneyer.

EXANCEASTER.
[Exeter.]

Type xxi.

79	✠ÆEL FREDRE XƩAXO NVM	E ∴X∴ Ā Wt. 24·3.	No Moneyer.
		[Pl. IV. 12.]	

GLEAPANCEASTER.
[Gloucester.]

Type xx.

80	ÆLFR ∴ EDX	ÆT GL EꓩⅤ Pꓥ· Wt. 24·5.	No Moneyer.
		[Pl. IV. 13.]	

LINCOLLA.
[Lincoln.]

Type viii.

81	⊢ERI BERT	(LINCOLLA) :* above, ⋎ ; below, ∴ Wt. 21·0.	Heribert.
		[Pl. IV. 14.]	
82	ERI ENER	,, below, cross pattée. Wt. 20·3.	

Type xi.

83	EL FR ED RE	L I I I I ✠ᚻꓭᛖE✠ Cᛙ LLꓥ Wt. 18·5.	Herebert ?
		[Pl. V. 1.]	

* Or LINCOLIA.

No.	Obverse.	Reverse.	Moneyer.
		LONDONIA. [London.] *Type* vi.	
84	ÆΓErD REX	(LONDONIA). Pellets in O; above, ⋮; below, ∴ Wt. 23·0. [Pl. V. 2.]	No Moneyer.
85	,, ,,	,, Wt. 25·0.	
86	ÆLFRE⋮⋮D REX	,, Pellets in O; above and on left, pyramid of dots; below, cross pat- tée. Wt. 23·4.	
87	ÆLFR ⋮⋮ ED REX	,, Pellets in O; above, cross pat- tée; below, pyra- mid of dots; on left, ⋮ Wt. 23·8.	
88	,, ,,	,, Wt. 25·5.	
89	ÆLFR ED REX	,, Pellets in O; above, cross pat- tée; below, pyra- mid of dots. Wt. 23·5.	
90	Æ ,, ,, ,,	,, Wt. 24·0.	
91	Æ ,, ,, ,,	,, Pellets in O; above, cross pat- tée; below, ...; on left, ⋮ Wt. 24·3.	
92	,, ,, ,,	,, One pellet only in O; above, cross pattée; below, ∴ Wt. 25·0.	
		[Pl. V. 3.]	

No.	Obverse.	Reverse.	Moneyer.
93	ÆLFR ED REX	₪ (LONDONIA). Two pellets in O; above, cross pattée; below, ∴. Wt. 25·6.	
		[Pl. V. 4.]	
94	ÆLF RED RE X	„ No pellet in O; above, cross pattée; below, ∴ Wt. 23·2.	
95	✠ÆГЬR ED RE	„ Pellets in O; above, ∷; below, ∴ Wt. 24·0.	
96	ÆLFR ED RE✠	„ No pellet in O; above, ▽; below, △; on left, pyramid of dots. Wt. 20·2.	
97	ELFR D RE✠	„ Pellets in O; above, cross pattée; below, ∴ Wt. 17·3.	
98	ELFR LD REX	„ Two pellets in O; above, ∴; below, cross pattée. Wt. 22·5.	
99	ÆLFR ED REX	„ No pellets in O and no ornaments in field. Wt. 21·2.	
100	∴ELFR ED RE	„ „ Wt. 18·5.	
101	ÆLIƆƐ E REX	„ Pellets in O; above, ∵; below, cross pattée. Wt. 21·5.	
102	✠EFRE ƷƆƷ	„ No pellets in O and no ornaments in field. Wt. 21·5.	
103	XELFꞀ ED RE	„ Pellets in O; above, ∵; below, cross pattée. Wt. 21·4.	

(Barbarous.)

No.	Obverse.	Reverse.	Moneyer.
		Fragments.	
104	ÆL . . . D REX	(LONDONIA) partly seen.	No Moneyer.
105	ÆLFR I	,, Pellets in O; above, cross pattée.	
106	ELFR . . . EX	,, Below, cross pattée.	
107	ELFR E	,, Pellets in O; below, .·.	
108	. . . . ED RE✠	,, No ornaments in field.	
	[Pl. V. 5.]		
109	ELFR . . . . +	,, Crossline of N runs upwards; pellets in O; below, cross pattée.	
110	. . FR	,, ,,	
		HALFPENNIES.	
111	ÆLFRED RE	(LONDONIA). Pellets in O; above, cross pattée; below, .·.; on left .· Wt. 8·0.	No Moneyer.
	[Pl. V. 6.]		
112	LF IE	,, No pellets in O; on left, .· Wt. 10·7.	
		Type vii.	
113	:: EROT .·. BOLT (Barbarous.)	(LONDONIA). Above and below, .·. Wt. 22·2.	Uncertain.
	[Pl. V. 7.]		

No.	Obverse.	Reverse.	Moneyer.
	Type ix.		
114	ÆLFR ·:· ✠ ED RE	AELF·:· [monogram] ✠ ƺTΛN Wt. 22·0.	Ælfstan.
		[Pl. V. 8.]	
115	ÆLFR✠ ✠ED REX	HEΛE✠ [monogram] ✠ VVLF✠ *Var.* Above monogram, cross pattée. Wt. 24 0.	Heauulf.
116	✠ΛELF RED REX	TILEVINE ✠ [monogram] ✠ M⊙NETA Wt. 23·2.	Tileuine.
117	ÆLF ... . EX	⌐I . . . . ✠ [monogram] IOHETΛ (Fragment.)	Uncertain.
		ORSNAFORDA. [Oxford.]	
		Type xviii.	
118	·:· ✠RSNΛ ÆLFRED F⊙RDΛ ·:·	·:· BERIV ✠·✠·✠ ΛLDIO ·:· Wt. 22·0.	Beriuald (Bernuald ?).
		[Pl. V. 9.]	
119	·:· ✠RSИΛ ELFRED✠ F✠RDΛ ·:·	·:· BERIV ✠ ✠ ✠ ΛLDM·⊙· ·:· Wt. 22·5.	Bernald (= Bernuald).
120	⊙RSNΛ ÆFRED✠ F⊙RÐΛ	BERIIΛ ✠·✠·✠ ΛLDMO Wt. 18·3	Bernald (= Bernuald).

No.	Obverse.	Reverse.	Moneyer.
121	✠ ⊙RSNⱯ ELFRED FORDⱯ ✠	✠ BERIIⱯ ✠ ✠ ✠ ⱯLDIIO ✠ Wt. 17·7.	
122	∴ ✠R☺IIⱯ ÆLFRED FORDⱯ	∴ BERNⱯ ✠ ✠ ✠ ⱯLDEIO ∴ Wt. 20·7.	
123	⊙R☺IIⱯ ÆLIⒸED F✠RDⱯ ∴	∴ BERNⱯ ✠ ✠ ✠ ⱯLEDMO ∴ Wt. 21·4.	
124	✠ ✠I☺IIⱯ✠ IELIRED F✠RNⱯ ∴	BERIIⱴ ✠ · ✠ ⱯDIIO Wt. 24·3.	
125	✠RSIIȺ ÆFRED E⊙RDⱯ	BERIIⱴ ✠ ✠ ✠ ⱯLDIIO Wt. 22·8.	Bernuald.
126	✠RSNⱯ ÆLFRED F⊙RDⱯ ∴	∴∴ BERIIⱴ ✠ ✠ ✠ ⱯLDII·✿· ∴ Wt. 22·3.	
127	∴ ✠HⱾNⱯ ÆLFRED F✠RDȺ ∴	BERNⱴ ✠ ✠ ✠ ⱯLDMO Wt. 25·6.	
128	OHⱾNⱯ ÆLFRED FORDⱯ ∴	∴ BERNⱴ ✠ ✠ ✠ ⱯLDHO ∴ Wt. 19·0.	
129	OWⱾNⱯ ÆLFRED FORDⱯ	BERNⱴ ✠ ✠ ✠ ⱯLDNO Wt. 22·5.	
130	⊙ℛⱾNⱯ ÆLFRED✠ E⊙RDⱯ	BERIIⱴ ✠ ✠ ✠ ⱯLDIIO Wt. 20·0.	

No	Obverse	Reverse	Moneyer
131	·ᴖᴢᴎᴧ ÆLFRED✠ EoRDᴧ	BERᴎᴗ ✠✠✠ ᴧLDMO Wt 21·7	
132	⸸Rɷllᴧ·✠ ÆᴦFRED F✠RDᴧ	BERᴎᴗ ✠✠✠ ᴧLDᴎO Wt 22·0	
133	,,	BERᴎᴗ ✠✠✠ ᴧᴦᴑMO Wt 21·9	
134	,,	BERᴎᴗ ✠✠✠ OMDᴦᴧ Wt 20·5	
135	oRᴢNᴧ ÆLFRED✠ FoRDᴧ ✠	BERIIᴗ ✠✠✠ ᴧLDIIO Wt 21·4.	
136	✦Rɷllᴧ ÆLFRED F✠RDᴧ ·	ᴧIIᴚƎB ✠✠✠ oᴖIᴑIᴋ Wt 19·0	
137	OHᴢIIᴧ ᴧᴦᴇRID EORDᴧ	BERIIᴗ ✠✠✠ ᴧLDIIO Wt 17·3	
138	✦ᴦɷllᴧ✠ ᴧᴦFRED F✦RDᴧ	BERᴎᴗ ✠✠✠ ᴧᴦᴑMO Wt 20·2	
139	✦ᴧɷᴎᴧ ᴧᴦFRED F✦IIᴧ	ᴗᴎᴚƎB ✠✠✠ ᴧᴦDIIO Wt 20·5	
140	✦Rɷᴎᴧ ELFRED✠ FoRDI	BERᴎᴗ ✠✠✠ ᴧLDIIO Wt 20·8	

No.	Obverse.	Reverse.	Moneyer.
141	⊹ R☾ᴎ⋀ ELFRED✠ F⊹RDI	BERIIV ✠ ✠ ✠ ⋀LDIIO Wt. 20·7.	
142	OVSII⋀ ELFRID✠ F☉RD⋀	BERᴎV · · · · ⋀LDᴎO Wt. 22·5.	
143	◎RSᴎ⋀ ELFRED✠ F☉RDI	BERIIV ✠ ✠ ✠ ⋀LDIIO Wt. 20·4.	
144	ORSN⋀ ELFRED FORD⋀	BERIIV ✠ ✠ ✠ ⋀LEDI Wt. 22·1.	
145	⊹ R☾ᴎ⋀ ELFRED✠ F⊹RDI	BERIV ✠ ✠ ✠ ⋀LEDIO Wt. 22·0.	
146	ORSN⋀ ELFRED FORD⋀	BERIIV ✠ ✠ ✠ ⋀LRDIIO Wt. 20·0.	
147	⊹RSᴎ⋀ ELFRED✠ F⊹RDI	BERIIV ✠ ✠ ✠ ⋀LRIIO Wt. 20·9.	

BLUNDERED PENNIES.

148	IꙄIꓤI ᗡIꓤꟻ⅃Ǝ FIꓤI⋎	BERᴎV ✠ ✠ ✠ ⋀LDᴎO Wt. 21·2.	Bernuald.
149	Oᴎ⋎II⋀ ᗡƎꓤꟻ⅃Ǝ ⱵORD⋀	VIꓱꓯIV ✠ ✠ ✠ ⋀LDMO Wt. 21·8.	
150	⊹ ⋏ꓤIIV \ƎⱵFRED F⋎☾IIV	ᗡƎꓤᴎⵏ ✠ ✠ ✠ ⋀⅃ᗡᴎO Wt. 20·7.	

No.	Obverse.	Reverse.	Moneyer.
151	IRIOI ECFRID FIRIΛ	ERDLS ✛✛✛ CRIEI Wt. 22·2.	Uncertain.
152	OIRFO ERIERII ERED	OIERR O✛✛ IDERI Wt. 22·0.	Uncertain.

HALFPENNY.

(Blundered: name of Moneyer on *obv.* and Mint on *rev.*)

153	IEIII ΛEFEO IDIIO	ONSII ✛✛✛ EOORΛ Wt. 9·7.	Uncertain.
	[Pl. V. 10.]		

Type xix.

154	✛ RSNΛ ELFRED FORDΛ	BERNV ΛLDNO Wt. 21·0.	Bernuald.
	[Pl. V. 11.]		

ROISENG?
[Castle Rising?]

Type xii.

155	ÆLFRED REX	ÆÐEL ⚏⚏E ⸪ VFMO Wt. 22·9.	Æðelaf or Æðelulf.
	[Pl. V. 12.]		

No.	Obverse.	Reverse.	Moneyer.

PINCEASTER.
[Winchester.]

Type xxi.

| 156 | ✠ÆL FREDR EX ƧÆX OИVM | P ∴ I ∴ N | No Moneyer. |
| | [Pl. V. 13.] | Wt. 24·6. | |

| 157 | ✠ÆL [F]RED R [EX]ƧÆX · · · · | [P] [✠] I ✠ N | (Fragment.) |

SERIES B. WITHOUT NAME OF MINT.

Type xxii.

OFFERING PENNIES.

158	✠AEL FREDRE XƧAXO NVM	· ELI · · · MO ·· ·	Eli.
	Var. Around, two circles, inner one of dots.	*Var.* Around, two circles, inner one of dots. Wt. 162·4.	
	[Pl. V. 14.]		

159	[✠AEL] [FRED]RE [XƧ]AXO NVM	E[LI] MO	
	Var. Around, two circles, inner one of dots.	*Var.* Around, two circles, inner one of dots. (Fragment.) Wt. 53·0.	
	[Pl. V. 15.]		

No.	Obverse.	Reverse.	Moneyer.
		Type i.	
160	✠ΛELBRED∴ REX	· MⵟN · ✠BO · ΣΛ ⵝ · ETΛ · (Broken.)	Bosa.
161	„ ∴ REX	· MON · ⵎΙΛLMOD · ETΛ ∵ Wt. 18·5.	Cialmod.
162	✠ΛELBRED RE ∷	· HⴸMO · DEIⵎMV · HETΛ · Wt. 20·3.	Deigmund.
163	„ REX	MON HEBEⵎΛ ETΛ Æ base (Broken).	Hebeca ?
164	✠ΛELFRED : REX	ⵎMⵟ MⵠNNIN NETΛ (Broken.)	Mannine.
165	✠ΛELBRED : REX	· MON · OꟅHERE · ETΛ ∵ Wt. 14·3.	Oshere.
166	„ „	· MON · ꟅEFREÐ · ETΛ ∵ Wt. 17·6.	Sefreð.
167	„ „	· MON · ꟅIⵎESTEF · ETΛ ∵ (Pierced.)	Sigestef.
168	✠ELFRED REX	FMO ꟍIⵎEꟍTE NETΛ Wt. 15·0.	Sigestef.
169	✠ΛEBBRED REX	· MON · TIDBΛLD · ETΛ · (Broken.)	Tidbald.

No.	Obverse.	Reverse.		Moneyer.
170	ELŁEREDREX	EMON TILEFEIN ETA ·.·		Tilefein (Tileuine ?).
	[Pl. VI. 1.]		Wt. 18·5.	
171	✠ÆELBRED : REX	·.· MON ·.· VVLFÆRD ·.· ETΛ ·.·		Uulfard.
			(Broken.)	
	WITH M–X *on obv.*			
172	✠ELFERED M‾X	·.· MOH ·.· ✠TΛTΛ : ·.· ETΛ ·.·		Tata.
	[Pl. VI. 2.]		Wt. 18·0.	
	Type i. *var. a.*			
173	✠ΛELBRED REX	· DM ✠ BIΛRNVL · NETA ·.·		Biarnuald.
			(Broken.)	
174	,, ,,	MON ✠DVNN ETΛ ·.·		Dunn.
	[Pl. VI. 3.]		Wt. 11·5.	
175	,, ,,	MON ƧIEEƧTEF ETΛ		Sigestef.
			Wt. 20·7.	
	Type i. *var. b.*			
176	✠ΛELBRED REX	MON MΛNNINⅭ ETΛ		Mannine.
	[Pl. VI. 4.]		Wt. 15·1.	
	Type i. *var. c.*			
177	✠ΛELBRED RE✠	FMO ⅭIΛLVL ΝETΛ		Cialulf ?
			Wt. 19·0.	

No.	Obverse.	Reverse.	Moneyer.
178	ΛELBRED RE✠	MON ✠DVINΣ ETΛ ∴ Wt. 15·5. [Pl. VI. 5.]	Duine (Dunine?).
		Type ii.	
179	[✠ΛELFR]ED REX	[EÐ ER] E · D M · [O NĒT] Λ (Fragment.) [Pl. VI. 6.]	Eðered?
		Type v.	
180	✗Λ⋯ELFRED REX	✠DI ΛR MV ND *Var.* Ends of bead- ed line floriated. Wt. 19·3. [Pl. VI. 7.]	Diarmund.
181	✠ÆLFRE D REX Ƨ	DVИ ИΛ ∴ MOИ ETΛ *Var.* Opposite each side of lozenge, ∴ (Broken.)	Dunna.
182	. . . . . . D REX∴ ƧΛX	EÐLE M . . . . . ETΛ *Var.* Opposite one side of lozenge, small cross. (Fragment.)	Eðelmod.
183	✠ΛELFRED REX ƧΛX (Legend undivided.)	LVL LΛ∴ MⵔN ETΛ Wt. 22·2.	Lulla.
184	ELFRE D REX	✠OT RH TM VND *Var.* Dot opposite each side of lo- zenge. Wt. 17·0.	Torhtmund.
185	. . . . . ED REX ƧΛX (Legend undivided.)	. . . . . LF MⵔN ET *Var.* Cross opposite each side of lo- zenge. (Fragment.)	Uncertain.
186	. . . . . . D R . .	. . . . LVV . . . . (Fragment.)	Uncertain.

No.	Obverse.	Reverse.	Moneyer.

Type v. *var. a.*

| 187 | ✠ÆLFRED REX ꝫΛX | ÆΛD VLF MOИ ETΛ
Var. ∴ outside one side of lozenge.
Wt. 21·3. | Eadulf. |
| | [Pl. VI. 8.] | | |

Type v. *var. b.*

| 188 | ELFR · ED RE · | ᕲIOL VVLF MON ETΛ
Wt. 20·7. | Cioluulf. |
| | [Pl. VI. 9.] | | |

Type xiii. *var. a.*

(St. Eadmund.)

| 189 | ꝺЯꝺƎꝶꝶƎꝶƎᕲ✠ | ✠CECΛDMVIIDRF
Var. Two pellets in type.
Wt. 19·5. | No Moneyer. |
| | [Pl. VI. 10.] | | |

Type xiv.

Pennies.

190	✠ED ER EL RE	ΛBE · ꝱEL Wt. 21·0.	Abenel
191	✠REIVFᕒVIDMEII‥	ΛDVÆ · ΛDM✠ · Wt. 22·6.	Aduard (Eadueard).
192	‥ ‥	ΛDVÆR · · · ΛDM✠ · Wt. 21·8.	
193	✠EL FR ED RE	ÆLF ∶ · VΛLD Wt. 20·3.	Ælfwald.

No	Obverse	Reverse		Moneyer
194	✠EL FR ED RE	ÆLFP ᚪLD	Wt 20 6	
195	ᚪEL FRE DREX	ÆÐEL✠ · ʃTᚪN	Wt 23 9	Æᵗelstan
196	,, ,, ,,	ÆÐER ✠ EDMO	Wt 21 0	Æᵗᵉred
197	✠EL FR ED RE	Iᗡ⅃ᗅ · IOᱭVᗅ ·	Wt 20 5	Uncertain
198	+ ,, ,, ,, ,,	ᚪLV · VDᗅ	Wt 21 0	Aluuada? (Luda?).
199	EL ᚱ ED ᱭE✠	BEᗅᒐ ZTᚪN	Wt 23 8	Beagstan
200	EL [ᚱ] ED ᱭE✠	BEᗅᒐ ZTᚪN	(Broken)	
201	ÆL ᚱ ED ᱭEX	BEᚪᒐ ZTᚪN	Wt 23 0	
202	✠EL FR ED RF	BEᒐᱭ · TᚪN	Wt 22 7	
203	ÆL FRE DRE	BEORM MERM	Wt 23 7	Beornmer
204	✠EL FR ED RE	BERH TEᱭE	Wt 17 5	Berhtere

No.	Obverse.	Reverse.	Moneyer.
205	✠EL FR ED RE	· BERh · · TERE ∴ Wt. 17·3.	
206	✶ ,, ,, ,, ,,	BERN · RED ∶· Wt. 23·0.	Bernred.
207	,, ,, ,, ,,	BERN ∶· · RED ∶∶· Wt. 23·5.	
208	✠ ,, ,, ,, ,,	BED ∶· · RERN Wt. 15·0.	
209	,, ,, ,, ,,	BEB ∶ BERH Wt. 14·4.	
210	,, ,, ,, ,,	BERNV ✠ ✠ ✠ ALDM⊙ Wt. 17·5.	Bernuald.
211	✶ ,, ,, ,, ,,	BIORH RED Wt. 23·0.	Biornred.
212	EL FR ED REX	,, Wt. 22·0.	
213	✶ ,, ,, ,, RE	BIORII · RED ∶· Wt. 23·2.	
214	EL FR ED RE ·	BRIϴ · · ·∶ ARD Wt. 20·0.	Briřard.
215	✠ ,, ,, ,, ,,	BOFA · MOИE Wt. 23·5.	Boga (= Buga).
216	✠ᛘEL FR ED RE	BOⳐA · MOII Wt. 24·0.	

No	Obverse		Reverse		Moneyer
217	✠ÆL FR ED RE		BVGA MON	Wt 214	
218	„ „		„ Var Orna- ments,	Wt 210	
219	„ „		„ „	Wt 210	
220	✠EL FRED RE		„ „	Wt 200	
221	✠EL FR ED RE		BPNH ERE	Wt 214	Burnhere or Byrnhere ?
222	✗ „ „ „ „		BVRN EREA	Wt 205	
223	ÆL FRE DREX		BYRN ELM✠	Wt 235	Burnelm or Byrnelm ?
224	ÆL „ „		BYRN ELM✠	Wt 240	
225	ÆL FRE DREX		„ Var Orna- ments,	Wt 244	

[Pl VI 11]

226	ÆL FRE DREX		BYRN ELM✠	Wt 237	
227	EL FR ED REX		CIRES ŒIEN	Wt 201	Ciresrien or Heirserie ?
228	+ÆL FR ED RE		CVDB ERNT	Wt 194	Cudberht or Cudberht

No	Obverse	Reverse	Moneyer
229	ÆL FRED REX	CVDB ERNT Wt 19 6	
230	✠ ÆLFRED RE	✠ „ Var Ornaments. ✠ Wt 24 0	
231	✠ ÆL FR ED RE	CVDB ERHT Wt 21 9	
232	✠ ÆL R E D F E	„ Var Orna-ments, Wt 25 9	
233	✠ ÆL FR ED RE	CVDB ERNT Wt 23 4	
234	„ „ „ „	„ Var Orna-ments, ✠ Wt 22 7	
235	✠ ÆLFR ED RE	CVDB ✠ ✠ ERNT Wt 21 4	
236	✠ ÆL FR ED RE	CVDB ERNT Wt 23 0	
237	✠ ÆLFRED RE	CVDB ERNT Wt 22 4	
238	„ „	„ Var Orna-ments, Wt 22 4	
239	ÆLFR ED REX Var Four pellets around cross	CVDB ERIIT Wt 19 0	
240	„ „ Var Four pellets around cross	„ Var Or-naments Wt 21 0	

No.	Obverse.	Reverse.	Moneyer.
211	+EL FR ED RE	CVDB ERIIT Wt. 20·7.	
212	✚ ,, ,, ,, ,,	CVDB ER·:·NT · Wt. 21·9.	
213	,, ,, ,, ,,	CVDB ERNT Wt. 21·9.	
214	✠ÆLIR ED REL	,, *Var.* Orna- ments, Wt. 20·0.	
215	✱ELFIEED ЯE	CVDB ERIII Wt. 16·0.	
216	✠ELF REDRE	ꓭꓯꓷꓛ ТНЯƎ Wt. 20·4.	
217	✠EL FR ED RE *Var.* Four pellets in angles of cross.	CYDB ERHT Wt. 23·3.	
218	,, ,, ,, ,,	CΛÐB ERHE:· Wt. 19·5.	
219	EL FR ED REX	CVÐB ERHT Wt. 21·5.	
250	,, ,,	CVÐB EꓭHꓕ ·: Wt. 18·2.	
251	✠EL FR ED RE	CVÐ VVLF Wt. 23·6.	Cu?uulf.
252	,, ,,	,, *Var.* Orna- ments, Wt. 23·8.	

No.	Obverse.	Reverse.	Moneyer.
253	ELFR ED REX	CVÐ VVLF Wt. 20·2.	
254	✠ELFR ED E	,, ,, Wt. 20·6.	
255	✠EL ER ED RE	CYN EVLF (Broken.)	Cyneulf.
256	✠EL FR ED RE	DEA LINE Wt. 23·0.	Dealinc or Dealing.
257	✠ ,, ,, ,, ,,	DEAL INE Wt. 22·4.	
258	EL FR ED REX	DEAL LAMO Wt. 23·0.	Dealla.
259	,, FR ,, ,,	DELA M✠N Wt. 22·2.	
260	✠EL RII R R E	DIAR LDM✠ Wt. 24·2.	Diarald. (Diaruald.)
261	✠EL FR ED RE	DIARV ALDM✠ Wt. 22·5.	Diaruald.
262	,, ,, ,, ,,	,, *Var.* Ornaments, Wt. 21·5.	
263	,, ,, ,, ,,	,, ,, Wt. 23·1.	
264	✠ÆL FR ED RE	DVDIG ✠ ✠ HON Wt. 24·0.	Dudig.

No	Obverse.	Reverse.	Moneyer.
265	✠ ÆL FR ED RE	DVDIG ✠✠✠ HON Wt. 21·2.	
266	✠EL FR ED RE	„ *Var.* Orna- ✠ · ✠ ments, Wt. 21·2.	
267	ÆL FRE DRE	DVN MAN Wt. 21·3.	Dunna.
268	„ „ „	DVN OAN Wt. 23·5.	
269	ÆL FRE DR EX	✠DVNNIA MOIETA Wt. 22·0.	
270	✠EL FR ED RE	DVNN NEM✠ Wt. 22·4.	Dunninc.
271	„ ER „ „	DVNN INEM✠ Wt. 22·0.	
272	✠ÆL FR ED RE	EADA VALD Wt. 21·5.	Eadueald.
273	✠EL FR EP RE	EAD VALD Wt. 20·5.	
274	„ „ ED „	∴ɑΛƎ VΛ1D Wt. 20·8.	
275	„ „ „ „	EADVA LDM✠ Wt. 22·3.	

No.	Obverse.	Reverse.	Moneyer.
276	✠EL FR ED RE	EⱯDVE ⱭLDM✠ Wt. 23·0.	
277	✠ÆLFR ED RE	EⱯDV VⱭLD Wt. 22·7.	
278	✠ÆL FR ED RE	EⱯDV VⱭLD Wt. 24·5.	
279	,, ,, ,, ,,	,, Wt. 24·5.	
280	✠ⱭELFRED RE	,, Wt. 23·9.	
281	,, ,,	,, Wt. 24·5.	
282	✠ÆLFREDRE *Var.* Pellet in each angle of cross. [Pl. VI. 12.]	EⱯDV VⱭLD Wt. 24·0.	
283	✠EL FR ED RE	EⱯDV VⱭLD Wt. 20·0.	
284	✠ELFR ED RE *Var.* Pellet in each angle of cross.	EⱯDV VⱭLD Wt. 24·0.	
285	,, ,, *Var.* Pellet in each angle of cross.	,, *Var.* Ornaments, Wt. 24·4.	
286	✠EL FR ED RE	EⱯE TⱭᴎ Wt. 18·5.	Eactan ? (Eadstan ?).
287	,, ,, ,, ,,	EⱭLD VVLF∴ Wt. 24·9.	Ealduulf.
288	✳ ,, ,, ,, ,,	ELBER H✠M (Double struck.) Wt. 19·5.	Ecberht.

No	Obverse	Reverse	Moneyer
289	ÆE LF RED RE	VLF ECV Wt 236	Ecwulf.
290	ÆEL FRE DRE	VLF ECV Wt 213	
291	ÆELFRED RE✠	ECVL FMON Wt 230	
292	ÆE LF RED RE	,, Wt 210	
293	ELF RE DR ÆA	,, Var Orna- ments, Wt 237	
294	ÆELFREDR Æ	,, ,, Wt 217.	
295	ÆE LF RED RE	FMON ECVL Wt 230	
296	ELF RED REX	ECVV· LFMO Wt 230	
297	DR EÆ ELF RE✠	ECVVLF MONE Wt 235	
298	ÆE LFR EDR E	ECÞ VLF Wt 210	
299	ÆELFR EDR Æ	,, Var Orna- ments, Wt 219	
300	ÆE LF RED RE	ECÞ MLF Wt 230	
301	ÆLF RED REX	ECÞ VLF Wt 235	

No.	Obverse.	Reverse.	Moneyer.
302	✠EÆELFR ∴ E✠	ECÐ ∴ MLF Wt. 24·0.	
303	EL FR ED REX	ELDA · MEFE Wt. 20·5.	Elda
304	✠EL FR ED RE	ELDA ∴ · MEFEC Wt. 22·3.	
305	✠EL EE „ „	ƎLDA ∴ (retrograde) · MEFEC · (retrograde) Wt. 24·1.	
306	ÆL FR ED REX	ELFVA · LDMC Wt. 23·2.	Elfuald.
307	✠EL FR EDR E	EЯICV ∴ · · VALD Wt. 21·7.	Ericuuald?
308	AEL FRE DREX	· EDEL ∴ · · ·STAN · Wt. 19·4.	Edelstan.
309	✠EL FR ED RE	EDEL S R. · GELDA Wt. 21·4.	Edelstan and Gelda.
310	✠AE LFR EDR E	· EÐELV · INEM ✠ · Wt. 23·0.	Eðeluine.
311	✠EL FR ED RE	· EÐELV · IIÆM ✠ · Wt. 23·2.	
312	✠ELFR ED REX	„ Wt. 23·0.	
313	✠ELFREDCE (retrograde)	· CDELV (retrograde) · · · IIEM ✠ (retrograde) Wt. 23·2.	

No.	Obverse.	Reverse.	Moneyer
314	✠EL FR ED RE	EÐELV ИEM✠ Wt. 21·2.	
315	✠·ΛE LFR ED RE	∴ EÐELV LFM✠ Wt. 24·3.	Eðelulf.
316	✠EL FR ED RE	„ Var. Ornaments, Wt 22·7.	
317	„ „ „ „	„ „ ∴ Wt. 24·5.	
318	✠EL ⊏R ED REX	„ „ ∴ Wt. 22·0.	
319	✠ΛE LFR EDR E	EDERE DWⵝИ Wt. 22·5.	Eðered.
320	✠EL FR ED RE	∴ EÐER EDM✠ Wt. 23·4.	
321	„ „ „ „	∴ EÐERE DM✠N Wt. 23·7.	
322	✠REFDⴥRHΛED REˉ	∴ EÐRⴥE EÐM✠ ∴ Wt. 20·5.	
323	✻EL FR ED RE	FER LVN Wt. 20·0.	Ferlun ?

No.	Obverse.	Reverse.	Moneyer.
324	✠EL FR ED RE	ĠARII · · · NEM✠ · Wt. 23·0.	Garuinc?
325	✠ ,, ,, ,, ,,	GOD · AM:: Wt. 23·3.	Goda.
326	✠ ,, ,, ,, ,,	· GOD ⁘ · ⁘AM · Wt. 23·7.	
327	✠[EL FR] ,, ,,	∴ GODA · MON (Fragment.)	
328	,, ,, ,, ,,	· GVÐ · HERE · Wt. 20·5.	Guðhere.
329	EL ꝒH RE ED	· GVD · ƎIƎH · Wt. 25·3.	
330	✠EL FR ED RE	hAΓD ⁘ · ⁘ BERE Wt. 20·5.	Haldberc or Berchald?
331	✠EL FR ED RE	· HEAV VLF · Wt. 22·5.	Heauulf.
332	✠EL FR ED RE	ИELI · IПП⊐ Wt. 19·6.	Helicau?
333	,, ,, ,, ,,	hERE · FERD∴ Wt. 17·0.	Hereferd or Hereferð.
334	ƎRDƎ Яꟻ ⅃Ǝ✠	hERE FERD Wt. 20·8.	

No.	Obverse	Reverse		Moneyer
335	✠EL FR ED RE	hERE FERÐ	Wt 219	
336	✠ ,, ,, ,	,, *Var Orna-* ment,	Wt 231	
337	, ,, , ,,	hERE FERÐ	Wt 217	
338	✠ELX ,, ,, ,,	hERE FERÐ	Wt 255	
339	✠EL , ,, ,,	hEREF ERÐ	Wt 235	
340	,, ,, ,, ,	hEREM ODM✠	Wt 228	Heremod
341	✠ELF RED RE	ИERE MVИD	Wt 236	Heremund
342	✠EL FR ED RE	hERE ЛVLF	Wt 212	Hereuulf
343	✠EL FR ED RE	HVNB ERHT	Wt 238	Hunbeaht
344	✠E LF RE DRE	,, *Var Orna-* ・ ment,	Wt 212	
345	✠ЛID ID D RE	IDЛ HOIE	(Broken)	Ida?
346	✠EL ED ED RE	IILE LIHE	Wt 205	Uncertain

No.	Obverse.	Reverse.	Moneyer.
347	✠ED FI IΛ RE	IILE ⁚ LIIE ⁚ Wt. 22·7.	
348	EL FR ED RE	IᕄDE LBΛRD Wt. 21·4.	Indelbard.
349	EL FR ED REX	LᕄDE EIM⊙ Wt. 20·4.	Ludeen, or Ludig.
350	,, ,, ,, ,,	LVDᑕ MON ⁚ Wt. 23·0.	
351	✸EL FR ED RE	LVD IᕄM Wt. 23·9.	
352	✠ÆL FR ED REX	LVD IᕄW Wt. 25·8.	
353	✸EL FR ED R	LVDI ᕄᑎO Wt. 20·9.	
354	✸E[L F]R ED RE	[L]VDI ᕄᑎ⊙ (Fragment.)	
355	ÆL FR ED REX	LVDIᕄ MON ⁚ Wt. 24·6.	
356	✸ÆL FR ED RE	LVDIᕄ NON Wt. 17·0.	
357	EL FR ED REX	LVDIᕄ MON Wt. 20·4.	
358	,, ,, ,, ,,	LVDIᕄ M⊙N ' Wt. 23·5.	

No.	Obverse.	Reverse.		Moneyer.
359	EL FR ED REX	LVDID M✧N	Wt. 24·6.	
360	„ „ „ „	LVDID MⓄN	Wt. 18·0.	
361	ELFRED REX Ƨ	LVLLΛ MOИET	Wt. 20·7.	Lulla.
362	✕EL EᴙED RE	ΛΛⓄEL ꟻHⓄINᒀ	Wt. 12·8.	Moelf?
363	✚EL FR ED RE	· Oꟻ⌐ · ᴙΛV	Wt. 20·8.	Uncertain.
364	„ „ „ „	OƧVV LꟻMO	Wt. 23·2.	Osuulf.
365	EL FR ED RE	OƧVVL ꟻMOИ	Wt. 23·1.	
366	„ „ „ REX	OƧVV ꟻMON	Wt. 23·0.	
367	✚EL FR ED RE	OƧVVL ꟻMOИE	Wt. 23·9.	
368	„ „ „ „	SÆRIS IHIVI	Wt. 20·2.	Særis?
369	EL FR ED REX	ZIⅭE VVⷱLD	Wt. 22·5.	Sigenuald.
370	„ „ „ „	SIMVN MEFEⅭ·	Wt. 20·0.	Simun.

[Pl. VI. 15.]

No	Obverse	Reverse		Moneyer
371	EL FR ED RE	ZTF AMVꟅ	Wt 19 4	Stefanus
372	✠EL FR ED RE	TILE VOIE	Wt 19 3	Tilenoie (Tilenmne ?)
373	,, ,, ,, ,,	TILE VVINE	Wt 21 0	Tilenmne
374	,, ,, , ,,	TILE VVNE	Wt 23 2	
375	✿ ,, ,, ,, ,,	TILE VVNE	Wt 25 0	
376	ELFRE DR EX	.,	Wt 19 6	
377	EL ER ED REX	TILE VVNE	Wt 21 2	
378	✠EL FR ED RE	TLE VVNE	Wt 21 9	
379	,, *Var* Four pellets around cross	TIRVA LDM✠	Wt 20 7	Tirwald
380	,, ,, ,, ,,	,, *Var* Ornaments, (Γ)	Wt 23 2	
381	✠ELFRED RE	,, ,,	Wt 21 1	
382	✠EL FR ED REX	., ,,	Wt 23 7	

No.	Obverse.	Reverse.	Moneyer.
383	✠EL FR ED RE	TIRVEΛ · LDM⌘ · Wt. 22·8.	
384	+ " " " "	VIC · BΛD·: Wt. 20·2.	Uigbald, or Uuigbald.
385	✠ " " " "	∴VIC· · ·BΛLD Wt. 21·5.	
386	+EL ER E[D] RE	VVIC · · BΛID (Fragment.)	
387	+EL FR ED RE	VVIC · ·: BALD Wt. 22·6.	
388	" " " "	ϘIVV ·: · ОJΑB Wt. 21·8.	
389	✠ " " " "	· VVIN · EM✠ · Wt. 24·4.	Uuine.
390	" " " "	VVIИ ·: ✱ :· EMOИ (Broken.)	
391	EL FR ED RE	VVIN · EMOИ Wt. 21·7.	
392	✠ " " " "	V-VINIC M✠IE Wt. 18·5.	Uuiniger.
393	✠ELFRED RE	·VVI·NI· · GE·RVS· Wt. 22·3.	

No	Obverse	Reverse	Moneyer
394	ÆELF RE D REX	VVLF RED Wt 195	Uulfred
395	ÆEL FRE DREX	VVLF RED ✚ Wt 214	
396	ÆEL FRE DREX	VVLF RED✚ Wt 213	
397	ÆEL FRE DREX	,, Wt 218	
398	,, ,, DREX	,, Wt 213	
399	✚ÆEL FRE DRE	VVLF RED Wt 210	
400	ÆEL FR ED RE	,, *for* Orna- ment, Wt 210	
401	ÆEL FRE DRE	VVLF RED✚ Wt 216	
402	,, ,, ,,	VVLF ✚ RED Wt 212	
403	,, ,, ,,	VVLF RED✚ Wt 217	
404	ÆEL ,, ,,	VVLF ✚RED Wt 217	
405	· ÆLF RED REX	VVLF RED Wt 208	

No	Obverse	Reverse		Moneyer
106	✠ÆL FR ED RE	VVLF RED ✠	Wt 230	
107	ÆL FRE DRE	VVLF RED	Wt 237	
108	ÆL FRE DRE	VVLF RED	Wt 210	
109	ÆL FRE DRE	Var Cina ments,	Wt 236	
110	✠ÆE LFR EDR E	VVLF REDM	Wt 232	
111	✠ÆL FR ED RE	ꟻⵡVV GƎꓣ	Wt 228	
112	✠ꓣEIH✠H CXI	✠ VVLF ✠ ✠ RIEDI ✠	Wt 107	
113	✠EL FR ED RE	VVNB ERHT	Wt 258	Wynbcrht
114	✠EL FR EDRE	VVYꟼ BERHT	Wt 228	
115	✠EL FR ED RE	ꟼ BE RET	Wt 241	
116	✠ÆL F ꓣEDRE	ꟼⵡNB ERHT	Wt 213	

No.	Obverse.	Reverse.	Moneyer.
417	✛EL FR EDRE	ΡΛИВ ∴ ∴ ÉRHT Wt. 20·8.	
418	„ „	„ *Var.* Orna- ∴ ∴ ments, Wt. 22·5.	
419	✛ИΛCXL✛REIИ	ΡΛИВ ∴ ∴ ÉRHT Wt. 19·0.	
420	✛EL FR ED RE *Var.* Pellet in each angle of cross.	ΡΛNB ∴ ∴ ERHT Wt. 21·6.	
421	✱EL FR EDE	„ Wt. 17 8.	
422	✛EL · FR ED RE	ΡYNB ∴ ∴ ÉRHT Wt. 21·5.	
423	✛EL FR ED RE *Var.* Pellet in each angle of cross.	ΡYhB∴ ∴ ERHT∴ Wt. 24·7.	

BLUNDERED PENNIES.

No.	Obverse.	Reverse.	Moneyer.
424	EL FR ED REX	BIΛY ∴ HOƎI Wt. 20·0.	Uncertain.
425	„ „ „ RE	ИRFΛ ⋯ EΛM · Wt. 20·5.	Uncertain.
426	EL FR ED R	ИRE DIƎꞀ Wt. 16·5.	Uncertain.
427	ꞀƎ FD ƎЯ ✛IЯ	IEИE ✛ ∴ RΛW Wt. 22·8.	Uncertain.

No.	Obverse.	Reverse.	Moneyer.

FRAGMENTS OR HALFPENNIES.

No.	Obverse.	Reverse.		Moneyer.
428	. . L FR ED . .	VRNV M ✖		Byrnuald ?
429	✚EL . . . . . E	∴ ⋮ ERHT [Pl. VI. 14]		Cudberht ?
430	. . . FR ED . .	∴ ⋮ RHT		
431	✚ . . . . ED RE	DVDIG ✚		Dudig.
432	. . . . . . D RE	ᗡOD		Goda.
433	ᴧEL . . . . REX	VVLF		Uulfred ?

HALFPENNIES.

No.	Obverse.	Reverse.		Moneyer.
434	✚EL · RF · DRE ·	ИRIꓭ ⅂ᗡM✚ [Pl. VI. 15.]	Wt. 10·0.	Birnuald ?
435	✚ᴁLFᴦ ED ᴦE	ᴄVDB ∴⋮⋮ ERHT ··	Wt. 9·5.	Cudberht.
436	ELF FD ᴦEX	IᗡVᴄ ∴✚·⋮ TIᴙꓱ	Wt. 7·4.	
437	✚ELFᴙDENAᴙᗡ (Inscription reading right to left, from below.)	DRᴧI · ADII✚	Wt. 9·0.	Uncertain.
438	✚ᴁLFᴦFDEE	EᴧDV ∴⋮⋮ VᴧᴌD	Wt. 7·7.	Eaduuald.

No.	Obverse.	Reverse.	Moneyer.
439	✠EIꞂ IꞂ ꞂIE	ƎVIꞀƎ ᗡᒐⱯꞀ Wt. 7·7.	
440	✠EL FRED RE	Ᵽ. BE RHT Wt. 8·6.	Wynberht.

Type xv.

441	ⱯEL FRE DREX	✠ⱯELF ✠✠✠ ꙄTⱯH Wt. 23·4.	Ælfstan.
442	„ „ DRE	ÆÐER ✠✠✠ EDMO Wt. 24·6.	Æðered.
443	„ „ DREX	ÆÐER ✠✠✠ EDMO✠ Wt. 24·2.	
444	„ „ „	✠ⱯÐEL ✠✠✠ VLFMO Wt. 24·2.	Aðelulf.

[Pl. VI. 16.]

445	„ „ „	„ Wt. 24·2.	
446	„ „ „	„ Wt. 24·6.	
447	„ „ DRE	„ Wt. 24·0.	
448	„ „ „	„ *Var.* No pellet above and below. Wt. 24·0.	
449	„ „ „	ⱯÐEL ✠✠✠ ✠VLFMO Wt. 24·2.	

No.	Obverse.	Reverse.	Moneyer.
450	ΛEL FRE DREX	BEORH ✠ ✠ ✠ MÆRИ Wt. 23·7.	Beornmaer.
451	,, ,, ,,	ꙅΛM ✠ ✠ ✠ ✠ꙅON Wt. 24·5.	Samson.
452	,, ,, DRE	,, Wt. 24·2.	
453	✠ÆL FRE DRE	✠ Ā ⅃⅃Ɍ ✠✠✠ SSC ✠ Wt. 22·3. [Pl. VI. 17.] Blundered.	Uncertain.
		Type xvi.	
454	✠ELFRED RE	C ∴ R V ✠ T ✠ N E Wt. 21·2. [Pl. VI. 18.]	No Moneyer.

EADWEARD THE ELDER

Succ A D 901, DIED A D 925

Moneyers

Abba
Adalberht
Aduald
Æðelfred?
Æðelred
Æðelstan, Eðelstan, &c
Æðeluuine
Æðeluulf, Aðelulf, &c
Æðel-, see also Eðel-
Æðered [Æðelred?]
Æðfrið
Agnes
Alhstan or Ealhstan
Aðulf
Badda
Beahstan
Beanred [= Beornred?]
Beornere
Beornferð
Beornred or Biornred
Beornuuald, Bernuuald, or Biornuuald,
&c
Beornuulf
Berhtred
Bernqar
Biorhald [Biornald? = Biornuuald?]
Biornard, Byrnard, &c [= Beornred?]
Biornhelm [= Byrnelm]
Boiga, Boga, &c
Brece or Brego
Briht (London)
Bryhtwald
Buga [cf Boiga]
Burden?
Burnelm or Byrnelm
Cenbriht
Ciolulf
Clip
Cudberht
Cuðferð?
Cynestan
Deora, Diora [Deoramod?]
Deormod, Deoramod
Deornred [=Beornred?]
Deoruuald
Dryhtwald [= Bryhtwald?]
Dudig
Durlac, see Þurlac
Eadered or Eadfred?
Eadhelm
Eadmund
Eaduuald
Ealhstan
Earduulf
Eared [Eadred?]
Earnuulf
Earuuard
Eauulf
Eclaf or Ellaf?
Edelgar
Eremund, Eigmund
Eorfrmund
Etile
Eðeluulf [see Æðeluulf]
Farmen
Framuuis
Frioðulf
Frið
Friðeberht, Friðelberht, &c
Gaeald?
Garcard
Garulf
Grimwald
Gunðberht
Gunne
Gunter
Hadebald or Haðebald
Heardber
Herebald
Heremfretia?
Heremod
Heðulf?
Hunfred
Hunlaf
Igereu
Iofermund
Irfara
Iua
Lamle?
Lanfer
Liofhelm
Maguard
Mann
Marbert
Odo
Ordulf
Oslac
Osulf
Pastor
Pitit
Rægenulf
Rennard, Renard, &c

Riornbed ? [or Riornred ?].
Samsun.
Sigebrand.
Sigeferð.
Sigot.
Spron[ald ?].
Stear.
Tila [or Tisa], see Etile.
Torhthelm.
Tuda.
Ulf.
Uualeman (Wallman).
Uuarmer.
Uucaldhelm.

Uuefred [Uuilfred ?].
Uilfred ?
Uuillaf [Uylla].
Uulfgar.
Uulfheard [Uulfard].
Uulfred.
Uulfsige.
Uynberht or Wynberht.
Waltere.
Warimer [= Uuarmer].
Wighard.
Winegear.
Þurlac.

DESCRIPTION OF TYPES.

Obverse.	Reverse.

Type i.

Name of king, &c., in four lines across field.	First three letters of mint across field; above and below, ornaments.

[Cf. Pl. VII. 1.]

Type ii.

Small cross pattée. Around, inscription between two circles.	Moneyer's name, &c., in two lines across field; crosses, pellets, &c., symmetrically arranged in field.

[Cf. Pl. VII. 2–5.]

Type iii.

Bust, l., generally diademed. Around, inscription between two circles.	Moneyer's name, &c., in two lines across field; crosses, pellets, &c., symmetrically arranged in field.

[Cf. Pl. VII. 6–9.]

Type iv.

Rude bust, r. Around, inscription between two circles.	Moneyer's name, &c., in two lines across field; crosses, pellets, &c. symmetrically arranged in field.

[Cf. Pl. VII. 10, 11.]

Obverse.	Reverse.

Type v.

Small cross pattée within circle. Around, inscription.

Moneyer's name across field, divided by saltire formed of rosette and four bars pommés; above and below, cross pattée.

[Trans. Chester Arch. Soc., 1864.]

Type vi.

Rosette within circle. Around, inscription.

Moneyer's name, &c., in two lines across field, divided by pellet between two rosettes of dots; above and below, curved lines pommés, enclosing pellets.

[Trans. Chester Arch. Soc., 1864.]

Type vii.

Small cross pattée. Around, inscription between two circles.

Moneyer's name, &c., across field and between two lines.

[Cf. Pl. VII. 12.]

Type vii. var. a.

Same.

Similar; no lines above and below moneyer's name.

[Cf. Pl. VII. 13.]

Type viii.

Small cross pattée. Around, inscription between two circles.

Moneyer's name across field; above and below, star of eight rays pommés.

[Cf. Pl. VIII. 1.]

Obverse.	Reverse.

Type ix.

Small cross pattée. Around, inscription between two circles.	Moneyer's name, &c., across field, surmounted or divided by floral design.

[Cf. Pl. VIII. 2-9.]

Type x.

Small cross pattée. Around, inscription between two circles: border of dots.	*Moneyer's name across field; above bird l., feeding from branch (Dove and olive branch); below,* ∵ *: border of dots.*

[Rud. Pl. 16, 7 and 16.]

Type xi.

Small cross pattée. Around, inscription between two circles.	Hand of Providence from clouds; moneyer's name, &c., in field.

[Cf. Pl. VIII. 10-12.]

Type xii.

Small cross pattée. Around, inscription between two circles.	Moneyer's name, &c., in two lines across field, divided by building (façade of church?).*

[Cf. Pl. VIII. 13, 14.]

Type xiii.

Small cross pattée. Around, inscription between two circles.	Moneyer's name, &c., across field; above, line, on which church; below, cross pattée.

[Cf. Pl. VIII. 15.]

Type xiv.

Rose formed by cross pommée with voided centre over cross moline. Around, inscription between two circles.	Moneyer's name, &c., in two lines across field; cross, voided in centre, between two circles dividing legend; above and below, Δ.

[Cf. Pl. VIII. 16.]

* This façade much resembles the type of the Prætorian Gate on coins of Constantine the Great and his successors.

DESCRIPTION OF COINS.

No.	Obverse.	Reverse.	Moneyer.
	SERIES A. WITH NAME OF MINT.		
	BAÐAN. [Bath.]		
	Type i.		
1	✠EĀD VVEĀRD REXꟅĀX OИVM	·✠· BĀÐ ·✠· [Pl. VII. 1.] Wt. 28·0.	No Moneyer.
	SERIES B. WITHOUT NAME OF MINT.		
	Type ii.		
2	✠EΛDVVEΛRD REX	ΛBBΛ ✠✠✠ MOŇ Wt. 25·3.	Abba.
3	✠EĀDVVEΛRD RE✠	IIEIEIIF ✠✠✠ ꞄEDIIO Wt. 24·4.	Æðelfred ?
4	✠EΛDVVEΛRD REX	ÆÐELꟅ TANM⁻O Wt. 23·8.	Æðelstan.
5	,, ,,	AEÐELꟅ TÁNMO Wt. 24·1.	Æðelstan.
6	✠ ,, ,,	ÆÐELV VIꞄEM⁻O Wt. 24·3.	Æðeluuine.

No.	Obverse.	Reverse.		Moneyer.
7	✠EADVVEARD REX	∧ĐEL✠ ✠ ✠ ✠ VLFMO	Wt. 24·5.	Æðeluulf.
8	✠E∆DVVE∆RD ,,	∆ĐEL✠ ✠ ✠ ✠ VLFM⁻⊙	Wt. 24·7.	
9	✠E∆DVVE∆RD ,,	∧EĐEL ✠ ✠ ✠ VVLFMO	Wt. 27·4.	
10	✠EADVVEARD ,,	ÆĐER ✠ ✠ ✠ EDM⁻O✠	Wt. 24·2.	Æðered.
11	E∧DVVE∧RD REX	ÆĐER ✠ ✠ ✠ EDMO✠	Wt. 24·5.	
12	✠E∆DVVE∆RD REX	ÆĐER ✠ ✠ ✠ EDMO	Wt. 24·3.	
13	✠E∧DVVE∧RD REX	,,	Wt. 24·5.	
14	,, ,,	ÆĐER ✠ ✠ ✠ EDM⊙	Wt. 25·0.	
15	E∆DVVE∆RD REX	ÆĐER EDMO	Wt. 24·4.	
16	,, ,,	,,	Wt. 24·5.	
17	✠EADVVEARD REX	BEAH⅄ ✠ ✠ ✠ TANMO	Wt. 26·2.	Beahstan.

[PL. VII. 2.]

No.	Obverse.	Reverse.	Moneyer.
18	✠EADVVEARD REX	BEORN ✠ ✠ ✠ EREM⁻O Wt. 24·8.	Beornero.
19	„ „	BEORN ✠ ✠ ✠ FERÐM⁻⊙ Wt. 24·0.	Beornferð.
20	✠E·ADVVEARD „	BEORNV ✠ ✠ ✠ VALDMO Wt. 25·2.	Beornuuald or Bernuuald.
21	✠EADVVEARD ⌐EX	BER NV ✠ ✠ ✠ ALDMO Wt. 24·2.	
22	✠EADVVEARD REX	BER Ħ ✠ ✠ ✠ REDM⁻O Wt. 24·5.	Berhtred.
23	✠EADVVEARD REX	BRE⊏ ✠ ✠ ✠ EM⁻O Wt. 25·3.	Brecc or Brege.
	[Pl. VII. 3.]		
24	✠EADVVEARD REX	BVGA ✠ · ✠ MON Wt. 23·7.	Buga.
	[Pl. VII. 4.]		
25	✠EADVVEARD REX	BVRH✠ ✠ ✠ ✠ ELMMO Wt. 24·7.	Burnelm or Byrnelm.
26	✠EADVVEARD REX	BYRN ELIMMO Wt. 24·4.	

No	Obverse	Reverse	Moneyer
27	EADVVEARD REX	CIOLV ✛⊙✛ LFM⁻O ∴ Wt 21 2	Ciolulf.
28	✛EADVVEARD REX	CLIP ✛✛✛ M⁻ONE ·· Wt 21 5	Clip
29	„　　　„	CLIPM ✛✛✛ ⊙NETA Wt 21 3	
30	✛EADVVEARD REX	CVDB ✛✛✛ ERNTO Wt 21 0	Cudberht
31	„　　　„	✛ DEORV ✛✛✛ VALDMO (Broken)	Deoruuald
32	✛EADVVEARD REX	DVDIC ✛·✛ MONE Wt 25 2	Dudig
33	„　　　„	DVDIC ✛ ✛ MONE Wt 21 0	
34	✛EADVVEARD REX	EADE ✛✛✛ REDI⁻O (Chipped)	Eadered or Eadfred.
35	✛EADVVEARD REX	EADNV ✛✛✛ NDM⁻O Wt 23 6	Eadmund
36	✕EADVVEARD RE✛	✛ EADV ✛·✛ VALD ✛ Wt 23 6	Eaduuald

No.	Obverse.	Reverse.		Moneyer.
37	✠EADVVEARD RE✠	✠ EADV VALD ✠	Wt. 24·5.	
38	✠EADVVEARD REX	EADV ✠ · ✠ VALD	Wt. 25·3.	
39	✠EADVVEARD REX	EALHS ✠✠✠ TANHO	Wt. 24·4.	Ealhstan.
40	,, ,,	ECLAF ✠✠✠ MONE	Wt. 23·7.	Eclaf.
41	✠EADVVEARD REX	EDELL ✠✠✠ ARFIˉO	Wt. 24·8.	Edelgar.
42	✠EADVVEARD REX··	EICMV ✠✠✠ NDMON	Wt. 21·2.	Eicmund.
43	EADVVEARD REX	FRIÐEB ✠✠✠ RHTMˉO	Wt. 24·5.	Friðeberht.
44	✠ ,, ,,	CARE ✠✠✠ ARDMˉ⊙	Wt. 25·6.	Garcard.
45	,, ,,	CRIMP ✠✠✠ ALDMˉ⊙	Wt. 24·0.	Grimwald.
46	,, ,,	HEARD ✠✠✠ HERMˉ⊙	Wt. 22·5.	Heardher.

No.	Obverse.	Reverse.	Moneyer.
47	✠EADVVEARD REX	IVAMO ✠ ✠ ✠ NETA✠ (Chipped.)	Iua.
48	✠EADVVEARD REX	MANNM ✠ ✠ ✠ ONETA Wt. 25·0.	Mann.
49	✠EADVVEARD REX	OEOIO ✠ ✠ ✠ DEVO Wt. 21·3.	Uncertain.
50	✠EADVVEARD REX	ORDV ✠ ✠ ✠ LFM‾O Wt. 24·6.	Ordulf.
51	,, ,,	PITIT ✠ ✠ ✠ ‾MONE Wt. 24·4.	Pitit.
52	,, ,,	RÆLEN ✠ ✠ ✠ VLF‾MO Wt. 24·2.	Rægenulf.
53	✠EADVVEARD REX	ΣILEBR ✠ ✠ ✠ ANĐ‾MO Wt. 22·1.	Sigebrand.
54	,, ,,	ΣILE ✠ ✠ ✠ FERĐ Wt. 23·3.	Sigeferð.
55	✠EADVVEARD REX	ΣILOT ✠ ✠ ✠ MONETA Wt. 24·3.	Sigot.

No.	Obverse.	Reverse.	Moneyer.
56	✠EADVVEARD REX	TILAM ✠✠✠ ONETA Wt. 24·7.	Tila.
57	✠EADVVEARD RE✠	VVALE ✠✠✠ IIAIITTO Wt. 26·2.	Uualeman.
58	✠EADVVEARD REX	VVAR ✠✠✠ MERMO Wt. 24·0.	Uuarmer.
59	„ „	VVEALD ✠✠✠ HELMMO Wt. 22·8.	Uucaldhelm.
60	EADVVEARD REX	VVLF ✠✠✠ ARD✠ Wt. 24·3.	Uulfheard.
61	✠EADVVEARD „	VVLF✠ ✠✠✠ ARDMO Wt. 24·0.	
62	✠EADVVEARD REX	VVLF ✠✠✠ ARDMO Wt. 24·3.	
63	✠EADVVEARD REX	VVLFE ✠✠✠ ARDMO Wt. 24·7.	
64	✠EADVVEARD REX	VVLFHE ✠✠✠ ARDMO Wt. 24·4.	
65	„ „	VVLFHE ✠✠✠ ARDM̄O Wt. 24·6.	

No	Obverse	Reverse	Moneyer
66	✠EADVVEARD REX	VVLF✠ ✠ REDMO Wt. 21·6	Uulfred.
67	·✠EADVVEARD REX	VVLF ✠ ·:· ✠ REDMO Wt 21·6	
68	✠EADVVEARD REX	VVEF ✠ ✠ ✠ REDMO · (Chipped)	
69	✠EADVVEARD REX *Var* Pellet in field	VYNB ✠ ✠ ERHT Wt 23·2	Uynberht
70	✠EADVVEARD REX	· PALT ✠ ✠ ✠ ERE·O · Wt 25·7	Waltere

HALFPENNIES

No	Obverse	Reverse	Moneyer
71	✠EADVVEARD REX [Pl VII 5]	BIORN ✠ ✠ ✠ VVALD · Wt 9·3	Biornuuald
72	✠EADVVEARD R[E]✠	VYNB ✠ ✠ ERNT (Chipped)	Uynberht

Type III

No	Obverse	Reverse	Moneyer
73	✠EADVVEARD REX	ÆÐER ✠ ✠ ✠ EDM·O Wt 25·0	Æðered.

No.	Obverse.	Reverse.	Moneyer.
74	✠EΛDVVEΛRD RX	BIORW ✠✠✠ VLDИO Wt. 19·3. [Pl. VII. 6.]	Biornuuald.
75	✠EADVVEĀRD REX	CVDB ✠·✠ ERNT✠ Wt. 25·7.	Cudberht.
76	Ā ,, ,,	DVDIC ✠·✠ MONE· Wt. 24·3. (Double struck.)	Dudig.
77	✠EADVVEARD REX	DVDIC ✠✠✠ MON· ✠ (Broken.)	
78	✠EΛDVVEARD REX	EALHS ✠✠✠ TANMO Wt. 25·4. [Pl. VII. 7.]	Ealhstan.
79	✠EADVVEARD REX	FRAMV ✠✠✠ VISM⁻O Wt. 24·8.	Framuuis.
80	✠EADVVEARDREX	ERAIIV ✠✠✠ OIISIV Wt. 27·7.	
81	✠EADVVEARD REX	CARE ✠✠✠ ARDM⁻O Wt. 23·4.	Gareard.
82	,, ,,	GRIMP ✠✠✠ ALDM⁻O Wt. 24·5.	Grimwald.

No	Obverse	Reverse		Moneyer
83	✠EADVVEARD REX	✠ IIEBEIED ✠ ✠ ✠ IIEEIEIC · · ✠ · ·	Wt 25·3	Uncertain
84	✠EADVVEARD REX	HERE ✠ ✠ ✠ MOD⁻M	Wt 24·3	Heremod.
		[Pl VII 8]		
85	✗ „ „	MEIOΛ ✠ ✠ ✠ ИCIET · ·	Wt 20·5	Uncertain
86	✠EΛDⱯⱯEΛR✠	ИIEICO ✠ ✠ ✠ ИIOICB ·	Wt 22·6	Uncertain
87	✠EΛDVVEΛRD REX	ИEIOIR ✠ ✠ ✠ OIIEICI · · ·	Wt 22·0	Uncertain
88	✠EADVVEARD REX	· ✠ · TILAM ✠ ✠ ✠ ONETA · ·	Wt 23·0	Tila.
89	„ „	VVLF · ✠ ✠ ✠ REDMO · ·	Wt 23·0	Uulfred
90	„ „	„	Wt 24·3	
91	„ „	· VVLF · ✠ ✠ ✠ REDM⁻O · ·	Wt 24·0	
		[Pl VII. 9]		

No.	Obverse.	Reverse.	Moneyer.

Type iv.

92	✠OЯᗡЯƎVᗡAƎ✠	⠒ IIDRI ✠ ✠ ✠ IRICI ⠒ Wt. 19·4. [Pl. VII. 10.]	Uncertain.
93	✠EADVVEARD RE *Var.* Before head, cross pattée.	⠒ BEDИ ✠ ✠ ✠ RIOIЯ ⠒ Wt. 25·7. [Pl. VII. 11.]	Biornred.

Type vii.

94	+EADVVEARD REX	ΛᗡVLFM Wt. 25·0. [Pl. VII. 12.]	Aðulf.
95	✠EΛDᑭER[E]X	LΛNFER Above and be- low, rose. (Broken.)	Lanfer.

Type vii. *var. a.*

96	✠EADVVEARD REX	ᑭBERHT · M̄O Wt. 24·0. [Pl. VII. 13.]	Wynberht.

Type viii.

97	✠EADVVEARD REX	BRE⋮CE✠ Wt. 24·5. [Pl. VIII. 1.]	Brece or Brege.

Type ix.

98	✠EADVVEARD REX	ADVLEMO Above, line on which floral design (bud be- tween two branches, rising from base on two steps); below, cross pattée. Wt. 27·0. [Pl. VIII. 2.]	Aðulf.

No	Obverse	Reverse	Moneyer
99	✠EADVVEARD REX	BOIGA Above and below, floral design rising from base on two steps Wt 25 0 [Pl VIII 3]	Boiga
100	✠EADVVEARD REX	BV GA Floreate stem with two branches enclosing legend Wt 21 0 [Pl VIII. 4]	Buga
101	✠EADV· ·RD REX·	[C]VDBERHT Above and below, three branches united at base (Broken) [Pl VIII 5]	Cudberht
102	✠EADVVEARD REX	HEREMOD Above, line terminating in two eight petalled flowers, from it springs rose between two branches; below, eight petalled flower Wt 24 0 [Pl VIII 6]	Heremod.
103	✠EADVVEARD REX	HVNLAF Above, rose between two branches rising from upper of two steps, below, bud between two branches rising from upper of two steps Wt 23 0 [Pl VIII 7]	Hunlaf
104	„ „	IOFERHN Above, line from which rises rose between two branches, under which H ▷, below, full - blown rose Wt 24 6 [Pl VIII 8]	Iofermund.

No.	Obverse.		Reverse.		Moneyer.
105	✠EADVVEARD REX	OƧVLF		Above and below, curved branches forming ꝫ. Wt. 24·6.	Osulf.
	[Pl. VIII. 9.]				
	Type xi.				
106	✠EADVVEARD REX	AL HꙄ TA N · MO ·		*Var.* Hand open, with cruciform nimbus. Wt. 21·8.	Alhstan (Ealhstan).
	[Pl. VIII. 10.]				
107	„ R REX	Λ Ꝿ L V F Ƨ		*Var.* Hand open, without nimbus. Wt. 24·4.	Aᵭulf.
	[Pl. VIII. 11.]				
108	„ R „	D X DE Oꞃ MO DM ✠		*Var.* Hand giving benediction (Latin—third and fourth fingers closed). Wt. 24·0.	Deormod
	[Pl. VIII. 12.]				
	Type xii.				
109	✠EADVVEARD REX	EA DV ꜧ ND		Wt. 25·6.	Eadmund.
	[Pl. VIII. 13.]				
110	✠EADVVEARD · REX	IR FA RA MO		Wt. 18·4.	Irfara.
	[Pl. VIII. 14.]				
	Type xiii.				
111	✠EADVVEARD REX	VVLFꝄAR		Wt. 24·6.	Uulfgar.
	[Pl. VIII. 15.]				

H 2

No.	Obverse.	Reverse.	Moneyer.

Type xiv.

No.	Obverse.	Reverse.	Moneyer.
112	✠EADVVEARD REX	△ EIEMV NDMON ▽ [Pl. VIII. 16.] Wt. 25·0.	Eiemund.
113	„ „	▽ VVLFHE ARDMO ▽ Wt. 24·6.	Uulfheard.

AETHELSTAN.

Succ A D 925, died A D 940 or 941

Moneyers

Abba [= Abun?] (Chester)
Abonel (Hertford, Maldon)
Abun (Exeter)
Adelbert (York)
Ælfnoð
Ælfred (Wareham)
Ælfric or Elfuc (Canterbury)
Ælfstan (London)
Ælfwald (London)
Ælfmine (Chester)
Ælf-, see also Elf-
Æðelberht
Æðelferð (Canterbury)
Æðelm [Æðelmod?] (Winchester)
Æðelmod [Aðelmod]
Æðelnoð or Eðelnoð (Derby, Nottingham)
Æðelred (York)
Æðelsige (Canterbury)
Æðelstan [Æðelstan]
Æðelwold [ef Haðelwold] (Gloucester)
Æðelwine (Shaftesbury)
Æðel-, see also Aðel-
Æðered (Chester, London)
Alet
Alfeah
Allstan
Amelric (Winchester)
Are [Ere?]
Arnulf, Arnalf, &c (York)
Asalf or Asulf
Aðelm [Aðelmod or Aðelmund] (Wallingford)
Aðelmod
Aðelmund
Aðelwold
Aðelwulf (Winchester)
Aðel-, see also Æðel
Aðulf (Winchester)
Baldric
Baldwine
Barbe (Norwich)
Bardel or Burdel (Norwich)
Barifeð [Barnferð?]
Beahred or Beanred (London)
Belge or Belge
Beorard [ef Beorneard] (Chester)
Beorhtulf or Biorhtulf (Bath, Dartmouth)
Beornwald and Byrnwald (Wallingford, Wareham)

Berhtelm [Berhthel] Byrhthelm, &c (Langport, Shrewsbury)
Bernard [ef Beorneard]
Bernere
Bernger
Biorhtric
Biorhtuald [= Bryhtuald]
Biorneard, Beorneard, &c (London)
Boiga or Boigalet (Chester, Derby)
Bryhtuald
Burhtelm [cf Berhtelm] (Wardborough)
Burdel [= Bardel?] (Norwich)
Burneld
Burnhelm
Bus?
Byrhtelm, see Berhtelm
Byrnwald (Wallingford)
Cenapa or Cnapa (Chester)
Cenberht or Cuberht (Shrewsbury)
Cudelm
Clae
Clael?
Cnað? (Chester)
Credard
Cristign
Cuqela?
Cugem?
Cunulf
Cynewald
Dequn
Deorerd (Chester)
Deorulf or Diorulf (Chester)
Deornuald, Diarunald, &c
Domnces, Dominic, &c [= Domnicu-]
Dorfie?
Dryhtuald [= Bryhtuald?]
Duriant
Eadgar (Norwich)
Eadgild (Canterbury)
Eadlif or Eadulf (Chester)
Eadmund or Edmund (Chester, Shrewsbury)
Ladru (Lewes?)
Eadstan
Eadulf
Edelstan
Eardulf (Oxford, Stafford)
Ernulf
Eelriht (York)
Feghud (Shrewsbury)
Eclaf or Ellaf (London)

Edred [Eadred] (Shrewsbury)
Efrard (Chester)
Egillorht [Ingellorht?]
Einard
Ele? (London).
Elfric, *see* Ælfric
Elfwin
Elf-, *see also* Ælf-
Ellaf, *see* Eclaf
Engillorht, Ingellorht, &c
Eofermund, *Efermund,* &c (Shrewsbury)
Erard [= Efrard?] (*Chester*)
Ere (London)
Eric
Etram (Canterbury)
Eðel-, *see* Æðel-, or Aðel-
Facle [Pawle?] (*London*)
Folcred
Fram
Frard [= Efrard] (Chester)
Fredard
Friðebriht
Frotger, *Froðger* (Shrewsbury)
Froterm?
Fugel
Fulrad
Garcard (London)
Garulf
Genard [= Conard?] (Exeter)
Gienceu?
Giongbald (Norwich)
Gis?
Gislemer
Gota
Grimwald (London)
Higenrede (Derby)
Harger [= Herigar?]
Haðelberht [Æðelberht?]
Haðelwold [Æðelwold?]
Heldalt (York)
Herdwit?
Heremod
Herne (Bath)
Hildulf [Hildulf]
Hrodear [= Hroðgar] (Norwich)
Hungar
Hunlat (Hereford)
Huurie
Igere or *Here (London)*
Ildeberht
Impi
Ingellorht
Ingelric (Oxford)
Iohann
Isnl [= Snel?]
Landac?
Leofric (Winchester)
Lifing, *Leuing,* &c (*Norwich*)
Liotholm (London)
Lutihram (London)

Maldomen (Chester)
Marten (Chester)
Magnard
Mali
Manna, Manne, Man, &c (*Canterbury, London, Norwich, Tamworth*)
Mannine.
Manticen (Norwich)
Maðelwold? [= Haðelwold or Æðelwold?] (*Oxford*)
Megenfreð (*Canterbury*)
Megred (Chester)
Monðign [Mon Þegn?] (Warwick)
Noðer
Nybald (Shrewsbury)
Oda or *Odo*
Oslac [= Oslaf?] (Chester)
Oslaf, *Osulf* (Chester)
Oswart
Otic (Winchester)
Paul, Paules or Paulus (Chester)
Pitit
Ragenald, Regnald, &c (*Exeter,* York)
Rægenulf and Rænulf (Chester, *Winchester*)
Regengrim
Regenward (Oxford)
Regnald, *see* Rægenald
Reinere
Renard or *Rinard (Exeter)*
Rinvald [= Regnald?)
Roghard
Rotberht (York)
Salces? (Chester)
Sandac, *see* Landac
Sigar[es], Sihares (Derby)
Sigebrand
Sigedrald?
Sigeferð (Chester)
Sigeland (Exeter, Oxford)
Sigenulf
Sigfold[es]
Siuard [=Siward] (York)
Smili
Snel (*Chester*)
Sota
Spromene
Stefanus
Steland
Tidgar, Tidger, &c (Chester)
Tda
Tuotes or *Totes (Chester)*
Torkthelm (Canterbury)
Turstan, *see* Þurstan
Uucaldhelm
Uuilluf or Uuillaf (*Shrewsbury*)
Uuidric
Uulfgar (Chester)
Uulfheard (Winchester)
Uulfsig or Uulfsige
Uulfstan or Wulfstan (Chester)

Uurnelm (Oxford)
Uuynsige (Langport)
Uðelric (Oxford)
Welnberht
Wiard (Chester)
Wihtemund, Wimund, &c (Stafford)
Wilebald
Wilne

Winele
Witil
Wulfhelm (London)
Wulfman or Uulfman
Wyltsig
Þurlac
Þurstan (Lincoln)

DESCRIPTION OF TYPES

Obverse	Reverse

Type I.

| Small cross pattée Around, inscription between two circles | Moneyer's name, &c, in two lines across field, crosses, pellets, &c, symmetrically arranged in field |

[Cf Pl X 5-6]

Type II

| Star of six points, between two pellets Around, inscription between two circles | Moneyer's name, &c, in two lines across field, crosses, pellets, &c, symmetrically arranged in field |

[Cf Pl X 7]

Type III

| Small cross pattée Around, inscription between two circles. | Moneyer's name in two lines across field, three pellets between, above and below, floral ornament |

[Cf Pl X 8]

Type IV

| Small cross pattée Around, inscription between two circles | Straight line dividing field, above, building (church?), moneyer's name, &c, above and below or wholly below the line |

[Cf Pl IX 2 & X 9]

Type V

| Small cross pattée Around, inscription between two circles | Small cross pattée Around, inscription between two circles |

[Cf Pl IX 1]

Type V var a

| Same | Small cross pattée surrounded by four pellets Around, inscription between two circles |

[Cf Pl IX 3]

Type V var b

| Same | Cross pattée voided Around, inscription between two circles |

[Cf Pl IX 11]

Obverse	Reverse

Type v *var c*

Same | Rosette of dots Around, inscription between two circles

[Cf Pl IX 8]

Type vi

Rosette of dots Around, inscription between two circles | Rosette of dots Around, inscription between two circles

[Cf Pl IX 9]

Type vi *var a*

Same | Small cross pattée Around, inscription between two circles

[Cf Pl IX 10]

Type vii

Bust r, diademed Around, inscription between two circles, divided by bust | Moneyer's name, &c, in two lines across field, crosses, pellets, &c, symmetrically arranged in field.

[Cf Pl X 10]

Type viii

Bust r, crowned Around, inscription between two circles, divided by bust | Small cross pattée Around, inscription between two circles

[Cf Pl IX 13 & X 2, 3, &c]

Type ix

Bust i, crowned Around, inscription between two circles | Small cross pattée Around, inscription between two circles

[Cf Pl X 4]

Type x

Bust r, in high relief, with traces of crown Around, inscription between two circles, divided by bust | Small cross pattée Around, inscription between two circles

[Cf Pl IX 1]

Type x *var a*

Same, but bust l | Same

[Cf Pl IX 5]

Type xi

Bust r, in high relief, with traces of crown Around, inscription between two circles, divided by bust | Cross crosslet Around, inscription between two circles

[Cf Pl IX 6]

Obverse	Reverse

Type xii

Bust r, helmeted and crowned Around, inscription between two circles, divided by bust

Cross crosslet Around, inscription between two circles

[Cf Pl X 13]

Type xiii

Head r, helmeted and crowned Around, inscription between two circles

Cross crosslet Around, inscription between two circles

[Cf Pl X 14]

Description of Coins

No	Obverse	Reverse	Moneyer
	SERIES A WITH NAME OF MINT		
	BAÐAN [Bath]		
	Type v		
1	✠ÆÐELƧTAN RE✠ TO BRANI	✠BIORHTVL Ł M ⊙N ᛒ AT CIVITATE *Var* Pellet in field Wt 22 5	Biorhtulf
	DEORABY [Derby]		
	Type v		
2	✠CDEIГTAIH RE ƧAX ORVM	✠BOIᚲA MOTET DEOR AIVI Wt 25 0	Boiga
	[Pl IX 1]		
3	✠ÆRELƧTAN DEX TO BRIT *Var* In field И ?	✠EDFˀHOT IN REOR ᚠBVI Wt 19 6	Eˀclnoð

No.	Obverse.	Reverse.	Moneyer.

DOROBERNIA.
[Canterbury.]

Type v.

| 4 | ✠EÐELꞀƬ∀N REX TO BRIT | ✠ELFRIꞆ · M⊙ D⊙R ꞆIVIT
Wt. 19·0. | Elfric. |

EAXANCEASTER.
[Exeter.]

Type x.

| 5 | ÆÐELꞀƬ∀N REX
Var. Bust, very rude. | ✠ꞆEN∀RD M⁻ON E✠E
Wt. 23·6. | Genard
(= Cenard). |

EBORACUM or EOFERPIC.
[York.]

Type iv.

| 6 | ✠∀EDEL · ꞀƬ∀N REX ·∵ | EB ●R
∀Ꞇ ∀Ꞇ
ꞀEꞆN∀ID
∵ M o N ∵
Wt. 22·0. | Regnald. |
| | [Pl. IX. 2.] | | |

Type v.

7	✠EÐELꞀƬ∀N REX TO BRIT	✠REꞆN∀⅃D M⊽ EFO RꝐIꞆ Wt. 23·0.	Regnald.
8	,, ,, ,,	,, ,, EFORꝐIꞆ∵ Wt. 24·0.	
9	,, ,, ,, BRIꝆ	,, ,, EFÖRꝐ.IꞆ Wt. 24·8.	.

No.	Obverse.	Reverse.	Moneyer.
10	✠EÐEL+ΣTAN REX Tŏ BRIΓ	✠REGNΛ·.·LD MŌ EFÖ RPI ⁝C Wt. 25·2.	
11	✠EÐELΣTΛN REX TO BRIΓ *Var.* Crescent and seven pellets below cross pattée.	✠REGNALD MŌ EFOR PIC Wt. 20·5.	
12	" " " *Var.* Above cross pattée, V.	✠REGИALD MŌ EFO RPIC Wt. 25·0.	
	Type v. *var. a.*		
13	✠EÐELΣTAN REX TO BRIΓ [Pl. IX. 3.]	✠REGNΛLD MŌ EFO RPIC Wt. 23·0.	
14	✠EÐLΣT·A·N REX TO BRIΓ	✠REGN·A·L·D· MŌ EFO RPIC Wt. 21·0.	
	Type x.		
15	✠ÆÐELSTVN RE [Pl. IX. 4.]	✠ΛRИVLF · ΠO EO · Wt. 22·5.	Arnulf.
16	✠ÆÐELSTΛИ REI	✠ROTBERT · ΠO EO Wt. 20·5.	Rotberht.
	Type x. *var. a.*		
17	XƎЯ ИΛTZJƎDƎ (retrograde) [Pl. IX. 5.]	✠ꓶBƎЯTƎƎNOƎO✠ (retrograde) Wt. 22·7.	Ecberht, or Rotberht?
18	✠ÆÐELSTΛN REX (Reading outwards.)	✠SIVERD ΠOIEITΛ OC* Wt. 22·3.	Siuard.
	Type xi.		
19	· ÆÐELΣTAИ REX [Pl. IX. 6.]	✠HEΓDAΓL EBRO✠ (Broken.)	Heldalt.

* Possibly Oxford.

No.	Obverse.	Reverse.	Moneyer.

GLEAPECEASTER.

[Gloucester.]

Type v.

No.	Obverse.	Reverse.	Moneyer.
20	✠ÆÐELꞀTⴹN RE✠ BRⴹE	✠ƎPÐEL⌐PO INO ⴹLEⴹꝃⴹZ Wt. 23·8.	Æðelwold?

HEREFORD.

Type v.

| 21 | ✠EÐELꞀTⴹN REX TO BRIT | ✠HVNLⴹF M⌐O HEREF- Wt. 22·9. | Hunlaf. |

LEGECEASTER, Etc.

[Chester.]

Type v.

22	✠ÆÐELꞀTⴹN RE TO BRⴹE	✠ⴹBBⴹ MO IN LEⴹE ⴹF Wt. 24·0.	Abba.
23	ÆÐELꞀTⴹN RE TO BRⴹE	BOIⴹ ✠ⴹLET MO LEⴹ ⴹF Wt. 25·5.	Boiga? (or Boigalet).
24	✠ÆÐELꞀTⴹN RE✠ TO BRT *Var.* Annulet above and below cross pattée.	✠ⴹNⴹꓭ M⌐O LEⴹ ⴹFI *Var.* On r. of cross pattée, S. Wt. 24·8.	Cnað.
25	✠EDꝧꞀOⴹH RE✠ TÐHDI *Var.* Small cross pattée above central one.	✠DEORERD MOH EIE ⴹIEI *Var.* Small cross pattée above central one. Wt. 16·4.	Deorerd.
26	✠ÆÐELꞀTⴹИ REX TO BRTI✠	✠DEORVLF M⌐O LEⴹE ⴹFI✠ Wt. 23·2.	Deorulf.
27	✠ÆÐELꞀTⴹN RE✠ TO⨀ BRT	✠EⴹDLFE M⌐O LEⴹ ⴹFI *Var.* S in field. Wt. 24·6.	Eadlaf.

[Pl. IX. 7.]

No.	Obverse.	Reverse.	Moneyer.
28	✠ÆÐELꙄ·TAN RE✠ TO BR	✠EADMVND MO LEᴄ ᴄF: Wt. 24·4.	Eadmund.
29	✠ÆÐELꙄTⱯИ REX TO BRT	✠EADMVИD M⁻O LEᴄᴄ Wt. 23·7.	
30	✠ÆÐELꙄTAN RE✠ TO BR	✠EFRARD M⁻O LEᴄ ᴄF Wt. 25·4.	Efrard.
31	✠ÆÐELꙄTAN RE✠ TO BRT *Var.* Annulet on either side of cross pattée.	✠MÆRTENE MO LEᴄE ᴄF Wt. 24·8.	Mærten.
32	,, ,, ,,	✠OꙄLFE M⁻O LEᴄE ᴄIF Wt. 25·2.	Oslaf or Osulf.
33	,, ,, ,,	✠PAVLEꙄ M⁻O LEᴄE ᴄIF✠ Wt. 24·2.	Paul(es).
34	,, ,, ,, BR	✠PAVLEꙄ M⁻O LEIᴄ ᴄF (Chipped.)	
35	,, ,, ,, BRT	✠RÆNVLF M⁻O LEᴄ ᴄF Wt. 24·0.	Rænulf.
36	ÆÐELꙄTⱯИ RE✠ TO BRIE	✠ꙄIᴄEFERÐ MOИ IEᴄE ᴄF Wt. 26·5.	Sigeferð.
37	✠ÆÐELꙄTAN RE✠ TO BR	✠ꙄIᴄFERÐ MO LEᴄE ᴄFI Wt. 24·2.	
38	ÆÐELꙄTAN RE✠ TO BRIE	✠TIDᴄER MO IN LEᴄE ᴄFI✠ Wt. 24·6.	Tidgar.
39	✠EÐELꙄTAN RE✠ TO BR	✠VVLFᴄAR MON LEᴄᴄE Wt. 25·6.	Uulfgar.
40	✠ÆÐELꙄTAN RE✠ TO BRT	✠VVLFꙄTAN M⁻O LEᴄᴄ Wt. 24·6.	Uulfstan or Wulfstan.
41	ÆÐELꙄTAN RE✠ TO BRI	✠ᴘLFꙄTAN M⁻O LEᴄᴄ Wt. 24·0.	

Type v. *var. c.*

No.	Obverse.	Reverse.	Moneyer.
42	ÆÐELꙄTAN RE TO EBLXE [Pl. IX. 8.]	✠ⱯBBA MO IN LEᴄE ᴄF Wt. 23·6.	Abba.

No.	Obverse.	Reverse.	Moneyer.
43	ÆÐELƧTʌN RE✠ TO BR	✠OƧLAC MON LEIEC✠ Wt. 24·4.	Oslac.
		Type vi.	
44	✠ÆÐEL·ƧT·ʌN RE✠ TO BR *Var.* Above rosette, ∞. [Pl. IX. 9.]	✠BE·O·R·ʌ·RD MON LEIE CF Wt. 24·5.	Beorard.
45	✠ÆÐELƧTʌN REX TO BR	✠DEORVLF MOI LEICC *Var.* To left of rosette, annulet. Wt. 23·5.	Deorulf.
46	*✠ÆÐELƧTʌN RE✠ TO BRI	✠E·ʌDMVND MON LEIE · Wt. 23·6.	Eadmund.
47	,, ,, ,, BR	✠EFRʌRD MON LECEC Wt. 25·2.	Efrard.
48	,, ,, ,,	✠FRʌRD M⁻O LEICE CIF Wt. 23·4.	
49	ÆÐEL·ƧTʌN ᴦEX TO BRI	✠MÆLDOMEN MO LECC Wt. 24·4.	Mældomen.
50	✠ÆÐELƧTʌN RE✠ TO BR	✠MECRED MON LECI CF Wt. 23·8.	Megred.
51	,, ,, ,,	✠OƧLAC M☉N LECEC Wt. 24·6.	Oslac.
52	,, ,, ,,	✠PʌVLEƧ MOI LEICC Wt. 23·3.	Paul(es).
53	✠ÆÐELƧʌN ᴦE✠ TO Bᴦ	✠TIDCʌR MON LEC CF Wt. 24·8.	Tidgar.
54	✠ÆÐEL'ƧTʌN RE✠ TO BR	✠TIDCER MONET LEIE CF Wt. 24·3.	
55	✠ÆÐELƧTʌN REX TO BR	✠ · VVLFCʌ·R M·ON · LEIE · Wt. 24·0.	Unlfgar
56	✠ÆÐELƧTʌN RE✠ TO BR	✠VVLFƧTʌN M⁻O LEICC Wt. 25·0.	Uulfstan.

* Struck on a coin of Ælfred?

No.	Obverse.	Reverse.	Moneyer.
	Type vi. *var. a.*		
57	✠ÆÐELSTAN REᛲ TO BᚱN	✠EADMVND MO LECC Wt. 24·7.	Eadmund.
58	„ „ „ [Pl. IX. 10.]	„ MON LECEC Wt. 24·2.	
	LONDONIA. [London.]		
	Type v.		
59	TOT ᛲƎᚱ NATƧIGƎᛰ TIRB	✠ERE ᚠONETA LVND CIVIƎT Wt. 19·3.	Ere.
60	✠ÆÐELSTAN REX TOT BRIT	✕CAREARD M⁻O LVND CIVITT Wt. 21·7.	Gareard.
	Type v. *var. b.*		
61	✠ÆÐELSTAN REX TOT BRIT [Pl. IX. 11.]	✕PVLFHELM M⁻O LVND CIVITT Wt. 21·8.	Wulfhelm.
	Type viii.		
62	✠ÆÐELSTAN REX	✠ÆLFSTAN MO LOND CI Wt. 24·6.	Ælfstan.
63	„ REX ⁚	✠ÆLFPALD M⁻O LOND CIVI Wt. 25·2.	Ælfwald.
64	„ REX	✠BEAHRED MO LOND CI Wt. 24·4.	Beahred.
65	„ „	✠BIORNEARD MO LOND CI Wt. 23·0.	Biorneard.
66	„ „	✠ELLAF MO LONDONI CI Wt. 22·7.	Ellaf (= Eclaf).
67	„ „	✠LIOFHELM MO LOND CI Wt. 23·9.	Liofhelm.

No	Obverse	Reverse	Moneyer
	LONGPORT. [Langport] *Type* v		
68	✠ÆÐELSTAN REX TO BRIT	✠VVYNSIGE · MO · LONGPORT Wt 23 5.	Uuynsige
	[Pl IX 12]		
	NORÐPIC. [Norwich] *Type* viii		
69	✠ÆÐELSTAN REX	✠BARBE MO NORÐPIC Wt 24 4	Barbe
70	✠ÆÐELNTAN REX	✠BARDEL NO NORP Wt 23 4	Bardel or Burdel
71	✠ÆÐELNTAH ,,	✠BVRDEL IIO NORÐ · I Wt 24 5	
72	✠ÆÐELNTAN RE✠	✠BVRDEL NORIÐP[I]C (Broken)	
73	✠ÆÐELSTAN REX	✠GIONGBALD MO NOR ÐPC Wt 24 5	Giongbald.
74	,, ,,	✠HRODEAR HO NORVC Wt 26 0	Hrodear (=Hroðgar)
75	✠ÆÐELSTAN REX	✠NANNE NO NORÐPE TI Wt. 24 8	Manne
76	✠ÆÐELSTAH REX	✠MANTICEH · MO NORPIC (Chipped)	Manticen
	OXNAFORD [Oxford] *Type* v		
77	✠ÆÐELSTAN REX TOT BRIT *Var* Pellet in field.	✠INGELRI▴M̄O▴OX▴ VRBI Wt 20 0	Ingelric

No.	Obverse.	Reverse.	Moneyer.

Type viii.

| 78 | ✠ÆÐELƧTⱯN REX | ✠VVYNELM · M·⊙ · ⊙X · VRBIƧ
Var. Four pellets in field opposite each end of cross.
Wt. 24·0.

[Pl. IX. 13.] | Uuynelm. |

SCROBBESBYRIG.
[Shrewsbury.]

Type v.

| 79 | ✠EÐELƧTⱯN REX TO BRIT | ✠BERHTELM ƧCROB
Wt. 24·3. | Berhtelm. |
| 80 | ,, ,, ,, BRIT
[Pl. IX. 14.] | ✠BERHTEL M⁻⊙
ƧCROB
Wt. 23·8. | |

Type vi.

81	EELZTⱯN RE✠ TO BꞒ	✠EDRED M⁻O ƧCꞒOB Wt. 20·4.	Edred.
82	✠ÆÐ · EL · ƧTⱯN REX TO⊙ B	✠E·O·FERMVND M ƧCROB Wt. 24·8.	Eofermund.
83	✠EÐELƧTⱯN · RE✠ TO BRIT	✠FROTꞒER MŌ ƧCROB Wt. 25·0.	Frotger.

SNOTINGAHAM.
[Nottingham.]

Type v.

| 84 | ✠EDECƧTⱯN RE ƧⱯ✠ORVM | ✠EÐELNOÐ ON ƧNꝊTENCEHⱯM
Wt. 22·7. | Eʒelnoð. |

[Pl. X. 1.]

No.	Obverse.	Reverse.	Moneyer.
		PÆRINCPIC. [Warwick.]	
		Type v. var. c.	
85	✠ÆÐELƧTAN REX TOI BR	✠MONÐICN MON VERI *Var.* On r. of ro-sette, S. Wt. 22·7.	Monðign (Mon Þegn?).
		PELINGAFORD. [Wallingford.]	
		Type viii.	
86	✠ÆÐELƧTAN REX	✠BEORNPÆLD · M⁻O · PEL Wt. 23·6.	Beornwald or Byrnwald.
87	✠ÆÐELƧTAN ,,	✠BYRNPÆLD MON · PE Wt. 21·6.	
88	✠ÆÐELƧTĀN ,,	✠BYRNPÆLD MO PELINCĀ Wt. 26·8.	
	[Pl. X. 2.]		
		PERHAM. [Wareham.]	
		Type viii.	
89	✠ÆÐELƧTAN REX	✠ÆLFRED MO · IN PERH·A Wt. 24·6.	Ælfred.
	[Pl. X. 3.]		

No.	Obverse.	Reverse.	Moneyer.

WINCEASTRE.
[Winchester.]

Type viii.

No.	Obverse.	Reverse.	Moneyer.
90	✠ÆÐELꞄTᴧN REX	✠AMELRIꓳ·M·O·VVINꓳI Wt. 24·6.	Amelric.
91	„ · REX	✠VVLFHEARD · MO VVIN · ꓳI *Var.* Pellet above cross. Wt. 24·6.	Uulfheard.

Type ix.

| 92 | ✠ÆÐELꞄTᴧN REX TO BR | ✠ÆÐELM⁻MO · VVIN · ꓳI · *Var.* Small cross pattée above central one. Wt. 23·0. | Æðelm. |

[Pl. X. 4.]

SERIES B.—WITHOUT NAME OF MINT.

Type i.

93	✠ÆÐELꞄTᴧN ꓨEX	ᴧBBᴧ ✠ ✠ ✠ MON̄ Wt. 24·4.	Abba.
94	✠ÆÐELꞄTᴧN REX	ÆLFꞄT· ✠ ✠ ✠ ᴧNM⁻O Wt. 20·7.	Ælfstan.
95	✠ÆÐELꞄTA·N REX	ᴧREM ✠ ✠ ✠ O‖ETᴧ Wt. 25·0.	Are (= Ere ?).
96	✠ÆÐELꞄ·TᴧИ RE	ᴧREM ✠ ✠ ✠ OИETᴧ Wt. 24·2.	

[Pl. X. 5.]

No.	Obverse.	Reverse.	Moneyer.
97	✠ÆEGLꟻTÆN REX	ÆREM ✠✠✠ OИETÆ (Chipped.)	
98	✠ÆÐEL·ꟻTÆN RE·	ΛRNY ✠✠✠ LFMOI Wt. 22·2.	Arnulf.
99	✠IÐEL·ꟻTÆN RE	ÆꟻVL ✠✠✠ FNEN Wt. 22·5.	Asalf or Asulf (cf. Oslaf).
100	✠ÆÐEL·ꟻTÆN RE	ᄃLÆᄃ ✠✠✠ MONE Wt. 23·7.	Clac.
101	✠ÆÐEL·ZTÆИ R	ᄃRIꟻ· ✠✠✠ TIᄃN Wt. 22·3.	Cristign.
102	ÆÐEL·ꟻTÆN REX	D⊙MEN ✠✠✠ CEꟻM⁻⊙ Wt. 22·0.	Domences or Dominic (= Dominicus).
103	,, ,,	DOMI ✠✠✠ NIᄃ⁻M Wt. 23·8.	
104	✠ÆÐELꟻTΛN REX	EΛDMV ✠✠✠ NDM⁻O Wt. 24·8.	Eadmund.
105	✝ÆÐELꟻTΛN REX TO BRIT·	EÆDV ✠✠✠ LFM⁻O Wt. 21·3.	Eadulf.
106	✠EÐELꟻTΛN ᱝEX	EᄃBE ✠✠✠ ᑭHT (Chipped.)	Ecberht.

No.	Obverse.	Reverse.	Moneyer.
107	✠ÆÐELƧTÃN REX	·ECLÃF ✠ ✠ ✠ M O N E · Wt. 27·0.	Eclaf.
108	ÆÐEL·ƧTÃN REX	FVᏀEL ✠ ✠ ✠ MONET ·.· Wt. 22·4.	Fugel.
109	✠ÆÐEL·ƧTΛИ RE	ᏀIƧLE ✠ ✠ ✠ ·MER ·.· Wt. 21·4.	Gislemer.
110	✠ÆÐELƧTΛИ REX	ᏀIƧLE ✠ ✠ ✠ MER · · Wt. 23·6.	*Var.* Annulet in field.
111	ÆÐEL·ƧTII REX	ᏀOTΛ ✠ ✠ ✠ IIONE· ·.· Wt. 22·6.	Gota.
112	\ЕÐEL·ƧTΛN · REX	HÃR ✠ ✠ ✠ GER ·.· Wt. 23·8.	Harger.
113	✠ÆÐELƧTΛN REX	HΛÐEL ✠ ✠ ✠ ᏢOLDM̄ · ·.· Wt. 25·3.	Haᵹelwold (Æðelwold?).
114	✠ÆÐELƧTΛN REX	IOHΛN ✠ ✠ ✠ NMONE ·.· Wt. 24·7.	Iohann.
115	✠ÆÐEL·ƧTÃN RE·	LÃИD ✠ ✠ ✠ ᵺᏟM̈O ·.· Wt. 26·0.	Landac?
116	✠ÆÐEL·ƧTΛИ RE	LI·TIL ✠ ✠ ✠ ᴡÃN · ·.· Wt. 19·0.	Litilman.

No.	Obverse.	Reverse.		Moneyer.
117	✠ÆÐELꟅTΛN REX	MEᄃEN ✠ ✠ ✠ FREÐ MO	Wt. 24·6.	Megenfreð.
	[Pl. X. 6.]			
118	ÆÐEL·ꟅTAN REX	NOÐEꝹ ✠ ✠ ✠ MOИ E	Wt. 23·4.	Noðer.
119	ÆÐELꟅTΛN ,,	NOÐE ✠ ✠ ✠ MONE	Wt. 25·0.	
120	ÆÐEL·ꟅTAN ,,	ODĀH ✠ ✠ ✠ ONETΛ	Wt. 24·8.	Oda.
121	,, ,,	,,	Wt. 23·2.	
122	✠ÆÐELꟅTAN REX	PĀVL ✠ ✠ ✠ ꟅMON	Wt. 23·6.	Paul(es).
123	ÆÐEL·ꟅTĀN REX	PITIT ✠ · ✠ · ✠ M͡ONE	Wt. 25·2.	Pitit.
124	✠ÆÐELꟅTĀN REX	RÆᄃEN· ✠ ✠ ✠ YLFM⊙	Wt. 24·6.	Rægenulf.
125	✠ÆÐELꟅTAN RE✠	ꟅIᄃEBR ✠ ✠ ✠ ANDMÖ	Wt. 23·2.	Sigebrand.
126	,, ,,	ꟅNEL·∶ ✠ ✠ ✠ MOM͡		Snel.

No.	Obverse.	Reverse.	Moneyer.
127	ÆÐEL·ƧTN REX	SOTA ✠✠✠ NOИE Wt. 23·4.	Sota.
128	✠ÆÐELƧTAN REX	VVEALD ✠✠✠ ҺELИMO⁻ Wt. 17·4.	Uuealdhelm.
129	ÆÐELƧTⱮN RE✠	VVIL ✠✠✠ LVFM Wt. 24·0.	Uilluf.
130	✠ÆÐELƧTⱮN REX	VVLFҺE ✠✠✠ ⱮRDM⁻O Wt. 23·8.	Uulfheard.
131	✠ÆÐELƧTⱮN ꓤE	VVLF ✠✠✠ ƧTⱮN Wt. 23·4.	Uulfstan.
132	„ „	PINE ✠✠✠ LEM⁻O Wt. 23·8.	Winele.
133	ÆÐELƧTAN REX	PINE ✠✠✠ ꓬEM⁻O (Chipped.)	
	BLUNDERED.		
134	ÆÐEL·ƧTⱮN REX	ⱮƧAEL ✠✠✠ NꓕAO Wt. 21·0.	Asalf?
135	✠EⱭDEꙅωTⱮИ REX	IEⱯꓱO ✠✠✠ DIOꓤ Wt. 23·5.	Diorulf?

No.	Obverse.	Reverse.	Moneyer.
	Type ii.		
136	✠ ÆÐELꙄTAN REX *Var.* Above star, D ; below, ⊥. [Pl. X. 7.]	⠒ PΛVIVꙄ ✠ ✠ ✠ MONETΛ ⠒ Wt. 23·7.	Paulus.
	Type iii.		
137	�֎ ÆÐELꙄTAN REX [Pl. X. 8.]	M O N • • • ÐELN Wt. 24·2.	MonÐegn (Mon Þegn ?).
	Type iv.		
138	✠ AEDELꙄTAN REˣ ▲ *Var.* Annulet on ▲▲ either side of cross. [Pl. X. 9.]	FR OT I E R M MON Wt. 21·0.	Frotger (Froðger)
139	✠ AEDLꙄTAN REX ▲ *Var.* In field, ⠒ ▲▲	⠒ ⠒ PѰLTSI9 • Wt. 21·4.	Wyltsig.
140	,, REˣ ▲ ▲▲	W̄ N̄ TVRꙄTAN ⠒ Wt. 21·3.	Turstan (Þurstan).
	Type v.		
141	✠ ÆÐELꙄTĀN REX TOT BRIT	✠Ǝꓤ NΛTꙄIGƎ✠ TIRB TOT Wt. 15·6.	No Moneyer.
142	✠ EÐEIꙄTΛH RE ꙄΛ✠ ORVꓨ	✠HRL · ꙄΛXORVM ΛTƎ Wt. 22·6.	
143	✠ EˇÐELˋꙄTAN REX TÔ BRIꓨ	✠ Eˇ·ÐEL·ꙄTΛN REX T8 BRIꓨ Wt. 25·6.	
	Type vii.		
144	✠ ÆÐELꙄTĀN REX	⠒⠒ VVLFꙄ ✠ ✠ ✠ ILEMO ⠒ Wt. 22·5.	Uulfsige.
	[Pl. X. 10.]		

No.	Obverse.	Reverse.	Moneyer.
	Type viii.		
145	✠ÆÐELΣTN REX	✠ÆÐELFREÐ MON Wt. 21·7.	Æðelfreð (Æðelferð).
146	✠ÆÐELΣTĀN REX	✠AÐELFRMD M⁻ONNE Wt. 17·4.	Æðelfreð?
147	✠ÆÐELΣTAͶREX.	✠ΛLFEAV MONET⁻ Wt. 21·0.	Alfeah.
148	✠ÆÐELΣTAN REX	✠DRYHTVALD MON Wt. 23·0.	Dryhtuald (= Bryhtuald?).
	[Pl. X. 11.]		
149	" "	✠LIFINC MONEИ Wt. 23·2.	Lifing.
	Type x.		
150	ÆDEL∾ꓕΛN REX	✠ΛDELПOD+ΛRNVLF Wt. 23·0.	Aðelmod and Arnulf.
	[Pl. X. 12.]		
	Type xii.		
151	✠ÆÐELΣTAͶREX	✠BALDRIC ИOMT Wt. 22·0.	Baldric.
	[Pl. X. 13.]		
152	✠ÆÐELΣTAͶREX	✠EINARD MOIETA Wt. 23·8.	Einard.
153	✠ÆÐEΓ∾T X	· EIИARD M⊙H . . (Broken.)	
154	ÆÐELΣTAN REX	✠ΣMALA MONETA Wt. 23·0.	Smala.
155	✠ÆÐELΣTAͶREX	✠ƿIARD MONETA Wt. 21·4.	Wiard.
	Type xiii.		
156	ÆÐ⁝ELΣTAN REX O	✠ωMALA MONETA Wt. 25·6.	Smala.
	[Pl. X. 14.]		

EADMUND.

Succ A D 940 or 941, died A D 946

Moneyers

Abban (Abba?)
Abenel
Addelerd
Addelme or Æðelwine
Adulf
Æðelric [= Ælfric]
A gnice?
Alfred
Alfric
Alfstan
Ælfwald or Elfwald
Alfwine
Alfwinig
Alf -, *see also* Elf -
Arnulf or Arnulf
Aðelm [= Aðelmund]
Aðelmod
Aðelmund or Aðelmund
Aðelric
Aðelulf or Aðelulf
Æðelwine or Aðelwine
Æðel -, *see also* Aðel -
Aðered [Aðelred]
Aglard[es?]
Alberic?
Amund or Amynd[es]
Arc
Arnulf or Arnulf
Asulf or Asulfuen
Aðan?
Aðelulf [= Aðelulf]
Aðelmund
Aðel -, *see also* Æðel -
Baciager or Bacialer
Baldric
Balduine
Barbe [Barbi] (Norwich)
Beahred
Benedictus
Beorwald (Wallingford)
Berhtelm
Berhtred
Berhtwig.
Bernað
Bernsige
Bese or Besel
Betunli
Biorhtulf or Biorhtulf
Birneard, Biorneard, &c
Boeg [= Boiga?] (York?)
Boiga, Boga, &c
Beonsult, Beonulf [= Biornulf?]
Bonsom
Burnhelm
Birnric or Byrnric

Byrnferð
Byrnwald
Cenberht
Ceolberht, Ceolberht, &c
Clac (Exeter, London)
Cnapa or Gnapa
Cundferð
Daoilulf
Demenec, Domenees, &c [= Domi-
　nieus]
Deorwald, Diarwald, &c
Diarelm
Dorulf
Dregel, Dregl, &c
Dudelet?
Dudig
Durant [= Durandes]
Durand[es]
Eadgar
Eadgild,
Eadmund
Eadred, Eldred, &c
Eadstan
Eaduueard
Ealgeart?
Eardulf
Eegbrīht
Eldreð
Eireeos?
Ererbrd [Eferwerd?]
Eferult
Elgeulf?
Egered
Einard
Elaet
Elferd
Elf -, *see also* Ælf -
Eofermund
Ercombald [= Ercimbald]
Erembald
Ereðic
Ergimbalt [= Ercimbald]
Erieil
Eulgart [= Ealgeart?]
Eðelsige
Eðel -, *see also* Æðel -
Faraman, Farman
Faromia? (Leicester)
Foleard, Fildered
Frard [= Etrard?]
Fredard [= Freðard]
Freða[es]
Fugel
Geundferd or Gundferð
Giongbald (Norwich),

Gis[lemer?].
Gnapa or Cnapa.
Gota or Gotaf.
Grimwald.
Hadebald.
Hana, Hanen, &c.
Hereman.
Heremod.
Hereuuig.
Hildeomert.
Hotaf.
Hrodear or Hroðgar (Norwich).
Hunlaf.
Hunsige.
Iedulf.
Igcre.
Ingelbert.
Ingelgar (York).
Landwine.
Leofric.
Liafinc.
Ligeberd [= Sigeberð?].
Liofhelm.
Litilman.
Mæld or Mældomen.
Mærten or Martin.
Man, Mana or Manna.
Maneta.
Manticen or Mannicen (Norwich).
Megred.
Nansige.
Oda.
Ondres?
Onunman?
Osferð.
Oslac.
Osmund.
Osulf or Oswulf.
Oswald.
Otic.
Oðelric [= Æðelric].

Oðetiorcel.
Paul, Paules, &c.
Pitit.
Prim.
Rægenold.
Randulf.
Regnulf [= Raegenulf].
Regðer.
Reingrim, or Regegrim (Oxford).
Rodberht.
Rodear or Rodgar (Norwich).
Salciarene?
Sarauuard.
Saxsa.
Scurua?
Siademan or Sideman.
Sigar[es] or Sigear[es].
Sigeberð?
Sigwold.
Smerel.
Stefhan.
Telia.
Ulf (Chester).
Ulgebert? [Ingelbert?].
Uuihtes or Uuihtseg.
Uuilaf.
Uuitelm.
Uulfstan.
Uuynsige.
Warn [= Warin].
Waringod.
Werlaf.
White.
Wigard, Wigeard, or Wigheard.
Winuc?
Wulfgar.
Wulfhelm.
Wulfric.
Wynhelm or Wynnelm.
Þeodulf.
Þermod.

DESCRIPTION OF TYPES.

Obverse.	Reverse.

Type i.

Small cross pattée. Around, inscription between two circles.	Moneyer's name, &c., in two lines across field; crosses, pellets, &c., symmetrically arranged in field.

[Cf. Pl. XI. 2-6.]

Type ii.

Small cross formed of pellets. Around, inscription between two circles.	Moneyer's name, &c., in two lines across field; rosette, pellets, and ornaments symmetrically arranged in field.

[Cf. Pl. XI. 7.]

Obverse	Reverse

Type III.

Rosette of pellets Around, inscription between two circles	Moneyer's name, &c, in two lines across field, five rosettes symmetrically arranged in field.

[Cf Pl XI 8]

Type IV

Small cross pattée Around, inscription between two circles	Rosette of dots Around, inscription between two circles

[Cf Pl. XI 1]

Type V

Small cross pattée Around, inscription between two circles	Moneyer's name in one line across field, above, straight line from which springs a rose between two curved branches, below, seven-petalled flower

[Cf. Pl XI 9]

Type VI

Bust r, crowned Around, inscription between two circles, divided by bust	Small cross pattée Around, inscription between two circles

[Cf Pl XI 10, 11]

Type VII

Rude bust r, helmeted and crowned Around, inscription between two circles, divided by bust.	Cross crosslet Around, inscription between two circles

[Cf Pl. XI 12]

DESCRIPTION OF COINS.

No	Obverse	Reverse	Moneyer
	SERIES A WITH NAME OF MINT		
	LEIGECEASTER, ETC [Chester]		
		Type IV	
1	EADMVND REX	✠VL⅃ MOИ LEIEFFI✠ (Barbarous) Wt 21 5 [Pl XI 1]	Ulf.

No.	Obverse.	Reverse.	Moneyer.
	LONDONIA. [London.] *Type* vi.		
2	✠EΛDMVND RE	✠ᗩLᗩᗤ MONE LON EIITX* Wt. 18·8.	Clac.
	NORÐᗱIᗤ. [Norwich.] *Type* vi.		
3	✠EΛDMVHD REX *Var.* Bust not crowned.	✠BΛRBE IIO NORÐᗱIᗤ (Chipped.)	Barbe.
4	✠EΛDMVN REX	✠MΛNTIEEN MO NORᗱI Wt. 24·8.	Manticen (or Mannicen).
	SERIES B. WITHOUT NAME OF MINT. *Type* i.		
5	✠EADMVND REX	. . . ᴁBBV ✠ ✠ ✠ N M⁻O . . . Wt. 22·4.	Abbun (Abla?).
6	,, ,,	⁙ ᴁLFƧ✠ ✠ ✠ ✠ TANM⁻O ⁙ Wt. 25·5.	Ælfstan.
7	EΛDMVND RE✠	⁙ ᴁLFV ✠ ✠ ✠ ·ΛLM⁻O ⁙ Wt. 23·3.	Ælfwald.
8	✠ᴁADMVND REX	⁙ ᴁLFᗱ ✠ ✠ ✠ ALDM⁻O ⁙ Wt. 25·0.	Ælfwald.

---

* Probably an abbreviation of "Civitas."

No.	Obverse	Reverse	Moneyer
9	✠ÆADMVND REX *Var Small cross pattée below central one*	ÆLFPA ✠✠✠ LDM⁻O ·· Wt 21 5	
10	✠EADMVND ,,	ÆLFP ✠✠✠ ALDM⁻O Wt 21·7	
11	✠ EA·DNVN D R	ÆELR ✠✠✠ ICH⁻O Wt 19 6	Æelric (= Ælfric)
12	✠EADMVND REX	ÆERN ✠✠✠ VLFⱵ⁻O Wt 22 7	Ærnulf (Arnulf)
13	✠EADMVND REX *Var Pellet in field*	ÆÐEL ✠✠✠ PINEM Wt 25 0	Æðelwine
14	✠EADMVND REX	AÐELM ✠✠✠ VNDM⁻O ·· Wt 22 3	Aðelmund (Æðel-mund)
15	✠EADMVND REX	ALB ✠✠✠ ERIM⁻O Wt 18 3	Alberi(c?)
16	,, ,,	,, Wt 19 0	
17	✠EADMVND PEX	✠AMYN ✠✠✠ DESMOT ∷ Wt 22 2	Amynd(es) (Amund)
18	✠E·ADMVND REX	AREM ✠✠✠ ONETA Wt. 23 5	Are (= Ere?)

No.	Obverse.	Reverse.	Moneyer.
19	✠ⵏEⵜDHVND RE	ⵜⵉⵜVL ✠✠✠ FNEN ·.· Wt. 19·6.	Asulfnen (Asulf).
20	✠·.· EⵜDMVND RE ·.·✠	ⵜⴹEⴺⵜ ✠✠✠ ⵜMⴺⵜV Wt. 18·0.	Aᵭelulf (= Æᵭelulf).
21	✠EⵜDMVND RE	BⵜCI ✠✠✠ ⵜⴹER ·.· Wt. 20·5.	Bacialer or Baciager.
22	✠EⵜDMVND RE✠	BEAHI ✠✠✠ REDMO ·.· Wt. 21·7.	Beahred.
23	✠EⵜDMVND · REX ·	BEⵜH· ✠✠✠ REDM̄ · ·.· Wt. 23·0.	
24	✠ⵏEⵜDMVND RE	BENE ✠✠✠ DICTVS ·.· Wt. 20·3.	Benedictus.
25	✠·E·A·D·M·V·N·D·R·E✠	BERHT· ✠✠✠ ELMM̄O ·.· Wt. 25·0.	Berhtelm.
26	✠EⵜDⴹVND REX	BERHT ✠✠✠ PⴺM̄O ·.· Wt. 16·5.	Berhtwig.
27	,, ,,	,, Wt. 16·0.	
28	✠EⵜDMVND REX	BERNⵉ ✠✠✠ IⴺEM̄O Wt. 15·0.	Bernsige.

No.	Obverse.	Reverse.	Moneyer.
29	✠E·A·DMVND RE✠	BIⓄRH ✠ ✠ ✠ TVLFM̄ Wt. 22·0.	Biorhtulf.
30	✠EADMVND REX	BIRNE ✠·✠ ✠ ARDM̄O Wt. 21·0.	Birneard.
31	✠EADMVND RE	BOIⅭ ✠ ✠ ✠ AM̄O Wt. 25·3.	Boiga.
32	✠EΛDMVN·D REX	BOEΛI ✠ ✠ ✠ MONETΛ Wt. 21·0.	Boiga ?
33	✠EΛMNDVD REX	BOEG ✠ ✠ ✠ EBBⅭ * (Chipped.)	Boeg (= Boiga ?).
34	Ω ⅁NVMⅅΛƎ✠	ꓭOIN ✠ ✠ ✠ ZYՐF (Chipped.)	Boinsulf.
35	✠EADMVND REX	BONΣ ✠ ✠ ✠ OMM̄O (Chipped.)	Bonsom.
	[Pl. XI. 2.]		
36	✠EꓤDMVND RE	ⅭLꓮⅭ ✠ ✠ ✠ ꓵONE Wt. 23·0.	Clac.
37	✠EΛDMVND RE ·	,, (Retrograde.) Wt. 21·5.	

* Hawkins (*Silver Coins of England*, 3rd Edit. p. 142) suggests that EBBⅭ may possibly be for Eoferwick.

No.	Obverse.	Reverse.	Moneyer.
38	✠EⱯDMVHD RE	ⱢⱢⱭ⫩ⱯⱢⱭ⫩⫩⫩ ⳤⱢⱭⱣ ⫩⫩⫩ Ɫ⫩ⱯⱣ ✠ ✠ ✠ ⱯMO⁻N ⫩⫩⫩	Cnapa.
		Wt. 24·8.	
39	✠EⱯDMVⱭD RE✠	DEMEN ✠ ✠ ✠ EⱢMOT	Demenec or Domences (=Dominicus).
		Wt. 22·0.	
40	,, ,,	DEMEN ✠ ✠ ✠ EⱢMOT	
		(Chipped.)	
41	✠EⱯDMVND · REX	DOMEN ✠ ✠ ✠ ⱢEⱢM⁻O	
		Wt. 24·0.	
	[Pl. XI. 3.]		
42	✠EADMVND REX	DIARE ✠ ✠ ✠ LMM⁻O	Diarelm.
		Wt. 20·0.	
43	✠EⱯDWVND RE	DORV ✠ ✠ ✠ LFM⁻O	Dorulf.
		Wt. 25·0.	
44	EⱯDMVHD REX	DORV ✠ ✠ ✠ LFEM	
		Wt. 24·9.	
45	✠E·Ʌ·DMVND RE	DREⱢ ✠ ✠ ✠ LMOT ·	Dregel.
		Wt. 20·0.	
46	✠EADMVND REX	DVDE ✠ ✠ ✠ LETM⁻O	Dudelet (=Dudig ?).
		Wt. 22·4.	

No.	Obverse.	Reverse.	Moneyer.
47	✠EΛDMVND RE	DVDI ✠✠✠ ᒐΠOE Wt. 21·9.	Dudig.
48	✠EΛDMVND RE	ᗡVRΛ ✠✠✠ I N T· Wt. 20·0.	Duraint (=Durand).
49	✠EΛDMVND RE✠	DVRΛN ✠✠✠ DEƩMOT Wt. 18·9.	Durand(es).
50	*✠EΛDMVND REX	EΛDM ✠✠✠ VNDM Wt. 23·6.	Eadmund.
51	,, ,,	,, Wt. 25·0.	
52	✠EΛDMVND REX	✠ EΛDR ✠✠✠ EDM⁻O ✠ Wt. 25·2.	Eadred.
53	✠EΛDMVND REX	EADR ✠✠✠ EDM⁻O Wt. 23·6.	
54	✠EΛDMVND · REX	✠ EADR · O ✠ O EDM⁻O ✠ Wt. 20·3.	
55	,, ,,	,, Wt. 22·2.	
56	✠EΛDMVN·D REX	EΛDƩ · ✠✠✠ TΛNM Wt. 21·8.	Eadstan.

* Struck on a coin of Eadweard the Elder.

No.	Obverse.	Reverse.		Moneyer.
57	✠EΛDMVND REX	EΛDΣ ✠ ✠ ✠ TANO	Wt. 23·8.	
58	✠EΛDMVND REX	EΛDVVE ✠ ✠ ✠ Λ R D M	Wt. 24·6.	Eaduucard.
		[Pl. XI. 4.]		
59	✠EΛDMVND RE✠	EΛRD VLFM	Wt. 21·6.	Eardulf.
60	✠EADMVND · REX ·	EARD ✠ ✠ ✠ YLFM¨O	(Clipped.)	
61	✠EADMVND REX	EFER ✠ ✠ ✠ VLFM¨O	Wt. 18·6.	Eferulf.
62	✠EAD·NVMD R	EFER ✠ ✠ ✠ VLFI¨O	Wt. 21·2.	
63	✠EΛDMVND REX	ECERED ✠ ✠ ✠ MONETΛ	Wt. 24·7.	Egered.
64	„ „	ECCERD ✠ ✠ ✠ MONETΛ	Wt. 23·8.	
65	„ „	EOFERM ✠ ✠ ✠ VИDM¨O	Wt. 25·0.	Eofermund.

No.	Obverse.	Reverse.		Moneyer.
66	✠EADMVND RE	EVL ✠✠✠ GART	Wt. 22·0.	Eulgart (= Ealgeart).
67	EADMVND REX	FRAR ✠✠✠ DMON	Wt. 22·0.	Frard (= Efrard).
68	*EADMVND „	„	Wt. 25·3.	
69	✠E·ADFIVND RE	FVGEL ✠✠✠ MONET	Wt. 22·8.	Fugel.
70	✠EADMVND RE	FVGEL ✠✠✠ MONEI	Wt. 20·3.	
71	EADMVND ERX	GEVN ✠✠✠ DFEÐO	Wt. 21·4.	Geundferð or Gundferð.
72	✠EADMVND RX	GVND ✠✠✠ FERÐIO	Wt. 21·6.	
73	✠EADMVND RE	GOTA ✠✠✠ MONE	Wt. 19·4.	Gota.
74	✠EADMVND RE	GOTAE ✠✠✠ MOIIE	Wt. 24·2.	
75	✠EADMVND REX·	HERE ✠✠✠ MODMO	Wt. 24·9.	Heremod.

* Struck on a coin of an earlier reign.

No	Obverse	Reverse	Moneyer
76	✠EADHVND RE✠	HERE ✠✠✠ VVICM̄ · Wt 22 0	Hercuuig
77	✠EADMVND REX	✠ ✠HVNL ✠✠✠ ĀFM̄·ʘ ✠ Wt 20 6	Hunlaf
78	" Var Pellet in field "	HVNSI ✠✠✠ CEN̄·ʘ · Wt 23 5	Hunsigo
79	✠EADMVND · REX	ICERE ✠✠✠ MONET Wt 22 8	Igere
80	✠EĀDMVND REX	INCEL ✠✠✠ CĀRM̄ Wt 20 0	Ingelgar
81	✠EĀDMVND REX:	,, ,, Wt 23 3	
82	✠EĀDMVND R·EX·EC	,, ,, Wt 22 3	
83	✠EADMVND REX *Var* Annulet in field	INCEL ✠✠✠ CAR̄M Wt 16 0	
84	✠E∵A·DMVND REX B	INCEL ✠✠✠ CARMO Wt 23 0	
85	✠EĀDMVND REX EB	INCEL ✠✠✠ CAR̄MO (Chipped)	
86	✠E∨Ā DMVND REX EB	INCEL ✠✠✠ CĀR M̄O Wt 21 0	

No.	Obverse.	Reverse.	Moneyer.
87	✠EADMVND REX H *Var.* Annulet in field.	INƉEL ✠ ✠ ✠ ⅬARMO Wt. 21·0.	
88	✠EADMVND RE✠·M	INƉEL ✠ ✠ ✠ ⅬAR·M⁻O Wt. 25·8.	
89	✠EADMVND REX	LANDⱣ ✠ ✠ ✠ INEM⁻O Wt. 19·2.	Landwine.
90	,, ,,	LEOF✠ ✠ ✠ ✠ RIⅬM⁻O Wt. 24·4.	Leofric.
91	✠ÆADMVND REX	✠ LIAFI ✠ ✠ ✠ NⅬM⁻O ✠ Wt. 18·3.	Liafinc.
92	✠EADMVND REX	LIAFI ✠ ✠ ✠ NⅬH⁻O Wt. 20·7.	
93	✠EADMVND RE✠	. LIⅬRBE ✠—✠—✠ RDꞱꞱ☉IE Wt. 24·0.	Ligeberd (= Sige- berð ?).
94	✠ÆADHVND REX	LIOFH· ✠ ✠ ✠ ELMM⁻O Wt. 21·8.	Liofhelm.
95	✠EADMVND RE	LIT·IL ✠ ✠ ✠ ИAⅯ Wt. 20·2.	Litilman.

No.	Obverse.	Reverse.		Moneyer.
96	✠EΛDMVND · RE	M ÆLD ✠ ✠ ✠ OMENE	Wt. 23·0.	Mældomen or Mæld.
97	✠EΛDMVND RE	M ÆLD ✠ ✠ ✠ OMEN	Wt. 25·0.	,,
98	✠EΛDMVND REX	M ÆRT ✠ ✠ ✠ ENM⁻O	Wt. 25·0.	Mærten or Martin.
99	✠EΛDMVND REX	M ÆRT ✠ ✠ ✠ ENEM	Wt. 24·2.	
100	,, ,,	M ÆRT ✠ ✠ ✠ E N E I	Wt. 21·6.	
101	✠EADMVND ,,	MART· ✠ ✠ ✠ INM⁻O	Wt. 22·6.	
102	✠EADMVND RE	MANA ✠ ✠ ✠ MONE	Wt. 22·8.	Mana or Manna.
103	✠EVDMΛND RE✠.	MΛИΛ ✠ ✠ ✠ MOИETΛ	Wt. 18·0.	
104	✠EVDMVND RE✠	ΛΛИИИ ✠ ✠ ✠ ΛΛOИET	Wt. 21·0.	

No.	Obverse.	Reverse.	Moneyer.
105	✠EΛDMVND RE	MAN✠ ✠ ✠ ✠ NANO Wt. 23·5.	
106	✠EΛDMVND REX	MĀN· ✠ ✠ ✠ ·NΛNO Wt. 21·0.	
107	,, ,,	MΛИ ✠ ✠ ✠ ИΛИO Wt. 21·4.	
108	✠EΛDMVND RE	NΛM ✠ ✠ ✠ NΛNO Wt. 19·7.	
109	,, ,,	,, Wt. 17·4.	
110	✠EΛDMVND REX	MEᴦ ✠ ✠ ✠ REDM̄ Wt. 25·0.	Megred.
111	,, ,,	ИOИO ✠ ✠ ✠ OΠNE Wt. 21·0.	Uncertain.
112	✠EΛDMVND ,,	ODAH ✠ ✠ ✠ ONETA Wt. 20·2.	Oda.
113	✠EΛDMVND RE·✠	OSLΛᴦ ✠—✠—✠ MON Wt. 24·2.	Oslac.
114	✠EĀDMVND RE·X	OZ·PĀ ✠ ✠ ✠ ·LDH⁻O Wt. 22·2.	Oswald.

No.	Obverse.	Reverse.	Moneyer.
115	✠EΛDMVND RE✠	OƧÞΛ ✠ ✠ ✠ ΓDMO Wt. 22·0.	
116	✠EΛDMVND RET✠	OZPΛ ✠ ✠ ✠ LDMO Wt. 23·0.	
117	,, REX	OTIᴄ✠ ✠ ✠ ✠ M·ON⁻E Wt. 25·0.	Otic.
118	,, ,,	OTIᴄ✠ ✠ ✠ ✠ MON⁻E· Wt. 25·0.	
119	✠EΛDMVND REX T⊙	PΛVL ✠ ✠ ✠ EƧM⁻O Wt. 23·6.	Paul(es).
120	✠EΛDMVND RE	PΛVE ✠ ✠ ✠ LƧMO Wt. 24·6.	
121	✠EΛDMVND REX	PITIT ✠ ✠ ✠ MONE Wt. 23·2.	Pitit.
	[Pl. XI. 5.]		
122	✠EΛDMVND ,,	REᴄN ✠ ✠ ✠ VLFM Wt. 24·8.	Regnulf.
123	,, ,,	,, Wt. 24·3.	
124	✠EΛDMVИD RED✠	REᴄÐE ✠ ✠ ✠ REƧM⊙T Wt. 19·2.	Regðer.

No.	Obverse.	Reverse.	Moneyer.
125	✠EΛDMVND RE	SΛ·RΛ ✠✠✠ VVΛRD Wt. 25·5.	Sarauuard.
126	✠EΛDMVND RE✠	SA̅XSΛ⊙ ✠✠✠ ·ƎƎ̅W Wt. 21·5.	Saxsa me fecit ?
127	✠EADMVND REX	ΣIADE ✠✠✠ MANM̅O Wt. 22·6.	Siademan (or Sideman).
128	EΛDMVND REX	ƧIGΛR ✠✠✠ EΓMOT [Pl. XI. 6.] Wt. 20·6.	Sigar.
129	EΛDMVN REX	VVIHT ✠✠✠ EΓWOI Wt. 24·7.	Uuiht(es) (or Uuihtseg ?).
130	✠EΛDMVND RE	VVILΛ ✠✠✠ FEMO Wt. 23·3.	Uuilaf.
131	EΛDMVND REX	VVLF· ✠✠✠ ΣTAN Wt. 24·4.	Uulfstan.
132	✠EADMVND · REX	VVYN ✠✠✠ ΣIGEM̅O Wt. 22·7.	Uuynsige.
133	„ RET	PΛRN ✠✠✠ MOIIE Wt. 22·4.	Warn (Warin).

No.	Obverse.	Reverse.		Moneyer.
134	✠EΛDMVN ⁚·D REX	PIᒪΛ ✠ ✠ ✠ RDM⁻O	Wt. 22·2.	Wigeard.
135	✠EΛDMVND RE✠	PIᒪE ✠ ✠ ✠ ΛRDN	Wt. 22·2.	
136	✠EΛDMVΛD RET	PIᒪE ✠ ✠ ✠ ΛRIN	Wt. 21·3.	
137	,,	,,	Wt. 21·2.	
138	✠IDИΛƎMDƎ✠	PINV ✠ ✠ ✠ ᒪIVIO (Blundered.)	Wt. 21·8.	Winuc ?
139	IƎᴚ DИVMDΛƎ✠	PVᒪFᒪΛ ✠ ✠ ✠ REƵMOT	Wt. 21·4.	Wulfgar.
140	✠EADMVND REX	PVLFH ✠ ✠ ✠ ELMM⁻O	Wt. 24·5.	Wulfhelm.
141	✠EΛDMVND R⁚·EX *Var.* In field ⁚	PϒNNE ✠ ✠ ✠ LMM⁻O	Wt. 25·3.	Wynhelm.
142	✠EΛDMV·⁚ND REX *Var.* In field ✠	PϒNNE ✠ ✠ ✠ LMM⁻O	Wt. 22·0.	
143	EADMVND REX	ᑲEOD· ✠ ✠ ✠ VLFM	Wt. 21·2.	Þeodulf.

No	Obverse	Reverse	Moneyer
114	EADMVND REX	ÐEOD ✠ ✠ ✠ YLFᴴM Wt 25 7	
115	EADMVND REX	ÐEOD ✠ ✠ ✠ VΓEᴍ Wt 22 2.	
116	✠EADMVND RE	✠ÐRM ✠ ✠ ✠ ODEM Wt. 25 9	Þermod
117	✠EADMYИD REX	*Type* ii ᛏ MΛИИ EMOT ꜪU [Pl XI. 7] Wt 19 6	Mann.
148	✠EADMVИD REX	*Type* iii PEᴚL ΛFMOT [Pl. XI 8] Wt. 21 4	Werlaf.
119	✠EADMVND REX	*Type* v ÆÐELMOD [Pl XI 9] Wt 24 6	Æ̃elmod.
150	✠EADMVND REX	*Type* vi ✠CL A⋅C MѺNEAWTD✠ Wt. 23 0 [Pl. XI 10]	Clac.
151	,, ,,	✠CLAC MONE MONE MON✠ Wt 21 2	
152	✠EADMVHD RE	✠EᴚCIꜪBΛLT WOИETΛ Wt 23 4	Ergumbalt (= Ereum- bald)

No.	Obverse.	Reverse.	Moneyer.
153	✠EΛDMVИD REX	✠FREDΛD ИOИEIT Wt. 23·0.	Fredard.
154	✠EΛDMVND REX *Var.* No traces of crown. [Pl. XI. 11.]	✠FREЬΛRЬ ИOИEIT Wt. 25·4.	
155	✠EΛDMVND RE✠	✠FVᕊEL IION · EII · Wt. 24·9.	Fugel.
156	,, ,,	✠REINᕊRIM MONETΛO Wt. 25·8.	Reingrim.

Type vii.

| 157 | ✠EΛDMVD REX | ✠BΛLDRIᕊ ИOIET
Wt. 15·0. | Baldric. |
| | [Pl. XI. 12.] | | |

EADRED.

Moneyers

Ælfsige or Ælfsic
Ælfstan
Æriger
Ætard[es] or Agtard[es]
Æðelm [Æðelmund?]
Æðelmund or Aðelmund
Æðelulf
Æðelwald
Eðel -, *see also* Aðel -
Æðered
Agtard[es] or Ætard[es]
Albert
Alsige [= Ælfsige?]
Anna
Anocret
Are
Arnulf
Aspler?
Aðelmund or *Æðelmund*
Aðelwerð
Aðel -, *see also* Æðel -
Baldric.
Balduuine
Bernard or Burnard
Bernere
Bernferð
Bese
Biorhtuulf
Boga or Boiga
Burnard
Cali
Calismert?
Canceret?
Cenberht
Cilient
Clic
Copman
Cristin
Culein [= Culfin?]
Demence [Dominicus]
Deorulf
Dreml?
Dudig
Duran
Eadmund
Eardulf
Ecerulf
Elfred
Engilbred
Eodin
Eorod [= Froð?]
Irimes [= Grimes?]

Eðelnoð
Frard [= Efrard?]
Fredard or Fredred
Freðic or Ferðic [*see* Froðric]
Froð [= Froðric?]
Froðric
Fynnelm [= Wynnelm?]
Gilles
Gislehelm
Gislemer
Godin
Grim
Heremod
Herigar
Hildulf.
Hroðgar.
Hunlaf
Hunred
Hunsaft
Huscbald
Ingelgar
Inguces [= Ingulf?]
Ive
Landferð
Leofric.
Lifine
Maneca [cf. Manncein].
Manna, &c (Norwich)
Manncein
Martin
Munred.
Norbert
Norðgar [= Hroðgar?]
Oeðrheri [= Oðelric?]
Osferð
Osgod
Oslaf
Oswald
Oswine
Oðelric
Prin
Ræduine
Reedes
Regðer
Reinferð
Reiðereil
Riculf
Rinuc [*Rinulf?*] cf Winne
Rinulf
Rodbert
Saruurd [= Saruard]
Sey丨丨丨丨?

Seege [= Seegestef ?] (Norwich) Uuilfred
Siefereð [cf Sifert] Uuinetin
Siegred Uulfstan
Sifert. Warin or Uuarin
Sigar[es] *Walter*
Smertcali *Wigeroð*
Suince Winuc [= Winulf ?]
Swerline ? *Wulfbald*
Swerting Wulgar[es]
Tyleadrex [= Tyleadred or *Wynnehelm* [*Wynnelm*]
 Wealdfred ?] Þeolberht
Unbein Þeodmær
Uualdfreð. Þeodred
Uuarin or Warin Þeodulf
Uuerstan Þurferð
Uuilaf Þurmod
Uuildaf [= *Uualdulf* ?] Þurulf [cf Deorulf]
Uuilebert

DESCRIPTION OF TYPES

Obverse	Reverse

Type i

Small cross pattée Around, inscription between two circles | Moneyer's name, &c, in two lines across field, crosses, rosettes, pellets, &c, symmetrically arranged in field

[Cf Pl XII 2-4]

Type ii

Small cross pattée Around, inscription between two circles | Floriate stem with two branches enclosing moneyer's name

[See No 103, p 151]

Type iii

Small cross pattee Around, inscription between two circles | Rosette of dots Around, inscription between two circles

[Cf Pl XII 5]

Type iv

Rosette of dots Around, inscription between two circles | Moneyers name, &c, in two lines across field rosettes of dots symmetrically arranged in field

[Cf Pl XII 6]

Type v

Bust r, crowned Around, inscription between two circles, divided by bust } Small cross pattee Around, inscription between two circles

[Cf Pl XII 1 & 7]

DESCRIPTION OF COINS.

No.	Obverse.	Reverse.	Moneyer.
	SERIES A. WITH NAME OF MINT.		
	NORÐƿIC. [Norwich.] *Type* v.		
1	✠EADRED REX	✠HĀNNE NO NORDÞ.·.X Wt. 22·3.	Manna.
2	✠EADRIƆ REX	✠ƧECCCE NO NORÞIC Wt. 21·8.	Secge (Secgestef?).
	[Pl. XII. 1.]		
	SERIES B. WITHOUT NAME OF MINT. *Type* i.		
3	EADRED REX	⁘ ÆLFΣ O ✠ O ICEM̄ ⁘ Wt. 23·8.	Ælfsige.
4	" "	⁘ ÆLFZI O ✠ O EMŌM ⁘ Wt. 23·3.	
5	✠EADRED RE✠	⁘ ÆLFƧ⊥ ⁘ ✠ ⁘ ANMO ⁘ Wt. 17·5.	Ælfstan.
6	✠EĀDRED REX M	∴ ÆRIC ✠ ✠ ✠ ERMŌ ·.· Wt. 19·5.	Æriger.
7	✠EĀDRED REX	∴ ÆÐE · ✠ ✠ ✠ LMMŌ ·.· Wt. 23·8.	Æðelm (Æðelmund?).

No.	Obverse.	Reverse.	Moneyer.
8	✠EΛDRED RE	·:· ΛETΛR ✠ ✠ ✠ DEƧMOT ·:· Wt. 21·5.	Ætard(es) or Agtard(es).
9	✖EΛDRED RE✠ *Var.* In field, **M**.	,, Wt. 20·0.	
10	EΛDRED REX	·:· ΛLTΛR ✠ ✠ ✠ DEƧMOT ·:· (Chipped.)	
11	EΛDRED REX *Var.* In field, **M**.	·:· ΛRNVL ✠ ✠ ✠ FMONT ·:· Wt. 20·5.	Arnulf.
12	✠EĀDRED REX	·.· ĀÐEL ✠ ✠ ✠ MVND· ·.· Wt. 23·2.	Aðelmund.
13	,, ,,	ĀÐELM ✠ ✠ ✠ VNDM⁻O ·.· Wt. 19·5.	
14	✠EADRED REX·:	·.· BALD ✠ ✠ ✠ RILM⁻O ·.· Wt. 18·0.	Baldric.
15	✠DИ EΛDRED REX	·.· BALDV ✠ ✠ ✠ IVINH⁻O ·.· Wt. 21·2.	Balduuine.
16	✠EĀLDRED REX *Var.* In field, three pellets.	·.· BALDV ✠ ✠ ✠ VNHO ·.· Wt. 21·2.	
17	EΛDRED REX	·:· BERN ✠ ✠ ✠ ΛRDM ·:· Wt. 20·7.	Bernard or Burnard.

No.	Obverse.	Reverse.	Moneyer.
18	✠EADRED REX	BVRИ ✠✠✠ ARDMᴏO Wt. 22·5.	
19	✠EADRED REX O	BERN ✠✠✠ EREH (Chipped.)	Bernere.
20	EADRED REX	BERИF ✠✠✠ ERÐMⵙ Wt. 23·0.	Bernferð.
21	✠EADRED REX	BEƩE ✠✠✠ MOIⵑT Wt. 21·5.	Bese.
22	EADRED REX	BOᒋA ✠✠✠ EƩMOT Wt. 21·0.	Boga or Boiga.
23	" Var. In field, M.	BOIᒋA ✠✠✠ EƩMOT Wt. 20·8.	
24	EADRED REX ANGLOR·⁻	ᒋENBE ✠✠✠ RHTMⵙ Wt. 24·8. [Pl. XII. 2.]	Cenberht.
25	EADRED RE✠	ᒋOPO ✠✠✠ ꟿAZO Wt. 19·0.	Copman.
26	" "	DEMEИ ✠✠✠ ᒋEMOT Wt. 19·0.	Demence (Dominicus).

No	Obverse	Reverse		Moneyer
27	EADRED RE	DEOR O ✛ O VLFM⁻O	Wt 18·2	Deorulf
28	EADRED REX	DORV O ✛ O LFMŌ	Wt 22·2	
29	✛EADRED REX I	DREM ✛✛✛ LNOT	Wt 19·7	Dreml?
30	✛EADRII REX	DVDI ✛✛✛ ⊏IIO⊏	Wt 20·4	Dudig
31	✛EADRED RE✛	DVDI⊏ ✛✛✛ MOIIT	Wt 21·4	
32	EADRED REX	EADM O ✛ O VNDM̄	Wt 23·4	Eadmund
33	✛EADRED REX	EVDW O ✛ ✛ ANDN	Wt 23·0.	
34	,, RE✛	EARO VLFM	(Chipped)	Eardulf
35	✛EADRED RE✛ O	EFER ✛✛✛ VLFIO	Wt 22·0	Eferulf
36	✳EADRED R E✛	ELFRED ✛✛✛ ESMŌN	(Broken)	Elfred

L 2

No.	Obverse.	Reverse.	Moneyer.
37	✠EⱯREⓄM BEX	⬩⬝⬩ ELFR ✠ ✠ EΣMOT ⬦ (Chipped.)	
38	✠EⱯDRED RE✠	⬩⬝⬩ ENᏟIB ✠ ✠ ✠ REDNO ⬝⬩⬝ (Wt. 18·0.)	Engilbred.
39	✠EⱯDRED RE✠ O	ENᏟLB ✠ ✠ ✠ REDHO ⬝⬩⬝ (Wt. 21·0.)	
40	EⱯDRED REX	⬦⬦ FRⱯR O ✠ O DMON ⬦⬦ (Wt. 25·2.)	Frard (= Efrard ?).
41	,, ,,	⬦⬦ FRⱯR O ✠ O DMNÖ ⬦⬦ (Wt. 22·0.)	
42	,, ,,	⬦⬦ FREÐI ✠ ✠ ✠ EΣMOT ⬦⬦ (Wt. 18·0.)	Freðic (= Froðric ?).
43	,, ,,	⬦⬦ EROÐ O ✠ O MON⁻ ⬦⬦ (Wt. 23·2.)	Froð(ric ?).
44	✠EⱯDRED RE	⬩⬝⬩ FROÐ ✠ ✠ O RIᏟM⁻ ⬦ (Wt. 23·5.)	Froðric.
45	,, RE✠	⬦⬦ FROÐ ⊙ ✠ ⊙ RIᏟMO ⬦⬦ (Wt. 23·6.)	
46	,, ,,	,, (Wt. 20·2.)	

No.	Obverse.	Reverse.		Moneyer.
47	✠EΛDRED RE✠	⊔IƩLE ✠✠✠ IIEΓM	Wt. 23·6.	Gislemer.
48	✠EΛDRED RE✠ O	⊔ODIN ✠✠✠ MOTI	Wt. 21·3.	Godin.
49	EΛDRED REX	⊔RIΠ ✠✠✠ EƩΠOT [Pl. XII. 3.]	Wt. 20·6.	Grim.
50	✠EADRED REX : :	HVN ✠✠✠ RE‾D :	Wt. 22·0.	Hunred.
51	✠EADRED REXⅩ	HVN ✠✠✠ RED̄Ⅹ	Wt. 22·0.	
52	✠EADRED RE··	HVN ✠✠✠ REDC	Wt. 20·3.	
53	✠EADRED REX	HVNR ✠✠✠ ED‾⋒O	Wt. 23·0.	
54	✠EADRED REXⅠ	HVNR ✠✠✠ ED⋒O⟩	Wt. 21·5.	
55	✠EADRED REX‾	HVNR ✠✠✠ ED⋒OT	Wt. 21·0.	

No.	Obverse.	Reverse.	Moneyer.
56	✠EADRED RE✠ O	∴ HVN ✠✠✠ ᛉΛFT ∴ Wt. 26·8.	Hunsaft.
57	✠EADRED REX · *Var.* In field, four pellets.	∴ HVᛉEB ✠ ✠ ✠ ΛLDII⁻O ∴ Wt. 23·0.	Husebald.
58	✠EADRED REX I	∴ INᏀEL ✠ ✠ ✠ ᏀΛR⁻MO ∴ Wt. 22·3.	Ingelgar.
59	✠EADRED RE✠:	∴ INGEL ✠ ✠ ✠ ᏀΛR⁻MO ∴ (Chipped.)	
60	✠EADRED · REXᵒ	,, Wt. 21·5.	
61	✠EADRED REX″	,, Wt. 22·5.	
62	EΛDRED REX	⠿ I NᏀ V ✠ ✠ ✠ ᏟEᛋMOT ⠿ Wt. 20·5.	Inguees (= Ingulf?)
63	✠EADRED RE✠	∴ LΛND ✠✠✠ FERÐ ∴ Wt. 20·0.	Landferð.
64	,, REX	∴ LEOF ✠✠✠ RIᏟM ∴ Wt. 23·3.	Leofric.
65	✠EADRED RE	✠LIF.I ✠✠✠ NᏟMO · Wt. 24·3.	Lifinc.

No.	Obverse.	Reverse.	Moneyer.
66	EADRED REX	MANE ✠ ✠ ✠ CAMOT Wt. 22·5.	Maneca.
67	✠EVDRED REX I	NAH ✠ ✠ ✠ NANO Wt. 19·0.	Manna.
68	✠EADRED RE	NORÐ ✠ ✠ ✠ CARM Wt. 19·8.	Norðgar.
69	„ Var. In field, S.	OSFE ✠ ✠ ✠ RÐMO Wt. 22·0.	Osferð.
70	✠EADRED REX	OSVV ✠ ✠ ✠ ALDM (Chipped.)	Oswald.
71	„ Var. In field, S.	OSPA ✠ ✠ ✠ ΓDMO Wt. 19·0.	Osferð.
72	EADRED REX	OÐELRI ✠ ✠ ✠ CESOMT Wt. 21·0.	Oðelric.
73	✠EADRED RE✠	.. Wt. 22·5.	
74	✠EADRED RE✠ O	RAEDV ✠ ✠ ✠ NEWO Wt. 21·0.	Raeduine.
75	✠EADRED REX	RECÐE ✠ ✠ ✠ RESMOT Wt. 21·7.	Regðer.*

* Ruding, Pl. 15, No. 6 (Aethelred I.), is no doubt a coin of this reign, similar to No. 75.

No.	Obverse.	Reverse.	Moneyer.
76	✠EΛDRED REX	REIN ✠ ✠ ✠ FIRÐ Wt. 16·2.	Reinfirð.
77	✠EADRED RE✠ O	∴ ∫IEF-E ✠ ✠ ✠ REÐIO ∵ (Chipped.)	Siefereð (cf. Sifert).
78	EΛDRED REX	⠿ ∫ILΛR ✠ ✠ ✠ E∫MOT ⠿ Wt. 20·3.	Sigar.
79	EΛDREÐΛEℲ✠	⠿ ⊥YLEΛD ✠ ✠ ✠ TOMXEℲ ⠿ (Broken.)	Tyleadrex (= Tylead- red or Wealdfred ?).
80	✠EADRED REX	∴ VVALD ✠ ✠ ✠ FREÐ ∵ Wt. 21·0. [Pl. XII. 4.]	Uualdfreð.
81	✠EΛDRED REX	∴ VVAR⁻ ✠ ✠ ✠ IИM⁻O ∵ Wt. 17·4.	Unarin or Warin.
82	„　　　„	∴ PΛRI ✠ ✠ ✠ NMŌN ∵ Wt. 20·6.	
83	✠EΛDRED RE	⠿ VVER∫ O ✠ O TΛNWO ⠿ Wt. 22·2.	Uuerstan.
84	EΛDRED REX	⠿ VVILⴷ O ✠ O FMON ⠿ Wt. 23·0.	Uuilaf.

No.	Obverse.	Reverse.	Moneyer.
85	✠EⱯDRED MON	⠿ VVLF O✠O ƩTⱯN̄ ⠿ (Chipped.)	Uulfstan.
86	,, ,,	⠿ VVLFƩ ✠✠✠ TⱯNM̄ ⠿ Wt. 24·2.	
87	EⱯDRED ꞂEX	⠿ VVLFƩ ✠✠✠ TNMO ⠿ Wt. 25·2.	
88	✠EⱯDRED RE *Var.* In field ⠆	⠿ ꟼIᴎV ✠✠✠ ᄃMO⁻ᴎ ⠿ Wt. 21·0.	Winuc (= Winulf?)
89	✠EⱯDRED REX	⠿ ꟼVLᄃⱯ ✠✠✠ REƩMOT ⠿ Wt. 22 2.	Wulgar.
90	✠EᵒADRED REX Eᵘ	∴ ĐEODM ✠✠✠ AER⁻M ∵ Wt. 20·8.	Þeodmær.
91	✠EAD·RED· REX F	,, Wt. 20·4.	
92	✠EADRED REX I♥	,, Wt. 20·5.	
93	✠EA·DRED REX⁻M·	,, Wt. 23·0.	
94	✠EAD·RED REX N	,, Wt. 20·5.	
95	✠E·ADRED REX N	,, Wt. 22·2.	
96	✠E·∴A·DRED REXꞮ	,, Wt. 23·5.	
97	✠E·A·D·R·E·D· R·EX⁻	,, Wt. 22·0.	

No.	Obverse.	Reverse.	Moneyer.
98	✠E·A·D·R·E·D· R·EX ⊤	⊕EODM ✠✠✠ AER⁻M Wt. 20·0.	
99	✳·EΛDRED REX	⊕EOD O✠✠ VLF⁻M Wt. 23·7.	Þeodulf.
100	✠EΛDRED REX	⊕RMO O✠O DEMO Wt. 25·4.	Þurmod.
101	EΛDRED REX	⊕VRM O✠O ODMO⁻И Wt. 21·8.	
102	✠EΛDRED REX	⊕YRM ✠✠✠ ODИ⁻ Wt. 22·2.	

Type ii.

103	✠EΛDRED RE✠	NOR BERT Wt. 17·5.	Norbert.

Type iii.

104	✠EΛDRED REX	✠CVLEIH HⁱⁿO Wt. 20·0. [Pl. XII. 5.]	Culein (Culfin?).

Type iv.

105	✠EΛDⲧED ⲧFX·	⊕VЛV FLmꞓ Wt. 20·6. [Pl. XII. 6.]	Þurulf (cf. Deorulf).

No.	Obverse.		Reverse.	Moneyer.
			Type v.	
106	✠EΛDRED RE		✠ΛLBERT ONΛEMI Wt. 18·6.	Albert.
107	,,	REX	✠ΛNNΛ HONETΛE·.· Wt. 15·2.	Anna.
108	,,	,,	✠ΛRE MT·ΛEWECIΛIIV (Blundered.) Wt. 22·4.	Are.
109	,,	RE	✠CΛLI ✠ωIIERT (Chipped.)	Cali and Sifert.
110	,,	REX	✠CLΛC MONETΛ MONET · Wt. 23·4.	Clac.
111	✠EΛDRED REX		✠CLΛC MON MONEVT Wt. 22·0	
112	✠EΛDRED RENEX		✠CL·Λ·C IIONE IIONE IIONEX Wt. 23·2.	
113	✠EΛDRED REX		✠FREDΛRD NONEIΛ Wt. 24·3.	Fredard or Fredred.
114	,,	RE✠	✠FREDRED MONETΛ Wt. 21·5.	
	[Pl. XII. 7.]			
115	,,	,,	✠II ✠IVE·IЯONETΛ (Blundered.) Wt. 19·5.	Ive.
116	[✠]EΛDRED RE		✕HΛИ[И]E NONOИ: (Broken.)	Manna.
117	✠EΛDRED REX		✠MΛNNECIN MONE Wt. 20·5.	Mannecin.
118	,,	,,	✠·.·ΣΛRVVRD MONE (Pierced.)	Saruurd.
119	,,	RE✠	✠VNBEIN MONETΛ Wt. 17·2.	Unbein.
120	,,	REX	✠VVILFRED MONE IIX Wt. 23·6.	Uuilfred.

EADWIG.

Succ. A.D. 955; died A.D. 959.

Moneyers.

Abonel (*Hereford* ?).
Ælfred.
Ælfsig[e].
Ælwig.
Æscuulf.
Ætard [= Agtard ?].
Æðelgar.
Æðelstan or Eðelstan.
Aðeluuerd or Ædeluward.
Agtard.
Amund[es].
Aðulf (*London*).
Baldric (*Southampton*).
Baldwine (Bedford).
Berenard.
Biruer.
Boiga or *Boga* (Bedford).
Briunine [= Brunine].
Cnape[es].
Clac (*Newark* ?).
Copman.
Crin . . .
Cutel or Cytel [= Gytel ?].
Demence [*Dominicus* ?].
Deorulf [= Þurulf ?] (*York*).
Driuning.
Dudema[n].
Dunn.
Dunine (Huntingdon).
Eadmund (York).
Eadulf.
Eacnolf [= Ecnolf ?].
Efrard.

Eofered (York).
Eoroð ?
Erim [= Grim ?]
Eðel.-, *see also* Æðel.-
Fanael ?
Frard [= Efrard ?] (York).
Freðic [= Froðric ?].
Froðgar (Bedford).
Froðric or Freðeric (York).
Godeferð.
Grim (Bedford).
Gytel, *see* Cytel.
Heremod.
Herewig.
Heriger.
Leofstan (Bedford).
Leuine [= Lifine ?].
Lifine.
Litelman.
Manngod or *Maneod* (Southampton, Winchester).
Mann or *Manna*.
Manolet.
Oswald.
Otic (Winchester).
Sedeman [= Sideman].
Uuærin [= Warin ?]
Wilebert.
Wilsig.
Wulfgar.
Þurmod (*York*).
Þurferð.
Þurulf [cf. Deorulf].

DESCRIPTION OF TYPES.

Obverse.	Reverse.
Type i.	
Small cross pattée. Around, inscription between two circles.	Moneyer's name, &c., in two lines across field; crosses, rosettes, pellets, &c., symmetrically arranged in field.

[Cf. Pl. XIII. 1, 2.]

Obverse.	Reverse.

Type ii.

Small cross pattée. Around, inscription between two circles.	Moneyer's name, &c., in two lines across field, divided by name of mint; crosses, rosettes, pellets, &c., symmetrically arranged in field.

[Cf. Pl. XII. 8–13.]

Type iii.

Small cross pattée. Around, inscription between two circles.	Moneyer's name between two lines across field. Above and below, rosette.

[Cf. Pl. XIII. 3.]

Type iv.

Small cross pattée. Around, inscription between two circles.	Moneyer's name in one line across field, divided by mitre-shaped ornament; below, T ⋮

[Cf. Pl. XIII. 4.]

Type v.

Small cross pattée. Around, inscription between two circles.	*Small cross pattée. Around, inscription (Moneyer's name, &c.) between two circles.*

[Lindsay, 'Coinage of the Heptarchy.' Pl. 5, 115.]

Type vi.

Bust, r., crowned. Around, inscription between two circles, divided by bust.	*Small cross pattée. Around, inscription (Moneyer's name, &c., and Mint) between two circles.*

[Rud. Pl. 20. 1.]

DESCRIPTION OF COINS.

No.	Obverse.	Reverse.	Moneyer.

SERIES A. WITH NAME OF MINT.

BEDANFORD.
[Bedford.]

Type ii.

No.	Obverse.	Reverse.	Moneyer.
1	✠EΛDVVIꞄ RE·✠	∴ BΛLD BE✠DΛ ꝂIÑE· ∴ [Pl. XII. 8.]	Wt. 23·3.	Baldwine.
2	✠EΛDVVIꞄ REX⁻∴	∴ BOIꞄΛ ✠BE✠DΛ✠ MONETΛ ∴	Wt. 22·2.	Boiga.
3	✠EΛDVVI·Ꞅ REX O	∴ FROD· BE✠DΛ ꞄΛR⁻M ∴	Wt. 15·0.	Froðgar.
4	✠EΛDVVIꞄ··RE·	∴ ꞄRIꞂ. BE✠DΛ MON⁻E ∴	Wt. 20·5.	Grim.
5	✠EΛD.VVIꞄ REX	∴ LEOFƧ BE✠DΛ TΛIⱵMO ∴	Wt. 18·2.	Leofstan.

EOFERꝂIC.
[York.]

Type ii.

No.	Obverse.	Reverse.	Moneyer.
6	✠EΛDVVIꞄE RE	⁖ DEOR OƷ✠NO VLFM̄ ⁖ [Pl. XII. 9.]	Wt. 22·3.	Deorulf (cf. Þurulf).

No.	Obverse.	Reverse.		Moneyer.
7	✠EΛDVVIᴄ RE✠	∴ EΛDM ON✠EO VNDM ∴	Wt. 23·3.	Eadmund.
8	✠EΛDVVIᴄE RE	∴ EOFE OE✠ИO RΛD⁻M ∴	Wt. 19·5.	Eofered.
9	✠EΛDVVIᴄ REX	∴ FRΛR OE✠NO DMO⁻И ∴	Wt. 21·0.	Frard (= Efrard ?).
10	✠EΛDVVIᴄE RE	∴ FROÐ ON✠ETO RIᴄM⁻O ∴	Wt. 23·0.	Froðric.

HAMTUNE.
[Southampton.]

Type ii.

| 11 | ✠EΛDVVIᴄ RE✠ | ∴ ᴜΛHᴄ ✠HΛ✠M✠ ODПO ∴ | Wt. 16·4. | Manngod. |
| [Pl. XII. 10.] | | | | |

HUNTANDUNE.
[Huntingdon.]

Type ii.

| 12 | ✠EΛDVVIᴄ RE✠∴ | ∴ DVN ✠HV✠N✠ NᴄMÖ ∴ | Wt. 19·8. | Dunninc. |
| [Pl. XII. 11.] | | | | |

No.	Obverse.	Reverse.	Moneyer.
	NEPE. [Newark* ?] *Type* ii.		
13	✠E∀DVVIᏟ RE✠	.·. ᏟL∀Ꮯ ✠IIE✠PE MONE .·. Wt. 14·2. [Pl. XII. 12.]	Clac.
	PINCEASTRE. [Winchester.] *Type* ii.		
14	✠E∀DVVIᏟ REX ·	.·. M̄ANN ✠PI✠N̄✠ ᏟODM̄O .·. Wt. 23·5. [Pl. XII. 13.]	Manngod.
	SERIES B. WITHOUT NAME OF MINT. *Type* i.		
15	✠E∀DPIᏟ REX I *Var.* In field, **M**	ⵗ ÆLFRED ✠ ✠ ✠ EƧM⊙N ⵗ Wt. 21·8. [Pl. XIII. 1.]	Ælfred.
16	✠E∀DPIᏟ REX ⁘	.·. ÆƧᏟVV· ✠ ✠ ✠ LFM̄O· .·. Wt. 18·0.	Æscuulf.
17	✠E∀DVVI RE	.·. ∀DEL ✠ ✠ ✠ VVERD .·. Wt. 20·7.	Aðeluuerd.
18	✠E∀DVVIᏟ RE✠	.·. BONᏳA· ✠ ✠ ✠ ·MOIĒT∀ .·. Wt. 13·0.	Boiga.

* In Northamptonshire.

No.	Obverse.	Reverse.	Moneyer.
19	✠EΛDVVI RE✠ I [Pl. XIII. 2.]	∴ BRIV· ✠✠✠ NINC ∵ Wt. 22·4.	Briunine (= Brunine).
20	✠EΛDVVIC REX	∴ CYTEL ✠✠✠ MONE̅ ∵ Wt. 20·7.	Cytel
21	✠EΛDPIC REX *Var.* In field, **M**.	⸪ DVNN ✠✠✠ EƩM̄ON ⸪ Wt. 18·8.	Dunn.
22	✠EΛDVVⲄ RE✠	∴ EÆH ✠✠✠ OLEM̄· ∵ Wt. 22·6.	Eaenolf?
23	✠EΛDVV[I]C REX	⸪ EFRΛ O✠O RDM̄ ⸪ (Broken.)	Efrard.
24	✠EΛDVVIC REX I	⸪ FREÐI·∴ ✠✠✠ CEƩMOT ⸪ Wt. 15·2.	Freðic(es).
25	✠EΛ·DVVIC R·E✠·∵	∴ FVⱵⱵ ✠✠✠ EELO̅ ∵ ∵ Wt. 15·4.	Uncertain.
26	✠EΛDVVIC REX·∵	∴ CODEF ✠✠✠ ERÐM·∵ ∵ Wt. 21·2.	Godeferð.
27	✠EΛDPIC REX̄	∴ IERIC ✠✠✠ ERM̄O ∵ Wt. 20·2.	Heriger.

No	Obverse	Reverse		Moneyer
28	✠EADPIC REX Γ	IIERIC ✠✠✠ ERM̄O .•	Wt 20 3	
29	„ REX E	• IERIC ✠✠✠ ERM̄O	(Clipped)	
30	✠EADVVI BE	LEVI ✠✠✠ NCMO	Wt 20 3	Leuinc (= Lifinc ?)
31	✠EADVVIC RE✠ •	•MANN ✠✠✠ HON̄E	Wt 18 0	Mann
32	✠EADVVI REX	SEDEM ✠✠✠ OM̄И Λ	(Broken)	Sedeman (= Sideman)
33	✠EADVVIC REX	VVÆR ✠✠✠ INM‾O •	(Clipped)	Uuærin (= Warin ?)
		Type III		
34	✠EADVVIC RE	BIRVER	Wt 19 7	Biruer
35	✠EADPIE EPE	CNAPEES	Wt 20 6	Cnape(es)
		[Pl XIII 3]		
		Type IV		
36	EADPIC REX	OSP ΛLD	Wt 15 0	Oswald
		[Pl XIII 4]		

KINGDOM OF ENGLAND

EADGAR.

King of Mercia a d 957, of all England a d 959, died a d 975

Moneyers

Adelauer or Aðelauer
Adelgar or Æðelgar
Adelwold [= Æðelwold] (London)
Aden
Ælfgar (Thetford)
Ælfnoð (*London, Winchelsea*)
Ælfred or Elfred
Ælfsige (Bedford, Chester, *Exeter, Stafford, Wilton, Winchester*)
Ælfstan or Elfstan (Chester, Derby, *Exeter*)
Æseman (Chester, *Exeter, Lincoln,* Stamford)
Æsculf
Ætferð.
Æðelauer or Adelauer
Æðelbrand
Æðelferð (*Ilchester*)
Æðelgar or Adelgar
Æðelred (London)
Æðelsie or Æðelsige (Bath, *London*)
Æðelstan (*Canterbury, Lymne*)
Æðelweard
Æðelwine (*Oxford*)
Æðelwold or Adelwold (London)
Æðered (London)
Albart? (*Cambridge*)
Albutic
Aldewine
Alferð
Andreas
Asferð
Azma? (*Lincoln*)
Aðel -, see Adel -, and Æðel -
Aðulf (*London*)
Baldric (*Bedford, Southampton*)
Baldwin
Benedictus
Beorhtric (*Wallingford*)
Berenard
Bernferð
Birgstan
Boga, *Bogea,* Boiga, &c , *see also* Fra-tolf (*Canterbury, Chester, Wilton*)

Britferð or *Brihtferð*
Brunine (*Norwich*)
Byrhferð [= Bernferð or *Brihtferð*] (*Maldon*)
Byrhtric (*Lymne*)
Byrhtwold (*Shaftesbury*)
Capelin
Carðen [= Parðen ?] or *Corðelin*
Cnapa (*Stamford*)
Colenard
Colgrim
Copman
Cylm ? (*Southampton*)
Cynsige (*Chichester*)
Demence [*Dominicus*]
Deorlaf [= Deorulf ?] (Chester)
Deorulf (*Tempsford ?*)
Dodnorð
Dudeman or *Dudseman*
Dun (York)
Durand
Eadmer (*Southampton*)
Eadmund (Chester)
Eaduli
Eadwine (*Wilton*)
Ealfsige
Eanred
Eanulf (*Lincoln*)
Eatstan [= Eadstan ?] (*Winchester*)
Eldon
Elfred or Ælfred
Elfstan
Eltwald
Elt -, *see also* Ælf -
Eoferard
Eogermund
Eoterulf (*Tempsford ?*)
Eorod (*Chester*)
Erembald (*Norwich*)
Erfein
Esclin
Esclune
Eðel -, *see also* Æðel -
Farman

Farðen or Farðine [= Carðen?]
Fastolf (York)
Fastolf and Boga
Fastolf and Oda
Fastolf and Rain
Fnolman
Fodger (Chester)
Folcnard (Norwich)
Forðgar (Bedford)
Froðric or Froðric [= Freðic?] (Chester)
Freðic[es] or Freðicin (Derby)
Fricsmund
Gillus, Gillys, *Gyllis*, &c (Chester, Hereford)
Gilu, see Cylm
Gird
Girm (Bedford)
Ginnulf (York)
Gunnerd
Hacult
Herebert
Heretes
Herman
Heramod (Wallingford)
Henger
Herolt (York)
Hebb
Haltune (London)
Hingolf or Ingolf
Hunbein or Unbein
Ingelberd
Ingelheres or Ingelres
Ingolf or Hingolf
Ingolferð
Iohan, see Iuhan
Ioles
Isembert
Iuðl
Iuhan [= Iohan] (Exeter)
Ive
Ieeferð
Letune, Leofine, *Lyðine*, &c (Ipswich)
Lenni
Leofgar (Dover)
Leofhelm
Leofnel [= Leofhelm?]
Leofric
Ledsige (Oxford, Southampton, *Walton*)
Leofwine (Tempsford?)
Leofwold (Walton)
Leofp?
Ludstan (Bedford)
Louman
Magrad (Winchester)
Melsuðin (Chester)
Man (Tempsford?, *Winchester*)
Maning

Manna, Manan, Manne, &c (*Leicester*, York)
Mansat or *Mantat* (Southampton)
Mantieen
Marcei
Marseale or *Marseeale* (Winchester)
Mertin [= Mertin]
Morgna [= Morena?]
Nunan, see Manna
Norðbard (*Norwich*)
Oda, *see* Fastolf
Oeeman [= Ogman?]
Oger (*Norwich*, Stamford)
Ogman
Osferð
Oslac or Oslaf (*Norwich*)
Osmund
Osulf (Derby)
Osward
Oðulsht
Pirim? *see* Wirim
Radstan
Raegnulf, &c (Winchester)
Rain, *see* Fastolf
Regenold (Winchester)
Riccolf or Ricolf
Sæydtine [= Saduting?]
Sedeman, Sideman, or *Sydeman* (Rochester)
Sexbyrht (Lewes)
Siterð
Styrcar (Leicester)
Tuma (York)
Unbein or Hunbein
Umferð or *Wiferd* [= Winferð?]
Unisig or Wilsig
Wihtsige (see Wynsige)
Wilsig or Uuilsig
Wine
Winemes
Winenr [= Winein]
Wirim? (Huntingdon)
Wode
Wulfbald (Bath)
Wulfgar or Wulgar (Stamford)
Wulfmaer
Wulfred (Orford)
Wulfric (York)
Wulfstan or Wulstan (*Leicester*, *Wallingford*)
Wynsige or Wihtsige (*Gloucester*, Winchester)
Wynstan or Wunstan (*Totness*, Winchester)
Peodgar (Lewes)
Pinern [= *Winern*]
Purferð
Purmod (Chester)
Purstan

DESCRIPTION OF TYPES.

Obverse.	Reverse.

Type i.

Small cross pattée. Around, inscription between two circles. | Moneyer's name, &c., in two lines across field, divided by three crosses pattées; above and below, triangle of dots

∴

✠ ✠ ✠

∵

[Cf. Pl. XIV. 1.]

Type i. *var. a.*

Same. | Similar: *ornaments varied* ✠ ✠ ✠
•

[Rud., Pl. 28, 2.]

Type i. *var. b.*

Same. | Similar: ornaments varied ✠ ✠ ✠ ✠

[Cf. Pl. XIV. 2.]

Type i. *var. c.*

Same. | Similar: ornaments varied ✠ ✠ ✠

[Cf. Pl. XIV. 3.]

Type i. *var. d.*

Same. | Similar: ornaments varied O ✠ O

[Cf. Pl. XIV. 4.]

Obverse	Reverse

Type 1 var c

Same | Similar   ornaments varied   O O O

[Cf Pl XIV 5]

Type 1 var f

Similar   rosette of dots in centre | Similar   ornaments varied   ·' :' :'

[Cf Pl XIV 6]

Type 1 var g

Same | Similar   ornaments varied   ·: . .·

[Cf Pl XIV. 7]

Type 11

Small cross pattée   Around, inscrip-tion between two circles | Moneyer's name, &c , in two lines across field, between which name of mint   ornaments   symmetrically arranged in field

O ✠ O

[Cf Pl XIII 10 & 12]

Type 111

Small cross pattée   Around, inscrip-tion between two circles | Small cross pattée   Around, inscrip-tion between two circles

[Cf Pl XIII 5]

Type 1v

Rosette of dots   Around, inscription between two circles | Rosette of dots   Around, inscription between two circles

[Cf Pl XIII 6]

Type v

Bust r , crowned   Around, inscription between two circles, divided by bust | Small cross pattée.   Around, inscrip-tion between two circles

[Cf Pl XIII 8-9]

Obverse.	Reverse.

*Type v. var. a.**

Same.	Similar: four crosses pattées arranged around central one.

[Rud., Pl. 20, 4.]

Type v. var. b.

Same.	*Similar: three pellets and cross pattée arranged around central cross pattée.*

[Rud., Pl. 28, 1.]

Type vi.

Bust l., diademed. Around, inscription between two circles.	Small cross pattée. Around, inscription between two circles.

[Cf. Pl. XIII. 7, 11 & 13.]

* The specimens of the type (Nos. 37 & 211) in the National Collection are too imperfect for illustration.

DESCRIPTION OF COINS.

No.	Obverse.	Reverse.	Moneyer.

SERIES A. WITH NAME OF MINT.

BAÐAN.
[Bath.]

Type iii.

| 1 | +EΛDGAR REX ΛNGLORVM ·∴ [Pl. XIII. 5.] | ✠:ÆÐELSIGE MO BAÐA GIFI Wt. 21·8. | Æðelsige. |

BEDANFORD.
[Bedford.]

Type v.

| 2 | ✠EADGAR REX | ✠ÆLFSIG MONETA BE *Var.* Small cross pattée above central one. (Broken.) | Ælfsige. |
| 3 | ✠EADG.. ... | ✠LI.........TA BE (Fragment.) | Liofstan ? |

Type vi.

| 4 | ✠EΛDGAR REX ΛNGLOX | +GRIM M⁻O BEDΛFO (Pierced.) | Grim. |

CÆNTPARABYRIG or CANTPARABYRIG.
[Canterbury.]

Type vi.

| 5 | ✠EΛDGAR REX ΛNGLOX | ✠BOGΛ M⁻O GÆTPΛRΛ Wt. 23·5. | Boga (or Boiga). |

No.	Obverse.	Reverse.	Moneyer.

DEORABY.
[Derby.]

Type iii.

| 6 | ✠EΛDᒑΛR REX ΛNᒑLO | ✠ÆLFƧTAN M⁻O VRDBY Wt. 19·8. | Ælfstan. |

Type iv.

| 7 | ✠EΛDᒑΛR REX T☉ BI [Pl. XIII. 6.] | ✠FREϑIᒑIN DE☉RBY Wt. 19·8. | Freᒑicin. |

Type vi.

| 8 | ✠EΛDᒑΛR REX ΛNGLOX [Pl. XIII. 7.] | ✠OƧVLF MO⁻ DEORBY Wt. 20·0. | Osulf. |

EAXANCEASTER.
[Exeter.]

Type vi.

| 9 | ✠EΛDᒑΛR REX ΛNᒑLOX | ✠IVHΛN M⁻O EΛXNᒑ· Wt. 23·8. | Iuhan (=Iohan). |

EOFERPIC.
[York.]

Type vi.

10	✠EΛDᒑΛR REX ΛNᒑLOX	✠DVN M⁻O EOFORPIᒑ· Wt. 22·0.	Dun.
11	✠EᴀDᒑᴀR⟩ REX ΛNᒑL	✠FΛƧTOLFˣ M⁻O EFER Wt. 22·5.	Fastolf.
12	✠EΛDᒑΛR REX ΛNᒑLOX	✠MΛNNΛ M⁻O EOFORPI· Wt. 22·7.	Manna.
13	✠EΛDᒑΛR REX ΛNᒑLOX	✠TVMΛ M⁻O EOFOR· Wt. 27·3.	Tuma.

No.	Obverse.	Reverse.	Moneyer.
		HAMTUNE.	
		[Southampton.]	
		Type v.	
14	✠EADGAR REX	✠EADMER MONETA H	Eadmer.
		Wt. 22·3.	
		[Pl. XIII. 8.]	
		Type vi.	
15	✠EADGAR REX ANGLOX	✠CYLM MO HANTVN·	Cylm?
		Wt. 20·5.	
16	,, ,, ,,	✠LEOFSIG M⁻O HAMT·	Leofsige.
		Wt. 21·2.	
17	,, ,, ,,	,, ,,	
		Wt. 19·10.	
18	,, ,, ,,	✠MANSAT M⁻⊙ HAM	Mansat?
		Wt. 20·0.	
		HUNTANDUNE.	
		[Huntingdon.]	
		Type v.	
19	✠EADGAR REX	PIRIM MONETA HVNTE	Wirim?
		Wt. 20·4.	
		[Pl. XIII. 9.]	
		LÆPES.	
		[Lewes.]	
		Type vi.	
20	✠EADGAR REX ANGLOX	✠ÐEODGAR M⁻O LÆPE·	Þeodgar.
		Wt. 23·8.	

No.	Obverse.		Reverse.		Moneyer.

LEIGECEASTER, Etc.
[Chester.]

Type ii.

21	✠EADCAR RE		⠿ ÆLF⟨ ⊙L✠EO I CM ⠿	Wt. 19·6.	Ælfsige.
22	” ”		⠿ ÆLF⟨ ⊙L✠EO TΛИ ⠿	(Chipped.)	Ælfstan.
23	” ”		⠿ DEOR ⊙L✠EO LΛFM ⠿	Wt. 22·5.	Deorlaf (= Deorulf?).
24	” ”		⠿ EOR OL✠EO OÐM ⠿	Wt. 23·7.	Eoroð.
25	” ”		⠿ FLOD OL✠EO CERM ⠿	Wt. 22·2.	Flodger.
26	” ”		⠿ FROÐ ⊙L✠EO RCMO ⠿	Wt. 17·8.	Froðric.
27	” ”		⠿ FROÐ ⊙L✠EO RICM ⠿	Wt. 20·2.	Froðric.
28	✠EADCAR RE✠		⠿ CIL ⊙L✠EO L V ⟨ ⠿	Wt. 18·6.	Gillus.

No.	Obverse.	Reverse.	Moneyer.
29	✠EADCAR RE✠	∴ MÆLꝜ ⊙L✠E⊙ VÐAN ∴　　Wt. 22·3.	Mælsuꝺan.
30	✠EADCAR RE	∴ ÐVRI ⊙L✠E⊙ MOD ∴　　Wt. 20·7.	Ꝺurmod.
31	✠CADEAR 　,,	∴ ÐVR OL✠E⊙ MOD ∴　　Wt. 17·4.	
32	✠EADCAR 　..	∴ ÐVR ⊙L✠E⊙ MODM ∴　　Wt. 22·0. [Pl. XIII. 10.]	

Type iv.

33	✠EADCAR REX LE	✠EADMVND MOИE 　Wt. 22·7.	Eadmund.
34	✠EADCAR REX TO Þ	✠ÐVRMOD MO LEX 　Wt. 22·9.	Ꝺurmod.
35	,,　　　,,　　　,,	,,　　　,, Wt. 19·0.	

LUNDENE.
[London.]

Type v.

36	✠EADCAR REX	✠ÆÐERED MⵔNETA LVN Wt. 25·0.	Æꝺered.

Type v. *var.* a.

37	✠EAD... ..X	✠ÆÐER.. .. ..ND CIFITA‾ (Broken.)	Æꝺered.

No.	Obverse.	Reverse.	Moneyer.
	Type vi.		
38	✠EADCAR REX ANCLOVX	✠ADELPOLD M⁻O VN· Wt. 24·8.	Adelwold.
39	✠EADCAR REX ANCLOVX	✠ÆÐELRED M⁻O LVN Wt. 21·7.	Æðelred.
	ROFECEASTRE. [Rochester.]		
	Type vi.		
40	✠EADCAR REX ANCLOVX	✠ΣIDEMAN M⁻OH ROF Wt. 18·4.	Sideman.
	STANFORD. [Stamford.]		
	Type vi.		
41	✠EADCAR REX ANCLOVX	✠ÆΣCMAN M⁻O STANF· Wt. 20·3.	Æscman.
42	,, ,, ,,	✠CNAPA M⁻O ΣTANFO· Wt. 22·3.	Cnapa.
43	,, ,, ,,	✠OCEA M⁻O ΣTANFORD· Wt. 21·5.	Ogea?
44	,, ,, .,	✠PVLCAR M⁻O ΣTANF· Wt. 21·0.	Wulgar.
	[Pl. XIII. 11.]		
	TÆMESEFORDA or TEMESANFORD? [Tempsford.]*		
	Type ii.		
45	✠EADCAR RE	⁙ DEOR OT✠EO VLFMO ⁙ Wt. 19·0.	Deorulf.
	[Pl. XIII. 12.]		

* A *burgh* built here by Eadweard the Elder, 921. See S. Chr.; cf. also S. C. 1010, &c.

No.	Obverse	Reverse	Moneyer.
46	✠EADCAR RE	EOFR OT✠EO LFNO ∴ (Chipped)	Eoferulf?
47	,, ,,	∴ MOИ OT✠Eⵔ ИΛM ∷ Wt 23 4	Man

PELEGAFORD or **PELIGAFORD**
[Wallingford]

Type III

| 48 | ✠EADCAR REX ΛNCLORVM | ✠HEREMOD MŌ PELEⵔΛFOR Wt 23 0 | Heremod |

PILTUNE
[Wilton]

Type VI

| 49 | ✠EADCAR REX ΛNCLOⵝ | ✠ÆLFⵝICE M⁻O PILTV (Pierced) | Ælfsige |
| 50 | ,, ,, ,, | ✠EADPINE M⁻O PILTVN Wt 25 0 | Eadwine |

[Pl XIII 13]

PINCELSEA
[Winchelsea]

Type VI

| 51 | ✠EADCAR REX ΛNCLOⵝ | ✠ÆLFNOÐ M⁻O PENⵔLEⵝ Wt 24 4 | Ælfnoð |

No.	Obverse.	Reverse.	Moneyer.

PINTONIA.
[Winchester.]

Type iii.

52	✠EADGAR REX ·· *Var.* Pellet in field.	✠EATZTAN M⁻O PINTO· *Var.* Small cross pattée, in field. Wt. 20·0.	Eatstan.
53	✠EADGAR RE✠ ANGLORVM	✠PVNSIGE MONETA PINⓉ·· (Chipped.)	Wynsige.
54	✠EADGAR REX ANGLOVM	✠PVNZTAN MO✠PNT✠ M✠ (Broken.)	Wynstan.

Type vi.

| 55 | ✠EADGAR REX
 ANGLOX | ✠MARZCALE M⁻O PIN.
 Wt. 22·6. | Marscale. |

ÐEOTFORD.
[Thetford.]

Type vi.

| 56 | ✠EADGAR REX
 ANGLOX | ✠ÆLFGAR M⁻O
 ÐEOTF⁻
 Wt. 24·8. | Ælfgar. |

SERIES B.   WITHOUT NAME OF MINT.

Type i.

| 57 | ✠E·ADG·AR RE✠ ⁝ | ADELA
 ✠ ✠ ✠
 VERN⊙
 ·· | Adelaver <br> or Aðelaver. |
| 58 | ✠E·ADG·A·R RE✠ ▽ | ADEL·A
 ✠ ✠ ✠
 VERNO
 ·· | |

No.	Obverse.	Reverse.		Moneyer.
59	✠E·Λ·DᏣ·ΛR RE	ΛƉELΛ ✠ ✠ ✠ VERꝋO	Wt. 20·2.	
60	✠E·ΛDᏣΛR RE✠⌣	ΛƉEL·Λ ✠ ✠ ✠ VEᏒꝋO	Wt. 19·3.	
61	✠EΛDᏣ·Λ·R REX:	ΛƉELΛ ✠ ✠ ✠ VERꝋO	Wt. 16·3.	
62	✠EΛDᏣAR R✠⌣	ΛƉELO ✠ ✠ ✠ VERꝂ	Wt. 14·8.	
63	✠EΛDᏣ·Λ·R REX ⁚	ΛƉEL ✠ ✠ ✠ ᏣEꝏO	Wt. 18·1.	Adelgar (=Æðelgar).
64	✠EΛDᏣAR RE	ΛƉEN ✠ ✠ ✠ NOꝋE	Wt. 20·0.	Aden.
65	✠EΛDᏣAR REX	ÆƧᏟV ✠ ✠ ✠ LFꝊO	Wt. 22·3.	Æsculf.
66	✠E·ΛDᏣAR RX⌣	ÆTFE ⁚ ✠ ✠ ✠ RNΛO	Wt. 18·8.	Ætferð.
67	✠EΛDᏣ·Λ·R R·✠:	ÆTFE· ✠ ✠ ✠ RDꝊO	Wt. 18·5.	

No.	Obverse.	Reverse.		Moneyer.
68	✠E·A·DC·A·R RE	ÆÐEL ✠ ✠ ✠ ZIEÑO	Wt. 18·1.	Æðelsie (= Æðelsige).
69	✠EADCAR RE	ÆÐEL ✠ ✠ ✠ ZIEÑO	Wt. 17·0.	
70	✠EADCAR RE✠	ALBV· ✠ ✠ ✠ TCMO	Wt. 15·5.	Albutic.
71	✠E·A·DCAR RE⌣	ALBV ✠ ✠ ✠ TCÑO	Wt. 18·5.	
72	✠EADC·A·R RE✠	ALBV ✠ ✠ ✠ TCÑO	Wt. 19·0.	
73	✠EADCAR REI	ASFER ✠ ✠ ✠ ᴅNON·	Wt. 14·6.	Asferð.
74	✠E·A·DCAR R·E✠⁚	ASFER ✠ ✠ ✠ ÐMOÑ·	Wt. 20·1.	
75	✠EADCA·R REX ▼	BENE ✠ ✠ ✠ ÐIHT⁚	Wt. 21·0.	Benedictus.
76	✠EADC·A·R· REX *Var.* In field ·⁚·	BERN ✠ ✠ ✠ FERÐ	Wt. 20·2.	Bernferð.

No.	Obverse.	Reverse.		Moneyer.
77	✠E·Ā·DC·Ā·R RE✠	BIRII.·. ✠ ✠ ✠ VIIIIO ·.·	Wt. 18·5.	Uncertain.
78	✠EⱭDCⱭR RE✠	BRIT ✠ ✠ ✠ FER̄O ·.·	Wt. 19·0.	Dritferð.
79	✠EⱭDC·Ɑ·R RE✠ ·.·	CⱭPE ✠ ✠ ✠ LIÑO ·.·	Wt. 16·7.	Capelin.
80	✠EⱭDC·Ɑ·R ꞂE✠	CⱭRÐ ✠ ✠ ✠ EIIM̄O ·.·.	Wt. 22·3.	Carðen (= Farðen?).
81	✠EⱭDCⱭR ꞂE✠O	CNⱭP ✠ ✠ ✠ EMŌI· ·.·	(Chipped.)	Cnapa.
82	„ ꞂE✠	CNⱭP ✠ ✠ ✠ EMŌI· ·.·	Wt. 19·0.	
83	„ ꞂE✠᷍	COPM ✠ ✠ ✠ ⱭNM̄ ·.·	Wt. 19·6.	Copman.
84	✠EⱭDCⱭR ꞂEX꒱	DVRⱭ ✠ ✠ ✠ NDM̄O ·.·	Wt. 18·8.	Durand.
85	✠EⱭDC·Ⱡ·R ꞂEX᷍	EⱭNV ✠ ✠ ✠ LFM̄O ·.·	Wt. 18·2.	Eanulf.

No.	Obverse.	Reverse.	Moneyer.
86	✠E·Λ·DC·Λ·R RE✠⦂	EΛNV ✠✠✠ Γ·FMO Wt. 20·0.	
87	✠EΛDCΛR RE✠	ELFⷠ ✠✠✠ ΛLDĬ· Wt. 21·6.	Elfwald.
88	✠EΛDCΛR RE✠	ELFV ✠✠✠ ΛLOĬ Wt. 15·5.	
89	✠EΛDC·Λ·R RE✠·	EĐEL ✠✠✠ ΛIÑEO Wt. 19·0.	Eðeluine.
90	✠E·Λ·DC·Λ·R RE✠	FΛR ✠✠✠ NΛÑO Wt. 19·5.	Farman.
91	✠EΛDCΛR RE∇	FΛR· ✠✠✠ ИΛÑO Wt. 17·8.	
92	✠E·Λ·DCΛR RE✠·	FΛRD ✠✠✠ EИHĬO Wt. 20·4.	Farðen.
93	✠E·Λ·D·C·Λ·R RE✠⦂	FΛRÐ ✠✠✠ EHÑO Wt. 16·0.	
94	✠E·ΛDCΛR REX ⌣	FΛRÐ ✠✠✠ EIИÑO Wt. 18·1.	

N 2

No.	Obverse.	Reverse.		Moneyer.
95	✠EADᴳA·Γ ΓE✠·	ᴳΓID ✠ ✠ ✠ MOÑE	Wt. 21·5.	Grid.
	[Pl. XIV. 1.]			
96	✠E·A·Dᴳ·AR ΓE	ᴳΓID ✠ ✠ ✠ NOÑE	Wt. 15·0.	
97	✠EADᴳAR ΓE	ᴳVNV ✠ ✠ ✠ ERÐO	Wt. 15·5.	Gunuerd.
98	✠EADᴳA·R RE✠	HAᴳV ✠ ✠ ✠ FMⳒO	Wt. 20·8.	Haculf.
99	✠EADᴳ·∴ AR RE✠⨯	IEΓEB ✠ ✠ ✠ ERⳒHO	Wt. 19·5.	Herebert.
100	✠E·A·DᴳA·R R·∴✠·∴	ᴎERE ✠ ✠ ✠ MAⳅO	Wt. 19·6.	Hereman.
101	✠EADᴳAR REX⁑	HERIᴳ ✠ ✠ ✠ ERⳂO	Wt. 20·9.	Heriger.
102	✠EADᴳAR · REX⁻	,,	Wt. 18·4.	
103	✠E·A·DᴳA·R REX I	HERIᴳ ✠ ✠ ✠ ERⳂO	Wt. 17·4.	

No.	Obverse.	Reverse.	Moneyer.
104	✠EADG·AR REX ⊗	HERIG ✠ ✠ ✠ ERMO Wt. 22·4.	
105	✠EADGAR REX ∵	HERIG ✠ ✠ ✠ ERMO· Wt. 22·2.	
106	✠EADG·AR REX	HERIG ✠ ✠ ✠ ERMO Wt. 18·4.	
107	✠EADG·A·R REX	HERIG ✠ ✠ ✠ ERMCI Wt. 21·4.	
108	✠E·A·DG·A·R RE✠:	H·VN· ✠ ✠ ✠ BEIÑO Wt. 20·0.	Hunbein or Unbein.
109	✠EADG·A·R RE✠:	VИBE ✠ ✠ ✠ INĦ⊙ Wt. 22·0.	
110	✠EADGAR RE✠ ⸫	IИGO ✠ ✠ ✠ LFHV̄ Wt. 19·6.	Ingolf or Hingolf.
111	,, ,,	,, Wt. 16·8.	
112	✠E·ΛDG·A·R RE✠×	HIG⊙ ✠ ✠ ✠ LFHV̄ Wt. 20·5.	
113	✠E·ΛDG·A·R RE✠	IZEW ✠ ✠ ✠ BERT Wt. 19·8.	Isembert.

No.	Obverse.	Reverse.		Moneyer.
114	✠EΛDᴳ·Λ·R RE✠◡	∴ IᴎEM ✠ ✠ ✠ ONET̄ ∵	Wt. 21·0.	Ive.
115	✠EΛ·DᴳΛ·R RE✠·	∴ ·IᴎEN ✠ ✠ ✠ ONĒM· ∵	Wt. 20·0.	
116	✠EΛDᴳ·Λ·R ᴙEᕼ	∴ IᴎEN ✠ ✠ ✠ ONĒN ∵	Wt. 18·2.	
117	✠EΛ·DᴳΛ·R ᴙE✠	∴ IᴎEN ✠ ✠ ✠ ONĒT ∵	Wt. 17·6.	
118	✠EΛDᴳΛᴙ ᴙEᕼ	∴ IᴎEN ✠ ✠ ✠ ·TEᴎ̄O ∵	Wt. 20·2.	
119	✠EΛ·DᴳΛᴙ ᴙ·E✠ ⁝	∴ LEᴎ ✠ ✠ ✠ ᴎΛᴎ̄O ∵	Wt. 19·5.	Lenna.
120	„ „	„	Wt. 17·4.	
121	✠EΛDᴳ·Λ·R ᴙE✠·	∴ MΛ̄MO ✠ ✠ ✠ IETM̄ ∵	Wt. 20·2.	Manna or Manan.
122	✠E·Λ·DᴳΛᴙ ᴙE✠ꞏ	∴ WΛN· ✠ ✠ ✠ ΛMM̄O ∵	Wt. 19·2.	
123	✠EΛDᴳΛᴙ ᴙE✠·	∴ WΛN ✠ ✠ ✠ ΛIM̄O ∵	Wt. 20·8.	

No.	Obverse.	Reverse.	Moneyer.
124	✠EⱯDᴄ·Ⱥ·R RE✠·	∴ NⱭN ✠ ✠ ✠ ⱯNH̄O ∴ Wt. 21·7.	
125	✠E·Ⱥ·DᴄⱯR RE✠·	,, (Chipped.)	
126	✠E·Ⱥ·Dᴄ·Ⱥ·R RE	∴ NⱭH· ✠ ✠ ✠ ⱯHN̄O ∴ Wt. 21·6.	
127	✠EⱯDᴄⱭR RE✠	∴ WⱭNI ✠ ✠ ✠ Nᴄ̄H· ∴ (Chipped.)	Maning.
128	✠EⱯDᴄⱭR REX ⤬	∴ WⱭRᴄ ✠ ✠ ✠ ERM̄O ∴ Wt. 16·2.	Marcer.
129	✠EⱯDᴄⱭR R✠ᴈ	∴ MORᴄ ✠ ✠ ✠ NⱭ̄IO ∴ Wt. 16·2.	Morgna? (= Morena?)
130	✠EⱯDᴄ·Ⱥ·R RE✠∴	∴ MORᴄ ✠ ✠ ✠ NⱯ̄N ∴ Wt. 19·3.	
131	··✠··E·Ⱥ·Dᴄ·Ⱥ·R RE✠··	∴ MORᴄ ✠ –✠ ✠ NⱯN ∴ Wt. 18·5.	
132	✠EⱯDᴄ·Ⱥ·R RE∵✠∵	∴ OEEN∵ ✠ –✠ ✠ ⱯNꞂ· ∴ Wt. 18·0.	Oeeman (= Ogeman?).
133	✠E·ⱯDᴄR RE✠﹏	∴ RIᴄᴄ ✠ –✠ ✠ OLᴇN ∴ Wt. 17·8.	Riccolf or Ricolf.

No.	Obverse.	Reverse.	Moneyer.
134	✠EꞀDꞬꞀR RE᛭	ꞀIꞒOL ✠ ✠ ✠ FMN Wt. 19·3.	
135	᛭EꞀDꞬꞀR ∴ RE᛭ +	ꞫEDE ✠ ✠ ✠ IIꞀM ∴ Wt. 20·9.	Sedeman.
136	✠EꞀDꞬ‾ꞀR · ꞀEX	VVIFE ✠ ✠ ✠ RÐMO Wt. 20·4.	Uuiferð (=Winferð ?).
137	✠EꞀ·DꞬꞀR · R·E᛭·∴	ÞIꞀE· ✠ ✠ ✠ ꞀRꞀO Wt. 19·8.	Winenr (Winern).
138	✠EꞀ·DꞬ·Ꞁ·R · RE᛭	,, (Chipped.)	

Type i. var. b.

No.	Obverse.	Reverse.	Moneyer.
139	᛭EADꞬꞀR RE᛭ [Pl. XIV. 2]	✠ · BEORH · ✠ ✠ ✠ TRIꞬM · ✠ Wt. 22·7.	Beorhtric.

Type i. var. c.

No.	Obverse.	Reverse.	Moneyer.
140	᛭EADꞬꞀR REX *Var.* In field, M [Pl. XIV. 3.]	DEMEꞀ ✠ ✠ ✠ ꞬEMOꞀ Wt. 21·0.	Demenco (Dominicus).
141	,, *Var.* In field, M	FREÐI ✠ ✠ ✠ ꞬEꞱMOT Wt. 22·5.	Freðic(es).

No.	Obverse.	Reverse.		Moneyer.
142	✠EADGAR REX	INGELB ✠ ✠ ✠ ERDMO		Ingelberd.
			Wt. 17·5.	
143	,, ,,	IOLES· ✠ ✠ ✠ MONET		Ioles.
			Wt. 18·4.	
144	✠EADGAR RE✠ *Var.* In field, M	LEFINC ✠ ✠ ✠ ESMON		Lefine.
			Wt. 16·0.	
145	EADGAR REX *Var.* In field, M	MANNE ✠ ✠ ✠ ESMOT		Manne.
			Wt. 17·2.	
146	,, RE *Var.* In field, M	OSPAR ✠ ✠ ✠ DESMOT		Osward.
			Wt. 19·6.	
	Type i. var. d.			
147	✠EADGARE✠	ÆLF O ✠ O RED		Ælfred or Elfred.
			Wt. 23·0.	
148	✠EVDEVRE	ELF ⊙ ✠ ⊙ RED		
			Wt. 16·1.	
149	✠EADGAR RE	ALDE O ✠ O PINE		Aldewine.
			Wt. 23·5	

No.	Obverse.	Reverse.	Moneyer.
150	✠EADGAR RE	⁘ ALDE ⊙ ✠ ⊙ ƿINEM ⁘ Wt. 23·4.	
151	„ RE✠	⁘ EAD ⊙ ✠ ⊙ MVИD ⁘ Wt. 20·0.	Eadmund.
	[Pl. XIV. 4.]		
152	„ RE	⁘ EAD O ✠ O NYN ⁘ Wt. 19·8.	
153	„ „	⁘ EALF O ✠ O ΣIGE ⁘ Wt. 21·2.	Ealfsige.
154	„ REX	⁘ EALFΣ O ✠ O IGEM ⁘ Wt. 20·9.	
155	✠EADG[A]R RE	⁘ EO[R] O ✠ [O] OÐM ⁘ (Broken.)	Eoroð.
156	✠EADGARE✠	⁘ FREO ⊙ ✠ ⊙ ÐRIC ⁘ Wt. 22·2.	Freoðric.
157	✠EADGARE	⁘ GIL O ✠ O LYΣ ⁘ Wt. 22·9.	Gillys.

No.	Obverse.	Reverse.	Moneyer.
158	✠EADGAR RE✠	⠿ ᴄILY O ✠ O ZMŌ ⠿ Wt. 23·5.	
159	✠EADGAR RE	⠿ MER O ✠ O TIN ⠿ Wt. 18·3.	Mertin.
160	✠EADGAR RE	⠿ ƩIFER O ✠ O ÐMON ⠿ (Chipped.)	Siferð.
161	„ „	⠿ ƩIFE O ✠ O RÐM ⠿ Wt. 23·7.	
162	✠EADGAR RE	⠿ ÐYR O ✠ O MOD ⠿ Wt. 19·4.	Þurmod.
163	✠EADGARE	⠿ ÐYR ⊙ ✠ ⊙ MOD ⠿ Wt. 20·8.	
164	*Type i. var. e.* ✠EADGAR R✠ [Pl. XIV. 5.]	⠿ ÐVRF O O O ERÐ∏O ⠿ Wt. 18·8.	Þurferð.
165	*Type i. var. f.* ✠EADGAR RE [Pl. XIV. 6.]	⠿ ⱣINE ⠿ ⠿ ⠿ EƩV⁻O ⠿ Wt. 23·6.	Wine.

No	Obverse	Reverse	Moneyer

Type i var g

166	✠EADGAR RE	✠ ÆÐER ⁝ ⁝ ⁝ EDM‾O ✠ Wt 19 8	Æðered

[Pl XIV 7]

Type iii

No	Obverse	Reverse	Moneyer
167	✠EADGAR REX TI	✠DVDEMV NOETII Wt 19 0.	Dudeman
168	✠EADGAR REX A	✠DVRAND ES MOT *Var* In field, . Wt 21 0	Durand
169	✠EADG AR REX ANG	✠DVRANDIES MONETA *Var* In field, . Wt 21 4	
170	✠EADGAR REX	✠FASTOLF MON (Chipped)	Fastolf
171	✠EADGAR! REX!	✠F A STOL··F MON Wt 21 4	
172	✠EADGAR REX	✠FASTOL F MON Wt 20 2	
173	✠E A DGAR REX ·S·	✠F A STOL F ✠MON Wt 20 2	
174	✠EADGAR REX⟩	✠FASTOLFI MONE Wt 21 8	
175	✠EADGARTRE X ANGL	✠FASTOLF! MONETA‾ *Var* In field —, above and below cross pattee Wt 20 3	
176	✠EADGAR· REX *Var* Pellet in field	✠FASTOLF HOI *Var* Pellet in field Wt 20 7	
177	✠EADG‾A R REX‾	✠FASTOLF ⟩X⟨ HOI Wt 21 8	
178	✠EADGAR REX AG	✠FASTOL F. ES MO T (Broken) Wt. 18 2.	
179	✠EADGAR REX·T·	✠FASTOLF⟩ES MOT Wt 24 0	

No.	Obverse.	Reverse.	Moneyer.
180	✠EADGAR·⸱ REX · Ƨ ·	✠FAƷTOLF✠ EƧ MO Wt. 22·2.	
181	✠EADGAR ◢ REX ᴄ	✠FA·ƧTOLF · BOIᴄA Wt. 19·5. [Pl. XIV. 8.]	Fastolf and Boiga.
182	✠EADGAR REX · Ƨ ·	✠FAƧTOLF · BOIᴄA Wt. 20·4.	
183	✠EADᴄ·A·R REX	✠FAƧTOLF ▽ OD · A · Wt. 20·9.	Fastolf and Oda
184	✠EADGAR · REX : Var. In field, —	✠FAƧTOLF RAFN Wt. 20·5.	Fastolf and Rafn.
185	✠EADGAR · REX · ANᴄLO Var. Cross pattée in field.	✠FIⵙDVAN MONETA ᴄ* Wt. 22·0.	Fioduan.
186	✠E·A·Dᴄ·A·R RE	✠ᴄRID NONE✠ⵙ Wt. 19·7.	Grid.
187	✠EADᴄA · R : REX I	✠HEROLF ⋏ MON : Var. Pellet in one angle of cross. Wt. 18·4.	Herolf.
188	✠EADGAR · REX ꝋ	✠HEROLF O MONE · Wt. 24·6.	
189	✠EADGAR! REXꝋ	✠HEROLF! MONE Wt. 20·4.	
190	✠EADGAR·⸱ REX Var. Pellet in field.	✠HEROLF : MONET Wt. 21·4.	
191	✠EADᴄ·A·R : REX I	✠HEROLF Ɔ MONE·T· Wt. 21·2.	
192	✠EADGAR · ꝛ·EX ⋏	✠HEROLF✠EƧ MOT Wt. 20·7.	
193	✠EADGAR · ꝛEX I	,, Wt. 22·2.	
194	✠EADGAR REX ANᴄ	✠Iᴄ OLFERÐ·EƧ MOT Wt. 18·8.	Ingolferᶊ.
195	✠EADGAR RE✠ MT·	✠LEOFNEL MⵙNET Wt. 18·2.	Leofhelm ?
196	✠EADGARƆ REX ANᴄ	✠LEOFINᴄ : EƧ MOT·I· Wt. 19·6.	Leofinc.

* This may be the initial of a mint, Gifeleeaster or Gipeswic. The moneyer's name *Fioduan* does not occur on the coinage of any subsequent reign.

No.	Obverse.	Reverse.	Moneyer.
197	✠EADᏟᴀR꜖ REX TI	✠ᏢVLFTᴧᴧ MOᴧET Wt. 20·7.	Wulfstan.
		Type iv.	
198	✠EᴧDᏟᴧR REX TO	✠ÆLFᏕIᏟE MOᴧE Wt. 21·8.	Ælfsige.
199	✠EᴧDᏟᴧREX TO	✠ᴧLDEYYIᴧEϴ Wt. 20·9.	Aldewine.
	[Pl. XIV. 9.]		
200	✠EᴧDᏟᴧR REX TOD	✠EᴧDMVND MOᴧ Wt. 20·7.	Eadmund.
201	✠EᴧDᏟᴧR REX TO BR	✠ELFᏕTᴧN MONETᴧ Wt. 17·4.	Elfstan.
202	✠EᴧDᏟᴧR RE✠	✠YYILᏒIᏟ MOT Wt. 22·9.	Uuilsig.
203	✠EᴧDᏟᴧR REX TOD	✠ꝊVRMOD MONET Wt. 20·5.	Þurmod.
204	,, RE✠ T	✠ꝊVRMϴD MOᴧI Wt. 21·9.	
		Type v.	
205	· · ADᏟᴧR REX	✠BAL · · IN MONETA *Var.* In field, ∴ (Fragment.)	Baldwin.
206	✠EᴧDᏟᴧR RE✠	✠BRVNINᏟ MONETᴧE (Chipped.)	Brunine.
	[Pl. XIV. 10.]		
207	,, REX	✠ᏟOLENARD MONET Wt. 22·5.	Colenard.
208	✠EᴧDᏟᴧR REX	✠LIOFᏕTᴧN MONETAI (Chipped.)	Liofstan.
209	,, RE	✠NᴧNTIEEN MONETᴧ Wt. 22·2.	Manticen.
210	✠EᴧDᏟᴧR · RE✠	✠SᴧYDTINE ✠MONV Wt. 22·8.	Saydtine? (Saduting?)
		Type v. *var. a.*	
211	✠EᴧDᏟᴧR [REX]	✠BIRᏟᏕ[TᴧN MO]NI (Fragment.)	Birgstan.

EADWEARD II.

(THE MARTYR.)

Succ. A D 975, Murd A D 979

Moneyers *

Adelaver
Ælfstan or Elfstan (Bedford, Canterbury)
Ælfwald or Elfwald (Stamford)
Ælfweard or Alfweard
Æseman or Eseman (Stamford)
Æðelred or Æðered (London)
Æðelstan, Æðestan, or Æðstan (Lymne)
Æðeluald or Aðelwold (London)
Alhstan
Aðelwold, see Æðelwald
Baldic [=Baldric] (Bedford)
Beaniene (York)
Bemene, Bermene, &c
Beala
Boga, Boia, Boiga, &c (Canterbury, Chester, London, Stamford)
Brantme (Norwich)
Brihtferð (Bath)
Burhstan or Burnstan (Gloucester)
Cnapa or Cnape (Stamford)
Colgrim
Culm
Cyne?
Deorulf
Dun (York)
Dunic
Eadnoð (Southampton)
Eaduene (Wilton)
Einulf (Lincoln)
Einnte?
Elf - see Ælf -
Eseman, see Æseman
Eðelm or Eðeln [=Æðelm?] (Luffwick?)
Facer, see Lacer
Fastolf
Glounulf?
Grim (Stamford)
Grind (Lincoln)
Gunnula
Hafgrim (Lincoln)
Hancrent, see Nancrent
Hangrim

Hild (Stamford)
Hustan
Indolf or Ingolf
Iohan (Exeter)
Isulf
Knapa, see Cnapa
Lacer or Sacer [cf Wacer] (Stamford)
Lafwold
Leofen or Leofrue (Ipswich)
Levig [=Liting?] (Lincoln)
Malsuðen
Mana, Manna, &c (Tamworth)
Mannic
Mantat (Southampton)
Megered (Winchester)
Milsion
Nancrent [=Hancrent?] (Southampton)
Odn
Ogea? (Stamford)
Oia, see Boia
Osmaer (Warwick)
Osulf (Derby)
Oswald (Southampton)
Ragenulf (Winchester)
Rodbert
Sacer, see Lacer
Schylgryht or Schxburht
Styrpar
Surelos, Surulos, &c (York)
Sienreline
Tunult (Buckingham)
Vulfred or Wulfred
Vulpar, see Wulfgar
Wacer [cf Lacer] (Stamford)
Wigferð
Wihtsige or Winsige (Winchester)
Wilebeart (Ipswich)
Wine (Canterbury Lymne, Stamford)
Wulfgar or Wulgar (Stamford)
Wulfmer (Hertford)
Wulfstan or Wulstan (Stamford, Winchester)
Winsige (Winchester)
Peolgar.

DESCRIPTION OF TYPES.

Obverse.	Reverse.

Type i.

Bust l., diademed. Around, inscription between two circles.	Small cross pattée. Around, inscription between two circles.

[Cf. Pl. XIV. 11-16.]

Type ii.*

Bust r., diademed. Around, inscription between two circles.	Hand of Providence, pointing downwards, between Ā ·Ꙍ. Around, inscription between two circles.

[Montagu Coll.]

DESCRIPTION OF COINS.

No.	Obverse.	Reverse.	Moneyer.
	BAĐAN. [Bath.]		
	Type i.		
1	✠EADPEARD REX ANᒪOX	✠BRIHFERĐ Mˉ O BAꝽA Wt. 24·2.	Brihtferð.
	[Pl. XIV. 11.]		
	BEDANFORD. [Bedford.]		
	Type i.		
2	✠EADPEARD REX ANᒪ	✠ÆLFƧTAN Mˉ O BEDA·.· Wt. 22·0.	Ælfstan.
3	✠EADPEᴀRD REX AN	✠BᴀLDIᒪ MONETA· BEDA· Wt. 22·5.	Baldie (= Baldric).

* This unique coin was probably struck at Canterbury, the inscription on the reverse being
PINE MO NAENTA (Caenta?).

No.	Obverse.	Reverse.	Moneyer.
	CÆNTƿARABYRIG. [Canterbury.]		
	Type i.		
4	✠EADƷEARD REX ANCLOX	✠ÆLFΣTAN M̄O CÆNT· Wt. 22·2.	Ælfstan.
	DEORABY. [Derby.]		
	Type i.		
5	✠EADƷEARD REX AN	✠OΣVLF M̄O DEORBY Wt. 19·0.	Osulf.
	EOFERƷIC. [York.]		
	Type i.		
6	✠EADƷEAED REX ANCL	✠BEANIENE (?) M̄OFERIC Wt. 22·2.	Beaniene?
7	✠EADƷEARD REX	✠DVN M̄O EOFORƷIC· Wt. 23·3.	Dun.
	GIPESƷIC. [Ipswich.]		
	Type i.		
8	✠EADƷEARD REX ANCLOX [Pl. XIV. 12.]	✠ƷILEBEART M̄O CIPE· Wt. 23·7.	Wilebeart.

No.	Obverse.	Reverse.	Moneyer.

HAMTUNE.
[Southampton.]

Type i.

| 9 | ✠EΛDPEΛRL R✠ ΛNEL | ✠NΛNCRENT NΛN Wt. 21·4. | Nancrent or Hancrent ? |

HEORTFORD.
[Hertford.]

Type i.

| 10 | ✠EΛDPEΛRD REX ANLO | ✠PVLFMÆR M⁻O IIERT Wt. 20·6. | Wulfmær. |

LIMENE.
[Lymne.]

Type i.

| 11 | ✠EΛDPEΛRD REX ΛNLOX | ✠ÆÐEZTΛN M⁻O LIMEN· Wt. 20·2. | ÆÐestan (Æðelstan). |
| 12 | ,,   ,, | ✠PINE M⁻O LIMENE· Wt. 22·5. | Wine. |

[Pl. XIV. 13.]

LINCOLNE.
[Lincoln.]

Type i.

13	✠EΛDVVΛRD E✠ ΛNLO⊙	✠EΛNVΓE M⁻⊙ LINDCOL Wt. 23·7.	Eanulf.
14	,, RE✠ ΛNLO	✠CRIND N⁻O ,, Wt. 22·2.	Grind.
15	✠EΛDPEΛR E✠ ΛNLOX	✠HΛFCRIM N⁻⊙ LINCOL Wt. 22·7.	Hafgrim.

No.	Obverse.	Reverse.	Moneyer.
16	✠E𝖠DVV𝖠RD RE✠ NᴦΓ	✠LEVᴌ Nᵒ⊙ LINDOLNE Wt. 21·6.	Levig (= Liting?).
17	✠E𝖠DPE𝖠RE✠ 𝖠NᴌLOᴊX	✠LEVIᴌ ᴎᵒO LNDᴌOL·⸴ Wt. 22·0.	
	[Pl. XIV. 14.]		
18	✠E𝖠DVV𝖠RD RE✠ NᴌLOᴊX	✠ᴦEVIᴌ Nᵒo LINDᴌOL·⸴ Wt. 21·7.	
		LUNDENE. [London.]	
	Type i.		
19	✠E𝖠DPE𝖠RD REX 𝖠NᴌLOᴊX	✠ÆÐELRED Mᵒo LVN· Wt. 21·0.	Æŏelred.
		LVVEIᴌ. [Luffwick?*].	
	Type i.		
20	✠E𝖠DPE𝖠RD REX 𝖠NᴌLOᴊX	✠EÐELN Mᵒo LVVEIᴌ·⸴ Wt. 20·7.	Eŏeln (= Æŏelm?).
	[Pl. XIV. 15.]		
		STANFORD. [Stamford.]	
	Type i.		
21	✠E𝖠DPE𝖠RD REX 𝖠NᴌLOᴊX	✠ÆLFPΛLD Mᵒo ΣTΛNFOR· Wt. 20·6.	Ælfwald.
22	✠E𝖠DPᴧRD REX 𝖠NᴌLOᴊX	✠ÆΣᴌMΛN Mᵒo ΣTΛNF· Wt. 19·3.	Æseman or Esemau.
23	✠E𝖠DPᴧRD REX 𝖠NᴌLᵀ	✠EΣᴌMAN Mᵒo ΣTΛNF· Wt. 21·3.	
	[Pl. XIV. 16.]		

* In Northamptonshire.

No.	Obverse.	Reverse.	Moneyer.
24	✠EADÞARD REX ANᴄ⁻	✠BOIΛ Mᴼ ΣTANF⁻ Wt. 21·2.	Boia (= Boiga).
25	✠EΛDPEΛRD REX ΛNᴄLOX	✠OIΛ Mᴼ ΣTANFORD· Wt. 20·8.	
26	✠EΛDÞΛRD REX ΛNᴄL	✠ᴄNΛPE Mᴼ ΣTΛNF⁻ Wt. 21·8.	Cnape.
27	✠EΛDPΛRD REX ΛNᴄLOX	✠ᴄRIM Mᴼ OTO ΣTΛNFOR Wt. 20·2.	Grim.
28	✠EΛDÞΛRD „ „	✠HILD Mᴼ ΣTΛNFORD Wt. 23·0.	Hild.
29	✠EΛDPEΛRD REX ΛNᴄLO	✠ΓΛᴄER Mᴼ ΣTΛNFO. Wt. 23·1.	Lacer or Sacer.
30	✠EΛDPΛRD „ „	✠*OᴄEΛ Mᴼ ΣTΛNF⊙RD·ᐧ Wt. 20·9.	Ogea?
31	✠EΛDPEΛRD REX ΛNᴄLO	✠PINE Mᴼ ΣTΛNFORD·ᐧ Wt. 21·4.	Wine.
32	✠EΛDPEΛRD REX ΛNᴄLOX	✠PVLFᴄΛR Mᴼ ΣTΛN· *Var.* Annulet in field. Wt. 20·4.	Wulfgar or Wulgar.
33	✠EΛDÞΛRD REX ΛNᴄLOX	✠PVLᴄΛR Mᴼ ΣTΛⅡF⁻ Wt. 20·4.	
34	✠EΛDPΛRD REX ΛNᴄLOX	✠PVLΣTΛN Mᴼ ΣTΛ·NF⁻ Wt. 22·6.	Wulstan (Wulfstan).

PINTONIA.
[Winchester.]

Type i.

No.	Obverse.	Reverse.	Moneyer.
35	✠EΛDPEΛRD REX ΛNᴄLOX	✠PIHTΣIᴄE �Πᴼ PINT Wt. 20·3.	Wihtsige or Wynsige.
36	„ „ „	✠PVHΣIᴄE Mᴼ PINT·ᐧ·ᐧ Wt. 23·3.	

---

* Or OEEΛ.

ÆTHELRÆD II.

Succ AD 979, DEP AD 1013, REST AD 1014, DIED AD 1016

Moneyers

Abnðorb (York)
Æad-, see Ead-
Ædwine, see Eadwine
Ælfic (Shrews)
Ælfrleh (Shrews)
Ægelric (Bath, Shaft)
Egelwine (Lond)
Ægenulf (Lond, Staff)
Ælewine or Llewine [= Ælfwine] (Chest)
Ælfcctel [= Ulfcctel] (Derby, Thetf)
Ælfelm (Bardn, Itch, Winchel, Winchest)
Ælfgar, Alfgar, &c (Aylesb, Lewes, Lond, Stamf, Tamw, Warch, Winchel, Winchest)
Ælfgrd, Alfgrt, Lfgrt, &c (Heref, Lond, Southamp, Stamf)
Ælfhenh, Elfrah, &c (Roch, Shrews, Winchest)
Ælimær (Exct, Oxf, Wallingf)
Ælmoð, Elfnoð, &c (Axminst, Chest, Exct, Hunt, Lewes, Lond, Salisb, Sudb)
Ælfred (Cant, Hast)
Ælfric (Bath, Cambr, Exct, Hunt, Luc, Lond, Norw, Southw, Sudb, Wallingf)
Ælfrid or Elfryð (Cant, Lond)
Ælfsige (Bardn, Itch, Linc, Lond, Warch, Wilt, Winchest)
Ælfstan, Llfstan, &c (Bedf, Chest, Exct, Heref, Lond, Lydf, Shrews, Totn, Winchest, York)
Ælfwald or Elfwold [see also Alfwold] (Lond, Stamf, Thetf)
Ælfweard or Llfwend [see also Alfweard] (Brist, Lewes, Lond, Wallingf, Wore)
Ælfwt [= Elfsig or Ælfwine?] (Bedf, Buck, Cambr, Chich, Lond, Sudb, Wallingf)
Ælfwig or Elfwig (Cambr, Lue, Lond)
Ælfwine or Alfwine (Cambr, Chest, Chich, Colch, Heref, Lond, Mald, Oxf, Shaft, Southw, Thetf)
Ælmær (Winchest)
Ælwine [= Elfwine?] (Cricll)
Ælrqred
Æseman (Linc, Stamf)

Eaðl, Eaðli, &c (Lond)
Earwig (Stamf)
Eadgar (Shaft, Winchest)
Eadelm (Chich)
Eadmer or Eadmær (Linc, Lond, Oxf, Shaft, Wore)
Eadman (Harie)
Eadnoð or Eaðnoð (Linc, Southamp)
Eadric (Bath, Itch, Lond, Milton, Oxf, Shaft, Warch, Harie, Wore)
Eadsigo (Bath, Crickl, Lond, Southamp)
Eadstan (Hunt, Winchest)
Eadwerd, &c (Harie, Hertf, Lond, Sudb)
Eaduet [= Eadwig or Eadwine] (Heref, Lond, Shaft)
Eadweg (Heref, Lew, Shaft, Wore)
Eadwine or Eaðwine (Crickl, Heref, Linc, Lond, Mald, Norw, Oxf, Romn, Stamf, Winchest)
Eadwold [= Eaðwold] (Lond, Thetf)
Eaðwold, Aðwold, &c (Lond, Thetf)
Eaðwyrd [= Eadweard?] (Stamf)
Eael-, see also Eðel-
Eaered or Eaeryd (Lond, Lydf)
Eaestan or Eaestan [= Eaðstan] (Bath, Bedf, Bruton, Chich, Crickl, Exct, Hunt, Lond, Lydf, Lymne, Shaft, Stamf, Harie, Winchest)
Aesige (Chest)
Ablred (Lond)
Algar, see Alfgar
Altold, see Altwold
Alstan, Alstan see Elfstan
Alward [= Alfweard] (Hast)
Altwald or Altwold [= Ælfwold] (Bath, Lond, Oxf, Staff, Stamf, Stanwick, Thetf, Wallingf, Warm, Winchest, Wore)
Arneytel (York)
Arnðor, Arnður, Arður, &c
Aseetel, Aseytel, &c (York)
Asel (Lond)
Asewig or Eswig (Stamf)
Asteið (York)

Asman (Linc)
Asml [= Asul?] (Lond)
Aulf or Aulf (York)
Axra? (Norw)
Aðulfi (Lond)
Aðel-, see also Æðel-
Baldic
Baldulf
Bapim
Badan (York)
Beorhno?, Berhtna?, Byrhtno?, &c (Sudb, Winchest)
Beorulf or Burnulf (Hertf, Lond)
Berhtmer, Brihtmer, Byrhtmer, &c, (Dors, Lond, Roch, Winchest)
Berhtna? [= Beorhtno?] (Winchest)
Berhtwine, Brihtwine, &c (York)
Berhtferð [see also Byrhtferð] (Lond)
Brihtsige, Byrhtsige, &c (Bardn, Exet, Lond, Warch, Ware, Winchest)
Blaceman (Derby)
Boga, Boge, Bonga, &c (Cant, Chest, Hertf, Linc, Lond, Southw, Thet)
Bora [= Boga] (Cant, Hertf, Linc, Stamf, Wilt)
Brantene (Ipsw, Norw, Southw)
Breston
Bretwed (York)
Brihtlaf or Byrhtlaf (Hertf, Lond, Sudb)
Brihtno?, &c [of Berhtno?, &c] (Lond, Southamp, Winchest, York)
Brihtric or Bryhtric (Warch, Winchest)
Brihtwine, Byrhtwine, &c (Orf, Totn, York)
Brihtwold or Byrhtwold (Lond, Shaft, Winchest)
Bruman (Lond)
Brun or Bruni (Exet, Ludf)
Brunger (Shrews)
Brunine or Bryuine (Southamp)
Brunstan (Lond, Winchest)
Bruntat (Linc, Lond)
Bruntes?
Brihtred (Winchest)
Brihtric, see Brihtric or Byrhtric
Burhstan [= Brunstan or Byrhstan?] (Winchest)
Bynn (Southamp)
Bynm (Dover)
Byrhsige [= Byrnsige] (Bardn, Exet, Lond, Warch, Ware, Winchest)
Byrhstan or Byrnstan (Exet, Heref)
Byrhtferð (Exet, Lond, Totn)
Byrhtlaf, see Brihtlaf
Byrhtelm (Sudb)
Byrhtno? [Byhtno?] (Rom?)
Byrhtlaf, see Brihtlaf
Byrhtmer, see Berhtmer

Byrhtno?, &c, see Beorhno?
Byrhtred (Winchest)
Byrhtric [= Brihtric] (Exet, Southw, Sudb, Thet, Wallingf, Warch, Winchest)
Byrhtwine, see Brihtwine
Byrhtwold, see Brihtwold
Byri [= Byrning?] (Southamp)
Byrning [= Bruning?] (Southamp)
Carig (Lond)
Carla (Exet)
Cawe (Lond)
Cawe (Dover, Norw)
Causige, Cawsige, &c (Dover)
Ceolno?, Ciolno?, or Colno? (Lond, Sudb)
Citel, see Cytel
Cina (Winchest)
Citelle [Cytel?] (York)
Clem (Cambr)
Cnut or Cynt [= Cnut?] (Cambr)
Congrim [= Colgrim?] (Lxna?)
Coldwine, see Goldwine
Coleman (Oxf)
Colgrim or Golgrim (Linc, York)
Crastgin, Cristin, or Cristðin (Stamf)
Cuili (Exet)
Cuna, Cunna, or Cynna (Chich, Winchest)
Cinsige or Cunsige (Dover, Lond)
Cynt, [see also Cnut] (Cambr)
Citel (Exet, York)
Cytlbern or Cytlern (Linc)
Cythæ [= Cytlbern?] (Linc)
Derul [= Derulf, Deorulf?] (Lond)
Deahn[x] (York)
Deorsige (Lond)
Dcmuhg? (Cant)
Dillun (Heref)
Dioreman or Dyreman (Lond)
Direwine or Dyrewine (Thet)
Dersi[ge?] [= Deorsige?] (Lond)
Doda or Dodda (Dover, Totn)
Doding
Dorewine, [see also Direwine] (Bedf)
Drantyng
Dreng (Linc)
Dreof? (Lond)
Drihwold [Drihtwold] (Lond)
Duda [see Doda] (Cant, Winchest)
Dudd or Dudde (Exet)
Durinelm [= Dyfnelm?] (Chest)
Dun (Linc)
Duneild (Guildf)
Dunstan (Chich, Exet, Guildf)
Duran [see Durtan] (York)
Durand or Durant (Worc)
Durtan [= Purstan?] (York)
Dureman, see Dioreman
Dyrewine (Thet)
Byrhtman

Eadeasge [= Eadsige] (Winchest)
Eadelm or Ldelm (Lond, Roch)
Eadgar (Lewes, Lond, Thett)
Eadlaf (Lond)
Ladmer (Exet)
Eadmund or Edmund (Cambr, Colch, Line, Lond, Noru, Southamp)
Eadnoð (Bridpu, Cinch, Lond, Roch, Winchest, York)
Eadric or Edric (Cambr, Chest, Exet, Ipsw, Lond, Taunt, Thetf, Wallingf, York)
Eadrinoð [= Eadnoð?] (Lond)
Eadsi[g?] (Dunw, Lond)
Eadsig, Ladsige, Edsige, &c (Dover, Hast, Lond, Roch, Shreus, Winchest)
Eadsme [= Eadsige?] (Lond)
Eadstan, Edstan, or Eatstan (Ashaban?, Bath, Exet, Lymne, York)
Eadwacer or Edeacer (Noru)
Eadwerd or Edwerd (Lond, Lymne, Roch, Thetf)
Eadwi or Edwi[ct Eadwine and Eduig] (Hertf, Lond, Roch, Stamf, Sudb, Thetf)
Eadwine, Edwine, &c (Cambr, Colch, Exet, Lond, Noru, Roch, Southue, Stamf, Thetf, Totn, Wilt, Winchest)
Eadwoi [= Eadwold] (Thetf)
Eadwold or Eldwold (Cant, Lond, Mald, Thetf)
Ealdgar (Lond)
Ealdred (Lond, Mald, Malm)
Ealhstan, Lalstan, &c (Lond)
Eamer (Lmc)
Eamund (Lond)
Eardnoð (Lond)
Eastulf [= Festulf] (Thetf)
Eatstan, see Eadstan
Ecferð (Lond)
Eduene, see Eadwine
Eelaf, see Eilaf
Eila (Cambr)
Eilelbriht (Line)
Eilelm (Lond)
Eilelric (Lond)
Ederei (Lond)
Edel-, see also Eðel-, and Eðel-
Eilferer? (York)
Edric, see Eadric
Edsige, see Eadsige
Eilstan [= Æðestan?] (Bath)
Edwerd, see Eadwerd
Edwi, see Eadwi
Eilwig (Lond, Thetf, Wallingf)
Edwine, see Eadwine
Eilwine? [= Lilwine?] (Hunt)
Eheuine [= Elfwine?] (Chest)
Eilaf or Eilof [= Lelaf?] (York)

Eilofuine (Southue)
Elebriht [= Elfbriht?] (Stamf)
Elenoð [= Llenoð or Elfnoð?] (Chest)
Elenoð [= Elfnoð?] (Chest, Lond)
Elewine [= Lilwine?] (Chest, Colch)
Elfgyt (Lond)
Lif-, see also Elf-
Linla (Wallingf)
Lolman [for Godman?]
Erewine (Derby, Thetf)
Escei (Stamf)
Eostulf [= Eostulf] (York)
Estle? (Lond)
Eswig, see Aswig
Eykard (Exet)
Eyesop (Warch)
Eðelune [Eðeluine] (Lond)
Eðel-, see also Edel-
Fallan (York)
Farðen (Line)
Fasðulf, see Fastulf
Faremun [= Farman?] (Line)
Farman (York)
Fastolf, Fastult, Fasulf, &c (Tamue, Thetf, York)
Fedineð? (Lymne)
Feresoh?
Folcard, Foleard, &c (Noru, Thetf)
Frostulf or Froðsulf (York)
Fryðemund (Winchest)
Fyhelle? (Thetf)
Gargun (Line)
Garult (Wore)
Gile (Line)
Godeuine, see Godwine
Goel (Cudb, Exet, Hch, Lond, Sudb)
Goda or Godda (Chest, Exet, Jedb, Lond, Lydf, Shaft, Totn, Wore)
Godeg, Goday, &c (Stamf)
Godgerð, Godyerð or Godeiryð (Cudb, Lewes)
Godbyt, Godeleof, Godlear, &c, (Stamf, Winchels)
Godeman or Godman (Cant, Crekl, Dover, Glouc, Harm, Herst, Lewes, Line, Lond, Thetf, Winchest)
Goder or Godere (Lond, Stamf)
Godeg or Godeg, see Godeg
Godine (Line, Oxf)
Godman, see Godeman
Godin (Lond)
Godrie (Bedf, Bridpn, Cambr, Cant, Colch, Hnt?, Ipsw, Lond, Lydf, Lymne, Staff, Stamf, Sudb)
Godune [= Godwine] (Sudbury)
Godure [= Godure?] (Ipsw)
Godwine (Cambr, Cant, Colch, Derby, Dover, Exet, Glouc, Ipsw, Line, Lond, Lydf, Roch, Salisb, Sedmorð, Stamf, Sudb, Thetf, Tom?, Totn, Warm, Wilt, Winchest)

Gola or Golla (York)
Goldstan (Lewes)
Goldus (Salisb, Wilt)
Goldwine (Cant, Lond, Roch, Winchest)
Golgrim, see Colgrim
Grim (Linc, Lond, Thetf)
Grind (Linc)
Gunar, Guner, &c (Derby)
Gunhwat (York)
Gunleof or Gunuleof (Chest)
Gunni (Bedf)
Gunstan? (Linc)
Hancrent, Mancrent, or Nancrent
Harmeytel, see Arneytel
Heawulf (Cholc, Lond, Southw, Sudb, Winchest)
Herebriht, Herebreht, Herebyrht, &c (Lewes)
Herulf or Herwulf (Winchest)
Heawlf [=Heawulf ?] (Cholc)
Hiardi ?
Hildolf or Hildult (York)
Hildsige (Bath)
Hundolf or Hundulf [= Hildulf?] (York)
Huneman (Totn)
Hunewine (Exet, Ipsw, Totn, Watch)
Hunna [Huniga] (Bardn)
Huniga (Bardn)
Hunstan (Cambr)
Hwasman [Hwateman] (Norw)
Hwateman, Hwateman, or Hwatman (Heref, Norw)
Hyse (Warw)
Ingelric (Winchest)
Ira, Ire, Irra, &c (York)
Iscgel (Harw)
Isegod, Isgod, or Isengod (Exet)
Iufine [=Lufine] (Worc)
Iulstan [=Iustan?] (Linc)
Iustan (Linc)
Kynsige, see Cynsige
Leof -, see Leof -
Lafe [cf Lefa] (Lond)
Lefa, Leta, Lefja, &c (Hast, Lewes)
Lehne, Leofine, see Lifine
Lof -, see also Leof -
Lefwine [= Leofwine ?] (Leng = Linc ?)
Leyðoð? (Oxford?)
Leofhelm [= Leofhelm ?] (Shrews)
Leofdag (Stamf)
Leofgar (Heref)
Leofget (Malm)
Leofgod (Crickl, Southamp, Worc)
Leothelm (Shrews)
Leofhese, Leofhysi, or Leofhuse (Dover, Ilch)
Leofine, see Lifine
Leofine [=Leofwine] (Winchest)

Leofman (Chest, Ipsw, Linc, Oxf)
Leofmer (Norw)
Leofmon (Chest)
Leofmoð [= Leofnoð ?] (Lond)
Leofn[oð?] (Hunt)
Leofnod, Leofnoð, Liofnoð, &c (Bedf, Cambr, Cant, Chest, Lewes, Lond, Malm, Shrews)
Leofred or Lufred (Colch, Lond, Sudb)
Leofric, Lefric, Liofric, &c (Cant, Dover, Exet, Hunt, Ilch, Ipsw, Linc, Lond, Lynne, Norw, Roch, Tamw, Thetf, Wallingf)
Leofrine, see Leofwine
Leofryð (Lond)
Leofsige (Cambr, Glouc, Ilch, Ipsw, Shrews, Southamp)
Leofstan, Liofstan, &c (Aylesb, Cant, Colch, Ipsw, Lewes, Lond, Norw, Romn, Southamp, Southw, Urtf?, York)
Leofsunu (Exet, Shrews, Winchest)
Leofwig (Colch)
Leofwine or Liofwine (Bath, Bedf, Chest, Dover, Lewes, Linc, Lond, Mald, Malm, Newr?, Norw, Romn, Southamp, Stamf, Sudb, Tamw, Tamst, Thetf, Wallingf, Walt, Winchest, York)
Leofwold or Liofwold (Cant, Colch, Guildf, Lond, Southamp, Warw, Wilt, Winchest)
Leofðegn (Thetf)
Leoman, see Leofman
Leousige, see Leofsige
Leva, see Lefa
Lifine, Lifing, Lefing, Leofine, Lufine, Lynne, &c (Bedf, Cant, Ipsw, Linc, Lond, Norw, Southamp, Stamf, Warw)
Lind (Lond)
Lioeri [= Liofric], see Leofric
Liof - see Leof -
Litman, see Lytelman
Liuegod or Liufgod (Lond, Stamf)
Liuing or Liuing (Lond, Norw)
Luda, Ludia, or Ludda (Exet)
Lufa [cf Lefa] (Shaft)
Lumar (Heref)
Lycfea or Lyva [cf Lefa] (Hast)
Lyine, see Lifine
Lufsye [= Lyfsige?] (Dover)
Lytelman, Lyteman, or Litman (Ipsw)
Martin or Martin (Shrews, Worc)
Man or Mann (Wallingf, Worc)
Mana or Manna (Exet, Linc, Romn, Thetf, Totn)
Mancrent, see Hancrent
Mangod (Exet)
Maning or Manning (Dover, Norw)
Manwine (Colch, Hunt)

Mereuine (Lewes)
Mua? (Thetf)
Nancrent, see Hancrent
Oban or Oslan [cf Osla] (York)
Osla, Oslu, Osla, &c (Ipsw, Lond, Wallingf, Warch, Winchest, Wore, York)
Osleated [= Osseted?] (York)
Odgrim, see Osgrim
Oslu [= Osla?] (York)
Ofe? (Stamf)
Oqu [= Oqu?] (Hunt)
Oterlid? (Corbridge?)
Oiga (York)
Onlaf (Lewes)
Ordbright (Winchest)
Osalf, Osolf, or Osulf (Derby, Ipsw, Lond, Thetf, York)
Osberen or Osbern (Thetf, Wilt)
Oscitel, Oscytel &c (Cambr, Chest, Lond, York)
Osferð (Dover, Leic, Lanc, Lond, Roch, Thetf)
Osfram? (Linc)
Osgar (Bedf, Derby)
Osgod, Osgot, Osgut, &c (Hunt, Linc, Lond, Winchest, York)
Osmær (Warch, Warw, Wore)
Osmund (Lanc, Lond, Stamf)
Osulf, see Osalf, &c
Osrerd
Oswi[g] (Bedf, Lond)
Oswold (Lewes, Lond, Norw, Nott, Shrews)
Ousgrim, see Osgrim
Osbern or Ousbern (Linc)
Osencar (Lond)
Osgrim or Ousgrim (Linc, York)
Osulf (Chest, York)
Regenbald
Regenulf (Winchest)
Regenold [= Regenold?] (Lanc)
Rofen (Linc)
Riculf (Chest, Shrews)
Rodbart or Rodbert (Linc)
Sælne? (Exet)
Seman (Salisb)
Serteg (Norw)
Sæwine or Sewine (Crickl, Exet, Hunt, Salisb, Shaft, Wilt)
Scot (Stamf)
Scertebrand (Stamf)
Scolen or Sydcn (Southamp, Winchest)
Sercloms [= Stercol or Sweetcol?] (York)
Siba [cf Siboda] (Winchest)
Sibda or Sibeda (Winchest)
Sibwine (Lond)
Sibsino? (Lond)
Suleman (Roch)
Sidewine, Sulwine, &c (Cambr, Colch, Greenwich, Lond, Roch)

Sigeferð (Wore)
Sigeric (Watch)
Sigulf or Suglaf (Wallingf)
Supreme (Chest, Wore)
Sihleald? (Maglmt?)
Siulf [= Sigulf?] (Wallingf)
Sircol (Colne)
Siro (Winchest)
Sirold or Sirold (Ipsw)
Siswine, see Sulwine
Sulme (Lew)
Smolf (Lanc)
Somund [= Somund?]
Stegenhat (Linc)
Stegenold (Lanc)
Storcar Storcer, Styrcar, &c (Linc, York)
Streol (York)
Sumerleda, Sumerleða, Sumerlid, &c (Linc, Nott, Thett, York)
Sunegod [= Godsunu?] (Linc, Lond)
Sunulf or Swunlf (York)
Swatgar, Swartcar, &c (Sandw, Stamf, York)
Swegen (Chest, Linc)
Swert [= Sweetgar?] (Stamf, York)
Swerteol, &c (York)
Swertine, Swyrtine, &c (Norw)
Swetine (Colch, Lond)
Swetman (Lond)
Swetun (Lond)
Swilemin or Swelman (Southamp, Winchest)
Swyrling [= Swerting?] (Thetf)
Sydcn, see Scolen
Toca or Toga (Colch, Crickl, Lond, Mald, Winchest)
Tumme [= Tumu?] (York)
Tuna (Exet)
Tunemin (Souther, Suolb)
Tunult (Buck)
Uthint [Welham?]
Unas, see Wuas
Uf [= Wulf?] (Cant, Linc, York)
Ulcetel, &c (Linc, Norw, Colch?, York)
Ulfgrim or Wulfgrim (Linc)
Ulfic (Southamp)
Unbegn, Unbein, &c (Linc)
Unsten (Shrews)
Uri (York)
Ulmund, see Wlmund
Walgist Walgist, Walost, &c (Thetf)
Walos [= Walgist?] (Thetf)
Walters (Ipsw)
Wanstan, see Wunstan
Weln
Wempes, see Wenpes
Wensep [- Wensep] (Wilt)
Weltsup (Colne)
Welmund (Cambr)

Win or Winn (Wallingf.).
Winu[s] [= Wine?] (Cadb., Crewk., Ilch.).
Wine (Bridgn., Lymne, Tamar.).
Winegos, Wynegos, &c. (York).
Winsige, Wynsige, &c. (Exet., Lond., Shrews.).
Winterleda (York).
Wulbearn, Wulfbeorn, &c. (Linc.).
Wulf [see also Ulf] (Cant.).
Wulfah (Linc.).
Wulfelm or Wulfhelm (Cadb., Ilch.).
Wulfgar, &c. (Cambr., Hunt., Linc., Lond., Stamf., Wilt.).
Wulfgeat, Wulfgit, &c. (Leic., Linc.).
Wulfgrim, see Ulfgrim.
Wulfmær, Wulmar, &c. (Bardn., Jedb., Linc., Lond., Norw., Shrews., Totn.).
Wulfnoð (Colch., Dorch., Hertf., Leic., Romn., Lond., Southamp., Thetf., Winchest.).
Wulfred, Wulford, or Wulfryd (Lond.).
Wulfric (Chest., Colch., Hertf., Leic., Linc., Lond., Southamp., Warch., Warw., Worc.).

Wulfsige (Cambr., Derby, Exet., Lond., York).
Wulfstan, &c. (Æt.?, Cant., Colch., Derby, Dover, Exet., Lewes, Lond., Stamf., Winchest.).
Wulfwi or Wulfwig (Cant.).
Wulfwine (Colch., Ilch., Linc., Lond., Orf., Wallingf.).
Wullaf or Wyllaf (Chest.).
Wulstan [see also Wulfstan] (Stamf.).
Wunstan or Wynstan (Bath, Chich., Winchest.).
Wynsige (Exet., Lond., Shrews.).
Þeodgar (Lewes).
Þeodgeld, Þeodgyld, &c. (Linc.).
Þeodred (Linc., Lond., York).
Þitulf (Lond.).
Þorald (Chest.).
Þorcetel, Þurcetel, &c. (Linc., Southamp., Torksey).
Þorel [= Þoreil ?] (Lond.).
Þorgrim (York).
Þorsige (Lond.).
Þorstan, Þorstan, Þurstan, &c. (Linc., Norw., Stamf., York).
Þorulf, Þurulf, &c. (Leic., York).
Þurgod (Exet.).

DESCRIPTION OF TYPES.

Obverse.	Reverse.

Type i.

Bust l., diademed. Around, inscription between two circles.	Small cross pattée. Around, inscription between two circles.

[Cf. Pl. XV. 2, &c.]

Type i. var. a.

Similar; bust r.	Same.

[Cf. Pl. XV. 6.]

Type i. var. b.

Similar; bust l.; in front, sceptre, cross pommée.	Same.

[Hild. Pl. 2. Type A. var. b.]

Obverse	Reverse

Type i var c

| Similar, no sceptre in front of bust | Similar, five crosses pattée arranged in form of cross, central one largest |

[Cf Pl XVI 13]

Type i var d

| Similar, bust l, diademed top not | Similar, small cross pattée, &c, as Type i |

[Hild, Pl 2, *Type A var e*]

Type i var e

| Similar, no inner circle around bust | Same |

[Hild, Pl 3, *Type A var f*]

Type ii

| Bust l, diademed Around, inscription between two circles | Hand of Providence issuing from clouds, on either side $\bar{A}$ $\bar{\omega}$ Around inscription between two circles |

[Hild, Pl 3, *Type B i var a*]

Type ii var a

| Similar, bust r | Same |

[Cf Pl XVI 8]

Obverse.	Reverse.

Type ii. *var. b.*

Obverse	Reverse
Similar.	Similar ; *on either side of Hand*, $\overline{\omega}$ $\overline{\Lambda}$.

[Hild., Pl. 3, *Type* B. 1, *var. c.*]

Type ii. *var. c.*

Obverse	Reverse
Similar ; *in front of bust, sceptre, cross pommée.*	Similar ; *on either side of Hand*, $\overline{\Lambda}$ $\overline{\omega}$.

[Hild., Pl. 3, *Type* B. 1, *var. b.*]

Type ii. *var. d.*

Obverse	Reverse
Similar.	Similar ; *lines curved outwards issuing from clouds*, and $\overline{\Lambda}$ $\underline{\omega}$.

[Cf. Pl. XVI. 10.]

Type ii. *var. e.*

Obverse	Reverse
Similar.	Similar ; *without letters on either side of Hand.*

[Hild., Pl. 3, *Type* B. 2, *var. a.*]

Type ii. *var. f.*

Obverse	Reverse
Similar ; *sceptre, cross pattée.*	Similar ; Hand of Providence giving the Latin benediction ; i.e. third and fourth fingers closed ; cross in clouds.

[Cf. Pl. XVI. 14.]

Obverse.	Reverse.

Type iii.

Bust l., diademed. Around, inscription between two circles.	Short cross, voided, frequently with pellet in centre : in angles, Ꞇ R V ✠. Around, inscription between two circles.

[Cf. Pl. XVI. 12.]

Type iii. var. a.

Similar; in front of bust, sceptre, cross pommée.	Same.

[Cf. Pl. XV. 3.]

Type iii. var. b.

Similar; bust r.	Same.

[Hild., Pl. 4, Type C. var. c.]

Type iii. var. c.

Similar; sceptre, cross pattée.	Same.

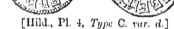

[Hild., Pl. 4, Type C. var. d.]

Type iv.

Bust l., diademed. Around, inscription between two circles.	Long cross, voided, frequently with pellet in centre; each limb terminating in three crescents. Around, inscription: outer circle.

[Hild., Pl. 4, Type D. var. a.]

Obverse.	Reverse.

Type iv. var. a.

Similar; rude bust l.; inscription divided by bust.	Same.

[Cf. Pl. XV. 4.]

Type v.

Bust l., in armour and radiate helmet. Around, inscription divided by bust.	*Small cross pattée. Around, inscription between two circles.*

[Hild., Pl. 4, Type E. var. a.]

Type vi.

Bust l., in armour and radiate helmet. Around, inscription divided by bust.	*Long cross, voided, each limb terminating in three crescents: pellet in centre. Around, inscription: outer circle.*

[Hild., Pl. 4, Type E. var. b.]

Type vii.

Bust l., in armour and radiate helmet. Around, inscription divided by bust: outer circle.	*Long cross, voided, reaching to edge of coin; pellet in centre; in angles, ⊏ R V X. Around, inscription: outer circle.*

[Hild., Pl. 4, Type E. var. c.]

Obverse.	Reverse.

Type viii.

| Bust l., in armour and radiate helmet. Around, inscription divided by bust: outer circle. | Square with three pellets at each corner: over it, bisecting the sides, long cross, voided, each limb terminating in three crescents; pellet in centre. Around, inscription: outer circle. |

[Cf. Pl. XV. 1.]

Type ix.*

| *Bust l., in armour and radiate helmet. Around, inscription divided by bust: outer circle.* | *Long cross, voided, each limb terminating in three crescents; in 1st and 4th angles, crescent. Around, inscription: outer circle.* |

[Hild., Pl. 4, *Type* F.]

Type ix. var. a.

| *Similar; rude bust l., dividing inscription.* | *Same.* |

[Hild. Pl. 5, *Type* F. *var. a.*]

Type x.

| *The Agnus Dei r.; below,* Λ · Ϲ : *within border of dots. Around, inscription: outer circle.* | *The Holy Dove. Around, inscription: outer circle.* |

[Hild., Pl. 5, *Type* G.]

---

* The style of this and the next type is certainly Danish.

Obverse.	Reverse.

Type xi.

The Agnus Dei r.; below, on tablet, AGN. Around, inscription: outer circle.	Small cross pattée. Around, inscription between two circles.

[Hild., Pl. 5, Type G. var. a.]

DESCRIPTION OF COINS.

No.	Obverse.	Reverse.	Moneyer.
	GOLD.		
	LÆPES.		
	[Lewes.]		
	Type viii.		
1	✠ÆÐELRÆD REX ANGL	✠LEOFPINE MO LÆPE·. Wt. 51·5.	Leofwine.
	[Pl. XV. 1.]		
	SILVER.		
	ÆGLESBYRIG.		
	[Aylesbury.]		
	Type iii. *var. a.*		
2	✠ÆÐELRÆD REX ANGLOX	✠ÆLFGAR M-O ÆGLX Wt. 20·3.	Ælfgar.
	BARDANIG.		
	[Bardney.]		
	Type ii. *var. d.*		
3	✠ÆÐELRÆD REX ANGLOX	✠BYRHXIGE M-O BARD Wt. 19·5.	Byrhsige (Byrnsige).

No.	Obverse.	Reverse.	Moneyer.
		BAÐAN. [Bath.]	
		Type i.	
4	✠ÆÐELRED REX AN	✠ÆÐESAN · ⊙N BAÐ Wt. 26·7.	Æþestan.
5	,, ,, ANC	✠ALFPOLD ON BAÐ Wt. 18·8.	Alfwold.
		[Pl. XV. 2.]	
		Type ii. *var. d.*	
6	✠ÆÐELRÆD REX ANCLOX	✠ÆÐELRIC M⁻O BAÐAN Wt. 21·1.	Æþelric.
		Type iv. *var. a.*	
7	✠ÆÐELRÆD REX ANCLOR	✠·ÆLFRIC MΩ⊙ BAÐ Wt. 26·7.	Ælfric.
8	,, ,, ANCL⊙	✠·ÆÐELRIC MΩO BAÐ (Pierced.)	Æþelric.
9	,, ,, ,,	✠EDSTAN MΩ⊙ BAÐ Wt. 26·5.	Edstan (= Æþestan?).
10	,, ,, ANCLOX	✠EDSTAN M·Ω·O BAÐ· Wt. 26·3.	
		BEDANFORD. [Bedford.]	
		Type ii. *var. a.*	
11	✠ÆÐELRED REX ANCLOX	✠OSPI MONETA BEDAF Wt. 25·8.	Oswi(g).
		Type iii. *var. a.*	
12	✠ÆÐELRÆD REX ANCLOX	✠ÆLFSTAN M⁻O BEDA Wt. 21·5.	Ælfstan.
		Type iv. *var. a.*	
13	✠ÆÐELRÆD REX ANCL⊙	✠CVNNI Mt⊙ BEDA Wt 27·2	Gunni.

No.	Obverse.	Reverse.	Moneyer.
	BUCCINGAHAM.		
	[Buckingham.]		
	Type iii. *var. a.*		
14	✠ÆÐELRÆD REX ANᴄLOX [Pl. XV. 3.]	✠TVNVLF M⊙ BVᴄIᴄ Wt. 22·3.	Tunulf.
	CÆNTPARABYRIG.		
	[Canterbury.]		
	Type i. *var. a.*		
15	✠ÆÐELRED REX ANᴄLOR·	✠ᴄODMAN MION ᴄANT Wt. 19·5.	Godman.
	Type ii. *var. a.*		
16	✠ÆÐELRED REX ANᴄLOX	✠BOIA П⁻O ᴄÆNTPA Wt. 21·9.	Boiga.
17	✠ÆÐELRÆD ,, ANᴄLOX	,, ,, ᴄÆNTPARE Wt. 20·6.	
18	,, ,, ,,	✠EADPOLD M⁻O ᴄÆNTPA Wt. 20·9.	Eadwold.
19	,, ,, ,,	,, ,, (Chipped.)	
20	,, ,, ,,	✠LIFINᴄ M⁻O ᴄÆNTPARA Wt. 25·2.	Lifine.
	Type iii. *var. a.*		
21	✠ÆÐELRÆD REX ANᴄLOX	✠EADPOLD M⁻O ᴄÆNT Wt. 22·4.	Eadwold.
22	,, ,, ,,	✠ᴄODPINE M⁻O ᴄÆNT Wt. 20·0.	Godwine.
23	,, ,, ,,	✠LEOFRIᴄ M⁻O ᴄÆNT Wt. 25·1.	Leofric.
24	,, ,, ,,	✠LEOFƧTAN M⁻O ᴄÆNT Wt. 21·0.	Leofstan.

No.	Obverse.	Reverse.	Moneyer.
25	✠ÆÐELRÆD REX ANGLOX	✠PVLFPI M·O CÆNT Wt. 21·2.	Wulfwi (= Wulfwig?).
	Type iv. *var. a.*		
26	✠ÆÐELRÆD REX ANGL⊙	✠·EADPOLD M⊙ CÆNT Wt. 25·8.	Eadwold.
27	✠ÆDELRED „ ANGL⊙	✠GODPINE M·⊙ CÆNT Wt. 22·3.	Godwine.
28	✠ÆÐELRÆD „ ANGLOX	✠GODPINE M·Ω·O CÆNT Wt. 26·0.	
29	„ „ „	✠LEOFRIC MΩO CÆNT Wt. 26·4.	Leofric.
30	„ R·EX „	✠LE⊙FZTAN M⊙ CÆNT Wt. 25·0.	Leofstan.
	[Pl. XV. 4.]		
	Type viii.		
31	✠ÆÐELRÆD REX ANC	✠GO:DMAN M⊙ CÆNT Wt. 18·2.	Godman.
32	„ „ ANGL	✠L·E⊙FZTAN M⊙ CÆNT Wt. 20·2.	Leofstan.

CISECEASTRE.
[Chichester.]

Type iv. *var. a.*

No.	Obverse.	Reverse.	Moneyer.
33	✠ÆÐELRÆD REX ANGLOX	✠EADN⊙Ð MΩO CIZE Wt. 27·0	Eadno8.
	[Pl. XV. 5.]		

COLENCEASTRE.
[Colchester.]

Type i.

No.	Obverse.	Reverse.	Moneyer.
34	✠ÆDELRÆD REX ANGL	✠ÆDPINE MΩN COLEN Wt. 19·3	Ædwine.

P 2

No.	Obverse.	Reverse.	Moneyer.
	Type iii. *var. a.*		
35	✠[ÆÐELRÆ]D REX ANCLOX	[✠TO]CA M⁻O COLE[N] (Broken.)	Toca (Toga).
36	,, ,, ,,	✠PVLFNOÐ M⁻O COLN Wt. 19·0.	Wulfnoð.
	Type iv. *var. a.*		
37	✠ÆÐELRÆD REX ANCLO⊙	✠LEⵔFPIC MΩ⊙ COLΥ Wt. 19·9.	Leofwig.
	DEORABY. [Derby.]		
	Type viii.		
38	✠·ÆÐELRÆD REX ANC	✠EREP·I·NE MO DE: Wt. 16·4.	Erewine.
	DOFERAN. [Dover.]		
	Type i. *var. a.*		
39	✠ÆÐELRED REX ANCL⊙R [Pl. XV. 6.]	✠CODMAN M⁻ON DOFR Wt. 20·4.	Godman.
	Type ii. *var. d.*		
40	✠ÆÐELRÆD REX ANCLOX	✠OΣFERÐ M⁻O DOFRA (Chipped.)	Osferð.
	Type iv. *var. a.*		
41	✠·ÆÐELRÆD REX ANCLO⊙	✠CODPINE Mⵔ⊙ DOFE Wt. 25·2.	Godwine.
42	,, ,, ANCLOX	✠CYNΣICE MΩO DOFER Wt. 25·2.	Cynsige.
	Type viii.		
43	✠·ÆÐELRÆD R·EX· ANCL	✠CYNΣICE MΩ⊙ DⵔFE Wt. 21·5.	Cynsigo.

No	Obverse	Reverse	Moneyer

EAXECEASTER
[Exeter]

Type i

44	✠ÆÐELRÆD· REX· A NGL	✠ ÆLFNOÐ ON EAXECƧER Wt 27 0	Ælfnoð
45	✠ÆÐELRÆD REX AN	✠IƧCOD ON EAXƧET Wt 17 5	I-god
46	„ „ ANC	✠Ƨ ÆILNE ON EAXCEƧTR Wt 20 0	Sæilne

Type ii var d

| 47 | ✠ÆÐELRÆD REX ANCLOX | ✠ÆL FNOÐ Mͦ EAXEC Wt 17 0 | Ælfnoð |
| 48 | ✠ÆÐELRÆD „ ANCCOX | ✠CODA Mͦ EAXEC Wt 17 2 | Goda |

Type iii var a

49	✠ÆÐELRÆD REX ANCLOX	✠ÆLFƧTAN Mͦ EAXE Wt 18 5	Ælfstan
50	„ „ „	„ Wt 20 7	
51	„ „ „	✠BYRHƧTAN Mͦ EAXE Wt 25 3	Byrhstan
52	„ „ „	✠CODA Mͦ EAXEC Wt 23 8	Goda
53	„ „ „	✠LVDA Mͦ EAXEC Wt 25 0	Luda
54	„ „	✠TVNA Mͦ EAXEC Wt 23 8	Tuna

Type iv var a

| 55 | ✠ÆÐELRÆD REX ANCLOX | ✠ÆLFNOÐ MΩO EAXE Wt 27 4 | Ælfnoð |
| 56 | „   „ A NCL | ✠C ARL A MtO EAXE Wt 22 2 | Carla |

No.	Obverse.	Reverse.	Moneyer.
57	✠ÆÐEL·RÆD REX ANGLO⊙	✠·DVNSTAN Mt⊙ EAXE Wt. 23·3.	Dunstan.
58	✠ÆÐELRÆD REX ANG	✠MANG⊙D Mt⊙ EAXE (Pierced.)	Mangod.
59	,, ,, ANGLO⊙	✠MANNA Mt⊙ EAXE Wt. 19·7.	Manna.
60	✠· ,, ,, ,,	✠ƿVLFΣIGE Mt⊙ EAXE Wt. 20·4.	Wulfsige.
61	✠ ,, ,, ,,	✠ƿYNΣIGE MΩ·⊙ EAXE Wt. 25·8.	Wynsige.
62	✠·ÆÐELRÆD REX A·NGL·	,, M·Ω·⊙ EAXE Wt. 21·2.	

Type viii.

No.	Obverse.	Reverse.	Moneyer.
63	✠·ÆÐELRÆD REX ANGL·	✠ÆLFN⊙Ð MΩ⊙ EAXE Wt. 22·5.	Ælfnoð.
64	✠EÐELRED REX ANGLO	✠ƿVLFΣ:IGE: MO E Wt. 19·5.	Wulfsige.
65	✠ÆÐELRÆD REX ANGL·	✠ƿVLFΣIGE MtO EAXE Wt. 18·5.	
66	✠· ,, ,, ,,	,, ,, ,, Wt. 19·5.	

EOFERƿIC.

[York.]

Type i.

No.	Obverse.	Reverse.	Moneyer.
67	✠EDELRED REX ANGLOR:	✠ABNÐORB: M˜O EOFR: Wt. 23·0.	Abnðorb.
68	,, ,, ANGLORVM	✠DAHFIN M˜O EOFRƿIC Wt. 24·5.	Danfin(x).
69	✠ÆDELRED RE✠ AE	✠FTΣT⊙LF И˜EFER Wt. 20·6.	Fastolf.
70	✠EÐELRED REX ANGLORV:	✠OΣGOT: MΩO EOFERPIC Wt. 25·0.	Osgot.
71	✠ÆÐELRÆD REX ANGLOR	✠VRI M·ONETĀ EFOR Wt. 20·0.	Uri.

No.	Obverse.	Reverse.	Moneyer.
72	✠ÆÐYRÆD REX ANCLO	✠ÐYRƧTAN MO EFER Wt. 21·6.	Þurstan.
	Type ii. *var. a.*		
73	✠EÐELRED REX ANCLO	✠EILAF M⁻O EOFER Wt. 20·4.	Eilaf.
74	✠ÆÐELRED REX ANCL	✠FÆLLAH M⁻⊙ EOFE Wt. 21·6.	Fællan.
75	✠ÆÐELRED REX ANCL	✠FAƧTVLF M⁻O EFOR Wt. 17·2.	Fastulf.
76	[✠]ÆÐELRED REX ANC··	✠[HV]NDOLF M⁻O EFO (Broken.)	Hundolf?
77	✠ÆÐELRÆD REX ANCLOX	✠⊙DA MONETA EFERPIC Wt. 22·5.	Oda.
78	✠ÆÐELRED REX ANCLOX	✠TVNПE П⁻O EFERPIC Wt. 23·2.	Tumme (= Tuma?).
	Type iii. *var. a.*		
79	✠ÆÐELRÆD REX ANCLOX	✠OBAN M⁻O EOFRPI Wt. 26·5.	Oban.
	Type iv. *var. a.*		
80	·✠·ÆÐEL·RÆD REX ÑNC	✠CYTEL MΩ⊙ E·⊙FR Wt. 22·2.	Cytel.
81	✠ÆÐELRÆD REX ANCL⊙	✠EÑDRIC MᛢO E⊙FR Wt. 22·0.	Eadric.
82	✠ÆÐELRED REX ÑNCL⊙	✠LEOFƧTAN Mᛢ⊙ EOFR Wt. 27·2.	Leofstan.
83	✠ÆÐELRÆD REX ÑNCLOX	✠⊙ÐCRIM MO E⊙FR Wt. 21·4.	Oðgrim.
84	✠EÐELRED REX ÑNCL	✠ƧVMERLDÑ Mᛢ⊙ E⊙FR *Var.* Cross pattée in one angle of cross, and pellet in another Wt. 21·4.	Sumerleda.
85	„ „ ÑNCL⊙	✠VLFCETL MO E⊙FR· *Var.* Annulet in field Wt. 25·2	Ulfcetel.

No.	Obverse.	Reverse.	Moneyer.
86	✠NIEVNCII ONT *Var.* Cross pattée behind bust.	✠ÐEODRED ON EO Wt. 17·0.	Ðeodred.
		Type viii.	
87	✠ÆÐELREÐ REX ANC	✠COLCRIM MO EO Wt. 21·8.	Colgrim.
88	✠ÆÐELRÆD ,, ANCLO	✠HILDVLF M : O EOF Wt. 21·4.	Hildulf.
89	,, ,, ANCL·	✠IRRA MO EOFR Wt. 21·8.	Irra.
90	✠\EÐELRED REX ANC	✠OBAN M⁻O E:·OFR Wt. 22·0.	Oban.
91	✠ÆÐELRÆD REX ANCLO	✠PVLFZICE MⲒO EOFR Wt. 19·2.	Wulfsige.
92	✠EDERED REX ANCLO	✠ÐO : RZT : AN MO EOF *Var.* Crescent in one angle of cross. Wt. 20·0.	Ðorstan.

GEOÐA.

[Jedburgh?]

Type viii.

93	✠ÆÐELRED REX ANCLO	✠PVLFMÆR MⲒ⊙ CE⊙ÐA Wt. 20·4.	Wulfmær

[Pl. XV. 7.]

GIFELCEASTER.

[Ilchester.]

Type iii. *var. a.*

94	✠EDELRÆD REX ANCLOⲬ	✠COD M⁻O CIFELC Wt. 22·3.	God.
95	✠ÆÐELRÆD ,, ,,	✠LEOFZICE M⁻O CIFEL Wt. 22·3.	Leofsige.
96	,, ,, ,,	✠PVLFELM M⁻O CIFEL Wt. 25·7.	Wulfelm.
97	,, ,, ,,	,, CIELC Wt. 18·7.	

No.	Obverse.	Reverse.	Moneyer.
	Type iv. *var. a.*		
98	✠ÆÐELRÆD REX ANCLO	✠COD MΩO CIFELC Wt. 27·3.	God.
		GIPESPIC. [Ipswich.]	
	Type ii. *var. a.*		
99	✠ÆÐELRED REX ANCLOX	✠PALTFERÐ M¯O CIP Wt. 25·0.	Waltferð.
100	,, ANCLOX	,, M¯O CYPES Wt. 22·3.	
	[Pl. XV. 8.]		
	Type iii. *var. a.*		
101	✠ÆÐELRÆD REX ANCLOX	✠LEOFSICE M¯O CIPES Wt. 25·0.	Leofsige.
102	,, ,, ,,	✠LYTLMAN M¯O CIPES Wt. 22·0.	Lytelman.
	Type viii.		
103	✠EÐEL··RÆD REX ANC	✠CODRIC NIOM CIPE Wt. 17·3.	Godric.
104	✠EÐELRED REX ANCL	✠L·EIOFSICE MO CIbZ Wt. 23·3.	Leofsige.
		GLEAPECEASTER. [Gloucester.]	
	Type iii. *var. a.*		
105	✠ÆÐELRÆD REX ANCLOX	✠CODPINE M¯O CLEA Wt. 25·3.	Godwine.
	Type iv. *var. a.*		
106	✠ÆÐELRÆD REX ANCLOX	✠CODPINE WΩO CLEA Wt. 22·0.	Godwine.
107	✠ÆÐELRÆD REX ANCLO	✠LEOFSICE MΩO CLEA Wt. 22·0.	Leofsige.

No	Obverse	Reverse	Moneyer
	Type viii		
108	✠ÆÐELRÆD REX ANCL	✠CODPINE MꞨO CLEA Wt 21·2	Godwine
	GRANTEBRYCGE. [Cambridge]		
	Type iii *var a*		
109	✠ÆÐELRÆD REX ANCLOX	✠EDRIC MꞨO CRANT Wt 23·4	Edric
	HAMTUNE [Southampton]		
	Type iii *var a*		
110	✠ÆÐELRED REX ANCLOX	✠BRVNINC MꞨO HAMTV Wt 24·6	Brunine
	Type iv *var a*		
111	·✠ ÆÐELRÆD REX ANCL	✠ÆÐELNOÐ MꞨO HAM Wt 22·8	Æðelnoð
	HEORTFORD [Hertford]		
	Type iii *var a*		
112	✠ÆÐELRÆD REX ANCLOX	✠BOCA MꞨO HEORT Wt 18·0	Boga
113	,, ,, ,,	✠BYRHTLAF MꞨO HEORT Wt 19·2	Byrhtlaf
114	,, ,, ,,	✠EDPI MꞨO HEORT Wt 19·2	Edwi

No.	Obverse.	Reverse.	Moneyer.

HEREFORD.
[Hereford.]

Type iv. *var. a.*

| 115 | ✠ÆÐELRÆD REX ANCLO | ✠BYRHƧTAN MꞙO HERE Wt. 21·8. | Byrhstan. |
| 116 | ·✠· „   ANCLOX | ✠DILION MΩO HERE Wt. 23·2. | Dilion. |

HUNTANDUNE.
[Huntingdon.]

Type ii. *var. a.*

| 117 | ✠ÆÐELRED REX ANCLOX | ✠PVLFCAR M⁻ON HVNTAN Wt. 21·4. | Wulfgar. |

Type iii. *var. a.*

| 118 | ✠ÆÐELRÆD REX ANCLOX | ✠ÆLFRIC M⁻O HVNT Wt. 21·2. | Ælfric. |

Type iv. *var. a.*

| 119 | ✠ÆÐELRÆD REX ANCLOX | ✠ÆLFRIC MΩO NVNT Wt. 22·5. | Ælfric. |
| 120 | ·✠· „   ANCL·O· | ✠OƧCVT MꞙO NVNT *Var.* Pellet in field. Wt. 25·0. | Osgut. |

Type viii.

| 121 | ✠EDELRÆD RE:X AHC | ✠EDELƧTAN MꞙO HV Wt. 22·0. | Ædelstan. |

LÆPES.
[Lewes.]

Type i.

| 122 | ✠EÐELRED REX ANCLO | ✠ÆLFPERD ON :LÆP:E: Wt. 26·7. | Ælfweard |

No.	Obverse.	Reverse.	Moneyer.
123	✠ÆÐELRÆD REX ANᴄLO	✠ÆLFᵽERD ⊙N :LÆᵽ:E: Wt. 21·6.	
124	✖　„　„ ⅄N	✖LEF⅄ ON LÆHᵽE·⅄ Wt. 19·5.	Lefa.
125	✠　„　„ ⅄Nᴄl	✠LEOFᵽINE ON LÆᵽE Wt. 18·7.	Leofwine.
126	✠EÐELRED REX ⅄NᴄL·	✠ONL⅄F MON LEᵽE (ᴁ base. Chipped.)	Onlaf.

Type ii. *var. a.*

| 127 | ✠ÆÐELRÆD REX ANᴄLOX | ✠E⅄Dᴄ⅄R Mˉ‌O · LÆᵽE (ᴁ base. Worn.) | Eadgar. |

Type ii. *var. d.*

| 128 | ✠ÆÐELRÆD REX ANᴄLOX | ✠HEREBREHT Mˉ‌O LÆᵽE Wt. 20·7. | Herebreht (Hereberht). |

Type iii. *var. a.*

129	✠ÆÐELRÆ[D] REX ANᴄLOX	✠LEOFNOÐ [M]ˉ‌O LÆᵽ (Broken.)	Leofnoð.
130	„　„　„	„　„ LÆᵽE Wt. 23·2.	
131	„　„　„	✠LEOFᵽINE Mˉ‌O LÆᵽE Wt. 24·5.	Leofwine.
132	„　„　„	„　„ Wt. 22·5.	
133	„　„　„	✠OƧPOLD Mˉ‌O LÆᵽ Wt. 26·4.	Oswold.

Type iv. *var. a.*

| 134 | ✠ÆÐELRÆD REX ANᴄLOX | ✠HEREBYRHT M⊙ LÆᵽ Wt. 24·0. | Herebyrht. |

LEIGECEASTER, Etc.
[Chester.]

Type i.

| 135 | ✠ÆÐEL·RED REX ANᴄ | ✠ÆLFNOÐ ON LEᴄ·ᴄ Wt. 20·0. | Ælfnoð. |

No.	Obverse.	Reverse.	Moneyer.
136	✠ÆÐELRED REX ANGL	✠LE·OFPINE· ON LEIG Wt. 20·7.	Leofwine.
137	„ „ AN	✠LIOFNOÐ: ON LEIGE Wt. 19·3.	Liofnoð (Leofnoð).
138	„ „ ANG	✠SPEGEN ON L·EIG Wt. 27·0.	Swegen.

Type iii. *var. a.*

| 139 | ✠ÆÐELRÆD REX ANGLOX | ✠EDRIC M⁻O LEGGEX Wt. 27·4. | Edric. |

Type iv. *var. a.*

140	✠ÆÐELRÆD REX ALO	✠ÆLEPINE MO LEIG Wt. 22·8.	Ælewine (=Ælfwine?).
141	✠·EÐELRÆD REX ANGLO	✠·ÆLEPINE M⊙ LEIG Wt. 26·5.	
142	✠EDELRED REX ANGLO	✠ELEPNE MO LEIG Wt. 22·8.	
143	✠EDELR·D R·EX AIGO	✠ELFXTAI M·ΩO LEGE Wt. 21·5.	Elfstan.
144	✠ÆÐELRÆD REX ANGL·	✠LEOFPINE M⊙ LEIG Wt. 27·1.	Leofwine.

Type viii.

| 145 | ✠·ÆÐELRÆD REX ANGL· | ✠ÆLFNOÐ MΩO LEIG Wt. 22·2. | Ælfnoð. |

LINCOLNE.
[Lincoln.]

Type i.

146	✠ÆÐELRED REX ANG	✠ÆÐELMÆR M⁻O LIIG *Var.* Pellet in field. Wt. 19·7.	Æðelmær.
147	✠ÆÐELRÆD REX ANGLOR	✠BRVNTAT M⁻O LINC Wt. 20·7.	Bruntat.
148	✠ÆÐELRED REX ANG	„ „ Wt. 19·0.	
149	✠ÆÐELRÆD REX ANGL	„ ⊙N LINC Wt. 25·5.	

No	Obverse	Reverse	Moneyer
150	✠ÆÐELRÆD REX ANGL	✠GODPINE · MΩO LINCOL· Wt 21 0	Godwine
151	✠ÆÐELRED REX ANGL [Pl XV 9]	✠GRIND M⁻O LINCL Wt 21 2	Grind
152	✠ÆÐELRED REX ANGL	✠OÐBERN MΩO LINC (Chipped)	Oðbern
153	✠ÆÐELRED RE✠ ANG	✠RODBERT M⁻O LIND Wt 22 4	Rodbert
154	✠ÆÐELRÆD REX ANGL	✠VLFCETEL MO LINC Wt 20 4	Ulfcetel
155	„ „ ANCLOR	✠PVLFRIC M⁻O LINCOI Wt 20 6	Wulfric
	Type ii var a		
156	✠ÆÐELRÆD REX ANCLOX	✠RODBART M⁻O LINDCO Wt 26 2	Rodbart (Rodbert)
157	✠ÆÐELRED REX ANCLO	✠VNBEGN M⁻O LINCOL Wt 20 2	Unbegn (Unbein)
	Type iii var a		
158	✠ÆÐELRÆD REX ANCLOX	✠STECENBIT M⁻O LIN Wt 22 2	Stegenbit
159	„ „ ANCOX	✠VNBEGN M⁻O LIN Wt 21 4	Unbegn (Unbein)
	Type iv var a		
160	✠ ÆÐL RED R E X Λ IO	✠Æ SCMAM NO L HC Wt 21 2	Æscman
161	✠ÆÐELRÆD REX ANCL	✠ÆÐELNOÐ M⊙ LINC Wt 20 3	Æðelnoð
162	„ „ ANCLOX	✠COLCRIM M Ω O LINC Wt 28 0	Colgrim
163	✠ÆÐELRED REX ANCLO	„ „ Wt 19 2	
164	✠ÆÐELRÆD REX ANCL	✠DRENC MΩO LINC Wt 25 2	Dreng

No.	Obverse.	Reverse.	Moneyer.
165	✠ÆÐELRÆD REX ANCLO	✠CRIM MΩ☉ LINCOL Wt. 26·4.	Grim.
166	✠ÆÐERED REX ANCLO	✠☉SCVT MΩ☉ LINC Wt. 19·5.	Osgut.
167	✠EÐELRED R[EX A]NCLO	✠[O]ÐCRIM MΩ☉ LIIIC (Broken.)	Oꝺgrim.
168	,, ,, ,,	✠VLFCETL MΩ☉ LINC Wt. 20·0.	Ulfcetel.
169	✠EÐELRÆD ,, ,,	✠VNBEIN MΩ☉ LINC Var. Pellet in field. Wt. 21·7.	Unbein.
170	✠ÆÐELRÆD REX ANCLOX	,, MΩ·O LINC Wt. 25·3.	

Type viii.

No.	Obverse.	Reverse.	Moneyer.
171	✠ÆÐELRÆD REX ANCL·	✠☉·S·CVT: MΩ☉ LINC Wt. 22·5.	Osgut.
172	✠ÆÐELRED REX A	✠☉ÐCRIM MΩ☉ LINC· Wt. 21·0.	Oꝺgrim.

LUNDENE.
[London.]

Type i.

No.	Obverse.	Reverse.	Moneyer.
173	✠ÆÐELRÆD REX ANCLOX	✠ÆLFNOÐ MΩ☉N LVNDE Wt. 21·7.	Ælfnoꝺ.
174	✠EÐELRED REX ANCLOX	✠CINMCO‾LVNCON Wt. 26·0.	Uncertain.
175	✠EÐELR·ED EX A·NC	✠EAÐSME MONE LVND Wt. 18·0.	Eadsme (= Eadsige?).
176	✠ÆÐEL[RED] REX ANCLO	✠EAÐPERD M[O LV]NO : (Broken.)	Eadwerd.
177	,, ,, ,,	✠EA·ÐPED MON LVND : Wt. 16·5.	
178	✠ÆÐELRÆD RÆX ,,	✠EAÐPINE MΩON LVND Wt 16·5	Eadwine.

No.	Obverse.	Reverse.	Moneyer.
179	✠ÆÐELRED REX ΛNᴄL	✠EΛDPOLD MON LVND Wt. 19·2.	Eadwold.
180	✠EÐELRED REX ΛNᴄLORV	✠EDELⱣINE NON LVNDEN : Wt. 19·6.	Edelwino (Æðelwine).
181	✠ÆÐELRÆD REX ΛNᴄLOⵒX	✠ᴄODERÆ MON LVNDEI Wt. 19·5.	Godcre.
182	✠ÆÐELRED REX ΛNᴄO	✠ᴄODMAN ⊙N LVN Wt. 26·2.	Godman.
183	,, ,, ΛNᴄL :	✠LEOFNOÐ M ⊥ O LVNDE Wt. 20·0.	Leofnoð.
184	,, ,, ΛNᴄLOⵒX	✠L·ÆOFƵTΛ M·Ω· ⊙N LVND Wt. 15·7.	Leofstan.
185	✠EÐELRÆD REX ΛNᴄLORV :	✠LEⵔFPINE M⊙ LVND : Wt. 19·8.	Leofwine.
186	✠ÆÐELRED RED REX ΛN	✠LI⊙FPOLD MΩ ⊙N LVND Wt. 20·0.	Liofwold.
187	✠ÆÐELRDE RÆX ΛNᴄ	✠ⱣVLFPINE M⊙N LVID Wt. 17·0.	Wulfwine.
188	✠ÆÐELRÆD REX ΛNᴄLO	✠Ᵽ·VLFPINE M:⊙N LVN Wt. 17·5.	Wulfwine.

Type ii. *var. a.*

No.	Obverse.	Reverse.	Moneyer.
189	✠EÐELRED REX ΛNᴄLOⵒX	✠ÆLFPINE ⊓⁻O LVND· Wt. 25·5.	Ælfwine.
190	✠ÆÐELRÆD ,, ,,	✠ÆÐERD M⁻O LVNDONI Wt. 22·6.	Æðered.
191	,, ,, ,,	✠ᴄYNƵIᴄE M⁻O LVNDONI Wt. 22·0.	Cynsige.
192	,, ,, ,,	✠EALHƵTΛN M⁻O LVND Wt. 22·2.	Ealhstan.
193	,, ,, ,,	✠EΛ·LNƵTΛN M⁻O LVND Wt. 24·5.	Ealhstan.

No	Obverse			Reverse	Moneyer
194	✠ÆÐELRÆD REX ANGLOX			✠GOD M⁻O LVN DONI Wt 220	Godl
195	„	„	„	✠LEOFZTAN M⁻O LVND Wt 237	Leof-tan
196	„	„	„	✠OZALF N⁻ON LVHHDI Wt 196	Osalf or Osulf
197	„	„	„	✠PVLFMÆR M⁻O LVNDON Wt 220	Wulfmær
198	„	„	„	✠PVLFRIC M⁻O LVNDONI Wt 227	Wulfric
199	„	„	„	✠PVLFZTAN M⁻O LVNDO Wt 207	Wulf-tan

Type n tar d

200	✠ÆÐELRÆD REX ANGLOX			✠ÆLFGAR M⁻O LVNDO Wt 213	Ælfgar
201	„	„	„	✠ÆÐERED „ „ Wt 230	Ælfred
202	„	„	„	✠X ÐEVLF[M⁻O]LVND (Broken)	Æthulf?
203	„	„	„	✠BYRHZIGE M⁻O LVND Wt 198	Byrh-ige
204	„	„	„	✠EALHZTAN M O LVN Wt 170	Ealhstan
205	„	„	,	✠EDPINE M⁻O LVND Wt 212	Edwine
206	✠ÆÐELRED „ .			„ „ Wt 193	
207	✠ÆÐELRÆD „ „			✠LEOFZTAN M⁻O LVND Wt 116	Leof-tan
208	„	„	„	✠OZCYTEL M⁻O LVND Wt 191	Oscytel
209	„	„	,	. Wt 196	

No.	Obverse.		Reverse.	Moneyer.
210	✠ÆÐELRÆD REX ANCLOX		✠OΣVLF MˉO LVNDO (Broken.)	Osulf.
211	,,	,, ,,	✠PVLFMÆR MˉO LVND. (Chipped.)	Wulfmœr.

Type iii. *var. a.*

212	✠ÆÐELRÆD REX ANCLOX		✠ÆLFNOÐ MˉO LVND Wt. 25·6.	Ælfnoð.
213	,,	,, ANCLO	✠ÆLFΣTAN MˉO LVN *Var.* Pellet in two angles of cross. Wt. 21·8.	Ælfstan.

[Pl. XV. 10.]

214	,,	,, ANCLOX	✠ÆÐELPERD MˉO LVN Wt. 22·6.	Æðelwerd.
215	,,	,, ,,	✠BYRHTLAF MˉO LVN Wt. 23·8.	Byrhtlaf (Brihtlaf).
216	,,	,, ,,	✠EADMVND MˉO LVN Wt. 22·0.	Eadmund.
217	,,	,, ,,	,, ,, LVD Wt. 21·2.	
218	,,	,, ,,	✠EADPOLD MˉO LVN Wt. 22·2.	Eadwold.
219	,,	,, ,,	✠EALHΣTAN MˉO LVN Wt. 23·6.	Ealhstan.
220	,,	,, ,,	✠EDPERD MˉO LVN Wt. 22·4.	Edwerd.
221	✠ÆÐELRED REX ANCL		✠EDPINE MˉO LVD Wt. 18·0.	Edwine.
222	✠ÆÐELRÆD REX ANCLOX		✠CODRIC MˉO LVND Wt. 25·2.	Godric.
223	,,	,, ,,	✠COLDPINE MˉO LVN Wt. 19·7.	Goldwine.
224	,,	,, ,,	✠LEOFΣTAN MˉO LVN (Pierced.)	Leofstan.
225	,,	,, ,,	✠LEOFPINE MˉO LVN Wt. 25·7.	Leofwine.
226	,,	,, ,,	✠LIFINC MˉO LVND Wt. 23·5.	Lifinc.

No.	Obverse.	Reverse.	Moneyer.
227	✠ÆÐELRÆD REX ANCLOX	✠PVLFPINE M⁻O LVN Wt. 20·8.	Wulfwine.
	Type iv. *var. a.*		
228	✠ÆÐELRÆD REX ANCL·	✠ÆLFR·ÝD M⦿ LVND Wt. 21·6.	Ælfryd.
229	·✠· ,, ,, ANCL	✠ÆLFPINE M⦿ LVND Wt. 21·2.	Ælfwine.
230	✠ ,, ,, ,,	✠ÆÐELPERD M·⦿ LVND Wt. 20·2.	Æðelwerd
231	,, ANCLOX	✠BRIHTLAF M⦿ LVND Wt. 25·0.	Brihtlaf (Byrhtlaf).
232	,, ,, ,,	✠BRVNZTAN M⦿ LVND Wt. 26·5.	Brunstan (= Byrnstan?).
233	·✠· ,, ,, ANCL·	✠EADPINE M⦿ LVND Wt. 19·7.	Eadwine.
234	✠ÆÐELRÆD REX AN	✠EADPOLD M⦿ LVN Wt. 20·6.	Eadwold.
235	✠ÆÐELRÆD REX ANCL	✠E·ADPOLD N·⦿ LVND Wt. 22·4.	
236	,, ANCLOX	✠EADPOLD M·Ω·O LVND Wt. 25·0.	
237	,, ,, ANCL⦿	✠EDZICE M·⦿ LVN (Broken.)	Edsige.
238	,, ,, ,,	✠C·⦿DEMAN M⦿ LVND Wt. 22·0.	Godeman.
239	,, ,, ,,	✠CODEMAN Wt. 23·0.	
240	,, ,, ,,	✠CODMAN M⦿ LVND Wt. 22·3.	
241	,, ,, ,,	,, Wt. 19·5.	
242	·✠· ,, ,, ,,	✠C·⦿DRIC M⦿ LVND Wt. 21·9.	Godric.
243	✠ ,, ,, ,,	✠C⦿DPINE M⦿ LVND Wt. 20·7.	Godwine.

No	Obverse	Reverse	Moneyer
214	✠ÆÐELRÆD REX ANCL	✠CODPINE MꞩO LVND Wt 20·5	
215	,, ,, ANCLO	✠HEAPVLF MꞩO ,, Wt 21·3	Heawulf
216	,, ,, ANCL	✠LEOFNOÐ ,, ,, Wt 20·6	Leofnoð
217	,, ,, A NCLO	✠LEOFRIC MΩO ,, Wt 23·5	Leofric
218	✠ ÆÐELRÆD REX ANCL	✠LEOFRIC MꞩO ,, Wt 19·5	
219	✠ÆÐELRÆD REX AN	,, ,, LVN (Broken) Wt 18·5	
250	✠ÆÐELRÆD REX ANCLO	✠LEOFRYD MꞩO LVND Wt 19·5	Leofryd (= Leofric ?)
251	,, ,, ,,	,, ,, Wt 19·8	
252	✠ ,, ,, ,,	✠LEOFSTAN MꞩO LVND Wt 20·0	Leofstan
253	✠ ,, ,, ,,	,, ,, Var Pellet in field Wt 22·8	
254	,, ,, ANCLO	✠LEOFPINE MꞩO LVND Wt 23·3	Leofwine
255	·✠ ,, ,, ANCL	✠LYFINC MꞩO LVND Wt 22·0	Lyfinc
256	✠ ,, ,, ,,	✠OSVL F MꞩO LVND Wt 21·2	Osulf
257	✠ ,, ,, ANCLO	✠SIBPINE ,, ,, Wt 25·6	Sibwine
258	✠ÆÐELRÆÐ RE✠ ANCO	✠SIBÐINE MꞩO LVND Wt 19·9	Sibðine (= Sibwine ?)
259	✠ÆÐELRÆD REX AN	✠SPETINC MꞩO LVND Wt 22·3	Swetine
260	·✠· ,, ,, ANCL	✠ ,, ,, LVND Wt 23·7	
261	✠ ,, ,, ANCLO	✠SPETINC MꞩO LVND Wt 23·7	

No.	Obverse.	Reverse.	Moneyer.
262	✠ÆÐELRÆD REX ANC	✠TOCA MΩO LVND Wt. 19·7.	Toga.
263	✠ÆÐELRÆD REX ANCL·	✠PVLFZTAN MC LVND Wt. 22·0.	Wulfstan.
264	,, ,, ANCLO·	✠PVLFPINE MΩO LVND Wt. 21·7.	Wulfwine.

Type viii.

No.	Obverse.	Reverse.	Moneyer.
265	✠ÆÐELRÆD REX ANCL	✠ÆÐELPERD MΩC LVND Wt. 23·7.	Æðelwerd.
266	,, ,, ,,	,, Wt. 19·6.	
267	,, ,, ANC·	,, MC ,, *Var.* Two annulets in field. Wt. 22·2.	
268	✠EÐELRED ,, ANCLO	✠BRVNZAN MC LVNDE Wt. 21·5.	Brunstan.
269	✠ÆÐELRÆD ,, ANCL·	✠EADPOLD M·Ω·O LVND Wt. 23·2.	Eadwold.
270	,, ,, ANCLO	✠C·ODA M·⊥O LVNDEN Wt. 22·1.	Goda.
271	,, ,, ANCL·	✠CODMAN MΩO LVND Wt. 22·0.	Godman.

[PL. XV. 11.]

No.	Obverse.	Reverse.	Moneyer.
272	·✠ÆÐEL·RÆD REX ANCLO	✠CODPINE MC LVND Wt. 21·6.	Godwine.
273	·✠·ÆÐELRÆD REX ANCL	✠LEOFPINE MC LVND Wt. 20·6.	Leofwine.
274	✠ÆÐEL·RRÆD REX AN	✠LVFINC MON L·VNDE Wt. 23·6.	Lufine (= Lifine).
275	✠ÆÐELRÆD REX ANCL·	✠OZVLF MC LVNDN Wt. 20·2.	Osulf.
276	·✠EÐELRED REX ANCL·	✠TOCA M⊥O LVNDENE Wt. 22·5.	Toga.

No.	Obverse.	Reverse.	Moneyer.
277	✠EÐELRED REX ANᴄLO	✠PVLFƧTAN Mᴵ☉ LVND Wt. 21·5.	Wulfstan.
278	·✠·ÆÐELRÆD ,, ,,	✠PVLFPINE Mᴵ☉: LVND Wt. 21·8.	Wulfwine.

LYDANFORD.
[Lydford.]

Type i.

279	✠ÆÐELRYD REX ·ANᴄ·	✠BRVNA ON LYD·A·FORD Wt. 23·0.	Bruna.
280	✠ÆÐELRÆD REX ANᴄ	✠ᴄ☉DA ☉N LYDAF☉R: Wt. 18·0.	Goda.

Type ii. *var. a.*

281	✠ÆÐELRED REX ANᴄLOⅩ	✠ÆÐERED M⁻O LYDAN· Wt. 26·2.	Æðered.
	[Pl. XV. 12.]		

Type iii. *var. a.*

282	✠ÆÐELRÆD REX ANᴄLOⅩ	✠ᴄODA M⁻ LⅩOA Wt. 18·5.	Goda.
283	,, ,, ,,	,, M⁻O LYDA Wt. 18·6.	

Type iv. *var. a.*

284	✠·ÆÐELRÆD REX ANᴄL	✠BRVNA Mᴵ☉ LYDA Wt. 20·0.	Bruna.

MÆLDUNE.
[Maldon.]

Type iii. *var. a.*

285	✠EDELRÆD REX ANᴄLOⅩ	✠ÆLFPINE M⁻O MÆLD Wt. 22·0.	Ælfwine.
286	✠·ÆÐELRÆD.. ,,	,, ,, MÆLDV Wt. 20·9.	

No.	Obverse.	Reverse.	Moneyer.
287	✠ÆÐELRÆD REX ANCLOX	✠EALDRED M⁻O MALD Wt. 23·0.	Ealdred.
		NORÐPIC. [Norwich.]	
	Type i.		
288	✠EDELRED REX ·A·NCL·OI [Pl. XV. 13.]	✠HPATEMN M⁻O NORÐP: Wt. 19·8.	Hwateman or Hwatman.
	Type ii. *var. a.*		
289	✠ÆÐELRED REX ANCLOX [Pl. XVI. 1.]	✠FOLCEARD M⁻O NORÐ Wt. 25·0.	Folceard.
290	,, ,, ANCLOX	✠MANNIC M⁻O NORÐPIC (Chipped.).	Manning.
	Type ii. *var. d.*		
291	✠ (*Inscription double struck.*)	✠MANINC M⁻O NORPI Wt. 21·0.	Maning.
292	✠ÆÐELRÆD REX ANCLOX	✠ƩPYRTINC M⁻O NORÐ Wt. 21·1.	Swyrtinc (or Swertine).
	Type iii. *var. a.*		
293	✠ÆÐELRÆD REX ANCLOX	✠ƩPERTINC M⁻O NORÐ Wt. 25·0.	Swertine.
	Type iv. *var. a.*		
294	✠ÆÐELRÆD REX ANCL	✠ÆLFRIC MΩ·☉ NORÐ Wt. 21·8.	Ælfric.
	Type viii.		
295	✠ÆÐELRÆD REX ANCL·	✠HPATM(MO NORÐ Wt. 22·7.	Hwateman.

No	Obverse	Reverse	Moneyer

OXNAFORD
[Oxford]

Type iii var a

No	Obverse	Reverse	Moneyer
296	✠ÆÐELRÆD REX ANLLOX	✠ÆÐELMÆR M⁻O OXNA Wt 26 0	Æðelmær
297	,, ,, ,,	✠ÆÐELPINE ,, ,, Wt 25 7	Æðelwine
298	,, ,, ,,	✠LODINL ,, ,, Wt 25 9	Godine

[Pl XVI 2]

ROFELEASTER
[Rochester]

Type ii var a

No	Obverse	Reverse	Moneyer
299	✠ÆÐELRED REX ANLLOX	✠ΣIDEPINE M⁻O ROF Wt 215	Sidewine

[Pl XVI 3]

| 300 | ✠ÆÐELRÆD REX ANLLOX | ,, M⁻O ROFE Wt 21 0 | |

Type ii var d

| 301 | ✠ÆÐELRÆD REX ANLLOI | ✠LEOFRIL M⁻O ROF Wt 14 6 | Leofric |

Type iii var a

| 302 | ✠ÆÐELRÆD REX ANLLOX | ✠EDΣILE N⁻O ROFE Wt 26 1 | Edsige |
| 303 | ,, ,, ,, | ✠ΣIDPINE M⁻O ROFEL Wt 25 6 | Sidewine |

Type iv var a

| 304 | ✠ÆÐELRÆD REX ANLO | ✠EADPERD MΩO ROFE Wt 23 8 | Eadwerd |
| 305 | ,, ,, ANLO | ✠EDΣILE MΩO ROF Wt 23 8 | Edsige. |

No.	Obverse.	Reverse.	Moneyer.
306	✠ÆÐELRÆD REX ANƉLOX	✠EDPINE MΩO ROFE Wt. 22·8.	Edwine.
307	,, ,, ANƉLO⊙	✠ƉOLDPINE M⊙ ROFE Wt. 22·4.	Goldwine.

RUMENEA.
[Romney.]

Type i.

| 308 | ✠ÆÐELRED REX ANƉL· | ✠PYLFNOÐ: ON RVME· Wt. 11·3. | Wulfnoð. |

SANDPIC.
[Sandwich.]

Type viii.

| 309 | ✠ÆÐELRÆD REX ANƉLO | ✠SPARTƉAR M⊙ SAN· Wt. 20·0. | Swartgar. |

SCEFTESBYRIG.
[Shaftesbury.]

Type ii. *var. d.*

| 310 | ✠ÆÐELRÆD REX ANƉLOX [Pl. XVI. 4.] | ✠ÆÐESTAN M·O ƉEFTEN (Pierced.) | ÆðEstan. |

Type iv. *var. a.*

| 311 | ✠ÆÐELRÆD REX NƉLOX | ✠ƉODA MΩO SƉEFT Wt. 25·8. | Goda. |

SCROBESBYRIG.
[Shrewsbury.]

Type ii. *var. a.*

| 312 | ✠ÆÐELRED REX ANƉLOX [Pl. XVI. 5.] | ✠LEOFÆLM O SƉOB Wt. 21·5. | Leofælm (Leofhelm?). |

No	Obverse	Reverse	Moneyer
	SIÐESTEBYRIG. [Sidbury ?]		
	Type 1		
313	✠ÆÐELRÆD REX ᚪ NᚳL OR	✠ᚳIⴲLNⴲÐ ⴲN ᛋIÐEᛋTEB Wt 21 3	Ciolnoð
	STANFORD [Stamford]		
	Type 1		
314	✠ÆÐELRÆD REX ᚪNᚳLO	✠ÆÐELPINE MO ᛋTᚪN Wt 23 0	Æðelwine
315	✠ÆÐELRED REX ᚪNᚳLO	✠ÆÐELPINE ON STᚪNF Wt 21 2	Æðelwine
316	„ „ ᚪN	✠EᛋPIᚳ Mᵔⴲ ᛋTᚪNE Wt 17 0	Eswig
317	✠ÆÐELRÆD „ ᚪNᚳ	✠ᚳODÆᚳ Mᵔⴲ ᛋTᚪN Wt 18 0	Godæg
318	„ „ ᚪNᚳL	✠ᚳⴲDELᚳⴲE ⴲN ᛋTᚪ NF Wt 25 2	Godcleof ?
319	✠ÆÐELRED REX ᚪNᚳ	✠ᚳODELEⴲE Mᵔⴲ ᛋTᚪ Wt 16 4	
320	„ „ ᚪNF	✠OEE Nᵔⴲ ᛋTᚪNFⴲ Wt 19 2	Ofe ?
	Type 11 var a		
321	✠ÆÐELRED REX ᚪNᚳLO [Pl XVI 6]	✠PVLᛋTᚪN Mᵔⴲ ᛋTᚪN Wt 26 4	Wulstan (Wulfstan)
322	✠ÆÐELRED REX ᚪNᚳL	Wt 26 2	

No.	Obverse.	Reverse.	Moneyer.
	Type iv. *var. a.*		
323	✠ÆÐELRED REX ANLLO	✠ΛΣCPIL M·O ΣTΛ Wt. 19 2.	Asewig.
324	,, ,, ,,	✠ELEBRIH[T M]tO· ΣTΛN (Broken.)	Elebriht (= Elfbriht ?).
325	✠ÆÐELRÆD REX ANLLO⊙	✠LODELOF M⊙ ΣTAN Wt. 17·8.	Godeleof.
	STANVIC? [Stanwick.]		
	Type ii. *var. a.*		
326	✠ÆÐELRED REX ANLLO'	✠ΛLFPΛLD M¯O ΣTANV Wt. 25·9.	Alfwald.
	SUÐBYRIG. [Sudbury.]		
	Type iii. *var. a.*		
327	✠ÆÐELRÆD REX [ANLL]OX	✠ÆLFNOÐ M¯O Σ[VÐB]Y (Broken.)	Ælfnoð.
328	,, ,, ,,	✠[Æ]LFRIC M¯O ΣVÐBY (Pierced.)	Ælfric.
329	✠ÆÐELRÆD ,, ,,	✠BYRHTLAF M¯O ΣVÐB· Wt. 21·7.	Byrhtlaf (Brihtlaf).
330	✠ÆÐELRÆD R[EX].,	✠L[OD]PINE M¯O ΣVÐBY (Broken.)	Godwine.
	SVÐGEPEORC. [Southwark.]		
	Type iii. *var. a.*		
331	✠ÆÐELRÆD REX ANLLOX	✠ÆLFRIC M¯O ΣVÐLE *Var.* Five pellets in angles of cross. Wt. 23·1	Ælfric.
	[Pl. XVI. 7.]		

No.	Obverse.	Reverse.	Moneyer.

TOTANÆS.
[Totness.]

Type i.

| 332 | ✠ · ÆÐEL· RÆD REX · ANᴄLO [Pl. XVI. 8.] | ✠ᴄODA ON TOTA NÆSSE Wt. 25·6. | Goda. |

Type ii. *var. a.*

| 333 | ✠ÆÐELRÆD REX ANᴄLOX | ✠MANNA M⁻O TOTAN· Wt. 22·2. | Manna. |

Type iii. *var. a.*

| 334 | ✠ÆÐELRÆD REX ANᴄLOX | ✠ÆLFƧTAN M⁻O TOTA Wt. 20·2. | Ælfstan. |

TVRᴄESIGE.
[Torksey.]

Type ii. *var. a.*

| 335 | ✠ÆÐELRÆD REX ANᴄLO [Pl. XVI. 9.] | ✠ÐVRᴄETEL M⁻O TVRᴄ Wt. 26·1. | Þurcetel. |

PEᴄEDPORT.
[Watchet.]

Type ii. *var. d.*

| 336 | ✠ÆÐEᖴRED REX ANᴄLOX [Pl. XVI. 10.] | ✠ƧIᴄERIᴄ M⁻⊙ PEᴄED Wt. 18·4. | Sigeric. |

Type iii. *var. a.*

| 337 | ✠ÆÐELRÆD REX ANᴄLOX | ✠ƧIᴄERIᴄ M⁻⊙ PEᴄED Wt. 25·0. | Sigeric. |

Type iv. *var. a.*

| 338 | ✠ÆÐELRÆD REX ANᴄLOX | ✠HVNEPINE Mt⊙ PEᴄED Wt. 24·7. | Hunewine. |

No	Obverse	Reverse	Moneyer

PELIGAFORD, PELINGAFORD, Etc
[Wallingford]

Type iv var a

| 309 | ✠ÆÐELRÆD REX ANGLOX | ✠PVLFPINE MꞍO PELIG Wt 20·6 | Wulfwine |

Type viii

| 310 | ✠ ÆÐELRÆD REX ANGL | ✠ ÆLFPERD MꞍO ꝥ ELIG Wt 16·6 | Ælfword |

[Pl XVI 11]

| 311 | „ „ „ | „ „ Wt 23·3 | |

PERHAM
[Wareham]

Type ii var a

| 312 | ✠ÆÐELRÆD REX ANGLOX | ✠PVLFRIC MꞍO PERHM Wt 24·0 | Wulfric |

Type iv var a

| 313 | ✠ÆÐELRÆD REX ANGLOX | ✠ÆLFSIGE MꞍO PER Wt 24·6 | Ælfsige |

| 314 | ✠ÆÐELRÆD „ „ | ✠ÆÐELRIC MꞍO PER Wt 24·6 | Æðelric |

PILTUNE
[Wilton]

Type iii var a

| 315 | ✠ÆÐELRÆD REX ANGLOX | ✠SÆPINE M O PILTV Wt 24·7 | Sæwine |

No.	Obverse.	Reverse.	Moneyer.
	Type iv. *var. a.*		
316	✠ÆÐELRÆD REX ANGLO	✠GOLDVS MΩ⊙ PILT Wt. 26·6.	Goldus.
317	✠· ,, ,, ANGLOX	✠SÆPINE MΩ⊙ PILT Wt. 26·2.	Sæwine.

PINCEASTRE or PINTONIA.
[Winchester.]

No.	Obverse.	Reverse.	Moneyer.
	Type i.		
348	✠ÆÐELRÆD REX ANGL·	✠ÆLFSIGE ON PINCES: Wt. 22·5.	Ælfsige.
349	✠ÆÐELRÆD REX ANG:	✠ÆLFSIGE ⊙N PINCST Wt. 21·4.	
350	✠ÆDELRÆD ·RE·✠ ANGL	✠CVNNA ON PINCSTR Wt. 18·4.	Cunna.
351	✠ÆÐELRÆD REX ANG	✠EADPINE ON PINCST Wt. 19·6.	Eadwine.
352	,, ,, ANGL	✠G⊙DMAN ⊙N: PINCS: Wt. 22·5.	Godman.
353	,, ,, ANGL⊙	✠ODA· ⊙N PINTCESRE Wt. 21·6.	Oda.
354	,, ,, ,,	✠ORDBRIHT ON PINCSR Wt. 20·7.	Ordbriht.
355	,, RE✠ ANGLOVM	✠SPILEMAN ⊙N PINTCSR Wt. 26·3.	Swileman.
	Type ii. *var. a.*		
356	✠ÆÐELRÆD REX ANGLOX	✠BE⊙RHN⊙Ð M˜⊙ PINTO Wt. 23·9.	Beorhnoð.
357	,, ,, ,,	✠EADSIGE M˜O RINTO (Clipped.)	Eadsige.
358	,, ,, ,,	✠FRYÐEMVND M˜O PIN· Wt. 25·0.	Fryðemund.
359	✠ÆÐELRED ,, ,,	✠INGELRI M˜O PINT· Wt. 25·5.	Ingelri(c).

No.	Obverse.	Reverse.	Moneyer.
360	✠ÆÐELRÆD REX ANGLOX	✠PVLFƩTAN MO PIN· Wt. 22·5.	Wulfstan.

Type ii. var. d.

No.	Obverse.	Reverse.	Moneyer.
361	✠ÆÐELRÆD RE·X ANGLOX	✠ÆLFƩIGE MO PINTO Wt. 23·8.	Ælfsige.
362	,, REX ,,	✠BEORHNOÐ MO PINT Wt. 22·4.	Beorhnoð.
363	,, ,, ,,	,, PINTO Wt. 24·5.	
364	,, ,, ,,	✠LEOFPOLD MO PINT Wt. 19·4.	Leofwold.

Type iii.

No.	Obverse.	Reverse.	Moneyer.
365	✠ÆÐELRÆD REX ANGLOX	✠GODPINE MO PINT Wt. 25·6.	Godwine.
366	,, ,, ,,	✠PVNƩTAN MO PIN Wt. 25·8. [Pl. XVI. 12.]	Wunstan (Wynstan).

Type iii. var. a.

No.	Obverse.	Reverse.	Moneyer.
367	✠ÆÐELRÆD REX ANGLOX	✠ÆLFƩIGE MO PINT Wt. 25·2.	Ælfsige.
368	,, ,, ,,	✠ÆÐEƩTAN MO PINT Wt. 25·4.	Æðestan.
369	,, ,, ,,	✠BERHTNAÐ MO PIN Wt. 25·7.	Berhtnað (Beorhtnoð).
370	,, ,, ,,	✠LEOFPOLD MO RINT Wt. 23·8.	Leofwold
371	,, ,, ,,	✠PYNƩTAN MO PIN Wt. 25·0.	Wynstan.

Type iv. var. a.

No.	Obverse.	Reverse.	Moneyer.
372	✠·ÆÐELRÆD REX ANGLO	✠·ÆÐELGAR MꙨ PINT Wt. 26·8.	Æðelgar.
373	,, ,, ANGLOX	✠BYRHƩIGE MꞐO PIN Wt. 27·0.	Byrhsige.
374	✳EDELRED RE✠ AIGIINꙨ	✠BYRHTIꙨÐ MꙨ RINI Wt. 24·2.	Byrhtnoð (= Beorhtnoð)

No.	Obverse.	Reverse.	Moneyer.
375	✠ÆÐELRÆD REX ANCLOX	✠BYRHTNOÐ M·ΩO PIN Wt. 26·6.	
376	,, ,, ,,	✠BYRHTPOLD MℓO PINT Wt. 26·6.	Byrhtwold.
377	,, ,, ANCL	✠·CODEMANMO PINT Wt. 27·0.	Godeman.
378	✠ ,, ,, ANCLX	✠CODPINE MℓO PINT Wt. 26·5.	Godwine.

Type viii.

379	✠ÆÐELRED REX ANCL	✠BRVNƩTAN MℓO PINT Wt. 20·3.	Brunstan.
380	✠ÆÐELRÆD ,, ,,	✠CYNNA MΩO PINT· Wt. 21·6.	Cynna (Cunna).
381	·✠· ,, ,, ANCL·	✠OƩCVT: MΩO PINC Wt. 22·3.	Osgut.
382	✠ ,, ,, ANCL	✠PVLFNOÐ MΩO PINT Wt. 21·3.	Wulfnoð.

PORICEASTER or PIHRACEASTER.
[Worcester.]

Type iv. *var. a.*

| 383 | ✠·ÆÐELRÆD REX ANCLOX | ✠ALFPOLD MℓO PORI Wt. 26·3. | Alfwold. |

ÐEODFORD.
[Thetford.]

Type i.

| 384 | ✠ÆÐELRED REX AIIC | ✠ÆLFPOLD IℓO ÐEO: Wt. 20·0. | Ælfwold. |
| 385 | ✠ÆÐELRÆD REX ANCLO | ✠ZVMERLID ON ÐEO: (Chipped.) | Sumerlid. |

Type i. *var. c.*

| 386 | ✠EÐELRÆD REX ANCLO [Pl. XVI. 13.] | ✠PELCIZT MON ÐEOD Wt. 22·2. | Welgist. |

No.	Obverse.	Reverse.	Moneyer.
	Type ii. var. a.		
387	✠ÆÐELRED REX ANCLOX	✠ÆADCAR M⁻O ÐE⊙TFOR Wt. 22·2.	Æadgar.
388	,, ,, ,,	✠ΣPYRLINC M⁻O ÐEODFO Wt. 25·2.	Swyrling (= Swerting?).
	Type ii. var. f.		
389	✠ÆÐELRÆD REX ANCLOX [Pl. XVI. 14.]	✠ΣPYRLINC M⁻O ÐEO Wt. 21·9.	Swyrling.
	Type iii. var. a.		
390	✠ÆÐELRÆD REX ANCLOX	✠BYRHTRIC M⁻O ÐEOD Wt. 26·0.	Byrhtric.
	Type iv. var. a.		
391	✠ÆÐELRÆD REX ANCLO	✠CRIM MΩ⊙ ÐEOD (Broken.)	Grim.
392	,, ,, ,,	✠ · ⊙ΣVLF MΩ⊙ ÐE⊙D (Pierced.)	Osulf.
	Type viii.		
393	✠ÆÐELRÆD REX ANC	✠AÐELP⊙LD M(⊙ ÐE⊙ Wt. 21·6.	Aðelwold.

UNCERTAIN MONEYERS AND MINTS.

INSCRIPTIONS BLUNDERED.

No.	Obverse.	Reverse.	Moneyer.
	Type i.		
394	✠EDCLRChI✠AHC	✠LFMAИ И⁻O LAL Wt. 19·5.	
	Type iii. var. a.		
395	✠ÆDEL· REX ƎVCOX	✠PIE ИO EVPΣECR·O Wt. 28·0.	

No.	Obverse.	Reverse.	Moneyer.
	Type iv. *var. a.*		
396	✠ÆÐELRÐ REX ANGN	✠NIⓄMNREN ⓄN M: Wt. 20·5.	
397	✠ÆÐELRDE REX AIGO	✠OΣGAEIA· DINMV Wt. 36·2.	

DOUBTFUL AND BLUNDERED COINS.

PROBABLY OF ÆTHELRÆD II.

No.	Obverse.	Reverse.	Moneyer.
	Type i.		
398	✠OAÐLÐNOÐ AOIIDMVIM	✠IIIÐNFⓄÐE ON DINRIN Wt. 32·6.	Uncertain.
399	✠EÐELRED REX ANGL·	(*Much blundered.*) Wt. 14·5.	
	Type iii. *var. a.*		
400	✠·.·ANEGMDX ENEROX	✠OAIRG M⁻O LÐAND Wt. 21·0.	
401	✠IAERMXDENGEOX	✠⁻NORDVNT NO FI Wt. 19·6.	
	Type iv. *var. a.*		
402	✠EÐEÐⓄNⓄEÐⓄPOPI	✠ ΑOLEOG✠Α II Wt. 30·0.	
403	✠IE : VE ·Ь· EL ·MVNL✠°O	✠EOONODIFR : Wt. 28·0.	
404	,, ,, ,,	,, ,, Wt. 38·8.	
405	ODPIᛉDO✠NOILIF (Retrograde.)	✠DIIONP✠PFOÐI Wt. 25·3.	
406	ODID✠PONDO✠IDO (Retrograde.)	✠IIDIL·OIIP L·OND* Wt. 18·7.	
407	✠OEDLOPꟻEDO✠✠	✠OIEREODI LN : Wt. 22·6.	
408	NLÐ : Ⓞ✠ · · · · · DON	✠PJIEÐIN IIIⓄNIP Wt. 22·4.	

* London.

CNUT *

SUCC A D 1016, DIED A D 1035

Moneyers

Ada or *Adea* (Cambr, Hunt)

Æad - *see* Ead -

Ælfman (Bedf)

Ehee [= Ælfric ?] (Exet, Norw)

Ægelbriht (Chich, Ipsw)

Ægelferð (Norw)

Ægelm (Chich)

Ægelmær (Bath, Bridpn, Linc)

Ægelric (Chest, Glouc, Oxf, Shaft, Southw, Winchest)

Ægelsige (Hast)

Ægelward or Ægelward (Lond)

Ægelwig or *Egelwig* (Ilch, Lewe, Winchest)

Ægelwine or Egelwine (Bath, Brist, Crickl, Lewe, Lond, Southw, Wore, York)

Ægfrye [= Ælfred ?] (Lond)

Ægesman or Æsman [= Æseman ?] (Stamf)

Æilbriht [= Ægelbriht] (Ipsw)

Ældfelm, Æltelm, &c (Brewt, Cadb, Cambr, Shrews, Winchest)

Ælfege (Roch)

Ælfeh or Ælfen (Lond, Roch, Stamf, Winchest)

Ælfere (York)

Ælferð (Norw)

Ælfgæt or Ælfget (Lond)

Ælfgar (Barda, Lond, Southw, Warw)

Ælfheah or Ælfheh (Shrews)

Ælfnoð (Chest, Hunt, Linc, Salisb)

Ælfred or Ælfryd (Cant, Hast, Lond, Salisb, Wilt)

Ælfric, Ælric, &c (Æxmunt, Bath, Brist, Cant, Chest, Chich, Exet, Linc, Lond, Norw, Shaft, Southw, Winchest)

Ælfric Moglu (Norw)

Ælfrye [= Ælfree ?] (Lond)

Ælfsige, Ælfsig *Ælfsw*, &c ("Ce85", Chest, Glouc, Hast, Ilch, Lewe, Lond, Southamp, Southw, Taunt, Wallingf, Winchest)

Ælfstan, *Ælstan, Alstan,* &c (Dover, Lond, Norw, Lewe, Wilt, Winchest, York)

Ælfweard, Ælfward, Ælfword, Ælward, &c (Aylesb, Chest, Hast, Jedb, Lewes, Lond, Romn, Southamp, Southw)

Ælfwi or *Ælfwi* [= Ælfwig, or Ælfwine ?] (Aylesb, Cambr, Cant, Heref, Lewe, Lond, Stamf, Thetf)

Ælfwi and Sigmel (Lond)

Ælfwig (Cambr, Cant, Heref, Ilch, Lond, Wallingf)

Ælfwine, Alwine, &c (Bath, Brest, Brist, Buck, Cant, Chest, Colch, Crickl, Exet, Heref, Ilch, Lond, Lydf, Maldn, Oxf, Salisb, Shaft, Southamp, Southw, Thetf, Totn, Wallingf, Wilt, Winchest, Wore, York)

Ælfwine Mus (Ilch)

Ælnoald, *see* Alfwold

Alphewine [= Ægelwine ?] (Crickl)

Almar [= Ælfmar] (Ilch, Wilt)

Æsemon (Stamf)

Æswine (Wallingf)

Æstan or Estan (Bath, Winchest)

Æstan Iuc (Winchest)

Æðelbreht or Æðelbriht (Ipsw)

Æðelm (Chich)

Æðelmer (Ilch, Linc)

Æðelman (Winchest)

Æðelnoð (Linc)

Æðelred (Winchest)

Æðelric or Æðeric (Bath, Chest, Oxf, Shaft, Winchest)

Æðelstan (Winchest)

Æðelweord (Hunt)

Æðelwr Æðelwi [= Æðelwig or Æðelwine] (Ilch, Lewe, Mald)

Æðelwine, Eðelwine, &c (Aylesb, Crickl, Ilch, Linc, Lewe, Lond, Mald, Southw, Winchest, York)

Æðelwold (Norw)

Æðere, *see* Æðelric

---

* No coins are known of Edmund "Ironside," son of Ethelred II who reigned, as rival king to Cnut, from April to November 1016. In November he obtained by treaty one half of the kingdom (Wessex, Essex, and East Anglia), and died the same month.

Æðestan [= Æðelstan] (Bath, Winchest)
Æðelstan [= Æðelstan?] (Stamf)
Alestan Hereʃ [Ælleg] (Chester)
Altwold, Altwold, or Ælwold (Bath, Oxf , Roch , Thetf , Winchest , Worc)
Alt — see also Æll—
Armested, Ærmgtel, Earmgtel, &c (Nott , Worc , York)
Arnold (York)
Asculʃ [Asculʃ = Asforð?] (York)
Asforð (Line , Lond , York)
Asgod, Asgout, Asguut, &c [= Osgod?] (York)
Aslac [= Oslac] (Line)
Æsric ʃ Nora)
Ata [d Adu] (Bardn)
Blacaman, see Blacaman
Bollu (Line)
Boda, Bolli, &c (Glouc , Shaft)
Beorn (York)
Blacaman, Blacaman, &c (Guild, Nott)
Blaman (Nott)
Boga [= Bonga] (Dover)
Bolli, see Boda
Bosing (Lond)
Brantine or Brantine (Line , Southa)
Brand (Stamf , York)
Brihtnoð, see Brihtnoð
Brenstan or Brihtstan [= Brunstan?] (Malm)
Brictcod (York)
Brixstan (Malm)
Bird (Hist)
Brihelm [= Brihtlelm] (Southa)
Brihstan or Brahstan [et Brenstan] (Malm)
Brihtred or Brihtred (Lond)
Brihtmer (Dover , Lond , Southa)
Brihtnoð, Byihtnoð, &c (Cluch , Hast , Lond , Malm , Thetf , Winchest , York)
Brihtred (Cant , Lond)
Brihtwi (Line)
Brihtwen (Oxf)
Brihtwi [= Brihtwine?] (Cant)
Brihtwin (Guild , Lond Oxf)
Brihtwold (Lond , Winchest)
Brunstan, see Brunstan
Bruuni [= Brunuin?] (Ipsf)
Brunin or Brunuin (Colch Lond)
Brun (Lond)
Brunston, see Brun-stan
Brunga Brynega, &c Lond , Shrews)
Bruning, Bruning Brunnu, &c (Bath , Lond Malm , Nott , York)
Brunuin, see Brunin
Brunstan Brunstan, &c (Lond Sand , Stamf Thetf Winchest)

Brndut [= Brunstan?] (Line)
Brunum (Stamf)
Brquut (Lond)
Brquuue, see Brunine
Burrum Bullouf)
Burkwold or Burrwold (Winchest)
Byrhstan or Byrnstan (Taunt)
Byrnst [= Byrnsige ?] (Bardn)
Cafel (Ilch)
Carla or Carla (Ixt , Jolb)
Catel, see Cetel
Cabbourne (Lew s)
Cadu (Lond)
Carel (Lond)
Carla, see Carla
Cas (Winchest)
Cauclin (Stamf)
Cima (Winchest)
Ceolnoð, Ceolnoð, Celnoð, &c (Chest , Derby, Malð , York)
Cetel or Cytel (York)
Cnuwig (Line)
Cinsige (Dover, Southamp)
Ceustan (Dover)
Cuht, see Cynuht
Cnothln (Richb)
Cnut (Line)
Cuvtel [= Cytel] (" Cnet ' = Cant ?)
Codric, see Godric
Coleman or Coleman (Lond , Oxf , Wallingf)
Colbern (Chest)
Coleman, see Coleman
Colgrim, Colcrim, &c (Line , York)
Collini [= Colling ?] (Lewes)
Coila
Creserine
Criman, Crinna, or Crunan (Line, Lond , Shrews , York)
Croc or Croal (Chest)
Croil [= Croal] (Chest)
Crucan or Grucan (York)
Crurn or Grurn (York)
Cuuloef, see Gunloef
Cauloin, see Cauclin
Cynuht or Cuht (Cambr)
Cynut (Winchest)
Cytel, see Cetel
Duunn[e] (York)
Dunin (Lond)
Deorsige or Dursige (Hert , York)
Derewne (Thetf)
Duddu (Ixt)
Dunn (Line)
Drops or Drows (Winchcombe)
Dunuuor [= Brungar] (Shrews)
Dunstan (Lond)
Dunuuy (Lond)
Eadgar or Edgar (Lond)
Eadmund or Edmund (Lond , Norw)
Ealnoð Ealnoð, &c, (Hast , Hunt , Lond Roch)

Eadred, Edred, &c (Lond)
Eadric (Aylesb, Lond)
Eadsi [= Eadsige?] (Dover, Lond)
Eadsige, Edsige, &c (Dover, Exet, Lond)
Eadulf [= Ladwulf?] (Lond)
Eaduuard, Eadwerd, Edward, &c (Lond, Southw, Stamf, Wallingf, Winchest)
Eaduuy or Edwig (Lond, Oxf, Thetf)
Eadwine, Edwine, &c (Cambr, Cant, Colch, Dover, Exet, Lewes, Lond, Oxf, Southamp, Southw, Stamf, Taunt, Thetf, Wallingf, Winchest)
Eadwold, Edwold, &c (Cant, Lond)
Eaein (Lond)
Eablabeard or Eablebord (Exet)
Ealdred (Lewes, Lond, Thetf)
Ealgar (Lond)
Eardnoð or Erdnoð [cf Eadnoð](Lond, Roum)
Earneytel, see Arnectel
Earngrim or Engrim (York)
Eene [= Elric?] (Steyn)
Edel-, see Æðel-
Edgar, see Eadgar
Edmer (Exet)
Edric or Edric [see also Eadric] (Heref, Ipsw, Lang, Linc, Lond, Taunt, Thetf)
Edsic or Edsic [= Edsige?] (Dover, Exet)
Edsige, see Eadsige
Edsigewine (Exet)
Eduta (Lond)
Edwald, see Eadwold
Edwar or Edward (Lewes)
Edwen [= Eadwerd?] (Norw)
Edwerd, see Eadweard
Edwig, see Eaduuy
Edwine, see Eadwine
Efic (Norw)
Eghing, see Egelwig
Egelwine, see Ægelwine
Eglent? (Bedf)
Eldise? [= Ælfwig?] (Thetf)
Eleaig [= Æltwig?] (Heref)
Elt- see Ælt-
Elst (Hast)
Embwern (Chest)
Eob (Olðus?)
Estan, see Æstan
Etsige, &c [see also Eadsige] (Dover, Exet, Hast, Lond, Salisb, Shrews)
Estan [cf Æstan] (Heref, Shrews)
Ettige [= Etsige] (Shrews)
Eðel-, see Æðel-
Fargrim, Fargim, &c (Stamf, York)
Faeirom, Fairou, Faiðom, &c (Hunt, York)

Falgau [= Ealgar?] (Lond)
Fastolf, Fastulf, &c, (Ipsw)
Feremin
Flocail (Heref)
Folherd or Folherd (Ipsw)
Freðen one or Friðiwine (Steyn)
Freði[e] (Lond)
Friðcol (York)
Garulf (Winchest)
Gerbof (Ipsw)
Gimulf, see Grimulf
Ginnine (Roch)
Goal, Goda, Godd, &c (Exet, Ilch, Lond, Shaft, Winchest, Worc)
Godanuin, see Godnun
Godan [= Godric or Godmun?] (Exet)
Godcild, Gotcild, &c (Watch)
Godcira (Lond)
Godefreð, Godetrið, &c (Cant, Lewes)
Godelað (Hunt)
Godeleof or Godleof (Hunt, Lond, Stamf)
Godeman, see Godmin
Godere, Goddere, &c (Lond, Mald)
Godgod [= Goal] (Lond)
Godie (Glouc)
Godine (Lond)
Godleof, see Godeleof
Godmun, Godaman, Godeman, or Goðman (Brist, Cant, Crickl, Dover, Hunt, Lewes, Lond, Oxf, Romr, Thetf, Winchest, York)
Godric, Godric, Godric, &c (Bedf, Cant, Chest, Colch, Derby, Glouc, Hunt, Ilch, Linc, Lond, Lydf, Lynne, Roum, Southamp, Stamf, Winchest, York)
Godric and Calic (Lond)
Godric and Swot (Linc)
Godsunu or Godsunu (Cambr, Cant)
Godwer [= Godwine?] (Chest, Lond)
Godwine, Godwen, &c (Bedf, Cambr, Cant, Chest, Crickl, Glouc, Ilch, Lane, Lang, Linc, Lond, Mald, Mylt, Norw, Oxf, Roch, Salisb, Shrews, Stamf, Thetf, Wallingf, Warw, Winchest)
Godwine Cas? (Winchest)
Godwine and Ceuca, &c (Winchest)
Godwine and Wulia (Winchest)
Goere [= Godere?] (Lond)
Gorm (Lond)
Goldus (Salisb)
Gomin [= Godman] (Lond)
Gomine, see Godwine
Gotsalin (Ipsw)
Grim (Cambr, Lond, Norw, Shrews)
Grimann
Grimcetel or Grimcytel (Linc)
Grimulf, Grimult, &c (York)
Grimun, see Grimun
Grimpu

Grurn, see Crurn
Gunhwat (York)
Gunhof or Cunhof (Chest)
Gunnal (Dover)
Gustan, Gustin, &c [see also Iustin] (Lane)
Haleman or Halman [= Healeman?] (Norw)
Hearsenul (Lane, York)
Hibbet or Hibbult (York)
Hildred (Crickl, York)
Hunt or Hunna (Malm)
Hunoman (Exet, Souther)
Hunewine (Exet, Lond, Watch)
Huvaleman or Healman (Dorch, Norw)
Huld (Lond)
Iannus (Lynn)
Ire (York)
Isopel (Exet)
Iserard (Winchest)
Iustigen, Iustein, Iustin, Iustan, &c (Lane)
Ladmer, see Leodmer
Lawlters
Lcouane [= Leofwine?] (Stamf)
Lere [= Leotric?] (Steyn)
Lifa, see Leofa
Lefa [= Leofa?] (Southamp)
Lefstan and Sreine (Lond)
Lemman, see Leomman
Lendun, see Leofden
Leodmer, Ladmer, Leomar, &c (Lane, Winchest)
Leofa, Leta, &c (Chest, Lewes)
Leofden [= Leofdegn?] (Stamf)
Leofdeg[n] (Stamf)
Leofoleg [= Leofdegn] (Stamf)
Leofgar or Leofger (Heref, Lond, Totn)
Leofhere (Heref)
Leofine or Leofing, see Lifine
Leofn [= Leofnod?] (Heref)
Leofnod, Leofnod, Leofnod, &c (Cant, Chest, Glouc, Heref, Lewes, Southamp, Winchest)
Leofred (Lond)
Leofred and Brun (Lond)
Leofric (Buck, Cant, Cluch, Dunie, Hert, Ipsic, Lane, Lond, Norw, Souther, Stamf, Thetf)
Leofsi, Leofsig, Leofsige, &c (Bath, Bedf, Cambr, Chest, Glouc, Ilch, Ipsic, Lewes, Lond, Stamf, Warw)
Leofstan, Leofstin, Leofstan, &c (Cant, Ipsic, Lond, Salisb, Shrews, Winchest, Wore)
Leofstorn (Ipsic)
Leofsunu (Winchest)
Leofter [q?] (Chest, Lane, Lond, Warch, Warw)
Leofwin (Cambr, Chest, Lond, Warw)

Leofwine, Lnofwine, &c ("Aexereo," Bath, Bedf, Brist, Cant, Chest, Chich, Colch, Dover, Exet, Hast, Hunt, Ilch, Leices, Line, Lond, Mald, Norw, Roch, Romn, Shrews, Sulb, Southamp, Stamf, Thetf, Wallingf, Walsingh, Warw, Winchest, York)
Leofwold (Lond, Shrews, Southamp, Stamf, Winchest)
Leomar [= Leodmer] (Jedb, Lond)
Leomman, Lemmin, &c (Lond)
Leomred [= Leofred?] (Lond)
Leonar [= Leofwig?] (Chest, Warw)
Leonoli (Chest)
Leosan (Lane)
Lermen (Totn)
Leuerd [cf Leofweard] (Lond)
Lifine, Leofing, &c (Chest, Crickl, Exet, Hert, Ipsw, Lane, Lond, Oxf, Retf, Souther, Thetf, Warw, Winchest)
Lifardyn (Norw)
Luf-, see also Leof-
Lindwin (Lane)
Liofhelm (Lane)
Liorman (Lond)
Liofn (Bedf)
Liofnen [= Liofhelm?] (Lane)
Liofweard (Lond)
Liuf-, see also Leof-
Liwine [= Liofwine?] (Chest)
Loc (Winchest)
Loda [= Goda?] (Cswa?)
Lufa (Shaft)
Luferic [= Leofric?] (Wore)
Lufestan [= Leofstan?] (Salisb)
Lufwine [= Leofwine?] (Dover)
Lyfine, see Lifine
Macsuda[n] [= Matesan?] (Chest)
Man, Mana, Mann, or Manna (Exet, Lane, Norw, Thetf, Wallingf, Welmesf)
Manqod [cf Godman] (Bedf)
Manine (Dover)
Mansige (Sulb)
Matan [= Matesan?] (Lane)
Matasan and Balluc (Lane)
Miteðan, Matsan, &c (Liue)
Moglu (Norw)
Moleman (Iond)
Mus (Ilch)
Nieies (Lond)
Norulf (Stamf).
Norðman (Lewes)
Obn? (Lond)
Oda, Odea, or Ode ("Dncennti" = Winchest?, Ipsic, "Meonre," Winchest)
Oidbriht (Winchest)
Odrie (Heref)
Orst, Orst &c (Cambr)

Osbarn or Osbern [see also Oðbern] (Dorch, York)
Osferð (Linc)
Osfrum [=Osgram?] (Linc)
Osgar (Dorch)
Osgod, Osgot, Osgut, &c (Linc, York)
Osgram, see Oðgrim
Oslac (Linc, Nora)
Oslaf (Lond)
Osmund (Linc)
Osulf (Lond, Thetf)
Osuard or Osuard (Stamf)
Oswi, Oswig, &c (Ilch)
Oswold (Norw, Nott, Stamf)
Oustman (York)
Oðgrim or Oðgrim (Linc, York)
Owulsige (Here)
Oðan, Oðin, Oððin, &c (York)
Oðbarn or Oðbern (Linc)
Oðbi (Norw)
Oðgrim, see Oðgrim
Oððencar (Lond)
Ræfen (York)
Rienulf, Rienulf, or Rinulf (Norw)
Runstan [=Brunstan?] (Thetf)
Sægrim (Nott, Thetf)
Seman (Salisb)
Sæwine (Brist, Exet, Hythe, Lydf, Oxf, Shaft, Totn)
Sculu or Sculun (Exet, York)
Secoll or Sulecul [cf Snecoll] (York)
Sedra (Winchest)
Sirtine [=Swertine?] (York)
Sibula, see Sigbula
Sebrikt (Lond)
Sabrine (Oxf)
Saleuine (Crukl)
Sigar or Segar (Winchest)
Sigbuda, Sigbula, or Sibule (Southamp, Winchest)
Sigodia [=Sigbula?] (Winchest)
Sinoð (Lond)
Snuend (Lond)
Sired (Gloue, Lond)
Sirie [=Sihtric?] (Norw, Richb)
Snewine or Snewuine (Gudl, Winchest)
Snecoll [see also Scoll, &c] (York)
Snel or Snell (Chest)
Snrling (Linc)
Sota [cf Swota] (Bedf)
Spot, see Swot
Spaiful (Winchest)
Stængrim or Stængrim (Cambr)
Stanei (Hunt)
Stenmer (Thetf)
Stirc, Stircan, or Stircer (York)
Stircol, Styrcol, &c (York)
Stiðulf (Lond)
Snartcol (Hugh)

Suetine, Sweline, &c (Lond, Mylt)
Sunolf [=Sunolf] (York)
Sumerleda, Sumerleða, Sumerlida, &c (Linc, Lond, Norw, Thetf)
Sunegod [cf Godsune] (Linc)
Sunolt (York)
Surtine, Syrtine, &c [=Swyrtine]? (Linc, York)
Snafa (Linc)
Swan (Lond)
Swerafuc or Swerafuc (Winchest)
Swart, Swearta, Swert, &c (Linc, Stamf)
Swartafa, Swartafa, &c (Dover)
Swartine, Sweartine, Swertine, &c (Chest, Derby, Linc, Norw, York)
Sweartabrand, Swertebrand, &c (Linc)
Swegen (Chest, Southw, York)
Suene, Swened, &c (Lond)
Suet or Sweta (Carlb, Dorch)
Swrtine, see Suetine
Swileman (Winchest)
Swot or Swota (Bedf, Linc, Shrews)
Swreline [=Swertine] (Southw)
Seruant (Thetf)
Sybula, see Sigbula
Syrtine, see Surtine
Tidred (Thetf)
Toca, Tooca, &c [=Toga?] (Crickl, Lond, Southw, York)
Trotan (Chest)
Uccade or Uccde (York)
Ulf (Linc, Richb)
Ulfhorn (Linc)
Uljcetel (Linc, Lond, "Ustla," York)
Ulfgrim (York)
Umerð (Linc)
Ustman (York)
Ualgist (Thetf)
Hallos, Wallos, &c (Linc)
Wadel (Bath)
Walgist (Thetf)
Walrefan, Walraffen, &c (Linc)
Ware? (Exet)
Watuman or Wateman (Bradgen, Norw)
Weddes, Wedles, &c (Linc)
Hedsit (Thetf)
Wesig (Lond)
Walut or Wudut (Stegn, Winchest)
Wulm [=Wulm?] (Stevn)
Wihred [cf Winred] (Cant)
Wihtsige or Wihtsie (Winchest)
Wilim (Lydf)
Wimus or Wimns [cf Wine] (Carlb, Crewk)
Wine or Winne (Exet, Winchest)
Winman [cf Wine] (Thetf)
Winedeig, Winedeig, Winedig, &c (Cant)
Winegod [=Godwine] (Warm)

Wineman (*Salisb.*, Thetf.).
Winred or *Wynred* [cf. *Wihred*] (Cant.).
Winsan [= Winstan] (*Heref.*).
Winsi [cf. *Wynsi*] (*Lond.*).
Winstan or *Wynstan* (Salisb.).
Winus, *see Winus*.
Wiðrin, Wiðerine, &c. (York).
Wlaneðegn or *Wlaeðegn* (Cant., Leic.).
Wudia, see Widia.
Wulbern, *Wulborn*, *Wulfbern*, &c.
   (Linc., Winchest.).
Wulfei [= Wulfsig?] (Dover).
Wulfeh (*Derby*).
Wulfelm (Ilch.).
Wulferd [= Wulfred] (*Lond.*)
Wulfgar (Lond.)
Wulfgat or *Wulfget* (Linc., Shrews.).
Wulfmær, Wulmær, &c. (*Cambr.*, *Jedb.*,
   Lond., Oxf., *Romn.*, Shrews.,
   Thetf., Worc.).
Wulfnoð, Wulnoð, *Wulnað*, &c. (Chest.,
   Glouc., Leic., Linc., Lond., Romn.,
   Shaft., Stamf., Winchest., York).
Wulfred, *Wulfryd*, &c. (Lond., Salisb.,
   Shrews.).
Wulfric ("Ecorne." = York?, Exet.,
   Hert., Linc., Lond., Southw.,
   Warw., Winchest., York?).
Wulfsi [cf. Wulfsig] (*Cambr.*, Chest.,
   Southw.).
Wulfsig, *Wulfsige*, Wulsige, &c.
   (Cambr., Guild., Heref., Lond.,
   Stamf., York).

Wulfstan, *Wulfstin*, or Wulstan (Brist.,
   Cant., Exet., Hunt., Leic., Lond.,
   Southw., York).
Wulfwerd (Exet., Glouc., Shrews.,
   "Totel.").
Wulfwig (Cant.).
Wulfwine or Wulwine (Brist., Colch.,
   Crickl., Leic., Linc., Lond., Oxf.,
   Wallingf.).
Wulmiod [= Wulfnoð?] (Lond.).
Wulwi [= Wulfwig or Wulfwine?]
   (Oxf.).
Wul.-, *see* also Wulf.-
Wunsi or *Wynsi* [= Wynsige?] (Lond.,
   Southw.).
Wynsige (Brist., Hunt., Lond.).
Wynstan (Lond.).
Wynwid (Cant.).
Þegenwine (Exet.).
Þeodred (Lond.).
Þeoræð or Þoreð [= Þeodred] (Lond.).
Þerman (Lond.).
Þorcetl, Þurcetl, &c. (Linc., Lond.,
   Torks.).
Þurcil [cf. Þurcetl] (Lond.).
Þureferð, Þurferd, &c. (Norw., Thetf.).
Þurgod (Exet.).
Þurgrim, Þurim, &c. (Linc., York).
Þurstan, Þurestan, &c. (Lond., Norw.,
   Stamf., Taunt.).
Þurulf (Linc., Stamf.).

Description of Types.[*]

Obverse.	Reverse.

† Type i.

Bust l., diademed. Around, inscription between two circles.	Small cross pattée. Around, inscription between two circles.

[Hild., Pl. 5, *Type A.*]

---

[*] Hildebrand, Pl. 6, Types D. and D. *var. a* are Danish, and are therefore not included in the following list.

[†] The single specimen of this coin (see No. 609, p. 300) in the National Collection, besides being of an uncertain mint, is too much worn to allow of being illustrated.

Obverse.	Reverse.

Type ii.

Bust l. Around, inscription: outer circle. | Long cross voided, each limb terminating in three crescents; pellet in centre. Around, inscription: outer circle.

[Hild., Pl. 6, Type B.]

Type iii.

Bust l., crowned; in front, shield. Around, inscription divided by bust: outer circle. | Quadrilateral ornament with three pellets at each angle, over which long cross voided, each limb terminating in three crescents; pellet in centre. Around, inscription: outer circle.

[Hild., Pl. 6, Type C.]

Type iv.

Bust l. Around, inscription divided by bust: outer circle. | Over quatrefoil with pellet at apex of each cusp, long cross voided, each limb terminating in three crescents; pellet in centre. Around, inscription: outer circle.

[Hild., Pl. 7, Type E. var. f.]

Obverse	Reverse

Type IV var a

Bust l., diademed. Around, inscription between two circles	Same as last

[Hild., Pl 7, Type E var g]

Type v

Bust l., crowned, within quatrefoil. Around, inscription outer circle	Small cross pattée. Around, inscription between two circles

[Hild., Pl 5, Type A var a]

Type v var a

Bust l., crowned. Around, inscription between two circles	Same.

[Hild., Pl 5, Type A var b]

Type vi

Bust l., diademed, sceptre in left hand. Around, inscription divided by bust outer circle	Small cross pattée. Around, inscription between two circles

[Hild., Pl 5, Type A var c]

Obverse.	Reverse.

Type vii.

Bust l., crowned, within quatrefoil. Around, inscription: outer circle.	*Long cross voided, each limb terminating in three crescents. Around, inscription: outer circle.*

[Hild., Pl. 7, *Type* E. *var. k.*]

Type viii.

Bust l., crowned, within quatrefoil;* with or without pellet inside each cusp. Around, inscription: outer circle.	On quatrefoil, with pellet at apex of each cusp, long cross voided, each limb terminating in three crescents; pellet in centre. Around, inscription: outer circle.

[Cf. Pl. XVII. 1–3, &c.]

Type viii. *var. a.*

Similar; bust r.	Same.

[Cf. Pl. XIX. 15.]

Type viii. *var. b.*

Similar; bust l.; in front, sceptre.	Same.

[Cf. No. 220, p. 271.]

Type viii. *var. c.*

Similar; quatrefoil broken by bust, which divides inscription.	*Similar; angles of quatrefoil slightly arched.*

[Hild., Pl. 6, *Type* E. *var. b.*]

---

* The quatrefoils on the obverse and reverse vary in form; on some specimens the angles are much arched; on others very slightly so that the quatrefoil approaches the form of a circle.

Obverse.	Reverse.

Type viii. var. d.

Similar; bust l., diademed, within quatrefoil.	Same as last.

[Cf. Pl. XVIII. 2.]

Type ix.

Bust l., wearing pointed helmet: in front, sceptre. Around, inscription between two circles, divided by bust.	On quatrefoil, with pellet at apex of each cusp, long cross voided, each limb terminating in three crescents; pellet in centre. Around, inscription: outer circle.

[Hild., Pl. 7, Type E. var. h.]

Type x.

Bust l., crowned, within quatrefoil. Around, inscription: outer circle.	On quatrefoil, with three pellets at apex of each cusp, long cross voided, each limb terminating in three crescents. Around, inscription: outer circle.

[Cf. Pl. XVII. 12.]

Type xi.

Bust l., crowned, within quatrefoil. Around, inscription: outer circle.	Long cross voided, each limb terminating in three crescents; in each angle, annulet enclosing pellet. Around, inscription: outer circle.

[Hild., Pl. 7, Type E. var. l.]

Type xii.

Bust l., diademed; sceptre in left hand. Around, inscription divided by bust: outer circle.	Long cross voided, each limb terminating in crescent; in centre, circle enclosing pellet; in angles, P A Ɛ X. Around, inscription: outer circle.

[Cf. Pl. XVIII. 15.]

Obverse.	Reverse.

Type xiii.

Bust l. *Around, inscription divided by bust: outer circle.* | Short cross voided, limbs united at base by two circles; in each angle, annulet enclosing pellet. *Around, inscription between two circles.*

[Hild., Pl. 7, *Type G. var. b.*]

Type xiv.

Bust l., wearing pointed helmet; in front, sceptre. *Around, inscription between two circles, divided by bust.* | Short cross voided, limbs united at base by two circles; in centre, pellet: in each angle, broken annulet enclosing pellet. *Around, inscription between two circles.*

[Cf. Pl. XVII. 5.]

Type xiv. var. a.

Similar; bust r. | Same.

[Cf. Pl. XVII. 13.]

Type xv.

Bust l., crowned. *Around, inscription between two circles.* | Short cross voided, limbs united at base by two circles; in centre, pellet; in each angle, broken annulet enclosing pellet. *Around, inscription between two circles.*

[Hild., Pl. 8, *Type G. var. c.*]

Type xvi.

Bust l., diademed; in front, sceptre.* *Around, inscription divided by bust: outer circle.* | Short cross voided; in centre, circle enclosing pellet. *Around, inscription between two circles.*

[Cf. Pl. XVII. 4.]

---

* The sceptre varies in form, terminating either in a fleur-de-lis, a finial, or a crozier (see Hildebrand, Pl. 8, Types H., H. *var. a*, and H. *var. b.*). The fleur-de-lis type is the only one represented in the National Collection.

Obverse.	Reverse.

Type xvi. *var. a.*

Similar; *before bust, pennon.* | Same.

[Hild., Pl. 8, *Type* II. *var. c.*]

Type xvi. *var. b.*

Similar; *rude bust without diadem; sceptre terminates in fleur-de-lis.* | Similar; *in centre, pellet only.*

[Hild., Pl. 8, *Type* II. *var. d.*]

Type xvii.

Bust l., diademed; sceptre in left hand. Around, inscription divided by bust: outer circle. | Over short cross voided, quadrilateral ornament with pellet at each angle and in centre. Around, inscription between two circles.

[Cf. Pl. XVII. 7.]

Type xvii. *var. a.*

Similar; *sceptre not held by hand.* | Same.

[Hild., Pl. 8, *Type* I. *var. a.*]

Type xviii.

Bust l., wearing pointed helmet; in front, sceptre. Around, inscription between two circles, divided by bust. | Over short cross voided, quadrilateral ornament with pellet at each angle and in centre. Around, inscription between two circles.

[Hild., Pl. 8, *Type* I. *var. c.*]

Obverse.	Reverse.

Type xix.

Bust l., diademed; in front, sceptre. Around, inscription divided by bust: outer circle. | Over short cross voided, quadrilateral ornament with three pellets at each angle and one in centre. Around, inscription between two circles.

[Cf. Pl. XIX. 3.]

Type xx.

Bust l., diademed. Around, inscription divided by bust: outer circle. | Cross, composed of four ovals united at base by two circles. Around, inscription : outer circle.

[Cf. Pl. XIX. 4.]

Type xx. *var. a.*

Similar; in front of bust, sceptre. | *Similar; in centre of cross, pellet.*

[Hild., Pl. 9, *Type* K. *var. a.*]

DESCRIPTION OF COINS.

No.	Obverse.	Reverse.	Moneyer.
	ÆGLESBYRIG. [Aylesbury.]		
	Type viii.		
1	✠CNVT REX ANGLOR· [Pl. XVII. 1.]	✠ÆL·FPI ⊙N ACL (Chipped.)	Ælfwi.
	BARDANIG. [Bardney.]		
	Type viii.		
2	✠CNVT REX ANGLO	✠BYRHΣI O BARD Wt. 11·4.	Byrnsi (= Byrnsige?).

No.	Obverse.	Reverse.	Moneyer.

BAÐAN.
[Bath.]

Type viii.

No.	Obverse.	Reverse.	Moneyer.
3	✠CNVT REX ANCL☉R :	✠ÆLFR·IC ☉N BEAÐN Wt. 22·3.	Ælfric.
4	„ RE✠ ANCLORVM	✠ÆÐELRIC ☉N B·AÐA Wt. 22·5.	Æðelric.
5	„ RE✠ „	✠ÆÐEƧTAN ☉N BAÐAN Wt. 22·7.	Æðestan.

[Pl. XVII. 2]

6	„ R[EX A]NCL·☉ RVM :	✠ÆÐE[ƧTA].N ☉N BAÐ (Broken.)	
7	„ ., ANCL·☉RV	✠AL·FPALD ☉N BAÐ Wt. 17·3.	Alfwald or Alfwold.
8	„ R·EX A·NCL☉ RVM	✠ALFP☉LD ☉N BEAÐN Wt. 22·0.	

Type xiv.

9	✠CNVT R·ECX :	✠ÆÐESTAN ON BA Wt. 15·3.	Æðestan.
10	✠CNVT R EX ANC :	✠ÆÐESTAN : ON BAÐA Wt. 17·0.	
11	„ „ „	✠ESTAN ON BAÐANN : Wt. 16·6.	Estan (= Æðestan ?).

Type xvi.

| 12 | ✠CNVT ·RECX. | ✠ÆLFRIC ON BAÐA Wt. 17·5. | Ælfric. |
| 13 | „ ·R·ECX ·. | ✠ÆÐESTAN ON BAÐ Wt. 18·5. | Æðestan. |

BEDEFORD.
[Bedford.]

Type viii.

| 14 | ✠ENVT REX ANCLO RVM | ✠CODPINE M BED Wt. 20·0. | Godwine. |

[Pl. XVII. 3]

No.	Obverse.	Reverse.	Moneyer.
		Type xvi.	
15	✠CNV T RECX	✠SPOTⱯ ON BEDEF: Wt. 17·2.	Swota.
		BRICGSTOP. [Bristol.]	
		Type viii. *rar. d.*	
16	✠CNVT REX ⱯNCLOR (Double struck.)	✠ÆCELPINE ON· BRIC Wt. 15·2.	Ægelwine.
17	,, ,, ANCLOL:	✠PVLPINE ON BRIC Wt. 15·0.	Wulwine (Wulfwine).
		Type xvi.	
18	✠CNVT ·RECX	✠ÆELPINE ON BRI Wt. 17·6.	Ægelwine.
19	✠CNV· ·T RE·C	✠ÆCEL·PINE ON BRIC Wt. 17·7. [Pl. XVII. 4.]	
20	✠CNV T REC:	✠PVLSTⱯN O BR Wt. 13·8.	Wulstan (Wulfstan).
		Type xvii.	
21	✠EC⊙I RECCE✠	✠ÆCELPINE OH BRICC: Wt. 15·0.	Ægelwine.
		BRIVTVNE. [Brewton.]	
		Type viii.	
22	✠CNVT ᴦEX ANCLO RVM	✠ÆLFELM ⊙N BRIV Wt. 16·8.	Ælfelm.
		Type xiv.	
23	✠CNV. T RECX Ɐ	✠ÆL·FELM ON B·RIVT Wt. 14·0. [Pl. XVII. 5.]	Ælfelm.

No.	Obverse.	Reverse.	Moneyer.

CADANBYRIG.
[Cadbury.]

Type viii.

| 24 | ✠CNVT REX ANCLO RVM [Pl. XVII. 6.] | ✠ÆLFEL·M ON CAD Wt. 14·7. | Ælfelm. |

CÆNTPARABYRIG.
[Canterbury.]

Type viii.

| 25 | ✠CNVT REX ANCLOR | ✠PINEDEIC ⊙N CEN· Wt. 12·3. | Winedeig. |

Type xiv.

| 26 | ✠CNVT REX ANCL | ✠LEOFNOÐ M·ON CENT: Wt. 16·8. | Leofnoð. |
| 27 | „   „   ANCLO | ✠PVLSTAN ON CENTPA: Wt. 15·8. | Wulstan (Wullstan). |

Type xvi.

28	✠CNVT ·RECX A·	✠BRHTRED ON CEN: Wt. 17·2.	Brihtred.
29	✠CNVT ·REC·X :	✠CODPINE ON CENT: Wt. 15·3.	Godwine.
30	„ RECX A··	✠PINEDÆI ON CENTP Wt. 16·0.	Winedæi(g) (Winedeig).
31	✠CNV: T RECX.	✠PINRED ON CENTPA: Wt. 18·2.	Winred.

CISECEASTRE.
[Chichester.]

Type viii.

| 32 | ✠CNVT REX ANCLO RVM | ✠BRIHTN⊙Ð ⊙NCIX Wt. 20·0. | Brihtnoð. |

No.	Obverse.	Reverse.	Moneyer.
	Type xiv.		
33	✠CNVT R EX ꓮNGL:	✠ꓮEGELM ON ᴄIᴄESTR: Wt. 16·0.	Ægelm.
	Type xvi.		
34	✠CNVT ·T REᴄX	✠LEOFRIᴄ ON ᴄIᴄᴄ·· Wt. 16·5.	Leofric.
	COLECEASTRE. [Colchester.]		
	Type xiv.		
35	✠CNVT REX ·ꓮ·	✠ꓮEL·FPINE·· ON ᴄOL·· Wt. 16·6.	Ælfwine.
36	✠CNV: T REX ꓮN	✠ᴄꙨDR·Iᴄ: ꙨN ᴄOL·ꓮ· Wt. 17·5.	Godric.
37	✠·CNVT ,, ,,	✠P.VL·FPINE: ꙨN ᴄOL·· Wt. 17·2.	Wulfwine.
	Type xvi.		
38	✠CNVT REᴄX ꓮ·	✠ᴄODRIᴄ ON ᴄOLEᴄ Wt. 17·0.	Godric.
39	✠CNV·· T REᴄX	✠PVLFPINE ON COL·· Wt. 15·2.	Wulfwine.
	Type xvii.		
40	✠CNVT R Eᴄ✠ AN [Pl. XVII. 7.]	✠PVL·FPINE ON ᴄOLE Wt. 17·0.	Wulfwine.
	CRECGELADE ᴏʀ **CROCGELADE.** [Cricklade.]		
	Type viii.		
41	✠CNVT· REX ꓮNGLꙨ RVM	✠ꓮELPINE ON ᴄRO·ᴄI: Wt. 15·0.	Ælwine (Ælfwine).

No.	Obverse	Reverse	Moneyer
42	✠ CNVT R EX ANGLO⊙ RVM	✠EÐELPINE ⊙N CROC　Wt. 16·0	Eðelwine
43	✠CNVT REX ANGLO⊙ RVM　[Pl XVII 8]	✠ GODMAN ⊙N CROC　Wt 23·2	Godeman (Godman)
44	„　　„ ANGLORV	✠TOCA ON CRO C CIL　Wt 11·8	Toca.

CRUCERN
[Crewkerne]

Type xvi

| 45 | ✠ CNVT RECX | ✠PINVS ON CRVCE　Wt 17·0 | Winus? |
| | [Pl XVII 9] | | |

DOFERAN.
[Dover]

Type viii

| 46 | ✠CNVT REX ANGLORV | ✠GODMAN DOF　Wt 16·5 | Godman |
| 47 | „　　„　[AN]GLOR | ✠PV[L]FC I ON DOF　(Broken) | Wulfci (= Wulfsige?) |

Type xiv

48	✠CNVT　RECX A	✠CINSIGE ON D⊙FRAN　Wt 15·5	Cinsige.
	[Pl XVII 10]		
49	✠ CNV T R EX A	✠L E⊙FPINE ON DOF　Wt 16·8	Leofwine

Type xvi

50	✠CNVT R ECX.	✠BOCA　ON DOFR .　Wt 16·2	Boga (Boiga)
51	✠CNVT · · RECX	✠CINSIGE ON DOFR　Wt 17·0	Cinsige.
52	✠CNV T RECX·	✠EDPINE ON DOFERA　Wt 14·6	Edwine

No.	Obverse.	Reverse.	Moneyer.
53	✠CNV ·T RECX:	✠ETSICE ON DOFRAN Wt. 17·6.	Etsige (Edsige).
54	✠CNVT ·RECX:	✠LEOFPINE ON DOF·.· Wt. 18·3.	Leofwine.

DORCEASTRE.

[Dorchester.]

Type viii.

| 55 | ✠CNVT REX ANCL⊙
RVM
[Pl. XVII. 11.] | ✠OƧBERN MO DOR
Wt. 16·0. | Osbern. |

EAXANCESTRE, EXCEASTER, Etc.

[Exeter.]

Type viii.

56	✠CNVT REX ANCLOR	✠ÆLFRIC ON EAXA Wt. 12·4.	Ælfric.
57	✠CN·VT R·EX ANCLOR	✠EDƧIE ON EXCE Wt. 13·0.	Edsie (= Edsige?).
58	✠CNVT REX ANCLOI	✠PVLFƧTAN ⊙ EX Wt. 13 3.	Wulfstan.
59	,, ,, ,,	✠ÐVRCOD O EAXC Wt. 11·7.	Þurgod.

Type x.

| 60 | ✠CNVT ᚱEX ANCLOI | ✠HVNEPINE ⊙ EX
Wt. 22·5. | Hunewine. |
| | [Pl. XVII. 12.] | | |

Type xiv.

61	✠CNVT RECX A	✠ÆLFPINE ⊙N ECXÆ: Wt. 16·0.	Ælfwine.
62	✠CNV T RECX A·	✠EALDABEARD ON EC Wt. 14·4.	Ealdabeard or Ealdeberd.
63	✠CNVT: EX ANCL·	✠EA·L·DEB·ERD ON ECX Wt. 13·7.	
64	✠CNVT RECX AN	✠EDMÆR ⊙N ECXCE: Wt. 12·0.	Edmær.

No.	Obverse.	Reverse.	Moneyer.
65	✠CNVT : ·RECX Λ	✠EDSIE ON ECXÆEST Wt. 12·4.	Edsie (= Edsige?).
66	✠CNVT : R·EX ΛN	✠EDSICE ON EXCEST: Wt. 18·0.	Edsige.
67	✠CNVT RECX ΛN	✠S·ÆPINE ☉N EC✠CES· Wt. 17·4.	Sæwine.
68	,, ,, ,,	,, ,, ,, Wt. 17·0.	
69	✠CNVT R EX ΛNC	,, ,, ECCXCE: Wt. 17·4.	
70	,, RECX Λ.	✠PVLSTΛN ON ECX: Wt. 15·0.	Wulstan (Wulfstan).
71	✠CNV T RECX Λ	✠PVLSTΛN ON ECXEC·· Wt. 15·0.	

Type xvi.

No.	Obverse.	Reverse.	Moneyer.
72	✠CNVT ·RECX Λ·	✠ÆFICC ON ECXECE·· Wt. 16·4.	Æficc (= Ælfric).
73	✠CNV·T: ·RECX Λ	✠ÆLFPINE ON EC·XE: Wt. 16·4.	Ælfwine.
74	✠CNVT ·RECX.	✠EDSICEPΛRE ON EC Wt. 16·6.	Edsigeware.
75	✠CNVT RECX··	✠EDPINE ON ECXEΛ: Wt. 17·0.	Edwine.
76	✠·CNVT. ·REC·X Λ:	,, ,, EC✠EC: Wt. 16·8.	
77	✠CNV:T ·RE·CX:	✠HVNEMΛN ON ECX· Wt. 17·4.	Huneman.
78	✠CNVT ·RECX	✠LEOFPINE ON ΛCX Wt. 19·5.	Leofwine.
79	✠CNV:T ·RECX Λ	✠ÐECENPINE ON ECX Wt. 17·0.	Þegenwine.

EOFERPIC.

[York.]

Type viii.

No.	Obverse.	Reverse.	Moneyer.
80	✠CNVT REX ΛNCLOR·	✠COLCRIM MO EO Wt. 14·2.	Colgrim.

No.	Obverse.	Reverse.	Moneyer.
81	✠CNVT REX A·NGLORV	✠COLCR·IM MO EOI Wt. 15·7.	
82	,, ,, ANGLORV	✠HI·LDOLF MO EO Wt. 16·0.	Hildolf.
83	,, ,, ANGLORV⊥	✠O:SGOT M–O EO: (Chipped.)	Osgot.
84	✠:CNVT REX ANGLO· RVI	✠STIRC:AR MO EOI Wt. 18·7.	Stircar.
		Type xiv.	
85	✠CNVT R E✠ ·ANG	✠ÆÐELPINE M⊤⊙ EO: Wt. 15·2.	Æðelwine.
86	,, ,, ,,	,, M⊤O EOL: Wt. 16·0.	
87	,, R EX ANG	,, M⊤⊙ E⊙FR Wt. 15·6.	
88	,, REX ,,	✠ARNCETL M–O E⊙FI Wt. 17·5.	Arncetel.
89	,, R EX ,,	✠ARNOLF M⊤⊙ E⊙FRPI Wt. 13·7.	Arnolf.
90	,, REX AN	✠ASGOD M⊤O EOFR Wt. 16·0.	Asgod, Asgout, &c. (= Osgod?).
91	✠CNVT: REX AI	✠ASGOVT M⊤O E⊙F: Wt. 16·0.	
92	✠CNVT REX ·A·IL (Barbarous.)	,, ,, Wt. 12·4.	
93	✠CNVT: REX AI	✠ASGOVT M⊤O EOFR· Wt. 15·4.	
94	✠CNVT REX AN	,, MO EOFRPIC Wt. 15·0.	
95	,, ,, ,,	✠ASGVVT M⊤O EOFRPI Wt. 17·0.	
96	,, ,, ANG	✠CETEL M⊤⊙ EOFRPIC Wt. 15·3.	Cetel.
97	✠CNVT R EX ANG·	✠CRINAN M⊤⊙ E⊙FR Wt. 15·5.	Crinan.
98	,, ,, ,,	,, ,, E⊙FRP Wt. 16·0.	

No.	Obverse.	Reverse.	Moneyer.
99	✠CNVT REX ANC·	✠CRVCAN MᵀO EO Wt. 15·0.	Crucan.
100	✠CNVT· „ AN :	„ „ EOF Wt. 15·2.	
101	„ „ AN·	„ „ EOFR Wt. 15·2.	
102	✠:CNVT REX ANC·	✠CRVRN MᵀO EOFR : Wt. 15·9.	Crurn or Grurn.
103	„ „ „	„ MΩⵔ EⵔCRP Var. Pellet in one angle of cross. Wt. 15·6.	
104	✠CNVT· REX AN :	✠GRVRN Mᵀⵔ EOFRPI : Wt. 14·8.	
105	✠CNVT R EX „	✠FARCRMᵀⵔ EⵔFRPI Var. Pellet in two angles of cross. Wt. 15·6.	Fargrim.
106	„ „ ANC	„ Wt. 15·3.	
107	„ „ ANI	✠FARCRIMᵀO EOFR Wt. 15·4.	
108	✠CNVT REX AN	„ EOFRI Wt. 15·5.	
109	✠CNVT: REX ANC	„ EOFRP Wt. 17·9.	
110	✠CNVT R EX ANCL :	✠FARÐEIN Mᵀⵔ EOF Wt. 16·6.	Farðein or Farðin.
111	„ REX ANC	✠FARÐIN MᵀO EOFR Wt. 16·6.	
112	„ R EX ANC	✠FRIÐCⵔL Mᵀⵔ EⵔF : Wt. 15·0.	Friðcol.
113	„ „ „	„ „ EOFR Wt. 15·6.	
114	✠CNV T REX AN	„ „ EⵔFRI : Var. Pellet in one angle of cross. Wt. 15·0.	
115	✠CNVT R EX AN :	„ „ EⵔFRP Wt. 14·8.	
116	✠CNVT REX AN	✠CODMAN MᵀO EO Wt. 15·7.	Godman.

No.	Obverse.	Reverse.	Moneyer.
117	✠CNVT REX ΛN	✠CODMAN M⊤O EOE Wt. 15·0.	
118	✠CNVT R EX ΛNC	„ „ EⓄFR Wt. 16·6.	
119	✠CNVT REX ΛN :	✠CRIM⊙LF M⊤O EOF Wt. 15·5.	Grimolf.
120	„ „ ΛN	„ „ EOFR Wt. 15·0.	
121	✠ : CNV T REX Λ·	„ „EOFRP : Wt. 16·0.	
122	✠CNVT R EX ΛC	✠HILDOLF M⊤O EO : Wt. 16·5.	Hildolf.
123	„ „ ΛNI	„ „ EOFR Wt. 15·2.	
124	✠CNVT REX ΛNC	✠HILDOLF M⊤⊙ EⓄFR : Wt. 16·4.	
125	✠CNVT R EX ΛNCL	„ „ ·EOFRPI Wt. 16·5.	
126	„ „ ΛNC	„ „ EⓄFRPIC Wt. 16·0.	
127	„ „ „	✠HILDOL·F M⊤O EOR Wt. 14·6.	
128	✠CNVT REX ΛN	✠IRE M⊤O EOFRPI ·.· Wt. 14·3.	Ire.
129	„ „ ΛI	„ M⊤⊙ EOFRPIC Wt. 16·0.	
130	✠CNVT R EX ΛNCL·.·	„ „ EOFRPICE Wt. 16·8.	
131	✠CNVT REX ⱭN	✠OƧCOD M⊤O EOFR : Wt. 15·8.	Osgod or Osgot.
132	„ „ „	✠OƧCOT M⊤O EOFRP Wt. 15·9.	
133	✠CNVT R ·EX ΛNCI	✠ƧTIRCⓄL M⊤⊙ EⓄFRI Wt. 15·3.	Stircol.
134	„ „ ΛNCL	✠ƧT·RCⓄL �Π⊤⊙ EⓄFRP Wt. 15·0.	
135	„ „ „	✠STRCⓄL M⊤⊙ „ Wt. 15·2.	

No	Obverse	Reverse	Moneyer
136	✠ CNVT R EX ANC	✠STYRCOL MͲ⊙ EOFR Wt 113	
137	✠CNVT REX AN	✠ΣVNOLF MͲ⊙ EOF Wt 155	Sunolf
138	✠CNVT REX ANCI	„ „ E⊙FR Wt 156	
139	✠CNVT R EX ANCL	„ MͲ⊙ EOFRP Wt 170	
140	„ R EX ANC	✠ΣVRTINC MͲ⊙ EOF Wt 116	Surtinc (= Swyrtinc ?)
141	„ „ „	✠ΣVRTINC MͲ⊙ EO Wt 157	
142	„ „ ANCL	✠TOC A MͲ⊙ EOFRPIC Wt 160	Toca
143	„ REX ANC	✠T⊙⊙CA MͲ⊙ E⊙FRP Wt 177	
144	„ „ ANC	✠ PIÐRIN MͲ⊙ EOFR Wt 150	Wiðrine
145	„ „ AI	✠PIÐRIN MͲ⊙ E⊙FRP Wt 158	
146	„ „ AN	✠PIÐRINE MͲ⊙ EOF Wt 155	
147	„ „ „	✠PIÐRINE MͲ⊙ EOF Wt 158	
148	„ „ AN·	„ „ EOFR Wt 153	
149	„ „ „	✠PIÐRN MͲ⊙ EOERP Wt 157	
150	„ „ ANO	✠PIÐRN MͲ⊙ EOERP Wt 160	
151	„ , ANCO	✠PVLF NOÐ MͲ⊙ EOF Wt 155	Wulfnoð
152	„ „ AN	✠PVLN⊙Ð MͲ⊙ EOF Wt 138.	
153	✠CNVT R EX „	✠PVLN⊙Ð MͲ⊙ EOFR Wt 156	
154	„ „ „	„ „ EOFRP Wt 161	

No.	Obverse.	Reverse.	Moneyer.
155	✠CNVT R REX ΛN	✠PVLNOÐ M⊤O EOFRPI Wt. 16·6.	
156	✠CNVT REX ΛI	✠PVLꟅTΛN M⊤O EOF Wt. 17·4.	Wulstan (Wulfstan).
157	,, ,, ΛNC	✠Þ·VL·ꟅT·Λ·N M⊤⊙ E⊙FR Wt. 15·0.	

Type xiv. var. a.

| 158 | ✠NVƎXꓘ TVNꓤ | ✠ZVRTINE N⊤O EO Wt. 13·2. | Surtine (= Swyrtine ?). |

[Pl. XVII. 13.]

Type xvi.

159	✠CNVT ·RECX :	✠ÆELPINE ON EOF : Wt. 17·2.	Ægelwine or Egelwine.
160	,, REC·X.	✠ÆCELPINE ON EOF : Wt. 16·8.	
161	,, ·RECX :	✠ÆCEL·PINE ON EOFE Wt. 17·0.	
162	,, ,,	✠ECELPINE ON EOF : Wt. 16·8.	
163	,, ,,	✠ÆLFPINE ON E⊙F : Wt. 17·0.	Ælfwine.
164	,, ·RECX Λ :	✠BEORN ON EOFER· Wt. 17·2.	Beorn.
165	✠CCNV T RECX ∴	✠COL·CR·RIM ON ·EOF : Wt. 17·7.	Colgrim.
166	✠CNV T RECX	✠CRVCΛN ON EO : Wt. 17·2.	Crucan or Grucan.
167	✠CN T RECX	,, ,, EOF : Wt. 16·8.	
168	✠CNV T REC	,, ,, EOEE Wt. 16·7.	
169	✠CN TRECX	,, ,, EOFE·: Wt. 16·7.	
170	✠CNV T REC	✠CRVCΛN ON EOFER : Wt. 17·4.	
171	✠CNV T REECX	✠DEORSICE ON EOR Wt. 17·7.	Deorsige.

No	Obverse	Reverse	Moneyer
172	✠CNVT REECX.	✠EARNCRIM ON EO Wt 17 1	Earngrim
173	„ „	✠FÆRÐEIN ON EOF Wt 16 8	Færðein.
174	✠CN T RECX	✠FA RÐEIN ON EOFE Wt 15 8	
175	✠CNVT R ECX A	✠FRIÐCOL ON EOFE Wt 15 4	Friðcol
176	„ „	„ „ Wt 17 0	
177	✠CNVT RCCX	✠CODMAN ON EOC Wt 15 0	Godman
178	✠CN T RCCX	✠CODMAN ON EOFE Wt 16 9	
179	✠CNVT REOFC	✠CODMAN ON EOFE Wt 16 2	
180	✠CN T RECX	✠CODMAN ON EOFFR Wt 18 2	
181	✠CNVT REOFE	✠CODMAN ON EORC Wt 16 3	
182	✠CNVT RECX Var Pellet behind head	✠CRIMVLF ON EOF Wt 16 5	Grimulf.
183	„ ·RECX	„ „ Wt 16 7	
184	✠CNVT RECX	✠CIMVLF ON E⊙FE Wt 17 0	
185	✠CNV T RECX	„ „ Wt 13 6	
186	✠CNV T RECX	✠ HIL DVLF ON EOFE Wt 14 0	Hildulf
187	✠CN T RE A	✠HILDVLF ON EOF Wt 17 4	
188	✠CNV T RCX	✠HLDVLF ON EOFE Wt 16 7	
189	✠CNV T RE X	✠OÐAN ON EOFER Wt 17 2	Oðan or Oðin
190	✠CNVT RECX	✠⊙ÐIN ON EOFER Wt 15 8	

No.	Obverse.	Reverse.	Moneyer.
191	✠CNVT· ·R·EC·X:	✠⊙ÐIN ON EOFERPI Wt. 17·2.	
192	✠CNV ·T RCX	✠OÐÐIN· ON EDFER·.· Wt. 16·0.	
193	,, RECX:	,, ,, EOFER·.· Wt. 16·7.	
194	✠CNV T REC·.·	✠R/EFEN ON EOFE: Wt. 17·0.	Ræfen.
195	✠CNV ·T REC:	,, ON EOFERPI Wt. 16·5.	
196	,, REC·X·	,, ,, Wt. 17·4.	
197	✠·CNVT ·R·EE·C·X.	✠VCEΛDC ON EOFER· (Double struck.) Wt. 16·4.	Uceade.
198	,, ·RE·C·X	✠VCEDE ON EDFER·P Wt. 17·3.	
199	✠CNVT ·R·EECX.	✠PVL·NOÐ ON EOFE·.· Wt. 16·0.	Wulnoð (Wulfnoð).
200	,, RCX ΛN	✠PVLNOÐ ON EOFER Wt. 16·9.	
201	,, ,, ,,	,, ,, Wt. 16·2.	
202	✠CNV T RECX:	✠ÐVRCRIM ON EOFE: Wt. 15·8.	Þurgrim.
203	✠CNV ·T RC·X	,, ONEOFE: Wt. 16·2.	
204	✠CNV T RECX:	✠ÐVRIM ON EODE Wt. 17·0.	

Type xvii.

205	✠CNV RECX ΛN	✠ÐVRCRIM ON EOFERPI Wt. 15·2.	Þurgrim.

GIFELCEASTER.

[Ilchester.]

Type viii.

206	✠CNVT REX ΛNCLOR	✠/ELFSICE ON CIFL Wt. 13·6.	.Elfsige.

No.	Obverse.	Reverse.	Moneyer.
207	✠CNVT REX ANCLORV	✠ÆLFPINE ☉ CIF Wt. 14·0.	Ælfwine.
208	,,　R·EX　　,,	✠ÆL·PINE ☉N CIFEL Wt. 21·6.	
209	,,　REX　　,,	✠☉ΣPI ☉ CIFELC Wt. 13·8.	Oswi or Oswig.
210	,,　　,,　　,,	✠☉ΣPIE ☉NCIFEL Wt. 13·2.	
211	,,　R·EX ANCLORVM ·.	✠PVLFELM ☉N CIFELC Wt. 21·6.	Wulfelm.
	[Pl. XVII. 14.]		

Type xvi.

| 212 | ✠CNV·T ·R·ECX·. | ✠CODRIC ON CIFEL·.·
Wt. 17·5. | Godric. |

GIPESPIC.
[Ipswich.]

Type viii.

| 213 | ✠CNVT REX ANCLOX | ✠FOLHED MO CIP
(Pierced.) | Folherd. |

Type xvi.

| 214 | ✠CNVT ·RECX A: | ✠LIFINC ON CIPESPI
Wt. 16·4. | Lifinc. |

GLEPECEASTER.
[Gloucester.]

Type viii.

215	✠CNVT REX ANCLORV:	✠CODPINE ☉NCL Wt. 23·4.	Godwine.
216	,,　R·EX A·NNCL· Var. Before bust, ·.·	✠CODPINE ☉ CLE Wt. 20·0.	
	[Pl. XVIII. 1.]		
217	,,　REX ANCLOR·	✠CODPI·NE ☉: CLE. Wt. 18·2.	
218	✠CNVT REX ANCLOR: Var. Before head, ✠	✠LEOFSICE ON CLE Wt. 16·2.	Leofsige.

No.	Obverse.	Reverse.	Moneyer.
219	✠CNVT REX ANCLOR *Var.* Before head, **G**	✠SIRED ON CLEP Wt. 16·6.	Sired.
	Type viii. *var. b.*		
220	✠CNV·T REX ANCL⊙:	✠CODPINE O CLE Wt. 15·8.	Godwine.
221	✠CNVT REX ANCL·OR	✠CODPINE: ⊙ CL·P *Var.* Pellet in each angle of cross. Wt. 17·3.	
	Type viii. *var. d.*		
222	✠CNVT REX ANCL·.·	✠CODPINE ON CLEP Wt. 17·4.	Godwine.
	[Pl. XVIII. 2.]		
	Type xiv.		
223	✠C·NV: T REX A·N·	✠BOL·L·A ON CL·EPE: Wt. 16·3.	Bolla.
224	✠C·NVT R·EX A·NC	✠COD·R·IC ⊙·N CL·EPE: Wt. 17·5.	Godric.
	Type xvi.		
225	✠CNV T RECX:	✠CODRIC ON CEPE: Wt. 18·8.	Godric.
226	✠CNV ·T R·ECX	✠SIRED ⊙N CL·EDE: Wt. 15·0.	Sired.
227	✠CNVT ·RECX ·.·	✠PVLNOÐ ON CLEP Wt. 17·5.	Wulnoð (Wulfnoð).
	GRANTEBRYCGE. [Cambridge.]		
	Type viii.		
228	✠CNVT REX ANCLO	✠STÆNCRIM O CRA Wt. 11·2.	Stængrim.
229	,, ,, ANCLOR	✠PVFZIC ON CRA Wt. 11·0.	Wulfsig.
	Type xiv.		
230	✠CNVT RECX A	✠ADA ON CRANTI Wt. 14·3.	Ada.

No.	Obverse.	Reverse.	Moneyer.
231	✠CNV. T RECX :	✠CRIM ON CRANTE Wt. 15·5.	Grim.
		[Pl. XVIII. 3.]	
232	✠CNVT EX ANCL·	✠L·EOFSICE : ON CR·A Wt. 15·2.	Leofsigo.
	Type xvi.		
233	✠CNVT ·CR·EC··	✠ÆLF·PIC ON CR·A : Wt. 17·7.	Ælfwig.
	Type xvii.		
234	✠CNVT: RECX ·:	✠CODPINE ON CR·AT Wt. 17·7.	Godwine.
		[Pl. XVIII. 4.]	

HÆSTINGA.
[Hastings.]

No.	Obverse.	Reverse.	Moneyer.
	Type xiv.		
235	✠CNVT RECX AN	✠ÆLFPERD ON HÆX Wt. 13·2.	Ælfweard.
	Type xvi.		
236	✠CNV: ·T RECX	✠BRID ON HÆSTINC: Wt. 16·7.	Brid.
		[Pl. XVIII. 5.]	

HAMTUNE.
[Southampton.]

No.	Obverse.	Reverse.	Moneyer.
	Type viii.		
237	✠CNVT REX ANCLORV	✠ÆLFPERD ON HAMT Wt. 15·0.	Ælfweard.
	Type xvi.		
238	✠CNV: ·T RECX	✠L·EOFPINE ON HAMT Wt. 15·6.	Leofwine.
		[Pl. XVIII. 6]	

No.	Obverse.	Reverse.	Moneyer.
	HEORTFORD. [Hertford.]		
	Type xvi.		
239	✠CNV· T REC :	✠ŒORSICE ON HEO Wt. 15·7.	Deorsige.
240	✠CNV T REC	✠LEOFRIC ON HEO : *Var.* Pellet only in centre of cross. Wt. 15·7.	Leofric.
241	„ R·ECX A	„ „ HEOR Wt. 15·5.	
242	„ ·REC·X :	✠CEOFRIC ON HEOR Wt. 14·7.	
243	✠CNVT: ·T REX ··	✠L·EORIC ON HE·ORT Wt. 17·8.	
244	✠CNV ·T REX ··	„ „ Wt. 17·4.	
	[Pl. XVIII. 7.]		
	HEREFORD. [Hereford.]		
	Type xiv.		
245	✠CNVT R EX AN·	✠:FLEC·ɃIFL ON HREN Wt. 13·5.	FlecŊifl?
246	✠C·NVT: R·EX A·NC :	✠OR·DR·IC: ON HER·E: Wt. 17·5.	Ordric.
	[Pl. XVIII 8.]		
	Type xvi.		
247	✠CNV T R·EC	✠ELEPII ON HEREF Wt. 18·0.	Ælfwine?
248	✠CNVT ·R· ECX :	✠PVLSICE ON HERE·: Wt. 18·3.	Wulsige (Wulfsige).

No.	Obverse.	Reverse.	Moneyer.

HUNTANDUNE.
[Huntingdon.]

Type viii.

| 249 | ✠CNVT REX ᚭNGL·O⟩ | ✠GODRIC MO HVN (Broken.) | Godric. |

Type xiv.

250	✠CNVT R·EX ᚭNG	✠GODL·EOF ON HVNT Wt. 16·5.	Godleof.
251	„ RECX ᚭ:	✠LTEOCDINE ON VN: Wt. 11·8.	Leofwine.
252	✠CNVT: RE·X ᚭN	✠PVNSICE: O VNTDNE Wt. 15·3.	Wynsige.

[Pl. XVIII. 9.]

HYÐA.
[Hythe.]

Type viii.

| 253 | ✠CNVT REX ᚭNGLORVM | ✠ΣᚭPINE OL HᚢÐA Wt. 14·2. | Sæwine. |

[Pl. XVIII. 10.]

LÆÞES.
[Lewes.]

Type viii.

| 254 | ✠CNVT. REX· ᚭNGLORV: | ✠GODEFREÐ: N LE Wt. 20·0. | Godefreð. |
| 255 | ✠CNVT: REX: ᚭNGLORV | ✠LEOFNOD M LÆÞ Wt. 20·6. | Leofnoð. |

[Pl. XVIII. 11.]

Type xiv.

| 256 | ✠CNVT= RECX ᚭ | ✠ÆLFPERD ON LÆÞE Wt. 15·7. | Ælfweard. |
| 257 | ✠CNVT· REX ᚭN | ✠COLLINI ON LÆÞ Wt. 13·4. | Collini (= Colling?). |

No.	Obverse.	Reverse.	Moneyer.
258	✠CNV T R·EX Λ:	✠GODEFRIÐ ☉ L·ÆPE Wt. 16·6.	Godefrið.
259	✠CNV T RECX ΛN	✠LEOFΛ ON L·ÆPEE·∴ Wt. 15·0.	Leofa.

Type xvi.

260	✠CNV T REC:	✠EDPINE ON L·ÆPE Wt. 16·0.	Edwine.
261	✠CNVT ·RECX·∴	✠GODEFRIÐ ON L·ÆPE Wt. 17·6.	Godefrið.
262	„ ·R·ECX·∴	„ „ LVÆ Wt. 14·2.	

LAG.
[Lancaster?]*

Type viii.

263	✠CNVT REX ΛNGLOR	✠ÆÐ..PINE O LΛG (Oxid sed.) Wt. 9·0.	Æðelwine.
264	„ „ ΛNGLOR·∴	✠GODPINE O LΛG Wt. 12·0.	Godwine.

LANGPORT.
[Langport.]

Type viii.

265	✠CNVT REX ΛNGLOR	✠GODPINE ON LΛN‍P (Chipped.)	Godwine.

Type xiv.

266	✠CNVT RECX ΛN	✠EDRIC ON LANCPOR· Wt. 13·8.	Edric.
	[Pl. XVIII. 12.]		

LEHERCEASTER.
[Leicester.]

Type xvi.

267	✠CNV: T REC:	✠ÆCELPIC ON L·EHR· Wt. 12·5.	Ægelwig.

* So attributed by Hildebrand; but very possibly for LANC = Langport.

T 2

No.	Obverse.	Reverse.	Moneyer.
268	✠CNVT: RECX A [Pl. XVIII. 13.]	✠PVLNOĐ ON LEHR Wt. 17·6.	Wulnoð (Wulfnoð).
269	✠CNV T REC:	✠PVLSTAN ON L·EHR· Wt. 16·2.	Wulstan (Wulfstan).

LEIGECEASTER, Etc.
[Chester.]

Type viii.

No.	Obverse.	Reverse.	Moneyer.
270	✠CNVT REX ANGLORV [Pl. XVIII. 14.]	✠ÆLFNOĐ ON LEI Wt. 20·0.	Ælfnoð.
271	✠CNT REX ANGLORVM *Var.* Pellet before head.	✠ÆLFSI ON LEI Wt. 18·0.	Ælfsige.
272	,, ,, ,, *Var.* Pellet before head.	✠ÆLFSIG ON LEI Wt. 20·2.	
273	✠CNVT ,, ,,	✠ÆĐERIC ON LEG Wt. 20·9.	Æðeric (= Æðelric).
274	,, ,, ,,	✠ÆĐRIC ON LE·GE Wt. 21·7.	
275	,, ,, ANGLORVM	✠ALCSI ON LEGE Wt. 15·3.	Alcsi(g) (= Alfsig or Ælfsig?).
276	,, ,, ANGLORV	✠CROFL ON LEI Wt. 14·2.	Crofl.
277	✠CNV.T REX ANGLOR	✠ELEPINE ON LEG (Chipped.)	Elfwine.
278	✠CNVT REX ANGLORVM	✠ELEPINE ⊙ LEGG Wt. 20·3.	
279	,, ,, ,, *Var.* Before head, ∵; behind, ∴	,, ,, Wt. 17·0.	
280	✠CNVT· ,, ,,	✠GO·DRIC· ON L·EGG Wt. 20·1.	Godric.
281	✠CNVT REX ANGLOR	✠GODPINE ⊙NLE Wt. 15·5.	Godwine.
282	,, ,, ,,	,, ON LEI Wt. 16·2.	

No.	Obverse.	Reverse.	Moneyer.
283	✠CNVT REX ANGLORVM *Var.* Before head, ∴; behind, pellet.	✠CVNLEOF ON LEC Wt. 17·3.	Gunleof.
284	,, ,, ANGLORV	,, ,, Wt. 21·0.	
285	✠CNVT· REX ANGLORVM	✠LEOFENOÐ ON LEI *Var.* Pellet in one angle of cross. Wt. 15·0.	Leofnoð.
286	✠CNVT REX ANGLORV	,, ,, Wt. 16·3.	
287	,, ,, ANGLORVM	✠L·Æ·OFPINE ON L·EC Wt. 21·8.	Leofwine.
288	,, ,, ANGLORV.	✠LIFIC· ON L·ECI· Wt. 14·6.	Lifinc.
289	,, ,, ANGLORV	✠LIPIN·E ON LEC Wt. 16·2.	Liwine (= Liofwine?).
290	✠CNVT ,, ANGLORVM	✠MACZVÐA ON LEI *Var.* Pellet in field. Wt. 17·3	Macsuða(n).
291	,, ,, ANGLORV·∴	✠ZPARTIC ON LEI Wt. 20·4.	Swartinc.
292	✠CNVT ,, ,,	✠ZPARTIN ON LEC Wt. 20·0.	
293	✠CNVT ,, ANGL⊙RV:	✠ZPECEN ON LEC Wt. 19·5.	Swegen.
294	✠CNVT ,, ANGLOR	✠TROTAN ON LEC Wt. 16·5.	Trotan.
295	,, ,, ANGLORV:	✠TROTA ∴ N ON LEI Wt. 16·0.	

Type xiv.

No.	Obverse.	Reverse.	Moneyer.
296	✠CNVT REX AN	✠ÆL·FSICE ⊙N L·EICE Wt. 15·5.	Ælfsige.
297	,, ,, ,,	,, ,, Wt. 17·2.	
298	,, RECX A	✠CE⊙LИ⊙Ð ⊙N LEIC Wt. 12·5.	Ceolnoð.
299	,, REX AN	✠C·R⊙C ⊙N L·EICE·S: Wt. 15·5.	Croc.

No.	Obverse.		Reverse.	Moneyer.
300	✠CNVT RECX AN		✠GOD·PINE ⊙N L·EIC : Wt. 17·8.	Godwine.
	Type xvii.			
301	✠CNVT· REX ANC		✠COLBEIIN ON LEIICEE Wt. 17·0.	Colbein.

LINCOLNE.
[Lincoln.]

Type viii.

No.	Obverse.		Reverse.	Moneyer.
302	✠CNVT REX ANCLORVM		✠ÆLFNⵔD MO LINC Wt. 15·0.	Ælfnoð.
303	„ „ ANCLORVI		✠ÆÐELMÆR MO LIN Wt. 16·2.	Æðelmær.
304	„ „ ANCLORV :		✠ÆÐELNOÐ MO LIN Wt. 21·4.	Æðelnoð.
305	„ „ ANCLORV		✠CODPINE M·O LINC Wt. 13·5.	Godwine.
306	„ „ „		✠CRIMCETEL MO LIN Wt. 16·0.	Grimcetel.
307	„ „ ANCLORVI		✠LEOFRIC MⵧO LINCO Wt. 22·1.	Leofric.
308	„ „ ANCLORV		✠LEOFPINE MⵧO LINCO Wt. 15·2.	Leofwine.
309	„ „ ANCLORVI		✠MATEÐAN MO LINC (Chipped.)	Mateðan?
310	„ „ ANC[LO]RV		✠OꟅFERÐ MO LIN . (Broken.)	Osferð.
311	„ „ ANCLORV : *Var.* Behind bust, cross pattée.		✠ꟅVMERLÐ MO LIN *Var.* Pellet in field. Wt. 15·7.	Sumerleða (Sumerleda, &c.).
312	„ „ ANCLORVI		✠ꟅVNEC : OD MO LIN Wt. 20·7.	Sunegod (= Godsune ?).

Type xii.

No.	Obverse.		Reverse.	Moneyer.
313	✠CNVT REX AN		✠VL·F ONLINCONLNC Wt. 15·7.	Ulf.

[Pl. XVIII. 15.]

No.	Obverse.	Reverse.	Moneyer.
		Type xiv.	
314	✠CNVT REX ΛN	✠ÆÐELMER ON LINC: Wt. 14·5.	Æðelmær.
315	,, ,, Λ	✠CVΣTIN ON LICOLNE Wt. 14·1.	Gustin (= Iustin).
316	✠CNVT R EX ΛNC:	✠IVSTECEN ON LINC: Wt. 17·6.	Iustegen.
317	✠CNVT·.· EX ΛNC:	✠IVSTEIN ⊙N LINCOL Wt. 17·0.	Iustein (= Iustegen).
318	✠CNVT REX ΛN	✠LEOFINC ⊙N LINC⊙ (Fragments.)	Leofinc.
319	✠CNVT·.· EX ΛNC:	✠LEOFINC MO LINCOL Wt. 18·0.	
320	✠·CNVT REX ΛN	✠LE⊙FPNE ⊙N LINCOL Wt. 14·3.	Leofwine.
321	✠CNVT REX ΛN	✠LEOÐΛN ON LINCVL Wt. 13·0.	Leoðan.
322	✠CNVT RECX Λ	✠LI⊙FNEN O L·ILC⊙LILE: Wt. 14·5.	Liofnen (= Lioflielm?).
323	✠CNVT R·.· EX ΛNC:	✠OΣFERÐ MO LINCOL Wt. 15·6.	Osferð.
324	✠CNVT·.· EX Λ..	✠[OSL]ΛC MO LINCOLN (Broken.)	Oslac?
325	✠CNVT·.· EX ΛNC	✠ΣVMERLIDΛ MO LII Wt. 17·6.	Sumerlida.
326	✠CNVT: EX ΛNC	✠SVMERL·IDΛ ON L·IN Wt. 17·0.	
327	✠CNVT R·.· EX ΛNC:	✠ΣVMERLIDΛ MO LINC Wt. 15·6.	
328	,, R EX ΛNC	✠PVLFPINE ON LINC Wt. 15·3.	Wulfwine.
		Type xvi.	
329	✠CNV T R·CX	✠ÆLFNOÐ ON LINC: Wt. 16·7.	Ælfnoð.
330	✠CNV ·T REX.	✠CNVT ON LINC⊙LN Wt. 17·0.	Cnut.

No.	Obverse.	Reverse.	Moneyer.
331	✠CNV T REC:	✠COLCRIM ON LIN Wt. 17·2.	Colgrim.
332	✠CИV T RECX	,, ,, Wt. 17·2.	
333	✠CNVT· ·RECX··	✠COLRIM ON LINCO Wt. 18·2.	
334	✠CNVT ·R·ECX:	✠CRINA ON LINCOL·: Wt. 17·8.	Crina (Crinan).
335	,, ·R·ECX:	✠CODRICSPOT ON LIN Wt. 17·2.	Godric and Swot (or Spot).
336	✠CNV ·T RECX:	✠LEOFPINE ON LIN Wt. 17·0.	Leofwine.
337	✠CNV ·T REX.	,, O LИCOL Wt. 18·0.	
338	✠CИ T REX	✠LEⵔPINE ONLИC· Wt. 12·5.	
339	✠CNVT RECX ··	✠L·IFINC ON LINCO Wt. 17·5.	Lifinc.
340	✠CNV ·RECX ··	,, ,, LINCOL·N Wt. 16·7.	
341	✠CNV T EC ··	✠MATĐAN ON LIN·· Wt. 16·9.	Matðan (cf. Mateðan).
342	✠CNVT ·RECX ··	✠ИAĐAN ON LINC·· Wt. 17·3.	
343	✠CNV ·T REX	✠OSLAC ON LINCO: Wt. 16·4.	Oslac.
344	✠CNVI· ·T RCX:	✠SPART ON LINCOL·· Wt. 15·6.	Swart.
345	✠CNVT ·RECX A	✠SPEARTA ON LINCO Wt. 17·2.	Swearta.
346	✠CNV ·T REC··	✠SPARTINC ⵔN LIN Wt. 17·0.	Swartinc, Sweartinc, &c.
347	✠CN T REC··	✠SPEARTINC ON LII Wt. 17·6.	
348	✠CNV ·T REC··	✠SPERTINC ON LIN Wt. 17·2.	
349	✠CNV ·T REC.	✠SPEARTBRAND LI Wt. 17·2.	Swearthrand or Swerte-braud.

No.	Obverse.	Reverse.	Moneyer.
350	✠CNV· ·T REX :	✠SPERTEBRAND ONLI Wt. 17·2.	
351	✠CNV ·T REC·	✠SPERTEBR ON L·I· Wt. 17·2.	
352	✠CИV T ·RECX	✠PEDDES ON LИИCOL Wt. 16·1.	Weddes.
353	✠CNVT ·RECX ··	✠PVL·BERN ON L·INC: Wt. 15·6.	Wulbern.
354	,, ,,	✠PVLFRIC ON LINCO Wt. 16·4.	Wulfric.
355	,, ·RECX :	✠PVLFPINE ON LIN Wt. 17·7.	Wulfwine.
	Type xvii.		
356	✠CNVT REX ∧N	✠OÐCRIИ OИ LIИCOL Wt. 17·9.	Oðgrim.

LUNDENE.
[London.]

Type viii.

No.	Obverse.	Reverse.	Moneyer.
357	✠CNVT REX ∧NCL	✠BORSTIC M LVND Wt. 21·3.	Borstig.
358	,, ,, ∧NCLOR	✠BRIHPOL·D LVN Wt. 21·5.	Brihtwold.
359	,, ,, ∧NCLOR :	✠BRVM∧N LVNDI Wt. 21·6.	Bruman.
360	,, ,, ∧NCLO·	✠EADMVND .⊙.ЛLVNDI Wt. 13·0.	Eadmund.
361	,, ,, ∧NCLORV	✠EADN⊙D. ⊙NLVNDEI Wt. 15·5.	Eadnoð.
362	,, ,, ∧NCLOR	✠EADPERD LVND Wt. 16·3.	Eadwerd.
363	,, ,, ,,	✠EADPIN O LVND Wt. 14·8.	Eadwine.
364	,, ,, ∧NCLO	✠EADPINE ONLVNDE· Wt. 11·6.	
365	,, RETX ∧NCLOR	✠EADPOLD O LVN Wt. 19·6.	Eadwold.

No	Obverse		Reverse	Moneyer
366	✠CNVT REX ANGLO		✠EADÐOLD N LVND Wt 15 9	
367	,,	,, ANGLOR	✠ELEÐINE ONLVND Wt 13 0	Elfwine
368	,,	,, ANGLOR	✠ELFPI ON LVNDENE· (Pierced)	
369	,,	,, ANGLO	✠FREÐI ON LVND Wt 21 8	Freði(c)
370	,,	,, ANGLOR	✠GODMAN ONLVNDE Wt 15 1	Godman
371	,,	,, ANGL	✠GODRIC ON LV NDE· Wt 16 2	Godric
372	,,	,, ANGLOR	✠LEOFSTAN LVN Wt 21 6	Leofstan
373	,,	,, ANGLORV	✠LIFINC MO LVN Wt 21 4	Lifinc
		[Pl XIX 1]		
374	,,	,, ANGL⊙	✠LIFINC ⊙N LVND Wt 13 4	
375	,,	,, ANGL⊙RVM	✠LIOFPINE ⊙ LVND (Oxidised)	Liofwine
376	,,	,, ANGLO	✠⊙SVLF ON LVND Wt 16 1	Osulf
377	,,	,, ANGLOR	✠OSVLF ON LVND Wt 16 5	
378	,,	,, ANGL⊙	✠OSVLF ON LVND Wt 11 3	
379	,,	,, ANGLORV	✠⊙SVLF ON LVNDEI Wt 15 0	
380	,,	,, ANGLOR	✠PVLFRIC LVND Wt 22 0	Wulfric
381	,	,, ANGLOR	✠PVLMIOD LVND Wt 20 2	Wulmiod (= (Wultnoð?)
		Type xiv		
382	✠CNVT R ECX A		✠ÆGELPERD ON LVN Wt 15 2	Ægelwerd
383	,	, ,,	✠ÆGELPINE ON LVN Wt 13 7	Ægelwine

No.	Obverse.	Reverse.	Moneyer.
384	✠CNV T: REEX ⴼ:	✠ÆCELPINE ON LVN: Wt. 13·0.	
385	✠CNVT R·EC·X ⴼ:	✠ÆCFR⳨E ON LVNDE: Wt. 13·5.	Ægfrye ?
386	✠CNVT RECX ⴷ	✠ÆLFCⴼR ON LVND Wt. 15·5.	Ælfgar.
387	✠CNV T RECX ⴷ:	„ „ LVNDN Wt. 16·1.	
388	✠CNV. REX ⴼNC	✠ÆL·FRIC ON LVNDE Wt. 17·2.	Ælfric.
389	✠CNVT. RECX ⴼ:	✠ÆLEPERD ON LVND: Wt. 16·0.	Ælfwerd.
390	✠C·NVT REX ⴼNC	✠ÆL·PER·D ON LVNDE Wt. 16·0.	
391	✠CNVT RECX ⴼ	✠ÆLEPIC ON LVNDE: Wt. 15·2.	Ælfwig.
392	✠CNVT: REX ⴼNC·	✠ÆL·FPIC: ON LVD·ENE Wt. 16·1.	
393	✠CNVT R·ECX.	✠ÆL·FPIIC ON LVND: Wt. 13·2.	
394	✠CNVT: RECX ⴼ	✠BRIHTMÆR ON LVN Wt. 15·6.	Brihtmær.
395	„ RECX ⴼ·.·	✠BRVNCⴼR ON LVN Wt. 15·6.	Brungar.
396	✠CNV T R·EX ⴷN·	✠BRVNINC ON LVN· (Chipped.)	Bruninc.
397	✠CNVT RECX ⴼ:	„ „ LVND Wt. 15·6.	
398	✠CNV: T REX ⴷN	✠EⴼDPOLⴐ ON LVND: Wt. 16·2.	Eadwold.
399	✠CNVT RECX ⴼ:	✠EDCⴼR ON LVND: Wt. 15·1.	Edgar.
400	„ „ ⴼ=	„ „ LVNDEN Wt. 15·5.	
401	„ „ ⴼN	✠EDRIC ON LVNDE·.· Wt. 16·0.	Edric.
402	„ R·ECX ⴷ	✠EDPNII ON LVND: Wt. 11·7.	Edwine.

No.	Obverse.	Reverse.	Moneyer.
403	✠CNVT·⸫ EX ANC	✠ETSICE ON LVNDEN Wt. 14·3.	Etsige (Edsige).
404	✠CNVT EX A·NCLⓄ	✠CⓄ·DDER·E ⓄN LVND Wt. 16·0.	God here (Godhere).
405	✠CNVT RECX A	✠CODERE ON LVDE: Wt. 15·6.	
406	,, ,, A	✠CODRIC ON LVNDEN Wt. 16·6.	Godric or Gotric.
407	✠EVNTN RIИTC	✠CODR·ICC ON· LVND: Wt. 13·4.	
408	✠CNVT REL·✠ A	✠GOTRIC ON LVNDИ Wt. 11·0.	
409	✠CИVTN: RIX A	,, ,, Wt. 12·8.	
410	✠CNV RECX AN	✠CODPINE ON LVND Wt. 16·9.	Godwine.
411	✠CNV·T: R·ECX A:	✠LEOFSTAN ON LVN Wt. 15·7.	Leofstan.
412	✠CNVT RECX·⸫	✠L·EOFSTAN ON LVND: Wt. 15·2.	
413	✠CCNⵎET R EX ANCL	✠LEⓄFIIⵏE ⓄN LVLD Wt. 13·2.	Leofwine.
414	✠CNVT RECX A	✠LEⓄFPINE ON LVN: Wt. 15·3.	
415	,, RECX·⸫	,, ⓄLVN· Wt. 17·1.	
416	✠·CNVT R·EX· A·⸫	,, ⓄN LVN Wt. 11·5.	
417	✠CNVT REX AN	✠L·EⓄFPⓄLD ⓄN LVN Wt. 14·9.	Leofwold.
418	,, RECX A	✠LIFINC: ON LVDDEN: Wt. 16·3.	Lifinc.
419	,, ,, A·⸫	✠LIⓄFSICI ⓄN LVND: Wt. 14·4.	Liofsige.
420	✠ⓄIИDCИ RCИC	✠S·IRⵍEIID ИCИ LNRИ Wt. 12·4.	Sirænd.
421	✠CNV T REX AN	✠STIꝊVL·F ON LVND: Wt. 14·8.	Stiðulf.

No.	Obverse.	Reverse.	Moneyer.
422	✠CNVT REX A	✠PYNSICE ON LVN Wt. 15·2.	Wynsige.
423	✠·CNV T R·E·C·X :	✠PYNSTAN ⊙N LVN : Wt. 15·3.	Wynstan.

HALFPENNY.

424	✠CNVT.	. . . . . .N LVNDN Wt. 7·5.	

Type xvi.

425	✠CNV T REXX :	✠ÆCELPINE ON LVN Wt. 16 6.	Ægelwine.
426	,, RECX	✠ÆLFPIC ON LVND Wt. 18·0.	Ælfwig.
427	✠CNV ·T ECX.	,, ,, LVND : Wt. 16·6.	
428	✠CNV· ·T REX :	✠ÆLPIINE ,, LVND. Wt. 11·3.	Ælfwine.
429	✠CNV T RECX	✠·ÆLPINE ON LVND : Wt. 16·0.	
430	,, ,,	✠BRIHTMÆR O LV Wt. 15·6.	Brihtmær.
431	✠CNV ·T RECX	✠BRVNCAR ON LV : Wt. 17·2.	Brungar or Bryngar.
432	✠CNV T RECX	✠BRVNCAR· ON LVN Wt. 15·7.	
433	,, R·ECX	✠BRYHCAR ON L Wt. 17·5.	
434	✠CИ· ΛT RCX :	✠BRVNMAN O LVИD Wt. 15·0.	Brunman.
435	✠CИ T RCCX	✠EADPⵙLD ON LV Wt. 17·2.	Eadwold.
436	✠CNV T RECX	✠EDRED ON LVND·.· Wt. 16·2.	Edred.
437	✠·CNV ·T RECX	,, ,, LVND Wt. 18·5.	
438	✠CNV T RECX	,, ,, LVNDE Wt. 17 0.	
439	,, REC :	✠EDPERD ,, ,, Vt. 17·8.	Edwerd.

No.	Obverse.	Reverse.	Moneyer.
440	✠CNV ·T R·EC:	✠EDPINE ON LVD: Wt. 14·5.	Edwine.
441	,, RECX	,, ,, LVND: Wt. 17·3.	
442	,, ,,	✠CODAMAN ON LVN Wt. 16·0.	Godaman, Godman, &c.
443	✠CNVT REC·X :	✠CODEMAN ON LV: Wt. 15·9.	
444	✠CNVT· ·RECX	✠CODMAN ON LVND Wt. 16·8.	
445	✠CNV T RECX	✠COMAN ON LVND: Wt. 17·1.	Goman (= Godman).
446	✠CNV T RECX	✠CODERE ON LVN Wt. 16·4.	Godere.
447	✠CNV ·T R·EC·	,, ,, LVND: Wt. 14·9.	
448	✠CNV T RECX	✠COERE ON LVND Wt. 15·5.	
449	✠CNV T REC ··	✠CODRIC ON ·LVN ·· Wt. 15·7.	Godric.
450	✠CN/· T RECX	,, ,, LVND Wt. 16·2.	
451	✠CNV T RC·X :	✠LEOFRED ON LVND Wt. 15·0.	Leofred.
452	✠CNV : T RE[CX]	,, O LVND: Wt. 16·5.	
453	✠CNV· ·T RECX	✠L·EOFPINE ON LVND Wt. 16·1.	Leofwine.
454	,, REC·	✠LEOFPOLD ON LV Wt. 17·6.	Leofwold.
455	✠CN/ T RECX	✠L·EOFPOLD ON LV: Wt. 16·0.	
456	✠CNV ·T R ·· E ··	✠SPAN MON LVND Wt. 17·1.	Swan ?
457	,, RECX	,, ON LVND·· Wt. 17·2.	
458	✠CNV T REC ··	,, ,, LVNDEN Wt. 18·2.	
459	✠CNVT ·REC ··	✠PVLFPINE ON LV: Wt. 17·7.	Wulfwine.

No.	Obverse.	Reverse.	Moneyer.
460	✠CNV [T] RECX	✠PYNSICE ON LVN Wt. 16·8.	Wynsige.
461	✠CNV· T RECX	✠PYNSICE ON LVND : Wt. 15·6.	
462	✠CNV T RECX	✠PYNSICIE ON LV Wt. 16·3.	
		Type xvii.	
463	✠CNVT· REX :	✠BRVNCAR ON LVND : Wt. 15·9.	Brungar.
464	✠CNVT R ECX ΛN :	,, ,, LVNDE : Wt. 15·7. [Pl. XIX. 2.]	
465	,, REC✠	✠PVLFRED ON LVNDEN Wt. 14·7.	Wulfred.
		Type xix.	
466	✠CNVTE : RER·X :	✠ÆLFRED ON LVNDE Wt. 17·0. [Pl. XIX. 3.]	Ælfred.
		Type xx.	
467	✠CNVT· RECX Λ	✠BRVNMΛN ON LVND Wt. 17·6. [Pl. XIX. 4.]	Brunman.
468	✠CNVT :RECX Λ.	✠PVLCΛR ON LVNDEN Wt. 15·3.	Wulgar (Wulfgar).
		MÆLDUNE.* [Maldon.]	
		Type viii.	
469	✠CNVT REX ΛNCLOR	✠C:ODPINE MEL Wt. 21·3.	Godwine.
		Type xiv.	
470	✠CNV T RECX :	✠CODERE ON MÆLD Wt. 16·2.	Godere.

* It is not possible to distinguish with certainty between the mints Maldon and Malmesbury
See *Introduction*.

No.	Obverse.	Reverse.	Moneyer.
	MEALMESBYRIG. [Malmesbury.]		
	Type viii.		
471	✠CNVT REX ANCL⊙ RVM· [Pl. XIX. 5.]	✠BREHSTAN ⊙N MEAL Wt. 22·7.	Brenstan (cf. Brunstan).
472	,, ,, ANCL⊙ RVM	✠BRVNIN ⊙N MEALE Wt. 20·0.	Bruning.
	NORÐPIC. [Norwich.]		
	Type xiv.		
473	✠CNVT R EX ANCL	✠RICNVL·F ON NORÐI Wt. 15·8.	Ricnulf.
	Type xvi.		
474	✠CNV ·R·CCX ·.·	✠MANA ON NORÐ: Wt. 17·2.	Mana.
475	✠CNVT ·RECX :	✠SIRIC ON NORÐ: Wt. 15·2.	Siric (=Sihtric ?).
	Type xvii.		
476	✠CNV T REX ANC	✠LEOFPINE ON NORPIC Wt. 17·3.	Leofwine.
477	✠CNV·.· RECX ANC	✠MANN ON NORRCÐ: Wt. 15·3.	Mann.
	OXENAFORD. [Oxford.]		
	Type viii.		
478	✠CNVT REX ANCL·O RVM	✠ÆÐELRIC· ON OXSN Wt. 17·3.	Æðelric.
479	,, ,, A·NCL⊙ RVM	✠BRIHTP·INE ⊙N ⊙XE· Wt. 22·1.	Brihtwine.

No.	Obverse.	Reverse.	Moneyer.
480	✠CNVT RE✠ ANCLO RVM	✠CODMAN ON OXN Wt. 17·5.	Godman.
481	✠CNVT R·EX ANCL⊙ RVM :	✠CODPINE ⊙N ⊙·XƧEN Wt. 20·9.	Godwine.
482	,, ,, ANCL⊙ RVM	✠PVLMÆR· ON ⊙XƧEN Wt. 21·0.	Wulmær (Wulfmær).
483	,, ,, A·NCLO RVM	,, ,, ⊙XƧENA Wt. 20·2.	

Type xiv.

No.	Obverse.	Reverse.	Moneyer.
484	✠CNVT R·EX ANC	✠ALFPOLD ⊙N ⊙CXE Wt. 17·5.	Alfwold.
485	✠CNV T RECX A :	✠CODPINE : ON ⊙CXA Wt. 16·0.	Godwine.

Type xvi.

No.	Obverse.	Reverse.	Moneyer.
486	✠CNV ·T RE :	✠ALFPOLD ON OC· Wt. 17·8.	Alfwold.
487	,, REX :	✠LIFINC ON OC✠ : Wt. 18·0.	Lifinc.
488	✠CN AT ЯAX	,, ,, OXEN· Wt. 17·7.	
489	✠CNVT : ·RECX :	✠LIIFINC ON OCXEN Wt. 17·7.	

Type xvii.

No.	Obverse.	Reverse.	Moneyer.
490	✠CNV T REX :	✠EDPIC ⊙N ⊙N ⊙CXEN Wt. 15·5.	Edwig.

RICYEBYRIG.

[Richborough ?]

Type viii.

No.	Obverse.	Reverse.	Moneyer.
491	✠INVT RNE✠ AICLORV	✠CNOFLN EN RIC Wt. 14·5.	Cnofcln ?

[Pl. XIX. 6.]

No.	Obverse.	Reverse.	Moneyer.

ROFECEASTER.
[Rochester.]

Type xvi.

492	✠CNV ·R·ECX·∴	✠CODPINE ON ROFE Wt. 14·8.	Godwine.

RUMENEA.
[Romney.]

Type viii.

493	✠CNVT REX ANCLOR [Pl. XIX. 7.]	✠ÆLFPIRD RVI Wt. 23·0.	Ælfwerd.
494	,, ,, ANCL	✠LEOFPINE ⊙NRVMN Wt. 14·0.	Leofwine.

Type xvi.

495	✠CNV T RECX :	✠L·EOFPINE ON RII Wt. 14·7.	Leofwine.

SCEFTESBYRIG.
[Shaftesbury.]

Type viii.

496	✠CNVT REX ANCLORV	✠ÆLRIC ON SCEA Wt. 12·6.	Ælric (Ælfric).
497	,, ,, ANCLORVM	✠ÆLPINE ⊙N SEFTE Wt. 23·5.	Ælwine (Ælfwine).
498	,, R·EX ANCLO RVM·∴	✠LVFA ON ÆSCFTES Wt. 18·8.	Lufa.

Type xiv.

499	✠CNVT RECX A	✠CODA ON SCEFTESB Wt. 15·5	Goda.

No	Obverse.	Reverse	Moneyer

Type xvi.

| 500 | ✠CNV T RECX | ✠LODA ON SCEFT Wt 162 | Goda |
| 501 | ✠CNVT R ECX. | „   ONN SCEFTE Wt 163 | |

SCROBESBYRIG
[Shrewsbury]

Type viii.

| 502 | ✠CNVT REX ANGLO | ✠CRINVT SCROBR Wt 178 | Crinna. |
| 503 | „   „   ANGLORV | ✠ETSIG ON SRO Wt 113 | Etsige (Edsige) |

Type xvi.

504	✠CNVT R ECX A	✠BRVNGAR ON SR O Wt 172	Brungar
505	✠CNV T RECX A	✠ETSILE ON S CR O Wt 170	Etsige (Edsige)
506	✠CNV T R ECX A	✠PVL FRED ON S R ⊙ Wt 172	Wulfred

[Pl XIX 8]

Type xvi

| 507 | ✠CNVT RECX | ✠PVLFMÆR ONN SCR Wt 166 | Wulfmær |

SEREBYRIG
[Salisbury]

Type xiv

| 508 | ✠CNV T R ECX | ✠PINSTAN ON SERE Wt 167 | Winstan |
| 509 | ✠CNVT   R EX A | ✠PINSTAN ON SER EB Wt 169 | |

No.	Obverse.	Reverse.	Moneyer.
	Type xvi.		
510	✠CNV T REX :	✠ÆLFRED ON SERE Wt. 15·3.	Ælfred.
511	✠CNV ·T REX :	✠CODPINE ON SER· Wt. 16·3.	Godwine.
512	✠CNVT RECX ∧N·.·	✠CODPINE ⊙N SERE : Wt. 11·5.	
	[Pl. XIX. 9.]		
513	✠CNV T RE·CX	✠COLDVS ON SER· Wt. 16·7.	Goldus.
	SIÐESTEBYRIG. [Sidbury.]		
	Type viii.		
514	✠CNVT REX ĀNCLO RVM	✠LE⊙FPINE ON· ΣIÐE Wt. 19·7.	Leofwine.
	[Pl. XIX. 10.]		
	SNOTINGAHAM. [Nottingham.]		
	Type viii.		
515	✠CNVT REX ∧VCLO RVM	✠BL∧CEMAN MO ΣNO Wt. 18·1.	Blaceman or Blacaman.
	Type xvi.		
516	✠CNV ·T RECX	✠BL·∧C∧M∧N ON SN Wt. 16·6.	Blacaman.
	[Pl. XIX. 11.]		
	STÆNIG. [Steyning.]		
	Type xvi.		
517	✠CNVT RECX	✠ECRIE ONN ΣTEC Wt. 13·0.	Ecrie (= Elric ?).
518	„ ·RECX	✠FRÐIPINE ⊙N STÆ : Wt. 17·3.	Friðiwine.

No.	Obverse.	Reverse.	Moneyer.
519	✠CNVT ·RECX	✠PIDNA ON ST÷ENII Wt. 13·7.	Widna (= Widia ?).

STANFORD.
[Stamford.]

Type viii.

520	✠CNVT REX ANCLO RVI	✠CODRIC MIO ꙅTA· Wt. 19·0.	Godric.
521	„ „ ANCLORV	✠CODPINE MO ꙅTA· Wt. 14·0.	Godwine.
522	„ „ ANCLORVM	„ MIO ꙅTA·· Wt. 21·7.	
523	„ „ „	✠ꙅPERT MIO ꙅTANF Wt. 21·9.	Swert.

Type xiv.

524	✠CNVT RECX A	✠ÆISMAN ⊙N STANF⊙ Wt. 15·6.	Æisman (= Æscman ?).
525	✠CNV T R·ECX A·	✠ÆÐEÐꙅTAN MO ꙅTAN Wt. 14·6.	Æðeðstan (= Æðelstan ?).
526	✠CNVT R·ECX A:	✠C⊙DPINE ⊙N STAN: Wt. 15·8.	Godwine.
527	„ „ „	✠LE⊙FP⊙LD ⊙N STAN Wt. 17·3.	Leofwold.

Type xvi.

528	✠CNVT ·RECX	✠EDPERD ON STANFO: Wt. 16·6.	Edwerd.
529	✠CNVT: ·REC·X:	✠CODPINE ONN STAN Wt. 17·5.	Godwine.
530	✠CNV ·T REC✠	··✠·L·EOFDÆII ON STA Wt. 15·8.	Leofdæn (= Leofdegn ?).
531	✠CNV ·T REX	✠LEOFEDEC ON STA Wt. 15·4.	Leofedeg (Leofdegn).
532	✠CNV T RECX	✠LEOFPINE ON STA Wt. 16·0.	Leofwine.
533	✠CNVT ·RECX·	✠LEOPINE ON STAN: Wt. 15·5.	

No.	Obverse.	Reverse.	Moneyer.
534	✠CNV· ·T REX :	✠NORVLF ON STAN Wt. 15·0.	Norulf.
535	✠CNV ·T REX :	„ „ STANF Wt. 16·0.	
536	✠CNV T RECX :	✠ÐVRSTAN ON STA Wt. 15·9.	Þurstan.
537	✠CNV· ·T REC :	„ „ ” Wt. 17·0.	
538	✠CNVT ·RECX.	✠ÐVSTAN ON STANFOR Wt. 17·0.	
539	✠CNV T REX :	✠ÐVRVLF ON STAN· Wt. 16·2.	Þurulf.

SUÐGEϷEORC.
[Southwark.]

Type xiv.

| 540 | ✠CNVT R EX ANC | ✠ÆLFCAR ⊙N ƩVÐC
Wt. 16·6. | Ælfgar. |

Type xvi.

| 541 | ✠CNV T RECX. | ✠ÆLPINE ON SVÐ
Wt. 16·5. | Ælwine
(Ælfwine). |
| 542 | ✠CNVT REC·X Λ : | ✠ÆωELPINE ON SV
Wt. 14·6. | Æðelwine. |

Type xvii.

| 543 | ✠CNV· T RECI | ✠ÆL·FRIC ONN
SVÐCC
Wt. 17·0. | Ælfric. |

TANTUNE.
[Taunton.]

Type viii.

| 544 | ✠CNVT REX ANCLOR | ✠EDRIC ⊙ TANTV
Wt. 13·2. | Edric. |

No.	Obverse.	Reverse.	Moneyer.

TOTANÆS.
[Totness.]

Type xiv.

| 545 | ✠·CNVT: RE·X Λ·N: | ✠ÆL·FPINE: ON TOTTΛ· Wt. 18·2. | Ælfwine. |
| 546 | ✠CN.V.T REX Λ·N | ✠SÆPIN·E O·N TOTΛ. Wt. 12·0. | Sæwine. |

ΡÆRINCΡIC.
[Warwick.]

Type viii.

| 547 | ✠CNVT REX ANCLORV | ✠LEOFPIN ·O ΡÆ·RINC Wt. 21·7. | Leofwine. |

Type xiv.

| 548 | ✠CNVT·· R·EX ΛN: | ✠LIFINC: ON ΡÆR·INC Wt. 17·4. | Lifinc. |

[Pl. XIX. 12.]

Type xvii.

| 549 | ✠CNVT R ECX A | ✠LEOPII ON ΡÆRIN: Wt. 16·1. | Leofwine. |

ΡECEDPORT.
[Watchet.]

Type xvi.

| 550 | ✠CNVT R·ECX ·∴ | ✠CODCIL·D ON PECED: Wt. 17·6. | Godcild. |

[Pl. XIX. 13.]

No.	Obverse.	Reverse.	Moneyer.

ꝥELINGAFORD.
[Wallingford.]

Type viii.

| 551 | ✠CNVT REX A·NCL·⊙ RVM | ✠COLEMA·N ⊙N ꝥELI Wt. 16·3. | Coleman. |

Type xvi.

552	✠CNV ·CNVT:	✠ÆLFꝥINE ON ꝥELII Wt. 17·5.	Ælfwine.
553	✠CNV: T RECX	,, ,, ꝥELIN Wt. 17·9.	
554	✠CNV· T R·EC·.·	✠EDꝥERD ON ꝥELIN Wt. 17·0.	Edwerd.
555	✠CN/ ·T REX	✠LEOFꝥINE ON ꝥELI Wt. 17·3.	Leofwine.

ꝥELMESFORD.
[Welmesford.]

Type viii.

| 556 | ✶CNVT REX ANCLORV | ✠MAN ON ꝥELMIAE Wt. 17·0. [Pl. XIX. 14.] | Man. |

ꝥIHRACEASTER or ꝥIGRACEASTER.
[Worcester.]

Type xiv.

| 557 | ✠CINVT R·EX AN | ✠ÆL·FꝥINE: ON PHRA·.· Wt. 16·9. | Ælfwine. |
| 558 | ✠·CNVT· REX A· | ✠·AR·NCTE·L· ⊙·N· PÐC: Wt. 13·2. | Arncetel. |

No.	Obverse.	Reverse.	Moneyer.
	PILTUNE. [Wilton.]		
	Type xvi.		
559	✠CNVT: T REC·X :	✠ÆL·FR·ED ⊙N PILTV Wt. 17·7.	Ælfred.
	PINCEASTRE. [Winchester.]		
	Type viii.		
560	✠CNVT R·EX ⱯNⅭL⊙ RVM	.✠ÆLFR·IC ⊙N PINCⱵTR Wt. 18·8.	Ælfric.
561	✠CNVT RE✠ ⱯNⅭL⊙ RVM ·.·	✠ÆLFⱵIⅭE ON PINCⱵT Wt. 22·2.	Ælfsige.
562	,, ,, ⱯNⅭLORV	✠ÆLFPINE ON PINCⱵT Wt. 13·4.	Ælfwine.
563	,, ,, ⱯNⅭLOR·	✠ⱯLFP⊙LD OᴎPI Wt. 17·0.	Alfwold.
564	,, ,, ⱯNⅭLORVM	✠BREHTNOⒹ ONPINCⱵT Wt. 20·0.	Brehtnoð (Brihtnoð).
565	,, R·EX ⱯNⅭ LⱰVM ·.·	✠LE⊙FⱵVNV ⊙N ÞINCⱵ Wt. 19·7.	Leofsunu.
566	,, REX ⱯNⅭL⊙ RVM :	✠⊙DⱯ ⊙N PINCⱵTR· Wt. 22·8.	Oda.
567	,, ,, ⱯNⅭLORV	✠ⱵIⅭⱯR ON PINCⱵR Wt. 17·2.	Sigar.
568	,, ,, ,,	✠ⱵIⅭODIⱯ ⊙NPINCⱵT Wt. 15·6.	Sigodia (= Sigboda?).
569	,, REX ⱯNⅭL⊙ RVM·	✠ⱵPRⱯFVL ⊙N P·INCⱵT Wt. 16·2.	Spraful.
570	,, R·EX ⱯNⅭLO RVM·	✠PIHTⱵIⅭE ⊙N PINCⱵT Wt. 19·7.	Wihtsige.
	Type xiv.		
571	✠CNVT RECX Ɐ ·.·	✠ÆLFⱵIⅭE ON PINCE: Wt. 15·5.	Ælfsige.

No.	Obverse.	Reverse.	Moneyer.
572	✠CNVT R EX ANGL·O	✠ÆL·FSTAN ☉N PINCE Wt. 17·7.	Ælfstan.
573	„ RECX Ⱥ:	✠ÆÐEƩTAN ☉N PIN Wt. 16·3.	Æðestan.
574	„ „ Ⱥ:	✠LADMÆR ON PINC: Wt. 15·4.	Ladmær.
575	✠CNV: R·EX AN	✠L·E☉FPINE ☉N PINC· Wt. 17·5.	Leofwine.
576	✠CNVT R: EX ANGL·	✠L·EOFPOL·D ON PINCEST Wt. 17·5.	Leofwold.
577	✠CNVT RECX Ⱥ·	✠PINE ON PNCESTR·⁖ Wt. 15·7.	Wine.
578	✠CNVT R EX ·Ⱥ·NC.	✠PINEE ON PINCEST Wt. 15·7.	
579	✠·CNVT REX AN	✠PVLBERN MO PINC: Wt. 15·0.	Wulbern.
580	✠CNVT ·⁖ EX ANC	„ „ Wt. 16·0.	
581	✠CNVT: EX ANGL·	✠PVLNOÐ: ON PINCES: Wt. 17·4.	Wulnoð (Wulfnoð).

Type xvi.

No.	Obverse.	Reverse.	Moneyer.
582	✠CNV T RECX	✠ÆCELRIC ON PINC· Wt. 17·9.	Ægelric.
583	✠CNVT RECX Ⱥ:	✠ÆLFEN ☉N PINC·⁖ Wt. 17·4.	Ælfen (= Ælfeh?).
584	„ „ „	„ „ PINCES: Wt. 18·3.	
585	✠CNVT RECX·⁖	✠ÆL·FSICE ☉N PINC· Wt. 18·3.	Ælfsige.
586	✠CNV T R·ECX ·Ⱥ:	✠CODPINE ON PINC·⁖ Wt. 17·3.	Godwine.
587	„ RECX	✠CODPINE CⱿS ON PI Wt. 17·3.	Godwine.*
588	„ „	✠LEODMÆR ON PIN Wt. 17·2.	Leodmær.
589	„ „	„ „ PINC Wt. 17·3.	

* Probably blundered for GODPINE ON PINCⱿS.

No.	Obverse.	Reverse.	Moneyer.
590	✠CNV· T RECX :	✠SPIL·EMAN ON PINC Wt. 17·8.	Swileman.
591	,, ,,	,, ,, PIN Wt. 17·8.	
592	✠CNV T RECX	✠PVLNOÐ ON PINC·.· Wt. 13·3.	Wulnoð (Wulfnoð).

Type xvii.

593	✠CNVT REX AN	✠CODEMAN ON PINCE: Wt. 15·1.	Godeman.
594	,, ,, A·M	✠CODMAN ON PINC· Wt. 15·5.	
595	,, : RECI	✠COPINE ON PINCE: Wt. 14·6.	Godwino.
596	,, REX AN	✠SPILEMANN ON PINC Wt. 15·0.	Swileman.

PINCELCUMB?
[Winchcombe.]

Type viii. *var. a.*

597	✠CNVT R·EX ANCL⊙R [Pl. XIX. 15.]	✠DROPA ON DINCL· Wt. 16·0.	Dropa or Drowa.

ÐEODFORD.
[Thetford.]

Type viii.

598	✠CNVT REX ANCLOⵝ	✠CODMAN M: ÐEO Wt. 18·9.	Godman.

Type xiv.

599	✠CNVT RECX A	✠ÆLFPI·NE ON Ð·E⊙: Wt. 17·7.	Ælfwine.
600	✠CNVT R EX ANCL :	✠ÆLFPINE : ON ÐEODF : Wt. 16·0.	

Type xvi.

601	✠CNVT ·RECX A	✠ÆL·FPIE ON ÐEOD : Wt. 16·0.	Ælfwine.

No.	Obverse.	Reverse.	Moneyer.
602	✠CNVT ·R·EC·X.	✠ÆLFPINE ON ÐEO Wt. 17·6.	
603	„ „	✠ΛLFPOLD ON ÐEO: Wt. 17·8.	Alfwold.
604	✠CNV·T ·RECX	✠BRVNSTΛN ON ÐE Wt. 17·0.	Brunstan.
605	„ „	„ ÐEOD: Wt. 17·5.	
606	✠CNVT ·REC·X:	✠RVNSTΛN ON ÐE Wt. 16·6.	
607	✠CNVT ·RECX·.·	✠PINEMΛN ON ÐE: Wt. 17·4.	Wineman.
		Type xvii.	
608	✠CNVT· RECX·.·	✠SÆCRIM ON ÐEOTFO: Wt. 17·9.	Sægrim.

UNCERTAIN MINTS.

No.	Obverse.	Reverse.	Moneyer.
		Type i.	
609	✠CNVT REX ΛNCLORV	✠ꝺIIIꙆOˉIIEIII ON ⌒COC Wt. 19·5.	Uncertain.
		Type viii.	
610	✠LИVT RE✠ ΛNCL·OR	✠NEOFNIORREN Wt. 13·8.	Uncertain.
		Type xiv.	
611	· · · ·· ···· Double struck on rev. of Type i.	✠EIIOEMÐIEX ON ИEÐVR: Wt. 19·4.	Uncertain.
612	✠CNVT REX ΛF	✠·L·O·D·Λ ON ·CⱳPΛ· (Chipped.)	Loda.
613	✠CNVT EX ΛNCL	✠:☉DΛ ON DNCENITI* *Var.* Two pellets in field. Wt. 13·2.	Oda.
		Type xvi.	
614	✠CNI· TI RCX N	✠L·EИOFPИCNVIEP Wt. 14·3.	Uncertain.

* Winchester?

No.	Obverse.	Reverse.	Moneyer.
	Type xvii.		
615	✠CNVT∴ RECF꞉	✠CNYTEL ON CNET∴* Wt. 17·0.	Cnytel (=Cytel).
616	✠CNVT REX AN	✠PVLFRIC ON †ECORNC∴ Wt. 13·9.	Wulfric.
	HALFPENNY.		
	Type xvi.		
617	✠ . . . . ·R·ECX∴	✠/EÐESTA . .. . Wt. 9·1.	Æðestan.

* Canterbury? † York?

HAROLD I.

SUCC A D 1035, DIED A D 1040

Moneyers

Æте (Norw)
Ægelwin, Ægelmer, &c (Bath, Thetf, York)
Ægelman (Bedf)
Ægelric (Glouc, Oxf, Shaft, Winchest)
Ægelwig (Oxf)
Ægelwine (Brist, Crickl, Ilch, Lanc, Worc, York)
Ælbricht (Ipsw)
Ælfe [= Ælfere] (York)
Ælfere (Colch, Roch, York)
Ælfgar (Barda)
Ælfin, see Ælfwine
Ælfnoð (Lanc, Lond)
Ælfred (Cant, Lond, Salisb)
Ælfric or Ælric (Cant, Chich, Dorch, Glouc, Lond, Lydf, Norw, Staff, Wallingf, Winchest)
Ælfsige (Chest, Glouc)
Ælfstan (Walt, Winchest)
Ælfwald or Ælfwold (Lond, Norw, Thetf)
Ælfward or Ælfwerd (Brist, Hast, Lanc, Norw, Winchest)
Ælfwi [= Ælfwig or Ælfwine] (Cambr)
Ælfwig or Elwig (Bath, Cambr, Oxf, Thetf, Wallingf, Winchest)
Ælfwine, Ælwine, Allwine, &c (Chest, Crickl, Derby, Lond, Lydf, Norw, Oxf, Southamp, Stamf, Thetf, Wallingf, Winchest, York)
Ælfwold, see Ælfwald
Ællman [= Ægelman?] (Bedf)
Ælmer [= Ægelmer?] (Bath, Oxf)
Ælnoð, see Ælfnoð
Ælric, see Ælfric
Elwig, see Ælfwig
Elwine, see Ælfwine
Æston (Winchest)
Æðelwin (Lond, York)
Æll-, see Ælf-
Alwing [= Alf-win?] (Tamw)
Ared, Areyl, or Irned [= Arncetel?] (Stamf, York)
Arneel (Stamf, York)
Asterð (Lanc)
Biörn or Biörn (York)

Blacaman (Nott)
Blacan [= Blacaman?] (Derby)
Boga (Dover, Norw)
Brid or Bridd (Hast)
Brihtmær, Brihtmær, &c (Lond)
Brihtred (Cant)
Brihtric (Creuk)
Brihtwine (Buck)
Brun (Lond)
Bruncar or Brungar (Lond)
Brunman (Lond)
Brunstan (Thetf, Winchest)
Brunwine, Brunwin, or Brunwine (Stamf, Wallingf)
Cæren m (Lond)
Cerla (Exet)
Caldewine (Cant)
Cnve (Winchest)
Cille (Chest)
Cineweg (Lond)
Cinewine (Hast)
Cinewold (Lond)
Cinstan, see Cunstan
Coleman (Oxf)
Coldsige or Coltsige, see Goldsige
Colgrim (Lond)
Conrim (Lanc)
Corf, Corfl, or Corrf (Lond)
Grucan [= Grucan ?] (York)
Cunstan or Cnnstan (Dover)
Cyldewine, see Gyldewine
Cytel (Cant)
Deorsig, Deorsie, &c (Hert)
Dudline [= Dudling] (Lond)
Dufacan [= Duracan ?] (York)
Duracan (York)
Eadwold, Edwald, or Edwold (Lond)
Edmer (Exet, Romn)
Edred (Lond)
Edric, Edrice, &c (Hythe, Lanc, Lond, Thett)
Edsine [= Edsige ?] (Exet)
Edwacer (Cambr)
Edwald, see Eadwold
Edwald and Pealda (Lond)
Edward, Edwerd, &c (Lewes, Lond, Wallingf)
Edwig, Edwuig, &c (Lond, Oxf)

Edwine, *Eduene*, &c (Dover, *Hast*, *Lewes*, *Lond*, Winchest)
Edwold, see *Eadwold*
Egelewne, see *Ægelwine*
Elbriht (Ipsw)
Elewig [= Ælfwig] (*Heref*)
Elewine, see Ælfwine
Elf -, see Ælf -
Eonred (Dorch)
Eowine [= *Eofwine*?] (*Lond*)
Erncytel [= *Arncutel*?] (*York*)
Erngrim or *Ergrim* (*York*)
Ernui (*Heref*)
Estan, see Æstan
Etsige [= *Eadsige*] (Dover)
Eðel -, see Æðel -
Fareman (*Lond*)
Fargrim or *Fargrim* (Stamf)
Friðewine (Steyn)
Gdacris or *Gdlacris* [= *Gillechrist*?] (*Chest*)
God, *Goda*, &c (Chich, Loud, Warw)
Godaman, *Godman*, or *Godmon* (*Hert*, *Lond*, *Malm*, *Winchest*, *York*)
Godan (*Wilt*)
Godedild (*Watch*)
Godinc or *Godinc*, see Godwine
Godric, *Goric*, &c (*Chich*, Colch, *Derby*, Glouc, *Rch*, *Linc*, *Lond*, Staml)
Goldsige, see Goldsige
Godsn, see Goldsige
Godwine, &c, see Godwine
Godwine, *Gowine*, &c (Dorch, Lewes, Lond, Oxf, Roch, *Salisb*, *Stamf*, *Winchest*, *York*)
Godwine and Caw (*Winchest*)
Godwine and Stener (*Lond*)
Godwine and Wili (*Winchest*)
Goldsige, *Goltsige*, &c (*Linc*, Lond, *Wilt*)
Gonwine [= Godwine ?] (Dorch)
Goric, see Godric
Gotedild, see *Godedild*
Grimulf (*York*)
Gyldewine (Cant, *Chest*)
Herra (Exet)
Harðacnut or *Harðecnut* (*Linc*)
Hunna (*Exet*, *Malm*)
Hwataman (Dorch)
Huhl (*Lond*)
Iscula (*York*)
Ladimer or *Lodiman* (Winchest)
Lefdic [= *Leofðegn*?] (*Linc*)
Lefenoð, see *Leofnoð*
Lef -, see also *Leof -*
Leofdai, *Lefedei*, &c (Stamf)
Leofmar or *Leomar* (Jedb)
Leofnoð, *Lefenoð*, &c (Cant, *Chest*, *Glouc*, *Heref*, *Linc*)
Leofred, *Lifred*, &c (*Lond*)

Leofric or Lefric (*Chich*, *Linc*, Lond, *Southu*, Stamf)
Leofstan, Lefstan, Leostan, &c (Cant, Lond, *Shaft*, *Shrews*, *Winchest*, *Wore*)
Leofwi [= Leofwig or Leofwine] (*Lond*)
Leofwig (Chest, *Linc*, *Waric*)
Leofwine, Leowine, &c (*Bedf*, Brist, *Buck*, Cant, *Chest*, Exet, *Linc*, Lond, Norw, Oxf, *Shrews*, *Southamp*, Thetf, *Wallingf*, *Winchest*)
Leofðegen (Bedf, *Malm*)
Liedrafen ? (*Linc*)
Lifinc, Living, *Lifinc*, &c (Cant, *Hast*, *Ipsw*, *Linc*, Lond, *Oxf*, *Southu*, *Stamf*, Wilt, *Winchest*)
Lifred, see Leofred
Lodimar, see Ladimer
Lufinc [= *Leofinc*?] (*Winchest*, *Wore*)
Mana or *Manni* (*Linc*, Norw)
Manbof (Exet)
Norðmn [= *Norðman*?] (*Linc*)
Norðman (Lewes)
Ordric (*Heref*)
Orferð (*Linc*)
Oslac (*Linc*)
Osmund (*Linc*)
Ouðncar [= *Ouðencarl*?] (Lond)
Oðbern or *Oðeran* [= *Oðbeorn*?] (*Linc*)
Oðgrim, *Oðgrim*, *Oðrim*, &c (*Linc*)
Oðin or *Oðina* (York)
Pororic, see *Wororic*
Rader ? (Lond)
Rincult (Thetf)
Ranulf [= *Rincolf*?] (Norw)
Sædman (*Heref*)
Saxgrim (Nott)
Seuerd (*Winchest*)
Sæwine (Brist, *Chest*)
Scula (York)
Snel, *Smel*, or *Snell* (*Chest*)
Stancr (*Lond*)
Stircenre (Cambr)
Stirred (*York*)
Sumerlad, *Sumerleda*, *Sumerlyd*, &c. (*Chest*, *Linc*)
Sumeilr [= *Sumerleda*?] (*Chest*)
Sumlad ? (*Cant*)
Sunrild, &c [= *Sumerleda*?] (*Linc*)
Swafa (*Linc*)
Swart or *Swert* (Stamf, York)
Swartebrand, *Swartefrand*, *Swartebrand*, &c (*Linc*)
Swartinc, *Swertinc*, &c (*Chest*, *Derby*, *Linc*, Thetf, *Wallingf*)
Swegen (*Chest*, *York*)
Swðeman (*Winchest*)
Swola or *Swole* (*Bedf*)

Swraculf [=Swartculf?] (Winchest.).
Ucede or Ueder (York).
Ulfcil or Ulftil (Lond.).
Wadlos or Waxlos (Linc.).
Waedell or Wedel (Bath).
Walrafen (Linc.).
Walfet (Linc.).
Wamanea (Lond.).
Wertine [=Swertine?] (Derby).
Widfara (Ipsw.).
Widia, Wudia, &c. (Lond., Winchest.).
Widig or Widige (Lond., Winchest.).
Wilgrim (Stamf.).
Winedwig (Cant.).
Winred (Cant.).
Winstan (Salisb.).
Witlos [=Wadlos?] (Linc.).
Wiðirinne or Wiðering (York).
Wororic (Linc.).
Wudia, see Widia.
Wulborn, Wulborn, &c. (Linc.).
Wulceet, see Wulfget.
Wulerine [=Wulfwine?] (York).
Wulfeh (Derby).
Wulfine, see Wulfwine.
Wulfget or Wulceet (Linc., Shrews.).
Wulfred (Shrews.).
Wulfric (Linc., Shaft.).
Wulfwerd (Lond.).

Walfwi or Wulfwis [=Wulfwig or Wulfwine] (Cant., Hunt., Lond.).
Wulfwine, Wulfwine, Wulwine, &c. (Brist., Cumbr., Cant., Chest., Colch., Hunt., Lond., Mald., Wallingf., York).
Wulgar [=Wulfgar] (Lond.).
Wulnoð [=Wulfnoð] (Brist., Cant., Chest., Exet., Leic., Romn., Winchest.).
Wulsie, Wulsige, &c. (Heref., Lond.).
Wulstan [=Wulfstan] (Cant., Lond., Leic., "Worime").
Wulward [=Wulfward] (Glouc.).
Wulwig [=Wulfwig] (Cant.).
Wulwii [=Wulfwig or Wulfwine] (Hunt., Lond.).
Wulwine, see Wulfwine.
Wunsige [=Wynsige] (Lond.).
Wydia, see Widia.
Wynsie, Wynsig, Wynsige, &c. (Lond.).
Wynsige and Wamanea (Lond.).
Þealda (Lond.).
Þerman (Lond.).
Þudinei? (Lond.).
Þurcet[l] (Stamf.).
Þurgrim (York).
Þurstan (Linc., Stamf.).
Þurulf (Stamf.).

DESCRIPTION OF TYPES.

Obverse.	Reverse.

Type i.

Bust l., diademed. Around, inscription divided by bust: outer circle.	Cross composed of four ovals, united at their bases by two circles enclosing pellet. Around, inscription: outer circle.

[Cf. Pl. XX. 1.]

Type i. var. a.

Same: but of rude work.	Similar; inscription between two circles.

[Hild., Pl. 9, Type A. var. a.]

Obverse.	Reverse.

Type ii.

Bust l., *diademed. Around, inscription divided by bust: outer circle.*

Long cross voided; in centre, circle enclosing pellet: in angles, P A C X. *Around, inscription: outer circle.*

[Hild., Pl. 10, *Type* E.]

Type iii.

Bust l., diademed. Around, inscription divided by bust: outer circle.

Short cross voided; in centre, circle enclosing pellet. Around, inscription between two circles.

[See No. 61, p. 313.]

Type iii. var. a.

Similar: in front of bust, sceptre. | Same.

[See No. 65, p. 314.]

Type iv.

Bust l., *diademed. Around, inscription divided by bust: outer circle.*

On short cross voided, quadrilateral ornament with pellet at each angle and in centre. Around, inscription between two circles.

[Hild., Pl. 10, *Type* D.]

Type iv. var. a.

Similar: bust in armour: in front, shield and sceptre. | *Same.*

[Hild., Pl. 10, *Type* D. *var. a.*]

Obverse.	Reverse.

Type v.

| Bust l., diademed, in armour; in front, shield and sceptre. Around, inscription divided by bust: outer circle. | Long cross voided, limbs united at their bases by circle, enclosing pellet: in each angle, trefoil of three pellets. Around, inscription: outer circle. |

[Cf. Pl. XX. 4.]

Type v. var a.

| Similar: bust r. | Same. |

[Montagu Coll.]

Type v. var. b.

| Similar: bust l. | Similar; in first angle of cross, trefoil of three pellets; in second and third, fleur-de-lis between two pellets; and in fourth, fleur-de-lis. |

[Cf. Pl. XX. 10.]

Type v. var. c.

| Same. | Similar: in each angle of cross, fleur-de-lis between two pellets. |

[Cf. Pl. XX. 2.]

Type vi.

| Bust l., helmeted, in armour: in front, shield and sceptre. Around, inscription divided by bust: outer circle. | Long cross voided; in centre, circle enclosing pellet: in each angle, fleur-de-lis between two pellets. Around, inscription: double outer circle. |

[Hild., Pl. 9, Type B. var. c.]

DESCRIPTION OF COINS.

No.	Obverse.	Reverse.	Moneyer.
	BAÐAN. [Bath.]		
	Type i.		
1	✠H·A·RO LD REX.	✠PÆDELL ON BAÐAN (Pierced.)	Wædell.
	[Pl. XX. 1.]		
	Type v. *var. c.*		
2	✠HAR OLD REC *Var.* Two pellets above head.	✠PÆDEL· ONN BA! Wt. 16·2.	Wædell.
	BEDEFORD. [Bedford.]		
	Type i.		
3	✠HAR· OLD REX	✠L·EOFÐECEN ONBED Wt. 17·0.	Leofðegen.
	Type v. *var. c.*		
4	✠HARO LD RECX	✠ÆLLMAN ON BED Wt. 18·5.	Ællman.
	[Pl. XX. 2.]		
	BRICGSTOP. [Bristol.]		
	Type v. *var. c.*		
5	✠ИLO D RCE✠	✠ÆLFPERD ONN BRI: Wt. 14·3.	Ælfwerd.
6	✠HAR OLD RE:	✠ÆLFPER·D ON BRIC Wt. 16·3.	
7	✠HARO LD RECX	✠L·EOFPINE ON BRIE Wt. 17·0.	Leofwine.
8	✠HAR: OLD REC:	✠SÆPINE ON BRIC: Wt. 17·0.	Sæwine.

No.	Obverse.	Reverse.	Moneyer.
9	✠HAR. OLD REC	✠DVLNOÐ ⊙N BRIC Wt. 15·0.	Wulnoð.
10	✠HAR OLD REC··	✠PVLPINE O BRIC Wt. 16·5.	Wulwine (Wulfwine).

CÆNTPARABYRIG.
[Canterbury.]

Type i.

| 11 | ✠HAR. OLD R : | ✠LEFENÆÐ ⊙NCAN
 Wt. 17·3. | Lefenað (=Leofnoð). |

Type v. *var. c.*

12	✠HИR : OLD RE	✠ÆLFRED ONO CEN Wt. 14·0.	Ælfred.
13	✠HÃRO. LD RECX.	✠CYLDEPINE O CE Wt. 16·4.	Gyldewine.
14	✠HAR LD REC	" " CE : Wt. 13·6.	
15	✠HAR ⊙LD RE	✠LEFSTAN O CEN (Broken.)	Lefstan.

CICESTRIE.
[Chichester.]

Type i.

| 16 | ✠HAR OVD R | ✠ÆLFRIC ON CICES
 Wt. 17·8. | Ælfric. |

COLENCEASTRE.
[Colchester.]

Type v. *var. c.*

| 17 | ✠HAR : ·OLD RE : | ✠CORIC ON CONC
 Wt. 15·3. | Goric (Godric). |
| 18 | ✠HAR·OL D RECX : | ✠PVLPINE ON COL·
 Wt. 13·8. | Wulwine (Wulfwine). |

No.	Obverse.	Reverse.	Moneyer.
	DOFERAN. [Dover.]		
	Type i.		
19	✠HⱯR OL·D R :	✠EDPINE ⊙NN DOFR·· Wt. 14·0.	Edwine.
	Type v. *var. c.*		
20	✠HⱯROL D REC :	✠CVИSTⱯИ ⊙И DOF : Wt. 14·7.	Cunstan.
	HALFPENNY.		
21	.... OLD RCE :	. . . . . . N DOFRⱯ : Wt. 7·5.	
	ECXECEASTER, ETC. [Exeter.]		
	Type i.		
22	✠HⱯR·O· L·D ·R·CX :	✠HÆRRⱯ ⊙N ECXECC Wt. 16·4.	Hærra.
	Type v. *var. c.*		
23	✠HⱯR OLD REX	✠EDⱖER ONECXC Wt. 16·5.	Edmær.
24	✠HⲠ⊙ LOD ᒋEC	L·EOFDINE ⊙N E✠ Wt. 13·8.	Leofwine.
	EOFERPIC. [York.]		
	Type i.		
25	✠HⱯRO : LD REX.	✠DVFⱯCⱯN ON EOFER Wt. 17·5.	Dufacan (= Duracan?).
26	✠H·ⱯR· OLD R·	✠SPECEN ⊙N EOFEᒋ Wt. 16·8.	Swegen.
27	✠HⱯR OLD RE	✠PIÐIRPINNE ON EO : Wt. 16·0.	Wiðirwinne (cf Wiðering)

[Pl. XX. 3.]

No	Obverse	Reverse	Moneyer

Type v

| 28 | ✠HAR OLD REC | ✠ÆL FERE ON EOE
Wt 166 | Ælfere. |
| 29 | ✠HAR·. OLD RÆ | ✠SP ECLII ON EOE
Wt 118 | Swegen? |

[Pl XX 4]

| 30 | ✠HAR OLD REX | ✠VCEDE ONEOFE
Wt 162 | Ucede. |
| 31 | ✠HAR OLD RECX | ✠PIIÐERINC ONEO
Wt 177 | Wiðering |

Type v var c

32	✠HAR OLD REC	✠OÐIN ON EOFER Wt 174	Oðin
33	✠HAR O· LD REC✠	✠SCVLA O NN EOFER Wt 178	Scula
34	✠NARO LD RE✠	✠SCVLA O N COPCN Wt 133	Scula
35	✠HAR OLD REC	✠ÐVRCRIM ON EO Wt 178	Þurgrim

GIPESPIC
[Ipswich]

Type v var c

| 36 | ✠HAROL D RECX | ✠ELBRIHT ON CII
Wt 154 | Elbriht. |
| 37 | ✠HARO L D REX | PIDFARA ON CIP
Wt 177 | Widfara. |

[Pl XX 5]

GRANTEBRYCGE
[Cambridge]

Type i

| 38 | ✠HAR OL D RECX | ✠EDPA CER ON
CRANT
Wt 170 | Edwacer |

No.	Obverse.	Reverse.	Moneyer.
	Type v. *var. c.*		
39	✠HARO LD RECX	✠ÆLFPIC ON CːRAN Wt. 17·6.	Ælfwig.
		HÆSTINGA. [Hastings.]	
	Type i.		
40	✠HARO LD REX	✠ÆL·FPERD ON HÆST Wt. 17·4. [Pl. XX. 6.]	Ælfwerd.
		HAMTUNE. [Southampton.]	
	Type i.		
41	✠HAROL D RECX	✠ÆL·FPINE ON HAMTVː· Wt. 17·8.	Ælfwine.
		LÆPES. [Lewes.]	
	Type v. *var. c.*		
42	✠HARO LD R·ECX	✠COPINE ON LÆPE Wt. 17·4.	Gowine (Godwine).
		LEHERCEASTER. [Leicester.]	
	Type v.		
43	✠HAR·O LD REX ː	✠PVLSTAN ON LEH Wt. 14·5.	Wulstan (Wulfstan)

No.	Obverse.	Reverse.	Moneyer.

LEIGECEASTER, Etc.
[Chester.]

Type i.

44	✠HAR OLD REX	✠ÆLFSIIGE ON LEIGE : Wt. 16·5.	Ælfsige.
45	✠HAR· OLD REX	✠ELEPINE ON L·EIGE·· Wt. 17·1.	Elwine (Ælfwine).

[Pl. XX. 7.]

46	✠HAR DLD REX	✠LEOFPIG ON LEGIEE Wt. 17·2.	Leofwig.

Type v. *var. c.*

47	✠HAR OLD REG	✠LEOFNOĐ ON LEIG Wt. 17·4.	Leofnoð.
48	,, ,, REX	✠PVLPNE : ON LEIOG Wt. 14·8.	Wulwine (Wulfwine).

LINCOLNE.
[Lincoln.]

Type i.

49	✠HAR OLD REX	✠GONRIH ON LINGOL Wt. 14·0.	Conrim.
50	✠HAR· OLD REX	✠SPAFA ON LINGOLN : Wt. 17·7.	Swafa.

[Pl. XX. 8.]

Type v. *var. c.*

51	✠HARO LD REGX	✠GODRIG ON LIN Wt. 17·0.	Godric.
52	✠HAR OLD RG	✠LIADRAFEN LING Wt. 15·5.	Liadrafen ?
53	✠HAR· OLD R·EX.	✠SPARTING O LING Wt. 15·7.	Swartinc.

No.	Obverse.	Reverse.	Moneyer.
54	✠HA·DO D RCX :	✠PORORIE O : LIN⊏ Wt. 15·0.	Wororie ?
55	✠HARD : LD REX	✠PVLBRN ⊙ LIN⊏ : Wt. 16·6.	Wulborn.

LUNDENE.
[London.]

Type i.

No.	Obverse.	Reverse.	Moneyer.
56	✠H·ⲦⲄ OLD RE	✠ÆL·FNOÐ ON LVND : Wt. 15·2.	Ælfnoð.
57	✠HARO· LD REX.	✠⊏ÆRENAN ON LVD. Wt. 16·2.	Cærenan.
58	✠HAR OL·D RE	✠⊏ODPINE ON LVNDE : Wt. 15·7.	Godwine.
59	✠HⲦR OLD ,,	✠⊏OLDSI⊏E ON LVN Wt. 15·8.	Goldsige.
60	✠HAR· OLD REX :	✠L·EOFPINE ON LVNDE : Wt. 17·6.	Leofwine.

[Pl. XX. 9.]

No.	Obverse.	Reverse.	Moneyer.
61	✠HARO· LD REX	✠L·EORI⊏ ON LVND·· Wt. 17·2.	Leofric.
62	✠HAR· OLD REX	✠P.V.L·FPINE ON L·VN Wt. 17·6.	Wulfwine.
63	✠HAR OLD ,,	✠PVL⊏·ⲦR ON L·VNDE Wt. 17·6.	Wulgar.

Type iii.

No.	Obverse.	Reverse.	Moneyer.
64	✠NAREII ✠RE	✠⊙VⱵN⊏AR ⊙N LV Wt. 20·0.	Ouðncar (= Ouðcncarl?).

No.	Obverse.	Reverse.	Moneyer.
	Type iii. *var. a.*		
65	✠HAR : ·OLD REΓX	✠LEIFINE OII LVND Wt. 11·5.	Lifing.
	Type v. *var. b.*		
66	✠HARO LD REC··	✠BRIHTMÆR O LV Wt. 15·5.	Brihtmær.
	[Pl. XX. 10.]		
	Type v. *var. c.*		
67	✠HAR OLD REC	✠BRVNCAR ON LV Wt. 13·6.	Bruncar or Brungar.
68	,, ,, ,,	VꓧꓛⱯ NO ꓤAꓒNVꓤB✠ Wt. 16·3.	
69	✠HAR·O· LD RECX	✠CORFF ONN : LVN Wt. 14·0.	Corff.
70	✠HARO : LD ,,	✠EDPOLD ON LVN Wt. 17·2.	Edwold.
71	✠HAR : OLD REX	,, ,, Wt. 15·5.	
72	✠ꓴARO L·D RECX	✠COD ON LVNDE : Wt. 11·5.	God.
73	✠HAR· OLD RE :	✠CODSIIE ON LVN Wt. 11·5.	Godsige (Goldsige).
74	✠HAR OLD REC··	✠CODPINE ON LVN Wt. 16·8.	Godwine.
75	,, ,, REC	✠LEOORED ON LVD : Wt. 12·7.	Leofred or Lifred.
76	,, ,, REC :	✠LIFRED ONN LVN Wt. 16·7.	
	[Pl. XX. 11.]		
77	✠HARO ·LD R·ECX	✠LEOFR·IC O : LVN Wt. 17·3.	Leofric.

No	Obverse	Reverse	Moneyer
78	✠HИR OLD RE	✠LEOFRIC ON LVN Wt 135	
79	✠HAR OLD REC	✠LEOFSTAN ON LVN Wt 160	Leofstan
80	✠NARO LD REX	✠PVNSICE ON L VИD (Partly retrograde and irregular) Wt 119	Wunsige

HALFPENNY

81	✠HAR RECX	✠RA[DER ON L]VND Wt 81	Rader ?

NORÐPIC

[Norwich]

Type i

82	✠HAR OLD REX	✠ÆLFFPALD ON NOR Wt 176	Ælfwald or Ælfwold
83	✠HARO LD RECX	✠ÆL FPOL D O NORÐPI Wt 160	

Type v var c

84	✠HAR OLD REC	✠LEOFPINE O ИORÐ Wt 147	Leofwine
85	✠HARO LD RCX	✠MA IIIA ON NORÐ Wt 117	Manna

OXENAFORD

[Oxford]

Type v var c

86	✠HARO D REX A	✠LEOFPINE ON O (Pierced)	Leofwine

ROFECEASTER

[Rochester]

Type v var c

87	✠HAR OLD REC	✠CODPIIN ⊙N R OC Wt 127	Godwine

No	Obverse	Reverse	Moneyer.

SCROBESBYRIG
[Shrewsbury]

Type v var c

| 88 | ✠HAROLD REX· | ✠PVFCT ON SEOB Wt 165 | Wulfget |

SNOTINGAHAM
[Nottingham]

Type v var c

| 89 | ✠HARLD REX | ✠BLACANAN O SN Wt 130 | Blacaman |

STANFORD.
[Stamford]

Type 1

| 90 | ✠HAROLD RE | ✠BRVNPINE ON STA Wt 124 | Brunwine |
| 91 | ✠HAROLD RE ✠. | ✠LEOFRIC ON STANF Wt 165 | Leofric |

Type v var c

| 92 | ✠HAROLD REX | ✠CODRIIC ON STA Wt 178 [Pl XX 12] | Godric |

PÆRINCPIC.
[Warwick]

Type 1

| 93 | ✠HAROLD REX | ✠CODD ON PÆRINCP Wt 163 | God |

No.	Obverse.	Reverse.	Moneyer.

PELINGAFORD.
[Wallingford.]

Type i.

| 94 | ✠HᴬROL D RECX | ✠ᴁL·PIC ⊙NN PEL·INCᴀ Wt. 16·3. [Pl. XX. 13.] | Ælfwig. |

Type v.

| 95 | ✠HᴬROL· D RECX ᴀ | ✠ᴁLPINE ON PELII Wt. 15·5. | Ælfwine. |

Type v. *var. c.*

| 96 | ✠HAR·.· OLD REC | ✠LEOFPI:NE O : PEL Wt. 15·7. | Leofwine. |

PILTUNE.
[Wilton.]

Type v.

| 97 | ✠NᴬRO LD RECX | ✠LIFINC ONN PILT Wt. 15·7. | Lifinc. |

PINCEASTRE.
[Winchester.]

Type i.

98	✠HARO· LD REX	✠ᴁCELRIC ON PICE· Wt. 16·0.	Ægelric.
99	✠NᴬROL D REX	✠BRVNSTᴀN ON PIN :· Wt. 16·6.	Brunstan.
100	✠HᴬRO LD. RCX	✠PVDIᴀ ON PINCEST·.· Wt. 17·2.	Wudin (Widin).

No.	Obverse.	Reverse.	Moneyer.

Type v. *var. c.*

101	✠HARO LD REX :	✠ALPINE ON PINC : Wt. 16·3.	Alfwine.
102	✠HAR OLD REC	✠ED PINE ON P:INC Wt. 15·2.	Edwine.
103	✠HAR. OLD REC··	✠LADMÆR ON PIN Wt. 17·4.	Ladmær.
104	✠HAROL D RECX	✠PIDIC ON PINC Wt. 16·3.	Widig.

ÐEODFORD.
[Thetford.]

Type i.

105	✠HARO LD RECX·:	✠BRVNNSTAN ON ÐEOTF : Wt. 17·3.	Brunstan.

Type v. *var. c.*

106	✠HAR OLD REC	✠ÆLFPICC ONN ÐEO (Broken.)	Ælfwig.
107	✠HAROL D RECX Λ	✠ÆLFPINE ON ÐEOD: Wt. 18·2.	Ælfwine.
108	✠NAR OLD REC	✠BRVNSTAN O ÐE Wt. 13·2.	Brunstan.
109	✠HAR OLD REC	✠EDRIC ON : ÐEO Wt. 14·4.	Edric.
110	✠HAR OLD REX	✠LEFPINE ON ÐEOD : Wt. 12·5.	Leofwine.
111	✠HAROL D RECX ΛN	✠LEOFPINE ON ÐEO Wt. 17·3.	

[Pl. XX. 14.]

112	,, ,, ,, ,,	✠LEOFPINE ,, ,, (Chipped.)	
113	✠HAD ⟩⟩⟩ D· R[EC]	✠[R]INCOLF ON Ð (Broken.)	Rincolf.

No.	Obverse.	Reverse.	Moneyer.
	UNCERTAIN MINTS.		
	HALFPENNIES.		
	Type v. *var. c.*		
114	. HAR	... PER·D ON .... Wt. 7·8.	Edwerd.
115	. ... RO LD R ..	... FPINE ON .... Wt. 7·6.	Lefwine (Leofwine).

HARTHACNUT.

Succ. A.D. 1040, died A.D. 1042

Moneyers

Æþlmær (Bath)
Æþlric (Dorch, Oxf, Shaft, Winchest)
Ægelward (Lond)
Ægelric [= Ægelwine?] (Ilch, Oxf)
Ægelwine (Brist, Cant, Crockl, Ilch, Linc, Oxf, Southw, Witham)
Ælerie or Ælric [= Ælfric?] (Glouc)
Ælfeh (Shrews)
Ælfnoð (Linc)
Ælfred (Cant, Winchest)
Ælfric or Alfric (Glouc, Linc, Wallingf)
Ælfsig[e] (Chest, Glouc)
Ælfstan (Chest, Exet)
Ælfwig (Cambr, Southw)
Ælfwine, Elwine, Alfwine, &c (Hunt, Lond, Oxf, Southamp, Thetf, Winchest)
Ælfwinea [= Ælfwine?] (Wallingf)
Ærngrim (York)
Æstan (Winchest)
Æðwine (Brist, Lond)
Alfward
Alfnoð (Linc)
Alfred (Hast)
Alfward (Lond)
Alf-, see also Ælf-
Alward [= Alfward] (Lond)
Arncetel (Lond)
Aslac (Lond)
Blacman (Guild, Nott)
Blacman [= Blacaman] (Dorch)
Boga (Dover)
Brdd (Hast)
Brun or Brunn (Lond)
Brunstan, see Brunstan
Brunred (Southw)
Brunstan or Brunstan (Thetf)
Brunwine or Brunwine (Stamf, Wallingf)
Calic (Lond)
Crof[ca] (Winchest)
Cillecrest [= Gillecrest] (Chest)
Cinstan or Cinstan (Dover)
Colgrim (Linc)
Coorneerf? (Linc)
Cort (Lond)
Dudda or Dod (Lict)
Dudine (Lond)

Dunberd (Langp)
Earnwi (Heref)
Edmær (Exet)
Edric (Lond)
Edwerd (Leices)
Edwig (Lond, Oxf)
Eldwine (Lond)
Elsige (Dover)
Eðestan
Færgrim or Fargrim (Stamf)
Friði (Steyn)
Godcild (Watch)
Godric (Glouc, Ilch, Linc, Lond, Southamp, Stamf)
Godric and Calic (Lond)
Godsune (Cumbr)
Godwine (Dorch, Exet, Lond, Oxf, Roch, Salisb, Stamf, Thetf, Winchest)
Godwine and Crof[ca] (Winchest)
Godwine and Wudi[a] (Winchest)
Golda (Exet)
Goldcetel (Lict)
Goldsige (Lond)
Havra (Exet)
Hildulf (Linc)
Hunna (Malm)
Huatreman (Brist)
Isulman [= Suleman?] (Ware)
Iudmær (Winchest)
Lifwi or Leofwi [= Leofwine?] (Cant)
Lef-, see Leof-
Leofnoð, Lefenoð, &c (Brist, Cant, Chest, Glouc, Heref)
Leofred (Lond)
Leofred and Brun (Lond)
Leofric (Cant, York)
Leofstan, Lefstan, &c (Lond, Ware)
Leofwine, Lotwine, &c (Cant, Chest, Chich, Dover, Noric, Stamf, Thetf, Ware)
Leofðegn
Leonig (Linc)
Litine (Ipsw, Linc, Lond, Oxf)
Manhog (Lict)
Norðman (Leices)
Ordric (Heref)
Osben (Sotun?)
Osferð (Linc)

Osmund (*Linc., Norw.*).
Oudcel or Ouðcel [= Ouðcetel] (*Lond.*).
Ouðencarl, Oððencar, &c. (*Lond.*).
Rinculf or Rinulf (*Norw.*).
Rulnoð [= Wulnoð?] (*Linc.*).
Rumeried?
Sævard (*Winchest.*).
Sæwine (*Brist.*, Leic., Winchest.).
Sincerd (*Warw.*).
Snell (*Chest.*).
Swert [= Swerting?] (*Stamf.*).
Swertinc (*Derby, Linc.*).
Swot (*Bedf.*).
Toci [= Toca?] (*Lond.*).
Ulfcetel (*Lond.*).
Wadel (*Bath*).
Windi[g] [= Winedeig] (*Cant.*).
Wiðerwinne (*York*).

Wraca (*Winchest.*).
Wudi[a] [= Widia?] (*Winchest.*).
Wulbern (*Linc.*).
Wulfch (*Derby*).
Wulfred [= cf. Wulfwerd] (*Glouc., Lond.*).
Wulfwi [= Wulfwine?] (*Hunt.*).
Wulfwine or Wulwine (*Langp., Leic.*).
Wulnoð (*Exet., Glouc., Nott.*).
Wulsiewod (*Heref.*).
Wulsige (*Heref.*).
Wulwine, see *Wulfwine*.
Wuwerd [= Wulfwerd] (*Glouc.*)
Þegenwine (*Exet.*).
Þorcetel (*Lond.*).
Þorstan or Þurstann (*Lond.*).
Þurcil [see also Þorcetel] (*Lond.*).
Þurgrim (*Linc.*).

DESCRIPTION OF TYPES.*

Obverse.	Reverse.

Type i.

| Bust, l., diademed. Around, inscription divided by bust: outer circle. | Cross composed of four ovals, united at their bases by two circles enclosing pellet. Around, inscription: outer circle. |

[See No. 12, p. 326.]

Type i. var. a.

| Similar; bust r. | Same. |

[Cf. Pl. XXI. 1.]

Type ii.

| Bust l., diademed; in front, sceptre in left hand. Around, inscription divided by bust: outer circle. | Over short cross voided, quadrilateral ornament with pellet at each angle and in centre. Around, inscription between two circles. |

[Cf. Pl. XXI. 2.]

Type ii. var. a.

| Similar; no sceptre. | Same. |

[Hild., Pl. 10, *Type* B, *var. a.*]

* Hildebrand Type E, Pl. 11, is not described as it is of Danish style and fabric. Type H, *var. b*, Pl. 11, and Type I, *var. a*, Pl. 12, may also be Danish copies of English coins, but as they resemble in their reverse types coins of the English mints, Norwich and York, they are included in the following list. They are given as Type ix. and Type vii. *var. a.*

Obverse.	Reverse.

Type iii.

Bust l., diademed. Around, inscription divided by bust : outer circle. | *Small cross pattée. Around, inscription between two circles.*

[Hild., Pl. 11, *Type* C.]

Type iv.

Bust l.; in front, sceptre. Around, inscription between two circles. | *Short cross voided, pellet in centre; in angles, ⊏ R V ✠. Around, inscription between two circles.*

[Hild., Pl. 11, *Type* D.]

Type v.

Bust l., in mitre-shaped helmet; in front, sceptre. Around, inscription between two circles, divided by bust. | *Short cross voided, limbs united by circle; in each angle, crescent enclosing pellet. Around, inscription between two circles.*

[Hild., Pl. 11, *Type* F.]

Type vi.

Bust l., diademed. Around, inscription divided by bust : outer circle. | *Short cross voided; limbs united by circle. Around, inscription between two circles.*

[Hild., Pl. 11, *Type* G.]

Obverse	Reverse

Type VI var a

Similar, in front, sceptre | Same

[Hild., Pl. 11, *Type* G *var* a]

Type VI var b

Similar, bust wearing mitre-shaped helmet, and inscription between two circles, divided by bust | Same

[Hild., Pl. 11, *Type* G *var* b]

Type VII

Bust l., diademed, in front, sceptre. Around, inscription divided by bust outer circle | Short cross voided, in centre, circle enclosing pellet in angles, P A C X Around, inscription outer circle

[Hild., Pl. 12, *Type* I]

Type VII var a

Similar, bust r., in armour and helmeted, no sceptre | Similar, the limbs of cross extend to edge of coin, each terminating in crescent

[Hild., Pl. 12, *Type* I *var* a]

Y 2

Obverse	Reverse

Type viii

| Bust l , diademed, divided by bust   Around, inscription outer circle | Long cross voided, limbs united by circle enclosing pellet; in each angle, fleur-de-lis between two pellets Around, inscription outer circle |

[Hild , Pl 11, *Type* II]

Type viii *var a*

| Similar , bust in armour , before, shield and sceptre | Similar , pellet at end of each limb of cross, and no pellet on either side of fleurs-de-lis in angles |

[Hild , Pl 11, *Type* II *var a*]

Type ix

| Bust r , helmeted, in armour   Around, inscription divided by bust   outer circle | Long cross voided, pellet in centre, in each angle, fleur de-lis between two pellets   Around, inscription . outer circle. |

[Hild , Pl 11, *Type* II *var b*]

DESCRIPTION OF COINS.

No.	Obverse.	Reverse.	Moneyer.
	ECXECEASTER, Etc. [Exeter.]		
	Type i. *var. a.*		
1	✠HARD CNVT RE	✠GOLDA ON AXSAP·.· Wt. 17·0. [Pl. XXI. 1.]	Golda.
2	✠HARÐA CNVT RE	✠GOLD·CYTA ON CAX·.· Wt. 17·0.	Goldcytel.
	GILDEFORDA. [Guildford.]		
	Type i. *var. a.*		
3	✠HARÐA CNVT RE	✠BLACAMAN ON CIL·.· (Chipped.)	Blacaman.
	GLEPECEASTER. [Gloucester.]		
	Type ii.		
4	✠HAÐAC NVT RE	✠ÆLERIC ON CL·EPEP: Wt. 17·2.	Æleric (=Ælfric?).
5	✠HARÐ ACNVT RE	✠GODRIC ON CLEPECE: Wt. 20·1. [Pl. XXI. 2.]	Godric.
	HEREFORD. [Hereford.]		
	Type ii.		
6	✠HAR: ÐCIV RE	✠LEFENOOÐ ON HERE Wt. 16·6. [Pl. XXI. 3]	Lefenoð (=Leofnoð).

No.	Obverse.	Reverse.	Moneyer.
7	✠HARÐE CNVT RE	✠ORDREC ON HEREFO Wt. 17·6.	Ordrec.

LEHERCEASTER.
[Leicester.]

Type ii.

| 8 | ✠HARÐ CNVT : | ✠S÷ÆVINE ON LEHER :
 Wt. 17·0. | Sæwine. |

LINCOLNE.
[Lincoln.]

Type ii.

| 9 | ✠HARÐ AC:NV | ✠COLCRIM ON LINC :
 Wt. 18·5. | Colgrim. |
| 10 | ✠HARÐ CNVT R : | ✠CODRIC ON LINCO
 Wt. 17·0. | Godric. |

[Pl. XXI. 4.]

| 11 | ✠HⲀRÐ ACNVT R | ✠LIFINC ONN LHCOC··
 Wt. 13·8. | Lifine. |

LUNDENE.
[London.]

Type i.

| 12 | ✠HARÐ· ·ACNVT | ✠LEOFSTAN ON LVND
 (Pierced.) | Leofstan. |

Type ii.

| 13 | ✠HAR· ÐCNV | ✠ÆCELPARD ON LV··
 Wt. 16·2. | Ægelward. |
| 14 | ✠HA RⲀV | ✠BRVN ON LVN·
 Wt. 14·0. | Brun. |

No	Obverse	Reverse	Moneyer
15	✠HARÐ ᴄNVTE	✠LEFSTAN ON LVNDE Wt 178	Lefstan (Leofstan)
	[Pl XXI 5]		
	OXENAFORD		
	[Oxford]		
	Type ii		
16	✠HARÐ ᴄNVT	✠ÆᴄELPINE ON OXA Wt 153	Ægelwine
	[Pl XXI 6]		
17	✠HᴧRDᴧ ᴄNVT RE	✠ÆᴄLPINE ON ᴄOX E Wt 158	
18	✠HARÐ ᴧᴄNVT	✠EDVIᴄ ON ᴆROXᴧNA Wt 157	Edwig
19	✠HᴧRÐ ᴧᴄNVT RE	✠ᴄODPINE ⊙N ᴄOXE· Wt 152	Godwine
	SNOTINGAHAM		
	[Nottingham]		
	Type ii		
20	✠HARÐ ᴧᴄN	✠PVLNOD ON ƧNOT Wt 150	Wulnoð (Wulfnoð)
	STÆNIG		
	[Steyning]		
	Type i var a		
21	✠HᴧRÐᴧ ᴄNVT RE	✠FRIÐI ON STÆNIᴄE Wt 165	Friði
	[Pl XXI 7]		
	SVÐGEᴘEORᴄ		
	[Southwark]		
	Type ii		
22	✠HARÐ ᴄNVT	✠ÆLVII ON SVÐᴄER Wt 183	Ælfwig?
	[Pl XXI 8]		

No.	Obverse	Reverse	Moneyer.

PINCEASTRE.

[Winchester.]

Type i. *var. a.*

23	✠HARÐA CNVT RE	✠ÆLFPINE ON PICE :　Wt. 16·6.	Ælfwine.
	[Pl. XXI. 9.]		
24	„　　　„　　　„	✠CODPINE· PVDI ON　　　　　　Pl·:　Wt. 16·8.	Godwine and Wudi(a).

Type ii.

25	✠HARÐ CNV REX	✠SÆPINE ON　　　　　PINEEST:　Wt. 18·0.	Sæwine.
	[Pl. XXI. 10.]		

EDWARD THE CONFESSOR

Succ A D 1012, died A D 1066

Moneyers

Æhtan [= Æstan ?] (Winchest)
Ædgar (Lond)
Ædric, Edric, &c (Cant , Linc , Lond , Thetf)
Edward, *see* Eadward
Æelric [*see also* Ælfric] (Glouc , Heref , Lond)
Egelmær (Bath)
Egelric or Egelric (Glouc , Leic , Lond , Oxf)
Egelsie (Thett)
Egelsig (Lond)
Egelward (Lond)
Egelwer [Egelwerd] (Lond)
Egelwig or Egelwig (Lond , Oxf)
Egelwine (*Agincor ?*, Crickl , Ilch , Leic , Lond , Oxf , Tamw , Winchest , Wore)
Eilsio (Thetf)
Eilwig (Wallingf)
Eilwine [*see also* Egelwine], (Crickl)
Ælfch (Shrews , *Stamf*)
Ælfere, Ælfhere, or Elfere (*Stamf*, York)
Ælflet (Lond)
Ælfgiu (Chest , Lond)
Ælfget (Linc)
Elfmere
Æltnoð, Elnoð, or Elfnoð (Linc , Lond)
Ælfred or Elfred (Cant , Lond , York)
Ælfric, Ælric, or Eltric (*Bardn*, Brist , Cant , Exet , *Glouc* , Guild , Leic , Lond , *Lydf* , *Southw* , Staf , Thetf)
Ælfsie, Alfsie, Elfsie, &c (Chest , Glouc , Lewes , Lond , Thetf , Warw)
Ælfsig, Ælfsige, Elfsige, *Elsig*, &c (Chest , *Glouc* , Lond)
Ælfstan, see Elfstan
Ælfwald, Ælfwold, Alfwald, &c (Lond , *Salisb* , Wilt)
Ælfward, Ælfweard, Ælfwerd, *Elfward*, &c (Brist , Cant , Lond , Shaft)

Ælfwi or *Elfwie* [= Ælfwig or Ælfwine], (*Cambr* , Heref , Lond , *Thetf*)
Ælfwig, Ælwig, &c (Brist , Cambr , Lond , Oxf , *Thetf*, *Wallingf*)
Ælfwine, Elwine, Elfwine, &c (Brist , Cambr , Chich , Colch , *Crickl* , Dover , Exet , Guild , Hert , Hunt , *Hythe*, Ilch , Ipsw , Linc , Lond , Norw , Oxf , Southamp , Southw , Thetf , Wilt , Winchest , Wore , York)
Ælfwold, *see* Ælfwald
Ælfwond [= Ælfwold ?] (Lond)
Elmar (Bath)
Elmon (Bedf)
Elræd, Elred, &c , (Cant)
Elric [= Ælfric ?] (Glouc , *Heref*, Leic)
Erfre [cf Arfra] (Stamf)
Estan, Astan, or Estan (*Brist* , Romn , Warw , Winchest)
Estan and Loc (Winchest)
Estmar or Estmar (Lond)
Eudt, see Eawulf
Eðelveard
Eðelwine (Thetf , York)
Eðestan (Brist , Winchest)
Agamund (Linc)
Aldgar (Lond)
Alcof (York)
Alfsie, *see* Ælfsie
Altwald or Alfwold, *see* Ælfwald
Alhmund (Nott)
Alric (Lond)
Alxxi [= Ælfsig ?] (Chest)
Anderboda or Anderbode (Winchest)
Ansera
Arbetel [= Arnecte l t] (York)
Arfra [= Erfara ?] (Stamf)
Arnecti, Arnectel, Arncytel, *Arletel*, &c (York)
Arngrim, Erngrim, or Erngrim (*Chest* , Nott , York)
Asefer [= Osfer ?] (Linc)
Astan, *see* Estan
At-ere (Thetf)

* The Moneyers' names without Mint places are chiefly taken from the list in Ruding

Authof *Aulfe* (Linc)
Baldwin (Stamf)
Beorn or Biorn (Warch , York)
Bmred (Lond)
Blaceman, Blacmin, or Blaceman (Dorch , Guild , Nott)
Blacer (Theff)
Blaceman [= Blaceman ?] (Dorch)
Blacer [cf Blacer] (Theff)
Bodric
Boga, Borg, or Boiga (Dover, Taunt)
Brand (Hast , Wallingt , Winchest)
Briesige (Lond)
Brid or *Bradd* (Hast)
Brightmær, Brihtmær, &c (Lond , Wallingf , Winchest)
Brihtne [= *Brihtine* ?]
Brihtnod (Glouc)
Brihtred (Lond , Oxf)
Brihtric, *Bristric*, &c (Colch , Ipsw , Linc , Read , Taunt , Wallingt)
Brihtwine (Lond , Malm , Oxf , Wallingf , York)
Brihtwold (Oxf , Winchest)
Brin
Brinut? (Stamf)
Brinwold (Oxf)
Brixi (Wilt)
Bristric, see Brihtric
Bruchyse, see Brunhyse
Brunne [= Brunwine] (Ipsw)
Brun (Ipsw)
Brunian, Brunnan, or *Brunman* (Cant , Ipsw , Lond)
Brun or *Brunn* (Ipsw , Winchest.)
Brundwine
Brungar (Lond , Romn)
Brunhyse [= Brunsige] (Colch)
Brunic, Brunine, Brunnine, Brynine, &c (Chest , Ipsw , Linc , Lond , Tamw)
Brunnese [= Brunhyse] (Colch)
Brunnusel [= Brunhusel ?] (Chest)
Brunstan (Theff)
Brunwine or *Brynwine* (Stamf , Wallingf)
Brynine, see Brunine
Bured or *Bufred* (Lond)
Burewine [= Brunwine ?] (Wallingf)
Burnhere (Lond)
Burnred
Cedeman (Shaft)
Cytel
Cenelm (Norw)
Centwine (Wilt)
Cuna or Coda (Winchest)
Coftan
Ceolwi or Cilwi (Dover)
Ceorl (Brist)
Cetel, see Cytell
Cewine [= Centwine] (Exet)

Cild (*Bulf*, Bedwin)
Cillerist (Taunt)
Cillon? (Linc)
Cilwi, see Ceolwi
Cinemer (Lond)
Cinstan (Dover)
Cityl
Clantu
Col or *Cola*
Colbin (Derby)
Colbrand (Chest)
Colgrim (Linc)
Coline (Tamw)
Colsi
Colstan
Colswegen (Hast)
Coltsne
Conli? (Linc)
Conna
Corff (Lond)
Cuðferð (Linc)
Cytell or Cetel (York)
Demmut (Aylesb , Mald)
Dehpn (Norw)
Deohen or Deorhan (Lond)
Deornau or Diorman (Colch , Lond , Steyn)
Deorsige (Hert , Linc)
Dermon [= Deorman ?] (Steyn)
Direman (Lond)
Direine
Dirine or *Dyrine* [= Wirine ?] (Cant , Chich)
Dodne [= Dudine ?] (Lond)
Dudine (Hornd , Lond)
Duducol (Shift)
Dulwic (Lond)
Dunine, Duning, Dunnine, &c (Chest , Hast)
Durberd (Ilch)
Durine (Lond)
Durreb (Lond)
Durul
Eadgar or Edgar (Berkel , *Lond*)
Eadmund (Lond)
Eadric (Lond)
Eadwald, Eadwold, Edwald, Edwold, &c (Lond)
Eadward, Eadweard, Edward, Edwerd, &c (Cambr , Cant , Exet , Lewes)
Eadwig or Edwig (Chich , Exet , Ipsw , Lewes, Lond)
Eadwine, Edwine, &c (Leic , Lewes, Linc , Lond , Norw , Oxf , Roch , Stamf)
Ealesi
Ealdgar (Lond)
Ealdulf (Lond)
Ealdwig (Mald , Malm)
Lantierd (Cant)
Eared (York)

Earnwi[g] (Heref, Shrews)
Eastmær (Wore)
Eawulf (Glouc)
Eewig (Lond)
Eblu
Edgar, *see Eadgar*
Edin ? (Lond)
Edmær (Exet)
Edmund (Line)
Edred (Lond)
Edric or *Edric, see Ædric*
Edsie [= Edsige ?] (Exet)
Edstan (Cambr)
Edwald or Edwold, *see Eadwald*
Edward or Edword, *see Eadward*
Edwic (Winchest)
Edwig, *see Eadwig*
Edwine, *see Eadwine*
Egelric, *see Ægelric*
Egelwine, *see Ægelwine*
Egel-, *see also Ægel -*
Eilnoð
Eilwine [= Ælfwine ?] (Langp)
Elewine (*Thetf*, York)
Elfred, *see Ælfred*
Elfsine
Eilstan or Ælfstan (Lond , Wilt , Win-
    chest)
Elf -, *see also Ælf -*
Elræd or Elred, *see Ælræd*
Elric [= Ælfric] (Heref)
Eltin [= Elfstan] (York)
Elwine [= Eilwine ?] (Oxf , Winchest)
Endru or Enru (Derby)
Eola (York)
Enð [= Cnut ?] (Read)
Erfric [= Ælfric ?] (Exet)
Ermæ (Heref)
Erncilor Ernestel[cf Arnestel](York)
Erngrim [cf Arngrim] (York)
Estan, *see Æstan*
Esther (Lond)
Estmær, see Æstmær
Estmund (Lond , Thetf)
Etsige [= Edsige] (Dover, Lond)
Etstan [= Edstan] (Cambr)
Euerard
Euuan, &c (Hert , Lond)
Exel-, *see Æxel -*
Farchir (Sandw)
Fargrim or Fergrim (Chest , Stamf)
Forlane (Stamf)
Folcerd (Thetf)
Folewine (Sudb)
Forman (Nott)
Friðmund (Winchest)
Friðwine (Stamf)
Fromm or Frome (Derby)
Fron [cf Fromm] (Derby)
Garfin (Line)
Garnui

Garulf (Winchest , Wore)
Geldewine, Gildewine, Guldewine, or
    Gyldewine (Cant , Leic)
Geola (York)
Gife or Gir (Line)
Gilpin (Oxf)
Gltwine (Lond)
Godedd (*Bdf*, Watch)
Godeleof (Thetf)
God-hydd
Godchan or Gohnin (Hert , Lond ,
    Southw , Warch , Winchest)
Godere (Lond)
Goderic *see Godric*
Godesbrand (Shaft)
Godesune, God-unu, Gotsunu, &c
    (Cambr , Cant , Lond)
Goda (Lond)
Godlamb (Cambr)
Godric, Godenc, &c (Bath , Bedf ,
    Chest , *Derby*, Glouc , Hunt ,
    Hch , Leic , Lewes , Line , Lond ,
    Lymn, Midd , *Oxf*, Salisb ,
    Shaft , Southw , Stamf , Thetf ,
    Winchest)
Godwi, Godwic, or Godwig (Lond)
Godwin, Godwinc, or Godwine (Bedf ,
    Brist , Cambr , Chich , Colch ,
    Dorch, Dover , Glouc , Hert ,
    Hunt , Lewes , Lond , Midd ,
    Norw , *Oxf*, Roch , *Salisb*,
    Shrews , Stamf , Steyn , Thetf ,
    Winchest , Wore , York)
Godwine and Coca (Winchest)
Godwine and Widia (Winchest)
Goht
Goldan (Lond)
Goldman (Colch)
Goldsie, Goldsige, or Goltsige (Lond)
Goldwine or Goldewine (Hert , Hythe ,
    Lond , Winchel , *Winchest*)
Goltsine (Lond)
Gotsunu, *see Godsunu*
Goum (Thetf)
Goðric, *see Godric*
Grimdy, Grimulf, Grinulu, &c (York)
Guldewine, *see Geldewine*
Guoltwine (Glouc)
Guðat
Guðred (Hythe)
Gwelic [= Godelif ?] (Thetf)
Gyldewine, *see Geldewine*
Hærgod or Hiregod (Oxf)
Herred or Herred (Wilt)
Hildene (Nott)
Harem [= Marem ?] (Stamf)
Heaðulf or Heðewulf (Winchest)
Hlmgulf (Norw)
Horn (Roch)
Hunewine (Exet)
Huscarl, &c (Chest)

Hwateman (Brist, Dorch)
Icacro or *Icoroff* (Lond)
Iline [= *Laline?*] (Winchest)
Iocctel, Iocitcl, Ioketcl, &c (York)
Iola, *Iolla*, or *Iole* (York)
Ioluna or *Ioualua* (York)
Iona
Iord
Iughlet [= Iugetel or Ioectel] (York)
Iulferð (Gloue)
Iurckel [= Iucctel?] (York)
Iadmer or *Iadmer* (Line, Winchest)
Lafatel
Lelenoð, *see* Leofnoð
Lei -, *see also* Leof -
Leofdeg
Leofman, Lofman, &c (Lewes)
Leofn (*Chest*, Gloue)
Leofnoð, Liofnoð, &c (Chest., *Cheh*, Gloue, Heref, Lond, York)
Leofred, Lifred, Laofred, &c (Crickl, Lond, Southw, Thett)
Leofric, Liofric, Lofric, &c (Hunt, Leic, Lond, Norw, Romn, Southamp, Stamf, Thetf, Warw, *Wore*)
Leofsie [= Leofsige] (Lond, *Nott*)
Leofsige or *Lofsig* (*Nott*)
Leofstan, Lefstan, Liofstan, &c (Cant, Gloue, Ipsw, Lond, Richb, *Salisb*, Shrews, Winchest, Wore)
Leofward, Leofword, or Liofweard (Colch, Lewes)
Leofwi or Lefwi [= Leofwig or Leofwine] (Chest, Lewes, Lond, *Noru*)
Leofwie, Leofwig, Lofwig, &c (*Chest*, Lond, Norw, *Warch*)
Leofwine (Exet)
Leofwine, Lifwine, Liofwine, &c (*Aylesb*, *Buch*, Cant, Chest, Derby, *Dorer*, Exet, Gloue, Hast, Hunt, Hythe, Ilch, Leic, Line, Lond, Norw, Oxf, Roch, Sandw, Shrews, Southamp, Southw, Stamf, Thetf, Wilt, Winchest)
Leofwold or Liofwold (Ipsw, Lewes, Line, Winchest)
Leofword, *see* Leofward
Leofðegen (Bedf)
Lafere
Lifie [= Lifine] (Ipsw, York)
Lifine, Lifing, Liofine, Luffine, &c (*Exet*, *Ipsw*, Line, Lond, *Warw*, Wilt, Winchest)
Lifred, *see* Leofred
Lifwine and Horn (Roch)
Liof -, *see* Leof -
Loc (Watch, Winchest)
Lucine [= Leuing] (Warw)

Luff [= *Luffine?*] (*Warw*).
Lufric, *see* Leofric
Lufstan, *see* Leofstan
Lufwine, *see* Leofwine
Man, Mana, Manna, Manne, &c (Cant, Line, *Norw*, *Thetf*, York)
Manue [= *Manna?*] (*Norw*)
Manwine (Dover)
Marcere or Morcere (St Edmunds)
Marcin [= Harcin?] (Stamf)
Morre
Omund, *see* Osmund
Orlaf (Lond)
Osferð, *Osfryð*, &c (Line)
Osmær (Bath)
Osmund, Omund, or Omynd (Lewes, Lond, Norw, Southw)
Osward (Ilch, Stamf)
Oswold (Lewes)
Oterine
Oðan, Oðen, Oðin, or Oðinne (York)
Osborn, Osbern, Osborn, or Ouðbearn (Line, York)
Oðgrim or Ouðgrim (Line, York)
Oðin, *see* Oðan
Oðolf, Ouðolf, or Ouðulf (York).
Oðslac (Line)
Price (Norw)
Rædulf (Hert)
Ræfen, Ræfin, Rafen, &c (York)
Raieman
Rinculf, Rinulf, &c (Norw)
Rudearl (Cant)
Sæcol or Sæcolf (Cambr, Cant)
Sæfucef [= *Sæfugel?*] (York)
Sæfugel (*York*)
Sæfuhel, Sefuel, &c. [= *Sæfugel*] (York)
Sæmær (Hert)
Sæwine or Siewine (Exet, Hunt, *Leic*, Southamp, Wilt)
Sbeiman? [= Swetman?] (Lond)
Sculn, Scule, &c (York)
Selewine (Gloue)
Sideman (Warch)
Siewine, *see* Sæwine
Sigebode (Salisb)
Sigod (Bedf)
Silac (Gloue)
Sired (Cant, Lond, Newp)
Snæborn, Sneaborn, Sneaburn, Sne-born, Snebearn, &c (York)
Snicine [= *Siewine?*] (*Brist*)
Snoter (Nott)
Spot, *see* Swot
Spraceline, Spraceling, Sprageline, Sprencaling, &c (Lond, Winchest)
Sprot, *see* Swot
Stanmær (Colch)
Stircol, Styrcol, &c (York)

Sumerleda, Sumerluda, &c (*Lanc*, Thetf)
Swafa (*Linc*)
Swarcolf [=Swartcol?] (Stamf)
Swartcol, Sweartcol, Swertcol, &c (Chest, York)
Swartinc or Swertinc (*Cant*, Derby, *Lanc.*)
Swatic (Derby)
Sweart or *Swert* [= Swertinc?] (*Stamf*).
Swearting (Winchest.)
Swegn (*York*)
Swertinc, see *Swartinc*
Swetman (Lond, Oxf, *Southamp*, Southw)
Swetric (Mald, Richb, Wilt)
Sweðan
Swileman (*Winchest*)
Swot or *Swota* (Bedf)
Swotric (*Bedf*)
Tidred (*Hert*, *Thetf*)
Tolsi
Udfe? (*Lanc*)
Uhtred [=Whitred] (Lond)
Ulf, *Ulfe*, or Ulff (Linc)
Ulfcetel, Ulfcytel, &c (Bedf, Hunt, York)
Ulfcil [=Ulfcetel] (York)
Unolf (York)
Urlewine (Bath)
Utti [cf Auti] (*Lanc*)
Wædel (Bath)
Walrafan (*Linc*)
Wibearn (Cambr)
Wicing (Exet, Worc)
Widia or Widica (Winchest)
Widred
Wigmær
Wilægrip or Wilgrip (Hert)
Wilerif (Stamf)
Wileric [=Wulfric?] (*Stamf*)
Wilfrid? (Hert)
Wilgrid [=Wilfrid?] (*Stamf*)
Wiltrand [=Wilfrid?] (Hert)
Windecild
Wineman (*Salisb*)
Winstan (Dover)
Winterfugel, Winterfuhel, &c (York)
Wintred (Thetf)
Winus (Wilt)
Wireina (Lond)
Wirinc [see also Dirinc] (Lewes)
Wiryn (Chest)
Wudeman (Shrews)
Wulbeorn, &c (Linc)
Wulcred [=Wulfred?] (Lond)
Wuldor [=Wulfgar?]
Wuldric [=Wulfric?] (Chich)
Wulcnnoð, see Wulfnoð

Wulf [*see also* Ulf] (Linc)
Wulfcetl [=Ulfcetel]
Wulfgar or Wulgar (Derch, Linc, Lond)
Wulfget or Wulget (*Cant*, Glouc, *Shrews*, Steyn)
Wulfmær, see Wulmær
Wulfnoð, Wulnoð, &c (Chest, Leic, *Nott*, Southamp, Stamf)
Wulfrard
Wulfred or Wulred (Aylesb, Cant, Lond)
Wulfric (Chich, Hast, *Ilch*, Leic, Linc, Lond, Roch, Shaft, Steyn, *Warch*)
Wulfsige, Wulsig, Wulsige, &c (*Ipsw*, Lond, Norw)
Wulfstan or Wulstan (Cant, Dorch, *Lond*)
Wulfulf (*Linc*)
Wultward, Wulfwerd, &c (Dover, Glouc, Lond)
Wulfwi [=Wulfwine?] (Bedf, *Cambr*, Dover, *Hunt*, *Worc*)
Wulfwig or Wulwig (Glouc, Hunt)
Wulfwine or Wulwine (*Brist*, *Cambr*, Cant, Colch, *Exet*, Heref, Hunt, Lewes, Lond, Oxf, *Stamf*, Wallingf, *Warch*)
Wulgar, see Wulfgar
Wulbed (Romn)
Wulmær or Wulmar (Exet, Romn, Shrews)
Wulnað or Wulnoð, see Wulfnoð
Wulsi or Wulsie [=Wulfsige] (Ipsw, Lond)
Wulstan, see Wulfstan
Wulwi, see Wulfwi
Wulwig, see Wulfwig
Wul-, see also Wulf-
Wurluid (Thetf)
Wurreb [=Þurreb] (Lond)
Wydecoc (*Shaft*)
Wynstan (Winchest)
Þeodric (Warw)
Þeoðred, Þreoðred, &c (Hast, *Hythe*)
Þor or Þori (Lond, York)
Þorcil, *Þorctel*, or Þurcil (*Lond*, Wilt)
Þorferð or Þorford (*Lond*, Norw)
Þorstin or Þurstan (Norw, *Stamf*, Warw)
Þorcil (Lond)
Þurturð or Þuruerð (Norw)
Þurgrim or *Þurmgrim* (Lanc, Lond, Norw, York)
Þurrim or *Þurrin* [=Þurgrim] (York)
Þurstan, see Þorstin
Þuruerð, see Þurfurð
Þurulf (*Stamf*)

DESCRIPTION OF TYPES.

Obverse.	Reverse.

Type i.

Bust l., with radiate crown. Around, inscription divided by bust: outer circle. | Small cross pattée. Around, inscription between two circles.

[Cf. Pl. XXVI. 10.]

Type i. var. a.

Same. | Similar: annulet in field.

[Cf. Pl. XXIV. 5.]

Type i. var. b.

Similar: bust l., diademed; in front, sceptre. | *Same as Type i.*

[Hild., Pl. 12, *Type A. var. a.*]

Type ii.

Bust l., diademed. Around, inscription divided by bust: outer circle. | Short cross voided; pellet in centre. Around, inscription: outer circle.

[Cf. Pl. XXII. 8.]

Type ii. var. a.

Same. | Similar: annulet in one angle of cross.

[Cf. Pl. XXIV. 6.]

Type ii. var. b.

Similar: in front of bust, sceptre. | Same as Type ii.

[See No. 1113, p. 420.]

Type iii.

Bust l., diademed; in front, sceptre (pommée). Around, inscription divided by bust: outer circle. | Over short cross voided quadrilateral ornament with three pellets at each angle and one in centre. Around, inscription between two circles.

[Cf. Pl. XXII. 7.]

Obverse.	Reverse.

Type iii. var. a.

Similar: bust r. | Same.

[Cf. Pl. XXVI. 13.]

Type iii. var. b.

Similar: bust l., with radiate crown; no sceptre. | Same.

[Cf. Pl. XXIV. 7.]

Type iii. var. c.

Bust l., diademed, &c., as Type iii.; but sceptre terminating in fleur-de-lis. | *Similar : one pellet only at each angle of quadrilateral ornament.*

[Hild., Pl. 13, *Type C. var. d.*]

Type iv.

Bust l., diademed: in front, sceptre. Around, inscription divided by bust: outer circle. | Long cross voided, each limb terminating in crescent; in centre, circle enclosing pellet, and in angles P A C X. Around, inscription: outer circle.

[Cf. Pl. XXVI. 14.]

Type iv. var. a.

Same. | Similar; short cross voided, with no crescents at ends of limbs.

[Cf. Pl. XXVII. 14.]

Type iv. var. b.

Same. | *Similar : pellet at end of each limb of short cross voided, and inscription between two circles.*

[Hild, Pl. 13, *Type D. var. b.*]

Obverse.	Reverse.

Type v.

| Bust 1, diademed; in front, sceptre (pommée). Around, inscription divided by bust: outer circle. | Short cross voided, the limbs gradually expanding and united at base by two circles. Around, inscription between two circles. |

[Cf. Pl. XXII. 4.]

Type v. var. a.

| Same. | Similar: annulet in one angle of cross. |

[Cf. Pl. XXIV. 8.]

Type v. var. b.

| Same. | Similar: cross pattée in each angle of cross. |

[See No. 1179, p. 427.]

Type vi.

| Bust 1, diademed; in front, sceptre. Around, inscription divided by bust: outer circle. | Short cross voided, each limb terminating in three crescents; in centre, annulet. Around, inscription between two circles. |

[Cf. Pl. XXX. 14.]

Type vii.

| Bust r., bearded, wearing pointed helmet and holding in r. hand sceptre, which terminates in cross,* fleur-de-lis or three pellets (pommée). Around, inscription divided by bust: outer circle. | Short cross voided, each limb terminating in three crescents; in centre, annulet, frequently enclosing pellet. Around, inscription between two circles. |

[Cf. Pl. XXII. 1.]

Type vii. var. a.

| Same. | Similar: annulet in one angle of cross. |

[Cf. Pl. XXIV. 9.]

Type vii. var. b.

| Similar; bust l. | Same as Type vii. |

[Cf. Pl. XXII. 2.]

Type viii.

| Bust r., bearded; wearing pointed helmet, and holding in r. hand sceptre. Around, inscription divided by bust: outer circle. | Short cross voided; annulet in centre; in each angle a martlet. Around, inscription between two circles. |

[Cf. Pl. XXVIII. 6.]

---

* In describing the coins of this type, unless otherwise stated, the sceptre terminates in a cross, that being the more common form.

Obverse	Reverse

Type ix

King seated towards r, on throne, generally bearded, wearing crown surmounted by three balls, he holds in r hand long sceptre, and in l orb surmounted by cross Around, inscription outer circle | Short cross voided, annulet or pellet frequently in centre, in each angle a martlet Around, inscription between two circles

[Cf Pl XXIII 2]

Type ix *var a*

Same | Similar annulet in two angles of cross

[Cf Pl XXIV 10]

Type x

King seated towards r, on throne, generally bearded, wearing crown surmounted by three balls, he holds in r hand long sceptre, and in l orb surmounted by cross Around, inscription outer circle | Short cross voided, each limb terminating in an incurved segment of a circle, in centre, pellet Around, inscription outer circle

[Cf Pl XXVI 8]

Type xi

Bust r, bearded, wearing crown of two arches, surmounted by three balls, in front, sceptre Around, inscription divided by bust outer circle. | Short cross voided, each limb terminating in an incurved segment of a circle, in centre, pellet Around, inscription outer circle

[Cf Pl XXII 3]

Type xi *var a*

Same | Similar, annulet in one angle of cross

[Cf Pl. XXIV 11]

Type xi *var b*

Same. | Similar to Type xi, but no incurved segments of circle at ends of limbs of cross

[Cf Pl XXV 6]

Type xii

Bust r, bearded, wearing crown of two arches, surmounted by three balls, in front, sceptre Around, inscription divided by bust outer circle | Small cross pattée Around, inscription between two circles

[Cf Pl XXVI 2]

Obverse	Reverse

Type XIII

| Bust facing, bearded, wearing arched crown, frequently surmounted by cross. Around, inscription between two circles, usually divided above by head | Small cross pattée. Around, inscription between two circles |

[Cf Pl XXII 9]

Type XIII *var a*

| Same | Similar annulet in field |

[Cf Pl XXIV 12]

Type XIII *var b*

| Same | Similar to Type XIII pellet at end of each limb of cross |

[Cf Pl XXV 7]

Type XIV

| Bust facing, bearded, wearing arched crown and holding sceptre directed over r shoulder in r hand and orb in l from each side of the crown depends a fillet terminating in three pellets. Around inscription divided by bust outer circle | Short cross voided, annulet or pellet frequently in centre, in each angle pyramid springing from inner circle and terminating in pellet Around, inscription between two circles |

[Cf Pl XXIII 8]

Type XV

| Bust r, wearing arched crown, from which depends a fillet, terminating in three pellets in front, sceptre Around, inscription divided by bust outer circle | Short cross voided, annulet or pellet frequently in centre, in each angle pyramid springing from inner circle and terminating in pellet. Around, inscription between two circles |

[Cf Pl XXII 10]

Type XV *var a*

| Same | Similar annulet instead of pyramid in one angle of cross |

[Cf Pl XXIV 13]

Type XV *var. b*

| Similar, bust l | Same as Type XV |

[Cf Pl XXVII 7]

Type XV *var c*

| Similar, bust r, no sceptre | Similar at end of each limb of cross, segment of circle curved outwards |

[Cf Pl XXIX 10]

Obverse.	Reverse.

Type xvi.

Bust r.; wearing arched crown, from which depends a fillet, terminating in three pellets; in front, sceptre. Around, inscription divided by bust: outer circle.	Short cross voided; each limb terminating in three crescents; annulet enclosing pellet in centre; in each angle, pyramid springing from centre and terminating in pellet. Around, inscription between two circles.

[Cf. Pl. XXVIII. 7.]

Type xvii.

Bust r.; wearing arched crown, from which depends a fillet, terminating in three pellets; in front, sceptre. Around, inscription divided by bust: outer circle.	Across field and between two dotted lines P A X. Around, inscription between two circles.

[Cf. Pl. XXIV. 14.]

DESCRIPTION OF COINS.

No.	Obverse.	Reverse.	Moneyer.
	ÆGLESBYRIG. [Aylesbury.]		
	Type vii.		
1	✠EDPER· D RE·	✠·PVL[F]RED ONECELE· Wt. 18·5.	Wulfred.
	[Pl. XXII. 1.]		
	BAÐAN. [Bath.]		
	Type i.		
2	✠EDPE: RD RE	✠·ÆCLM/ER ON BAÐ: Wt. 16·3.	Ægelmær.
	Type iv.		
3	✠EDPERD RECX A	✠·P/EDEL· ON BAÐA Wt. 16·5.	Wædel.

z 2

No.	Obverse.	Reverse.	Moneyer.
	Type v.		
4	✠EDPE RD REX	✠ÆIELMÆR ON BAÐ: Wt. 26·2.	Ægelmær.
5	,, ,, ,,	,, ,, BAÐ *Var.* Limbs of cross united by one circle only. Wt. 17·2.	
	Type vii.		
6	✠EDPAR· D REX	✠GODRIC ☉N BAÐAN: Wt. 21·0.	Godric.
7	,, RE	✠GODRICC ONN BAÐANN: Wt. 20·8.	
8	,, REX	✠OSMÆR ON BAÐANN: Wt. 20·2.	Osmær.
9	,, ,,	,, ,, ,, Wt. 20·7.	
	Type vii. *var. b.*		
10	✠EAD PERD REX *Var.* Sceptre, pom- mée. [Pl. XXII. 2.]	✠GODRICC ONN BAÐANN: Wt 20·4.	Godric.
	Type ix.		
11	✠EADVVEARDVS REX ANCLO	✠GODRIC ON BAÐAN Wt. 20·7.	Godric.
	Type xi.		
12	✠EADPAR RD RE	✠GODRIC ON BAÐEN: Wt. 20·8.	Godric.
13	✠EADPAR ,, ,, [Pl. XXII. 3.]	✠OꟹMÆR ☉N BAÐEN Wt. 20·5.	Osmær.
14	.✠.EADPAR,, ,,	,, ON BAÐEN Wt. 20·2.	
15	✠ ,, ,, ,,	✠OꟹMÆR: ON BAÐEN Wt. 20·7.	
16	✠EADPARD RD RE	✠VRLL·EPINE ON BAÐEN Wt. 20·0.	Urlewine?

No.	Obverse.	Reverse.	Moneyer.
	Type xiii.		
17	✠EΛDPΛRD REX Λ··	✠OSMÆR O·N BÆÐE Wt. 18·0.	Osmær.
18	✠EADRARD REX Λ	✠OωMÆR ON „ Wt. 17·2.	
	BEDEFORD. [Bedford.]		
	Type ii.		
19	✠EDPAD RE	✠VL·CHTEL ONB Wt. 13·5.	Ulfcctel ?
	Type v.		
20	✠EDPE: ·RD REX:	✠ÆLMON ON BEDEFO. Wt. 24·5.	Ælmon.
21	„ „ REX·	✠SPOT ON BEDEFOR Wt. 25·7.	Spot or Swot.
	[Pl. XXII. 4.]		
	Type vii.		
22	✠EDPER· D REX	✠PVLFPI ON BEDEFOR Wt. 20·0.	Wulfwi (= Wulfwine ?).
	Type ix.		
23	EΛDPΛRD REX ΛИGL·	✠CODRIC OИИ BEDE Wt. 22·0.	Godric.
	Type xi.		
24	✠EΛDPΛR RD RE	✠CODPIИE ON BEDEFO Wt. 20·6.	Godwine.
	[Pl. XXII. 5.]		
25	„ *Var.* „ „ Sceptre ter- minating in fleur- de-lis.	✠ωICOD ON BEDEFOR Wt. 18·5.	Sigod.

No	Obverse	Reverse	Moneyer.
	Type XIII.		
26	EADPARDI REX A	✠LEOFÐEGN ON BED Wt 15 4	Leofðegn.
27	✠EADPARD REX AN	✠SIGOD ON BEDEFOR Wt 16 5	Sigod

BEDEPINE
[Bedwin *]

	Type XI		
28	✠EADPAR RD RE	✠CILD ON BEDEPIND Wt 18 6	Cild
29	″ ″ ″	✠CILD ON BEDEPINNE Wt 19 7 [Pl XXII 6]	
30	″ ″ ″	″ ″ Wt 20 4	

BEORCLEA
[Berkeley]

	Type III		
31	✠DDE RDEX	✠EDCAR ON BEORC Wt 17 4 [Pl XXII 7]	Edgar.

BRICGSTOP
[Bristol]

	Type II		
32	✠EDPA RD RE	✠HPATEMAN ONBR Wt 15 0 [Pl XXII 8]	Hwateman
	Type IV		
33	✠EDPE RD REX	✠ÆL PIC ON BRIC Wt 15 0	Ælfwig

* Great Bedwin in Wiltshire

No.	Obverse.	Reverse.	Moneyer.
	Type v.		
34	✠EDPE: ·RD REX··	✠ÆLFPƛRD ON BRICST· Wt. 26·4.	Ælfward.
35	✠EDP RD REX	✠ÆÐESTƛN ON BRI Wt. 17·6.	Æðestan.
	Type xi.		
36	✠EADPƛR· RD RE	✠ÆLFRIC ON BRVCωTO Wt. 20·5.	Ælfric.
37	✠EADPƛR „ „	✠ÆLFPINE· ON BRE: Wt. 20·2.	Ælfwine or Elfwine.
38	„ „ „	✠ELFPINE ONBRVCSTO Wt. 20·6.	
39	✠EADPƛR „ „	✠CODPINE ON BREEC· Wt. 20·0.	Godwine.
	Type xiii.		
40	✠EADPƛRD REX ƛ	✠GODPINE ON BRVCE Wt. 16·7.	Godwine.
	[Pl. XXII. 9.]		
41	·EIIDDIIRI REC✠·	„ „ BRVC Wt. 17·2.	
	Type xv.		
42	✠EƛDPƛRD REX	✠IELFPINE ON BREC: Wt. 19·7.	Ælfwine.
	[Pl. XXII. 10.]		
43	✠CADPƛRD RE	✠CEORL ON BRVCC: Wt. 20·4.	Ceorl.
	CÆNTPARABYRIG, Etc. [Canterbury.]		
	Type ii.		
44	✠EDPH·· D RE	✠BRVHAN OPCEN Wt. 16·0.	Druman.
	[Pl. XXII. 11.]		

No.	Obverse.	Reverse.	Moneyer.
45	✠EDPE RD RE	✠DIRINC ONCE Wt. 14·5.	Dirine (= Wirine ?).
46	✠EDPE RD RE	✠EDPARD ON CEN Wt. 13·0.	Edward.
47	✠EDPH· RD E	✠ELFRED ON CÆNT Wt. 11·8.	Elfred.
48	✠EDPE RD RE	✠CVLDEPINE ONC. Wt. 11·6.	Guldewine.
49	✠ÆDRE RD RE	✠LEFSTAN ONCEN Wt. 15·7.	Lefstan or Lifstan (Leofstan).
50	✠EDPE RD RE	✠L·IFSTAN ONCEN Wt. 11·5.	
51	,, ,, ,,	✠LEOFPINE OH CENT Wt. 12·7.	Leofwine.
52	,, ,, ,,	✠MANA ONCENT : Wt. 12·6.	Mana.

Type iii.

No.	Obverse.	Reverse.	Moneyer.
53	✠EDPND RD EX V	✠BRVMNAN ON CENT Wt. 14·5.	Brumnan (Bruman).
54	✠EDPHDR RD E	✠EADPERD ON CECTN Wt. 17·2.	Eadwerd.
55	✠EDPN RD EX V	✠ELFRED ON EENCT·· Wt. 14·5.	Elfred.
56	✠EDPNDE : D RE· *Var.* Sceptre terminating in fleur-de-lis.	✠CVLDEPNE ON CENT : Wt. 17·0.	Gyldewine.
57	✠EDPE : RD RCX :	✠CYLDEDINE ON CE Wt. 15·4.	
58	,, ,, ,, *Var.* Sceptre terminating in fleur-de-lis.	✠CYLPINE ON CENT Wt. 16·2.	
59	✠EDPNER RD E	✠MAN : ON CENCTE : Wt. 16·2.	Man.

[Pl. XXII. 12.]

No.	Obverse.	Reverse.	Moneyer.
60	✠EDPNE·· RER	✠RVDCARL ON CENT : Wt. 16·2.	Rudcarl.

No	Obverse	Reverse	Moneyer
		Type v	
61	✠EDPER D REEX	✠ÆLFRED ON ᴄENTPΛ Wt 28 4	Ælfred
62	✠EDPE RD REX	✠EDPERD ON ᴄETPEREᴄO Wt 19 7	Edwerd.
63	✠EDPNR·· RD RE	✠LIFPINE ON ᴄÆNT Wt 16 0 [Pl XXII 13]	Lifwine (Leofwine)
64	✠EDPE· RD REX.	✠MANNA ON ᴄANTPA Wt 25 7	Manna
65	✠EDPER D R REE	✠PVLFRED ON ᴄETPERE Wt 19 7	Wulfred.
		Type vii	
66	✠EPDE D PEX *Var* Sceptre terminating in fleur-de-lis	✠EADPARD ON ᴄENT· Wt 20 0	Eadward.
67	✠EDPE RD RE	✠EИDPARD ON ᴄÆNT Wt 20 6	
68	✠EDPER D REX *Var* Sceptre terminating in fleur-de-lis	✠EDPERD ⊙N ᴄENT Wt 21 5	
69	✠ EDPE RD RE	✠EL RÆD ON ᴄÆNTᴄÆ Wt 21 5	Elræd
70	✠EDPER D RE✠	✠ELRED O N ᴄENTPΛ Wt 19 0	
71	„ „ REX *Var* Sceptre terminating in fleur-de-lis	✠GˣLDEPINE ON ᴄENT Wt 20 5	Gyldewine
72	✠EDPN RD REX *Var* Sceptre terminating in fleur-de-lis	✠L EOFꟅTAN ONᴄÆNT Wt 15 4	Leofstan
73	✠EDPE RD RE	✠MANNΛ ON ᴄANTP Wt 21 0	Manna

No.	Obverse.	Reverse.	Moneyer.
74	✳EDPER D RE	✢PVLSTAN ON CENT.∴ Wt. 19·0.	Wulstan.

Type ix.

No.	Obverse.	Reverse.	Moneyer.
75	EADPARD RDX ANG	✢ÆL·RED OИИ FEИT Wt. 22·4.	Ælred or Elred.
76	READPRD RX ΛИGⱺ	✢ELRED ONN FENTNP Wt. 19·8.	
77	„ „ ΛNG·O·	„ „ Wt. 20·7.	
78	EADPEARD REX ANGLO·	✢EL·RED ONN FENTN Wt. 19·0.	
79	EADPARD REX ΛИGL	✢EADPEARD OIⱯИE Wt. 21·9.	Eadweard.
80	EADPIRD RAX ANⱯORV	✢ⱯELDEPIИE ON CÆNTN Wt. 21·2.	Geldewine or Guldewine.
81	„ „ „	✢ⱯVDEPIИE ON CENTPИ Wt. 19·0.	
82	EADPRD RX ANⱯOR·	✢MΛИИΛ OИ ⱯИET. Wt. 20·3.	Manna.

Type xi.

No.	Obverse.	Reverse.	Moneyer.
83	✢EADPΛ RD RE	✢ÆL·EREARD ON ⱯVETN Wt. 16·5.	Ælfweard ?
84	✢EADPAR RD RE	✢ÆLRÆD: ON CÆNTN Wt. 19·5.	Ælræd.
85	✢EADPAR· RD RE	✢ÆLRÆD·· ON CÆNTPΛ Wt. 19·2.	
86	✢EADPAR RD RE	✢EADPARD ON CÆNT·∴ Wt. 21·9.	Eadward.
87	„ „ „	✢ELFRIC: ON CÆNTN Wt. 18·8.	Elfric.
88	✢EAEDPΛ RD RE	✢ⱯVLDEPIИE ON CÆNT: Wt. 20·2.	Guldewine.

No	Obverse	Reverse	Moneyer
89	✠EADPΛR RD RE	✠LIOFꞶTAN ON CÆNT Wt 21 5	Liofstan
90	,, ,, ,,	✠LIOFPINE ON CÆNTN Wt 18 5	Liofwine
91	,, ,, ,,	,, ,, EÆNT Wt 21 3	
92	✠EΛDPΛR RD RE	✠MΛNNE ON CÆNT Wt 20 4	Manne (Manna)
93	✠EΛDPΛR RD RE	✠MΛNNE ON CÆNTNE Wt 20 2	
94	✠EΛDPΛR RD RE	✠ꞶÆCOLF ON CΛNT.. Wt 19 0	Sæcolf
95	✠EΛDPΛR RD RE	✠PVLFPINE ON CΛNTC Wt 22 0	Wulfwine

Type XIII

No	Obverse	Reverse	Moneyer
96	EΛDPΛRD REX	✠ÆDRIC ON CΛNTV Wt 14 8	Ædric
97	EΛDPΛRD REX	✠GILDEPINE ON CΛ Wt 17 4	Gildewine (Gyldewine)
98	EΛDPRD RE X	✠LEOFPNE ON CΛN Wt. 18 0	Leofwine
99	EΛD[P]RD RE X	✠LEOFPINE ,, ,, (Broken)	
100	EΛDPΛRD RE	✠MΛN· ON CΛNTVR Wt 15 9	Man
101	EΛDÞRD REX	✠SIRED ON CΛNTV Wt 15 6	Sired

Type XV

No	Obverse	Reverse	Moneyer
102	EVDPRVD EX	✠ÆLFPEΛRD ON KEN Wt 20 0	Ælfweard
103	EΛDPΛRD REX	✠MΛNΛ ON CΛNT Wt 20 9	Mana

No.	Obverse.	Reverse.	Moneyer.

CICESTRIE.
[Chichester.]

Type ii.

| 101 | ✠EDPE RD R·· | ✠EDPI ON CICESI Wt. 11·3. | Edwig. |

Type v.

105	✠EDPHE· RD RE	✠ÆLFPINE ON CICEST : Wt. 17·2.	Ælfwine.
106	✠EDPE :· RD RE	,, ,, CICLST Wt. 16·8.	
107	✠EDPE : ·RD REX	✠ÆLFPINE ON CI[CE]STR : Wt. 20·0.	
108	,, ,, REX :	✠ÆLPIN·E ON CICEST:R: Wt. 25·7.	

[Pl. XXII. 14.]

Type vii.

| 109 | ✠EDPE D RE : X· | ✠ÆLFPINE ON CICEIE· Wt. 20·0. | Ælfwine. |
| 110 | ✠EDPER· D RE· | ,,   ,,   CICEϩT Wt. 20·5. | |

[Pl. XXIII. 1.]

111	✠EDPE D RE : X·	✠EILFPINE ON CNCEIE·· Wt. 20·0.	
112	✠EDPER D REX	✠CODPINE ON CICE : Wt. 20·5.	Godwine.
113	,, ,, RE·	,, ,, CICCϩT Wt. 20·7.	
114	✠EDPER· D REX· *Var.* Sceptre termi- nating in fleur- de-lis.	✠PVLFRIC ON CICEϩT Wt. 20·3.	Wulfric.
115	✠EDPA· ID REX *Var.* Sceptre termi- nating in fleur- de-lis.	,, ,, CICCϩT Wt. 20·8.	

No.	Obverse.	Reverse.	Moneyer.
	Type ix.		
116	EADPARD REX· ANGLO	✠ÆL·FPINE ON CICES.· Wt. 20·7.	Ælfwine.
117	,, ,, ANGLO	✠ÆLFPINE: ON CICEωT·· Wt. 20·5.	
118	,, ,, ,,	✠CODPINE ON CICE·· Wt. 20·2.	Godwine.
119	EADPPRD R:✠ ANCORV	✠CODPINE·· ON CICEωIT: Wt. 20·0.	
120	,, ,, ,,	✠CODPINE : ON CICEωTN Wt. 20·3.	
121	EADPARD REX ANG·	✠PVLFRIC ON CICES· Wt. 20·3.	Wulfric.
122	EADPEARD REX ANGLO⁻	,, ON CICEωT: Wt. 20·5.	
	[Pl. XXIII. 2.]		
	Type xi.		
123	✠EADPAR· RD RE	✠ÆLFPINE ON CICEAω Wt. 20·3.	Ælfwine.
124	,, ,, ,,	✠ÆLFPINE ON CICEN. Wt. 20·7.	
	[Pl. XXIII. 3.]		
125	,, ,, ,,	✠ÆLFPINE ON CICEST Wt. 20·0.	
126	✠EADPAR ,, ,,	✠CODPINE ☉N CICEIT. Wt. 20·5.	Godwine.
127	,, ,, ,,	✠GODPINE ON CICEωT Wt. 20·5.	
128	,, ,, ,,	✠PVLFRIC ON CICEIT Wt. 20·4.	Wulfric.
	Type xiii.		
129	EADPARD REX A	✠ÆLFPINE ON CIC· Wt. 17·5.	Ælfwine.

No.	Obverse.	Reverse.	Moneyer.
130	EADPARD REX Λ	✠PVLFRIC ON CIC Wt. 17·0. [Pl. XXIII. 4.]	Wulfric.
131	,, ,,	,, ,, Wt. 18·0	

Type xv.

No.	Obverse.	Reverse.	Moneyer.
132	EADPARD REX	✠ÆLFPINE ON CICEꞶ Wt. 20·4.	Ælfwine.
133	,, ,,	,, ,, CICEꞶT Wt. 21·0.	
134	,, ,,	✠IELFPINE ON CICES Wt. 20·9.	
135	,, ,,	✠PVLDRIC ⊙N CIC Wt. 14·5.	Wuldric (= Wulfric ?).
136	,, ,,	✠PVLFRIC ON CICEST Wt. 21·2.	Wulfric.

COLECEASTRE.
[Colchester.]

Type iii.

No.	Obverse.	Reverse.	Moneyer.
137	✠EDPE·. ·RD REX	✠BRVNHYSE ON COL·Λ (Twice pierced.)	Brunhyse.
138	✠EDPER RD RE	✠ELEPINE ON COLI Wt. 15·7.	Elfwine.
139	✠EDPE: RD REX	✠LEOFPARD ON COLE Wt. 16·5.	Leofward.
140	✠EDPER· D REX.	✠PVLFPINE ON COL·ΛE Wt. 17·2.	Wulfwine.

Type vii.

No.	Obverse.	Reverse.	Moneyer.
141	✠EDPEA· D REX·	✠BRIHTRIC ON COLECE: Wt. 15·2.	Brihtric.
142	✠EDPER D RD R· *Var.* Sceptre termi- nating in fleur- de-lis.	✠BRVNNEꞶE ON COLEC Wt. 21·0.	Brunnese (cf. Brun- hyse).

No.	Obverse.	Reverse.	Moneyer.
143	✠EDPER D REX	✠DEORMAN ON COLECE Wt. 20·0.	Deorman.
144	✠EDPER D REX	✠LEOFPORD ON COLEEE Wt. 16·7.	Leofword.
145	✠EDPER D REX	✠ΣTANMÆR ON COL· Wt. 20·0.	Stanmær.
146	✠EDPE: D REX	✠PVLFPINE ON COLECT Wt. 19·8.	Wulfwine.

Type ix.

147	EADPARD EX ANGOL	✠PVLFPINE ON COLECET: Wt. 20·7.	Wulfwine.

Type xi.

148	✠EADPARD RD RE	✠CODPINE ON COLECE: Wt. 21·3.	Godwine.
149	✠EADPAR RD RE	✠COLDMAN ON COLECE Wt. 21·0.	Goldman.

Type xv.

150	✠EADPARD REX	✠PVLFPINE ON COLECE Wt. 19·0.	Wulfwine.

[Pl. XXIII. 5.]

CRECGELADE, CROCGELADE. Etc.
[Cricklade.]

Type v.

151	✠EDPE·· ·RD REX:	✠ÆILPINF ON CRECELA Wt. 26·5.	Æilwine (Ægelwine).

[Pl. XXIII. 6.]

Type vii.

152	✠EDPER D REX·	✠ÆIELPINE ON CREC: Wt. 19·6.	Ægelwine.

No.	Obverse.	Reverse.	Moneyer.
153	✠EDPAR· D REX	✠LEOFRED ON CROC: Wt. 20·7.	Leofred.
	[Pl. XXIII. 7.]		
	Type ix.		
154	EADPARD REX ANGL·	✠ÆGELPI: ON CRECCELAD· Wt. 19·6.	Ægelwi[ne].
155	EDPARD REX AGORVM	✠LEOFRED ON CREECA Wt. 21·3.	Leofred.
	Type xi.		
156	✠EADPAR RD RE	✠LIOFRED ON CRECEL Wt. 20·6.	Liofred (Leofred).
	Type xiv.		
157	EADPARD REX	✠LEOFRED ON CRECLA Wt. 20·0.	Leofred.
	[Pl. XXIII. 8.]		
	Type xv.		
158	EADPARD REX	✠LEOFRED ON CRECLA Wt. 19·8.	Leofred.

DEORABY.
[Derby.]

No.	Obverse.	Reverse.	Moneyer.
	Type ii.		
159	✠EDPE RD R	✠FRON ON DEOR Wt. 16·9.	Fron (Froma).
	Type iii.		
160	✠EDPER ·D REX··	✠SPATIC ON DERBII: Wt. 18·0.	Swatic.
	[Pl. XXIII. 9.]		
	Type v.		
161	✠EDPE: ·RD REX.	✠FROME ON DEORBE Wt. 24·7.	Frome.

No.	Obverse.	Reverse.	Moneyer.
162	✠EDPE RD REX	✠LEDFPINE ON DEOR : Wt. 22·2.	Leofwine.
163	✠·EDPE: ·RD REX	✠SPERTINC ON DEORB Wt. 27·7. [Pl. XXIII. 10.]	Swertinc.
		Type vii.	
164	✠EDPE RD RE	✠FROME ON DOREBI (Broken.)	Frome.
165	✠EDPE RD R	✠SPRTINC ON DORB Wt. 21·0.	Swertinc.
		Type xi.	
166	✠EADPAR RD RE	✠FROMA ON DOR· Wt. 22·0. [Pl. XXIII. 11.]	Froma.
		Type xiii.	
167	·EADPARD REX·	✠COLBIN ON DREB Wt. 17·9.	Colbin.
	DOFERAN or DOFEREN. [Dover.]		
		Type i.	
168	✠EDPER· DREX :·	✠·BOCA ONNDOFRAN : Wt. 18·5.	Boga.
		Type ii.	
169	✠EDPA RD R.	✠CINSTAN ONDOF Wt. 18·2. [Pl. XXIII. 12.]	Cinstan.
170	✠EDR RD RE	✠PINS·· TAN ON DOFR Wt. 12·0.	Winstan.
		Type iii.	
171	✠EDPA RD REX :	✠CINSTAN ON DOIRI Wt. 17·3. [Pl. XXIII. 13.]	Cinstan.
172	✠EDPNR D RE	✠ETSICE ON DOFRR·· Wt. 16·6.	Etsige (Eadsige).

No.	Obverse.	Reverse.	Moneyer.
		Type v.	
173	✠EDDA RD REX	✠CINSTAN ON DOF : Wt. 26·8.	Cinstan.
174	✠EDP : RD REX :	✠CNωTAN ON DOFER Wt. 17·0.	
		Type vii.	
175	✠EDPR· D REX A	✠CILPI : ON DOFCREN (Broken.)	Cilwi (= Ceolwi).
176	✠EDPER D REX	✠CNωTA·N ON DOFER Wt. 19·4.	Cinstan.
177	✠EDPER· D PEX *Var.* Sceptre termi- nating in fleur- de-lis.	✠CNSTAN ⊙N DOFER : Wt. 17·4.	
178	‥ D REX *Var.* Sceptre termi- nating in fleur- de-lis.	„ „ Wt. 18·6.	
179	‥ „ RE·	✠CNωTAN ON DOFERE· Wt. 19·2.	
180	✠EDPER D REX	„ „ DOFERER Wt. 20·0.	
181	✠EDPR· D REX	✠CODPINE ON DOFER : Wt. 19·7.	Godwine.
182	✠EDPE·· D REX	„ „ DOFERE Wt. 19·6.	
		Type ix.	
183	EADPADD RX AИG·	✠CILPI : ON DOFERENN Wt. 19·8.	Cilwi (= Ceolwi).
184	EADPERD RAX AИCORV	✠CN~TAN : ⊙N DOFERE Wt. 20·5.	Cinstan.
185	EADPEARD REX AИGLO	✠GODPINE ON DOFER Wt. 21·0.	Godwine.
		Type xi.	
186	✠EADPAR· RD RE	✠CILPI : ON DOFCRE Wt. 20·4.	Cilwi (= Ceolwi).

No.	Obverse.	Reverse.	Moneyer.
187	EⱯDPⱯRD ANGL☉	✠G☉DPINE : ☉N D☉FER: Wt. 20·3.	Godwine.
	Type xiii.		
188	✠EⱯDPⱯRD RE	✠CIN∞TⱯN ON DOFE Wt. 15·7.	Cinstan.
189	✠EⱯDPⱯRD RE· ⱭN	✠MⱭNPINE ON DOFR· Wt. 18·0.	Manwine.
190	,, ,, ,,	,, ,, ,, (Broken.)	,,
191	EⱯDDⱯRD PEX	✠PVL·FPVRD ON DO Wt. 16·6. [Pl. XXIII. 14.]	Wulfward.
	Type xv.		
192	EⱯDPⱯRD REX	✠CEOLPI ON DOFERE Wt. 20·0.	Ceolwi (cf. Cilwi).
193	,, ,,	✠MⱭNPINE ON DOFER: Wt. 18·6.	Manwine.

DORCEASTRE.
[Dorchester.]

No.	Obverse.	Reverse.	Moneyer.
	Type ii.		
194	✠EDPE·· RD RC:	✠PVLSTⱭN OⱭ DOR *Var.* Pellet in field. Wt. 17·0.	Wulstan.
	Type iv.		
195	✠EⱭREDR D RE	✠BIⱭCⱭMⱭN DOR Wt. 16·5.	Blacaman.
	Type v.		
196	✠EDPE: ·RD REX	✠HPȂTEMAN ON DORC Wt. 25·6. [Pl. XXIV. 1.]	Hwateman.
	Type xi.		
197	✠EⱯDPⱯR RD RE	✠BLAREMAN ONDOR Wt. 20·1.	Blareman (= Blacaman ?).

No.	Obverse.	Reverse.	Moneyer.
		Type xiii.	
198	: EADPARD REX :	✠BLACAMON ON DO Wt. 17·0.	Blacaman.
199	EADRARD REX AN	✠BLAREMAN ONDORC *Var.* Two crosses saltire in field. Wt. 16·4.	Blareman (= Blacaman?).
	[Pl. XXIV. 2.]		

DYRHAM or DEORHAM.*
[Dereham.]

No.	Obverse.	Reverse.	Moneyer.
		Type ii.	
200	✠ÆDA RD R	PVLCAR O DYR·· Wt. 11·2.	Wulgar (Wulfgar).
	[Pl. XXIV. 3.]		
201	„ „ „	„ „ „ Wt. 9·2.	
202	✠EDPE RD R··	„ „ „ Wt. 10·4.	

EADMUNDSBYRIG.
[St. Edmundsbury.]

No.	Obverse.	Reverse.	Moneyer.
		Type v.	
203	✠EDPER ·D REEX :	✠MORCEREE ON EDMVN Wt. 25·0.	Morcere.
		Type xi.	
204	✠EADPARD RD RE	✠MORCRE ON EADMVN Wt. 19·5.	Morcere.
		Type xiii.	
205	·EADPARD REX·	✠MARCERE ON EAD Wt. 17·6.	Marcere (Morcere).

* See Introduction.

No.	Obverse.	Reverse.	Moneyer.
	ECXECEASTER or EXECESTER. [Exeter.]		
	Type i.		
206	✠EDPER RE·X Ⲁ·.·	✠EDMÆR ON ⊏XⅭEST Wt. 18·0.	Edmær.
	Type ii.		
207	✠EDPE RD REX	✠PVLMAR ONⅭEX Wt. 17·3.	Wulmær.
	Type iii.		
208	✠EDPE RD RE	✠PVLMÆR ON ECXE·.· Wt. 19·0.	Wulmær.
	Type iv.		
209	✠EDPER D REX·.·	✠LE:OFP.INⅭ O EⅭ Wt. 17·0.	Leofwine.
	Type v.		
210	✠EDPE: ·RD REX:	✠EDSIE ON EXⅭESTR· Wt. 26·2.	Edsie.
211	,, ,, ,,	✠EDPII ON EX·EⅭEST· Wt. 26·8.	Edwi(g).
212	,, ,, ,,	✠HVNEPINE ON EXⅭ: Wt. 26·8.	Hunewine.
213	✠EDPRE·.· RD REX:	✠S٩·PINE ON EXSⅭEX: Wt. 17·0.	Sæwine.
214	✠EDPA·.· RD RE	✠PVLMÆR ON EXSⅭEX Wt. 17·6.	Wulmær.
	Type vii.		
215	·✠EDPER· D REI· *Var.* Sceptre terminating in fleur-de-lis.	✠ÆL·FRIⅭ ON EXⅭES Wt. 21·0.	Ælfric.
216	✠EDPER D REX·	✠ⅭEPINE ON EXEⅭEꝏT Wt. 20·6.	Cewine.
217	✠EDPAR D REX	✠ERFRIⅭ OИ ⅭXⅭESTR Wt. 17·3.	Erfric (cf. Ælfric).

No	Obverse.	Reverse.	Moneyer.
218	✠EDPER· D REI· *Var.* Sceptre terminating in fleur-de-lis.	✠LIFINC ON EXECESTR Wt. 20·6.	Lifinc.
219	✠EDPER D REX·	✠ɷÆPINE ON EXECEɷ Wt. 18·4.	Sæwinc.
220	„ „ „	✠PVLMER ON ECXECE· Wt. 20·6.	Wulmær.
221	✠EDPER· D REX *Var.* Sceptre terminating in fleur-de-lis.	„ „ EXECEE Wt. 20·8.	

Type ix.

222	EADPARD REX ANGLOV	✠ÆL·FRIC OИИ EX·EC·· Wt. 20·2.	Ælfric.
223	„ „ „	✠ÆLFRIC ⊙N EXECES· Wt. 20·0.	
224	„ „ ANGLOR	✠LIF·И·IC OИИ EXECES: Wt. 20·6.	Lifinc.
225	„ „ ANGL·	✠PVLNÆR OИИ EXC: Wt. 20·4.	Wulmær.

Type xi.

226	✠EADPAR RD RE A	✠ÆLFRIC ON EXECEɷ Wt. 18·7.	Ælfric.
227	✠EADPARD RD RE	✠ÆL·FRIC ON EXECEɷT Wt. 22·4.	
228	✠EADPAR RD RE A	✠ÆL·FRIC ON EXECEɷTE: Wt. 20·0.	
229	✠EADPAR RD RE	✠LIFINC ON EXECEɷT Wt. 20·0.	Lifing.
230	„ „ „	✠PICINC ON EXECEɷT: Wt. 21·3.	Wicing.

[Pl. XXIV. 4.]

231	„ „ REI	✠PVLMÆR ON EXECEɷT Wt. 20·0.	Wulmær.

No.	Obverse.	Reverse.	Moneyer.
		Type xiii.	
232	·EΛDPΛRD RE:	✠EΛDPΛRD ☉N E Wt. 18·0.	Eadward.
233	,,　　REX·:·	✠LIFING ON EXECE Wt. 16·0.	Lifing.
		Type xv.	
234	EΛDPΛRD REX:	✠SIEPINE ON EXEEE Wt. 22·6.	Sæwine.
235	,,　　REX·	✠PVLFPINE ON E✠ECE Wt. 18·4.	Wulfwine.
236	,,　　REX A	,,　　　,, Wt. 19·0.	
		EOFERPIC. [York.]	
		Type i.	
237	✠DPΛ P REX Λ	✠OÐNNIE ON EOFE : Wt. 16·0.	Oðinne (Oðin).
		Type i. *var. a.*	
238	EDPΛR D RE✠ Λ	✠ÆLFPINE ON EOFER Wt. 16·6.	Ælfwine.
239	✠EDPΛR P RE ·✠· Λ	✠ARBETEL　,,　　,, Wt. 16·2.	Arbetel (= Arncetel?).
240	✠EDP: P RE✠:	✠ĀRNCETEL· ON EOFERPIC Wt. 15·7.	Arncetel.
241	✠FDDER D RE✠ Λ	✠ARNCETEI·　,,　,, Wt. 15·7.	
	[Pl. XXIV. 5.]		
242	✠DPER P REX Λ	✠ARNCRIN ON EOF Wt. 16·5.	Arngrim.
243	✠PPE P REX Λ	✠ELEPINE ON EOFEPI Wt. 16·3.	Elewine.
244	✠EDPER D RE✠ A	✠IOL·ANA OH EOFER· Wt. 15·7.	Iolana.

No.	Obverse.	Reverse.	Moneyer.
245	✠DPER P REX Λ	✠OĐIN ONN EOEFRIIC Wt. 16·4.	Oðin.
246	✠EDPER D RE✠:	✠RÆFEN ON EOFER· Wt. 16·2.	Ræfen.
247	✠DPER R RE✠ Λ	„ „ „ Wt. 14·7.	
248	✠·PPER P RE·✠ Λ	✠·RÆFN ON EOFEI Wt. 16·3.	
249	✠DPER D RE✠ Λ	✠SÆFVHEL ON EOF: Wt. 13·2.	Sæfuhel (=Sæfugel?).
250	✠PIER P REX Λ	✠SEFVEL ON EOFER Wt. 15·5.	
251	✠EDPER D REX Λ··	✠SCVLΛ ONN EOEER Wt. 16·0.	Scula.
252	„ „ „	✠SCVL·ΛΛ ONN EOEFR Wt. 15·8.	
253	✠EDPE: P RE✠:	✠STIRCOLL ON EOFE· Wt. 15·9.	Stircol.
254	✠EDPER: D RE✠	„ „ „ Wt. 16·0.	
255	EDPER P RE✠ Λ·	✠VLFCETEL ON EOF· Wt. 16·5.	Ulfcetel.
256	✠EDPE· P REX Λ·	✠VNOLF ON EOFER· Wt. 14·4.	Unolf.
257	✠EDPΛR· D REX	✠ĐVRRIM ON EOF· Wt. 16·5.	Þurrim (Þurgrim).

Type ii.

258	✠ERI RD RE	✠L·CI O·N EIOER Wt. 11·8.	Lifie (=Lifine?).
259	„ „ „	„ „ „ Wt. 11·0.	
260	✠EDPI RD RE	✠LIFICE ON EOF: Wt. 12·0.	

HALFPENNY.

| 261 | … DR … … | … CEN ON EO Wt. 6·0. | |

No.	Obverse.	Reverse.	Moneyer.
	Type ii. *var. a.*		
262	✠EDPI RD RE	✠ÆLFER ONEOF: Wt. 17·5.	Ælfere.
263	✠EDPE RD RE	✠ARNCEL· ONEOFE Wt. 18·0. [Pl. XXIV. 6.]	Arncel (Arncetel).
264	,, ,, ,,	✠ARNCRIM ON EO Wt. 16·7.	Arngrim.
265	✠EDPA RD RE	,, ONEOF Wt. 17·4.	
266	✠EDP RD RE✠	✠ELFERE ON ECR Wt. 17·8.	Elfere (Ælfere).
267	✠EDPE RD RE	✠ELFPINE ONEOFI Wt. 16·8.	Elfwine.
268	✠EDPER RD RE	✠EOLA ⊙N EOFER· Wt. 16·9.	Eola.
269	✠EDPI RD RE	✠IVCBTEL ON EOF Wt. 17·2.	Iugblet (=Iugetel? cf. Iocetel).
270	✠EDPE RD RE	✠LEOFNOÐ ONEO Wt. 19·3.	Leofnoð.
271	✠EDP: RD RE	✠ωÆFVCEF ONEO Wt. 17·3.	Sæfucef (= Sæfugel?).
272	✠EDPA RD R:	,, ,, Wt. 16·6.	
273	✠EDPA RD R:	✠ωCVLA ON EOF: Wt. 17·3.	Scula.
274	✠EDPI RD RE	✠ÐOR ON EOFER Wt. 18·7.	Þor.
	Type iii.		
275	✠EADPE REX	✠ÆLFNERC ON EOFR· Wt. 14·4.	Ælfhere.
276	✠EDPER D REX:	✠ÆLFPINE OIEOF: Wt. 16·7.	Ælfwine.
277	✠EDPE RD REX:	✠ÆLFPINE ON EOF Wt. 16·0.	
278	·✠·EDPER D REX	✠ÆLFDINE ON EONCR· Wt. 17·4.	

No.	Obverse.	Reverse.	Moneyer.
279	✠EDPER· D REX·.·	✠ÆRNCRIM ON EOFERP Wt. 18·7.	Ærngrim.
280	✠EDP·.· ·ERD ERX	✠EL·TAИ OИ EOFEERI·: Wt. 17·5.	Eltan.
281	✠EDPE RD RE·:·	„ „ „ Wt. 17·7.	
282	✠EDPER D RE✠	✠ELTAN ON EOFRPI Wt. 15·4.	
283	„ „ „	✠ER·ИCIL OИ EOFER Wt. 15·6.	Erncil (Erncytel).
284	„ „ REX	✠ERNCYTEL ON EOF: Wt. 18·2.	Erncytel.
285	✠EDPE·.· D RE✠:	✠IVRELEL· OH EOFER· Wt. 16·4.	Iurelel? (=Iucetel?).
286	✠EDP·:· E RE·X	✠RÆFEN ON EONEO Wt. 18·0.	Ræfen.
287	·:·EDPER ERX	✠SÆFVHEL OИ EOFR Wt. 14·0.	Sæfuhel (= Sæfugel?).
288	✠EDPE ·D REX:	✠SCVLA ON EOFER· Wt. 17·3.	Scula.
289	✠EDP D REX	✠ÐO:R ON EOFEERPI Wt. 16·2.	Þor.
290	✠EDPE ·RD RE:X·.·	✠ÐVRCRIH ON EOFE: Wt. 16·6.	Þurgrim.
291	✠EDPE D RE✠:	✠ÐVRICRIH ON EOF Wt. 16·5.	
	Halfpenny.		
292	.... PER R ...	✠ERN ...... .OFER Wt. 7·7.	Erngrim? (Arngrim).
	Type iii. *var. b.*		
293	✠EDP· ERD REX Λ [Pl. XXIV. 7.]	✠OÐEИ OИ EFRPPIC·: Wt. 16·0.	Oðen.
	Type v. *var. a.*		
294	✠EDP ·RD RE✠: [Pl. XXIV. 8.]	✠ÆLFPINEE ON EOFERI Wt. 26·8.	Ælfwine.

No.	Obverse.	Reverse.	Moneyer.
295	✠EDPAR D RECX·⋮ *Var.* Sceptre terminating in fleur-de-lis.	✠ARCXTEL ☉N EOFERPI Wt. 26·2.	Arncytel.
296	✠EDPAR ·D RECX·	✠ĀRNCRIM ON EOF Wt. 17·6.	Arngrim or Erngrim.
297	,, ,, RECX·⋅ *Var.* Sceptre terminating in fleur-de-lis.	,, ,, EOFE Wt. 17·6.	
298	,, D RECX·⋮ *Var.* Sceptre terminating in fleur-de-lis.	,, ,, EOFER⋮ Wt. 24·7.	
299	✠EDPER· ·D REEX	✠ĀR·NCRIM ON EOFER Wt. 27·2.	
300	✠EDPERN RD REX :	✠ARNCRIM ON EOFERPI Wt. 27·0.	
301	✠EDPAR D RECX	✠ARNCRIML OA ONEO Wt. 18·0.	
302	✠EDRER· ·D REEX :	✠ERNCRIH ON EOFER⋮ Wt. 26·8.	
303	✠EDPR RD REX :	✠ERNCRIM ON EOFERPI : Wt. 26·5.	
304	✠EDPAR ·D RECX·	✠CEOLA ON EOFERPI Wt. 18·0.	Gcola.
305	✠EDPR RD REX :	✠IOLĀ ON EOFERPICC: Wt. 22·5.	Iola.
306	✠EDPE: ·RD REX.	✠LE☉FENOÐ ON EOFE : Wt. 28·3.	Leofnoð.
307	✠EDPĀR D RE·X : *Var.* Sceptre terminating in fleur-de-lis.	✠ɷCVLA ON EOFERI Wt. 26·4.	Scula.
308	✠EDPAᴧ ·D RECX.	✠SCVL·A ON EOFERP Wt. 18·5.	
309	✠EDPĀR ·DRD RE	,, ,, EOFERP. Wt. 18·0.	
310	✠DPEI ·RD RE✠ :	✠ɷCVLA ON EOFERPIC Wt. 26·0.	

No	Obverse	Reverse	Moneyer
311	✠EDPAR D REEX.	✠STYRCOL ON EOFER Wt 16·5	Styrcol
312	✠EDP RD REX	✠STYRCOL ON EOFERP. Wt. 27·3	
313	✠EDPAR RECX Var Sceptre terminating in fleur-de-lis	✠SPERTCOL ONEOF Wt 17·5	Swertcol
314	✠EDPA RD RE	✠VLFCIL ON EOFER Wt 17·0	Ulfcil (Ulfcetel)
315	✠EDPAR D RECX	✠VLFCIL· ON EOFERPI Wt 18·3	
316	✠EDPA RD RCX	✠PINTEFVHEL ONE⊙ Wt 17·5	Winterfuhel (Winter-fugel)
317	✠EDPA RD RE	✠PINTERFVH. ONEOF Wt 17·3	
318	✠EDPAR D REX	✠ÐORR ON EOFRPIC Wt 18·7	Þorr
		Type vii	
319	✠EDPER D REX	✠GODPINE ON EOFER (Broken)	Godwine.
		Type vii var a	
320	✠EDPAR D RE	✠ ĀRNCEL ON EOFER Wt 21·2	Arncetel
321	✠EDPA RD R	✠ARNCTEL· ON EOFE Wt 20·7	
322	,, ,, ,	,, , EOFER Wt 21·7	
323	✠EDPER D REX	✠ARNGRIM ON EOEE Wt 20·3	Arngrim
324	✠EDPA RD R	,, EOFER Wt 21·0.	
325	✠EDPAR D RE	,, ,, EOFR Wt 21·7	
326	✠EDP RD E·.·	✠ARNCRIM ON EOFRPIC Wt 21·5	

No.	Obverse.	Reverse.	Moneyer.
327	✠EDPAR D RE·	✠IOL·E ON EOFERPIC Wt. 21·7.	Iole.
328	✠EDPA RD DX	✠LEOFENOÐ ONEOF Wt. 22·0.	Leofnoð.
329	✠EDPERD REX··	,, ON EOFE Wt. 21·7.	
330	✠EDPER·· D RX	✠RAFEN ON EOFERP Wt. 21·0.	Rafen.
331	✠EDPAE· RD RX	✠R·AFEN ON EOFERPI Wt. 20·2.	
332	✠EDPAR· D R·	✠SCVLE ON EOFERICC Wt. 19·8.	Scule (Scula).
333	✠EDPAR· D REX	✠ωCVLE ON EOFERPII Wt. 21·7.	
334	✠EDRER· D REI·	✠ƩTIRCOL ON EOFER Wt. 21·5.	Stircol.
335	✠EDPÆ· D RD	✠STIRCOL ON EOFERPIC Wt. 20·2.	
336	✠EDPER D REX	,, ,, EOFRP Wt. 18·5.	
337	✠EDP· ARD X	✠SPARTCOL ON EOFER Wt. 21·0.	Swarteol.
		[Pl. XXIV. 9.]	
338	✠EDPER· D REX	✠SPARTCOL ON EOER Wt. 21·0.	
339	✠EDPA· RD R	✠VLFCETEL ON EOFR Wt. 20·7.	Ulfcetel.
340	✠EDPEA·· RD X	✠VLFCTEL ON EOFERPIC Wt. 22·4.	
341	✠EDPER· D REI·	✠PINTERFVGEL· ON EO Wt. 21·3.	Winterfugel.
342	✠EDPAR· D RI·	✠PINTERFVGL ON EOF Wt. 20·3.	
343	✠EDPER· D REX	✠ÐORR ON EOFERPI Wt. 19·2.	Þorr.

No.	Obverse	Reverse	Moneyer

Type IX

No.	Obverse	Reverse	Moneyer
344	EADVEARDVS REX AN	✠ARИGRIM ON EⵔFR· Wt 11·5	Arngrim
345	EDPAD RX ANGORA	✠ARNCRIM ON EOFR Wt 22·5	
346	EADPARD REX ANGORV	✠IOLA OИ EOFER Wt 22·0	Iola
347	EADPARD REX AИGL	✠SCVLA ON EOFRPIC Wt 21·5	Scula
348	„ RCX ANG	✠SИEABVRИ OИ EOFE Wt 21·0	Sneaburn (Snæburn)

Type IX var a

No.	Obverse	Reverse	Moneyer
349	EDPARD X ACLORO	✠IOKETEL ON EOFE Wt 20·4	Ioketel (Iocetel)
350	EDPR RX ANGLOP	✠OⵔCRIM ON EFRPI Wt 21·0	Oꝺgrim
351	EDPAD X AN[GL]ORA·	✠VLFCETL ON EOFRP Wt 21·7	Ulfcetl
352	„ RX ANGLOR	✠VLFCIL ON EOFRPIC Wt 20·5	Ulfcil (Ulfcetl)
353	EDPAD RX ANGLOR	✠DORR ONN EOFRPC Wt 19·7	Þorr

[Pl XXIV 10]

No.	Obverse	Reverse	Moneyer
354	EADPARD REX AИGL	„ ON EOFERPIC Wt 20·7	
355	EDPAD RX ANGLOR	„ ON EOFRPIC Wt 20·7	

Type XI

No.	Obverse	Reverse	Moneyer
356	✠EADPAR RD RE	✠OⵔCRIM ON EOFI Wt 19·2	Oꝺgrim

Type XI var a

No.	Obverse	Reverse	Moneyer
357	✠EDPARD REX	✠ARCETL ON EOFRP Wt 20·2	Arncetel
358	✠EDPAER D R	✠ARNCTEL ON EOFR Wt 19·0	

No.	Obverse.	Reverse.	Moneyer.
359	✠EDPAR· D RE	✠ARNGRIM ON EOFER Wt. 18·0.	Arngrim.
360	✠EDPARD D RE·	✠IOCITEL ON EOFRP Wt. 20·0.	Iocitel.
361	✠EADPA· RD RE	✠IOCTEL ON EOFR Wt. 20·6.	
362	✠EADPR· D RE	✠OÐBERN ON EOFER Wt. 20·4.	Oðbern.
363	✠EADPRD D RE	✠OÐBORN ON EⵙFR Wt. 21·2.	
364	✠EDPAED D RE	✠OÐGRIM ON EOFER Wt. 20·4.	Oðgrim.
365	✠EDPAR D RE·	✠SCVLA ON EOFRPICE Wt. 20·3.	Scula.
366	✠EADPAR D RE·	✠SCVLAE ON EOFRPI Wt. 21·7.	

[Pl. XXIV. 11.]

No.	Obverse.	Reverse.	Moneyer.
367	✠EDPAR D RE	✠SNEBORN ON EOF Wt. 21·7.	Sneborn.
368	✠EADPAR D RE·	✠SPARTCOL ON EO Wt. 21·0.	Swartcol.
369	✠EDPARD D RE·	✠VLFCTEL ON EOFER Wt. 20·0.	Ulfcetel.
370	✠EDPARD „	„ „ EOFP Wt. 20·6.	
371	„ „	„ „ EOFRP Wt. 20·6.	
372	✠EDPARI D RE	✠ÐORR ON EOFERPI Wt. 21·9.	Þorr.
373	✠EDPARD D RE·	„ „ EOFERPIC Wt. 20·3.	

Type xiii. var. a.

No.	Obverse.	Reverse.	Moneyer.
374	✠EDPARDE REX	✠ARCEL ON EOFRPI Wt. 17·8.	Arcel (= Arncetel?).
375	„ „	ARCIL ON EOFRP Wt. 18·7.	
376	„ „	✠ARNCTEL ONEOF Wt. 20·0.	Arncetel.

No.	Obverse.	Reverse.	Moneyer.
377	✠EADPARED RE	✠ARNCRIM ON E· Wt. 18·4.	Arngrim.
378	✠EADPARD RE·	,, ,, EOI Wt. 18·0.	
379	✠EDPARDE REX	✠IOCTEL ON EOFR Wt. 17·0.	Iocetel.
380	,, ,,	,, ,, EOFRPI Wt. 17·6.	

[Pl. XXIV. 12.]

No.	Obverse.	Reverse.	Moneyer.
381	✠EADPARD RE✠	,, ,, EORP Wt. 18·4.	
382	✠EADPARD RE	✠OVÐOLF ON EOFCR Wt. 15·3.	Onðolf or Oðolf.
383	✠EDPARD REX AN	✠OÐOLF ON EOFER Wt. 18·0.	
384	EADPARD RE✠ AN	✠OÐBEN ON EOFRI Wt. 17·0.	Oðbeorn.
385	,, ,, ,,	✠OÐBEORN ON EOFR Wt. 15·0.	
386	·EDPARD REXX·	✠OÐBOREN ON EO Wt. 17·2.	
387	✠EADPARD REX	✠OÐCRIM ON EOF Wt. 16·2.	Oðgrim.
388	·EADPARD REX AN·	,, ,, EOFR Wt. 18·1.	
389	,, ,, ,,	,, ,, EOFRR Wt. 16·6.	
390	✠EAD[PA]RD REX	,, [ON]EOFRP (Broken.)	
391	·✠EADPARD RE✠ A·	✠SCVLA ON EOF Wt. 16·8.	Scula.
392	·EADPARD ,, ,,	,, ,, EOFRP Wt. 18·0.	
393	✠EDPARDE REX·	,, ,, EOFERP Wt. 18·0.	
394	✠EDPARED REHX	✠SNÆBORN ON EOF Wt. 18·6.	Snæborn.
395	,, ,,	✠SNEBORN ,, ,, Wt. 15·4.	

No.	Obverse.	Reverse.	Moneyer.
396	✠EΛDPΛRD REX Λ	✠SNEBORN ON EOFR Wt. 15 9.	
397	✠EDPΛRDE REX Λ	✠SPΛRTCOL ON EOF Wt. 16·3.	Swartcol.
398	✠EΛDPΛRD RE✠ Λ·	,, ,, EOFR Wt. 14·0.	
399	· ,, REX	✠SPRTCOL ONEOFR Wt. 17·6.	
400	·EΛDPΛRD REX Λ	✠VLFCIL ON EOFER· Wt. 12·0.	Ulfcil (Ulfcetel).
401	ÆΛDPΛRD REX ΛI·	✠VLFCTEL ON EOFR Wt. 15·5.	Ulfcetel.
402	✠EΛDPΛRD REH✠	,, ,, Wt. 18·6.	
403	,, REX	✠ÐORR ON EOFR· Wt. 18·0.	Þorr.
404	·EΛDPΛRD RE✠ Λ·	,, ,, EOFERP Wt. 18·6.	
405	ÆΛDPΛRD REX ΛN :	,, ,, EOFRP Wt. 17·5.	

Type xv. *var. a.*

No.	Obverse.	Reverse.	Moneyer.
406	EΛDPΛRD REX	✠ΛLEIF ON EOFRPICC Wt. 19·6.	Aleof.
407	,, REX :	✠ΛLEOF ON EOFERP Wt. 20·9.	
408	,, REX	✠EΛRCIL ON EOFERP: Wt. 20·6.	Earcil.
409	,, ,,	,, ,, Wt. 22·5.	
410	,, ,,	,, ,, EOFRPIC Wt. 20·8.	

[Pl. XXIV. 13.]

No.	Obverse.	Reverse.	Moneyer.
411	,, ,,	✠IOCCETEL ON EOFE Wt. 20·7.	Iocetel.
412	,, ,,	,, ,, Wt. 22·2.	
413	,, ,,	✠OVÐBEΛRN ON EO Wt. 21·4.	Ouðbearn, Oðborn, &c.

No.	Obverse.		Reverse.	Moneyer.
411	EADPARD REX		✠OVÐBORN ON EOFR Wt. 19·0.	
415	,,	,,	✠OÐBORN ON EOFRR Wt. 20·6.	
416	EDRRDI	,,	✠OVÐGRIM ON EOF Wt. 22·0.	Ouðgrim.
417	EADPARD	,,	✠OVÐVLF ON EOFEI Wt. 21·0.	Ouðulf.
418	,,	RX	✠OVÐÐVLF ON EOFE Wt. 22·6.	
419	,,	REX	✠SCVLA ON EOFER· Wt. 22·2.	Scula.
420	,,	RX	,, ,, EOFR Wt. 22·0.	
421	,,	REX	✠SENEBRN ON EOFR Wt. 22·0.	Snebearn (Snæborn).
422	,,	,,	✠SNEBEARN ON EO Wt. 23·2.	
423	,,	,,	✠SNEBRN ON EOFRPIC Wt. 20·2.	
424	,,	X	✠SPEARTCOL ON EO· Wt. 20·8.	Sweartcol (Swartcol).
425	,,	REX	,, ,, EOF Wt. 21·6.	
426	,,	RX	✠VLFCETL ON EOFER Wt. 18·5.	Ulfcetel.
427	,,	REX	✠ÐOR ON EOFERPIC : Wt. 19·8.	Þor or Þorr.
428	,,	,,	✠ÐORR ON EOFRPIEC Wt 20·0.	

Type xvii.

429	EADPARD REX		✠SENEBRN ON EOFR Wt. 21·0.	Snebearn (Snæborn).

[Pl. XXIV. 14.]

No.	Obverse.	Reverse.	Moneyer.

GIFELCEASTER.
[Ilchester.]

Type iii.

| 430 | ✠ED[PE] ΛRD· R | [✠]L·EOFPINE ON ꟼIF... (Broken.) | Leofwine. |

Type v.

| 431 | ✠EDPE: RD REX: | ✠OSPARD ON GIFELꟼ: Wt. 25·5. | Osward. |

Type vii.

| 432 | ✠EDPER REX *Var.* Sceptre terminating in fleur-de-lis. | ✠ꟼODRIꟼ ON ꟼIFELꟼ: *Var.* A straight line across one limb of cross. Wt. 20·6. | Godric. |

Type xi.

| 433 | ✠EΛDPΛRD RD RE | ✠ꟼODRIꟼ ON ꟼIEELꟼ *Var.* A straight line across one limb of cross. Wt. 20·5. | Godric. |
| 434 | ,, ,, ,, | ,, ,, ꟼIEELꟼ *Var.* A straight line across one limb of cross. Wt. 20·0. | |

Type xiii.

| 435 | ✠EΛDPΛRD RE·X ΛN | ✠ÆGLPINE ON GIFEL *Var.* A straight line above and below cross. Wt. 16·4. | Ægelwine. |

GIPESꟼIC.
[Ipswich.]

Type i.

| 436 | ✠EDPER D REX ·Λ· | ✠LEOFSTΛH ON ꟼIPE: Wt. 17·7. | Leofstan. |

No.	Obverse.	Reverse.	Moneyer.
		Type ii.	
437	✠EDPE RD RE·	✠BVNINC ON CIP Wt. 17·7.	Brunine.
438	,, ,, R··	✠EDPI ON CIPESI Wt. 13·3.	Edwi[g].
439	,, ,, RE	✠P.VL·SIE ON CIP Wt. 17·3.	Wulsie.
		Type v.	
440	✠.EDPE ·RD REX :	✠LIFIC ONO GIPESPIIC : Wt. 27·0.	Lifie (Lifine).
		[Pl. XXV. 1.]	
		Type xi.	
441	✠EADPARD RD RE	✠BRVMAN ONCIPEꟾPI Wt. 20·7.	Bruman.
		Type xiii.	
442	EDPARD RX	✠ÆLFPINE ON GIPPE Wt. 16·0.	Ælfwine.
443	·EADPARD RE··	✠BRIHTRIC· ON GIPP Wt. 15·6.	Brihtric.
444	EADPARD REX	✠BRINTRIC ON GIPE *Var.* Crescent in field. Wt. 15·0.	
445	·EADPARD RX	✠BRVM ON· GIPPES	Brum(an).
446	·EADꟾARD RE·	✠BRVNINC ON GIPPE Wt. 16·6.	Brunine.
447	,, ,,	✠LEOFꟾOLD· ,, ,, Wt. 16·3.	Leofwold.
		Type xv.	
448	EADPARD REX	✠IELFPINE ON GIPP Wt. 20·9.	Ælfwine.
449	EAPARD REX E°	,, ,, ,, Wt. 18·9.	

No.	Obverse.	Reverse.	Moneyer.

GLEPECEASTER.
[Gloucester.]

Type i.

450	✠EDPE RD REX	✠PVL·FPERD ON ELEP Wt. 17·2.	Wulfwerd.

Type ii.

| 451 | ✠EDPE RD RE | ✠LEOFNOÐ ON ELE
 Wt. 17·0. | Leofnoð. |
| 452 | ✠EDP· ARD·· | ✠PVLPIE ON ,,
 Wt. 14·0. | Wulwig. |

Type v.

453	✠EDP RD RE	✠ÆIELRIE ON GLEPE Wt. 17·4.	Ægelric.
454	✠EDPE: ·RD REX:	✠EAPVLF ON GLEPEEE: Wt. 24·4.	Eawulf.
455	✠EDPE ·RD REX	✠LEOFN ON ELEAEE Wt. 16·9.	Leofn.

Type vii.

456	✠EDPA· RD RE	✠ÆILRIE ON GL·EPEE: Wt. 20·7.	Ælric (Ægelric).
457	✠EDPAR· D REX	✠ÆLESIIE ON GLEPEE Wt. 20·0.	Ælfsiie (cf. Ælfsige).
458	✠EDPA· RD RE·	✠GODRIE ON GLEPE: Wt. 21·3.	Godric.
459	✠EDPE D RE· *Var.* Pellet behind bust.	✠IVLFERD O EL·EP: Wt. 21·0.	Iulferð.
460	(*Double struck.*)	✠PVLFEET ON ELEPE: Wt. 20·2.	Wulfget.

Type ix.

| 461 | EADVVEARDVS REX
 ANGL | ✠GODPINE ON
 GLEPEEST
 Wt. 16·3. | Godwine. |

No.	Obverse.	Reverse.	Moneyer.
462	EADY·RD REX [ANꟼLORX	✠LEOFSTAꟼ ON ꞒLEP Wt. 18·8.	Leofstan.
463	·EADPEARD REX AN·	✠SELꞒPINE ON ꞬLEPEꞒ Wt. 19·7.	Selewine.
464	EADPEARD REX ANꞬLO·	✠ƧILAꞒ ON ꞒLEPL Wt. 20·0.	Silac.

Type xi.

No.	Obverse.	Reverse.	Moneyer.
465	✠EADPAR RD RE	✠BRIHTNONƉ ONꞒLEP: (Pierced.)	Brihtnoð?
466	✠EDPARD· RD RE	✠ꞬVOLFPIꟼE ON ꞒLEPꞒ: Wt. 20·6.	Guolfwine.
467	✠EADPAR RD RE	✠LIOFPINE ON ꞒLEPEꞒE Wt. 20·2.	Liofwine.
468	✠EADP RD RE	✠PVLFPARD ONꞒLEPEꞒꞒ Wt. 20·6.	Wulfward.

[Pl. XXV. 2.]

Type xiii.

No.	Obverse.	Reverse.	Moneyer.
469	·EADPARD RE·	✠SILAꞒ· ON ꞬLEÞE Wt. 17·0.	Silac.

Type xv.

No.	Obverse.	Reverse.	Moneyer.
470	EADPARD RE	✠SIL·AꞒ ON ꞬLEÞE Wt. 18·4.	Silac.

GRANTEBRYCGE.
[Cambridge.]

Type ii.

No.	Obverse.	Reverse.	Moneyer.
471	✠EDPE RD RE	✠ETƧTAN ON ꞒRA Wt. 18·0.	Etstan (Edstan).

Type iii.

No.	Obverse.	Reverse.	Moneyer.
472	✠EDPER ·D REX	✠ÆLFPINE ONꞒ ONꞒR· Wt. 16·8.	Ælfwine.

No.	Obverse.	Reverse.	Moneyer.
		Type v.	
473	✠EDPER· ·D REEX: (Double struck.)	✠ELFPINON ᴌRᴀ·NTE· Wt. 26·6.	Elfwine.
474	✠EDPE: ·RD REX:	✠ᴌOTSVNV ON ᴌRᴀNTE Wt. 26·7.	Gotsunu.
		Type vii.	
475	✠EDPER D REX [Pl. XXV. 3.]	✠ᴌODPINE ON ᴌRᴀNT Wt. 18·3.	Godwine.
		Type ix.	
476	EᴀDPARD REX ᴧNᴌLO·	✠ᴧELFPIᴌ ⊙NN ᴌRᴀ Wt. 20·6.	Ælfwig.
477	EᴀDPRD REX ANᴌOR	✠ᴌODPINE ON ᴌRANT: Wt. 20·3.	Godwine.
		Type xi.	
478	✠EDPᴀR· RD REX	✠EᴀDI‾ERD ONᴌRᴧN Wt. 19·8.	Eadwerd.
		Type xiii.	
479	EADPARD REX AD	✠GODLAMB ONᴌRA: Wt. 16·2.	Godlamb.
480	,, RE:	✠SÆᴌOL ON 6RᴧNIV Wt. 16·0.	Sæcol.
481	,, REX ᴧ	✠PIBEARN ONᴌRᴧ Wt. 15·2.	Wibearn.

GULDEFORDA or GILDEFORDA.
[Guildford.]

No.	Obverse.	Reverse.	Moneyer.
		Type ii.	
482	✠EDP RD R·	✠ELFPINE ON 6V. Wt. 16·9.	Elfwine.
		Type v.	
483	✠EDPA ·RD RE:	✠BLAᴌEMAN ON 6YL Wt. 18·0.	Blaceman.
484	✠EDPE·· RD RE	✠BLAᴌEMAN ON ᴌVL Wt. 16·0.	Blaceman.

No.	Obverse.	Reverse.	Moneyer.
	Type vii.		
485	✠EDPNR D REX·	✠BLACMAN ON CVLD: Wt. 19·3.	Blacman (Blaceman).
486	,, ,, ,,	✠BLACMAN ON CYLD. Wt. 20·3.	
	Type ix.		
487	EADVVERDVS REX ANGLO	✠BLACEMAN ON GIL Wt. 21·0.	Blaceman.
488	,, ,, ,,	,, ,, GYLDEOR Wt. 19·9.	
	Type xi.		
489	✠EADPA· RD RE	✠ÆLFRIC: ON GLLDEFOR Wt. 19·4.	Ælfric.
490	✠EADPAR· RD RE	,, ,, ,, Wt. 20·1.	
	[Pl. XXV. 4.]		
491	✠EADPAR· RD RE	✠BLAEEMAN ON GLDE Wt. 19·5.	Blaceman.
	Type xiii.		
492	·EADPARD REX:	✠ÆLFRIC· ON GILDE Wt. 16·7.	Ælfric.
493	✠ ,, REX AN	OꟻƎꟽꟼI� NO ꓛIꓤꟻꟼƎꟻ✠ Wt. 14·0.	
	HÆSTINGA ᴏʀ HESTINGPORT. [Hastings.]		
	Type ii.		
494	✠EDPAR D RE	✠BRID ON HÆSTI Wt. 17·5.	Brid (cf. Brand).
	Type iii.		
495	EDPNDR R DEX	✠BRID: ON HESTST: Wt. 24·3.	Brid.

No	Obverse	Reverse	Moneyer

Type v

No	Obverse	Reverse	Moneyer
496	✠EDPE RD RE✠	✠BRID ON HEⱷTINPO Wt 15 9	Brid
497	✠EDPNER D RE	,, ,, HESTINPOR *Var* Pellet in one angle of cross Wt 18 0.	
498	✠EDDE . RE	✠LEOFPINE ON HÆS Wt 26 0	Leofwine or Lifwine
499	✠EDPN . RD RE	✠LEⓄFPINE ⓄN HÆSTC Wt 17 4	
500	✠EDPE RD RE	✠LEOFPINE ON HÆSTICC Wt 17 0	
501	✠EDPE RD REX	✠LIFPINE ON HAⱷT Wt 17 4	

Type vii

No	Obverse	Reverse	Moneyer
502	✠EDPER· D REX	✠BRID O N HÆⱷTIEN Wt 17 5	Brid
503	,, ,, ,,	,, ,, ⸚ Wt 19 8	
504	✠EDPE RD REX *Var* Sceptre termi- nating in fleur- de-lis	✠BRID ON HÆSTINC Wt 18 0	
505	,, ,, REI *Var* Sceptre termi- nating in fleur- de-lis	,, ,, HÆSTNC Wt 19 6	
506	✠EDPER D REX	✠DVINNC ON HÆⱷTIE Wt 21 1	Duninc
507	✠EDPE ,, ,,	,, ,, HÆƩTIN Wt 19 5	

Type ix

No	Obverse	Reverse	Moneyer
508	EⱯDPⱯRD REX ⱯNGL	BRID OⱯ HÆ SÐIⱯ Wt 20 7	Brid
509	,, ,, ,,	,, ,, ⸚ Wt 20 2	

No.	Obverse.	Reverse.	Moneyer.
510	EADPRD RIX ANCORV	✠BRND ON HÆ∞TIEN: Wt. 20·6.	Brand (cf. Brid).
511	EADPARD REX ANCLOⅩ	✠DVNNINC OИИ HÆS· Wt. 20·0.	Dunninc.

Type xi.

512	✠EADPAR RD RE	✠BRID: ON HÆ∞TI Wt. 19·6.	Brid.
513	✠EADRΛ : DD RE	✠BRND ON NEOSTIEN Wt. 19·0.	Brand.

[Pl. XXV. 5.]

514	EADPΛ: RD REX	✠DVNINC ON Æ∞TIN·: Wt. 19·0.	Dunninc.
515	✠EADPΛR RD RE	„ „ HÆ∞T *Var.* Pellet in field. Wt. 20·6.	
516	✠EADPΛ· RD RE	✠DVNNINC ON HÆ∞ Wt. 19·0.	
517	✠EADPΛP RD RE	✠PVLFRIC ON HÆ∞TI Wt. 20·0.	Wulfric.

Type xiii.

518	✠EADPARD REX ANG :	✠COLSPCGEN ON HÆS *Var.* Four wedge-shaped pellets attached to inner circle. Wt. 16·4.	Colswegen.
519	·EADPARD REX	✠DVNNINC ON HÆ Wt. 17·4.	Dunninc.
520	„ RE✠·	✠DVNNINC ON HEST Wt. 17·4.	
521	✠EADPARD REX ᚱN·	✠ÐREꙨDRED ⊙N HÆS *Var.* Two pellets in field. Wt. 14·4.	Þreodred (Þeodred).
522	·EADPARD RE	✠ÐREOÐRED ON H *Var.* Two pellets in field. Wt. 17·3.	

No	Obverse	Reverse	Moneyer

HAMTUNE

[Southampton]

Type i

| 523 | ✠EDPERER D REX A | ✠LEOFPINE ON NAMTV (Pierced) | Leofwine. |

Type iii

| 521 | ✠EDPE RD REX | ✠ÆL FPINE ON HAM Wt 17 4 | Ælfwine |

Type vii

| 525 | ✠EDPAR D REX | ✠LEOFRIC ON HAMTV Wt 21 0 | Leofric |

Type vii *var a*

| 526 | EDPE RD RE *Var* Sceptre terminating in three pellets | ✠ÆLFPINE ON HA Wt 21 0 | Ælfwine |

Type ix

| 527 | EADPARD REX ANGLO | ✠PVLNOÐ ON HAM Wt 20 3 | Wulnoð (Wulfnoð) |
| 528 | ,, ,, ANGL | ✠PVLИOÐ OИИ HAM Wt 21 2 | |

Type xi

| 529 | ✠EADPARD RD RE | ✠ѠÆPINE ON HAMTV Wt 22 2 | Sæwine |

Type xi *var b*

| 530 | ✠EADPAR RD RE [Pl. XXV 6] | ✠PVLFNOD ON HAMTV Wt 19 7 | Wulfnoð |

HEORTFORD

[Hertford]

Type i

| 531 | ✠EDPNRD REC | ✠DEORSIGE ON IEON* Wt 14 6 | Deorsige |

---

* Hertford ?

No.	Obverse	Reverse	Moneyer
		Type III	
532	✠EDPA RD R E	✠ÆLFPINE ON HERTF Wt 110	Ælfwine
533	✠EDPE RD REX	✠GODMAN ON HEOR Wt 160	Godman
534	✠EDPNE RER ✠	✠GODPINE ON HIR ·· Wt 145	Godwine
535	✠EDPND D RE *For Sceptre terminating in fleur-de-lis*	✠GOLDPINE ON HEOR Wt 137	Goldwine
536	✠ EDPE RD RE	✠RÆÐVL F ON HER·· Wt 162	Rædulf
		FARTHING	
537	P.E	✠ . . HIR. Wt 40	
		Type VII	
538	✠EDPER D REX	✠PILTRND ON HEORT Wt 172	Wiltrand (pos Wilfrid)
		Type XI	
539	✠EADPAP RD RE	✠ꟾÆMÆR ON HERTFO Wt. 195	Sæmær
		Type XIII *var b*	
540	EADPARD RE	✠PILÆGRIP ON HEOR Wt 172 [Pl XXV 7]	Wilægrip or Wilgrip
541	" "	✠PILGIRP ON HIRT Wt 156	
		HEREFORD [Hereford]	
		Type II	
542	✠EDPE RD RE	✠ERNDII ON HERE Wt 174	Earnwi

No	Obverse	Reverse	Moneyer

Type III

| 543 | ✠EDPE RD REX· | ✠EIEL RIC ON HERE Wt 16 7 | Æchic |

Type VII.

| 544 | ✠EDPRD D REX *Var* Sceptre termi- nating in fleur- de-lis | ✠PVLFPINE ON HER Wt 21 4 | Wulfwine |

Type VII *var b*

| 545 | ✠EDPE R D R EX *Var* Sceptre termi- nating in three pellets [Pl XXV 8] | ✠ERNPI ON HERE Wt 20 6 | Earnwi |

Type IX

| 546 | EADPEARD REX ANGL | ✠LEFENOÐ ON HEREFO Wt 21 6 | Lefenoð. |

Type XI

547	EADPERD REX *Var* Inscription begins behind bust	✠ÆLFPI ON HEREFOR Wt 19 7	Ælfwi(g)
548	✠EADPARD RD RE	✠EAꟼPI ON HEREFOdE Wt 20 5	Earnwi
549	✠EADPARD RD RE	✠EARNPI ON HERE Wt 19 0	
550	„ „ „	„ „ HEREFO Wt 20 1	
551	✠EADPAR RD RE	✠ELRIE ON HL RELOE Wt 19 8	Elric (cf Ælric)
552	✠EADPAR· RD RE	✠LIOFENOD ON HEREFO Wt 20 0 [Pl XXV 9]	Liofuoð

Type XIII

| 553 | EADPARD RE | ✠ÆLFꟼI ON HERE Wt 16 9 | Ælfwi(g) |

No.	Obverse.	Reverse.	Moneyer.

HORNINDUNA.
[Horndon.]

Type ix.

| 551 | ✠EADVVRD RAX ANGORV: [Pl. XXV. 10.] | ✠DVDINE ON HORNIDVNE: Wt. 19·9. | Dudine. |

HUNTENDUNE.
[Huntingdon.]

Type i.

| 555 | ✠EDPΛ RD REX | ✠PVLFPIC ON HVNT: Wt. 16·7. | Wulfwig. |

Type ii.

| 556 | ✠EDPE RD REX | ✠ÆLFPINE ON HV Wt. 17·1. | Ælfwine. |
| 557 | ✠EDPΛ· D RE | ✠VLFCTL ON HVNT Wt. 9·7. | Ulfcctel. |

FARTHING.

| 558 | . . . . PE . . . . . . | ✠ . . . . . . HV Wt. 4·2. | |

Type iii.

| 559 | ✠EDPERD ·REX Λ | ✠ÆL·FPINE ON HVNTE *Var.* Pellet in two angles of cross. Wt. 17·2. | Ælfwine. |

Type iv.

| 560 | ✠EÐPΛ RD REX | ✠P.V.LFPINE O HVN Wt. 16·2. | Wulfwine. |

Type v.

| 561 | ✠EDPER: ·D REX: | ✠ÆLFPINE ON HVNT·EN: Wt. 25·4. | Ælfwine. |
| 562 | ” ” ” | ✠CODRIC ON HVNTEN Wt. 25·4. | Godric. |

No	Obverse	Reverse	Moneyer
		Type xi	
563	✠EΛDPΛR RD RE	✠GODPINE ON HVNTE Wt 20 6 [Pl XXV 11]	Godwine
564	✠EΛDPΛR RD RE	✠LIOFRIC ON HVNTE Wt 21 4	Liofric
565	,, ,, ,,	✠LIOFPINE ON MVNT Wt 20 0	Liofwine
		Type xiii	
566	EΛDPΛRD RE	✠GODPINE ON HVNT Wt 16 7	Godwine
		Type xv	
567	EΛDPΛRD REX	✠SÆPINE ON HVN *Var* Pyramid in one angle of cross terminates in three pellets Wt 20 7	Sæwine
		HYĐE [Hythe]	
		Type ii	
568	✠EDP ΛRD RC	✠LIOFUINE ONHY * Wt 14 1	Liofwine
		Type vii	
569	·EDPR D REX	✠CVĐRED ON HYĐE Wt 19 7	Guðred
570	✠EDPER D RE	✠GVĐRED ON HYĐE Wt 19 9	Guðred
		Type xi	
571	✠EΛDPΛR RD RE	✠COLDPINE ON HEĐE Wt 18 5	Goldwine

* Possibly Huntingdon

No	Obverse	Reverse	Moneyer

LÆPES

[Lewes]

Type II

| 572 | ✠EDPE D RE Ⴑ | ✠EADPIC ON LÆPEN Wt 9 6 | Eadwig |

[Pl XXV 12]

573	✠CDPE ND RC	✠EDPINE ON LÆY Wt 15 4	Edwine
574	✠EDPⴑ RD RE	✠LEFMⴑN O LÆPE Wt 12 2	Leofman
575	✠EDI RD RX	✠LEOFPI ON LÆP Wt 13 2	Leofwi (= Leofwig?)
576	✠EDPI RD RE	✠PIRINC ON LÆPENEN Wt 13 6	Wirinc

Type III

| 577 | ✠EDP E RD REX | ✠CODRICC ON LEPEEI Wt 15 5 | Godric |
| 578 | (Type effaced) | ✠OSHVND ONN LEPE Wt 18 0 | Osmund |

Type V

| 579 | ✠EDPⴑE. RD RE | ✠ÆLFⴢIE ON LÆPEE Wt 17 3 | Ælfsic |

[Pl XXV 13]

580	✠EDPE RD REX	✠ÆLFSIE ONN LÆPEE Wt. 26 3	
581	✠EDPE RD RE	✠EDPERD ON LÆPEE· Wt 17 5	Edward
582	✠EDPE RD REX	„ ONN LÆPE Wt 23 7	
583	✠EDP R D REX	✠CODPINCE ON LÆ Far Limbs of cross united by one circle only Wt 17 0	Godwine
584	✠EDPA RD REX	✠GODPINE ON LÆPE Wt 16 7	

No	Obverse	Reverse	Moneyer
		Type vii	
585	✠EDPER D REX *Var* Sceptre termi-nating in fleur-de-lis	✠ÆDPARD ON LÆPE Wt 20 2	Edward
586	„ „ „ *Var* Sceptre termi-nating in fleur-de-lis	✠EADPARD ON LÆPE Wt 20 2	Eadward
587	„ „ REX	✠EDPINE ON LÆPE Wt 21 8	Edwine
588	✠EDPE D RE *Var* Sceptre termi-nating in fleur-de-lis	„ „ LÆPEE Wt 20 8.	
589	✠EDPER D RE✠	✠GODPINE ON LÆPI Wt 20 8	Godwine
590	„ „ „ *Var* Sceptre termi-nating in fleur-de-lis	✠OSPOL D ON LÆPE Wt 20 1	Oswold
591	✠EDPA D REX	✠OSPOL D ON LÆPEE Wt 21 3	
		Type ix	
592	EAPPARP REX ANGL	✠EADPARD ONN LÆPE Wt 20 1	Eadward
593	„ „ „	, ON LÆPE Wt 20 7	
594	EAD PARD REX ANGLOV	✠EADPINE ON LÆPE Wt 20 7	Eadwine
595	„ „ „	✠EADPINE ON LÆPE Wt 20 7	
596	EAPPARD REX ANGLO	✠GODPINE ONN LÆPE Wt 20 7	Godwine
597	EADPRD RX ANGOR	✠OSPOLD ON LÆPEN Wt 20 7	Oswold
598	EADPARD REX ANGL	✠OSPOLD ONN LÆPE Wt 21 0	

No.	Obverse.	Reverse.	Moneyer.
		Type xi.	
599	✠EADPAR RD RE	✠GODPINE ON L.ÆPE·.· Wt. 20·9.	Godwine.
600	✠EADPAR RD RE·	✠LIOFPÆRD ON LÆPE Wt. 20·6.	Liofweard.
601	✠ADPAR RD RE	✠OσPOLD: ON LÆPE·.· Wt. 20·4.	Oswold.
602	✠EADPAR RD RE	✠PVLFPINE ON LÆPE Wt. 20·4.	Wulfwine.
		Type xiii.	
603	·EADPARD RE·	✠GODPINE· ON LÆPE Wt. 17·6.	Godwine.
	[Pl. XXV. 14.]		
604	✠DREDPDCDD RIΛ	✠LEOFPORD ON LÆ *Var.* Three pellets in field. Wt. 17·3.	Leofword (= Leofweard?).
605	EADPARD RE✠	✠OSPOLD· ON LÆPE Wt. 18·0.	Oswold.
		Type xv.	
606	EADPARD REX	✠GODPINE ON L·ÆP Wt. 21·0.	Godwine.
607	,, ,,	✠LEOFPORD ON LÆP· Wt. 20·3.	Leofword (= Leofweard?).
608	DDPARD · · · ΛEIPDI·	✠OσPO·LD ON LÆPE Wt. 20·7.	Oswold.
	LANCPORT. [Langport.]		
		Type v.	
609	✠EDPEΛ ·D REX·	✠EIL·PINE ON LANCP Wt. 26·0.	Eilwine.

No	Obverse	Reverse	Moneyer

LEHERCEASTER

[Leicester]

Type I.

No	Obverse	Reverse	Moneyer
610	✠EPDER D REX A	✠PVLFRIC ON LEHR Wt 17 5	Wulfric

Type II

| 611 | ✠EDPE RD RE | ✠CODRIE ONLEHER
 Wt 18 2 | Godric |

Type V

| 612 | ✠IDRIPA I RI | ✠EDPNE ON
 LE RICDII
 Wt 21 0 | Edwine |

Type VII

| 613 | EDPA RD RE
 Var Sceptre termi-nating in fleur-de-lis | ✠CLLDEPINE ON
 LEH
 Wt 18 6 | Gildewine |
| 614 | ✠EDPER D REX
 Var Sceptre termi-nating in fleur-de-lis | ✠CODRIC ON LEHER
 Wt 21 3 | Godric. |

[Pl XXVI 1]

615	✠E[D]PEI D RE	✠PVL[E]NNOÐ ON LEH (Broken)	Wulennoð or Wulnað (Wulfnoð)
616	✠EDPARD REX *Var* Sceptre termi-nating in fleur-de-lis	✠[PV]L ENOID ON LE Wt 18 5	
617	✠EDPAR D RE *Var* Sceptre termi-nating in fleur-de-lis	✠PVLNAÐ ON LEGR Wt 21 0	

Type IX.

| 618 | EADPARD REX ANGLO | ✠ÆGELRIC ON LEH
 Wt 20 4 | Ægelric. |
| 619 | „ „ „ | Wt 21 3 | |

2 C 2

No.	Obverse.	Reverse.	Moneyer.
620	EADPARD EX ANGL·	✠ÆGLPINE ON LEGR Wt. 18·4.	Ægelwine.
621	,, ,, ANGL	✠LEOFPINE ON LEH Wt. 20·0.	Leofwine.

Type xi.

No.	Obverse.	Reverse.	Moneyer.
622	✠EADPAR· RD RE	✠ÆLRIC ON LEHRECE Wt. 20·0.	Ælric (Ælfric).
623	✠EADPAR RD RE	✠GODRIC ON L·EHRECE Wt. 19·7.	Godric.
624	(Illegible.)	✠LIOFRIC ON LEHREC Wt. 19·0.	Liofric.

Type xii.

No.	Obverse.	Reverse.	Moneyer.
625	EADPAR RD REX	✠AGLRIC ON LEHR· Wt. 16·6.	Ægelric.

[Pl. XXVI. 2.]

Type xiii.

No.	Obverse.	Reverse.	Moneyer.
626	✠EADPARD REX	✠AGLRIC ON LEHR· Wt. 16·7.	Ægelric.
627	,, ,,	✠GODRIC ,, ,, Wt. 16·3.	Godric.

LEIGECEASTER, Etc.
[Chester.]

Type ii.

No.	Obverse.	Reverse.	Moneyer.
628	✠EDPE RD RE	✠AFFSIE ON IEII: Wt. 16·8.	Alfsie (cf. Elfsie).
629	✠EDPA RD R:	✠LEOFPINE ONLEI: Wt. 15·4.	Leofwine.
630	✠EDPER D REX	✠P[I]RYIN ON LEICEI (Pierced.)	Wiryn.

Type iii.

No.	Obverse.	Reverse.	Moneyer.
631	✠EDPE∴ ·R·D REX	✠COLBRAND ON LIC Wt. 16·8.	Colbrand.
632	,, ·RD REX·	✠ELFSIE ON LEICEST Wt. 16·4.	Elfsie.

No.	Obverse.	Reverse.	Moneyer.
	FARTHING.		
633	✠E.... X	... ... ON LE Wt. 4·5.	
	Type iv.		
634	✠EDᴘER D REX··	✠LEFPI ON LEᴅEᴄESR Wt. 16·9.	Lefwi (= Leofwine?).
	FARTHING.		
635	..... RE ..	..... .N LE .... Wt. 3·3.	
	Type v.		
636	✠EDPI RD REX	✠ELFSIE ON LEIᴄEST Wt. 17·4.	Elfsie.
637	✠EDPE: ·RD REX :	✠FĀRGRIM ON LEIᴄ·E·· Wt. 15·4.	Fargrim.
638	✠EDPER ·D REX··	✠LEOFPINE ON LEIᴄE Wt. 15·4.	Leofwine.
	Type vii.		
639	✠EDPAR D REX Var. Sceptre terminating in three pellets.	✠ÆLFᴄAR ON LEIᴄE· (Broken.)	Ælfgar.
640	·✠EDPAR D REX : Var. Sceptre terminating in fleur-de-lis.	✠BRVNINᴄ ONᴌEIᴄE Wt. 19·2.	Bruninc.
641	✠EDPA·R· D RE·· Var. Sceptre terminating in three pellets.	✠BRVNNIᴄ ON LEIᴄ Wt. 20·6.	Brunnic.
642	✠EDPAR D REX	✠ᴄOLBRAND OИ ,, Wt. 19·8.	Colbrand.
643	✠EDPAR D RE· Var. Sceptre terminating in three pellets.	✠ᴎVSᴄAR ON LEIᴄ: Wt. 19·7.	Huscarl.
644	,, ,, REX Var. Sceptre terminating in fleur-de-lis.	✠HVSᴄARL ONᴌEIᴄE Wt. 20·6.	

No.	Obverse.	Reverse.	Moneyer.
	Type vii. *var. b.*		
645	✠NDE RᴧIX *Var.* Sceptre termi- nating in fleur- de-lis. [Pl. XXVI. 3.]	✠COLBRᴧND ON LEI Wt. 20·9.	Colbrand.
	Type ix.		
646	EᴧDPᴧR RX ANGLO	✠ÆLFSIC ONN LEICE *Var.* Annulets on the limbs of cross. Wt. 20·3.	Ælfsig.
647	EᴧDPRD REX ANGLO	✠BR·YNNIC ON LEC: Wt. 19·2.	Brunninc.
	[Pl. XXVI. 4.]		
648	EᴧDPᴧRD REX ᴧNGLO	✠BRYNNIC ON[N] LEIC·∴ Wt. 21·0.	
649	,,　　　,,　ᴧNG·	✠COLBRᴧND ON LEI (Pierced.)	Colbrand.
650	EᴧDPRD RX ANGOR	✠DVNNIC ON LEGECES Wt. 18·6.	Dunninc.
651	EᴧDPᴧRD REX ᴧNGLO·	✠CODRIC ON LECA Wt. 21·6.	Godric.
652	,,　　,,　ᴧNGL·	✠LEOFNOD ON LEIC Wt. 19·6.	Leofnoð.
653	,,　　,,　　,,	✠SPEᴧRTCOL ON LEI. Wt. 20·5.	Sweartcol.
	Type xi.		
654	✠EᴧDPᴧRD RD RE	✠ÆLFωI ON LECECEω Wt. 20·6.	Ælfsig ?
655	✠EᴧDPᴧR RD RE	✠BRVNINC ON LECECC Wt. 19·0.	Bruning (Bruninc).
	[Pl. XXVI. 5.]		
656	✠EᴧDPᴧR· ,,　,,	✠DVNINC ON LECECE Wt. 20·6.	Duning (Duninc).
657	✠EᴧDPᴧR ,,　,,	✠HVωCᴧLR ONLECECC Wt. 16·0.	Huscarl.
658	✠EᴧDPᴧR· ,,　,,	✠LIOFEN◎P ON LECECC: Wt. 19·0.	Liofnoð.

No.	Obverse.	Reverse.	Moneyer.
		Type xiii.	
659	·EADPARD RE·	✠BRVNNVSEL· O LE Wt. 18·2.	Brunnusel (= Brunhusel ?).
		Type xv.	
660	✠EADPA RD RE	✠ÆLFS ON LE6EEE·· Wt. 20·8.	Ælfsig.
661	EADPARD REX	✠ALXXI ON LE6EEE Wt. 21·0.	Alxxi (Ælfsig ?).
662	,, ,,	✠HVSCARL ON LE6E Wt. 21·0.	Huscarl.
	[Pl. XXVI. 6.]		
663	,, ,, Λ·	✠HVωRALR ONLE6E Wt. 19·6.	
		LINCOLNE. [Lincoln.]	
		Type i.	
664	✠EPDAREC ECX	✠ÆLFNOÐ ONN LINCOL Wt. 15·0.	Ælfnoð.
665	✠EDPER D REX:	✠COLCRIM ON LINC Wt. 16·0.	Colgrim.
666	✠EADPAR ECCX	✠CODRIC ON LVCC Wt. 12·8.	Godric.
667	✠EDPER D REX	✠OSEFRÐ ON LINCOL: Wt. 17·5.	Osferð.
668	✠EDPE RD REX·	✠VLFF ONN LINCO: Wt. 16·6.	Ulff.
		HALFPENNY.	
669	✠EDPE .. .EX:	✠EDRI. .. ...C Wt. 6·7.	Edric.
		Type i. *var. a.*	
670	✠EADRD ECCX	✠CODRIC ON LWCL Wt. 14·0.	Godric.

No.	Obverse.	Reverse.	Moneyer.

Type ii.

No.	Obverse.	Reverse.	Moneyer.
671	✠EDPA RD RE	✠BRIHTRIC O L· Wt. 12·8.	Brihtric.
672	✠EDPI RD RE	✠BRITHRIC ON LI Wt. 15·0.	
673	✠EDPE RD RE	✠EDRIC ON LINC· Wt. 18·5.	Edric.
674	✠CDP RD RX	✠GODRIC ON LI *Var.* Pellet in field. Wt. 17·0.	Godric.
675	✠EDPA RD RX	,, ,, LIN Wt. 17·0.	
676	✠EDP RD RE	✠OÐCRIN ON LIN Wt. 13·6.	Oðgrim.

FARTHING.

No.	Obverse.	Reverse.	Moneyer.
677	✠ED..	✠..... .. ...COL Wt. 4·0.	

Type iii.

No.	Obverse.	Reverse.	Moneyer.
678	✠EDPER D REX:	✠ÆDRICC ON LINCOLE: Wt. 15·0.	Ædric.
679	✠EDPE·· RD R··	✠BRITHRIC ONINCOL Wt. 18·3.	Brihtric.
680	✠EDPEI: RD REX:	✠COLCRIM ON L·INCO Wt. 16·7.	Colgrim.
681	,, ,, ,,	,, ON LINCOL Wt. 16·2.	
682	✠EDPE ·RD REX:	✠CODRIC ON L·IHCOL Wt. 16·6.	Godric.
683	✠EDPE·· ·RD REEX	,, ,, LINCOLN· Wt. 17·6.	
684	,, ,, RE✠	✠CODRICC ON LINCOL Wt. 17·4.	
685	✠EDP: ED REX:	✠LEFPINE ON LINCOLE Wt. 17·4.	Leofwine.
686	✠EDPERI D RE✠:	✠LEOFPINE ON LINC Wt. 16·0.	

No.	Obverse.	Reverse.	Moneyer.
687	✠EDPE: ·RD REX·	✠OSFERÐ ON LINCOL· Wt. 17·3.	Osferð.
688	✠EDPE· RD REX:	✠VLFF ON LINCOLEI· Wt. 16·6.	Ulff (cf. Wulf).
689	✠EDPER· D REX:	✠PVLF ON LINCOLEI·.· Wt. 15·7.	Wulf.
690	·✠·EDPE ·RD REX	✠PVL·F ONN LINCOL·N: Wt. 18·0.	
691	✠EDPE :RD REX	✠PVLCAR ON LINCO Wt. 11·5.	Wulgar.
692	✠EDPER· D REX	✠ÐVRCRIM OИ LIИ Wt. 16·6.	Þurgrim.
693	✠EDPE· D REX:	✠ÐVRICRIM ONLINCO Wt. 15·8.	
	Halfpenny.		
694	✠EDPE X	[✠BRI]HTRIC ON L... Wt. 8·0.	Brihtric.
	Farthing.		
695	✠EDPA	✠.... .. .INCO Wt. 4·0.	
	Type iv.		
696	✠EDPA· REC✠	✠CODRVC ON· LINC Wt. 18·0.	Godric.
697	✠EDPA „	✠OSFERÐ ON L·INC: Wt. 17·3.	Osferð.
698	✠:EDPA P REE	✠VL·F ONLINCOLINA Wt. 16·2.	Ulf.
	Type iv. *var. a.*		
699	✠EDPERD REX A·.·	✠CILLIИ ONN LNCOLNN: *Var.* P A X X in angles of cross. Wt. 16·0.	Cillin?
	Type v.		
700	✠EDPE ·RD REX·	✠COLGRM ON LINCO Wt. 26·0.	Colgrim.

[Pl. XXVI. 7.]

No	Obverse	Reverse	Moneyer
701	✠EDP RD R EX	✠ĐODRIC ON LINĐO Wt 25·1	Godric
702	✠EDPE RD REX	,,　　　,,　LINĐOL Wt 27·2	
703	✠EDPAR D REĐX	✠OĐĐRIM ON LINĐO Wt 15·0	Oðbern
704	✠EDPE RD REX	✠VLF ON LINĐOLNE Wt 25·3	Ulf

Type VII

705	✠EDPE RD R	✠ASEFERĐ ⊙N LINĐO Wt 22·0	Aseferð (cf Osferð)
706	✠EDP ERD ✠	✠ĐOLĐRIM ON LIN Wt 21·2	Colgrim
707	✠EDP RD X	✠ELFN⊙Đ ⊙N LINĐO Wt 20·8	Elfnoð
708	✠EDPER D REI *Var* Sceptre terminating in fleur-de-lis	✠ĐODRIĐ ON LINĐO Wt 22·2	Godric
709	✠EDPE RD R	✠ĐODRIĐ ON LINĐOL· Wt 18·8	
710	,,　　　,, R✠	MĀNNĀ ⊙N LINĐOLL Wt 21·3	Manna
711	✠EDP ERD	✠OSFERĐ ⊙N LINĐ⊙ Wt 18·5	Osferð.
712	✠EDPAR D REI *Var* Sceptre terminating in fleur-de-lis	✠OĐBEORN ON LINĐ Wt 21·6	Oðbeorn
713	✠EDPA RD RX	✠OĐBERN ON LINĐO Wt 21·3	Oðbern
714	✠EDP ERD ✠	✠OĐĐRIM ON LINĐ Wt 24·0	Oðgrim
715	✠EDPER D REI *Var* Sceptre terminating in fleur-de-lis	,,　　,, LINĐO Wt 16·7	

Type VII *var a*

| 716 | ✠EDPER D REI *Var* Sceptre terminating in fleur-de-lis | ✠OĐĐRIM ON LINĐOL Wt 21·0 | Oðgrim |

No.	Obverse.	Reverse.	Moneyer.
		Type ix.	
717	EΛDPΛP RX ΛNGLOR·	✠ELFNOÐ ON LINƆO Wt. 20·0.	Elfnoð.
718	EDPΛR· DX ΛNGO	✠ƆODRIƆ ON LINƆO Wt. 20·5.	Godric.
719	EΛDPΛRD REX ΛИG·	✠MΛNNΛ ,, ,, Wt. 19·0.	Manna.
720	EΛDPΛD REX ΛNGLO	✠ODƆRIM OИ LINƆO Wt. 20·0.	Oðgrim.
721	EDPΛRD X. ΛNGLO·	✠PVLBEREN ON LIN Wt. 18·5.	Wulbeorn.
722	EΛDPΛRD X ,,	✠PVLFRIƆ ON LINƆO Wt. 21·2.	Wulfric.
		Type x.	
723	EDPΛD X ΛNGLOR·	✠ELFNOÐ ON LINƆ⊙ Wt. 20·4.	Elfnoð.
	[Pl. XXVI. 8.]		
		Type xi.	
724	✠EDPΛRD REX	✠ΛVTI ON LINƆOLNN Wt. 22·3.	Auti?
725	✠EΛDPΛR D RE·	✠ELFN⊙Ð OИ LINƆO Wt. 20·8.	Elfnoð.
726	✠EDPΛR· D RE:	✠ƆIFE ON LINƆOLL Wt. 17·0.	Gife.
727	✠EΛDPΛR RD RE	✠ƆODRƆ ON LINƆOL· Wt. 20·3.	Godric.
728	✠EDPΛRD REI·	✠ODƆRIM ON LINƆO Wt. 20·8.	Oðgrim.
729	✠EΛDPΛR· RD RE	✠OÐωL·ΛƆ ON LINƆO (Broken.)	Oðslac (Oðlac).
730	✠EΛDPΛR RD RE	✠VLF ON LINƆOLИE Wt. 22·0.	Ulf.
731	,, ,, ,,	✠PVLBEORN ⊙NLINƆOL· Wt. 21·5.	Wulbeorn.
732	,, ,, ,,	,, ,, Wt. 21·0.	

No.	Obverse	Reverse	Moneyer.
733	✠EDPAR D R	✠PVLFRIC ON LIN (Broken)	Wulfric

Type xiii

734	·EADPAD RE✠ ANC	✠EDRIC ON LINCO Wt 17 6	Edric
735	✠EADPARED REX	✠GARFIN ON LINCOL Wt 17 3	Garfin
736	✠EADPARE D R✠ *Var* Frontal-band of crown omitted	✠OÐCRIM ON LINC Wt 16 5	Oðgrim
737	✠EADPARD RX	✠VLF ON LINCOL *Var* Four pellets on inner circle Wt 17 5	Ulf.
738	✠EADPARD REX *Var* Frontal-band of crown omitted	✠PVL BRN ON LINC Wt 17 7	Wulbeorn

Type xiii *var a*

| 739 | ✠EADPARD REX *Var* Frontal band of crown omitted [Pl XXVI 9] | ✠PVL BRN ⊙ON LINCO Wt 17 5 | Wulbeorn. |

Type xv.

740	EADPARD REX	✠IEFGEHT ON LIN Wt 21 8	Ælfget?
741	„ „ A	✠IELFGEHT ON LINC Wt 22 0	
742	„ „	✠AGAMVND ON LINC Wt 20 8	Agamund.
743	EADARD REX IO	✠EDRIC ON LINCOL Wt 21 2	Edric.
744	EADPARD „	✠LEOFPOLD ON LINC Wt 19 2	Leofwold
745	„ RE	✠PVLGHR ON LNI Wt 16 3	Wulgar.

No.	Obverse.	Reverse.	Moneyer.

LUNDENE.
[London.]

Type i.

No.	Obverse.	Reverse.	Moneyer.
746	✠EDPE: RD REX :	✠ÆLFRED ON LVNDE Wt. 16·0.	Ælfred.
747	✠EDPΣR D REX Λ:	✠ÆLFPERD ,, ,, Wt. 16·7.	Ælfwerd.
748	✠EDPNRD D REႠ	✠BRIHTMÆR ON LVD Wt. 12·5.	Brihtmær.
749	✠EDPER D REX.·.	✠DVDINႠ ONN LVN Wt. 15·0.	Dudinc.
750	✠EDPNR. REႠ.	✠EΛDPOLD ON LVN Wt. 16·5.	Eadwold.
751	✠EDDE· RD REX :	✠FDIII OIIN LVIIDE: Wt. 13·0.	Edin?
752	✠EDPER· D REX	✠ESTHER ON LVND: Wt. 14·0.	Esther.
753	EDPΛ: REႠ:✠ ·Λ·	✠ᏀODESVNE ON LVD: Wt. 15·0.	Godesunc.
754	✠·EDPNRD REI:	✠ႠODPINE ON LVD Wt. 11·3.	Godwiue.
755	✠EDPЄR: D REX.	✠ႠODPINE ON LVND: Wt. 17·3.	
	[Pl. XXVI. 10.]		
756	✠EDPER· D REX·.·	✠LEOFRED ONN LVND Wt. 14·0.	Leofred.
757	✠E[DP]ER D REX:	✠LEOFSTΛ[N] ON LVN (Broken.)	Leofstan.
758	,, ,, REX Λ:	✠LEOFSTΛN ON LVND Wt. 16·6.	
759	✠EDPΛR D REX·.·	✠PVLFRED ON LVND Wt. 14·9.	Wulfred.
760	✠·VEDNRD: D RE	✠PVLSIႠE ON LVDE Wt. 12·6.	Wulsige.

No.	Obverse	Reverse	Moneyer

HALFPENNIES

761	✠EDPNR	✠BRIHTM ND Wt 6·3	Brihtmær
762	✠EADPN .	✠CODPI . ND Wt 7·5	Godwine.
763	... PNRD	✠S . . N LVND Wt 7·5	
764	✠EDPN C	✠ NE ON LV Wt 5·8	

Type II

765	✠EDEA RD RE	✠ÆCELIC ON LVN Wt 12·7	Ægelwig
766	✠EDPА „ „	„ „ Wt 11·5	
767	✠EDNA RDE	✠ÆCELPI ON LVN Wt 15·5	
768	✠EDPA D RE	✠ÆCLPIC ON LVN Wt 11·7	
769	✠EDPA RD RE	✠ÆLFFET ON LVИ Wt 11·0	Ælfiet (Ælfeeh)
770	✠EDPE „ „	„ „ Wt 10·2	
771	„ „ „	✠ÆLFRED ON LVND Wt 13·0	Ælfred
772	✠EDP RD R	✠ÆLFP ON LVND Wt 15·5	Ælfw (= Ælfwald or Ælfwig)
773	✠EDPN RDE	„ „ LVNDE Wt 9·0	
774	✠EPD RD REX	✠ÆLFPALD OH LV Wt 13·7	Ælfwald
775	✠EDPA RD RE	✠ÆLFPIC OИ LVИ Wt 17·3	Ælfwig
776	„ „ „	„ „ Wt 17·8	
777	✠EDPА RD RE	✠ÆLFPIC OИ LVИ Wt 11·3	

No.	Obverse.	Reverse.	Moneyer.
778	✠EDPA RD R	✠.ÆL·P.IC ON LVN Wt. 9·5.	
779	✠EDPN : RDE✠ :	✠ÆEFPINE „ „ Wt. 11·3.	Ælfwine.
780	✠EDPA RD R	✠ÆLFPINE ON LVND Wt. 17·5.	
781	✠EDP RD RE	✠ÆL·PINE ON LVN : Wt. 11·5.	
782	✠EDPV RPD	✠ELFPINE ON LVD Wt. 9·6.	
783	✠EDHP : RDE	„ O LVN Wt. 14·8.	
784	✠EPA RD R :	„ ON LVND Wt. 11·2.	
785	✠EDPA· RDE	✠ÆLFPOND ON LVD Wt. 16·8.	Ælfwond ? (cf. Ælfwald).
786	✠EPD RD RE·X	✠ALDCAR ON LV Wt. 12·0.	Aldgar.
787	✠EPDI RD REX	„ „ LVN Wt. 10·2.	
788	✠EDPN·.· RDE	✠NLDCAR ON LVN : Wt. 12·0.	
789	✠EDP.·. E REEX	✠BINRED ON LVN Wt. 14·5.	Binred (=Winred or Brihtred).
790	„ „	„ „ „ Wt. 14·8.	
791	✠ED PAR R	✠BRINTRED ON LV Wt. 11·2.	Brihtred.
792	✠EDPE RD· R··	✠BRINTRED ON LVN Wt. 13·0.	
793	✠EDRA RD RX	✠BVRHREI OH LVN Wt. 15·0.	Burnhere?
794	✠EPA·R· D REX	✠CINENÆR ONLV Wt. 10·4.	Cinemær.
795	„ „ „	„ „ Wt. 10·0.	
796	✠EDPA· D RE	✠DEOHEN ON LVN Wt. 10·5.	Deohen (Deorhan).
797	✠EDPA RD RE	✠DEORHAN ONLV Wt. 17·2.	Deorhan.

No	Obverse	Reverse	Moneyer
798	✠EDPA D RE	✠DEORHAN ON LV Wt 150	
799	✠EDPH RDE	✠DIREMA ON LVN Wt 142	Direma(n)
800	✠EDPA RD R	„　　„　LVN Wt 94	
801	✠EDPER D REC	„　　„　„ Wt 131	
802	✠EDPE RD RE	✠DVLPC ON LVND Wt 170	Dulwic? (cf Wulfric).
803	✠EDPN RDE	✠DVRREB ON LVN Wt 141	Durreb?

[Pl XXVI 11]

No	Obverse	Reverse	Moneyer
804	✠EDP RD R·E	✠EADPIC ON LVN Wt 92	Eadwig
805	✠EDPA RD REX	✠EDPALD ON LVND Wt 116	Edwald
806	✠EDPI RD RE	✠EDPINE ON LV Wt 107	Edwine
807	✠EDP RD R	„　ONLVND Wt 157	
808	✠TIRIPI EDI	✠EDPINNE ON LVNI Wt 135	
809	✠EDPA RD E	✠ECELRIC ON LVN Wt 130	Egelric (Ægelric)
810	✠EDPNR· RD E	„　„　LVND Wt 153	
811	✠ED RD RE	✠ECLPIC ON LV Wt 121	Egelwig (Ægelwig)
812	✠EDPER D REX	✠ELFRIC ONN LVD Wt 174	Elfric
813	✠EDP ARI	✠ELFSTAN ON L D Wt 110	Elfstan
814	✠EDP. ARD RC	✠ELFSTAN ON IVDI Wt 86	
815	✠EDPA RD E	✠CODRIC ON LVND Wt 138	Godric
816	✠EDPA RD RE	✠ CODPI ON LVND Wt 98	Godwine

No.	Obverse.	Reverse.	Moneyer.
817	✠EPD RD REX	✠CODPINE ON LV Wt. 14·6.	
818	✠EDPE RD RE	,, ,, LVN Wt. 16·9.	
819	✠EDPH·.· RD E	✠CODPINE ON LVND Wt. 12·0.	
820	✠EDPN· RD E	✠COLDSIE ON LVN Wt. 14·0.	Goldsie.
821	,, ,, ,,	,, ,, ,, Wt. 11·3.	
822	,, RD E	✠COLDSI ON LVND Wt. 12·0.	
823	✠EDPE· RD R·	✠COLTSINE ON LX Wt. 9·6.	Goltsine (= Goltsige?).
824	✠EDPΛ RD E	·✠L·EOCNO : EI ON LV· Wt. 12·0.	Leofnoð?
825	,, ,, ,,	,, ,, ,, ,, Wt. 8·0.	
826	✠EDPE RD RE	✠LEOEPL· ON LVND Wt. 15·0.	Leofwi?
827	✠EPD RD REX	✠LICNFC ON L·VNI· Wt. 13·5.	Lifinc?
828	✠VD: REEPR	,, ,, LVND·.· Wt. 10·0.	
829	✠EP RD RE·	✠LICNI ON LVND·· Wt. 14·0.	
830	✠EDPΛ· RD RE	✠LIFINC ON LVND. Wt. 9·7.	Lifinc.
831	✠EDPΛ ,, ,,	,, ,, ,, Wt. 14·6.	
832	,, ,, ,,	,, ,, ,, Wt. 14·5.	
833	✠EDPE D REX	,, ,, LINDI Wt. 14·2.	
834	✠EDPNR R DEX·	✠LIFINEC ON IVN Wt. 12·5.	
835	✠EPI RD REX	✠L·IFRED ON LVN Wt. 11·2.	Liofred.

No.	Obverse.	Reverse.	Moneyer.
836	✠EDPN· RDE	✠LIOFRED ON LVN Wt. 15·2.	
837	✠EDPNA· D RE	✠PIREMA ON LVN Wt. 12·0.	Wirema.
838	,, ,,	,, ,, Wt. 10·7.	
839	✠EDPHR· D RE	✠PVLCRED ON LVHD Wt. 15·2.	Wulcred (= Wulfred?)
840	✠EDPH·· RD E	,, ,, LVN Wt. 14·2.	
841	✠ED·.·E RD RE·.·	✠PVLFRIC ON LVE Wt. 15·3.	Wulfric.
842	✠EDPN· D RE	✠PVLωI ON LVND Wt. 13·8.	Wulsige?
843	✠EDPNA· D RE	✠PVLPINE ON LVN Wt. 14·8.	Wulwine (Wulfwine).
844	✠EDPNR· RD E	✠PVRREB ,, ,, Wt. 13·5.	Wurreb (= Þurreb?).
845	✠EDPI RD RE	✠ĐOR ON LVNDI Wt. 10·0.	Þor.

HALFPENNIES.

No.	Obverse.	Reverse.	Moneyer.
846	..... RD RE·.·	✠BRI..... .N LV Wt. 5·8.	Brihtmaer.
847	....A RD ..	✠EL... .. LVИ Wt. 5·5.	Elfric?
848	✠EPD X	✠......E ON LV Wt. 7·0.	Godwine?
849	✠EDPE RD E	✠ᏟOL.... .. .VND : Wt. 8·8.	Goltsige?
850	✠EDP. .D E	...LSI ON LV.. Wt. 6·5.	Wulsig (= Wulfsig).
851	✠EDPΛ ...	✠.... ON LVN Wt. 7·2.	
852	...ER . .	✠.... O·N L·VN Wt. 7·2.	
853	✠EDP: ...	✠.... .. LVND : Wt. 4·7.	
854	✠EDPEI· ...	...... N LVND Wt. 4·8.	

No.	Obverse.	Reverse.	Moneyer.
		FARTHING.	
855	..... .D ...	..... ON LV Wt. 4·2.	
		Type iii.	
856	✠EDPE: R ERX·	✠ÆEELPI ON LVNDE Wt. 13·7.	Ægelwig ?
857	✠EDPND: D ER·	✠ÆGELPI ON LVNDE: Wt. 15·5.	Ægelwig.
858	✠EDPNR D RE·	✠ÆGL·PI·. ON LVND Wt. 14·3.	
859	✠EDPNER·· RD E	✠ÆGEL·PIG ON LVND Wt. 15·0.	
860	✠EDPN RD EX A	✠ÆGELPIG ON LVND Wt. 13·0.	
861	✠EDPHED: RD E	✠ÆLESISE ON LVND: (Chipped.)	Ælfsige.
862	✠EDPE ·D REX	✠ÆLFGAR ON LVNDE Wt. 14·0.	Ælfgar.
863	✠EDPNR· RDE	✠ÆLFRED ON LVND Wt. 14·2.	Ælfred.
864	·✠·EDPE·· ·RD REX	✠ÆLFRED ON LVND·· Wt. 17·0.	
865	✠EDPN: RD EX V	✠ÆLFPI: ON LVNDE· Wt. 13·0.	Ælfwig.
866	✠EDP ERD RE *Var.* Sceptre termi- nating in fleur- de-lis.	✠ÆL·FPIG ON LVND Wt. 16·0.	
867	✠·EDPE·: ·RD REX	✠ÆLFPINE ON LVNDE Wt. 16·3.	Ælfwine.
868	✠EDPED· ·D REX	✠ELFPINE ON LVND Wt. 15·5.	
869	✠EDPIIR: D RE·	✠ÆLFPN ON LVNDE: Wt. 14·5.	Ælfwine ?
870	✠EDPN· RD EX A	✠ALRIG ON LVNDE Wt. 15·0.	Alric.
871	✠EDPER RD RE·	✠BRINTRED ON LVND Wt. 13·2.	Brihtred.

No.	Obverse.	Reverse.	Moneyer.
872	✠EDPD: ·D RE✠ A	✠EADRIC: ON LVND Wt. 15·5.	Eadric.
873	✠EDPNE· RER	✠EDRIC ON LVNDE· Wt. 15·0.	
874	✠EDPE ·RD REX	✠ED·PINE ON LVNDE· Wt. 15·2.	Edwine.
875	✠EDPNE: RER	✠LODSVNNV ON LVND Wt. 13·2.	Godsunu.
	[Pl. XXVI. 12.]		
876	„ „	„ „ Wt. 14·8.	
877	„ „	✠LODSVMIV „ „ Wt. 12·0.	
878	✠EDPNR· D RE	✠LODPIC ON LVND Wt. 12·3.	Godwic.
879	✠EDPE··· ·RD REX	✠LODPINE „ „ Wt. 17·7.	Godwine.
880	✠EDPN: RD EX A	✠LOLDPINE ON LVND Wt. 15·3.	Goldwine.
881	✠EDPER ·D REX:	✠LOLTSILE ON LVNDE Wt. 13·0.	Goltsige.
882	✠EDPE: ·D REX··	✠LOLTSIIE ON LVND Wt. 17·5.	
883	✠EDPNDE: RD E	✠LOVSIV ON LVND: Wt. 12·0.	Uncertain.
884	✠EDPA RD R·EX	✠LEOFPIL ON LVNDN Wt. 15·2.	Leofwig.
885	✠EDPAR D RE Var. Sceptre terminating in fleur-de-lis.	✠LEOFPINE O LVND: Wt. 13·8.	Leofwine.
886	✠EDPE: RD REX	✠L·IFRED ON LVND Wt. 17·2.	Lifred.
887	✠EDPN·· R DEX V	✠SBEIMAN ON LVND Wt. 12·3.	Sbeiman (= Swetman?).
888	„ „ „	✠SPETMAN ON LVND Wt. 12·8.	Swetman.
889	✠EDPNE R DEX A	✠VHITRED ON LVND Wt. 16·0.	Uhitred (Whitred).
890	„ R DE:	✠PVLCRED ON LVND Wt. 14·3.	Wulcred (Wulfred?).

No.	Obverse.	Reverse.	Moneyer.
891	✠EDPEᴄ: D RE✠	✠PVLᴄRED ON LVND: Wt. 14·5.	
892	✠EDPNE RDE	✠PVLᴄPINE ON LVND Wt. 14·5.	Wulfwine.
893	✠EDPN·· RDE✠	✠PVLᴄPINE ON LVND: Wt. 13·2.	
894	✠EDPER·· D REX	✠PVLFPINE ON LVND Wt. 15·5.	
895	✠DPNR RDE·X ᴧ	✠PVLSIᴄ ON LVND Wt. 13·0.	Wulsig (Wulfsig).

HALFPENNIES.

No.	Obverse.	Reverse.	Moneyer.
896	✠EDP ·· .EX V *Var.* Sceptre termi- nating in fleur- de-lis.	· · · · RIᴄ: ON LV Wt. 5·4.	Godric ?
897	· · · · ᴧD RD · · ·	✠ᴄOD· · · · ·· · ·ND: Wt. 8·0.	Godwine ?
898	· · · ·PN·· R · · · ·	✠PVL· · · · ·· · ·ND: Wt. 7·0.	Wulfwine ?
899	· · · ·Pᴧ RD · · ·	·· Oᴄᴧ·T ON L·· · · · Wt. 6·5.	
900	· · · · ·D RE:X	✠· · · · ·ᴄ ON LVNDN Wt. 5·3.	
901	· · · ·E·· ·P. · · ·	· · · · · · · LVNDENN Wt. 7·0.	

FARTHINGS.

No.	Obverse.	Reverse.	Moneyer.
902	.EDPE ·· · · ·	✠· · · · · ·· LVN Wt. 4·2.	
903	· · ·ND ·· · · ·	✠· · · · · · ·· · VᴎD Wt. 4·5.	
904	· · · · · R RE✠ V	✠· · · · · · ·· · ·ND: Wt. 4·0.	

Type iii. *var. a.*

No.	Obverse.	Reverse.	Moneyer.
905	:XƎЯ D�7· ·ƎꟼDƎ✠	IᴎƎDIV7 ᴎᴎO ƎISꟼ7Ǝ✠ Wt. 17·5.	Elfsie.

[Pl. XXVI. 13.]

No.	Obverse.	Reverse.	Moneyer.
	Type iv.		
906	✠EDP· ·RD RE·	✠ÆC:ELPARÐ ON LVN Wt. 12·5.	Ægelward.
907	✠EDPAD· D REX	✠ED : POLD ONLVNDE Wt. 11·0.	Edwold.
908	✠EDPER D REX :	✠LEOFRIC ONLVNDE Wt. 14·0.	Leofric.
	[Pl. XXVI. 14.]		
909	✠EDPERD REX Λ·	✠ORLΛF ON LVND : Wt. 15·0.	Orlaf.
	HALFPENNY.		
910	.EDPER	. . . . . ONLVNDE Wt. 7·3.	
	Type iv. *var. a.* HALFPENNY.		
911	✠E . . . . D REX :·	. . . . IC ONN LVND Wt. 7·3.	
	Type v.		
912	✠EDPE: ·RD REX	✠ÆLFRED ON LVNDEN : Wt. 14·2.	Ælfred.
913	✠EDPND RDEX V	✠ÆLFRED ON LVNDENE· Wt. 16·0.	
914	✠EDPE RD REX	✠ÆLREDD ON LVND : Wt. 16·5.	
915	✠EDPE ·RD REX	✠ÆL·FPINE ON LVND Wt. 25·7.	Ælfwine.
916	✠EDPE: ·RD REEX :	✠ÆLFPINE ON LVNDENE : Wt. 23·8.	
917	✠EDPE ·RD REX :	✠BRICSIE ON LVND : Wt. 27·0.	Bricsige.
918	✠EDPER D REX :	✠BRICSICE ON LVND : Wt. 25·7.	

No.	Obverse.	Reverse.	Moneyer.
919	✚EDPER· ·D REEX·∴	✚BRIXSIE ON LVNDENE Wt. 25·7.	
920	✚EDPE RD RE	✚BRIИTRED ON LVИD Wt. 13·7.	Brihtred.
921	✚EDPE ·RD R:EX	✚BVRED ON LVND·∴ *Var.* Limbs of cross united by one circle only. Wt. 23·7.	Bured.
922	,, ,, REX	✚DVDIИE ON LVNDE· Wt. 17·0.	Dudinc.
923	✚EDP·· RD RE✚	✚EADMVND ON LVD Wt. 14·8.	Eadmund.
924	✚EDPER· ·D REEX:	✚EDRED ON LVNDE: Wt. 26·7.	Edred.
925	✚EDPER :D R·EX·∴	✚EPII OИM LVNDNDNE: Wt. 25·4.	Edwine?
926	✚EDPE ·RD REX	✚EDPINE ON LVNDE: Wt. 17·4.	Edwine.
927	✚EDP· ED REE·	✚ELFSIEE ON LVNDEN· Wt. 16·5.	Elfsige.
928	✚EDPE RD·· RE	✚ELFSIE OH LVNDENE·∴ Wt. 15·6.	
929	✖EDPR· RD REX	✚ETSE ONN LVNDE· Wt. 15·5.	Etsige (Eadsige).
930	✚EDPE RD REX	✚ETSIEE ON LVND·∴ *Var.* Limbs of cross united by one circle only. Wt. 24·9.	
931	✚EDP·∴ ·RD REX·	✚L·TSE ONN LVNDE·∴ Wt. 16·1.	
932	✚EDP: ·RD RX.	✚EODRIE ON LVNDEE·∴ Wt. 26·2.	Godric.
933	✚EDPE ·RD REX·	✚EODPINE ON LVN: Wt. 26·7.	Godwine.
934	,, R.D REX	,, ,, LVND·∴ Wt. 25·7.	
935	✚EDP ,, ,,	,, ,, LVNDE Wt. 18·2.	

No.	Obverse.	Reverse.	Moneyer.
936	✠EDD ·RD RE✠:	✠ꝆODDINE ON LVNEI: Wt. 24·0.	
937	✠EDP· RD ,,	✠ꝆOLTSNE ON LVNDE·.· (Broken.)	Goltsine.
938	✠EDPE: ·RD REX:	✠LEOFRED ON LVN: Wt. 26·3.	Leofred.
939	✠EDPE·.· ·RD REEX	,, ,, LVNDE Wt. 24·8.	
	[Pl. XXVII. 1.]		
940	✠EDPER: ·D REEX	✠LEOFSIE ON LVND·.· Wt. 27·4.	Leofsie (Leofsige).
941	✠EDP ·R·D R·EX·	✠LIFINꝆꝆ ONN LVNDEN: *Var.* Limbs of cross united by one circle only. Wt. 25·4.	Lifine.
942	✠EDP RD REX·	✠LIFIND ON LVNDE: Wt. 14·0.	
943	✠EDPER RD REEX	✠LIOFPINE ON LVND Wt. 21·0.	Liofwine.
944	✠EDPE·.· ·RD REX:	✠SPRAꝆELINꝆ ON LVND: Wt. 25·5.	Sprageline.
945	✠EDP· ·RD R·EX	✠PVLꝆRDD ON LVIIDE·.· Wt. 16·8.	Wulfred.
946	✠EDPI RD REX	✠ꞄVLꝆRED ON LVND: Wt. 17·7.	
947	✠EDPE ,, ,,	✠PVLFPINE ON LVNDEN Wt. 13·7.	Wulfwine.
948	✠EDP ·RD RE·X	✠P.VL·INEE ON LVDN Wt. 17·2.	
	Type v. *var. a.*		
949	✠EDPE ·RD REX	✠ꝆODPINE ONN LVND: *Var.* Limbs of cross united by one circle only. Wt. 24·0.	Godwine
	[Pl. XXVII. 2.]		

No.	Obverse.	Reverse.	Moneyer.
		Type vii.	
950	✠EDPERD REX· *Var.* Sceptre termi- nating in fleur- de-lis.	✠ÆIELRIꞒ ON LVND: Wt. 21·5.	Ægelric?
951	✠EDPER.·. D REX	„ „ „ Wt. 20·7.	Ægelwig.
952	✠EDPER· D RE· *Var.* Sceptre termi- nating in fleur- de-lis.	„ ON LVNDEE Wt. 20·5.	
953	✠EDPER·.· D REꞒ *Var.* Sceptre termi- nating in fleur- de-lis.	✠ÆLFRED ON LVND: Wt. 21·7.	Ælfred.
954	✠EDPERD REꞒ· *Var.* Sceptre termi- nating in fleur- de-lis.	✠ÆLFPERD ON LVND: Wt. 16·9.	Ælfwerd.
955	✠EDPER D RꞒX	„ „ LVNDE Wt. 17·7.	
956	✠EDPER· D REX·	✠ÆLFPORD „ „ Wt. 19·3.	
957	✠EDPER· D REX *Var.* Sceptre termi- nating in fleur- de-lis.	✠ÆLPERD: ON LVNDENE Wt. 19·7.	
958	„ „ „ *Var.* Sceptre termi- nating in fleur- de-lis.	✠ÆLFPINE : ON LVNDE : Wt. 19·7.	Ælfwine.
959	✠EDPER·.· D RERX	✠ÆLPINE ON LVNDE Wt. 18·2.	
960	✠EDPA·.· D REX	✠BRIHTPINE ON LV Wt. 18·8.	Brihtwine.
961	✠EDPER· „ „	„ „ LVND: Wt. 16·0.	
962	„ „ „ *Var.* Sceptre termi- nating in fleur- de-lis.	✠BRVNꞒAR ON LVND: Wt. 21·5.	Brungar.
963	✠EDPER·.· „ „	„ „ LVNDE Wt. 20·0.	

No.	Obverse.	Reverse.	Moneyer.
964	✠EDPER D REX	✠BRVNⒼAR ON LVNDE: Wt. 21·4.	
965	✠EDPER· „ „	✠EⱯDPOLD ON LVND : Wt. 19·2.	Eadwold.
966	✠EⱯDPE RD RE[X]	✠EⱯLDVLF ON LVNDENE Wt. 16·2.	Ealdulf.
967	✠EDPER· D REX	✠EⒸPIⒸ ONN ᒪVNDENE: Wt. 19·9.	Ecwig.
968	✠EDPE· D REX Var. Sceptre terminating in fleur-de-lis.	✠EDRED ON LVNDE: Wt. 20·5.	Edred.
969	✠EDPER D REX	✠EDRIⒸ ONN LVNDENE: Wt. 14·7.	Edric.
970	✠EDPER· D REX	✠EDPINE ON LVNDE: Wt. 21·0.	Edwine.
971	EADPE RD REX	✠ESTMVND ON LVɅE Wt. 20·5.	Estmund.
972	✠EⱯP ERD· Var. Sceptre terminating in fleur-de-lis.	✠ⒸLIFPINE ON LVNDE·· Wt. 16·7.	Glifwine.
973	✠EDPER· D REX Var. Sceptre terminating in fleur-de-lis. [Pl. XXVII. 3.]	✠ⒸODERE „ „ Wt. 20·7.	Godere.
974	„ Var. „ „ Sceptre terminating in fleur-de-lis.	✠ⒸODMⱯN ON LVN Wt. 20·7.	Godman.
975	„ „ „	✠ⒼODMAN ON LVND: Wt. 20·1.	
976	✠EDPE D R[EX]	✠ⒸODRIⒸ ON LVNDENE: Wt. 18·7.	Godric.
977	✠EDPER· D REX Var. Sceptre terminating in fleur-de-lis.	✠ⒸODPINE ON LVND Wt. 21·5.	Godwine.

No.	Obverse.	Reverse.	Moneyer.
978	✠EDPER· D REX *Var.* Sceptre terminating in three pellets.	✠ᴅODPINE ON LVNDE Wt. 19·5.	
979	„ „ „ *Var.* Sceptre terminating in fleur-de-lis.	✠ᴅOLDSIE „ „ Wt. 20·2.	Goldsige.
980	✠EDRER· D REI· *Var.* Sceptre terminating in fleur-de-lis.	✠LEOFRED ON LVND: Wt. 19·7.	Leofred or Liofred.
981	✠EDPER· „ „ *Var.* Sceptre terminating in fleur-de-lis.	„ „ LVNI: Wt. 21·9.	
982	✠EDPER· D REX· *Var.* Sceptre terminating in fleur-de-lis.	✠LIOFRED ON LVNDEN Wt. 15·2.	
983	✠EDPE· ·D REX *Var.* Sceptre terminating in fleur-de-lis.	✠:L·EORIᴅ ON L·VNDE Wt. 16·0.	Leofric.
984	✠EDPER· D REI· *Var.* Sceptre terminating in fleur-de-lis.	✠LEOFPINE ON LVND Wt. 21·2.	Leofwine.
985	„ „ „ *Var.* Sceptre terminating in fleur-de-lis.	✠LEOPINE ON LVND Wt. 20·5.	
986	EADPE RD REX	✠OMVND ON LVNDEI Wt. 17·4.	Omund (Osmund).
987	✠EDPER D „	„ ONN L·VNDEN Wt. 17·0.	
988	EⱭDPE RD REX	✠ഗIRED: ON LVDEN Wt. 19·6.	Sired.
989	„ „ „	✠SIRED: ON LVNDENE Wt. 18·9.	
990	✠EADP: ERD Rᴅ *Var.* Sceptre terminating in fleur-de-lis.	✠ƩPETMⱯN ON LVN Wt. 20·7.	Swetman.

No.	Obverse.	Reverse.	Moneyer.
991	✠EΛDPE RD RE	✠PVLFPINE ON LVNDENE Wt. 19·8.	Wulfwine.
992	,, ,, REX	✠PVLCΛR: ON LVNDEN Wt. 19·7.	Wulgar.
	Type vii. *var. b.*		
993	✠EΛDPE ·ΛR·D REX·	✠EΛDPOLD ONN LVND: Wt. 18·3.	Eadwold.
	Type ix.		
994	EΛDPΛRD REX ΛGORV	✠ÆCELPER OИ LVИD·: Wt. 19·4.	Ægelwer (cf. Ægelwerd).
995	EΛDVVEΛRDV REX ΛNCLO	✠ÆLFRED OИ LVИD: Wt. 21·3.	Ælfred.
996	EΛDVVERDVS REX ΛNCLO	✠ÆLFSICE ON LVNDEN Wt. 21·3.	Ælfsige.
997	EΛDPEΛRD REX ΛNGLOR	✠ÆLFPERD ON LVND Wt. 20·5.	Ælfwerd.
998	EΛDPPRD RΛX ANGORV	✠ÆLPERD ON LVND: Wt. 20·5.	
999	EADPΛ REX ΛNGLO	✠DEORMAN ,, ,, (Broken.)	Deorman.
1000	EΛDPEΛRD REX ΛNGLO	,, ,, LVNDE: Wt. 17·4.	
1001	EΛDPPRD RΛE:X ΛNGOR	✠DIREMΛN ON LVDENLDE Wt. 18·7.	Direman.
1002	EΛDPΛRD R✠ ΛNGLOR	✠EALDGΛR ON LVNDE Wt. 17·5.	Ealdgar.
1003	✠EΛDRPΛRD REX ΛNLCꓤ	,, ,, LVNDEI Wt. 17·4.	
1004	EΛDPΛRD REX ΛNCLO	✠EDPI ON LVNDENEN·· Wt. 21·0.	Edwig.
1005	EDPΛRD RE ΛNGLORVM	✠GODRIC ON LVND Wt. 20·3.	Godric.
1006	EΛDPΛ REX ΛNGLO·	,, ,, LVNDE Wt. 19·3.	

No.	Obverse.	Reverse.	Moneyer.
1007	EADPEARD REX ANGLO⊙··	✠GODRIC ON LVNDEN Wt. 20·0.	
1008	EADPEARD REX ANGLO	✠GODPINE ON LVND Wt. 20·3.	Godwine.
1009	EAVVARD REX ANGLORV	✠GODPNE „ „ Wt. 21·0.	
1010	EADPARD RX ANGLO·	✠LEFPINE ON LVND·· Wt. 18·4.	Lefwine (Leofwine).
1011	EADPPEARD SEX ANGLO	✠LIFIND: ON LVNDEEN·· Wt. 20·7.	Lifinc or Liofinc.
1012	EADPARD REX ANGLOE	✠LIOFINC ON LVNDEN Wt. 16·2.	
1013	EADVVEARDVS REX ANGL	✠OMYИD OИИ LVИD: Wt. 21·3.	Omynd (cf. Osmund).
1014	EADPPRD RIX ANGORV	✠OMYND: O:N LVNDNED Wt. 21·5.	
1015	EAPPRD REX ANGLOVM	✠PVLFCAR ON LVND Wt. 21·2.	Wulfgar or Wulgar.
1016	EADPEARD REX ANGLOƠX	✠PVLGAR „ „ Wt. 21·1.	
1017	EADPEA REX ANGLO	✠P.VL·GA·R ON LVNDE Wt. 19·8.	
1018	EADPEARD REX ANGLO	✠PVL·GAR „ „ Wt. 17·7.	
1019	EADPEARD REX ANGLO	✠PVLGAR ON LVNDEИE Wt. 17·1.	
1020	EADPRD R✠ ANCORV	✠PVLFRED ON LVND Wt. 22·1.	Wulfred.
1021	EADPARD RX ANGLOR	✠PLVFRED ON LVNDE·· Wt. 18·4.	

[Pl. XXVII. 4.]

| 1022 | ✠DREDND PENDREDRE | ✠RVLFRIIX OИ LVИИII Wt. 18·3. | Wulfric. |
| 1023 | EADPRD R✠ ANGO· | ✠PVLFPINE ON LVND Wt. 19·0. | Wulfwine. |

No.	Obverse.	Reverse.	Moneyer.
1024	EADPARD REX ANGORV	✠PVLFPINE ON LVNDEN Wt. 20·8.	
1025	EADPEARD REX ANGL	✠PVL·FPINE ON LVNDENE Wt. 16·6.	

Type xi.

No.	Obverse.	Reverse.	Moneyer.
1026	✠EADPARD RD RE	✠AEDCAR ON LVNDE: Wt. 16·9.	Ædgar.
1027	✠EADPAR· ,, ,,	✠ÆLFRED ,, ,, Wt. 19·6.	Ælfred.
1028	✠EADRAR ,, ,,	✠ÆLFϖICE ON LVNDE Wt. 21·0.	Ælfsige.
1029	✠EADPAR ,, ,,	✠ÆÆLFPARD ON LVND Wt. 19·5.	Ælfweard.
1030	✠EADARD RD RE	✠ÆLFPEARD ON LVND Wt. 15·3.	
1031	✠EADPAR ,, ,,	✠ÆLFPINE ON LVND: Wt. 19·7.	Ælfwine.
1032	,, ,, ,,	,, ,, LVNDE·· (Chipped.)	
1033	✠EADPARD· ,, ,,	,, ,, LVNDEN. Wt. 17·2.	
1034	✠EADPAR· ,, ,,	✠ÆLFPINE ON LVNDO: Wt. 17·2.	
1035	,, ,, REX A	✠ÆLPINE ON LVNDEN Wt. 15·0.	
1036	✠EADPAR RD RE	✠DVRIC: ON LVNDE·· Wt. 20·0.	Durinc.
1037	,, ,, ,,	✠DVRINC: ON LVNDE: Wt. 21·2.	
1038	✠EADPAR· ,, ,,	✠EDPINE ON LVNDE Wt. 22·0.	Edwine.
1039	✠EADPAR ,, ,,	✠GODRIC ON LVND: Wt. 17·0.	Godric.
1040	✠EADPAR ,, ,,	,, ,, LVNDE: Wt. 16·8.	
1041	✠EADPAR ,, ,,	✠GODPINE ON LVDND: Wt. 20·5.	Godwine.

No.	Obverse.	Reverse.	Moneyer.
1042	✠EADPAR· RD RE	✠GODPINE ON LVNDE Wt. 15·8.	
1043	✠EADD ,, ,,	✠OMMVИD ON LVИDE Wt. 17·8.	Osmund.
1044	✠EADPAR· ,, ,,	✠O:SMVND ,, ,, Wt. 18·8.	
1045	✠EADPARD ,, ,,	✠PVLFCAR ON LVND : Wt. 18·0.	Wulfgar.
1046	✠EADPARD ,, ,,	✠PVLFCAR ON LVNDE Wt. 20·6.	
1047	✠EDPERD : RECEX	✠PVLFCER ON LVNDEИE Wt. 20·7.	

Type xiii.

1048	✠EADPARD REX Λ · ·	✠ÆCELPI ON LVND Wt. 17·6.	Ægelwine.
1049	EADPARD ,, ANC	,, ,, LVNDE Wt. 17·3.	
1050	✠ ,, ,, Λ :	✠ÆGLPI ON LVNDEN Wt. 15·3.	
1051	,, ,, ,,	✠ÆGLPIN· ON LVNDE Wt. 12·3.	
1052	EADPARD· REX Λ :	✠ÆLFPARD N ,, Wt. 15·4.	Ælfward.
1053	: EADPARD REX Λ	✠ÆL·FDĀRD ON LVND Wt. 14·8.	
1054	EADPARD REX Λ·.·	✠EADPIИE ON LVND : Wt. 17·6.	Eadwine or Edwine.
1055	EADPARD REX ANC·.·	✠EDPINC ON LVND Wt. 16·0.	
1056	·EADPARD REX ΛG·	✠EDPINE· ON LVNDE· Wt. 16·6.	
1057	EADPARD REX :	✠EDPINE· O LVNDE Wt. 17·6.	
1058	·EADPARD REX Λ	✠GODRIC ON LVND Wt. 15·8.	Godric.
1059	,, ,, ANCL	✠ωPETMAN ⊙N LVN : Wt. 17·6.	Swetman.

No.	Obverse.	Reverse.	Moneyer.
1060	✠EΛDPΛRD REX ·Λ	✠SPETMAN· ON LVN Wt. 17·2.	
1061	EΛDPΛRD REX Λ	✠PVLFGΛR ON LVND Wt. 11·2.	Wulfgar.
1062	·EΛDPΛRD REX :	✠PVLGΛR „ „ Wt. 15·6.	
1063	„ REX Λ	✠PVLGΛR ON LVNDE *Var.* Four crescents in field. Wt. 16·9.	
1064	✠EΛDPΛRD REX ΛN:	✠DVLFωI ON LVNDE Wt. 18·0.	Wulfsige.
1065	✠EΛDRΛRD REX Λ·	✠DVLFDΛRD ONLVND Wt. 17·0.	Wulfward.
	[Pl. XXVII. 5.]		
1066	„ „ „	„ Wt. 16·6.	
1067	EΛDRΛRD REX Λ	„ ONLV Wt. 15·2.	

HALFPENNY.

No.	Obverse.	Reverse.	Moneyer.
1068	.....RD REX Λ	....PINE ON LV Wt. 8·3.	Eadwine?

Type xv.

No.	Obverse.	Reverse.	Moneyer.
1069	EΛDPΛRD REX Λ	✠ÆLFSI ON LVNDE:: Wt. 20·0.	Ælfsige.
1070	EΛDRΛRD „	✠GODRIC ON LVND Wt. 20·3.	Godric.
1071	EΛDPΛRD REX Λ	✠PVLFPΛRD ON LVN Wt. 19·5.	Wulfward.
	[Pl. XXVII. 6.]		
1072	EΛDPΛRD „ „	✠PVL·GΛR ON LVИ Wt. 20·4.	Wulgar.

Type xv. *rar. b.*

No.	Obverse.	Reverse.	Moneyer.
1073	✠ERDR D ΛC	✠ωPETMΛN ON LVI Wt. 17·0.	Swetman.
	[Pl. XXVII. 7.]		

No.	Obverse.	Reverse.	Moneyer.

MÆLDUNE.
[Maldon.]

Type ii.

| 1074 | ✠EDPAR D REX | ✠DÆININT ONMÆL
 Wt. 16·9. | Dæinint. |

[Pl. XXVII. 8.]

HALFPENNY.

| 1075 | ✠..... D REX | ✠DÆI... .. MÆL
 Wt. 8·5. | Dæinint. |

Type vii.

| 1076 | ✠EDPE Λ RE | ✠GODRIC ON MÆLD:
 Wt. 19·6. | Godric. |
| 1077 | ✠EDPER· D R[EX] | ✠GODPINE ON MEL·
 Wt. 19·7. | Godwine. |

Type ix.

| 1078 | EΛDPEΛRD REX
 ΛNGLOR | ✠GODPINE ON
 MÆLDVN
 Wt. 21·3. | Godwine. |
| 1079 | EΛDPΛRD REX ΛNGL· | ✠SPETRIC ON MEL
 Wt. 19·3. | Swetric. · |

Type xi.

| 1080 | ✠EADPAR· RD RE | ✠CODPINE ON
 MÆLDVN
 Wt. 19·0. | Godwine. |

Type xiii.

| 1081 | EADPARD REX AN: | ✠GODPINE ON
 MΛELDV:
 Var. Pellet in field.
 Wt. 17·6. | Godwine. |

No.	Obverse.	Reverse.	Moneyer.

MEALMESBYRIG.
[Malmesbury.]

Type vii.

1082	✠EDPΛR D REI·	✠EΛL·DPIG ON MEΛL·∴ Wt. 19·0.	Ealdwig.
1083	✠EDPE ∴ D. REX	✠EΛL·DPI ON MEΛ·L·D· Wt. 19·4.	
1084	✠EDPΛR D REI·	✠EΛL·DPIL ONN MEΛLM· Wt. 19·3.	

Type xi.

1085	✠EΛDPΛR RD RE	✠BRIHPI ON MELME *Var.* In opposite angles of cross, I and crescent. Wt. 20·0. [Pl. XXVII. 9.]	Brihtwine ?
1086	✠·E·DR· RDE	✠BRIHPI ON MELME *Var.* In opposite angles of cross, I and crescent. Wt. 20·3.	

NIPEPORTE.
[Newport.]

Type vii.

1087	✠EΛDPE RD RE	✠·SIRED ON NIPEPORTE· Wt. 19·2. [Pl. XXVII. 10.]	Sired.
1088	✠EDPE· D RE·	✠ωIREDD ON NIPEPO: Wt. 16·0.	

NORÐPIC.
[Norwich.]

Type i.

1089	✠EDDER D RE✠ Λ	✠L·EOLDINE ON NOR :∴ Wt. 14·4. [Pl. XXVII. 11.]	Leofwine.

No.	Obverse.	Reverse.	Moneyer.
1090	✠EDPER D RE✠ ⋀.	✠OSMVNDD O NORÐ: Wt. 17·6.	Osmund.
	Type ii.		
1091	✠EDPE RD RC	✠LEOPIC ON HOR Wt. 17·2.	Leofwic.
	Type iii.		
1092	✠·CDPE RD RE✠	✠LEOFPINE ON NORÐ· Wt. 17·3.	Leofwine.
	Type iv.		
1093	✠ELDDI ID PXII	✠OS:MVID ON NOR Wt. 14·5.	Osmund.
1094	✠EDPERD ·REX ⋀	✠RINVLF „ „ *Var.* PACS Wt. 17·7.	Rinulf.
	[Pl. XXVII. 12.]		
	Type v.		
1095	✠EDPE· RD REX	✠CCNELM ON NORÐ Wt. 25·7.	Cenelm.
1096	✠EDPER: ·D REX:	✠.L·EOFPINE ON NORÐ: Wt. 25·0.	Leofwine.
1097	✠EDP· ERD R✠	✠ÐORFRÐ O NORÐP Wt. 25·3.	Þorferð.
1098	✠EDPE: ·RD RE:	✠ÐVREVERÐ OИ ИOR· Wt. 25·1.	Þurucrð (= Þurferð?).
	Type vii.		
1099	·✠EDPER D REX· *Var.* Sceptre terminating in fleur-de-lis.	✠HLANGVLF ON NOR Wt. 20·4.	Hlangulf?
1100	·✠EDPR D REX *Var.* Sceptre terminating in fleur-de-lis.	✠ÐORSTAN O NORÐP Wt. 18·0.	Þorstan.
1101	✠EDPER D REX *Var.* Sceptre terminating in fleur-de-lis.	✠:ÐVRFVÐ ON NORÐ Wt. 19·7.	Þurfurð.

No.	Obverse.	Reverse.	Moneyer.

Type xi.

No.	Obverse.	Reverse.	Moneyer.
1102	✠EADPAR RD RE:	✠ELFPINE ON NORÐ[P] Wt. 17·4.	Elfwine.
1103	✠EDPARD D RE··	✠LEFPINE O NORÐPI Wt. 17·4.	Lefwine or Liofwine.
1104	✠EADPA· RD RE	✠LIOFPINE ON NORÐ Wt. 20·4.	
1105	✠EADPAR RD R	✠LIOFRIC: ON NORPPI Wt. 19·8.	Liofric.
1106	✠EADPAR RD RE·	✠PVLFϭI: ON NORPPIC Wt. 19·0.	Wulfsi (Wulfsige).

Type xiii.

No.	Obverse.	Reverse.	Moneyer.
1107	EADPARD RE	✠EDPINE ON ᴎORÐ Wt. 14·3.	Edwine.
1108	·EADPARD REX	✠CODPINE O NOR Wt. 12·3.	Godwine.

[Pl. XXVII. 13.]

1109	,, ,,	✠PRICE O NORÐ Wt. 14·0.	Price.

Type xv.

No.	Obverse.	Reverse.	Moneyer.
1110	EADPARD RX	✠ÐVRGRIM ONNORÐ Wt. 14·8.	Þurgrim.
1111	,, [D R]E	✠ÐVRSTAN ON NOR Wt. 19·6.	Þurstan.

OXENAFORD.
[Oxford.]

Type ii.

No.	Obverse.	Reverse.	Moneyer.
1112	✠EDPE RD RE	✠CLPIN ON OCX· Wt. 17·3.	Gilpin.

Type ii. var. b.

No.	Obverse.	Reverse.	Moneyer.
1113	✠EDPE RE·C	✠LEOFPINE OXF Wt. 17·2.	Leofwine.

No.	Obverse.	Reverse.	Moneyer.
	Type iv. *var. a.*		
1114	✠EDDE D REX··	✠BRIИPOLD OИИ ⊙ᕦXE: Wt. 17·7.	Brinwold.
	[Pl. XXVII. 14.]		
	Type v.		
1115	✠EDPE: ·RD REX:	✠EIELPIИE ON OXENE· Wt. 23·9.	Elfwine.
	Type vii.		
1116	✠EDPER· D REX	✠ÆLFPIᕦᕦ ON Oᕦ··XᕦИE Wt. 21·2.	Ælfwig.
1117	✠EDPER·· „ „ *Var.* Sceptre terminating in fleur-de-lis.	✠ÆLPIᕦ ON OᕦEXENAF Wt. 20·2.	
1118	✠EDPΛR D REI *Var.* Sceptre terminating in fleur-de-lis.	✠ÆLPII ON OᕦXENEFO Wt. 20·1.	
	Type ix.		
1119	EΛDPEΛRD REX ΛNGO	✠ÆLFPIᕦ ON OX: Wt. 20·6.	Ælfwig.
1120	EΛDPΛRD REX Λ·ИGLOV	✠EΛDPIИE OИИ OXИE: Wt. 21·4.	Eadwino.
	[Pl. XXVIII. 1.]		
1121	EΛDPΛRD REX ΛИGLO	✠ELPIИE OИИ OXИE·· Wt. 20·4.	Elwino.
1122	„ „ ΛNGL·	✠HÆRGOD ON O✠NEF: Wt. 21·1.	Hærgod (cf. Haregod).
1123	EΛDΛRD REX ΛNGLOV	✠SETMΛN ON OXEN·· Wt. 21·4.	Swetman.
	Type xi.		
1124	✠EΛDPΛRD RD RE	✠ÆᕦELPIИE ON OXENEX: Wt. 21·5.	Ægelwino.

No	Obverse	Reverse	Moneyer
1125	✠EADPAR RD DE	✠ÆLFPIC ONN ⊙XN E Wt 20 6	Ælfwig
1126	✠EADPARD „ „	✠ÆLFPI ON OXENEXFO Wt 20 0	
	[Pl XXVIII 2]		
1127	✠EADPAR „ „	„ ⊙N OXENEX Wt 20 2	
1128	✠EADPARD „ „	✠BRIHTRED ON OXENE Wt 19 2	Brihtred.
1129	✠EADPAR „ „	✠HARECOD ON OXENEX Wt 21 0	Haregod.

Type xiii

| 1130 | ✠EADPARD REX ANG | ✠PVLFPI ON OXENE Wt 16 2 | Wulfwine? |

RICYEBYRIG

[Richborough]

Type ix

| 1131 | EADPARD REX ANGLO | ✠LEOFSTAN ON RIC Wt 21 0 | Leofstan |
| 1132 | EADVVEARDVS REX ANCLO | ✠SPETRIC ON RIC Wt 19 8 | Swetric |

ROFECEASTER

[Rochester]

Type i

| 1133 | ✠EDPNR D PEC | ✠EDPINE ON ROFE Wt 14 2 | Edwine |

Type iii

| 1134 | ✠ EDPE RD REX | ✠EDPINE ON ROFE Wt 15 6 | Edwine |

No.	Obverse.	Reverse.	Moneyer.
1135	✠·EDPE: ·RD REX·	✠ᏞODPIИE ON ROFE Wt. 16·7.	Godwine.
1136	✠EDPE: ·RD REX	✠PVLFRIᏞ ON ROF Wt. 13·3.	Wulfric.

Type iv.

| 1137 | ✠EDPERD ·REᏞX· | ✠ᏞODPI:NE ON RO *Var.* Crescent at end of each limb of cross enclosing pellet. Wt. 13 0. | Godwine. |

Type vii.

| 1138 | ✠EDPER D REX *Var.* Sceptre terminating in fleur-de-lis. | ✠EDPINE ONN ROF: Wt. 19·6. | Edwine. |

Type xi.

| 1139 | ✠EΛDPΛR RD RE [Pl. XXVIII. 3.] | ✠LIFPINE: ON ROFE·· Wt. 21·7. | Lifwine. |
| 1140 | „   „   „ | ✠LIFPINE HORN OИ ROF Wt. 21·7. | Lifwine and Horn. |

RUMENEA.
[Romney.]

Type i.

| 1141 | ✠EDPERD REX Λ | ✠BRVNᏟΛR ON RV Wt. 15·5. | Brungar. |

Type ii.

| 1142 | ✠EDRE RD RE | ✠Eω̃TIN ON RHV Wt. 11·0. | Estan. |
| 1143 | ✠EDPE „   „ | ✠PVLHED ON RVM Wt. 14·5. | Wulhed. |

HALFPENNY.

| 1144 | ✠.... .D RE | ✠....ED OИRV Wt. 6·5. | Wulhed? |

No.	Obverse.	Reverse.	Moneyer.
	Type iv.		
1115	✠EDDER: D REX··	✠PVLMÆR ON RVM	Wulmær.
		Var. Crescent at end of each limb of cross enclosing pellet. Wt. 14·4.	
	[Pl. XXVIII. 4.]		
	Type vii.		
1146	✠EDRED D RE·	✠LEOFRC ON· RVM:	Leofric.
	Var. Sceptre terminating in fleur-de-lis.	Wt. 21·0.	
1147	✠EDPE·· D RE·	✠PVLMÆR ON RVMEE·	Wulmær.
	Var. Sceptre terminating in fleur-de-lis.	Wt. 19·5.	
	Type ix.		
1148	EADPARD EX ANGLO·	✠PVLMÆR ONN RVM	Wulmær.
		Wt. 22·0.	
	Type xi.		
1149	✠EADPAR RD RE	✠PVLMÆR ON RVMED	Wulmær.
		Wt. 21·5.	
	SANDPIC. [Sandwich.]		
	Type i.		
1150	✠EDPNR·· REC:	✠LIOFPINE ON SAND	Liofwine.
		Wt. 15·0.	
	Type ii.		
1151	✠EDPE RD RE	✠FAREhIR ON SA	Farehir.
		Wt. 14·5.	
1152	✠EDP ERD R·	✠LEFPINE ON SA	Lefwine, Leofwine, &c.
		Wt. 12·4.	
1153	✠EDP· ARD··	✠L·EOFDINE ON SA	
		Wt. 10·5.	

No.	Obverse.	Reverse.	Moneyer.
1154	✠EDPE RD RE	✠LEOFPINE ON SΛ Wt. 15·6.	
1155	✠EDP· ΛRD··	✠LIFPINE ON ƵΛN Wt. 12·4.	
1156	✠EDPE RD RE	,, ,, ƵAN Wt. 11·2.	

Type iii.

1157	✠EDPE RD EX V	✠LIOEPINE ON SAN Wt. 15·9.	Liofwine.

Type vii.

1158	✠EDPER· D RE·E	✠LIFPINE ON ᴡANEI Wt. 18·7.	Lifwine.
1159	··✠EDPR D RE·	,, ,, SANDP Wt. 16·0.	

Type xi.

1160	··✠EΛDPA RD RE· ·	✠LIOFPINE ON SA: Wt. 16·0.	Liofwine.

[Pl. XXVIII. 5.]

1161	✠EADPARD RD RE	,, ,, ᴡANCE Wt. 16·9.	

SCEAFTESBYRIG or SCEFTESBYRIG.
[Shaftesbury.]

Type i.

1162	✠EDP D RE✠:	✠ÆL·PERD N SCEFT:· Wt. 15·2.	Ælfwerd.

Type v.

1163	✠CDΛCE DCΓ RICCX	✠CEDEMAИDI OIL ƧCᵻECE* Wt. 12·3.	Cedeman.

* The limbs of the cross on the reverse are not expanded; but as it is a blundered coin it has not been made into a new type.

No.	Obverse.	Reverse.	Moneyer.
1164	✠EDPE RD REX	✠ᘰODESBRAND ON Sᘰ *Var.* Limbs of cross united by one circle only. Wt. 17·5.	Godesbrand.
1165	✠EDPE: ·RD REX·	✠PVLFRIᘰ ON SᘰEFTE: Wt. 25·0.	Wulfric.

Type vii.

| 1166 | ✠EDPΛR D REX· | ✠DVDVᘰOᘰ ON SᘰEFT· Wt. 21·0. | Duducol? |
| 1167 | ,, ,, ,, | ,, ,, Wt. 20·2. | |

Type vii. *var. b.*

| 1168 | ✠EADP RD REX ΛN | ✠P·VLFRIᘰ ·ONN: SᘰEF Wt. 19·2. | Wulfric. |

Type viii.

| 1169 | ✠EDP ED RE : | ✠PVLFRIᘰ ON SᘰEΛ·F Wt. 19·2. [Pl. XXVIII. 6.] | Wulfric. |

Type ix.

| 1170 | ✠EΛDPEΛRD REX ΛNGLO | ✠PVLFRIᘰ ON SᘰEF Wt. 20·2. | Wulfric. |

Type xi.

1171	✠EΛDPΛR· RD RE	✠ÆLFPÆRD ON ᘰᘰÆTᘰ Wt. 20·2.	Ælfweard.
1172	,, ,, ,,	,, ,, Wt. 20·2.	
1173	,, ,, ,,	✠ᘰODEᘰBRAND ON ᘰᘰ Wt. 20·0.	Godesbrand.

Type xv.

| 1174 | EΛDPΛRD RE | ✠GODRIᘰ ON SᘰEΛFI Wt. 20·0. | Godric. |

Type xvi.

| 1175 | EΛDPΛRD REX | ✠GODESBRAND ON S Wt. 20·0. [Pl. XXVIII. 7.] | Godesbrand. |

No.	Obverse.	Reverse.	Moneyer.

SCROBESBYRIG.
[Shrewsbury.]

Type v.

1176	✠EDPE ·RD REX··	✠ÆLFEH ON SCREOBE Wt. 25·2.	Ælfeh.
1177	✠EDPE: ·RD REX:	✠LEOFSTĀN ON SCREO Wt. 23·0.	Leofstan.
1178	✠EDRE: ·RD REX:	✠LEOFPINE ON SCREO: Wt. 25·0.	Leofwine.

Type v. *var. b.*

1179	✠EDPE: ·RD REX:	✠PVLMÆR ON SCREOB: Wt. 19·6.	Wulmær.

Type vii.

1180	·✠EDPE D RE·	✠LEOFƧTAN ON ᗡCRO Wt. 16·0.	Leofstan.

Type ix.

1181	EADPΛRD REX ΛИGL·	✠LEOFSTΛИ OИ SCRO Wt. 20·8.	Leofstan.

Type xi.

1182	✠EADPΛR RD RE	✠GODPINE ON ᗡCRO Wt. 22·0.	Godwine.
1183	✠EADPΛR· ,, ,,	✠PVDEMAN ON[ᗡ]COB (Pierced.)	Wudeman.
1184	,, ,, ,,	,, ,, ᗡEOB Wt. 18·0.	
1185	,, ,, ,,	,, ,, ,, Wt. 20·2.	

No.	Obverse.	Reverse.	Moneyer.
1186	✠EADPAR RD RE	✠PVLMÆR ON ⲱⲤOBE Wt. 20·6.	Wulmær.

Type xv.

| 1187 | EADPARD REX | ✠EARNPI ⊙N SRⲰP
 Wt. 20·4. | Earnwig? |

[Pl. XXVIII. 8.]

SEREBYRIG, Etc.
[Salisbury.]

Type ix.

1188	EADEARD REX ANGLO·	✠GODERIC ON IERBIRGE : Wt. 18·4.	Goderic or Godric.
1189	,, ,, ,,	,, ,, (Broken.)	
1190	EADPARD REX ANGLO	,, ,, SERBIRGE Wt. 20·2.	
1191	,, ,, ,,	,, ,, Wt. 20·4.	
1192	EADVVEARDVS EX NGLO	✠GODRIC ON SEARBIR Wt. 16·4.	

Type xi.

| 1193 | ✠EADPAR RD RE | ✠CODRIC ON ⲱERBV
 Wt. 19·5. | Godric. |

[Pl. XXVIII. 9.]

| 1194 | ,, ,, ,, | ✠GODRIC: ON
  ⲱERBVR :
 Wt. 19·0. | |

Type xv.

| 1195 | EADPARD REX | ✠SIEBODE ON SEAI
 Wt. 17·0. | Sigebode. |
| 1196 | ,, REX: | ,, ,, SERB:
 Wt. 18·5. | |

No.	Obverse.	Reverse.	Moneyer.

SNOTINGAHAM.
[Nottingham.]

Type ii.

1197	✠EDPR· RD RE	✠ALHHVND Λ SNO Wt. 12·9.	Alhmund.
	[Pl. XXVIII. 10.]		
1198	✠EDD : ,, ,,	✠ωNOTER ON ωN Wt. 16·6.	Snoter.

Type iii.

| 1199 | ✠EDPE D RE✠: | ✠BL·ΛCMΛN ON SNOTI
Wt. 16·2. | Blacman. |
| 1200 | ✠EDPER ,, ,,
Var. Pellet before
head. | ✠BLΛCMAN ON
SNOTIH
Wt. 17·5. | |

Type v.

| 1201 | ✠EDPER ·D REE·X: | ✠HALDENE ON SNOT·:
Wt. 26·5. | Haldene. |
| | [Pl. XXVIII. 11.] | | |

Type xiii.

| 1202 | ✠EΛDPΛ[RD] RE | ✠ΛRNCRI[M] ON SN
(Broken.) | Arngrim. |
| 1203 | ,,   REX Λ | ✠FORMΛN ON SNO
Wt. 16·0. | Forman. |

STÆFFORDA.
[Stafford.]

Type v.

| 1204 | ✠·EDPE : ·RD REX: | ✠ELFRIC ON
STÆFORDE
Wt. 17·5. | Elfric. |
| | [Pl. XXVIII. 12.] | | |

No	Obverse	Reverse	Moneyer

STÆNIG
[Steyning]

Type v

| 1205 | ✠EDPE RD REX | ✠PVLFCET ON STÆN
Wt 25 0 | Wulfget. |
| 1206 | ✠EDPNR RD RE | ✠PVLCET ON ωTENI ·
Wt 1G 7 | |

Type vii

1207	✠EDPA D REX	✠PVFERIC ON ωTÆ Wt 18 7	Wulfric.
1208	✠EDREI D REX *Var* Sceptre termi- nating in fleui- de-lis	✠PVLFRIC ON STÆ Wt 20 5	
1209	✠EDPR DER	„ ON STÆNI Wt 20 4	

Type ix

1210	EADPARD REX ANGLO [Pl XXVIII 13]	✠PVLFRIC ONN STÆ Wt 20 4	Wulfric
1211	„ „ „	„ „ Wt 20 4	
1212	EADPRD E X ANGOR	„ ON ωTÆN· Wt 18 0	

Type xi

| 1213 | EADPAR RD RE A
[Pl XXVIII. 11] | ✠DIORMAN ON
ωTÆNIC
Wt 19 0 | Diorman |
| 1214 | „   „   „ | „   „   Wt 18 5 | |

Type xiii

| 1215 | EADPARD RE | ✠DERMON ON STÆ
Wt 16 2 | Dermon |

No.	Obverse.	Reverse.	Moneyer.
1216	✠EΛDRΛRΛRD RE✠ Λ	✠DIORMΛN O.N ωTÆ Wt. 16·7.	Diorman.

Type xv.

1217	EΛDPΛRD REX Λ [Pl. XXIX. 1.]	✠DERMON ON STÆN Wt. 19·0.	Dermon.
1218	,, RE	✠GODPINE ON STÆ Wt. 20·4.	Godwine.

STANFORD.
[Stamford.]

Type ii.

1219	✠EDPE RD RE	✠ARFRA ON STA: Wt. 15·4.	Arfra (= Ærfara ?).
1220	✠EDE·· ,, ,,	✠�
GODDINE ON S·· Wt. 14·0.	Godwine.
1221	✠EDPI ,, ,,	✠�
GODPINE ON S: Wt. 15·7.	
1222	✠EDP ,, ,,	✠LEFPINE ON STAI: Wt. 13·7.	Leofwine.
1223	✠EDPE ,, ,,	✠LEOFPINE ON STΛ Wt. 15·7.	

Type iii.

1224	✠EDPER D REX	✠BRVИPIИE ON STΛ Wt. 14·0.	Brunwine.
1225	✠EDPE: D REX	✠EDPIИN ON STΛNFOR Wt. 14·5.	Edwine.
1226	✠EDPER: D RE✠	✠L·EOᎰRIИE ON ᏕTΛNF: Wt. 17·3.	Leofwine.
1227	✠EDRER ,, ,,	✠LEOFPINE ON ᏕTΛNF Wt. 13·6.	
1228	✠EDPE·· RD RE✠ [Pl. XXIX. 2.]	✠WΛRᎶIN OИᎻ STΛN Wt. 17·2.	Marcin or Harcin (Martin).

No.	Obverse.	Reverse.	Moneyer.
1229	✠EDPE RD RE✠	✠PILCRIF ON STANF: Wt. 14·0.	Wilcrif.
	HALFPENNY.		
1230	.EDPER:	✠. . . . . . N STA·NI: Wt. 6·0.	
	Type iv.		
1231	✠EPD ·PPNXAC	✠PVL·NO:Ð ON STAI: Wt. 14·7.	Wulnoð.
	Type v.		
1232	✠EDPE· ·RD REX	✠ÆRFRE ON STANFOR: Wt. 27·7.	Ærfre (cf. Arfra).
1233	✠EDPER ·D REEX·	✠FÆRGRIN ON STANEFO Wt. 26·5.	Færgrim.
	Type vii.		
1234	✠EDPER D REX *Var.* Sceptre terminating in fleur-de-lis.	✠BRVNPINE ON ΣTA Wt. 21·5.	Brunwine.
	Type ix.		
1235	EADPARD REX ANGLOV	✠CODPIHE ON STANF Wt. 20·9.	Godwine.
1236	EADPARD ,, ,,	✠LEOFRIC ON STANF: Wt. 22·0.	Leofric.
	Type xi.		
1237	✠EADPAR RD RE	✠OωPARD ON ωTAN Wt. 19·4.	Osward.
	Type xv.		
1238	EADPARP REX	✠BRVNPINE ON ST: Wt. 21·4.	Brunwine.
1239	EADPARD ,,	,, ,, STA Wt. 20·0.	
1240	,, ,,	✠GODPINE ON STA Wt. 21·5.	Godwine.
1241	,, ,,	✠SPARCOLF ON ST: Wt. 19·2.	Swarcolf (= Swartcol?).

No.	Obverse.	Reverse.	Moneyer.
	SUÐBYRIG. [Sudbury.]		
	Type xi.		
1242	✠EADPARD RD RE	✠FOLCPINE ON ⍵VPBVC Wt. 19·0.	Folcwine.
	SUÐGEPEORC. [Southwark.]		
	Type ii.		
1243	✠EDPN: RD E✠:	✠ELFPINE ON SVÐE Wt. 14·7.	Elfwine.
1244	✠EDPA RD E	✠LIOFPINE ON SVÐ Wt. 11·7.	Liofwine (Leofwine).
	Type iii.		
1245	✠EDPAR D RE·✠	✠L·EOFPINE ON SVÐ·: Wt. 14·5.	Leofwine.
	Type v.		
1246	✠EDPR RD R·E✠	✠CIOFRED ON ⍵VÐE: Wt. 14·2.	Liofred (Leofred).
	Type vii.		
1247	✠EDPER· D REX *Var.* Sceptre terminating in fleur-de-lis.	✠LEOFRED ON ƧVÐC Wt. 21·0.	Leofred.
1248	✠EDPE· D REX *Var.* Sceptre terminating in fleur-de-lis. [Pl. XXIX. 3.]	✠O·⍵MVND ON SVÐE·: Wt. 18·0.	Osmund.
1249	✠EDPAR· D REX *Var.* Sceptre terminating in fleur-de-lis.	✠OƧMVND ON ƧVÐC: Wt. 19·5.	
1250	„ „ „	„ „ Wt. 20·3.	

No	Obverse	Reverse	Moneyer
1251	✠EDPER D RE	✠SPETMAN ON SVÐG Wt 20 6	Swetman.
		Type ix	
1252	EΛDPEΛRD REX ANGLOX	✠CODMAN ON SVÐIE Wt 17 6	Codman.
1253	EΛDPΛR REX ΛИGLOX	✠OSMVИD OИ SVÐC Wt 20 6	Osmund.
		Type xi	
1254	✠EDDRD D D E	✠OꞶMΛND ON ƧIÐI Wt 20 2	Osmund.
1255	✠EΛDPΛR RD RE	✠ꞶPETMAN ON ꞶVÐG Wt 20 4	Swetman
		Type xiii	
1256	EΛDRΛRD RE·	✠GODRIC ON SVDP Wt 16 5	Godric
1257	✠EΛDPΛRD REX Λ	✠OꞶMVND ON ꞶVÐE Wt 14 8	Osmund.

TAMPEORÐ

[Tamworth]

No	Obverse	Reverse	Moneyer
		Type v	
1258	✠ EDP E RD RE	✠ÆCELPIИE ON TAMP Wt 20 9	Ægelwine.
		Type xi	
1259	✠EDPΛR D RE	✠COLINC ON TΛM Wt 20 9	Coline
	[Pl XXIX 4]		
		Type xiii	
1260	EΛDPΛRD RE	✠BRVNINC ON TΛ Wt 11 0	Brunine

No.	Obverse	Reverse	Moneyer

TANTUNE
[Taunton]

Type ii

| 1261 | ✠EDPE RD RE | ✠BOLA ON TANT
 Wt 16 0 | Boga |

Type iii

| 1262 | ✠EDPER D RE X | ✠BOIA ON TANTVNE
 Wt 17 6 | Boga |

[Pl XXIX 5]

Type iv (a) a

| 1263 | ✠EDPAR D RECX | ✠CILLECRIST OH TAH
 Var PAXX
 Wt 14 3 | Cilleerist |

Type ix

| 1264 | EADVVEARDVS REX
 ANCLO^ | ✠BRIHTRIC ON
 TANTVNE
 Wt 20 5 | Brihtric |

Type xi

| 1265 | ✠EADPAR RD RE | ✠BRIHRIC ON TANT
 Wt 20 5 | Brihtric |

PÆRINCPIC
[Warwick]

Type i

| 1266 | ✠EDPER D REX | ✠ÆLFSHE ON PÆRINC
 Wt 16 8 | Ælfsne |

[Pl XXIX 6]

Type v

| 1267 | ✠EDPRD RE X | ✠LEOFRICIOC O PER'
 Var Pellet in angle <br> of cross
 Wt 18 0 | Leofric |
| 1268 | ✠EDPE RD RE X | ✠LVEINC ON PÆRIN
 Var Pellet in angle <br> of cross
 Wt 21 0 | Lueine
 (Leuing) |

2 i 2

No.	Obverse.	Reverse.	Moneyer.

Type xi.

| 1269 | ✠EADPAR RD RE | ✠AῶTAN: ON PERINI:
Wt. 20·5. | Astan
(cf. Æstan). |
| 1270 | ✠EADPA[R] RD RE | ✠ÐVRῶTA[N ON PÆ]RI
(Broken.) | Þurstan. |

Type xv.

| 1271 | ✠EADPARD REX | ✠ÐEODRIC OИ PÆR
Wt. 19·5. | Þeodric. |

ℙALINGAFORD.
[Wallingford.]

Type iii.

| 1272 | ✠·EDPE: ·RD REX | ✠BRIHTRIC ON PELIN
Wt. 26·8. | Brihtric. |

Type v.

| 1273 | ✠EDPER ·D REEX: | ✠ÆILPII ON PALINGE:
Wt. 24·8. | Æilwig? |
| | [Pl. XXIX. 7.] | | |

| 1274 | ,, ,, ,, | ✠BRIHTRC ON PAL
Wt. 25·2. | Brihtric. |
| 1275 | ✠EDPE ·RD RE.X: | ✠BRVNPINE ON PÃ
Wt. 26·5. | Brunwine. |

Type vii.

1276	✠EDPER· D REX· *Var.* Sceptre termi- nating in fleur- de-lis.	✠BRAND ON PALING Wt. 21·0.	Brand.
1277	✠EDPR·: D REX *Var.* Sceptre termi- nating iu fleur- de-lis.	✠BRANND ON PELINC: Wt. 20·5.	
1278	✠EDPÃ RD REI·	✠BRIHTRIIC ON PÃL·I Wt. 21·0.	Brihtric.
1279	✠EDPR·: D REX *Var.* Sceptre termi- nating in fleur- de-lis	✠BRIHTPIИE ON PALI Wt. 20·2.	Brihtwine.

No	Obverse	Reverse	Moneyer
1280	✠EDPA RD R	✠BRVNPNE ON PAL Wt 20 4	Brunwine
1281	✠EDPA RD RE *Var* Pellet behind bust	✠BVREPINE ⊙N PALIN Wt 20 5	Burewine

Type ix

1282	EADPA R✠ ANGLO	✠BRAND ON PALI Wt 20 3	Brand
1283	EADPARD REX ANGL	✠BRAND ON PAL IN Wt 21 0	
1284	,, ,, ANGL	✠BRIHTRIC ON PAL I Wt 21 0	Brihtric
	[Pl XXIX 8]		
1285	,, ,, ,,	✠BRIHTPIN ON PALI Wt 20 5	Brihtwine
1286	,, ,, ANGL	✠BRVNPINE ON PÆL Wt 20 5	Brunwine
1287	,, ,, ANGLO	✠BRVNPIIE ON PALI Wt 20 4	

Type xi

1288	✠EADPAR RD RE	✠BRAD ON PALINCE Wt 21 0	Brand
1289	EADPA RD R EX	✠BRAND ON PALLI Wt 20 5	
1290	✠EADPAR RD RE	✠BRIHTMÆR ON PALI Wt 20 7.	Brihtmær.

Type xiii

1291	EADPARD REX A ·	✠BRAND ON PALI Wt 16 5	Brand
	[Pl XXIX 9]		
1292	,, ,, A	✠BRIHTMÆR ON PA Wt 17 0	Brihtmær
1293	,, ,, A	✠BVREPINE ON PA Wt 17 5	Burewine
1294	,, ,,	,, Wt 17 0	

No	Obverse	Reverse	Moneyer
1295	EADPARD RE	✠ PVLFPINE· ON PEA Wt 16 4	Wulfwine
		Type xv	
1296	EADPARD RE[X]	✠BVREPINE ON PA Wt 19 8	Burewine
		Type xv *var c*	
1297	EADPARD REX Λ	✠BRIHTMÆR ON PA Wt 20 5 [Pl XXIX 10]	Brihtmær

PECEDPORT
[Watchet]

		Type ii	
1298	✠VD REE RE	✠L C ON CEPOR I Wt 10 7	Loc
		Type vii	
1299	✠EDPER D REX *Var* Sceptre termi- nating in fleur- de-lis [Pl XXIX 11]	✠CODCIL D ON PECE Wt 21 7	Godcild
1300	” *Var* Sceptre termi- nating in fleur- de-lis	” ”Wt 20 0	

PERHAM
[Wareham]

		Type i	
1301	✠EDPER D REX	✠SIDENAN ON PER Wt 16 5	Sideman
		Type ii	
1302	✠EDP RD REX	✠ADCCNTEP ON PE Wt 11 2	Uncertain.
		Type vii	
1303	✠EDPAR D RE	✠SIDEMAN ON PERHAI Wt 19 7	Sideman.

No.	Obverse.	Reverse.	Moneyer.
1304	✠EΛDR· RD REI· *Var.* Sceptre termi- nating in fleur- de-lis.	✠SIDEMΛN ON PERI Wt. 19·3.	

Type ix.

1305	EΛDPΛRD REX ΛNGLO	✠SIDEMΛN ON PARN Wt. 20·8.	Sideman.

Type xi.

1306	✠EΛDPΛR· RD RE	✠BIORN· ON PERHΛM Wt. 20·8.	Biorn.
1307	✠EΛDPΛR ,, ,,	✠BIORN ON PERHΛM: *Var.* In two angles of cross Λ X. Wt. 18·0.	
1308	✠EΛDPΛR· ,, ,,	✠CODEMΛN ON PERH Wt. 17·3.	Godeman.
1309	✠EΛDPΛR ,, ,,	✠ωIDEMΛN ON PERHΛ Wt. 20·0.	Sideman.

[Pl. XXIX. 12.]

Type xiii.

1310	✠EΛDRΛRD RE II	✠SIDEMΛN PERHΛ Wt. 15·2.	Sideman.

Type xv.

1311	EΛDPΛRD REX	✠SIDEMΛN ON PER: Wt. 20·0.	Sideman.
1312	,, ,,	,, ,, PER Wt. 17·7.	

PIHRACEASTER or PIGRACEASTER.

[Worcester.]

Type i.

1313	✠EPDER· D REX·Λ·	✠LEOFSTΛN ON PIHR·.· Wt. 18·2.	Leofstan.

Type ii.

1314	✠EDPΛ RD RE	✠CODPINE O PIHE· Wt. 12·2.	Godwine.

No	Obverse	Reverse	Moneyer

Type VII

| 1315 | ✠EDPAR D REI
Var Sceptre termi-
nating in fleur-
de-lis

[Pl XXIX 13] | ✠GARVLF ON DIHEREC
Wt 20 2 | Garulf |
| 1316 | ✠EDPARD REX
Var Sceptre termi-
nating in fleur-
de-lis | ✠PIICINNC ON PIHER
Wt 20 2 | Wicing |

Type IX

| 1317 | EADPARD REX ANGLO | ✠ÆCEPINE ON PICR
Wt 20 6 | Ægelwine |
| 1318 | „   „   „ | „   „ Wt 21 4 | |

Type XI

1319	✠EADPAR RD RE	✠ÆCELPNE ONPIHREC Wt 21 2	Ægelwine
1320	„ „ „ [Pl XXIX 14]	✠LIOFωTAN ON PIHRE Wt 20 4	Liofstan
1321	„ „ „	✠PICINC ON PINRECE Wt 20 1	Wicing

Type XIII.

| 1322 | ✠EADPARD REX A | ✠ÆLFPINE ON PIHR
Wt 16 0 | Ælfwine. |
| 1323 | „   RE | ✠EASTMÆR ON PIH
Wt 16 0 | Eastmær |

PILTUNE

[Wilton]

Type I

| 1324 | ✠EPDER D REX A·
[Pl XXX I] | ✠LIFINCC ON PILTVN
Wt 16 8 | Lifinc |

No.	Obverse.	Reverse.	Moneyer.

Type iii.

| 1325 | ✠EDPE: ·RD RE.X | ✠ELFSTЛN ON PIL·TV: Wt. 17·0. | Elfstan. |
| 1326 | ✠EDPE· ·RD RE : X | ✠LIFINCC ON PILTVN Wt. 17·6. | Lifinc. |

Type v.

| 1327 | ✠EDPE: ·RD REX. | ✠ÆLFPINE ON PILT *Var.* 6 in one angle of cross. Wt. 17·2. | Ælfwine. |

Type vii.

1328	✠EDPE D REX	✠·ÆL·FPI·N·E ON PIL·T Wt. 19·8.	Ælfwine.
1329	,, ,, ,,	✠ÆLFPINE ON PIL·TE·· Wt. 19·8.	
1330	✠EDPAR· D REI·	✠ALFPOLD ON PILTVN Wt. 19·8.	Alfwold.
1331	,, ,, ,,	,, ,, PILTVNE Wt. 19·8.	
1332	,, ,, ,, *Var.* Sceptre terminating in fleur-de-lis.	✠ÐVRCIL ,, ,, Wt. 20·5.	Þurcil.
1333	✠EDPE· D RE	✠ÐVRECIL ON PILT Wt. 20·0.	

Type ix.

1334	EЛDPЛRD REX ANGLOV	✠ÆLFPINE ON PILT Wt. 19·8.	Ælfwine.
1335	EЛDPEЛRD REX ANGLO·	✠ELFPINE ON PILTVNEIC Wt. 14·0.	
1336	EЛDVVEЛRDVS REX ANGL	✠EFDPINE ON DILTVNEN Wt. 16·4.	
1337	EЛDPЛRD REX ЛNGLOX : [Pl. XXX. 2.]	✠ЛLFPOLD ON PILT Wt. 20·2.	Alfwold.
1338	EЛDPEЛRD REX ЛNGLO	,, ,, PILTVNE· Wt. 18·0.	

No.	Obverse.	Reverse.	Moneyer.
1339	EDAYE[RD] RAE✠ ANGORV	✠HÆRR[E]D ON PILTV Wt. 19·9.	Hærred.
1340	EADPARD REX ANGLOR·	✠HÆRRED ∴ ON PILTVN : Wt. 19·3.	
1341	,, ., ANGL·	✠HÆRRED : ON PILTVNE Wt. 19·7.	
1342	EADPEÆRD ,, ,,	✠SÆPINE ON PILT· Wt. 19·7.	Sæwine.
1343	,, EX ANGLO	✠SÆPINE : ON PILTVNE (Broken.)	
1344	EADVVEARD[VS] REX ANGLO	✠SPETRIC ON PILT: Wt. 20·4.	Swetric.
1345	EADPEARD REX ANGLO	,, ,, Wt. 19·9.	
1346	EADVVEARD[VS] REX ANDLO	✠SPETRIC ON PILTV Wt. 20·1.	
1347	EADPEARD REX ANGLO	✠ÐVRCIL ON PIL Wt. 20·1.	Þurcil.
1348	,, ., ANGLO·	✠ÐVRCILI: ON PILTVNE Wt. 17·8.	
1349	,, ,, ,,	,, ,, Wt. 18·7.	

Type xi.

No.	Obverse.	Reverse.	Moneyer.
1350	✠EADPA RD RE	✠ÆLFPOLD ON PILTV: Wt. 19·1.	Ælfwold or Alfwold.
1351	EADPEARD REX	✠ALFPOD· ON PILT: Wt. 19·4.	

[Pl. XXX. 3.]

No.	Obverse.	Reverse.	Moneyer.
1352	✠EADPAR RD RE	✠ALFPOLD ON PILTVNE Wt. 18·2.	
1353	✠EADPARD ,, ,,	✠BRIXI: ON PILTVNE·∵ Wt. 18·6.	Brixi.
1354	,, ,, ,,	✠HÆRRD : ON PILTVN·∵ Wt. 19·4.	Hærred.
1355	✠EADPAR ., ,,	✠HÆRRED : ON PILTVND Wt. 18·9.	

No.	Obverse.	Reverse.	Moneyer.
1356	✠EΛDPΛR RD RE	✠DVRCIL ON PILTVNE Wt. 19·1.	Þurcil.
		Type xiii.	
1357	·EΛDPΛRD REX·	✠ALPOLD ON PILTI Wt. 14·4.	Alfwold.
1358	EDPΛRD RE[X]	✠EL[F]PINE· ON PILT Wt. 15·9.	Elfwine.
1359	·EΛDPΛRD RE·	✠HERRED ON PILT: Wt. 16·3.	Herred (Hærred).
1360	·EΛDPΛRD ,,	,, ,, PILTV Wt. 16·0.	
1361	✠EΛDPΛRD REX·	✠LEOFPINE ON PILV Wt. 14·6.	Leofwine.
		Type xv.	
1362	EΛDPΛRD RE✠ Λ	✠ALFPOLD ON PILTV Wt. 19·5.	Alfwold.
1363	,, RE	✠CENTPINE ON PIL Wt. 15·6.	Centwine.
1364	,, RE:	,, ,, PIL Wt. 17·6.	
1365	,, ,,	✠PINVS ON PILTVN. Wt. 18·5.	Winus.
1366	,, REX	,, ,, PILTVNE Wt. 18·7.	

PINCEASTRE.
[Winchester.]

Type i.

No.	Obverse.	Reverse.	Moneyer.
1367	✠EDPER: D REX :	✠C·ODRIC ON PINCE Wt. 16·4.	Godric.
1368	✠EDPERD REX ΛN	✠L·ADMÆR ON PINC: Wt. 17·2.	Ladmær.
1369	✠EDPΛE RD REX	✠LEOFSTΛN ON PI Wt. 15·0.	Leofstan.
1370	✠EPDER D REX··	✠LFINC ONN PINCES: Wt. 17·4.	Lifinc.
1371	✠EDPER D RE·X :	✠LIFINCC ON PINCE Wt. 17·0.	

No.	Obverse	Reverse	Moneyer
		Type ii	
1372	✠EDPN RD E	✠ÆSTAN ON PIN Wt 10 9.	Æstan
1373	✠EDPA D ЯE	✠BRVN ON DINC Wt 12 2	Brun
1374	✠EDPA RD RE	✠EDPIE ON PIN Wt 12 0	Edwic
1375	✠EDPER RD RE	✠ELFSTAN ONPIN Wt 17 4	Elfstan
1376	✠EDPA ., ,,	✠LEOFPINE ON PIN Wt 11 4	Leofwine
1377	✠EDPEI RD RE	,, ,, PI Wt 11 2	
1378	✠EDP ,, ,,	✠IFINC ON PINC Wt 15 0	Lifinc
1379	(Legend barbarous)	✠LIFINC ON PIND Wt 12 1	
		HALFPENNIES	
1380	E R D	✠LOC NC Wt 6 5	Loc.
1381	✠ RD RE	IN ONPIN Wt 7 3	
		Type iii	
1382	✠EDPER D REX	✠CODPINE ON PINCE Wt 17 0	Godwine.
1383	,, ,, REX	✠LIFINC ON PINCEC Wt 15 8	Lifinc
		[Pl XXX 4]	
		Type iv	
1384	✠EDPERD REX ANC	✠ELPINE ON PINC Wt 16 4	Elwine
		Type v	
1385	✠EDP RD REX	✠ÆLFPINE ON PINCE Wt 25 0	Ælfwine

No	Obverse	Reverse	Moneyer.
1386	✠EDPE RD REX	✠ÆSTAN ON PINC *Var* Limbs of cross united by one circle only Wt 17 0	Æst in or Estan
1387	✠EDPR RD RE✠	✠ESTAN ON PINCEST Wt 15 8	
1388	✠EDPI RD REX	✠ÆالسTANN LOC ON PI Wt 1G 8	Estan and Loc
1389	✠EDPER D REEX	✠BRAND ON PINCESTR Wt 2ᴏ4	Brand
1390	„ „ „	„ „ Wt˝2G 0	
1391	✠ED RE R I D REX	✠BRIHTPOLD ON PINCE Wt 25 0	Brihtwold.
	[Pl XXX 5]		
1392	✠EDPER RD REX *Var* Sceptre terminating in fleur-de-lis	✠GODPINE ON PINC *Var* Limbs of cross united by one circle only Wt 17 0	Godwine
1393	✠EDPR RD REX	✠LEOFPINE ON PINC *Var* Pellet in one angle of cross (Broken)	Leofwine
1394	✠EDPE RD REX	✠LIFINC ON PINCES Wt 15 8	Lifinc
1395	✠EDPER D REX	✠LIOFINC ON PINCEωT Wt 1ᴏ8	
1396	✠EDPER D REX	✠LOC ON PINCEST *Var* Limbs of cross united by one circle only and pellet in one angle Wt 1G 8	Loc
1397	✗EPPE RD REX	✠L OC ON PINCEωT Wt 17 0	
1398	✠EDPE RD REX	✠LOC ON PINCESTR *Var* Limbs of cross united by one circle only Wt 21 8	

No	Obverse	Reverse	Moneyer
1099	✠EADP ARD RE	✠PIDICA ON PINCEST Wt 170	Widica.
1100	✠EDPE RD REX	✠PYNSTAN ON PINCEST Wt 201	Wynstan

Type XII

1101	✠EDPER D REI *Var Sceptre termi- nating in fleur- de-lis*	✠ÆLFPINE ON PINCEꟽ Wt 200	Ælfwine
1102	✠EDPER D REX *Var Sceptre termi- nating in fleur- de-lis*	✠ÆLFPINE ON PINCEꟽ Wt 207	
1103	„ „ RE	„ „ PNCES Wt 205	
1104	✠EDPER D REX	✠ÆꟽTAN ON PINCEꟽT Wt 200	Æstan
1105	„ „ RE *Var Sceptre termi- nating in fleur- de-lis*	✠ÆSTAN ON PINCEꟽT Wt 205	
1106	✠ „ „ REX *Var Sceptre termi- nating in fleur- de-lis*	✠ÆSTAN ON PINCESTI Wt 198	
1107	✠EDPER D RE *Var Sceptre termi- nating in fleur- de-lis*	✠ÆÐEꟽTAN ON PINCEꟽ Wt 208	Æðestan
1108	✠EDPER „ „	✠BRIHTMÆR ON PINCE Wt 211	Brihtmær
1109	✠EDPE „ „	✠DRIHTNÆR ON PIN Wt 184	
1110	✠EDPER D REX	✠CR TAN ON PINCCI Wt 184	Estan?
1111	EDPER „ „	✠ERT AN ON PINCEI Wt 212	
1112	✠EDPER D REX	„ „ Wt 173	
1113	✠EPDER REIEI	✠CODMAN ON PINC I Wt 158	Godman

No.	Obverse.	Reverse.	Moneyer.
1414	✠EDRDE D RE✠ *Var.* Sceptre termi- nating in fleur- de-lis.	✠ᴄODMAN ON PINEEω Wt. 20·2.	
1415	·✠EDPAR D REX· *Var.* Sceptre termi- nating in fleur- de-lis.	✠ᴄODMⱯNN ON PINᴄE Wt. 20·2.	
1416	✠ ,, ,, ,, *Var.* Sceptre termi- nating in fleur- de-lis.	✠ᴄODMⱯNN ON PINᴄ·EƧ· Wt. 20·2.	
1417	✠EDPE· D REX	✠ᴄODN·Ʌ·N ON PI Wt. 16·8.	
1418	✠EDPE D RIX	,, ,, PNᴄ Wt. 20·2.	
1419	✠EDPERV D REX·	✠ᴄODPIDIⱰ O PINI Wt. 20·0.	Godwine and Widia.
1420	✠EDPE· D RE·	✠·ᴄODPI·D·I·Ɒ O· PINI Wt. 20·7.	
1421	✠EDPE· D REX·	✠ᴄ·ODPIDIⱰ O PIN·II· Wt. 20·2.	
1422	✠EDPERV ,, ,,	,, ,, Wt. 20·0.	
1423	,, ,, ,,	,, ,, Wt. 20·0.	
1424	✠EDPE· D RE·	✠GODPIИE OИ PIIᴄ· Wt. 20·1.	Godwine.
1425	✠EADPE RD REX	✠ᴄODDINE ON DINᴄY Wt. 20·2.	
1426	✠EDPER· D REI·	✠ᴄODPIИE PIDIⱰ OИPIN Wt. 19·4.	Godwine and Widia.
1427	,, ,, REI *Var.* Sceptre termi- nating in fleur- de-lis.	,, ,, Wt. 19·6.	
1428	✠EDPERV D REX·	✠ᴄODPINE PIDIA ON PINᴄ Wt. 20·0.	

[Pl. XXX. 6.]

No.	Obverse.	Reverse.	Moneyer.
1429	✠EDPER· D REI *Var.* Sceptre termi- nating in fleur- de-lis.	✠LADMÆR ON PINᴄ Wt. 20·4.	Ladmær.

No.	Obverse.	Reverse.	Moneyer.
1430	✠EDPER· D REX *Var.* Sceptre terminating in fleur-de-lis.	✠L·ADMÆR ON PINCE: Wt. 20·7.	
1431	✠EDPERD· REX· *Var.* Sceptre terminating in fleur-de-lis.	✠LIFINC ON PINCEƧ Wt. 20·2.	Lifinc.
1432	EDDER·∵ D REX *Var.* Sceptre terminating in fleur-de-lis.	✠LICINC ON PINCEωT: Wt. 19·8.	
1433	✠EDPE·∵ „ „	✠L·IFINC ON PINCEST. Wt. 18·4.	
1434	✠EDPAR D REX· *Var.* Sceptre terminating in fleur-de-lis.	✠LIFINC ON PINCESTR Wt. 20·0.	
1435	·✠EDPER „ „ *Var.* Sceptre terminating in fleur-de-lis.	✠LIFIND ON PINCEωT Wt. 20·0.	
1436	✠EDPE D RE· *Var.* Sceptre terminating in fleur-de-lis.	✠PIDꓮ ON PINCESI: Wt. 20·5.	Widia.
1437	„ „ „ *Var.* Sceptre terminating in fleur-de-lis.	✠PIDꓮ DN PINCESI: Wt. 20·7.	
1438	✠EDPER D REX *Var.* Sceptre terminating in fleur-de-lis.	✠PIDIꓮ ON PINCESTI Wt. 19·4.	

Type vii. *var. b.*

1439	✠EADPE RD REX AN [Pl. XXX. 7.]	✠GARVLF ON PINCRE: Wt. 20·0.	Garulf.

Type ix.

1440	EADPEARD REX ANGL·:	✠ÆLFPINE ON PINCE Wt. 19·8.	Ælfwine.
1441	EADVVEARDVS REX ANCLO	„ „ PINCES Wt. 21·4.	

No.	Obverse.	Reverse.	Moneyer.
1442	EADPEARD REX ANGL·::	✠ÆLFPINE ON PINES: Wt. 17·7.	
1443	EᴀDVVEᴀRDVS REX ANGL	✠ÆSTᴀN ON PIINCEꟅ Wt. 21·2.	Æstan.
1444	„ „ ANGLO	✠ÆÐESTᴀN ON PNᴄEꟅ Wt. 21·0.	Æꝥestan.
1445	EADPEARD REX ANGL·:	✠ANDERBOD ON PIN Wt. 21·4.	Anderboda.
1446	„ „ „	✠ANDERBODᴧ: ON PI: Wt. 20·0.	
1447	„ „ ANG·	✠ANDERBODᴧ ON PINᴄE Wt. 18·8.	
1448	„ „ ANGL·	✠ANDERODᴧ· ON PINᴄ Wt. 19·8.	
1449	EᴀDVVEᴀRDVS REX ANGLO	✠BIRIHTMÆR· ON PINᴄE Wt. 20·0.	Brihtmær.
1450	„ „ ANGLO	✠BRIHTMÆR· ON PINᴄ Wt. 21·0.	
1451	„ REX:	✠BRIꟼMEHR· ON PINᴄES Wt. 18·7.	
1452	EADPARD EX HNGL	✠ᴄODPINE ON PINᴄ: Wt. 19·8.	Godwine.
1453	EADPEARD REX ANGL·:	:ONIꟼ NO ·ƎNIꟼᗡOᴄ✠ Wt. 19·0.	
1454	EᴀDRPARD REX ᴧN	✠ᴄODPINE ON P:INᴄ: Wt. 20·0.	
1455	EADPEARD REX ANGL·:	✠ᴄODPINEꞀ ON PINE:· Wt. 18·4.	
1456	EᴀDVVEᴀRDVS REX VᴄLO [Pl. XXX, 8.]	✠GODPINE ON PINGES Wt. 21·0.	
1457	„ „ ANGLO	✠LIFINᴄ ONN PINᴄE Wt. 21·0.	Lifinc.
1458	„ „ „	✠LIFINᴄ ON PINᴄEꟅT Wt. 21·4.	
1459	„ „ „	✠SPRᴧᴄELINᴄ ON PINᴄ: Wt. 21·6.	Spracelinc.

No.	Obverse	Reverse	Moneyer

Type XI

No.	Obverse	Reverse	Moneyer
1160	✠EADPAR RD RE	✠ÆLFPINE ON PINCE Wt 18.8	Ælfwine
1161	,, ,, ,,	,, ONPINCEꟼ Wt 20.1	
1162	,, ,, ,,	,, ON PINCEꟼT Wt 19.6	
1163	,, ,, ,,	,, ,, PINCꟼ Wt 20.0	
1164	✠EADPARD ,, ,,	✠ANDERBODA ON PIN Wt 19.4	Anderboda
1165	✠EADPAR ,, ,,	✠ANDERBODE ONPIN Wt 18.2	
1166	✠EADPAR ,, ,,	,, ONPINCE Wt 20.4	
1167	,, ,, ,,	✠BRIHTMÆR ON PINC Wt 20.4	Brihtmær
1168	,, ,, ,,	✠GODPINE ON PINCE Wt 20.4	Godwine
1169	, ,, ,,	✠CODPINE ON PINCꟼ Wt 19.2	
1170	,, ,, ,,	✠GODPINE ON PINE Wt 20.4	
1171	,, ,, ,,	,, ,, Wt 20.0	
1172	LADPA RD REX	✠LEOFPOLD ON PINC Wt 19.8	Leofwold or Liofwoll
1173	EADPEARD REX ANG (the Inscription con- tinuous from left to right)	,, ,, PINCE Wt 19.8	
1174	✠EDPAR RD RE	✠LEOPOLD ON PINCE Wt 20.0	
1175	✠EADPA ,,	✠LIOFPOLD ONPINCE Wt 19.2	
1176	EADPARDE RD R	,, ONPINCEꟼ Wt 19.0	
1177	✠EADPAR RD RE	,, ON PINCꟼT Wt 19.4	

No	Obverse	Reverse	Moneyer
1178	EADPEARD REX ANG *Var Inscription continuous from left to right*	✠LIOFPOLD ON PINCEωT Wt 194	
1179	✠EDPARD RD RE	✠ωPRARELINC ONPINCE Wt 194	Spraeclinc or Spraeclint
1180	✠EADPAR· ,, ,,	✠ωPRACELINC ONPINCE Wt 197	
1181	✠EADPARD ,, ,,	✠ωPRAELIHC ON PINCE Wt 190	

Type XIII.

No	Obverse	Reverse	Moneyer
1182	EADPARD RE	✠ÆLFPINE ON PI Wt 167	Ælfwine
1183	✠EADPARD REX D	✠ANDERBODA ON P Wt 158	Anderboda
1184	EADPARD RE	✠ANDERBODE· ON PI Wt 177	
1185	,, ,,	,, Wt 174	
1186	,, RE	✠HEÐEPVLF ON PIC Wt 164	Heðewulf
1187	✠ ,, REX	✠LEOFPOLD ON PIN Wt 164	Leofwold
1488	,, ,,	,, PN Wt 179	
1489	EADPARD REX A	✠LIFING ON PINC Wt 163	Lifing or Lifinc.
1490	,, REX	✠LIFNC ,, PINCE Wt 162	
1491	EADPARD RE✠	✠LIFNC ON PINCES Wt 172	

[Pl. XXX 9]

No	Obverse	Reverse	Moneyer
1492	,, RE·	✠SPRACALNG ON PI Wt 166	Spracalng or Spraeclinc
1493	,, REX	✠SPRACELINC ON P Wt 153	

2 G 2

No	Obverse		Reverse	Moneyer
1494	✠ EADPARD REX A		✠SPRACLEIIN ON PIN Wt 167	
1495	EAPPARD RE·		✠ωPRARELNC ONPIN Wt 138	

Type xv

1496	EADPARD RE		✠IELFPINE ON PII Wt 150	Ælfwine
1497	,,	,,	,, ,, PIN Wt 170	
1498	,,	RE	,, ,, PINC Wt 173	
1499	,,	REX	,, ,, ,, Wt 193	
1500	,,	,,	✠ANDERBODA ON PIN Wt 171	Anderboda
1501	,,	,,	✠ANDERBODE ON Wt 175	
1502	,,	RE✠	✠ANDERBODE ON P Wt 153	
1503	,,	REX	,, ,, PI Wt 190	
1504	EADPИRD RE		✠ANDRBODE ON I Wt 188	
1505	EADPARD RE		✠LEOEPOLD ON PCI Wt 188	Leofwold
1506	,,	,,	✠LEOFPOLD ON PCN Wt 188	
1507	EAPARD REX		✠LEOFPOLD ON PI Wt 175	
1508	EAPDARD R		,, ,, Wt 177	
1509	EADPARD RE		✠LEOFPOLLD ON PIN Wt 183	
1510	EAPARD REX A		✠LEOFPOLD ON PINC Wt 193	
1511	EADPARD RE		✠LFINE ON PINCE Wt 175	Lifinc

[Pl XXX 10]

No	Obverse	Reverse	Moneyer
1512	EADPARD RE	✠LIFINC ON PINCE Wt 16 1	
1513	„ RE ·	„ „ Wt 18 0	
1514	„ RE	„ „ PINPII Wt 18 0	
1515	„ R	✠SPRACELINC ON P Wt 18 6	Spracclinc
1516	„ „	✠SPRACELING ON Wt 19 1	
1517	„ „	✠SPRACELING ON PI Wt 16 1	
1518	„ „	„ „ PIN Wt 19 5	

Type xvii

| 1519 | EADPARD RE | ✠SPEARTING ON PI Wt 18 5 | Swcarting |

PINCELSEA
[Winchelsea]

Type xi

| 1520 | ✠EADPAR D RE | ✠COLDPINE ONPINCELE Wt 20 2 | Goldwiuc. |
| | [Pl XXX 11] | | |

ÐEODFORD
[Thetford]

Type i

| 1521 | ✠EDPER D REX A | ✠ELSIIE ONN ÐEO Wt 11 3 | Elfsic? |
| | [Pl XXX 12] | | |

| 1522 | „ „ „ A | ✠ESTMVND ON ÐEO Wt 17 0 | Estmund |

Type ii

| 1523 | ✠E DPE RD RI | ✠ELFRIC ON ÐE Wt 16 6 | Elfric |

No.	Obverse	Reverse	Moneyer
1524	✠EDPE RD RE	✠ESTMVND Ⰰ ÐE Wt 175	Estmund
1525	„ „ „	„ Wt 172	
1526	✠EDP „ „	✠LEFRIC ON ÐE Wt 177	Lefric (cf Elfric)

Type III

1527	✠ EDPE RD REX	✠ÆCLSIE ON ÐEOD Wt 177	Ægelsie
1528	✠EDPE „ „	✠BRVNSTAN ON Ð Wt 175	Brunstan
1529	✠EDPE RD REX	✠LECCFREDE ON ÐEO Wt 170	Leofred

Farthing

1530	RD	ON ÐE Wt 35	

Type IV

1531	✠EDP REX ON	✠EDRIC OИ ÐEPOI Wt 112 [Pl XXX 13]	Edric
1532	✠EDPI I RE CX	✠ED RIC O N ÐEOD Wt 130	
1533	✠IIEDP PD XCN	✠EDRIC C ON ÐEO Wt 137	
1534	✠EDPA D REX	✠L EOFPIN ÐEOD Wt 139	Leofwine
1535	✠EDPAR D RECX	✠LEOFPIN ÐEOD Wt 149	
1536	✠EDP DNTNCI	✠TN DRED ON ÐED Wt 137	Wintred?

Halfpennies

1537	✠NEDP	✠ED ÐEO Wt 65	Edric?
1538	D RX NT	· NE ÐEOD Wt 65	Leofwine?

No	Obverse	Reverse	Moneyer
		Type v	
1509	✠EDPER D REX	✠ÆILSIE ON ÐEODFO Wt 219	Eilsic
1510	✠EDPE RD REX	✠ESTMVND ON ÐEO Wt 268	Estmund
1511	,, ,, ,,	✠ES✠MVND ON ÐEO Wt 258	
		Type vi	
1512	✠EDPER D REEX	✠GODELEOF ON ÐEOT Wt 178	Godeleof
	[Pl XXX 11]		
		Type vii	
1513	✠ED[P]ER D RE	✠BL ARERE ON ÐITFOR Wt 170	Blarere (or Blaeer)
1514	✠EDPE D REX *Var Sceptre termi- nating in fleur- de-lis*	✠GODELEOF ON ÐEOT Wt 207	Godeleof
1515	✠EDPER D RE *Var Sceptre termi- nating in fleur- de-lis*	✠LEOFPINE ON ÐEOT Wt 202	Leofwine or Litwine
1516	✠EDDER D RE	✠LIFPINE ON ÐIDFOR Wt 196	
		Type vi	
1517	✠EADPER RD RE	✠ATⱲERE ON PIODFOI Wt 196	Atsere
1518	✠ EDPAI D RE	✠BLAⱢER ON ÐETFO Wt 191	Blaeer
1519	✠EADPAR RD RE	✠FOLⱢERD ON ÐATFOR Wt 192	Folcerd
1550	✠EDPARD ERE	✠ⱢÐELIⱢ ON PIODFOD Wt 175	Gwelc (=Godelif?)
1551	✠EADPAR RD REX	✠ⱲVMERLIDE ONPIODFO Wt 210	Sumerled
1552	✠EDPARD RD RE	✠SVMRED ON ÐET Wt 190	

No.	Obverse.	Reverse.	Moneyer.
1553	✠EAD·PAR RD RE	✠SVMRLEÐ ON ÐET: Wt. 19·2.	
1554	✠EADPAR RD REX	✠PVRFVRP ON PIODFO Wt. 19·0.	Wurfurd (cf. Þurfurð).

Type xiii.

1555	✠EADPARED REX·	✠ÆLFPINE ON ÐETF Wt. 18·3.	Ælfwine.
1556	EADPARD REX·	✠ATSER ON ÐETF Wt. 16·0.	Atsere.
1557	✠EADPARED REX	✠GODRIC ON ÐETFO Wt. 16·0.	Godric.
1558	✠EADPARD REX✠	✠SVMRD ON ÐETFOR Wt. 17·7.	Sumerleda.

Type xv.

1559	EADPARD REX	✠GODPI ON ÐETFORDI Wt. 18·5.	Godwine.

UNCERTAIN MINTS.

Type ii.

1560	✠DERE RD RE	✠ELEIPREИPHIO Wt. 12·5.	Uncertain.
1561	✠EDPE RD RE	✠HORCEP ON CD *Var.* Pellet in one angle of cross. Wt. 15·0.	Uncertain.
1562	✠EDPA·· RD E	✠PIDRED ON RTF: Wt. 10·4.	Widred.

Type iv.

1563	✠EDPER D REX··	✠L·IFINC ON SPES* *Var.* Crescent at end of each limb of cross enclosing pellet. Wt. 15·6.	Lifinc.

Type v.

1564	✠EDPE· RD REX:	✠HLIHHHOCHFHIII· Wt. 18·0.	Uncertain.

* Ipswich?

No.	Obverse.	Reverse.	Moneyer.
	Type vii.		
1565	✠EDPER· D REX	✠ÆLFPINE ON HTIMC: Wt. 20·1.	Ælfwine.
1566	✠ΛEDP ꝺREI	„ „ HTIMN Wt. 19·7.	
1567	✠EDPE· D RE·	✠ᴄODPINECC OON Wt. 19·0.	Godwine.
	Type ix.		
1568	EΛDPEΛRD REX ΛNGLO	✠EΛDPEΛRD O IENE Wt. 19·1.	Eadweard.
1569	„ „ „	„ „ Wt. 21·0.	
1570	EΛDPΛPD X ΛN6OR:	„ O IENENE: Wt. 20·0.	
1571	EΛDRND ·EX IIIO✠	✠EILNOĐ ON CINE Wt. 17·0.	Eilnoð.
	HALFPENNIES.		
	Type i.		
1572	. . DPERD . . .	. . . IHTRED O· . . . . Wt. 5·2.	Brihtred ?
1573	✠EDP . . . RЄC··	. PLFSICE O . . . . Wt. 6·5.	Wulfsige.
1574	. . . PER· D . . .	. . VLSICE ON . . . Wt. 6·8.	
	Type ii.		
1575	. . . P ER . . .	✠ÆLFRE . . . . . . Wt. 6·5.	Ælfred.
1576	✠ED·· . . . D RE··	✠BRIHTRE . . . . . . Wt. 6·0.	Brihtred.
1577	✠EDP . . . RDE	✠DIREME . . . . . Wt. 7·2.	Direme.
1578	. . . PE RD . .	✠EDPAR . . . . . . Wt. 8·6.	Edward.
1579	✠EDP . . D RE	✠LEOFPI . . . . Wt. 7·5.	Leofwine.

No	Obverse	Reverse	Moneyer
1580	✠EDPE	. OFPINE ON Wt 7 2	
1581	✠EDPE	. PINE ON . Wt 5 5	
1582	✠EDP D RE	✠LIFINC . Wt 6 0	Lifinc

Type III

1583	RD REX	✠ÆLFCAR Wt 7 0	Ælfgar
1584	[✠]EDPNER	✠CODSVNE Wt 5 5	Godsune
1585	✠ RE R✠	✠HARCIN ON Wt 6 3	Harcin or Marcin
1586	RD REX	. EFPINE ON Wt 8 5	Lefwine
1587	✠EDPE	✠PVLCPIN . Wt 7 5	Wulfwine

Type IV

| 1588 | ✠EDPAR . | ✠BVRNR For Crescent at end of each limb of cross enclosing pellet Wt 8 7 | Burnred |
| 1589 | [✠]EDPER | FPICNE O . For Crescent at end of each limb of cross enclosing pellet Wt 7 7 | Leofwine ? |

FARTHINGS

Type II

1590	D RE	✠E . . N Wt 2 0	
1591	✠ED	NA Wt 1 2	
1592	✠EDP .	. REC . Wt 3 0	
1593		RIN Wt 3 9	

No.	Obverse.	Reverse.	Moneyer.
1594	✠ED	. . . SBR . . . . Wt. 3·0.	

Type iii.

1595	[✠]EDPE	✠PVL	Wulfwine. Wt. 4·0.
1596	. . . . . RE . . .	. . . . . . INE . . . . . . Wt. 3·6.	
1597	. . . . E	. . . . . PINE . . . . . Wt. 2·7.	
1598	. . . . ΛR	. . . . NE ON . . . Wt. 3·0.	
1599	✠ED	. . . . E ON M . . . . . . Wt. 5·0.	
1600	. . . . . RD . . .	. . . . . E ON N . . Wt. 3·0.	

HAROLD II.

Moneyers

Ægelwine (Ilch , Leic , Thetf)
Ælfwine [= .Elfwine] (Thetf)
Ælfgeat (Line)
Ælfnoð [" Cant" = Chelsea ?]
Ælfwi[g] (Oxf)
Ælfwine or Elfwine (Brist , Cant ,
    Chich , Ipsw , Winchest)
Ælfwold or Alfwold (Wilt)
Ælger [ct Aldgar] (Lond)
Agemund
Aldgar (Lond)
Alcot (York)
Alfred
Alf - see also Ælf -
Almer [= Ulmer ? of Wulmer] (Line)
Alvvi [= .Elfwig ?] (Chest)
Anderboda (Winchest)
Blaceman
Brihtmær (Wallingf)
Brihtnoð (Glouc)
Brihtric (Exct , Taunt)
Brihtui [= Brihtwine]
Brihtwold (Oxf)
Brununion (Ipsw)
Brunwine (Stamf)
Burgwine (Wallingf)
Centwine or Cantwine (Wilt)
Ceorl (Brist)
Cinstan (Dover)
Colman
Colre
Dermen [= Permon ?] (Steyn)
Eadward
Eastner (Winchest)
Edue (Heref)
Edwine (Cant , Heref , Lond)
Eluui [= Elfwig or Elfwine] (Heref)
Elfwine, see Ælfwine
Egred
Erncetel [= Arncetel] (York)
Estre
Forna (Nott)
ForSu
Froin [= Froma ?] (Derby)
Gerran
Godesbrand
Godric (Lond , Shaft , Thetf)
Godwine (Chich , Hunt , Lewes, Mald ,
    Norw)
Goldman
Goldwine (Winchest)
Heawi (Winchest)
Ilei (Oxf)

Iocctel or Iocctel (York)
Leisine [= Leifine ?] (York)
Leofuic (Worc)
Leofsi [= Leofsige] (Lond)
Leotstan (Roch , Southamp)
Leofward (Lewes)
Leofwine (Brist , Exct , Roch , Stamf)
Leofwold (Guild , Winchest)
Lifinc or Lufinc (Exct , Warw , Win-
    chest)
Manna (Nott)
Orðric (Glouc)
Osmund (Lond , Southw)
Oswold (Lewes)
Ouðbearn (York)
Ouðgrim (York)
Ouðulf (York)
Rentwine [= Kentwine or Centwine ?]
    (Wilt)
Roscelf (York)
Sæwine (Southamp)
Sentwine, see Centwine.
Sigod (Bedf)
Snebeorn or Snebeorn (Colch , York)
Spraeling (Winchest)
Sueman [see also Swetman] (Lond)
Sutere (York)
Swearling, see Swearting
Sweartcol or Suartcol (York)
Swearting, Sweartling, &c. (Wallingf ,
    Winchest)
Swetman or Sueman (Lond , South-
    amp , Warch)
Ulfcetel (York)
Urstan, see Purstan
Wateman (Worc)
Winne
Winus (Wilt)
Wulfgeat (Glouc)
Wulfi or Wulfwi [= Wulfwig or
    Wulfwine] (Cambr , Colch)
Wulfmar, Wulmær, &c (Linc , Romn ,
    Shrews)
Wulfred (Cant)
Wulfward (Dover, Lond)
Wulgar [Wulfgar] (Lond).
Wulmer, see Wulfmær
Pealred (Hast)
Permon [= Dermon ?] (Steyn)
Purul
Purgel (Thetf)
Purstan (Norw)

DESCRIPTION OF TYPES

Obverse	Reverse

Type 1

Head 1, wearing arched crown from which depend two fillets, in front, sceptre, pommée Around, inscription outer circle	Across field and between two lines, P A X Around, inscription between two circles

[Cf Pl XXXI 1]

Type 1 var a

Similar no sceptre	Same

[Cf Pl XXXI 4]

Type 1, var b

Similar, head r, in front, sceptre, pommée	Similar, inscription in field, retrograde

[Cf Pl XXXII 5]

DESCRIPTION OF COINS.

No	Obverse	Reverse	Moneyer
	BEDEFORD [Bedford]		
	Type 1		
1	✠HAROL D REX ANGL	✠SIGOD ON BEDEFORD Wt 21 0	Sigod
	[Pl XXXI 1]		
	BRICGSTOP [Bristol]		
	Type 1		
2	✠HAROLD REX ANG	✠LEOFPINE ON BRI Wt 20 5	Leofwine

No.	Obverse	Reverse	Moneyer

CÆNTPARABYRIG
[Canterbury]

Type 1

3	✠HAROLD REX ANGLO	✠EDPINE ON CANTI Wt 20·8	Edwine
	[Pl XXXI 2]		
4	„ „ ANG	✠ELFPINE ON CAN Wt 21·7	Elfwine

CICESTRIE
[Chichester]

Type 1

5	✠HAROLD REX ANC *Var* No fillets to crown	✠ÆLFPINE ON CICEI Wt 20·3	Ælfwine
	[Pl XXXI 3]		
6	„ „ AI	✠GODPINE ON CICE Wt 21·7	Godwine

COLECEASTRE
[Colchester]

Type 1 var a

| 7 | ✠HAROLD REX ANGL | ✠PVLFPI ON COLEC
Wt 20·2 | Wulfwi
(Wulfwig or Wulfwine) |
| 8 | „   „   „ | „   „ COLEICST
Wt 19·5 | |

DEORABY
[Derby]

Type 1

| 9 | ✠HAROLD REX AG | ✠FRON ON DEORBI
Wt 21·0 | Fron
(= Frona ?) |

No.	Obverse.	Reverse.	Moneyer.

DOFERAN.

[Dover.]

Type i. *var. a.*

| 10 | ✠HAROLD REX ANGLORVI *Var.* Inner circle around bust. | ✠CINSTAN ON DOFI Wt. 20·8. | Cinstan. |
| 11 | ✠HAROLD REX ANGL | ✠PVLFPVRD ON DO *Var.* X Λ 9 Wt. 20·3. | Wulfward. |

[Pl. XXXI. 4.]

EOFERPIC.

[York.]

Type i.

12	✠HAROLD REX ANGI	✠ALEOF ON EOFER Wt. 17·5.	Aleof.
13	„ „ ANGL	✠ERNCETEL ON EOF Wt. 20·3.	Erncetel (= Arncetel).
14	„ „ ANGI	✠IOCETEL ON EOFER: Wt. 21·5.	Iocetel.
15	„ „ ANGL	✠IOCETL ON EOFER Wt. 22·7.	
16	„ „ „	✠LEISINC ON EOFRI Wt. 21·5.	Leisinc (= Leifinc?).

[Pl. XXXI. 5.]

17	✠MAROLD REX ANG	✠OVEGRIM ON EOF Wt. 22·0.	OuƷgrim.
18	✠HAROLD REXI [AN]GL	✠OVDVLF ON EOFERP Wt. 21·2.	Ouðulf.
19	„ „ ANGL	✠ƵNÆBEORN ON EON Wt. 20·2.	Snæbeorn.
20	„ „ „	„ Wt. 21·5.	
21	„ „ ANGLO	✠ƵVTERE ON EOFER Wt. 21·2.	Sutere.

No.	Obverse.	Reverse.	Moneyer.
22	✠HAROLD REX ANGLO	✠SVTERE ON EOFER Wt. 21·2.	
23	„ „ ANGL	✠SPEARTCOL ON EOI Wt. 20·7.	Sweartcol.
24	„ „ ANG	✠VLFCETEL ON EOF Wt. 20·0.	Ulfcetel.

EXECESTER.
[Exeter.]

Type i.

| 25 | ✠HAROLD REX AN | ✠LEOFDINE ON EXEC Wt. 21·0. | Leofwine. |

Type i. *var. a.*

| 26 | ✠HAROLD REX ANGL·· | ✠BRIHTRIC ON EXE Wt. 20·0. | Brihtric. |
| 27 | „ „ ANGL | ✠LIFINE ON EXECESTR Wt. 20·5. | Lifine. |

GIFELCEASTER.
[Ilchester.]

Type i.

| 28 | ✠HAROLD REX ANGL | ✠ÆGLPINE ON GIFELC Wt. 20·0. | Ægelwine. |
| 29 | ✠HAROLD REX AG | ✠ICGLPINE ON GIF Wt. 20·0. | |

Type i. *var. a.*

| 30 | ✠HAROLD REX ANGLO [Pl. XXXI. 6.] | ✠ÆGLPINE ON GIFE : Wt. 20·2. | Ægelwine. |

GILDEFORDA.
[Guildford.]

Type i.

| 31 | ✠HAROLDE ANGL· [Pl. XXXI. 7.] | ✠LEOFPOLD ON GILDI Wt. 19·3. | Leofwold. |

No.	Obverse.	Reverse.	Moneyer.

GIPESPIC.
[Ipswich.]

Type i.

| 32 | ✠HAROLD REX ANG· | ✠ÆLFPINE ON GIPPES Wt. 20·0. | Ælfwine. |
| 33 | ✠HAROLD REX ANG· | ✠BRVMMON ON GIPE Wt. 21·0. | Brummon. |

GLEPECEASTER.
[Gloucester.]

Type i.

| 34 | ✠NAROLD REX ANGRO | ✠ORÐRIC ON GL·EPEC Wt. 20·3. [Pl. XXXI. 8.] | Orðric. |
| 35 | ✠HAROLD REX ANGL : | ✠PNLFGEAT ON GLE Wt. 20·0. | Wulfgeat. |

GRANTEBRYCGE.
[Cambridge.]

Type i.

| 36 | ✠HAROLD REX AI | ✠PVLFPI ON GRANTI Wt. 20·6. | Wulfwi (Wulfwig or Wulfwine). |

HAMTUNE.
[Southampton.]

Type i.

| 37 | ✠HAROLD REX ANG | ✠SÆPINE ON HAMT Wt. 20·0. | Sæwine. |
| 38 | „ „ AI | ✠SPETMAN ON HA Wt. 20·3. [Pl. XXXI. 9.] | Swetman. |

No.	Obverse.	Reverse.	Moneyer.
	Type i. var. a.		
39	✠HAROLD REX ANGLO	✠LEOFSTAN ON HA Wt. 21·2.	Leofstan.
	[Pl. XXXI. 10.]		
	HÆSTINGA. [Hastings.]		
	Type i.		
40	✠HAROLD REX ANGLO	✠ÐEODRED ON ÆST Wt. 19·7.	Ðeodred.
	HEREFORD. [Hereford.]		
	Type i.		
41	✠HAROLD REX ANG	✠EDRIC ON HEREFOR Wt. 20·6.	Edric.
	HUNTENDUNE. [Huntingdon.]		
	Type i. var. a.		
42	✠HAROLD REX ANG:	✠GODYINE ON HVNIED Wt. 21·3.	Godwine.
	[Pl. XXXI. 11]		
	LÆPES. [Lewes.]		
	Type i.		
43	✠HAROLD REX AN:	✠GODPINE ON LEPE: Wt. 21·0.	Godwine.
44	,, ,, ANCO	✠LEOFPARD ON LEPE: Wt. 20·8.	Leofward.
	[Pl. XXXI 12.]		

No.	Obverse.	Reverse.	Moneyer.
45	✠HAROLD REX ANGL·	✠OƧPOLD ON LEƤEI Wt. 21·0.	Oswold.
46	✠HΛLOLD REX ΛNG	✠OƧPOLD ON LEƤEEI Wt. 21·0.	

LEHERCEASTER.
[Leicester.]

Type i.

47	✠HAROLD REX ΛI [Pl. XXXII. 1.]	✠ÆGLƤINE ON LEHRI Wt. 20·2.	Ægelwine.

LEIGECEASTER.
[Chester.]

Type i.

48	✠HAROLD REX ΛN· [Pl. XXXII. 2.]	✠ΛLXXI ON LLEGEC Wt. 21·0.	Alxxi (= Ælfsig ?).

LINCOLNE.
[Lincoln.]

Type i.

49	✠HΛROLD REX ΛI	✠ÆLFGEΛT ON LINCOI Wt. 20·0.	Ælfgeat.
50	,, ,, ,,	,, ,, ,, Wt. 19·0.	
51	✠HAROLD REX ΛNGL :	✠ΛLMER ON LINCO Wt. 22·0.	Almer (= Ulmer? cf. Wulmer).
52	,, ,, ΛNGL [Pl. XXXII. 3.]	✠PVLMER ,, ,, Wt. 23·1.	Wulmer (Wulfmær).

No.	Obverse.	Reverse.	Moneyer.
	LUNDENE. [London.]		
	Type i.		
53	✠HAROLD REX ANGOL	✠ÆLCÆR ON LVNDI Wt. 19·8.	Ælgær (cf. Aldgar).
54	„ „ ANG:	✠ALDGAR „ „ Wt. 19·2.	Aldgar.
55	✠HAROLD REX ANGLORI *Var.* Inner circle around bust.	✠EDPINE ON· LVND Wt. 17·5.	Edwine.
56	✠HAROLD REX ANGL	„ ON LVNDE: Wt. 20·2.	
57	„ „ ANGL∴	„ „ LVNDEI: Wt. 20·2.	
58	„ RE✠ ANGLO:	„ „ „ Wt. 22·0.	
59	„ REX ANGL	„ „ LVNDEN Wt. 18·5.	
60	„ „ ANGL *Var.* No fillets to crown.	„ „ LVNDI. Wt. 19·0.	
61	„ „ ANGLO	✠GODRIC ON LVNDE: Wt. 19·8.	Godric.
62	„ „ „	„ „ „ Wt. 18·3.	
63	„ „ AI	„ „ LVNDEI Wt. 22·0.	
64	„ „ ANG	✠LEOFSI ON LVND Wt. 21·5.	Leofsi(ge).
65	„ „ ANGI	„ „ LVNDE Wt. 21·0.	
66	„ „ ANGO *Var.* Inner circle around bust. [Pl XXXII. 4.]	„ „ LVNDEI Wt. 22·7.	

No.	Obverse.			Reverse.			Moneyer.
67	✠HAROLD REX ANGLO:			LEOFSI ON LVNDEN Wt. 19·7.			
68	,,	,,	ANGLO	✠OSMVND ON LVN Wt. 19·0.			Osmund.
69	,,	,,	ANG:	✠SVEMAN DE LVN Wt. 18·2.			Sueman (cf. Swetman).
70	,,	,,	,,	✠SPETMAN ON LVN Wt. 20·6.			Swetman.
71	,,	,,	,,	✠SPETMAN ON LVND Wt. 19·3.			
72	,,	,,	AN	✠PVLGAR ,, ,, Wt. 21·0.			Wulgar (Wulfgar).
73	,,	,,	ANGLO:	,,	,,	LVND Wt. 21·9.	
74	,,	,,	ANGIO	,,	,,	LIINDE· Wt. 19·8.	

Type i. var. b.

75	✠NVROLD REX VNG	✠PVLCPVRD ON LVDI Wt. 15·2.			Wulfward.

[Pl. XXXII. 5.]

NORÐPIC.
[Norwich.]

Type i. var. a.

76	✠HAROLD REX ANGLO	✠ÐVRSTAN ON NOI Wt. 20·5.	Þurstan.

OXENAFORD.
[Oxford.]

Type i.

77	✠HAROLD REX ANG	✠ÆLFPI ON OXENEFO Wt. 19·5.	Ælfwi(g).
78	,,	,, AG	✠BRIHTPOLD ON OXEI Wt. 19·5.	Brihtwold.

No.	Obverse.	Reverse.	Moneyer.

ROFECEASTER.

[Rochester.]

Type i.

79	✠HAROLD REX ANGL·:	✠LEOFωTAN ON ROFI	Leofstan.
		Wt. 21·0.	

[Pl. XXXII. 6.]

RUMENEA.

[Romney.]

Type i. *var. a.*

80	✠HAROLD REX ANGL	✠ΡVLMÆR ON RVMEI	Wulmær
		Wt. 18·5.	(Wulfmær).

SCEFTESBYRIG.

[Shaftesbury.]

Type i.

81	✠HAROLD REX TNGO	✠GODRIE ON SCEFTES	Godric.
		Wt. 18·0.	

[Pl. XXXII. 7.]

SNOTINGAHAM.

[Nottingham.]

Type i.

82	✠HAROLD REX ANGL:	✠FORNA ON SNOTIh	Forna ?
		Wt. 20·0.	
83	,, ,, ANG·L	✠MANNA ON ZNOT	Manna.
		Wt. 17·3.	

STÆNIG.

[Steyning.]

Type i.

84	✠HAROLD REX ANGLO	✠DERMON ON STÆNI	Dermon
		Wt. 21·5.	(Þermon ?).

[Pl. XXXII. 8.]

No.	Obverse.	Reverse.	Moneyer.

STANFORD.
[Stamford.]

Type i.

85	✠HAROLD REX ANGL·	✠BRVNPINE ON STΛ	Brunwine.
		Wt. 21·3.	
86	✠HΛROLD REX ĀN	✠LEOFPINE ON STΛN	Loofwine.
		Wt. 21·8.	

SUÐGEPEORC.
[Southwark.]

Type i.

87	✠HΛROLD REX ANGLO	✠OꙄMVND ON ꙄVDEP	Osmund.
		Wt. 17·7.	

PÆRINCPIC.
[Warwick.]

Type i.

88	✠HΛROLD REX ANGLO	✠LVFFINC ON PEARP	Luffinc
		Wt. 21·2.	(=Lifinc).
	[Pl. XXXII. 9.]		

PALINGAFORD.
[Wallingford.]

Type i.

89	✠HΛROLD REX ANGLO	✠BVRCPINE ON PΛLIN	Burgwine.
		Wt. 20·0.	
	[Pl. XXXII. 10.]		
90	✠HΛROLD REX ANG	✠SPEARTLINC ON PAL	Sweartling.
		Wt. 20·5.	

No	Obverse	Reverse	Moneyer

PERHAM
[Wareham]

Type 1

| 91 | ✠HAROLD REX AN | ✠SPEMAN ON PERH
Wt 190 | Swetman |

PILTUNE
[Wilton]

Type 1

92	✠HAROLD REX AN	✠ÆLFPOLD ON PILT Wt 20 0.	Ælfwold or Altwold.
93	,, ,, ANGL	✠ÆLFPOLD ON PILTI Wt 19 2	
94	,, ,, ANGL	,, ,, PILTV Wt 18 0	
95	✠HAROLD REX ANI	,, ⊙ON PITV Wt 18 5	
96	✠HAROLD REX ANGL	,, ON PITVI Wt 20 0	
97	✠HAROLD REX ANI	✠ÆLPOLD ON PILTVI Wt 19 4	
98	,, ,, AN	✠ALFPOLD ON PILTV Wt 19 7	
99	✠HAROLD REX ANG L	✠ALPOLD ,, ,, Wt 19 4	
100	✠HAROLD REX ANGL	✠CENTPINE ON PITI Wt 18 8	Centwine
	[Pl XXXII 11]		
101	✠HAROLD REX AI	,, ,, PITAI Wt 19 5	
102	✠HAROLD REX ANGL	✠CENPINE ON PILT Wt. 19 0	
103	✠HAROLD REX AI	✠GÆNTPINE OH PI Wt 20 1	

No	Obverse	Reverse	Moneyer
104	✠HAROLD REX ᛁ	✠RENTPINE ON PILTVN Wt 201	Rentwine (= Kentwine?)
105	✠HAROLD REX ANGOL	✠PINVS ON PILTIA Wt 199	Winus
106	„ „ ᛁ	✠PINVS ON PILTVN Wt 204	

PINCEASTRE
[Winchester]

Type 1

107	✠HAROLD REX ᛁN	✠ÆLFPINE ON PINC Wt 160	Ælfwine
108	„ „ ANGL	✠ANDERBODE ON P Wt 197	Anderboda
109	„ „ ᛁII	✠ANDERBODE ON PI Wt 171	
110	„ „ „	„ „ PII Wt 180	
111	„ „ ANGL	✠EᛁSTNÆR ON PIN Wt 195	Eastnær
112	„ „ ANLO	✠GOLDPIN PINCECI Wt 198	Goldwine
113	✠HAROLD REX ANGL	✠HEᛁÐEÞI ON ÞIC Wt 210	Heaðewi
114	„ „ ANG	✠LEOFPOLD ON PIN Wt 212	Leofwold

[Pl XXXII 12]

115	✠HAROLD EX AN	✠LEOFPOLD ON PINI Wt 180	
116	✠HAROLD REX ANGL	✠LIFIC ON PINCEƷT Wt 154	Lifinc
117	„ . ᛁII	✠SPRACELING ON P Wt 214	Spraceling
118	„ „ ᛁNG	✠SPEARLING ON PI Wt 210	Swearling or Sweartling (t Swearting)
119	✠HAROLD REX ANGL	✠SPEARTLING ON PI Wt 200	

No	Obverse	Reverse	Moneyer
120	✠HAROLD REX ANGL	✠SPEARTING ON PI Wt 195	Swearting

ÐEOTFORD.
[Thetford]

Type 1

No	Obverse	Reverse	Moneyer
121	✠HAROLD REX NGLI	✠ÆLEPINE ON ÐITFO Wt 200	Ægelwine
122	,, ,, ANG	✠GODRIL ON ÐEOTI Wt 207	Godric
123	,, ,, ,,	✠ÐVRGOD ON ÐEOT. Wt 187.	Ðurgod

UNCERTAIN MINT.

Type 1

No	Obverse	Reverse	Moneyer
124	✠HAROLD REX ANG	✠BLAGEMAN ON I (Broken)	Blaceman
125	,, ,, ,,	✠BRIHTMÆR ON I Wt. 200	Brihtmær

INDEXES.

I.—GENERAL INDEX.

*** The numbers in this Index, and in the following Indexes, refer to the *page* in the Catalogue.

A.

Ælfgifu, first wife of Æthelred II., lxxvii.

Ælfgifu (Alfífa), first wife or mistress of Cnut, lxxxvii.

Ælfgifu (Emma), second wife of Æthelred II., and of Cnut. *See* Emma.

Ælfheah, Abp. of Canterbury, martyrdom of, lxxix.

Ælfred, battle of Ashdown, xxxii.; besieges Vikings in Nottingham, *ib.*; accession, xxxii., xxxiii.; defeated at Wilton, xxxiii.; attacks Guðorm in Wareham, xxxiv.; destroys Viking fleet, *ib.*; retires to Æthelney, xxxv.; defeats Guðorm at Æthandune, and divides kingdom, *ib.*; his government, xxxvi.; rebuilds London, xxxvii.; siege of Exeter, xxxviii.

—— Coinage:—types of, imitated by Vikings, &c., xxxiii., xli.–xliii., xlvi., xlvii.; with monogram of London, xxxiv., xxxvii., xxxix.; causes of large issues, xxxvi.; issues and types of coins, xxxviii.–xlviii.; moneyers, list of, 32; coin-types, 33; coins, 38–82 (with mint name, 38; without mint name, 55).

Ælfred, the Ætheling, takes refuge in Normandy, lxxix.; his murder, lxxxvii.

Ælfric, the ealdorman, his treachery, lxxiii.

Ælfwyn, dau. of Æthelflæd, betrothed to Régnald of Northumbria, li. *n.*; lix.

Æthandune, battle of, xxxv.

Æthelbald, k. of Wessex, defeated at Ockley, xxiv.; rebellion of, xxiv., xxvi. *n.*, xxvii.; receives kingdom of Wessex, xxv., xxvi. *n.*, lxix.; his marriage, xxvii.; death, *ib.*

—— Coinage:—rarity of his coins, xxvii., 21 *n.*; moneyers and coins, 21.

Æthelbearht, marriage with Berchta, dau. of Charibert, xxv.; accession to throne of Kent, xxvii.; and Wessex, xxviii.; Viking raids, *ib.*

—— Coinage:—moneyers, list of, 22; coin-types, *ib.*; coins, 23–26.

Æthelflæd, Lady of the Mercians, marriage, xxxvii.; building of the burgs, li., lii.; death, li.

Æthelney, refuge of Ælfred in, xxxv.

Æthelred I., accession, xxviii.; battle of Ashdown and siege of Nottingham, xxxii.; death, *ib.*

—— Coinage:—moneyers, list of, 27; coin-types, *ib.*; coins, 28–31 (with bust, 28; without bust, 31).

Æthelred II., accession, lxx.; his sobriquet of 'Unready,' *ib.*; causes of decline of power, lxxi.; opposition to Vikings, lxxiii.; treachery of thanes and ealdormen, lxxv.; attacks Cumberland and the Isle of Man, *ib.*; massacre of St. Brice, lxxvi.; marriage, lxxvii.; bribes the

Danes, lxxviii , flight to Normandy and return, lxxix , death, lxxx

Æthelred II, Coinage — moneyers largely Scandinavian, xlvi , coinage, lxxx , coins of, found in Scandinavia, lxxxi , their wide circulation and imitation by Scandinavians, lxxxii , cxxv , with name of Dublin, lxxxiii , double cross type, lxxxix , moneyers, list of, 197, coin-types, 202 , coins, 208–212 (blundered coins, 241)

Æthelred, Lord of Mercia, marriage, xxxvii , no coins of, ib , defeats Vikings at Buttington, xxxviii , Governor of London, xxxix , death, li

Æthelstan, accession, lvi , war with Northumbria, lx , adds York to his kingdom, ib , opposed by British princes, ib , his power, lxi , relations with Harald of Norway, ib , war with Scotland and battle of Brunanburg, lxiii , death, ib

—— Coinage —strikes no coins for Kent, xxvi. n , moneyers, Frankish and Scandinavian, xlv , titles on coins and charters, lxi , lxii , coinage marks extent of conquests, lxii , coins of York, lxvii , lxviii , laws relating to mints, cviii , list of moneyers, 101 , coin-types, 103 , coins, 105–131 (with mint name, 105 , without mint name, 115)

Æthelstan, son of Æthelwulf, his rule in Kent, xxvi. n

Æthelwald, son of Æthelred I , rebellion of, xlviii , elected king of Northumbria, ib , defeated at Holme, xlix

Æthelwulf, k of Wessex, defeats Baldred, k of Kent, xiv , accession, xxiii , battle of Ockley, xxiv ; pilgrimage to Rome and marriage with

Judith, dau of Charles the Bald, xxv., divides kingdom with Æthelbald, xxv , xxvi n

—— Coinage —moneyers of xvii ; classification of coin-types, xxvi , xxvii , coins struck in Kent, ib ; list of moneyers, 9 , coin-types, ib ; coins, 13–20 (with mint name, 13; without mint name, 15).

Æthered, Abp of Canterbury, coin-types similar to Ælfred's, xxxviii.

Alphabetical forms used in Catalogue, ci

Army, standing, instituted by Cnut, lxxxiv

'Army,' the, of Vikings, its constitution and leadership, xxx

Arnulf, Emp of Germany, defeats Vikings, xlix

Arrangement of coins in Catalogue, xi.

Art of later Ang -Saxon coins, cause of decadence of, cxxiv , of earlier coinages, sceattas and pennies, cxxvi.

Asbjorn, Earl, killed at Ashdown, xxxii

Ashdown, battle of, xxxii ; mint of, notice, cxi.

Assandune, battle of, lxxx

Austin, Mr , his coin of Æthelbald, 21n.

B.

Bægseeg, Viking king, killed at Ashdown, xxxii

Bakewell, burg built by Eadweard I , lii.

Baldred, k of Kent, defeated by Æthelwulf, xiv., coins of, imitated by Ecgbeorht, xix

Baldwin, Count of Flanders, marriage with Judith, widow of Æthelbald, xxviii

Bamborough stormed by Danes, lxxiii

Bath, coins of, struck by Ælfred, xl., xli. *See also* Index of Mints.

Beaduheard, the port-reeve, slain by the Vikings, xxi.

Beda, and the title of Bretwalda, xv.

Bedford, 'army of,' xxx.; burg built by Eadweard I., lii.; Moneyers of, under Eadwig, Eadred, &c., lxix.

Bedwin, mint of, cix.; notice of, cxi.

Beorhtric, k. of Wessex, marriage and death, xiii.

Beorhtwulf, k. of Mercia, defeated by Rorik, the Dane, xxiv.

Beornwulf, k. of Mercia, defeated at Ellandune, xiv.; death, xv.

Berchta, dau. of Charibert, marriage with Æthelbearht of Kent, xxv.

Blundered pennies, of Ælfred, xli., xlii., 41–45, 79, 82; of Æthelstan, 119; of Æthelred II., 242.

Boyne, W., his coin of Ecgbeorht, 5.

Bremesbury (Bramsbury), burg built by Æthelflæd, li., lii.

Bretwalda, title of, xv.

Brewton, mint of, cix.; notice of, cxi.

Bribes to Vikings and Danes, xxxii., xxxiii., lxxiii., lxxv., lxxviii.

Brice, Mr. W., his coin of Æthelbald, 21 n.

Bridgnorth, burg built by Æthelflæd, li., lii; mint of, notice, cxii.

Brihtnoth, the caldorman, defeated at Maldon, lxxii.

Brunanburg, battle of, lxiii.

Bruton. *See* Brewton.

Buckingham, burg built by Eadweard I., lii.

Buildings, types of, on coins, lvi., cvii.

Burgred, k. of Mercia, attacked by Vikings, xxxii.; deposed by Halfdan, xxxiii.

Burgs, building of, in England, France, and Germany, xlix., l.; by Ead-weard I. and Æthelflæd l.–liii.; list of, lii.; illustrated by coins of Eadweard I., lvi.

Burgs,' the 'Five, jurisdiction and list of, xliv., xliv. *n.*, lix.; form of government, republican, liv.; increased to 'Seven Burgs,' *ib.*; incorporated into the West-Saxon kingdom, lv., lxv., lxviii.

Bust on coins, origin of type, cvii.; portraiture of, *ib.*

Buttington, battle of, xxxviii.

C.

Cadbury, mint of, notice, cxii.

Cambridge, taken by Guthorm, xxxv.; 'army' of, submits to Eadweard I., liv.

Camelford, battle of, xiv.

CANT and DORIBI, on coins of Æthelwulf, xxvi.

Canterbury, types of coins, imitated by Ecgbeorht, xix., xx.; attacked by Rorik, the Dane, xxiii.; mint of, and edict of Greatley, cix.

Carolingian coinage, its early influence on English coinage, xc., cxxiii.

Carolus-monogram of Charlemagne copied by Ecgbeorht, xx., xc.

Castle Rising, mint of, notice, cxii. *See also* Roiseng.

Ceolnoð, Abp. of Canterbury, copies monogram type of Ecgbeorht, xx.

Ceolwulf I., k. of Mercia, types of coins imitated by Ecgbeorht, xix.

Ceolwulf II., k. of Mercia, accession, xxxiii., xxxiv.; coin-type also used by Halfdan, xxxiv., xxxviii.; and by Ælfred, xxxviii., xxxix.

Charibert, k. of Paris, marriage of his dau. Berchta to Æthelbearht, xxv.

Charlemagne receives Ecgbeorht, xiii. ; coin-types imitated by Ecgbeorht, xx. ; 'Xristiana Religio' type, 27 n.

Charles the Bald revives Karolus-monogram type, xx. ; marriage of Judith to Æthelwulf, xxv.

Charles the Simple, marriage to Eadgifu, lxi.

Charmouth, defeat of the English by Vikings at, xxii.

Charters, titles of Æthelstan on, lxi., lxii. ; accuracy of names in, xcviii.

Cherbury, burg built by Æthelflæd, li., lii.

Chester, restored by Æthelflæd, li. ; coins of Æthelstan struck at, li., lxii. ; ravaged by Vikings, lxxii.

Chester or Leicester, coins of, lv. n.

Chichester, mint of, and edict of Greatley, cix.

Chippenham taken by Guthorm, xxxv.

Cledemutha (Gladmouth), burg built by Eadweard I., lii.

Cnut, invasion of, xxix. ; proclaimed king, lxxix. ; returns to England, ib. battle of Assandune, lxxx. ; treaty of Olney and king of all England, ib. ; extent of rule, lxxxii., lxxxiii. ; institutes standing army and fleet, lxxxiv. ; his policy and government, lxxxiv.-lxxxvi. ; endowment of churches and monasteries, lxxxv. ; division of his dominions, lxxxvii.

—— Coinage :— coins with his name struck at Dublin, lxxxiii. ; types of coins (helmeted head and crowned bust) lxxxix., xci., cvii., cxxv. ; mints of, xc. ; coin-types, their chronological order, xci. ; types copied by Scandinavians, cxxiv. ; list of moneyers, 213 ; coin-types, 248 ; coins, 255-301 (uncertain mints, 301).

CNUT on coins of Ælfred, xl. ; on coins in Cuerdale Find, xlvii.

Coenwulf, son of Offa, coinage for Mercia, xiii. ; coin-type imitated by Ecgbeorht, xix.

Coinage, its historical value, &c., xiii. ; right of not exercised by under-kings, xxvi.

Coins, arrangement of, in Catalogue, xi. ; number of Anglo-Saxon coins in National Collection, xi., xii. ; issues of, for payment of taxes, tributes, &c., lxxxi., cxxiv.

Colchester, burg built by Eadweard I., lii. ; mint of, and edict of Greatley, cix.

Combe, Taylor, on coin of Æthelbald, 21 n.

Conn's Half. See Leth-Cuind.

Constantine III., k. of Scotland, joins coalition against Æthelstan, lx. ; rebellion of, lxiii.

Corbridge, mint of, notice, cxiii.

Cross, double, on coins, its fiscal significance, lxxxix.

Crown on coins of Cnut, its origin, lxxxix., xci., cvii., cxxv.

Cuerdale Hoard, Viking imitations in, xxxix. ; coins of, xlii., xlvi. ; Northumbrian coins in, xlvii. ; debased penny of Ælfred in, 37 n.

Cumberland, granted to Malcolm I. of Scotland, lxix. ; attacked by Æthelred II., lxxv., lxxvi.

D.

Danebrog, on coins of Cnut, xcii.

Danegeld, nature of, and origin, xxxiii., lxxviii. ; levy of, by Harthacnut, lxxxviii.

Danish invasions of England, lxxii., lxxiii., lxxv.-lxxx. ; (attacks on

Southhampton, Chester, Thanet, Padstow, Dorchester, London, and Watchet, lxxii , on Ipswich and Bamborough, lxxiii . defeat at Maldon, *ib* , landing in the Isle of Wight and Kent, lxxv , return of Svend and siege of Exeter lxxvii. , conquest of England, lxxix , arrival of Cnut, *ib* , battles of Pen Selwood and Assandune and treaty of Olney, lxxx) *See also under* Vikings, invasions of

Danish kings in England, coinages of, lxxxix

Danish and Viking invasions distinguished, xxxi

Danish, Viking, and Norman invasions contrasted, xxviii , xxix

Darenth, mint of, cix , notice of, cxiii

Delgany Hoard, monogram-type coins of Egbeorht in, xx , account of, xxii

Denmark, early coin-types of, copied from English coins, lxxxii

Derby, coins of Æthelstan struck at, lvii

Dereham, mint of, notice, cxiii

Dies, how supplied, xcvii , civ , cx , process of engraving inscriptions on, xcix

Domesday, on supply of dies to Worcester, Hereford, &c , civ *n*

Dorchester, mint of, notice, cxiii

Dore, submission of Northumbrians to Egbeorht at, xv

DORIBI and CANT on coins of Æthelwulf, xxvi

'Dorobernia' on coins of Ælfred, xl

Dorstat, Swedish copies of coins of, xlvi

Double-cross type, its fiscal significance, lxxxix

Dublin, coins of, with names of Æthelred II and Cnut, lxxxiii

Dufnall, k of Strathclyde, rows Eadgar on the Dee, lxx

Dunstan, Abp of Canterbury, death, lxxiii

E

Eadgar, accession to throne of Mercia, lxix , king of all England, *ib* , assists Howel in North Wales, *ib* , confirms Cumberland to Malcolm of Scotland, lxx , the row on the Dee, *ib* , laws of, confirmed by Cnut, lxxxiv

—— Coinage —mints of, lxx , list of moneyers, 163 , coin-types, 165 , coins, 168–190 (with mint name 168 , without mint name, 175)

Eadgifu, marriage to Charles the Simple of France, lxi

Eadgith, marriage to Otto I , Emperor, lxi

Eadhild, marriage to Hugh the Great, duke of France, lxi

Eadmund, the 'Five Burgs,' subjection of, lv , accession, lxiii , attacked by Olaf Quaran and Wulfstan of York, lxiv , treaty with, *ib* , baptism of Olaf Quaran, lxiv , adds East Anglia and the Five Burgs to his dominions, lxv , defeat of Olaf and Ragnald of Northumbria, *ib* , murder of, *ib* , extent of power in Northumbria, lxvi

—— Coinage —Frankish and Scandinavian moneyers, xlv , xlvi , coins struck at York, lxvii, lxviii , list of moneyers, 122 , coin-types, 123 , coins 124–141 (with mint name, 124 , without mint name, 125)

Eadmund (Ironside) opposes the Danes, lxxix , accession, lxxx , battles of Pen Selwood, Shoiston, and Assandune, *ib.*; treaty of Olney, *ib.*; death, *ib.*

Eadmund (Ironside), Coinage:—no coins extant, 213 *n.*

Eadred, accession, lxvi.; allegiance of Wulfstan, Abp. of York, *ib.*; Erik Blöðöx driven from Northumbria, *ib.*; death, *ib.*

—— Coinage:—Frankish and Scandinavian moneyers, xlv., xlvi.; coins of York, lxvii., lxviii.; list of moneyers, 142; coin-types, 143; coins, 144–155 (with mint name, 144; without mint name, 144).

Eadred, of Bernicia, joins coalition against Æthelstan, lx.

Eadric Striona, treachery at Assandune, lxxx.; accused of murder of Eadmund Ironside, *ib.*; death, lxxxiii.; made Earl of Mercia, lxxxvi.

Eadweard the Elder, battle of Buttington, xxxviii.; accession, xlviii.; defeats Æthelwald of Northumbria at Holme, xlix.; treaty with Guthorm Eiriksson, l., liii.; his royal titles, l.; incorporates Mercia, *ib.*; building of the burgs, l.–liii.; list of burgs, lii.; captures Tempsford from Vikings, liv.; submission of the Danes, *ib.*; character of reign reflected by coinage, lv.

—— Coinage:—Frankish and Scandinavian moneyers, xlv.; titles on coins, l.; types of coins and inscriptions, lv., lvi.; list of moneyers, 83; coin-types, 84; coins, 87–100 (with mint name, 87; without mint name, 87).

Eadweard II., accession, lxx.

—— Coinage:—list of moneyers, 191; coin-types, 192; coins, 192–196.

Eadwig, accession, lxviii.; his unpopularity, lxix.; death, *ib.*

—— Coinage:—Frankish and Scandinavian moneyers, xlvi.; coins struck at York, lxviii.; list of moneyers, 156; coin-types, 156; coins, 158–162 (with mint name, 158; without mint name, 160).

Eadwine, earl of Mercia, rivalry of Tostig, xciv.

Ealgifu, marriage to Louis, k. of Provence, lxi.

Ealhstan, bp. of Sherborne, defeat of Baldred, k. of Kent, xiv.

Earldoms established in England by Cnut, lxxxvi., xc.; rivalry of, xciv.

East Anglia, kings of, their relation to Mercia, xiii.; supremacy of Ecgbeorht over, xv.; ravaged by Vikings, xxiii., xxxii.; Viking settlement in (A.D. 866), xxviii.; foundation of Viking kingdom in, xxxv., xxxvi.; Frankish moneyers' names on coins of, xliv.; submission of Vikings of, to Eadweard I., liv.; incorporated into Wessex, lxv.; government of the earls, *ib.*; earldom of, established, lxxxiv.; rivalry of, xciv.

Ecgbeorht, flight to France, xiii., xiv.; his conquests, xiii.; his policy and wars with Wales, xiv.; battle of Ellandune, *ib.*; extent of rule, xv.; submission of Northumbrians at Dore, *ib.*; supremacy over East Anglia and Northumbria, *ib.*; defeats Vikings at 'Hengestdune,' xxii.; death, xxiii.

—— Coinage:—probable date of first coinage, xii., xvii., xx., xxi.; his moneyers of Kentish origin, xvii.; early types of coins, xvii., xx.; coin-types derived from issues of Mercia, Kent, &c., xix., xx.; Carlovingian influence on early coin-type, xx ; list of moneyers, 1, coin-types, 1, coins, 6-8 (with mint name, 6, without mint name, 7)

Ecgbor, monogram of, 1 *n*

Eddesbury, burg built by Æthelflæd, li lii

Edward the Confessor, flight to Normandy, lxxix , claim to English throne supported, lxxxviii , receives support of Godwin, xcii , accession, *ib* , increase of Norman influence, xciii

—— Coinage.—Norman influence not traceable in coinage, xciii , coinage of, xcvi , chronological order of coin types, xcvii , list of moneyers, 329 , coin types, 334 , coins, 339-459 (uncertain mints, 456)

Ellandune, battle of, xiv , xvi , marks probable date of Ecgbeorht's first coinage, xii , xvii , xx , xxi

Emma (Ælfgifu) of Normandy, marriage to Æthelred II , lxxvii , flies to Normandy, lxxix , married to Cnut, lxxxvii

England, state of, under Æthelred II , lxxi , and wealth, lxxxi , under Cnut, lxxxvi , xcv , under Cnut's successors, xcv.

England, kingdom of, coins, 163-474

English coinage, its earliest types, cxxii , cxxiii , derived from Merovingian and Carolingian issues, cxxii ; distinctive nature of, *ib*

English and Frankish coinages, their early connection and separation, xviii

Engravers of dies, their process of engraving and errors, xcix -cii , whether moneyers, xcix , cxi

Erik Blôox, succession to throne of Norway, xxv *n* , k. of Northumbria, lxvi , expelled, *ib* , restored, *ib* , his moneyers, lxvii

Erik, earl of Norway, joins coalition against Olaf Tryggvason, lxxvi ; receives part of Norway, lxxvii , aids Cnut, lxxx , made earl of Northumbria, lxxxvi

Essex, added to Wessex, xv , Danes of, submit to Eadweard I , liv.

Evans, Sir John, account of the Delgany Hoard, xxii *n* , on mint of Newport, cxvii , coin of Ecgbeorht belonging to, 1

Exeter, retreat of Guthorm to, xxxv , captured by Vikings, xxxviii , coins of, struck by Ælfred, xl , xli , taken by Svend of Denmark, lxxvii

F.

Fastolfs, moneyers at Thetford and Lincoln, ciii

'Five Burgs' See Burgs,' the 'Five.

Fleet, building of, by Ælfred, xxxv , xxxvi , lvii , by Vikings, lvii ; standing, instituted by Cnut, lxxxiv

Floral designs on coins of Eadweard I , cvii

Forts, building of See Burgs

Frœne, Earl, killed at Ashdown, xxxii.

France, raid of Vikings in, xxiii

France and Germany, early coinages of, divergence of types, xc

Frankish coin-types in Cuerdale Hoard, xlvii

Frankish moneyers' names on coins of Wessex, East Anglia, &c , xliii -xlvi

Frankish and English coinages, their early connection, xviii , ceases with reign of Ecgbeorht, xviii , xxi

Freeman, on title of 'Rex Saxonum,' xix *n*

G.

Geddabuth (Jedburgh), mint of, notice, cxiv

Germany, raids of Vikings in, xxii, defeat of Vikings by Arnulf, emp, xlix coinage of, its influence on types of Cnut, xc

Gibbs, Mr H, his coin of Æthelbald, 21 n

Glelmouth See Cledemutha

Gloucester, coins of, struck by Ælfred, xl

Godwine, Earl, appointed earl of Wessex, lxxxvi, opposes claim of Harold I, lxxxvii murder of Ælfred, the Ætheling, ib, supports cause of Edward the Conf, xcii, his power, xcii, xciii, death, xciii

Gold coin of Æthelred II, 208

Greatley, synod of, its decree relating to mints, cviii

Green, J R, on 'Orsnaforda coins, xxxvii n

Guthfrid, k of Dublin claims Northumbria, lx

Guthmund, the Viking, attacks Ipswich, lxxiii

Guthorm (Æthelstan), k of East Anglia, invades Wessex, xxxv, battle of Æthandune and baptism at Wedmore, ib, receives East Anglia, xxxv, xxxvi

—— Coinage —copies coin-types of Ælfred, xl, coins of, xli, xlvi, moneyers chiefly Franks, xlii, xliv, coins of, in Cuerdale Hoard, xlvii

Guthorm Eiriksson, k of East Anglia, treaties with Eadweard I, l, lii

Guthred-Cnut, k of Northumbria, coin-types as Ælfred's, xl xlii, death, xlviii

Guðrum See Guthorm (Æthelstan)

Gyda, wife of Harald Fairhair, her taunt, xxx, xxxi.

Gyda, sister of Cnut, lxxxvi

H.

Hafirsfjord, battle of, xxxi n

Hakon, son of Harald, godson of Æthelstan, lxi, k of Norway, lxvi

Hakon, Earl, attempted conversion of, xliv, lxxiv, and Harald, k of Denmark, lxxiv, expelled from Norway, ib

Hakon Eriksson, Earl, coins of, lxxxii; made earl of Norway, lxxxvi

Halfdan, Viking king, defeated at Ashdown, xxxii, deposes Burgred of Mercia, &c, xxxiii, takes London, xxxiv, coin with London monogram, xxxiv, xxxvii–xxxix, king of Northumbria, xxxiv

Hamtune (Southampton), mint of and edict of Greatley, cix, notice of mint, cxv

Harald Harfagr (Fairhair), k of Norway, marriage and succession, xxv. n, reproached by Gyda, xxx, xxxi, and the Vikings of the West, xxxi, his relations with Æthelstan, lxi

Harald, Earl, killed at Ashdown, xxxii

Harald Blaatand, k of Denmark, his attempted conversion of Earl Hakon, xliv, lxxiv, conversion of, lxxiv

Harald Hardrada, claims throne of Norway, xciv and of England xcv, assists Tostig, ib, his invasion of England and death, xcvi.

Harold I, accession, lxxxvii, murder of Ælfred, the Ætheling, ib his character lxxxviii

—— Coinage —coin-types, order of, xcii, list of moneyers, 302, coin-types, 304, coins of, 307–319 (uncertain mints, 319)

Harold II, his influence under Edward the Conf, xciv, accession, ib, rebellion of the Earls, xciv, opposes Tostig, ib, the rival claimants, xcv, battles of Stamford Bridge and Hastings, xcvi, death, ib

—— Coinage —type of coins, xcvii, list of moneyers, 460, coin-types, 461, coins of, 461–474 (uncertain mints, 474)

Harthacnut, obtains crown of Denmark, lxxxvi, his right to English throne, lxxxvii, character, lxxxviii, war with Magnus of Denmark, ib, accession, ib, levy of danegeld, ib, death, ib

—— Coinage —types of coins, xcii, list of moneyers, 320, coin-types, 321, coins of, 325–328

Hasting, the Viking, takes Exeter, xxxviii

Hastings, battle of, xcvi, mint of and edict of Greatley, cix

Helmet, pointed, on coins of Cnut, lxxxix, xci, cvii

Hengstone (Hengestdune), battle of, xxii

Henry the Fowler, Emperor, his liberality to the Church, lxxxv

Heptarchic Kingdoms, xi, struggles of, terminated, xiii.

Hereford, new dies for coins, how supplied to, cix n

Hertford, burg built by Eadweard I, li, lii

Hincmar, Abp of Rheims, marriage of Æthelwulf to Judith, xxv

Hoards of English coins, found in Scandinavia, lxxxi, see also under Cuerdale, Delgany, and Skye

Holme, battle of, xlix

Horndon, mint of, notice, cxv

Howel, k of N Wales, joins coalition against Æthelstan, lx, receives assistance from Eadgar, lxix, rows Eadgar on the Dee, lxx

Hugh the Great, duke of France, marriage to Eadhild, dau of Eadweard I, lxi

Hugo, Count, betrays Exeter to Svend, lxxvii

Hunt, Mr William, on the Huscarls and the Comitatus, lxxxiv n

Huntingdon, burg built by Eadweard I, lii

Huscarls, their origin and duties, lxxxiv, massacre of, at Worcester, lxxxviii

I.

Iceland, conversion of, to Christianity, lxxv

Imitation of coins by Vikings, of Ælfred, xxxiii, xli, xlii, xlvi, of St Eadmund, Abp Plegmund, &c, xlii, xlvi, xlvii

Ine, k of Wessex, laws of, relating to fines, xviii

Inheritance, law of, among Scandinavians, its effect on succession to English throne, lxxxvi

Inscriptions, nature of, on reverses of coins, cv.

Ipswich attacked by Vikings, lxxiii

Ireland, invasion of, by Vikings, xxi, xxiii, Vikings establish kingdom there, xxii, xxiii, English coins brought by Vikings to, xlvi

Irish coinage, when initiated, xlvi

Isle of Man attacked by Æthelred II., lxxv.

Isle of Wight attacked by Danes, lxxv.; settlement of, in, lxxviii.

Ivar, House of, coins of, struck in Northumbria, lxvi.

J.

Jacob (Jago?), k. of North Wales, rows Eadgar on the Dee, lxx.

Jago, claim to the throne of Wales, lxix.

Jedburgh. *See* Geotaburh.

Juchill, k. of Westmoreland, rows Eadgar on the Dee, lxx.

Judith, dau. of Charles the Bald, marriage to Æthelwulf, xxv.; to Æthelbald, xxvii.; to Baldwin, Count of Flanders, xxviii.

Jumieges, Robert of, Abp. of Canterbury, his influence, xciii.

Justin, the Viking, attacks Ipswich, lxxiii.

K.

Karolus-monogram of Charlemagne copied by Eegbeorht, xx., xc.

Kenneth, k. of Scotland, rows Eadgar on the Dee, lxx.

Kent, under kings of Wessex, xvi.; a separate kingdom, *ib.*; ravaged by Vikings, xxiii., xxxviii.; kingdom of, united with Wessex, xxxvi.

—— Coinage:—types of coins imitated by Eegbeorht, xix.; predominant in the south till death of Æthelbald, xviii.; under-kings of, strike no coins, xxvi.

Kent, kings of, their relation to Mercia, xiii.

King, meaning of title of, among Vikings, xxx., xlvii., n.

L.

Laws relating to coinage of Ine and Wessex, xviii.; of Æthelstan, cviii.

Leicester, Viking raids from, liii.

Leicester and Chester, coins of, lv. *n.*

Leofa murders Eadmund at Pucklechurch, lxv.

Leth-Cuind, or Conn's Half of Ireland, invaded by Vikings, xxii.

Lewes, mint of, and edict of Greatley, cix.

Lincoln, monogram of, on coins of Ælfred, xxxix. *See also* Index of Types.

Lincolnshire ravaged by Vikings, xxiii.

Lindsay plundered by the Danes, lxxiii.

Llandaff, Bp. of, taken prisoner by Vikings, liv.

London plundered by Vikings, xxiii.; by Rorik the Dane, xxiv.; taken by Halfdan, xxxiv.; rebuilt by Ælfred, xxxvii., xxxix.; burnt by Vikings, lxxii.; relieved by Eadmund Ironside, lxxx.; heavily taxed by Cnut, lxxxiii.

—— Coinage:—monogram of, on coin of Halfdan, xxxiv., xxxvii.-xxxix.; on coins of Ælfred, xxxiv., xxxvii., xxxix.; mint of, and edict of Greatley, cix.

Louis, k. of Provence, marriage to Ealgifu, sister of Eadweard I., lxi.

Louis d'Outremer, k. of West Franks, lxi.

Louis the Pious, "Xristiana Religio" type on coins of, 27, *n.*

Lowick, mint of, notice, cxvi.

Ludican, k. of Mercia, death, xv.

Luffwick. *See* Lowick.

Lymne, mint of, notice, cxvi.

M.

Maccus, k of Man, assists Jago in Wales, lxix, lxxii. his allegiance to Eadgar, lxix, rows Eadgar on the Dee, lxx

Magnus Maximus, type of solidus imitated by Halfdan, xxxiv, xxxviii, and by Ælfred and Ceolwulf II of Mercia, xxxviii

Magnus the Good, k of Norway, &c, accession, lxxxviii, his compact with Harthacnut, ib, claims throne of Denmark, xcii, divides kingdom with Harald Hardrada, xciv, death, ib, claims English throne, ib

Malcolm receives Cumberland from Eadgar, lxx, rows Eadgar on the Dee, ib

Maldon, burg built by Eadweard I, lii, battle of lxxiii, mint of, notice, cxvi

Malmesbury, mint of, notice, cxvii

Manchester, burg built by Eadweard I, lii

Matilda, wife of William I, her descent from Judith, wife of Baldwin, Ct of Flanders, xxxiii

Mercia its pre-eminence under Offa, xiii, invasion of Wessex by, xiv, its position after battle of Ellandune, xvi attacked by Vikings, xxxii, incorporated into Wessex, xxxvi, xxxvii, l, li, separated from Wessex, lxix, Eadgar, king of, ib, an earldom, lxxxvi, rivalry of, xciv

—— Coinage —coins of, struck in Kent, xvii, moneyers of, Kentish, ib, coin-types copied by Ecgbeorht, xix

Mercia, Western, supremacy of Wessex over, xxxvi, xxxvii

Mercia and Northumbria, rivalry of, xiii

Mercia and Wessex, rivalry of, xiii

Merovingian coins, their types copied on English coins, cxxii, cxxiii

Mints, classification of coins of Wessex with mint names, xxvi, increase of, in reign of Eadgar, lxx, of Æthelstan mark conquests of Eadweard I, lxii, names of, earliest forms, cv, mint places, &c, cviii –cxvi (growth of, cviii –cx, laws of Æthelstan relating to, cviii, Synod of Greatley, ib, right of coinage granted to religious houses, cix, difficulties of identification, cx, a source of revenue, ib, uncertain and new mints, notices of, cxi –cxx), historical importance of, cxxiii See also Index of Mints

Mints, notices of, &c Ashdown, cxi, Bath, xl, xli, Bedwin, cxi, Brewton, ib, Bridgnorth, cxii, Cadbury, cxii, Canterbury, cix, Castle Rising, cxii, Chester, li lv n, lxii, Chichester, cix, Colchester, ib, Corbridge, cxii, Darenth, ib, Derby, lxii, Dereham, cxii, Dorchester, cxiii, cxiv Dublin, lxxvii, Exeter, xl, xli, Godasburh, cxiv, Gloucester, xl, Hamtune, cix, cxv, Hastings, cix, Hereford, civ n, Horndon, cxv, Jedburgh, cxiv, Leicester, lv n, Lewes, cix, Lincoln, xxxix, London, xxxiv, xxxvii –xxxix, cix, Lowick, cxvi, Lymne, ib, Maldon, ib, Malmesbury cxvii, Newark, ib, Newport, ib, Northampton, cxv, cxvii, Nottingham, lxii, Otford, cxvii Oxford, xxvii, xl, Richborough, cxviii, Roiseng, xxxix, cxii, Shaftesbury, cix, Sidbury, cxviii, Sidmouth, ib, Southampton, cix, cxv, cxix Tempsford,

cxix., Tonbridge, ib., Totleigh, ib.,
Wardborough, cix., cxix., Wareham,
cix., Warmington, cxx., Welmesford, ib., Weybridge, ib., Winchester, xl., xli., cix., Winchcombe,
cxxi., Witham, ib., York, lxii.,
lxvii., lxviii

Mon., Moneta (Moneta or Mone-
arius ?), cv

Moneyers, names of, not in National
Collection, xii., of Ecgbeorht, of
Kentish origin, xvii., of Vikings,
their mixed nationality, xxix., confusion and varieties of names of, xlii–
xliv., Scandinavian, Frankish and
English, xliii–xlvi., of York and
Northumbria under Æthelstan, Eadmund, &c., lxvii., whether local,
lxvii., of Bedford under Eadwig,
Eadred, &c., lxix., their status,
xcviii., ciii., civ., cxi., blundered
names of, xcviii–cii., early names
of English etymology, cii., rarity
of Latin and biblical names, cii.,
chiefly Frankish and Scandinavian
on Viking coinages, cii., punishment of, civ., whether itinerary, cv.,
names of, in possessive case, cvi.,
not engravers of dies, cv

Monkwearmouth, wreck of Vikings at,
xxi

Monogram types, of Ecgbeorht, their
origin, xx., of Canterbury on coins
of Ecgbeorht, ib., of 'Doribi' and
'Cant' on coins of Æthelwulf,
xxvi., of mints, inaugurated, xxvii.,
xxxix., a Frankish device, xxxix.,
&c., of London, xxxix., xxxvii.,
xxxix., of Lincoln, xxxix., of
Roiseng, ib

Montagu, Mr H., on coins of Chester
and Leicester, lv. n., on Castle
Rising mint, cxii., coin of Æthelwulf

belonging to, 12, of Æthelbald, 21,
of Ælfred, 31, of Eadweard II,
192, of Harold I, 306

Morkere, earl of Northumbria, rivalry
with Tostig, xciv.

Murchison Collection, coin of Ecgbeorht in, 5, of Ælfred, 35, n

M—x on coins of Ælfred, 57

N

Newark, mint of, notice, cxvii

Newport, mint of, notice, cxvii

Norman coinage in England uninfluenced by that of Normandy,
xciii

Norman influence during reign of
Edward the Confessor, xciii., little
or no trace of, on coinage, cxxv

Norman, Viking, and Danish invasions contrasted, xxviii., xxix

Normandy, invasion of, by Æthelred II, lxxvi

Norse invasion of Ireland, xxii.,
coinage, initiation of, xlvi

Northampton, Viking 'army' of, xxx;
Viking raids from, liii., submission
of Vikings of, liv., attacked by Olaf
Quaran, lxiv

Northampton, mint of (?), cxv.　See
Hamtune

Northumbria, submission of, to Ecgbeorht, xv., attacked by Vikings,
xxxii., foundation of Viking kingdom in, xxxiv., accession of Æthelwald, son of Æthelred I, xlviii.,
accession of Olaf Quaran, lxiii.,
division of, between Olaf Quaran
and Olaf Godfredsson, lxiv., later
earls of, lxv., conquered by Eadmund and divided with Malcolm of
Scotland, ib., its allegiance to Eadred, and revolt, lxvi., accession of

Erik Blóᵗox, *ib* , rule of Eadmund and Eadred in, lxvi , lxvii , united to England, lxviii , an earldom, lxxxvi , rivalry of, xciv

—— Coinage —continued after submission to Ecgbeorht, xv , coins of, in Cuerdale hoard, xli , xlvii . a Viking coinage, xlii , coins of, during reigns of Eadmund and Eadred, lxvi

Northumbria and Mercia, rivalry of, xiii

Norway, conversion of, to Christianity, lxxv , partition of, after death of Olaf Tryggvason, lxxvii , early coin-types copied from English, lxxxii

Norwich burnt by Svend, lxxvii

Nottingham, siege of, by Æthelred I and Ælfred, xxxii , burg, built by Eadweard I, lii , coins of Æthelstan struck at, lxii

O.

OCCIDENTALIVM, SAXONIORVM on coins of Æthelwulf, 10

Ockley, battle of, xxiv

Odo, Abp of Canterbury, treaty between Eadmund and Olaf Quaran, lxiv

Offa, introduction of penny coinage into England, xiii , cxxii

'Offering Pennies' of Ælfred, xl , xli, 55

Olaf, k. of Sweden, joins coalition against Olaf Tryggvason, lxxvi , assists Cnut, lxxix ; his coinage, lxxxii

Olaf Godfredsson, k of Northumbria, battle of Brunanburg, lxiii , divides Northumbria with Olaf Quaran, lxiv , his death, *ib*

Olaf Haraldsson (St Olaf) conveys Æthelred II to England, lxxix

Olaf Quaran, k of Northumbria, marriage, lxiii , battle of Brunanburg, *ib* , made k of Northumbria, *ib* , attack on Northampton and Tamworth, lxiv , peace with Eadmund and baptism, *ib* , divides Northumbria with Olaf Godfredsson, *ib* , driven from kingdom, lxv , restored to his throne, lxvi , his moneyers, lxvii

Olaf Skotkonung, k of Sweden, his assistance to Cnut, lxxix , institutes coinage in Sweden, lxxxii

Olaf Tryggvason, k of Norway, lxiii , attacks Ipswich, lxxiii , converted to Christianity, lxxiv , accession, *ib* , death, lxxvii

OBSVAFORDA on coins of Ælfred, xxvii , xl , 50

Otford, mint of, cix , notice of cxviii

Otto I , Emperor, marriage to Eadgith, sister of Eadweard I , lxi

Owen, k of Cumberland, attacks Æthelstan, lxiii , battle of Brunanburg, *ib*

Oxford, coins of, struck by Ælfred, xxxvii , xl , 50, meeting of Witenagemot at, lxxxiv , lxxxv

P.

PACX on coins of Cnut, lxxxv , of Edward the Conf, xcvii.

Padstow harried by Vikings, lxxii

Paris, siege of, and defeat of Vikings, xlix

Pen Selwood, battle of, lxxx

Penny, origin and introduction of, xiii , cxxii

Pied-forts of Ælfred, xl , xli , 55

Piffard, Mr. E. J. G., coin of Ecgbeorht belonging to, 3.

Pîtres, Edict of, and the Karolus-monogram type, xx. n.

Plegmund, Abp. of Canterbury, coin-types as Ælfred's, xl.; Viking imitations of coins of, xlii., xlvi.

Portraiture on English coins, cvii.

Portsmouth, victory of Vikings at, xxiii.

Prætorian gate?, type of, on English coins, 86.

Primogeniture and succession among Teutons, xxv.

Providence, hand of, on coins of Eadweard I., lvi. n.; as a coin-type, cvii.

Pucklechurch, murder of Eadmund at, lxv.

R.

Ragnald or Regnald, k. of Northumbria, betrothed to Ælfwyn, dau. of Æthelflæd, li. n., lix.: accession, lix.

Ragnhild, marriage to Harald Hárfagr, xxv. n.

Reading, encampment of Vikings at, and flight of Halfdan to, xxxii.

Regnald, son of Godfred, k. of Northumbria, lxiv.; driven out by Eadmund, lxv.

Religious divisions in England and Scandinavia, lxxiv.

Religious houses receive right of coinage, cix.

Rex Saxonvm on coins of Ælfred and Eadweard I., xix. n., xl., l.

'Rex totius Britanniæ' on coins of Æthelstan, lxi., lxii.

Richborough, mint of, notice, cxviii.

Ripon Cathedral burnt by Eadred, lxvi.

Robert of Jumièges, Abp. of Canterbury, his influence, xciii.

Rochester plundered by Vikings, xxiii.

Roiseng, monogram of, on coin of Ælfred, xxxix.

Roiseng, mint of. See Castle Rising.

Rorik, the Dane, attacks Canterbury and London, xxiii., xxiv.

Runcorn, burg built by Æthelflæd, li., lii.

S.

St. Andrew, coinage of, 7.

St. Brice, massacre of, lxxvi., lxxvii.

St. Clair-en-Epte, treaty of, lvii.

St. Eadmund coinage, imitated by Ælfred, xl.; date of, xli., xliv.; struck by Vikings, xlii., xlvi., xlvii.; moneyers, names on, xliii.; coins of, 38, 59.

Sandwich attacked by Danes, lxxviii.

Saxoniorvm on coins of Ecgbeorht, xix.

Scandinavia, coinages of, when initiated, xlvi.; early, imitated from English, lxxxii., cxxiii., cxxiv.; from Frankish, cxxiii.; extent of circulation, cxxv.

Scandinavia, greater, kingdoms of, in the 10th cent., lvii., lviii.

Scandinavian moneyers, names of, on coins, xliii.–xlvi.

Sceattas, coinage of, extent of circulation, cxxii.; types derived from Merovingian coins, cxxiii.

Scergeat, burg built by Æthelflæd, li., lii.

'Seven Burgs,' liv. See also under 'Burgs, Five.'

Shaftesbury, mint of, and edict of Greatley, cix.

Sheppey, island of, attacked by Vikings, xxii.

Shoiston, battle of, lxxx.

Sidbury, mint of, cix, notice of, cxviii

Sidmouth, mint of, notice, cxviii

Sicferð or Sicfred, k of Wales, rows Eadgar on the Dee, lxx

Siefred, k of Northumbria, assists Hasting, the Viking, xxxviii., coin-type as Ælfred's, xl, coins of, in Cuerdale hoard, xlvii

Sigvald, the Viking, betrays Olaf Tryggvason, lxxvi

Sihtric the Elder, Earl, killed at Ashdown, xxxii

Sihtric the Younger, Earl, killed at Ashdown, xxxii

Sihtric Gale, k of Northumbria, war with Æthelstan and death, lx

Skye, hoard of coins found in, cix, cxx

Solidus, a money of account in West-Saxon laws, xviii, type of, on coin of Halfdan, xxxiv, xxxviii, and on coin of Ælfred, xxxviii, 34

Southampton, defeat of Vikings at, xxiii, attacked by Vikings, lxvii, mint of, and edict of Greatley, cix

Southampton, mint of See Hamtune

Spink and Sons, Messrs, coin of Æthelbald belonging to, 21 n

Stafford, burg built by Æthelflæd, li, lii

Stamford, burg built by Eadweard I, liii

Stamford Bridge, battle of, xcvi

Steenstrup, his list of burgs founded by Æthelflæd and Eadweard I, lii

Stockholm Museum, its series of Anglo-Saxon coins, xii, lxxvi

Styeas, coinage of, cxxii

Surrey, under supremacy of Wessex, after battle of Ellandune, xvi

Sussex, under supremacy of Wessex, after battle of Ellandune, xvi

Svend, k of Denmark, invasion of England, xxix, attacks Bamborough, lxxiii, opposition to Christianity, lxxiv, invasions of Germany, lxxv, joins coalition against Olaf Tryggvason, lxxvi, receives part of Norway, lxxvii, revenges massacre of St Brice, ib, besieges Exeter, Norwich, &c, lxxvii, lxxviii, conquest of England and death, lxxix; his coinage, lxxxii

Svend, son of Cnut, k of Norway, lxxxvi, lxxxvii

Svend Estrid's son, claims throne of Denmark, lxxxviii, offer of English crown to, xcii

Svold, battle of, lxxvi

Sweden, coinage of, imitations of coins of Dorstat, xlvi, date of first coinage, ib, coin-types copied from English, lxxxii

T.

Tamworth, burg built by Æthelflæd, li, lii, besieged by Olaf Quaran, lxiv

Taxes, forced levies of, lxxviii, lxxxiii, lxxxviii

Temple type, its Carolingian origin, xc

Tempsford, built by Vikings, liv; taken by Eadweard I, ib, mint of, notice, cxix

Tettenhall, battle of, liii

Thanet, winter quarters of Vikings at, xxviii, attacked by Vikings, lxvii

Thelwall, burg built by Eadweard I, lii

Thetford, burnt by Svend, k of Denmark, lxxvii

Thorgisl, the Viking, his invasion of Ireland, xxi, xxii

Thurkill, Earl of East Anglia, lxxxvi

Tonbridge, mint of, notice, cxix

Tostig, Earl of Northumbria, his rivalry with Earls Morkere and Eadwine, xciv, banishment of, ib, seeks aid from William of Normandy and Harald of Norway, xcv, battle of Stamford Bridge and death, xcvi

Totleigh, mint of, notice, cxix

Towcester, burg built by Eadweard I, lii

Turferð, his unsuccessful invasion of Northumbria, lx

Turgesius See Thorgisl

Types of coins, not in the National Collection, xii, of Ecgbeorht, derived from Mercia, Kent, Canterbury and Charlemagne, xix, xx, xc, London monogram coins of Halfdan and Ælfred, xxxiv, xxxviii–xxxix, monogram types of Ælfred, xxxix, of Wessex, principle of classification, xxxvi, of Ælfred with mint names, xl, xli, Viking imitations of types of Ælfred, &c, xliii, xlv; hand of Providence, buildings, &c, on coins of Eadweard I, lvi, cvii, Scandinavian coin-types copied from Æthelred II's, lxxii, Agnus Dei and Dove types of Æthelred II, ib, PACS, its reference, lxxxv, double-cross type, its fiscal significance, lxxxix, pointed helmet and crowned types of Cnut, lxxxix, xci, cvii, cxxv, monogram (Ecgbeorht) and temple types, origin of, xc, king holding Danebrog, xcii, Sovereign type of Edward Conf, xcvii, types, their general character on Anglo-Saxon coins, cvi–cviii (chiefly religious, cvii, hand of

Providence, buildings, &c, ib, busts on coins, cvii, cviii, portraiture, cvii)

U.

Ulf, Earl, his rule over Denmark, lxxxv, his treachery to Cnut and death, ib, his son, Svend, claims throne of Denmark, lxxxviii

Ulfketil, Earl of East Anglia, his opposition to the Danes, lxxvi–lxxviii, death, lxxx

V.

Valentinian I, type of coin of, imitated by Halfdan, xxiv, and by Ælfred, 31

Verberie, marriage of Æthelwulf at, xxv

Viking, etymology of, lviii n

Viking Ages, First and Second, contrasted, lvi–lviii, lxxii, First Viking Age, states created by, lvii, Second Viking Age, warnings of, lxxii

Viking and Danish invasions distinguished, xxxi

Viking, Danish, and Norman invasions contrasted, xxviii, xxix

Vikings, first invasions of, xxi, attack Lindisfarne, xxi, invade Ireland, xxi, xxii, attack Island of Sheppey, xxii; and Charmouth, ib, defeated by Ecgbeorht at 'Hengistdune,' ib, defeated at Southampton, xxiii, victorious at Portsmouth, in Lincolnshire, East Anglia and Kent, ib, plunder London and Rochester, ib, raids in France and Germany, ib, attack Canterbury, ib, and

London, xxiv , defeated by Beorhtwulf, k of Mercia, ib , their first
settlement in Kent, ib , defeat Æthelbald at Ockley, ib , raids on Winchester, &c , during reign of Æthel-
beorht, xxviii , winter in Thanet,
and settle in East Anglia, ib , their
'armies,' laws and constitution of,
xxix , xxx , take York, xxvi ,
xxvii , invade Mercia, xxxii , en-
camp at Reading, defeated at Ashdown, ib , defend Nottingham, ib ,
invade Northumbria, Mercia and
East Anglia, ib , defeat Ælfred
at Wilton, xxxiii , take London,
xxxiv , settle in Northumbria, ib ,
land in Kent and defeated by Ælfred,
xxxvii , capture Exeter, xxxviii ,
defeated at Buttington, ib , defeated
at Holme, xlix , at Paris, ib , settle
in Normandy, ib , defeated in
Germany, ib , defeat at Tettenhall,
lii , raids and defeat of, in A D 911,
ib , division of territories in England
and forms of government, lii , liv ,
lv , raid on Wales A D 915, liv ,
defeat of, ib , build Tempsford, ib ,
march on Bedford, ib , submission
to Eadweard I , ib , invasions, eras
of, contrasted, (First and Second
Viking Ages) lvi -lviii , lxxii , First
Viking Age, states of, lvii , kingdoms
of, extent in England in 10th cent
lix , lx , cessation of raids, lxviii ,
First and Second Viking Ages, resemblance of, lxxii renewal of
attacks under Æthelred II (Second
Viking Age) lxxix -lxxx See also
under Danish invasions of England
Vikings, Coinage —imitations of coins
of Ælfred, xxxiii , xl , xli, xlii ,
xlvi , of coins of the Franks, xxxix ,
of St Edmund and Plegmund, Abp

of Canterbury, xlii , xlvi , xlvii ,
during reign of Ælfred, xlvi , established under Guthorm (Æthelstan),
xlvii

W.

Wales attacked by Ecgbeorht, xiv ,
by Vikings, xxi , liv , lxii , allegiance of Howel, king of, lxix
Wardborough, burg built by Æthelflæd, li n , coin of, in Skye Find,
cix , cxx , mint of, notice, cxix
Wareham, taken by Guthorm, xxxv ,
mint of, and edict of Greatley, cix
Warmington, mint of, notice, cxx
Warwick, burg built by Æthelflæd,
li , lii
Watchet ravaged by Vikings, lxxii
Waymere, burg built by Eadweard I ,
lii
Wedensborough (Wardborough ?), burg
built by Æthelflæd, li , lii
Wedmore, baptism of Guthorm at,
xxxv , Peace of, xxxv , xliv , lxxx ,
coins issued subsequent to Peace of
Wedmore, xli
Weland, Viking chief, plunders Winchester, xxviii , his defeat, ib ·
Welmesford, mint of, cix ; notice of,
cxx
Wessex, invaded by Mercia, xiv ,
supremacy of, xiv , xvi , absorbs
Kent and Western Mercia, xxxvi ,
extent of, under Eadweard I and
his sons, lxviii , an earldom, lxxxvi ,
rivalry of, xciv
—— Coinage —its extent, xi, xii ,
when first issued, xii , first coinage
of, xv , xix , xx , its origin, xvi ,
xvii , primarily Kentish, xvii , no
native currency before Ecgbeorht,
xviii , laws of, and payments by
kind, ib types of Ecgbeorht s

Wessex coins, xix , classification of early coins of, xxvi , Frankish and Scandinavian moneyers of, xli , supremacy of, south of the Humber, cxxii , kingdom of, coins, 1-162

Wessex and Mercia, rivalry of, xiii.

West-Saxon Kingdom, extent of, under Æthelstan, lix

Western Mercia, supremacy of Wessex over, xxxvi, xxxvii

Weybridge, mint of, notice, cxx

White, Mr John, coin of Æthelbald, 21 n

Willett, Mr Ernest, his statistics on moneyers of Edward the Confessor, cv n

William, Duke of Normandy, claims English throne, xcv , assists Tostig, ib , invades England and battle of Hastings, xcvi

Wilton, battle of, xxxiii

Wimborne, retreat to of Æthelwald, son of Æthelred I , xlviii

Winchcombe, mint of, notice, cxxi

Winchester plundered by Weland, the Viking, xxviii , coins of, struck by Ælfred, xl , xli , mint of, and edict of Greatley, cix

Witham, burg built by Eadweard I li , lii , liii , mint of, cix ; notice of, cxxi

Worcester, its refusal to pay danegeld, and massacre of huscarls, lxxxviii , new dies for coins supplied to, civ n , cx

Wulfheard, Earl, defeats Baldred, k of Kent, xix

Wulfstan, Abp of York, joins Olaf Quaran and attacks Eadmund, lxiv ; his escape, ib , allegiance to Eadred, lxvi.

X.

XRISTIANA RELIGIO coin-type of Charlemagne, 27 n

Y.

York taken by Vikings, xxxi , xxxii
—— Coinage —coins of Æthelstan struck at, lxii , lxviii , moneyers and coins of, under Æthelstan, Eadmund and Eadred, lxvii , lxviii
York, kingdom of, added to West-Saxon Kingdom, lx

II.—INDEX OF MONEYERS.

₊ The *numbers* printed in italics in the accompanying list correspond to the *names* in italics in the lists of moneyers under each king. They are of moneyers not represented in the Museum Collection.

A.

Abba, 83, 87, 101, 108, 109, 115.

Abbun, 122, 125.

Abenel, 32, 59, *122, 156.*

Abnᵹorb, 197. 214.

Abonel, *101.*

Abun, *101.*

Ada or Aden, 243, 271.

Adalbert, *83.*

Adelaver or Aᵹelaver, 163, 175, *191.*

Adelberht, *101.*

Adelgar, 163, 176. *See also* Æᵹelgar.

Adelover. *See* Adelaver.

Adelwerd, *122.*

Adelwine, *122. See* Æᵹelwine.

Adelwold, 163, 173. *See also* Aᵹelwold.

Aden, 163, 176.

Aduald, *83.*

Aducard, 32, 59.

Æadgar, 241. *See* Eadgar.

Æatan, *329.*

Ædgar, 329, 414. *See also* Eadgar.

Ædric, 329, 317, *392. See also* Eadric and Edric.

Ædulf, *122.*

Ædward, 329, 385. *See also* Eadward.

Ædwine, 197, 211. *See also* Eadwine.

Æelman, *243.*

Æelric, 122, 126, *320,* 329, 381. *See also* Æleric and Ælfric.

Æfie or Æfice, *197,* 213, 262, *302.*

Æilrheh, *197.*

Ægelbriht, *243.*

Ægelferᵹ, *243.*

Ægelm, 243, 259.

Ægelmær, Ægelmer, &c., *243, 302, 320,* 329, 339, 310.

Ægelman, *302.*

Ægelric or Egelric, *197,* 243, 298, 302, 317, *320,* 329, 331, 373, 387, 388, 400, 409.

Ægelsie, 329, 454. *See also* Ægelsig.

Ægelsig or Ægelsige, *243,* 329.

Ægelward or Ægelwerd, 243, 282, 320, 326, 329, 406.

Ægelwer, 320, 412.

Ægelwi, *320,* 352, 403, 415. *See also* Ægelwig and Ægelwine.

Ægelwig or Egelwig, 243, 275, *302,* 329, 331, 398, 400, 403, 409.

Ægelwine or Egelwine, *197,* 243, 245, 257, 267, 282, 285, *302, 303,* 320, 327, 329, 331, 351, 352, 371, 388, 415, 421, 434, 440, 460, 464, 466, 474.

Ægenulf, *197.*

Ægfrye, 243, 283.

Ægisman, *243. See* Æisman.

Ægnuce, *122.*

Æilsie, 329, 455.

Æilwig, 329, 436.

Æilwine, 329, 351.

Æisman, 243, 293. *See also* Ægisman.

Ælbriht, 243, 402
Ælfelm or Ælfelm, 197, 243, 257, 258
Ælere, 402
Ælere, 320, 425 See also Ælric and Elfru
Ælewig See Ælfwig
Ælewine, 197, 221, 460 See also Elwine
Ælfcetel, 197
Ælfeah, 197 See Ælfheah
Ælfege, 243
Ælfeh or Ælfen, 243, 298, 329, 427
Ælfelm, 197, 243, 257, 258 See also Ælfelm
Ælfere, Ælfhere, or Elfere, 243, 302, 310, 329, 361
Ælfers, 243
Ælfeh, 320
Ælfet, 329, 398
Ælfget, Ælfgeat, Ælfget, or Elfget, 197, 199, 243, 329, 396, 460, 467
Ælfgar, Alfgar &c., 163, 175, 197, 208, 225, 243, 283, 294, 302, 329, 389, 403 458
Ælfged, 197 See Ælfget
Ælfheah Ælfheh, or Ælfeah, 197, 243
Ælfhere, 329, 361 See also Ælfere
Ælfine, 302 See Ælfwine
Ælfmer, 197
Ælfmere, 329
Ælfnoð Ælnoð, Elfnoð, &c., 101, 163, 174, 197, 243, 244, 220, 221, 223, 226, 245, 243, 276, 278, 279, 302, 313, 320, 329, 391, 394, 395, 460
Ælfred or Elfred, 101, 102, 114, 122, 142, 147, 156, 160, 163, 185, 197, 243, 287, 292, 297, 302, 308, 320, 329, 331, 344 345, 397, 398 403, 406, 409, 412 414, 457
Ælfric, Alfric or Elfric, 101, 102, 106, 122, 197 209 219 231 245, 243

256, 261, 283, 294, 297, 302, 308, 320, 329, 313, 316, 357, 358, 376, 400, 402, 429, 453 See also Ælric.
Ælfric Moglu, 243
Ælfryd or Ælfryð, 197, 227, 243
Ælfryc, 243
Ælfsi, Ælfsic, Alfsic, Elfsic, &c., 142, 243, 329, 373, 381, 388, 389, 390, 405, 407, 416, 435, 453 See also Ælfsige
Ælfsig, Ælfsige, Elfsige, Elsige, &c., 142, 144, 156, 163, 168, 171, 174, 190, 197, 237, 238, 239, 243, 269, 276, 277, 297, 298, 302, 312, 320, 329, 390, 391, 403, 407, 412, 414, 416
Ælfstan, Ælstan, Alfstan, Elfstan, &c., 32, 44, 50, 81, 101, 111, 115, 122, 125, 142, 144, 163, 169, 171, 190, 191, 192, 193, 197, 209, 213, 221, 226, 236, 243, 298, 302, 320, 329, 331, 400, 411, 444
Ælfwald or Ælfwold, 32, 59, 101, 111, 122, 125, 191, 195, 197, 210, 243, 244, 302, 315, 329, 398, 399, 442, 460, 472 See also Alfwald and Elfwald
Ælfward, Ælfweard, Ælfwerd, Ælweard, &c., 191, 197, 219, 237, 243, 272 274, 283, 290, 302, 307, 311, 329, 343, 346, 347, 397, 409, 412, 414, 415, 425, 426 See also Alfward.
Ælfwi, Ælfwie, or Elfwi, 102, 197, 243, 255, 282, 299, 302, 329, 381, 398, 403, 422, 460, 469
Ælfwi and Swencel, 243
Ælfwig, Ælwig, or Elfwig, 156, 197, 243, 272, 283, 285, 302, 311, 317, 318, 320, 327, 329, 342, 375, 381, 398, 403, 421, 422
Ælfwine, Ælwine, Alfwine, Elfwine, &c., 101, 122, 197, 221, 227, 230,

243, 259, 261, 262, 267, 270, 273, 276, 282, 285, 290, 294, 295, 296, 297, 299, 302, 311, 312, 317, 318, 320, 328, 329, 343, 348, 349, 350, 359, 361, 362, 372, 374, 375, 379, 380, 382, 399, 403, 406, 409, 414, 420, 421, 433, 440, 441, 443, 444, 446, 448, 450, 451, 452, 456, 457, 460, 462, 465, 473.

Ælfwine Mus, *243*.

Ælfwinig, *122*.

Ælfwold, 197, 240, *243, 244*, 302, 315, 329, 442, 460, 472. *See also* Ælfwald.

Ælfwond, 329, 399.

Ælfword, 409. *See* Ælfward.

Ælgær, 460, 468.

Ælgelwine, *243*. *See* Ægelwine.

Ællman, 302, 307.

Ælmær, *197, 243, 302, 329*.

Ælmon, 329, 341.

Ælnot, *302*. *See* Ælfnoð.

Ælnoð, 329. *See* Ælfnoð.

Ælræd, Elræd, &c., 329, 331, 345, 346.

Ælric, 243, 290, *302*, 329, 373, 388. *See also* Ælfric.

Ælstan, *243*. *See* Ælfstan.

Ælvii, 327. *See* Ælfwig.

Ælvionwii, *320*.

Ælweard or Ælwerd, *243*, 409, 412, 425. *See also* Ælfweard.

Ælwig, *156*, 302, 317, 329, 342, 421. *See also* Ælfwig.

Ælwine, *197*, 243, 259, 270, 285, 290, 294, 302, 317, *320*, 329, 348, 399, 409, 414. *See also* Ælfwine.

Ænred, *1*.

Ærfre, 329, 432.

Ærgred, *197*.

Æriger, 142, 144.

Ærngrim, *320*, 329, 362. *See also* Arngrim.

Ærnulf, 122, 126. *See* Arnulf.

Æscman or Escman, 163, 173, 191, 195, 197, 222, *243*.

Æsctl or Æsctli, *197*.

Æseulf or Æscuulf, 156, 160, 163, 176.

Æsewig, *197*.

Æsewine, *243*.

Æstan, Astan, or Estan, 243, 245, 256, *302, 303, 320*, 329, 331, 423, 436, 444, 445, 446, 449.

Æstann and Loc, *243*, 329, 445.

Æstmær or Estmær, 329. *See also* Eastmær.

Ætard or Ætardes, 142, 145, *156*. *See also* Agtard.

Ætferð, 163, 176.

Æwulf, *329*. *See* Eawulf.

Æðelaf, 32, 54. *See also* Æðelulf.

Æðelaver, *163, 191*. *See also* Adelaver.

Æðelberht, *101, 243*.

Æðelbrand, *163*.

Æðelbriht, *243*.

Æðelferð or Æthelfreð, 101, 121, *163*.

Æðelfred, 83, 87.

Æðelgar or Adelgar, *156*, 163, 176, 197, 239.

Æðelm, 101, 115, *122*, 142, 144, *197, 243*.

Æðelmær or Eðelmær, 197, 221, 232, 243, 278, 279.

Æðelman, *197, 243*.

Æðelmod or Aðelmod, 101, 121, 122, 140.

Æðelmund or Aðelmund, *101*, 122, 126, 142, 145.

Æðelnoð or Eðelnoð, 9, 18, 22, 24, 101, 105, 113, *142*, 197, 218, 222, *243*, 278.

Æðelred, 83, *101*, 163, 173, 191, 195, *243*. *See also* Æðered and Eðelred.

Æðelric or Æðeric, *122*, 197, 209, 237, 243, 256, 276, 288.

Æðelsie or Æðelsige, *101*, 163, 168, 177, *197*.

Æðelstan, Æðestan, Æðstan, Eðelstan, or Eðestan, 32, 10, 60, 83, 87,
101, 156, 163, 191, 194, 197, 209,
219, 233, 240, 243, 244, 256, 298,
301, 320, 329, 313, 416, 419

Æðelulf, Æðelualf, Aðelulf, &c, 32,
54, 81, 83, 88, 122, 127, 142, 198,
225 See also Æðelaf

Æðelwald, 142, 191. See also Æðelwold and Aðelwold

Æðelweard or Æðelwerd, 156, 163,
197, 226, 227, 229, 243, 329 See
also Aðelweard

Æðelwi or Aðelwi, 197, 243.

Æðelwig, 197

Æðelwine, Eðelwine, &c, 32, 15, 69,
83, 87, 101, 122, 126, 163, 179, 197,
224, 232, 234, 243, 260, 263, 275,
294, 302, 329

Æðelwod, 197.

Æðelwold or Aðelwold, 101, 108, 163,
191, 197, 241, 243 See also Æðelwald

Æðelwynd, 197

Æðered or Eðered, 22, 24, 32, 45, 58,
60, 70, 81, 83, 88, 94, 101, 122, 142,
163, 172, 188, 191, 197, 224, 225,
230 See also Æðelred

Æðeric, 243, 276 See also Æðelric.

Æðeryd, 197

Æðestan or Eðestan, 191, 194, 197,
209, 233, 239, 2 4, 256, 298, 301,
320, 329, 313, 416, 419

Æðowine, 320.

Æðeðstan, 244, 293

Æðfrið, 83.

Æðric. See Æðeric

Aðstan, 191 See Æðelstan

Agamund, 329, 396, 460

Aglric, 388 See Egelric

Agnes, 83

Agtard or Agtardes, 122, 142, 145
156 See also Etard

Albart, 163.

Alberic, 122, 126

Albert, 112, 155

Albutic, 163, 177

Alest or Alfsi, 244, 276

Alesige or Alsige, 112, 197

Aldewine, 163, 185, 190

Aldgar, 329, 399, 460, 468

Aldred, 197

Alcof, 329, 369, 460, 463.

Alet, 101

Alfeah, 101, 121 See also Ælfheah.

Alfeard, 320

Alferð, 163.

Alfgar, 197 See Ælfgar

Alfnoð, 320

Alfold, 197 See Alfwold

Alfred, 320.

Alfric, 320 See Ælfric

Alfried, 460

Alfsi, 244 See Alesi

Alfsie, 329, 388. See also Ælfsie

Alfstan or Alfstean, 197, 243 See
Ælfstan

Alfwald or Alfwold, 197, 209, 235,
240, 244, 256, 289, 297, 300, 329,
441, 442, 443, 460, 472 See also
Ælfwald

Alfward, Alfweard, or Alfwerd, 191,
197, 320

Alfwine, 197, 302, 318, 320. See also
Ælfwine

Alfwold, 197, 209, 240, 244, 256, 289,
297, 300, 441, 442, 443, 460, 472 See
also Alfwald

Alhmund, 329, 429

Alhstan, 83, 99, 101, 191 See also
Ealhstan

Almer, 460, 467.

Alric, 329, 403

Alsanf, 302.

Alsige, 142 See Alesige

Aluuulu, 32, 60

Alward, *320*

Alxxi, 329, 391, 400, 407

Amelric, 101, 115

Amund, Amundes, or Amyndes, 122, 126, *156*

Anderboda or Anderbode, 329, 449, 450, 451, 452, 400, 473

Andreas, *163.*

Andred, 1, 7

Anna, 112, 155.

Anocret, *142*

Ansern, *329*

Arbctel, 329, 350

Arcil or Arcyl, *302* *See also* Arncel

Arc, 101, 115, 122, 126, 142, 155

Arfra, 329, 431

Arkctel, *329.*

Arnalf, *101. See* Arnulf

Arncel, Arncil, Arncetel, Arncitil, Arncytel, &c , *197*, 244, 263, 296, *302*, 320, 329, 359, 361, 363, 364, 366, 367

Arncytel *See* Arncel

Arngrim, Ærngrim, or Erngrim, *245*, *303*, 320, 329, 331, 359, 361, 362, 363, 364, 366, 367, 368, 429. *See also* Earngrim

Arnolf or Arnulf, 101, 107, 116, 121, *122*, 112, 115, 211, 263 *See also* Ærnulf

Arnðor, Arnðar, or Arður, *197*

Asalf, Asolf, Asulf, or Asulfncn, 101, 116, 119, 122, 127, *198*

Ascctel, Ascytel, &c , *197*

Ascil, *197.*

Ascutr, *214*

Asewig or Eswig, 197, 234, 235

Asferð or Aseferð, 163, 177, *197*, *244*, *302*, 329, 394

Asgod, Asgout, Asguut, &c , 244, 263

Aslac, *214*, *320*

Asman, *198*

Asoil, *198*

Asolf, *198 See* Asalf

Asplcr, *112.*

Astan, 329, 436 *See also* Æstan

Asulf, 101, 116, *122*, *198* *See also* Asalf

Asulfncn, 122, 127 *See also* Asulf.

Asðrið, *198*, *244*

Ata, *244.*

Atsere, 329, 455, 456

Auti or Autti, 330, 393

Azma, *163.*

Aðcan, *122*

Aðclaver, 163, 175 *See also* Adclaver.

Aðclm, *101.*

Aðelmod, 101, 121.

Aðclmund, *101*, 122, 126, 142, 145 *See also* Æðclmund

Aðclulf, 32, 81, 83, 88, 122, 127, 198, 225 *See also* Æðclulf

Aðclwcard or Aðclwcrd, *122*, *142*, 156, 160 *See also* Æðclwcard.

Aðclwi, *243 See* Æðclwi

Aðelwine, *122 See* Æðclwine

Aðclwold, *101*, *191*, 197, 241 *See also* Adelwold and Æðclwold

Aðclwulf, *101*

Aðulf, 83, 97, 99, *101*, *156*, *163*

B.

Bacaman, *244 See* Blacaman

Baciager or Bacialer, 122, 127

Badda, *83*

Bademund, 22, 23

Badenoð, 22, 23

Baldic, 191, 192, *198.*

Baldric, 101, 121, 122, 144, 142, 145, *156*, *163*

Baldwine or Baldwin, *101*, *122*, 112, 115, 156, 158, 163, 190, *330*

Balluc, *244*

Barbe, 101, 112, 122, 125

Bardel or Burdel, 101, 112.

Barifer&, *101*.

Beagmund, *1*, 9, 16, 19, 22, 23. *See also* Beahmund.

Beagstan, 32, 60.

Beahmund, *21*, 22, 23. *See also* Beagmund.

Beahred or Beanred, *83*, 101, 111, 122, 127.

Beahstan, 83, 88.

Bealdulf, *198*.

Beaniene, 191, 193.

Beanred, *83*, *101*. *See also* Beahred.

Begam, *198*.

Belga or Belge, *101*.

Bemene, Bermene, &c., *191*.

Benedictus, 122, 127, 163, 177.

Beola, Beolan, Bolla, &c., *191*, *198*, 244, 271.

Beorard, 101, 110.

Beorhno&, Berhtna&, Byrhtno&, &c., 198, 238, 239, *244*.

Beorhtric, 163, 184.

Beorhtulf, *101*. *See also* Biorhtulf.

Beorn, Beornn, or Biorn, 244, 267, *302*, 330, 439.

Beorneah or Biarneah, 27, 28.

Beornere, 83, 89.

Beornfer&, 83, 89.

Beornhae, 27, 31.

Beornhart, 1, 8.

Beornheard, 1, 8.

Beornmær or Beornmer, 32, 60, 82.

Beornm d, Biornmod, &c., 1, 6.

Beornred or Biornred, 32, 61, 83, 97.

Beornulf, Beornuulf, or Biornulf, *83*, *198*.

Beornuuald, Beornwald, Bernuuald, Biornuuald, Byrnwald, &c., 83, 89, 94, 95, 101, 114, *122*.

Beorwald, *122*. *See* Beornwald.

Berel ald, 32, 71.

Berenard, *156*, *163*.

Berhtelm or Byrhtelm, 101, 113, 122, 127, *198*.

Berhtere, 32, 60.

Berhtmær or Byrhtmær, *198*. *See also* Brihtmær.

Berhtna&, 198, 239. *See also* Beorhno&.

Berhtred, 83, 89, *122*.

Berhtwig, 122, 127.

Berhtwine or Brehtwine, *198*.

Beriuald, 32, 50.

Bermene, *191*. *See* Bemene.

Bernald, 32, 50. *See also* Bernuald.

Bernard or Burnard, *101*, 142, 145.

Berna&, *122*.

Bernere, *101*, 142, 146.

Berufer&, 142, 146, 163, 177.

Berngar, *83*, *101*.

Berured or Birnred, 32, 61. *See also* Beornred.

Bernsige, 122, 127.

Bernuald or Birnuald, 32, 38, 43, 45, 50, 51, 53, 54, 61, 80. *See also* Biarnuald and Burnuald.

Bernuuald, 83, 89. *See also* Beornuuald.

Bese or Besel, *122*, 142, 146.

Bianulf (Biarnulf), *122*.

Biare&, 32, 38.

Biarmod, 9. *See* Biarnmod.

Biarneah, 27, 28. *See also* Beorneah.

Biarneard, *101*. *See* Biorneard.

Biarnmod or Biarmod, 9, 22, 23, 27, 28.

Biarnno&, 9, 13, 16.

Biarnred or Biornred, 32, 41, 42, 45, 61, 83, 97.

Biarnuald, 32, 42, 43, 57. *See also* Birnuald.

Biarnuine, 22, 23.

Biarnuulf, *32*.

Binred, 330, 399.

Biorhald, *83*.

Biorhtric, *101*.

Biorhtulf or Biorhtwulf, 101, 105, 122, 128, *142*.

Biorhtwald, *101*.

Biorhtwulf, *122, 142*.

Biorn, 330, 439. *See also* Beorn.

Biornard, Biorneard, Biarneard, or Byrnard, *83*, 101, 111, *122*. *See also* Birneard.

Biornhelm, *83*.

Biornmod, 1, 6.

Biornred, 32, 61, 83, 97. *See also* Beornred and Biarnred.

Biornulf, *198*. *See* Beornulf.

Biornuuald, 83, 94, 95. *See also* Beornuuald.

Biosel or Bosel, 1, 6.

Birgstan, 163, 190.

Birhtferð, *198*.

Birhtsige, Byrhtsige, &c., *198*.

Birneard, 122, 128. *See also* Biorneard.

Birned or Birnred, 32.

Birnuald, 32, 38, 43, 45, 80. *See also* Bernuald, &c.

Biruer, 156, 162.

Blacaman, Blaceman, or Blacman, *198*, 244, 292, 302, 316, 320, 325, 330, 355, 356, 375, 376, 429, 460, 474.

Blacan, *302*.

Blaceman, *198*, 244, 292, 330, 375, 376. *See also* Blacaman.

Blacer, 330, 455.

Blacman, 330, 376, 429. *See also* Blacaman.

Blacman, *320*.

Blamian, *244*.

Blareman, 330, 355, 356.

Blarere, 330, 455.

Bodric, *330*.

Boeg, 122, 128.

Boga, Bogea, Boiga, or Boia, 32, 61, 83, 98, 101, 105, 108, 122, 128, 142, 146, 156, 158, 160, 163, 168, 189, 191, 196, 198, 210, 218, 244, 260, *302, 320, 330*, 353, 435.

Boigalet, 101, 108.

Boinsulf or Boinulf, 122, 128.

Bolla, 244, 271. *See also* Beola.

Bonsom, 122, 128.

Borstig, 244, 281.

Bosa, 1, 8, 32, 56.

Bosel, 1, 6. *See also* Biosel.

Brad, 437. *See* Brand.

Bræntine, *244*. *See also* Brantine.

Brahstan, *244*. *See* Brihstan.

Brand, *244*, 330, 378, 436, 437, 445.

Brantine, *191, 198, 244*.

Brece or Brege, 83, 89, 97.

Brehstan, 244, 288. *See also* Brenstan.

Brehtuoð, 244, 297. *See also* Brihtnoð.

Brehtwine, *198*.

Brened, 42. *See also* Biarnred.

Brenstan or Brehstan, 244, 288.

Brestan, *198*.

Bretecol, *198, 244*.

Bricsie. *See* Bricsige.

Bricsige, 330, 406.

Bricstan, *244*.

Brid or Bridd, 9, 13, 19, 244, 272, *302, 320*, 330, 376, 377, 378.

Brightmær, *330*. *See* Brihtmær.

Brihelm, *244*.

Brihine, *330*.

Brihstan, *244*.

Briht, *83*.

Brihtferð or Brihtfræð, *163*, 191, 192, *244*.

Brihtlaf or Byrhtlaf, 198, 218, 226, 227, 235.

Brihtmær, Brihttmær, &c., *198*, 244, 283, 285, 302, 314, 330, 397, 398, 402, 437, 438, 446, 449, 450, 460, 474.

Brihtnoð, *198*, 244, 258, 297, 330, 374, *460*.

Brihtred, 211, 258, 302, 330, 399, 103, 107, 122, 157
Brihtric, Brixric, or Bryhtric, 198, 211, 302, 330, 350, 372, 392, 393, 135, 136, 137, 160, 161
Brihtmær, 302   See Brihtmær
Brihtwen, 211
Brihtwi, 211, 160
Brihtwine or Byrhtwine, 198, 214, 288, 302, 330, 409, 118, 436, 437.
Brihtwold or Byrhtwold, 163, 198, 240, 211, 281, 330, 115, 460, 469
Brihwi, 418   See Brihtwine
Brin, 330.
Brimt, 330
Brinstan, 244   See Brunstan
Brintred   See Brihtred
Brinwold, 330, 421
Britferð or Brihtferð, 163, 178.
Briuning, 156, 161.
Brixi, 330, 412
Brixsic   See Briesige.
Brixard, 32, 61
Brixric, 330   See Brihtric
Bruchyse, 330   See Brunhyse.
Bruinne, 330
Brum, 330, 372.
Bruma, 244
Bruman, Brumnan, or Brunman, 198, 211, 281, 285, 287, 302, 330, 313, 314, 372
Brummon (= Brumnan), 460, 465
Brumnan, 330, 314   See also Bruman
Brun, Brunn, or Bruna 198, 230, 244, 302, 320, 326, 330, 444
Bruncar, 302, 314   See also Brungar.
Brunctan, 244, 320   See Brunstan
Brundwine, 330
Bruned, 32, 41, 42, 45
Brungar, Bryngar, &c, 198, 214, 283, 285, 287, 291, 302, 314, 330, 409, 423
Brunhyse, 330, 350

Brunic, Brunine, Bruning, Brunnine, Brynine, &c, 163, 190, 198, 218, 214, 283, 288, 330, 372, 389, 390, 431
Brunman, 214, 285, 287, 302, 330   See also Bruman
Brunn.   See Brun
Brunnese, 330, 350   See also Brunhyse.
Brunnic, 244   See Brunic
Brunnine   See Brunic.
Brunnstan   See Brunstan.
Brunnusel, 330, 391
Brunred, 320
Brunstan, Branctan, or Brinstan, 198, 227, 229, 240, 244, 300, 302, 317, 318, 320, 330, 454
Bruntat, 198, 221, 244
Bruntið, 198
Brunwine, Bruwin, Brynwine, or Burwine, 244, 302, 316, 320, 330, 431, 432, 436, 437, 460, 471
Bruwin, 302   See Brunwine.
Bryhtred, 198
Bryhtric, 198.   See Brihtric
Bryhtuald or Bryhtwald, 83, 101, 121
Bryngar, 244, 285   See also Brungar.
Brynia, 244.
Brynine, 198, 244, 330, 390   See also Brunine
Brynwine, 330   See Brunwine
Bugn, 32, 61, 83, 89, 98
Bulered, 330   See Bured
Burdel, 101, 112
Burden, 83
Bured or Bulered, 330, 407
Burewine, 244, 330, 437, 438
Burgnoð, 27, 28, 32
Burgwine, 460, 471
Burhstan or Burnstan, 191, 198.
Burhtelm, 101
Burhwold or Burwold, 244
Burnard, 142, 145   See also Bernard.
Burneld, 101

Burnelm, Burnhelm, or Byrnelm, 32, 62, 83, 89, *101, 122*.

Burnhere or Byrnhere, 32, 62, 330, 399

Burnred, 330, 458

Burnric or Byrnwic, *122*

Burnstan, *191 See* Burhstan

Burnuald, Burnuuald, or Byrnuald, 22, 23, 32, 38, 39, 80

Burwiine or Burwine, *302, 320 See* Brunwine

Burwold, *244*

Bus, *101.*

Bynic, *198.*

Byoga, *198*

Byrhferð, *163 See also* Byrhtferð.

Byrhsige, 198, 208, 225, 239.

Byrhstan or Byrnstan, 198, 213, 219, *244*

Byrhtalf, *199 See* Byrhtlaf

Byrhtcalm, Byrhtelm, or Byrhthelm, *101, 198*

Byrhtferð, *198.*

Byrhtioð, *198.*

Byrhtlaf, 198, 218, 226, 235 *See also* Brihtlaf

Byrhtmær, *199. See* Berhtmær

Byrhtnoð, 198, 239, *244 See* Beorhnoð or Brihtnoð

Byrhtred, *198*

Byrhtric, *163*, 198, 241

Byrhtsige, *199. See* Birhtsige

Byrhtwine, *198 See* Brihtwine

Byrhtwold, *163*, 198, 210 *See also* Brihtwold

Byri, *198*

Byrnard, *83. See* Biornard

Byrnelm, 32, 62, 83, 89 *See also* Burnelm

Byrnferð, *122*

Byrnhere, 32, 62 *See also* Burnhere

Byrning, *198*

Byrnsi, 244, 255

Byrnstan, *198*, *244 See* Byrhstan

Byrnuald, 32, 39, 80 *See also* Burnuald

Byrnwald, 101, 114, *122 See* Beornwald

Byrnwic, *122 See* Burnric

C.

Cæfel, *244*

Cærenan, 302, 313

Cærla, *244, 302 See also* Carla

Cæntwine, *460 See* Centwine

Cætel, *244. See* Cetel

Caldewine, *244, 302.*

Cali, 142, 155

Cali and Sifert, 142, 155

Calic, *244, 320*

Calismert, *142.*

Canceret, *142*

Capelin, 163, 178

Carel, *244*

Carig, *199.*

Carla, 198, 213, *244 See also* Cærla

Carðen, 163, 178.

Cas, 244, 298

Cawe, *198*

Cawelin, *244*

Cealcard, 22, 23

Cedeman, 330, 425

Ceftel, *330*

Cenapa, *101*

Ceuberht, *101*, *122*, 112, 116.

Ceubriht, *83*

Cenelm, 330, 419.

Cenred, 22, 23, *32.*

Cenric, *198*

Censige, *198 See also* Cinsige

Centwine or Cæntwine, 330 413, 460, 472

Cenucald, 22, 23, 26

Ceoc or Ceoca, *244, 302, 320 330.*

Ceoftan, *330*

Ceolu, *330*

Ceolna꞉, *211*   *See* Ceolno꞉

Ceolno꞉, Cilno꞉, Ciolno꞉, Colno꞉, &c , 198, 231, 211, 277

Ceolwi or Cilwi, 330, 351, 355

Ceorl, 330, 313, *460*

Cerman, 32, 41

Cetcel, *330*

Cetel, *198*, 211, 263   *See also* Cytel

Cewine, 330, 357

Cialberht, Ciolberht, &c , *122*

Cialclm, *101*

Cialmod or Ciolmod, 32, 56

Cialulf, 32, 57.   *See also* Ciolulf

Cild, 330, 312

Cilwni, *112*

Cille, *302*

Cilleerist, *320*, 330, 435

Cilhn, 330, 393

Cilno꞉, *211*   *See* Ceolno꞉

Cilwi, 330, 351   *See also* Ceolwi

Cina, *198*

Cincmær or Cincnær, 330, 399

Cincstan, *320*   *See* Cinstan

Cincwig or Ciniwig, *211*, *302*

Cincwine, *302.*

Cincwold, *302*

Ciniwig, *211*   *See also* Cincwig

Cinsige, *198*, 211, 260   *See also* Censige

Cinstan, *211*, *302*, *320*, 330, 353, 354, 355, 460, 463

Ciolberht, *122*   *See* Cialberht

Ciolmod, 32, 56   *See also* Cialmod

Ciolno꞉, *198*, 234   *See also* Ceolno꞉

Ciolulf or Ciolnulf, 32, 59, 83, 90

Ciresricn, 32, 62

Citelbe, *198*

Citgil, *330*

Clac, 101, 116, 122, 125, 128, 140, 142, 155, 156, 160

Clacl, *101*

Clern, *198*

Clewine, *330.*

Clip, 83, 90

Cnapa, Cnape, Cnapes, or Gnapa, *101*, 122, *123*, 129, 156, 162, 163, 173, 178, 191, 196.

Cna꞉, 101, 108

Cniht, *211*   *See* Cyniht

Cnit or Cynt, *198*

Cnofeln, 211, 289

Cnut, 211, 279

Cnytel, 211, 301

Codric, *211*   *See* Godric

Coigrim, *198*   *See* Colgrim

Col or Cola, *330*

Colaman, Coleman, or Colman, *198*, 211, 296, *302*, *460*

Colbein or Colbin, 211, 278, 330, 353.

Colbrand, 330, 388, 389, 390.

Colcrim, *211*   *See* Colgrim

Coldsige, *302*   *See* Goldsige

Coldwine, *198*.   *See* Goldwine

Coleman, *198*, 211, 296   *See also* Colaman.

Colenard, 163, 190

Colgrim, *163*, *191*, 198, 216, 222, 244, 262, 267, 280, *302*, 320, 326, 330, 391, 392, 393, 394

Colinc, 330, 434

Collini, 211, 271

Colman, *460*   *See also* Colaman.

Colno꞉, *198*   *See* Ceolno꞉

Colric, *460*

Colrim   *See* Colgrim.

Colsi, *330.*

Colstan, *330*

Colswegen, 330, 378

Coltsige, *302*   *See* Goldsige

Coltsue, *330*

Couli, *330.*

Conna, *330*

Conrim, 302, 313

Conrinccof, *320.*

Copman, 142, 146, *156*, 163, 178.

Corf, Corff, or Corrf, 302, 314, *320*, *330*.

Corlac, *244*.

Corrf, *302*. *See* Corf.

Credard, *101*.

Creðewine, *244*.

Crin . . ., *156*.

Crina, Crinan, Crinna, or Crunan, 244, 263, 280, 291.

Cristgin, Cristin, or Cristðin, *142*, *198*.

Cristign, 101, 116.

Cristin, *142*, *198*.

Cristðin, *198*. *See* Cristgin.

Croc, Croce, or Crocl, 244, 277, *302*.

Crofl, 244, 276.

Crucan or Grucan, 244, 245, 264, 267, *302*.

Crunan, *244*. *See* Crinan.

Crurn or Grurn, 244, 246, 264.

Cudberht or Cuðberht, 32, 62, 80, 83, 90, 95, 98.

Cudi, *198*.

Cugeli, *101*.

Cugem, *101*.

Culein, 142, 154.

Culm, *191*.

Cuna, Cunna, or Cynna, 198, 238, 240, *244*.

Cundferð, *122*.

Cunefreð, 22, 23, 26.

Cuneulf or Cyneulf, 32, 65.

Cunleof, *244*. *See also* Gunleof.

Cunna, 198, 238. *See also* Cuna.

Cunsige, *198*. *See* Cynsige.

Cunstan, 302, 309. *See also* Cinstan.

Cunulf, *101*.

Cutel, *156*. *See also* Cytel.

Cutferð, *83*.

Cuðberht, 32, 62. *See also* Cudberht.

Cuðferð, *330*.

Cuðhelm, 27, 31.

Cuðuulf, 32, 64.

Cwalin, *244*. *See* Cawelin.

Cyldewine, *302*. *See* Gyldewine.

Cylm, 163, 170.

Cyne, *191*.

Cynestan, *83*.

Cyneulf, 32, 65. *See also* Cuneulf.

Cynewald, *101*.

Cyniht or Cniht, *244*.

Cynna, 198, 240, *244*. *See also* Cuna.

Cynsige or Cunsige, *163*, 198, 212, 224.

Cynt, *198*.

Cytel or Cytell, 156, 161, 198, 215, *244*, *302*, *330*. *See also* Cetel and Cutel.

Cytlbern or Cytlern, *198*.

Cytlræ, *198*.

D.

Dæinint, 330, 417.

Dæodulf, *122*.

Dærul, *198*.

Danfinx, 198. 214, *244*.

Dealinc or Dealing, 32, 65.

Dealla or Dela, 22, 23, 27, 28, 32, 65.

Debis, *1*.

Degbearht, 9, 18, 22, 23.

Deglaf, 22, 24.

Degn, *101*.

Dehfin, *330*.

Deigmund, 32, 56.

Deineah, 9, 13, 15, 16.

Dela, 32, 65. *See also* Dealla.

Demence, 142, 146, *156*, 163, 184.

Demenec, 122, 129. *See also* Domences.

Denemund, 22, 24.

Denenald, 27, 28.

Deohen or Deorhan, 330, 399.

Deora or Diora, *83*.

Deoramod, *83*. *See* Deormod.

Deorerd, 101, 108.

Deorhan or Deohen, 330, 399.

Deorinc, *244*.

Deorlaf, 163, 171.

Deorman or Diorman, 330, 351, 412, 430, 431.

Deormod or Deoramod, 83, 99.

Deornred, 83.

Deorsie, Deorsig, Deorsige, or Dyrsige, 198, 244, 267, 273, 302, 330, 379.

Deoruhg, 198.

Deorulf or Diorulf, 101, 108, 110, 119, 142, 147, 156, 158, 163, 173, 191.

Deoruuald or Diaruuald, 83, 90, 101, 122.

Dermon, 330, 430, 431, 460, 470.

Derwine, 244.

Diar, 9, 14, 15, 16, 17, 18.

Diarald, 32, 65. See also Diaruald.

Diarelm, 122, 129.

Diarhelm, 32.

Diarmod, 22, 24.

Diarmund, 32, 58.

Diaruald, 32, 39, 44, 65.

Diarulf, 27, 28.

Diaruuald, 101, 122. See Deoruuald.

Diga, 27, 29.

Dilion, 198, 219.

Diora, 83. See Deora.

Dioreman or Dyreman, 198.

Diorman, 330, 430, 431. See also Deorman.

Diormod, 1, 6, 7.

Diorulf, 101, 119. See also Deorulf.

Direman, 330, 400, 412.

Direme, 330, 457.

Direwine or Dyrewine, 198.

Dirine or Dyrine, 330, 344.

Dirsige, 198.

Doda, Dodda, or Dode, 198, 244, 320.

Dodnie, 330.

Dodnor, 163.

Dodrig, 198.

Domences, 101, 116, 122, 129. See also Demenec.

Dominic, 101, 116. See also Domences.

Dorlfe, 101.

Dorulf, 122, 129, 147. See also Deorulf.

Dorwine, 198.

Dranting, 198.

Dregel, Dregl, &c., 122, 129.

Dreml, 142, 147.

Dreng, 198, 222, 244.

Dreolf, 198.

Drhwold, 198. See Dryhtuald.

Driuning, 156.

Dropa or Drowa, 244, 299.

Drungar, 244.

Dryhtuald or Dryhtwald, 83, 101, 121.

Duda, 198.

Dudda or Dudd, 27, 29, 32.

Duddine, 302.

Dudel or Dudele, 198.

Dudelet, 122, 129.

Dudeman, 156, 163, 168.

Dudewine, 32.

Dudig, 32, 65, 80, 83, 90, 95, 122, 130, 142, 147.

Dudine, 330, 382, 397, 407.

Dudinic, 320.

Dudsemon, 163.

Duducol, 330, 426.

Duduine, 9, 18, 22, 24.

Dufacan, 302, 309.

Dufnelm, 198.

Duine, 32, 58.

Dulwie, 330, 400.

Dun, 9, 19, 20, 163, 169, 191, 193, 198. See also Dunn.

Dunberd, 320.

Duneild, 198.

Dunic, 191.

Dunine, Duning, Dunnine, &c., 32, 40, 58, 66, 156, 159, 330, 377, 378, 390.

Dunn or Dunna, 27, 29, 32, 57, 58, 66, 156, 161. See also Dun.

Dunstan, 198, 214, 244.

Duracan, 302.

Duraint, 122, 130.

Duran, *142, 198.* ·

Durand, Durandes, or Durant, 122, 130, 163, 178, 188, *198.*

Durberd, *330.*

Duriant, *101.*

Durinc, 330, 414.

Durlac, *83.*

Durreb, 330, 400.

Durtan, *198.*

Durul, *330.*

Durwig, *244.*

Dynyn, 1, 7.

Dyreman, *198.* See Dioreman.

Dyrewine, *198.*

Dyrhtmær, *198.*

Dyrinc, *330.* See Dirinc.

Dyrsige, *244.* See Deorsige.

Dyyn, 20. See Dun.

E.

Eadeasge, *199.*

Eadelm or Edelm, *199.*

Eadered, 83, 90.

Eadfred, 83, 90.

Eadgar or Edgar, *101, 122,* 199, 220, 241, 244, 245, 283, 330, 331, 342.

Eadgild, *101, 122.*

Eadhelm, *32, 83.*

Eadlaf, 101, 108, *199.*

Eadmœr or Eadmer, 163, 170, *199.* See also Edmœr

Eadmund or Edmund, 83, 90, 99, 101, 109, 110, 111, 116, 122, 130, 142, 147, 156, 159, 163, 172, 186, 190, 199, 226, 244, 281, 330, *331,* 407.

Eadnoð, *191,* 199, 211, 244, 281.

Eadred, Edred, or Edired, *83,* 102, 113, 122, 130, 245, 285, 331, 407, 410.

Eadric or Edric, *101,* 199, 215, 218, 221, 245, 275, 283, 291, 302, 318, *320,* 329, 330, 331, 391, 392, 396,

404, 410, 454, 460, 466. *See also* Ædric.

Eadrnoð, *199.*

Eadsi, *199, 245.*

Eadsig, Eadsige, Edsige, &c., 199, 227, 232, 238, 245, 262.

Eadsme, 199, 223.

Eadstan or Edstan, 32, 67, *101,* 122, 130, 199, 209, *331.*

Eaduald or Eadueald, 32, 40, 66. *See also* Eadwald.

Eadueard, 32, 59. *See also* Adueard.

Eadulf or Eaduulf, 22, 24, 32, 59, 101, 116, *156, 163, 245.*

Eaduuald. *See* Eadwald.

Eadwacer or Edwacer, *199,* 302, 310.

Eadwald, Eadweald, or Edwald, 32, 80, 83, 90, *245,* 302, 330, 331, 400. *See also* Eadwold.

Eadward, Eadweard, Eadwerd, Edward, Edwerd, &c., 122, 131, 199, 223, 226, 232, 245, 281, 285, 293, 296, 302, 319, *320,* 330, 331, 344, 345, 346, 359, 375, 384, 385, 457, *460.*

Eadwi, *199. See also* Edwi.

Eadwig or Edwig, *199,* 245, 289, *302,* 320, 327, 330, 331, 348, 357, 372, 384, 400, 412.

Eadwine or Edwine, 163, 174, *191,* 199, ·. 223, 225, 226, 227, 233, 238, 245, 260, 262, 275, 281, 283, 286, 303, 309, 318, *320,* 330, 331, 384, 385, 387, 400, 404, 407, 410, 414, 415, 416, 420, 421, 422, 423, 431, 460, 462, 468.

Eadwod, *199.*

Eadwold or Edwold, 199, 210, 211, 224, 226, 227, 229, 245, 281, 283, 285, 302, 314, 330, 331, 397, 406, 410, 412. *See also* Eadwald.

Eaenolf, 156, 161.

Eaern, *245.*

Eaetan, 32, 67.

Eagmund, 13. *See* Ealgmund.

Ealesi, *330*.

Ealdabeard or Ealdeberd, 245, 261.

Ealdgar, *199, 245, 330*, 412.

Ealdred, 22, 24, 199, 231, *245*.

Ealdulf or Ealduulf, 32, 67, *330*, 410.

Ealdwig, 330, 418.

Ealfsige, 163, 186.

Ealgar, *245*. *See* Ealdgar.

Ealgeart, *122*.

Ealgmund, 9, 13.

Eallstan, 83, 91, 95, 99, *101*, 199, 224, 225, 226. *See also* Alhstan.

Ealstan, *199*. *See also* Euhlstan.

Eamer, *199*.

Eamund, *199*.

Eanmund, 9, 13, 16.

Eanred, *163*.

Eanulf, 163, 178, 191, 194.

Eanute, *191*.

Eanwald, 9, 15.

Eanwerd, *330*.

Earcil, 330, 369.

Eardnoð or Erdnoð, *199, 245*.

Eardulf, *101*, 122, 131, 142, 147.

Eardwulf, *9*, 83.

Eared, *83*.

Earncytel, *245*. *See* Arncetel.

Earngrim, 245, 268. *See also* Erngrim.

Earnulf, *101*. *See* Arnulf.

Earnwi, *320*, 331, 380, 381, 428.

Earnwulf, *83*. *See* Earnulf.

Earward, *83*.

Eastmær, 331, 440.

Eastnær, 460, 473.

Eastulf, *199*. *See also* Fastolf.

Eatstan, 163, 175, *199*. *See also* Eadstan.

Eawulf, *83*, 331, 373.

Eaðnoð, *244*. *See* Eadnoð.

Eeberht, 32, 67, 101, 107, 116.

Eeferð, *199*.

Eegbriht, *122*.

Eegherd, *101*.

Eclaf or Ellaf, 83, 91, 101, 102, 111, 117, *199*. *See also* Eilaf.

Ecrie, 245, 292.

Ecuulf or Eewulf, 32, 68.

Eewig, 331, 410.

Eewulf, 32, 68. *See also* Ecuulf.

Eda, *199*.

Edælbriht, *199*.

Edeulf, 32, 45.

Edelgar, 83, 91.

Edelic, *331*.

Edelm, *199*. *See* Eadelm.

Edelric, *199*.

Edelstan, 32, 69.

Edelstan and Gelda, 69.

Edelwine, 224. *See* Æðelwine.

Edered, *199*.

Edfecer, *199*.

Edgar, 244, 245, 283, 330, 331, 342. *See also* Eadgar.

Edhie, *302*.

Edin, 331, 397.

Edired, *122*. *See* Eadred.

Edireð, *122*.

Ediric, *245*. *See* Edric.

Edmær, 245, 261, 302, 309, *320*, 331, 357. *See also* Eadmær.

Edmund, *101, 199, 244, 331*. *See also* Eadmund.

Edraed, *302*.

Edred, 102, 113, 245, 285, 331, 407, 410. *See also* Eadred.

Edric, 199, 218, 221, 245, 275, 283, 294, 302, 318, *320*, 329, 331, 391, 392, 396, 404, 410, 454, 460, 466. *See also* Ædric and Eadric.

Edrice (= Edric), *245*.

Edriee (= Edric), *331*.

Edsie or Edsii, 245, 261, 262, 331, 357.

Edsieie, *302*.

Edsige, 199, 227, 232, 245, 262. *See also* Eadsige.

Edsigeware, 215, 262

Edstan, 199, 200, *331 See also* Eadstan.

Eduta, *215*

Edwacer, *199*, 302, 310 *See also* Eadwacer

Edwald, *215*, *302*, 331, 400 *See also* Eadwald.

Edwald and Þcalda, *302*

Edwar (= Edward), *215*

Edward or Edwerd, 199, 226, 245, 285, 293, 296, 302, 319, *320*, 330, 331, 344, 315, 384, 457 *See also* Eadward.

Edwear (= Edweard), *215*.

Edwene, *303 See* Edwine

Edwerd *See* Edward.

Edwi or Edwin, 199, 218, 318, 357, 372, 412 *See also* Edwig

Edwie, 331, 444

Edwig or Edwug, *199*, 245, 289, *302*, 320, 327, 330, 331, 348, 357, 372, 412 *See also* Eadwig

Edwine or Edwene, 199, 225, 226, 233, 245, 260, 262, 275, 283, 286, 303, 309, 318, *320*, 330, 331, 384, 385, 387, 400, 401, 407, 410, 414, 415, 420, 422, 423, 431, 460, 462, 468 *See also* Eadwine

Edwinei, *199*

Edwinne, *199 See* Edwine

Edwold, *199*, *215*, 302, 314, 330, 331, 406 *See also* Eadwold

Efeircos, *122*

Eferbrd, *122*

Efermund, *102 See* Eofermund

Eferulf, 122, 131, 112, 147

Efgeulf, *122*

Efic, *215*

Efrard, 102, 109, 110, 156, 161

Egelric, 329, 331, 400 *See also* Ægelric

Egelwig, *215*, 329, 331, 400 *See also* Ægelwig

Egelwine, 243, 215, 267, *303*, *331 See also* Ægelwine

Egered, 122, 131

Egilberht, *102*

Egligt, *215*

Ehewine, *199*

Eicmund or Eigmund, 83, 91, 100

Eielwine (= Elfwine), 421

Eilaf or Eilof, 199, 215 *See also* Eclaf

Eilfwine (= Elfwine), 348

Eilnoð, 341, 457

Eilofwine, *199*

Eilwige, *215*

Eilwine, 331, 386

Einard, 102, 121, *123*

Elact, *122*

Elbere, 27, 29, *32*

Elbriht or Elebriht, 199, 235, 303, 310

Elda, 32, 69

Ele, *102*

Elebriht, 199, 235 *See also* Elbriht

Eleden, *163*

Elemod, *199*

Elenoð, *199*

Elewig, *215*, *303*

Elewin, 273

Elewine, 197, 199, 221, 276, 282, 303, 312, 331, 350, 359 *See also* Ælewine and Ælfwine

Elferd, *122*

Elfere, 329, 361 *See also* Ælfere

Elfget, *197*, *199 See also* Ælfgæt

Elfnoð, *197*, 329, 394, 395 *See also* Ælfnoð

Elfred, 142, 147, 163, 185, 329, 331, 344 *See also* Ælfred

Elfric, 102, 106, 329, 346, 400, 402, 429, 453 *See also* Ælfric

Elfsic, 329, 388, 389, 405, 407, 453 *See also* Ælfsic

Elfsige, 329, 407 *See also* Ælfsige

Elfsine, *331*

Elfstan, 32, 44, 163, 190, *191*, 197, 221,

329, 331, 400, 441, 444. *See also* Ælfstan.

Elfuald or Elfwald, 32, 69, *122*, 163, 179, *191*. *See also* Ælfwald.

Elfwerd, *329*. *See* Ælfward.

Elfwi or Elfwie, *102*, 243, 282, *460*. *See also* Ælfwi.

Elfwig, *197*. *See* Ælfwig.

Elfwine, 273, 276, 282, 329, 343, 350, 361, 375, 399, 403, 420, 421, 433, 441, 443, 444, 460, 462. *See also* Ælfwine.

Eli, 32, 38, 55.

Ella, 27, 29.

Ellaf, *83*, 102, 111. *See also* Eclaf.

Elræd or Elred, 329, 331, 345, 346. *See also* Ælræd.

Elric, 331, 381.

Elsice, 453. *See* Elfsie.

Elsige, *329*. *See* Ælfsige.

Elst. *245*.

Eltan, 331, 362.

Elwine, 331, 421, 444.

Euberht, *101*. *See also* Cenberht.

Endiwern, 245.

Endric or Enric, *331*.

Engilberht, *102*.

Engilbred, 142, 148.

Enric, *331*.

Eoda, *199*.

Eodlin, *142*.

Eodman, *199*.

Eoferard, *163*.

Eofered, 156, 159.

Eofermund or Efermund, *83*, 102, 113, 122, 131. *163*.

Eoferulf, 163, 174.

Eofred, *400*.

Eola, 331, 361.

Eolð, *245*.

Eonred, *303*.

Eorff, *331*.

Eorod or Eoroð, *142*, *156*, 160, 171, 186.

Eowine, *303*.

Erard, *102*. *See* Efrard.

Erconbald, *122*, *163*.

Erdnoð, *245*. *See* Eardnoð.

Ere, 102, 111.

Erembald, *122*.

Erewine, 199, 212.

Ereðic, *122*. *See* Freðic.

Erfric, 331, 357.

Ergimbalt, 122, 140.

Ergrim, *303*. *See* Erngrim.

Eric, *102*.

Ericil, *122*.

Ericuuald, 32, 69.

Erim or Erimes, *142*, *156*.

Ermwi, *331*.

Erncetel, Erncytel, or Erncil, *303*, 331, 362, 460, 463. *See also* Arncetel and Earncytel.

Erngrim or Ergrim, *245*, *303*, 329, 331, 362, 363. *See also* Arngrim and Earngrim.

Ernwi, *303*.

Erostulf, *199*.

Eroð, 148. *See* Froðric.

Ertan, 446. *See* Estan.

Escea, *199*.

Escman, 191, 195. *See also* Æscman.

Esctli, *199*.

Estan, 243, 245, 256, *303*, 329, 331, 423, 445, 446. *See also* Æstan.

Esther, 331, 397.

Estmær, *331*. *See* Æstmær.

Estmund, 331, 410, 453, 454, 455.

Eswig, 199, 234. *See also* Ascwig.

Etfern, *163*.

Etile, *83*.

Etram, *102*.

Etsige, 245, 261, 284, 291, *303*, *320*, 331, 353, 407. *See also* Eadsige.

Etstan, *245*, 331, 374. *See also* Eadstan.

Ettige, *245*. *See* Etsige.

Eturcol (= Styrcol ?), *331*.

Eulgart, 122, 132

Ewiewii. *331*

Eyrhied, *199*

Eyrsige, *199*

Eðelgeard, 9, 18, 22, 24

Eðelheab, *32*

Eðelheard, *9*

Eðelhere, 9, 17, 20, 22, 24.

Eðelm or Eðeln, *163*, 191, 195

Eðelmær, *197*   See Æðelmær

Eðelmod, 1, 7, 8, 9, 18, 32, 58

Eðelmund, 9, 13, *32.*

Eðeln, 191, 195   See also Eðelm

Eðelnoð, 9, 18, 22, 24, 101, 105, 113, *142*, *197*   See also Æðelnoð

Eðelred, 9, 13, 22, 24, 27, 29, *32*   See also Æðelred

Eðelrine, *199*

Eðelsige, *122*

Eðelstan, 32, 40, *83*, *156*   See also Æðelstan

Eðelueald, 22, 24

Eðeluine or Eðelwine, 32, 45, 69, 163, 179, 197, 221, 243, 260   See also Æðelwine

Eðelulf or Eðelwulf, 22, 24, 32, 70, *83*

Eðelwine, 197, 224, 243, 260   See also Æðelwine and Eðeluine

Eðelwulf, *83*   See also Eðelulf

Eðered, 22, 24, 32, 45, 58, 70   See also Æðered

Eðestan, *197, 320*   See also Æðestan

F.

Facer, 191   See Lacer

Fællan, 199, 215

Færeman, *303*   See also Farman

Fœrgrim, Fœrgrin, or Fargrim, 245, 264, *303*, *320*, 331, 389, 432

Færðan, Færðin, or Færðein, *199*, 215, 268   See also Farðen

Fœsðulf (= Fastulf), *199*

Falgar, *245.*

Fanael, *156.*

Faraman or Fareman, *122. 199.   See also* Farman

Farehir, 331, 421

Fargrim, 215, 264, 331, 389   See also Fœrgrim

Farman or Farmen, *83, 122*, 163, 179, 199   See also Faraman

Faromia, *122*

Farðen, Farðein, or Farðin, 164, 179, 215, 264, 268   See also Fœrðan

Fastolf or Fastulf, 164, 169, 188, *191*, 199, 214, 215, *245*

Fastolf and Boiga, 164, 189

Fastolf and Oda, 164, 189.

Fastolf and Rafn, 164, 189

Fastulf, 199, 215, *245*   See also Fastolf

Fasulf, *199*   See Fastulf.

Fawle, *102*

Fereman, *245*   See also Faraman and Farman

Ferlun, 32, 70

Ferðic, *142*   See Froðic.

Fieelnið, *199*

Fiersih, *199.*

Fioduan, 164, 189.

Fleeðifl, 215, 273

Flodger, 164, 171.

Fodwine, *331*

Folcard, Folecard, or Folcerd, *32*, *122*, 199, 231, 331, 455

Folenard, *164*

Folcred, *102*, *122*

Folewine, 331, 433.

Folhed, Folherd, or Follhred, 215, 270

Folric, *460*

Forman, 331, 429

Forna, 460, 470

Forða, *460*

Forðgar, *164*

Fram, *102*

Framuuis, 83, 95

Franbald, 32

Frard, 102, 110, 122, 132, 142, 148, 156, 159

Fredard or Fredred, 122, 141, 142, 155

Freðric, 164, 186   See also Froðric

Freðard, 102   See also Fredard

Freðeric, 156   See Froðric

Freðewine, 245   See Friðewine

Freðic, Freðices, or Freðicin, 122, 142, 148, 156, 161, 164, 169, 184, 215, 282

Frioðulf, 83

Frið, 63

Friðeol, 215, 264, 268

Friðeberht, Friðebriht, or Friðelberht, 83, 91, 102

Friðemund, 331

Friðewine or Friðiwine, 245, 202, 303, 331   See also Freðewine

Friði, 320, 327

Fromn or Frome, 331, 352, 353

Fron, 331, 352, 460, 462

Frostulf or Frosðulf, 199

Frotgar or Frotger, 102, 113, 120   See also Froðgar

Froticrm, 102

Froð, 142, 148

Froðgar or Froðger, 102, 156, 158   See also Frotgar

Froðric or Freðeric, 112, 148, 156, 159, 164, 171   See also Freoðric

Fryðemund, 164, 190, 238

Fugel, 102, 117, 122, 132, 141

Fulrad, 102

Fyheltæ, 199

Fynnelm, 142

G.

Gaeald, 83

Garcard, 83, 91, 95, 102, 111

Garfin, 199, 331, 396

Garnwi, 331

Garnine, 32, 71

Garulf, 83, 102, 199, 245, 331, 410, 418

Georlaf, 245

Gelda, 32, 69

Geldewine, Gildewine, Guldewine, or Gyldewine, 303, 308, 331, 314, 315, 316, 317, 387

Genard, 102, 106

Geola, 331, 363

Gercfin, 460.

Geundferd or Gundferð, 122, 132

Giencea, 102

Gife or Gire, 102, 199, 331, 395

Gilacris or Gillacris, 303

Gildewine, 331, 347, 387   See also Geldewine

Gilles, Gillus, Gillys, or Gyllis, 142, 164, 171, 186

Gilm, 164   See also Cylm

Gilpin, 331, 420

Gimulf, 245, 268   See also Grimulf

Giodwine, 199   See Godwine

Giolwulf (Ciolwulf?), 32

Giongball, 102, 112, 122

Gire, 331   See Gife

Gis, 102

Gislehelm, 142.

Gislemer, 102, 117, 123, 142, 149

Glifwine, 331, 410

Glonnulf, 191

Gnapa, 123   See Cnapa

Gnorine, 245

God or Godd, 199, 216, 217, 225, 245, 303, 314, 316

Goda or Godda, 32, 71, 80, 199, 213, 229, 230, 233, 236, 245, 290, 291, 303.

Godæg, Godeg, or Godieg, 199, 234.

Godaman, 245, 286, 303   See also Godman

Godan, 245, 303

Godeild, Godeildd, or Goteild, 245, 295, 303, 320, 331, 438

Godeirea, 245

Gold, 245, 316   See also God

Goddere, 215, 284   See also Godere
Godeferð, Godefreð, Godefnð, Gode-fryð, or Godferð, 156, 161, 199, 215, 274, 275
Godeg, 199   See Godæg
Godelað, 245
Godelef, Godeleof, Godleof, or Godleow, 199, 231, 235, 245, 274, 331, 155
Godelfold, 331
Godeman, 199, 227, 215, 260, 286, 299, 331, 439   See also Godman
Goder, Godere, or Goddere, 199, 224, 215, 284, 286, 287, 331, 410
Goderic, 331, 428   See also Godric
Godesbrand, 331, 426, 460
Godesune, Godsune, Godsunu, or Gotsunu, 245, 320, 331, 375, 397, 104, 458
Godferð, 199   See Godeferð
Godgod, 245
Godi, 331
Godic, 245
Godieg, 199   See Godeg
Godin or Godine, 142, 149, 303   See also Godwine
Godinc, 199, 232, 245, 303.   See also Godine
Godlamb, 331, 375
Godleof, 215, 271   See also Godelef
Godleow, 199   See Godclef
Godman, Godaman, Godeman, Godmon, or Goðman, 199, 210, 211, 212, 224, 227, 229, 238, 240, 215, 260, 261, 268, 282, 286, 289, 299, 303, 331, 380, 110, 431, 439, 446
Godra, 199
Godric, Goderic, Goodric, Goric, or Gotric, 199, 217, 226, 227, 245, 259, 270, 271, 274, 276, 280, 282, 284, 286, 293, 303, 308, 312, 316, 320, 325, 326, 331, 340, 341, 371, 373, 382, 384, 387, 388, 390, 391, 392,

393, 394, 395, 400, 405, 407, 410, 412, 414, 415, 416, 417, 126, 428, 431, 443, 456, 160, 168, 170, 471
Godric and Calic, 215, 320
Godric and Swot, 215, 280
Godrinc, 199
Godsic, 303, 314   See also Goldsic
Godsige, 303, 314   See also Goldsige
Godsune or Godsunu, 245, 320, 331, 101, 158   See also Godesune
Godwi, 245, 331, 400, 456
Godwic or Godwig, 199, 331, 101
Godwin, 245, 331
Godwine or Godwincc, 303, 331, 384
Godwine and Ceoca, 331
Godwine, 199, 210, 211, 212, 217, 218, 222, 227, 229, 235, 239, 240, 245, 256, 258, 270, 271, 272, 275, 276, 278, 284, 287, 289, 290, 292, 293, 298, 299, 303, 311, 313, 314, 315, 320, 327, 328, 331, 341, 343, 348, 319, 351, 354, 355, 364, 373, 375, 380, 383, 384, 385, 386, 397, 398, 400, 402, 404, 405, 107, 408, 410, 413, 414, 417, 420, 423, 427, 431, 432, 439, 441, 445, 447, 449, 450, 456, 457, 460, 462, 466
Godwine and Cas, 215, 298
Godwine and Ceoca, 245, 303, 329
Godwine and Stewer, 303
Godwine and Widia (Wudia), 245, 303, 331, 447
Godwine and Wudia, 320, 328
Goere, 245, 286   See also Godere
Gome, 245
Gola or Golla, 200, 331
Golda, 320, 325
Goldan, 331
Goldcytel, 320, 325
Goldman, 331, 351, 400
Goldsic, Goldsige, or Goltsige, 303, 313, 314, 320, 331, 401, 102, 404, 111

2 L

Goldstan, *200*.

Goldus, 200, 238, 215, 292.

Goldwine, 200, 226, 233, 331, 380, 383, 404, 453, 460, 473.

Golgrim, *200*. *See* Colgrim.

Golla, *200*. *See also* Gola.

Goltsige, *303, 331*, 401, 402, 404. *See also* Goldsige.

Goltsine, 331, 401, 408.

Goman, 215, 286.

Gonwine, *245, 303*. *See* Godwine.

Goodric, *245*. *See* Godric.

Goric, 303, 308. *See also* Godric.

Gota or Gotaf, 102, 117, 123, 132.

Goteild, *245, 303*. *See* Godcild.

Gotric, 245, 284. *See also* Godric.

Gotsalin, *245*.

Gotsunu, 331, 375. *See also* Godesune.

Gowine, 299, 303, 311. *See also* Godwine.

Gowne, *331*.

Goðman, *245*. *See* Godman.

Goðric, *331*. *See* Godric.

Grid, 164, 180, 189.

Grim, 142, 149, 156, 158, 164, 168, 191, 196, 200, 223, 241, 245, 272.

Griman, *245*.

Grimcetel or Grimcytel, 245, 278.

Grimolf or Grimulf, 245, 265, 268, *303, 331*.

Grimwald, 83, 91, 95, *102, 123*.

Grind, 191, 194, 200, 222.

Grinule, *331*. *See* Grimulf.

Grucan, 245, 267. *See also* Crucan.

Grungar, *245*.

Grurn, 246, 264. *See also* Crurn.

Guldewine, 331, 344, 346. *See also* Geldewine.

Gunar or Guner, *200*.

Gundberht, *83*.

Gundferð, 122, 132. *See also* Geundferð.

Gunhwat, *200, 246*.

Gunleof or Gunnleof, *200*, 246, 277.

Gunne, *83*.

Gunni, 200, 209.

Gunnula, *191*.

Gunnulf, *164*.

Gunsig, *246*.

Gunstan, *200*.

Gunter, *83*.

Gunnerd, 164, 180.

Guolfwine, *331*, 374.

Gustan or Gustin, 246, 279.

Guðhere, 32, 71.

Guðort, *331*.

Guðred, 331, 383.

Gwelic, 331, 455.

Gyldewine, 303, 308, 331, 344, 345. *See also* Geldewine.

Gyllis, *164*. *See* Gilles.

Gynsige. *See* Cynsige.

Gytel, *156*. *See* Cytel.

H.

Haculf, 164, 180.

Hadebald, *83, 123*.

Hægenrede, *102*.

Hærgod or Haregod, 331, 421, 422.

Hærra, 303, 309, *320*.

Hærred or Herred, 331, 442, 443.

Hafgrim, 191, 194.

Haldbere, 32, 71.

Haldene, 331, 429.

Hana or Hanen, *123*.

Hancrent, 191, 194, *200*. *See also* Mancrent or Nancrent.

Hangrim, *191*.

Harcin, 331, 431, 458. *See also* Marcin.

Haregod, 331, 422. *See also* Hærgod.

Harger, 102, 117.

Harneytel, *200*. *See* Arneytel.

Harðacnut, Harðecnut, or Hearðcnut, 246, *303*.

Hateman or Hatman, 246   See also
    Hwateman
Haðebald, 83
Haðelberht, 102.
Haðelwold, 102, 117
Heabearht, 22, 24   See also Here-
    bearht
Heahmod, 27, 31
Healf, 32
Heardher, 83, 91
Hearðccnut, 246   See Harðacnut
Heauulf, 32, 50, 71   See also Heawulf
Heawulf or Heauulf, 32, 50, 71, 200,
    228
Heaðewi, 460, 473
Heaðulf or Heðewulf, 331, 451
Hebeca, 9, 14, 32, 56
Hedebeald, 9
Heirseric, (Ciresrien ?) 32, 62
Heldalt, 102, 107.
Helican, 32, 71
Herebald or Herebeald, 9, 14, 15, 17,
    22, 24, 27, 30, 32, 83
Herebearht, Hereberht, Herebert,
    Heriberht, Herebreht, or Herebyrht,
    9, 17, 24, 32, 46, 164, 180, 200, 220
Herebeav, 102
Hereberht, 200   See Herebearht
Herebert, 32, 46, 164, 180   See also
    Herebearht
Herebreht or Herebyrht, 200, 220
    See also Herebearht
Hereferd, Hereferð, or Herefreð, 22,
    24, 32, 40, 71, 164
Heregeard, 22, 24
Hereman, 123, 164, 180
Heremfretin, 83
Heremod, 32, 72, 83, 96, 98, 102, 123,
    132, 142, 156, 164, 174
Heremund, 22, 25, 32, 72
Hereulf or Hereuulf, 27, 30, 32, 72
Herewig, 123, 133, 156
Heriberht, 32, 46   See also Herebearht

Herigar or Heriger, 142, 156, 161, 164,
    180
Herolf or Herolfes, 164, 189
Herred, 331, 443   See also Hærred
Herric, 102
Herulf or Herwulf, 200.   See also
    Hereulf
Hewulf, 200   See Heawulf
Heðewulf, 331, 451   See also Heaðulf
Heðul, 83
Hiardi, 200
Higolf   See Hingolf
Hild, 191, 196
Hible, 164
Hildeomert, 123
Hildolf or Hildulf, 102, 142, 200, 216,
    246, 263, 265, 268, 320
Hildred, 246
Hildsige, 200
Hildulf   See Hildolf
Hiltwine, 164
Hingolf or Ingolf, 164, 181, 191
Hlangulf, 331, 419
Horn, 331, 423
Hotaf, 123
Hrodear or Hroðgar, 102, 112, 123,
    142
Hunna, 246   See Hunna
Hunbearht or Hunberht, 9, 13, 14, 17,
    18, 22, 25, 32, 72
Hunbein, 164, 181   See also Unbein
Hundolf or Hundulf, 200, 215
Huneman, 200, 246, 262
Hunewine, 200, 236, 246, 261, 331,
    357
Hunfred or Hunfreð, 32, 40, 83
Hungar, 102
Hunia, 200
Huniga, 200
Hunlaf, 83, 98, 102, 108, 123, 133,
    142
Hunna, 246, 303, 320
Hunred, 9, 18, 22, 25, 112, 149

Hunric, 102
Hunswit, 112, 150
Hunsige, 123, 143
Hunstan, 200
Hunwrd, 331, 389, 390, 391
Husebald, 112, 150
Husca, 27
Hustin, 191
Hwæteman, 200
Hwatman, Hwateman, or Hwatman,
   200, 241, 246, 303, 320, 332, 342, 355
   See also Hateman and Wataman
Hysa, 200

I

Ieserce, 332
Icorill, 332
Ida, 32, 72
Iedulf, 123
Iolfgeht, 390   See Ælfgæt
Ielm, 100
Ielfwine (= Ælfwine), 350, 372, 152
Ifa, 1
Iline (Iline?), 332
Igere, 102, 123, 133
Igeren, 83
Ihleberht, 102
Ilere, 102   See Igere
Iluhl, 246, 303
Indolf, 191   See also Ingolf
Inga, 102
Ingelberd, 164, 185
Ingelberht or Ingelbert, 102, 123
Ingelbrics, 164   See also Ingelric
Ingelgar, 123, 133, 112, 150
Ingelric or Ingelrics, 102, 112, 164, 200,
   248
Ingolf, 164, 181, 191   See also Indolf
   and Hingolf
Ingolferð, 164, 189
Inguers, 112, 150
Ioctel, Ioctlel, or Ioketel, 332, 366, 367,
   368, 463, 460, 463

Iofermund, 83, 98
Iohann or Iohan, 102, 117, 164, 191
   See also Iuhan
Ioketel, 332, 366   See also Ioctel
Iola, Iolla, or Iole, 332, 363, 365, 366
Iolana or Ionana, 332, 359
Ioles, 164, 185
Iolla, 332   See Iola
Ionana, 332   See Iolana
Iora, 332
Iorl, 332
Iounus, 246
Ira, Ire, or Irra, 200, 216, 246, 265
Irfara, 83, 99
Irra, 200, 216   See also Ira
Iscula, 303
Isegel, 200
Isegod, Isgod, or Isengod, 200, 213,
   216
Isembert, 164, 181
Iseward, 246
Isgod   See Isegod
Isideman, 320
Isuel (= Snel?), 102
Isulf, 164, 191
Iua, 83, 92
Iudelbard, 32, 73
Iufiue, 200.
Iugblet, 332, 361
Iuhan, 164, 169   See also Iohan
Iulferð, 332, 373
Iulstan, 200
Iurelel, 332, 362.
Iustan, 200, 246   See Iustegen
Iustegen, Iustein, or Iustin, 246 279
Iustin, 246, 279   See Iustegen
Ive, 142, 155, 164, 182

K.

Knapa, 191   See Cnapa
Kynsige, 200   See Cynsige

L.

Lacer or Sacer, 191, 196

Ladmær, Ladmer, or Lodmær, 246, 298, 303, 318, *320*, 332, 443, 447

Læfwi, *320*   *See* Leofwi

Lafe, *200*

Landac, 102, 117

Landæ, *83*

Landferð, 112, 150, *246*

Landwine, 123, 134.

Lanfer, *83*, 97

Leoewine (= Leofwine ?), *246*

Lerie, *246*

Lecferð, *164*

Lefa, Leofa, or Leva, 200, 220, 246, 275

Lefcetel, *332*

Lefden, *303*

Lefedei, *303*.   *See* Leofdæi

Lefei, *246*

Lefenað or Lefenoð, 303, 308, *320*, 325, 332, 381   *See also* Leofenað and Leofnoð

Lefine or Lefing, 164, 185, *200*   *See also* Leofine and Lifine

Lefman, 332, 381   *See* Leofman

Lefric, *200*, 303, 454   *See also* Leofric

Lefstan, 303, 308, *320*, 327, 332, 344   *See also* Leofstan

Lefstan and Sweue, *246*

Lefwi, 332, 389   *See also* Leofwi

Lefwine, 318, 319, 392, 413, 420, 421, 431, 458   *See also* Leofwine

Lofwold, *191*   *See* Leofwold

Leifine, 344   *See* Lifing

Leifwine, *200*   *See also* Leofwine

Leifðoð, *200*

Leisine, 460, 463

Lemman, *246*   *See* Leomman

Lenna, 164, 182

Leuerine, 434   *See* Leofwine

Leodæu, *246*   *See* Leofdi n

Leodmær or Leomær, 246, 298, *303*   *See also* Ladmær

Leofa, *200*, 246, 275   *See* Lefa

Leofælm, 200, 233

Leofdæg, *332*   *See also* Leofedæg

Leofdæi or Lefedei, *303*

Leofdæn, 246, 293   *See also* Leofdegn

Leofdag, *200*

Leofdeg or Leofdegn, 246, 293   *See also* Leofðegn

Leofedæg, *246*   *See also* Leofdæg

Leofen or Leofrne, *191*

Leofenað or Leofenoð, 277, *303*, 363, 365   *See also* Lefenað and Leofnoð

Leofgar or Leofgær, *164*, *200*, *246*

Leofget, *200*

Leofgod, 200.

Leofhelm, 164, 189, *200*, 233   *See also* Liofhelm

Leofhere, *246*

Leofhese, Leofhyse, or Leofhuse, *200*

Leofine, Leofinces, or Leofing, 164, 189, *200*, 246, 279   *See also* Lefine and Lifine

Leofine, *200*

Leofmær or Leomær, 246, *303*

Leofman or Lefman, *200*, 332, 381

Leofiner, *200*

Leofmon, *200*

Leofmoð, *200*

Leofn, *200*, 246, 332, 373.

Leofnað, *246*.   *See* Leofenað and Leofnoð

Leofnel, 164, 189

Leofnod, *200*   *See* Leofnoð

Leofnoð or Liofnoð, 200, 220, 221, 224, 228, 246, 258, 271, 277, 303, 308, 312, *320*, 332, 361, 363, 365, 373, 381, 390, 401   *See also* Lefenað and Leofenað

Leofred, Lifred, or Liofred, *200*, 246, 286, 303, 311, *320*, 332, 352, 397, 401, 404, 408, 441, 443, 454

Leofred and Brun, *246, 329*

Leofric, Leofric, or Lefric, *102*, 123, 131, 142, 150, *164*, 200, 210, 211, 228, 232, 246, 269, 274, 278, 304, 314, 314, 316, *329*, 332, 379, 383, 388, 406, 411, 420, 421, 432, 435, *460*

Leofrine, *200* See Leofwine

Leofryd, 200, 228

Leofsi, *246*, 160, 468 See also Leofsige

Leofsic, 332, 108

Leofsig or Leofsige, 164, 170, 200, 216, 217, 246, 270, 272, 284, *332*

Leofstan, Leostan, or Liofstan, 156, 158, 164, 168, 190, 200, 210, 211, 215, 224, 225, 226, 228, 246, 282, 284, 303, 315, 320, 326, 327, 332, 344, 345, 347, 371, 374, 397, 422, 427, 439, 440, 443, 460, 466, 470 See also Lefstan and Lifstan

Leofstegen, *246*

Leofsunu, *200*, 246, 297

Leofward, Leofword, Liofweard, or Liofwerd, *246*, 332, 350, 351, 386, 460, 466

Leofwi, *246*, 303, *329*, 332, 384, 401 See also Lefwi and Lafwi

Leofwie, 332, 419 See also Leofwig

Leofwig or Iofwig, 200, 212, *246*, 303, 312, 332, 404

Leofwine, 332, 357

Leofwine, Leowine, Lifwine, or Liofwine, *164*, 200, 208, 220, 221, 224, 226, 228, 229, 246, 260, 261, 262, 272, 274, 277, 278, 279, 280, 282, 284, 286, 288, 290, 292, 293, 295, 296, 298, 303, 307, 309, 313, 315, 317, 318, 319, *320*, 332, 344, 345, 347, 353, 371, 374, 377, 379, 383, 388, 389, 392, 404, 408, 411, 415, 418, 419, 420, 423, 424, 425, 427, 431, 433, 443, 444, 445, 454, 455, 457, 458, 460, 464, 466, 471

Leofwold or Liofwold, *164*, 200, 224, 239, 246, 284, 286, 293, 298, 332, 372, 396, 450, 451, 452, 460, 464, 473

Leofword, 332, 351, 386 See also Leofward

Leofðegen or Leofðegn, *200*, 303, 307, 320, 332, 312 See also Leofðegn

Leomær, *246*, 303 See also Leofmær

Leoman, *200* See Leofman

Leomman or Lemman, *246*

Leomred, *246*

Leonig, 320

Leoric See Leofric

Leostan, *246*, 303 See Leofstan

Leowi or Leown, *246*, 295

Leowie See Leofwie

Leowidn, *246*

Leowine, 280, 293, 303, 411 See also Leofwine

Leowsige, *200* See Leofsige.

Leoðan, 246, 279

Lerman, *246*

Leuine, 156, 162

Leva, *200* See Lefa

Levig, *164*, 191, 195

Lewerd, *246*

Liaba or Liuba, 9, 16, 17

Liabine or Liabineg, 22, 25, 27, 30, *32*

Liidrafen, 303 312

Liafine, 123, 134

Liafwald, *32*

Lifere, *332*

Lifie or Lifice, 277, 332, 360, 372, 473 See also Lifine

Lifine, Lifing, or Lyfine, 102, 121, 142, 150, *156*, *164*, 200, 210, 226, 228, 229, 246 270, 277, 280, 282, 284, 289, 295, 303, 314, 317, 320, 326, 332, 358, 359, 401, 408, 413, 410, 441, 443 444, 415, 418, 419, 451, 452, 456, 458, 460, 464, 471, 473 See also Lefine, Leofine, Liofine, and Lufine

Lifine, 303, 358 See Lifine

Lifred, 303, 314, 332, 401, 404. *See also* Leofred and Liofred.

Lifsig, *332. See* Leofsige.

Lifstan, 344. *See* Leofstan.

Lifwidya, *246.*

Lifwine, 332, 345, 377, 383, 423, 425, 455. *See also* Leofwine.

Lifwine and Horn, 332, 423.

Ligeberd, 123, 134.

Lind, *200.*

Lindwin, *246.*

Lioeri, *200. See* Leofric.

Liofenod, 381, 390. *See also* Liofnoð.

Liofhelm, *83,* 102, 111, 123, 134, *246,* 279. *See also* Leofhelm.

Liofinc, 332, 413, 445. *See also* Lifinc.

Liofman, *246.*

Liofn, *246.*

Liofuen, 246, 279.

Liofnoð, 200, 221, *246,* 332, 381, 390. *See also* Leofnoð.

Liofred, *200,* 332, 352, 401, 411, 433. *See also* Leofred.

Liofric, *200,* 332, 383, 388, 420. *See also* Leofric.

Liofsige, 284. *See also* Leofsige.

Liofstan, 164, 168, 190, *200, 246,* 332, 347, 440. *See also* Leofstan.

Liofweard or Liofwerd, *246,* 332, 386. *See also* Leofward.

Liofwine, 200, 246, 277, 282, 332, 347, 374, 383, 408, 420, 424, 425, 433. *See also* Leofwine.

Liofwold, 200, 221, 332, 450. *See also* Leofwold.

Liouing, *102.*

Litelman or Litilman, 102, 117, 123, 134, *156. See also* Lytelman.

Litman, *200. See* Lytelman.

Liuba, 9, 16. *See* Liaba.

Liufgod, *200. See* Livegod.

Livegod, *200.*

Living or Liwing, *200.*

Liwine, 246, 277.

Liwing, *200. See* Living.

Loc, *246,* 332, 438, 444, 445.

Loda, 246, 300.

Lodmær, *303. See* Ladmær.

Lofman, *332. See* Leofman.

Lofric, *332. See* Leofric.

Lofwig, *332. See* Leofwig.

Lofwine, *320. See* Leofwine.

Lowman, *164.*

Luceman or Lyceman, 22, 25.

Luda, Lude, Ludia, or Ludda, *32,* 200, 213.

Ludeca, 33, 73.

Ludig, 33, 73.

Lucinc, 332, 435.

Lufa, *200,* 216, 290.

Luferic, *246.*

Lufestan, *246.*

Luffe, *332.*

Luffinc or Lufinc, 200, 229, *332,* 460, 471. *See also* Lifinc.

Lufric, *303, 332. See* Leofric.

Lufstan, *332. See* Leofstan.

Lufwine, *246,* 332. *See* Leofwine.

Lulla, 27, 30, 33, 58, 74.

Lumar, *200.*

Luning, *33.*

Lyceman, 22, 25. *See also* Luceman.

Lycfea or Lyva, *200.*

Lyfinc, *164,* 200, 228, *246. See also* Lifinc.

Lyfsye, *200.*

Lytelman, Lyteman, or Litman, 200, 217. *See also* Litelman.

Lyva, *200. See* Lycfea.

M.

Macsuðan, 246, 277.

Mægred, *164.*

Mæld or Mældomen, 102, 110, 123, 135.

Mælsuðan or Mælsuðen, 164, 172, *191.*

Mærten or Mærtin, 102, 109, 123, 135, 200 See also Martin and Mertin

Magnard, 83, 102

Mah, 102

Man Mann, Mana, Manan, Manna, or Manne, 9 15, 16, 17, 19, 27, 30, 83, 92, 102, 112, 123, 135, 140, 142, 144, 151, 155, 156 162, 164, 169, 171, 182, 185, 191, 200, 214, 236, 246, 288, 296, 303, 315, 332, 344, 345, 346, 347, 394, 395, 460, 470

Mann See Man

Manne, 332

Manan See Man

Mancrent, 200 See also Hancrent

Maneca, 142, 151

Mancod, 156 See Manngod

Manctu, 123

Mangod, 200, 214, 246

Manne or Mannine, 9, 13, 18, 19, 22, 25 27, 30 33, 56, 57, 102, 246 See also Maning

Maning or Manning, 164, 183, 200, 231

Manleof 303, 320

Mann See Man

Manna See Man

Manne See Man

Mannecin, 142, 155

Manngod, 156, 159, 160 See also Mangod

Mannie, 191 See also Manine

Mannicen, 123, 125 See also Manticen

Mannine See Manine

Manning See Maning

Manolet, 156

Mansat, 164, 170

Mansige, 246

Mantat, 164, 191 See also Mansat

Manticen, 102, 112, 123, 125, 164, 190

Manwine, 200, 332, 355

Marbert, 83

Marcer or Marcere, 164, 183, 332 356 See also Morcere

Marcin, 332, 431, 458

Marscale or Marsceale, 164, 175

Martin, 123, 135, 142, 200 See also Mærtin and Mertin

Matan, 246 See also Mateðan

Mataðan and Balluc, 246

Mateǂan or Matðan, 246, 278, 280

Maǂelwold, 102

Megenfreð, 102, 118

Megered, 191 See also Megred

Megred, 102, 110, 123, 136

Melsdon, 191

Merewine, 201

Mertin, 164, 187 See also Mærtin and Martin

Mna, 201

Moelf, 33, 74

Moglu, 246

Moleman, 246

Monðegen or Monðign, 102, 114, 120

Morcere, 332, 356 See also Marcere

Morgna, 164, 183

Morre, 332

Munred, 142

Mus, 246

N.

Nanan, 164, 183

Nancrent, 191, 194, 201 See also Hancrent

Nanne, 112 See Manne

Nansige, 123

Nauðwn, 303

Naǂan, 280 See Matðan

Nebeca, 14, 33 See Hebeca

Nelican, 71 See Helican

Nerebeald, 17 See Herebeald

Nercbeuer, 17. See Herebearht

Nicici, 246

Norbert, 142, 154

Norulf, 246, 294

Norðberd, 164

Norðgar, 142, 151
Norðman, 246, 303, 327
Noðer, 102, 118
Noðulf, 22, 25
Nunbeant or Nunbeurht, 14, 17 See Hunbearht
Nybald, 102

O.

Oba, 1, 6.
Oban, 201, 215, 216
Obn, 216
Oda, 102, 118, 123 135, 164, 189 191, 201, 215, 238, 246, 297, 300
Odan, 201 See Oban
Odcotel, 201
Odda, 201 See Oda
Ode, 216 See Oda
Odea, 201, 246 See Oda
Odgrim, 201 See Oðgrim
Odo, 83, 102 See also Oda
Odu, 201 See Oda
Oeeman, 164, 183
Oeðrhern [= Oðelric?], 142
Ofe, 201, 234
Ogea, 164, 173, 191, 196
Ogeman, 164
Ogu, 201
Ora, 191, 196 See Borga
Orerbd, 201
Oign, 201
Omund or Ommund, 332, 411, 415 See also Osmund
Omynd, 332, 413 See also Omund
Ondres, 123
Onlat, 201, 220
Onuman, 123
Ordbright or Ordbriht, 201, 238, 246
Ordrec, 320, 326
Ordric, 246, 273 303 See also Orðric
Ordulf, 83, 92

Orist or Orst, 246
Orlaf, 332, 406
Orðric, 160, 465 See also Ordric
Osalf, 201, 225 See also Osulf
Osbarn, 247 See also Osbern
Osbearht, 22, 25
Osbern or Osberen, 201, 217, 261, 320
Oscetel or Oscytel, 201, 225
Osferð, 123, 142. 151, 161, 201, 212, 247, 278, 279, 303, 320, 332, 391, 393, 394
Osfram, 201, 247
Ostryð, 332 See Osferð
Osgar, 201, 247
Osgeard, 33
Osgod or Osgot, 142, 201, 214, 217, 263, 265 See also Osgut
Osgrim, 247
Osgut, 201, 219, 223, 240, 241, 247 See also Osgod
Oshere, 22, 25, 26, 27, 31, 33, 56
Oslac, 83, 102, 110, 123, 136, 164, 217, 279, 280, 303
Oslaf, 102, 109, 142, 164, 247
Osmær, 191, 201, 332, 340, 341
Osmund, 1, 6, 9, 11, 15, 17, 123, 164, 201, 247, 303, 321, 332, 384, 415, 419, 133, 431, 460, 469, 471 See also Omund
Osolf, 201 See Osalf
Osric, 33
Osuerd, 201 See also Osward
Osulf, Osuulf, or Oswulf, 33 74, 83, 93, 102, 123, 164, 169, 191, 193, 201, 226, 228, 229, 241, 247, 282 See also Osalf
Oswald, 123, 136, 142 151, 156, 162, 191 See also Oswold
Osward, 164, 185, 247, 332, 371, 432
Oswart, 102
Oswerd, 247
Oswi or Oswie, 201, 209, 247, 270
Oswig 201, 209 247 270

Oswine, 112
Oswold, 201, 220, 217, 332, 385, 386, 460, 467　See also Oswald
Oswulf 123　See also Osulf
Ottu, 102, 123, 137, 156
Otwine, 332
Oudecl or Ouðecl, 321
Oustman 217
Ouðbearn or Ouðbern, 201, 332, 369, 460　See also Osbeorn
Ouðecl, 321
Ouðenearl, 321
Ouðgrim, 201, 217, 332, 370, 460, 463　See also Osgrim
Ouðnear or Ouððenear, 217, 303, 313, 321　See also Ouðenearl
Ouðolf, Ouðulf, or Ouððulf, 332, 368, 370, 460, 463
Owulsige, 217
Oðan, Oðen, Oðin, Oðinne, or Oðð in, 217, 268, 269, 303, 310, 332, 359, 360, 362
Oðbarn, 217
Oðbeorn, Oðbern, or Oðborn, 201, 222, 247, 332, 367, 368, 369, 394　See also Ouðbearn
Oðberan, 303
Oðbi, 247
Oðborn　See Oðbeorn
Oðelric, 123, 112, 151
Oðelriht, 164
Oðen, 332, 362　See also Oðan
Oðenear, 201　See also Ouðenearl and Oððenear
Oðeran, 303
Oðethorcel, 123
Oðgrim, 201, 215, 223, 217, 281, 303, 332, 366, 367, 368, 369, 392, 394, 395, 396　See also Ouðgrim
Oðin, Oðinn, or Oðinne, 247, 268, 303, 310, 332, 359, 360　See also Oðan
Oðolf 332, 368　See also Ouðolf
Oðrim 303　See Oðgrim

Oðshu, 332, 395.
Oðulf, 201
Oðurim, 303　See Oðgrim
Oððenear, 217, 321　See also Ouðenearl and Oðenear
Oððin, 217, 269　See also Oðin

P.

Pastor, 83.
Paul, Paules, or Paulus, 102, 109, 110, 118, 120, 123, 137
Pirim, 164　See Wirim
Pitit, 83, 92, 102, 118, 123, 137
Pororic, 303　See Wororic
Price, 332, 420
Prim, 123
Prin, 142

R.

Rader, 303, 315
Radstan, 164
Ræduine, 142, 151
Rædulf, 332, 380
Ræfen, Ræfin, or Rafen, 164, 189, 201, 217, 269, 332, 360, 362, 365
Rægenald, 102.　See Regenold and Regnald
Rægenbald, 201
Rægenold, 123
Regenulf or Rænulf, 83, 92, 102, 109, 118, 164, 191, 201
Raienold, 201
Renulf, 102, 109　See also Rægenulf
Rafn or Rafen, 164, 189, 201, 332, 365　See also Ræfen
Randulf, 123
Reedes, 142
Regengrim or Regegrim, 102, 123　See also Reingrim
Regenold, 164
Regenward, 102
Regingæd 33

Regnald, 102, 106
Regnulf, 123, 137   See also Rægenulf
Regðer, 123, 137, 142, 151
Reinere, 102
Reinfirð, 112, 152
Reingrim, 123, 141
Reiðereil, 142
Renard, 102
Rentwine, 160, 173
Resaud, 33, 45
Riueman, 342
Riccolf or Ricolf, 161, 183
Ricnulf or Rienulf, 217, 288   See also Rinulf
Riculf, 142, 201
Ricnulf, 247   See Ricnulf
Rinard, 83, 102
Rincolf or Rincull, 303, 318, 321, 332   See also Rinulf
Rintald, 102
Rinnard, 83
Rinue, 142
Rinulf, 142, 217, 303, 321, 332, 419
Riornbed, 84
Rodbart, 201, 222
Rodbert or Rodberht, 123, 142, 191, 201, 222
Rodear or Rodgar, 123
Roghard, 102
Roscetf, 460
Rotberht, 102, 107
Rudearl, 332, 344
Rulnoð, 321
Rumeried, 321
Runstan, 217, 300   See also Brunstan

S.

Saeer, 191, 196
Saecol or Secolf, 332, 347, 375   See also Secol
Sedeman, 307   See also Sedeman

Saefueef (= Saefugel), 332, 361
Saefugel, 332
Saefuhel or Sefuel, 332, 360, 362
Saegrim, 217, 300, 303
Saeilne, 201, 213
Saemaer, 332, 380
Saeman, 201, 247
Saeris, 33, 74
Saerteg, 201
Saeuard, 321
Saeword, 303
Saewine, Sewine, or Siewine, 201, 237, 238, 217, 262, 274, 295, 303, 307, 321, 326, 328, 332, 357, 358, 359, 379, 383, 412, 460, 465
Salees, 102
Salciarene, 123
Samson, 33, 82
Samsun, 84
Saudac, 102   See Landac
Sarauuard, Saruuard, or Saruurd, 123, 138, 142, 155
Saxsa, 123, 138
Saydtine, 161, 190
Sbeiman, 332, 401
Scot, 201
Scula, Sculaa, or Scule, 247, 303, 310, 332, 360, 361, 362, 363, 365, 366, 367, 368, 370
Scurua, 123
Seyrua, 112   See Scurua
Seege, 143, 144
Secoll or Schcol, 247   See also Saecol
Sedeman, 156, 162, 164, 184   See also Siudeman, Suleman, and Sydeman
Seertebrand, 201
Sefreð or Selfred, 22, 25, 33, 56
Sefuel, 332, 360   See also Saefuhel
Schalauriht, 191   See also Schybyryht
Schybyryht, 191
Selewine, 332, 374
Selcol, 247   See Secol
Selered, 22, 25

Selfred, 22, 25   See also Setred
Sentwine, 160   See also Centwine
Seolca or Syolca, 201, 217
Sereloms, 201
Sertine, 217
Setman, 121   See Swetman
Sewine, 201   See Sæwine
Seaberht, 161
Sodeman, 123, 138   See also Sideman
Siba, 201
Siboda, Siboda, or Sibodi, 201, 217   See also Sigboda
Sibriht, 217
Sidewine, 201, 228, 217
Sidwine, 201, 228
Sideman, 123, 138, 164, 173, 201, 332, 138, 139   See also Sodeman and Sidemin
Sidewine or Sidwine, 201, 232, 217
Siefereð, 113, 152
Siegred, 143
Siestef, 33, 57   See also Sigestef
Siewine, 332, 359   See also Sæwine
Sifert, 113, 155
Siferð, 164, 187
Sigar, Sigares, Sigear, Sigeares, or Sihares, 102, 123, 138, 143, 152, 247, 297
Sigboda or Sigebode, 217, 332, 428   See also Siboda
Sigear or Sigeares, 123, 247   See also Sigar
Sigeberð, 123
Sigebrand, 84, 92, 102, 118
Sigedrald, 102
Sigeferð, 84, 92, 102, 109, 201
Sigehere, 22, 25
Sigelaud, 102
Sigeric, 201, 236
Sigestef or Siestef, 1, 33, 56, 57
Sigeulf or Sigeluf, 201
Sigenulfd, 33, 71

Sigewine, 201
Sigewulf, 102
Sigtoldes, 102
Sigol, 332, 311, 312, 160, 161
Sigodia, 217, 297.
Sigot, 84, 92
Sigwold, 123
Sihares, 102   See Sigar
Sihlodil, 201
Silac, 332, 374
Simun, 33, 71
Sinoð, 247
Siolf, 201
Sipoda, 247   See Siboda
Sirænd, 247, 284
Sired or Siredd, 201, 247, 271, 332, 317, 411, 418
Siric, 201, 247, 288
Siuard or Siuerd, 102, 107.
Siwald or Siwold, 201
Siwerd, 321
Siwold, 201
Sioðwine, 201   See Sidwine
Smala, 102, 121
Smerel, 123
Smertcali, 143
Snæbeorn, Snæborn, Sucaborn, Sucaburn, Snebearn, Snebcorn, or Sneborn, 332, 366, 367, 368, 370, 400, 403
Snæwine, Sneawine, or Suewine, 247, 332
Sneaborn or Sneaburn, 332, 366   See also Snæbeorn
Snebearn, Snebcorn, or Sneborn, 332, 367, 368, 370, 460   See also Snæbeorn
Snecoll, 247
Sneil, 303
Snel or Snell, 102, 118, 247, 303, 321
Sneling, 201, 247.
Snewine, 332   See also Snæwine
Snolf 201
Snoter 332, 429

Soemud, *201*

Sota, 102, 119, *247*

Spot, 247, 280, 332, 311   *See also* Swot.

Spraecline, Spraceling, Spraecaling, or Spragcline, 332, 408, 419, 451, 453, 460, 473

Spraecaling, 332, 450   *See also* Spraecline

Spraful, 247, 297

Spragcline, 332, 408   *See also* Spraecline

Spronene, *102*

Sprot, *332*   *See* Spot

Sprould, *84*

Stængrim or Steingrim, 247, 271

Stancr, *247*

Stanmær, 247, 332, 351

Stear, *84*

Stefanus, 33, 75, *102*

Stefhan, *123*

Stegenbit, 201, 222

Stegeneiel, *201*

Steingrim, *247*   *See* Stængrim

Steland, *102*

Steorcer, *201*   *See also* Stircer, &c

Stewer, *303*

Stirc, *247*   *See* Stircar

Stircar or Stircer, *201*, 247, 263

Stirceere, *303*

Stircer, *201*, *247*   *See also* Stircar and Steorcer

Stircol or Styrcol, *201*, 217, 265, 266, *303*, 332, 360, 364, 365.

Stiðulf, 217, 281

Styrcar, *161*, *201*   *See* Steorcer, Stircer, &c

Styrcol, 217, 266, 332, 364   *See also* Stircol

Styrgar, *191*

Suartcol, *217*   *See also* Swartcol

Sueman, 460, 469

Suetine, *247*   *See also* Swetine

Suince, *143*

Suinolf, *247*

Sumerled, Sumerleda, Sumerleša, Sumerlida, Sumerluda, or Sumerlyd, 201, 215, 240, 247, 278, 279, *303*, *333*, 455, 456

Sumerlr, *303*

Sumerluda, *333*   *See* Sumerleda

Sumerlyd, *303*   *See* Sumerled

Sumred, 455   *See* Sumerled

Sundeid, *303*

Sunegod, *201*, 247, 278

Sunolf, *201*, 247, 266

Sunrdde, *303*

Sunulf, *201*

Surclos, *191*

Surnlos, *191*

Surtine or Svrtine, 217, 266, 267   *See also* Swartine

Sutere, 460, 463

Swafa, *217*, *303*, 312, *333*

Swan, 247, 286

Swarafuc or Swerafuc, *247*

Swarcolf, 333, 432

Swart, Sweart, Swearta, or Swert, *201*, 247, 280, 293, *303*, *321*, *333*.

Swartafa or Swertafa, *247*

Swartcol, Sweartcol, or Swertcol, *201*, 333, 364, 365, 367, 369, 370, 390, 460, 464

Swartebrand or Swartefrand, *303*.

Swartgar or Sweartear, 201, 233

Swartic, Swartine, Sweartine, Swertine, or Swyrtine, 201, 231, 247, 277, 280, 303, 312, *321*, 333, 353

Swatic, *333*, 352

Swearling, 460, 473   *See also* Swearling

Sweart, *333*   *See also* Swart

Swearta, 247, 280   *See also* Swart.

Sweartabrand or Sweetebrand, 247, 280, *303*.

Sweartear, *201*   *See* Swartgar

Sweartcol, *333*, 370, 390, 460, 464   *See also* Swartcol

Sweartinc, 217, 280   See also Swartinc
Swearting or Sweartling, 333, 153,
   160, 171, 173, 174   See also Swearl-
   ing
Swefheard or Swefherd, 1, 6, 7
Swegen 201, 221, 217, 277, 303, 309,
   310
Swegn, 111
Sweiman, 160   See Swetman
Swene, 217
Swenced, 217
Swene, 1
Swerafue, 217   See also Swarafue
Swerlinc, 111
Swert, 201, 217, 203, 303, 321, 333
   See also Swart and Swearta
Swertafu, 217   See Swartafa
Swertcol, 201, 333, 361   See Swartcol
Swertebrand, 217, 280, 303   See
   Sweartabrand
Swertinc or Swyrtinc, 201, 231, 217,
   280, 303, 321, 333, 353   See also
   Swartinc
Swerting, 143   See also Swearting
Swet or Sweta, 217
Swetinc, 201, 228, 217   See also
   Suetinc
Swetman, 201, 333, 101, 411, 115, 116,
   121, 131, 160, 465, 469, 472
Swetric, 333, 117, 422, 142
Swetys, 201
Sweðan, 333
Swileman or Swilman, 201, 238, 217,
   299, 303, 333
Swot, Swota, or Swote, 217, 257, 280,
   303, 321, 333, 311   See also Spot
Swotric, 333
Swraculf, 304
Swrelinc, 217
Swrunt, 217
Swyrelinc, 191
Swyrling, 201, 241
Swyrtinc, 201, 231   See also Swertinc

Syboda, 217   See Sigboda
Sydeman, 161   See Sedeman.
Syolen, 201   See Seolen
Syrtinc, 217   See Surtinc

T.

Tata, 33, 57
Teha, 123
Tidbald, 33, 56
Tideman, 1
Tidgar or Tidger, 102, 109, 110
Tidred, 217, 333
Tila, 84, 93, 96, 102
Tilefein, 33, 57
Tileuine, Tileuuine, or Tilunine, 1, 6,
   33, 50, 51, 75
Tileuore, 33, 75
Timbearht, 1, 6
Tiotes or Totes, 102
Tiruald or Tirucald, 9, 19, 33, 40,
   75
Tiðbearht, 1
Toca, Toga, or Tooca, 201, 212, 229,
   217, 260, 266
Toci, 321
Toga, 201, 212, 229   See also Toca
Tulsi, 333
Tooca, 217, 266   See also Toca
Toihthelm, 84, 102
Torhtmund, 22, 25, 26, 27, 31, 33, 58,
Torhtulf, 9, 19, 21, 22, 25
Torhtwald, 9, 15
Totes, 102   See also Tiotes
Trotan, 217, 277
Tuda, 84
Tuma, 164, 169
Tumme, 201, 215
Tuna, 201, 213
Tuneman, 201
Tunulf, 191, 201, 210
Turstan, 102, 120   See also Þurstan
Tyleadrex, 143, 152

U.

Uccade, Uccde, and Uccdee, 217, 269, 304, 310.

Udfe, 333

Uermund, 9, 19, 22, 25

Uhitred, 333, 401

Uigbald or Uuigbald, 33, 76

Uihtmund, 22, 26

Uilfred, 84

Uilhemt, 201

Uillaf, 84

Uilnoð, 22, 26   See also Uinoð

Uinas, 201   See Winas

Uinoð, 22, 26

Ulanceard, 22, 26

Ulf, Ulfe, or Ulff, 84, 123, 124, 201, 217, 278, 333, 391, 392, 394, 395, 396

Ulfbeorn, 247

Ulfcetel or Ulfcytel, 201, 215, 222, 223, 247, 321, 333, 341, 360, 365, 366, 367, 369, 370, 382, 400, 401

Ulfcil or Ulftil, 304, 333, 364, 366, 369   See also Ulfcetel

Ulfcytel   See Ulfcetel

Ulfe or Ulff   See Ulf

Ulfgrim or Wulfgrim, 201, 202, 247

Ulfhi, 201

Ulftil, 304   See Ulfcil

Ulgebert, 123

Umerð, 217

Unbegn, 201, 222

Unbein, 143, 155, 164, 181, 201, 223   See also Unbegn and Hunbein

Unolf, 333, 360

Unswac, 201

Uri, 201, 211

Urlewine, 333, 310

Urstan, 460   See Þurstan

Ustman, 247

Utti, 333

Uu erin (Waru?), 156, 162

Uualdfreð, 113, 152

Uualeman, 84, 93

Uuarin or Warin, 143, 152   See also Uuærin

Uuarmer, 84, 93

Uucaldheard or Uuelheard, 9, 14, 20

Uucaldhelm, 84, 93, 102, 119

Uuefred, 84

Uuelheard, 9, 20   See also Uucaldheard

Uuelmheard, 9, 20

Uuerstan, 143, 152

Uuiferð or Wiferd, 164, 181

Uuigbald, 33, 76   See also Uigbald

Uuihtes or Uuihtseg, 123, 138

Uuilaf, 123, 138, 143, 152   See also Uillaf

Uuildaf, 113

Uuilebert, 143

Uuilfred, 143, 155.

Uuilheah, 9, 14, 16, 19   See also Wilheah.

Uuillaf or Uuilluf, 84, 102, 119   See also Uuilaf

Uuilric, 102

Uuilsig or Wilsig, 156, 164, 190

Uuinc, 27, 31, 33, 76

Uuinetin, 143

Uuinier or Uuiniger, 33, 76

Uuitelm, 123

Uulfard or Uulfeard, 26, 33, 57, 84, 93   See also Uuifheard

Uulfgar, 84, 99, 102, 109, 110   See also Wulfgar

Uulfheard, 22, 26, 84, 93, 100, 102, 115, 119

Uulfman, 103   See Wulfman

Uulfred or Uulfreð, 33, 77, 80, 84, 94, 96, 191   See also Wulfred

Uulfsig or Uulfsige, 84, 102, 120   See also Wulfsig

Uulfstan, 102, 109, 110, 119, 123, 138, 143, 153   See also Wulfstan

Uulgar, 191

Uulgist, 247

Uolmund, 201   See also Wilmund
Uunbearht, 22, 26   See also Uynbearht
Uuynberht or Wynberat, 53, 78, 81, 84, 91, 97
Uuuielm, 103, 113
Uuunsige, 103, 112, 123, 138   See also Wynsige
Uynbearht or Uynberht, 22, 26, 84, 91   See also Uuynberht and Wynberht
USclric, 103   See also OSclric

W.

Wacer, 191
Wadlos or Waðlos, 217, 301
Wæckl or Wædell, 217, 304, 307, 321, 333, 339
Wælgist, Wdeist, or Welgist, 201, 210, 217
Wielisð, 201
Welræfen, Welrefan, Walræften, or Walrafen, 217, 304, 333
Walerst, 201   See Welgist
Wallet, 304
Walræften, 217   See Welræfen
Walrafen, 333   See Welræfen
Walter or Waltere, 84, 91, 143
Walttreð, 201, 217
Wamanea, 304
Wanstan, 201   See Wunstan
Ware, 217, 262
Warimer, 84
Warin or Uuirin, 143, 152   See also Uuuerin
Waringod, 123
Warn, 123, 138
Wataman or Wateman, 247, 460   See also Hwataman.
Waðlos, 304   See Wadlos
Weddes, 217, 281
Wedel, 304.   See Wædel
Wedles, 247   See Wadlos
Wedles, 247   See Wadlos and Wedles
Weineah, 9

Welgist, 201, 210   See also Wælgist
Welnberht, 103
Welric, 201
Welsit, 217
Wengos, 201   See Wingos
Wensige, 201
Werheard, 1, 7
Werlaf, 123, 140
Wertinc, 301   See also Swertinc
Wesig, 217.
White, 123
Wiard, 33, 103, 121
Wibearn, 333, 375
Wicing, 333, 358, 440
Wida, 448   See Widia
Widfara, 304, 310
Widia or Widica, 217, 304, 333, 446, 447, 448   See also Wudia and Wydia
Widig or Widige, 304, 318
Widuna, 217, 293
Widred, 333, 456
Wiferd, 164
Wigard, Wigeard, Wighard, or Wigheard, 84, 123, 139
Wigeroð, 143
Wigferð, 191
Wighard or Wigheard, 84, 123
Wigmær, 333
Wihred, 247   See Winred
Wihtemund, 103
Wihtsige or Wihtsic, 164, 191, 196, 201, 247, 297   See also Wynsige
Wilægrip or Wilgrip, 333, 380
Wilerif, 333, 432
Wilebald, 103
Wilebeart, 191, 193
Wilebert, 156
Wileric, 333
Wilfrid, 333, 380
Wilgrid, 333
Wilgrim, 304
Wilgrip, 333, 380   See also Wilægrip
Wilheah, 9, 19   See also Uuilheah

Wiline, 247
Wilmund, 201
Wilne, 103
Wilnoð, 22
Wilsig, 156, 164 See also Uuilsig
Wiltrand, 333, 380
Wimund, 103
Win or Winn, 202
Winas, 202, 217 See also Winus
Windecild, 333
Windig, 321 See also Winedæig
Wine or Winne, 164, 187, 191, 194, 196, 202, 247, 298, 460
Winean, 247
Winedæig, Winedeig, or Winedig, 247, 258, 304
Winegear, 84
Winegod, 247
Winegos or Wynegos, 202 See also Wengos
Winele, 103, 119
Wineman, 218, 300, 333
Winemes, 164
Winenr, 164, 184
Winn, 202 See Win
Winno, 247, 460 See also Wine
Winred or Wynred, 248, 258, 304
Winsan, 248. See Winstan
Winsi, 248
Winsige, 202 See Wynsige
Winstan, 248, 291, 304, 333, 353 See also Wunstan and Wynstan
Winterfugel or Winterfuhel, 333, 364, 365
Winterleda, 202
Wintred, 333, 454
Winuc, 123, 139, 143, 153.
Winus, 217, 218, 260, 333, 113, 160, 473 See also Winas
Wirema, 333, 102
Wirim, 164, 170
Wirine, 333, 384
Wiryn, 333, 388

Witil, 103
Witlos, 304 See Wadlos
Wiðering, 304, 310 See also Wiðir-winne
Wiðerwinne, 321
Wiðirwinne, 304, 309 See also Wiðering
Wiðrin or Wiðrine, 248, 266
Wlacðegen or Wlancðegn, 248
Wode, 164
Worono, 304, 313
Wraca, 321
Wudeman, 333, 127
Wudia, 248, 304, 317, 321, 328 See also Widia
Wulbcorn, Wulbern, or Wulborn, 202, 218, 281, 298, 304, 313, 321, 333, 395, 396 See also Wulfbcorn
Wulccet, 304 See Wulfget
Wulcred, 333, 402, 404, 408
Wuldar, 333
Wuldric, 333, 350
Wulennoð, 333, 387 See also Wulfnoð
Wulerine, 304
Wulf, 202, 333, 393
Wulfah, 202
Wulfbald, 143, 164
Wulfbcorn or Wulfbern, 202, 248. See also Wulbcorn
Wulfcetl, 333
Wulfci, 218, 260
Wulfch, 248, 304, 321
Wulfcln, 202, 216, 218, 270
Wulferd, 248
Wulffinc, 304 See Wulfwine
Wulfgar or Wulgar, 1, 123, 139, 143, 153, 156, 164, 173, 191, 196, 202, 219, 248, 287, 304, 313, 333, 356, 393, 396, 412, 413, 415, 416, 460, 469 See also Uulfgar and Uulgar
Wulfgat, Wulfgeat, Wulfget, or Wulf-git, 202, 248, 304, 316, 333, 373, 430, 160, 165.

Wulfger, 415. *See* Wulfgar.

Wulfgrim, 202. *See* Ulfgrim.

Wulfhelm, 103, 111, 123, 139, *202*. *See also* Wulfelm.

Wulfi, *460*. *See* Wulfwi.

Wulfmær, *164*, 191, 194, 202, 216, 225, 226, 248, 291, *333*, *460*. *See also* Wulmær.

Wulfman or Uulfman, *103*.

Wulfnoð or Wulnoð, 202, 212, 233, 240, 248, 266, 269, 271, 276, 298, 299, 301, 308, 321, 327, 333, 379, 387, 432. *See also* Wulennoð.

Wulford, 202. *See* Wulfred.

Wulfrard, *333*.

Wulfred, *164*, *191*, 202, 248, 287, 291, *301*, *321*, *333*, 339, 345, 397, 408, 413, *460*. *See also* Uulfred.

Wulfric, *123*, *164*, 202, 222, 225, 237, 248, 281, 282, 301, *304*, *333*, 348, 349, 350, 378, 387, 395, 396, 402, 413, 423, 426, 430.

Wulfryd, *202*, 248. *See* Wulfred.

Wulfsi, 248, 416, 420.

Wulfsig, Wulfsige, Wulsig, or Wulsige, 202, 214, 216, 248, 271, 273, *304*, *321*, *333*, 397, 402, 405, 416, 420 457. *See also* Uulfsig.

Wulfstan, Wulfstin, or Wulstan, 102, 109, 164, 190, 191, 196, 202, 225, 229, 230, 234, 239, 248, 257, 258, 261, 262, 267, 276, 301, 311, 333, 346, 355. *See also* Uulfstan.

Wulfulf, *333*.

Wulfward, *333*, 355, 374, 416, 460, 463, 469.

Wulfwerd, *248*, *304*, *333*, 373.

Wulfwi, 202, 211, *304*, *321*, *333*, 341, 422, 460, 462, 465.

Wulfwic, *304*.

Wulfwig or Wulwig, *202*, 248, *333*, 373, 382.

Wulfwine, Wullfwine, or Wulwine, 202,

224, 227, 229, 230, 237, 248, 257, 259, 270, 281, 286, 304, 308, 312, 313, *321*, *333*, 347, 350, 351, 359, 381, 382, 386, 402, 405, 408, 412, 413, 422, 438, 458, 459.

Wulfwurd, 355. *See* Wulfward.

Wulgar or Wulgares, *1*, 143, 153, 164, 173, 191, 196, 287, 304, 313, 333, 356, 393, 396, 412, 413, 416, 460, 469. *See also* Wulfgar.

Wulget, 333, 430. *See also* Wulfget.

Wulhed, 333, 423.

Wullaf or Wyllaf, 202.

Wullfwine, *304*. *See* Wulfwine.

Wulmær, Wulmar, or Wulmer, *202*, 248, 280, 333, 357, 358, 424, 427, 428, 460, 467, 470. *See also* Wulfmær.

Wulmiod, 248, 282.

Wulnað, *248*, 333, 387. *See also* Wulfnoð and Wulnoð.

Wulnoð, 248, 266, 269, 271, 276, 298, 299, 304, 308, 321, 327, 333, 379, 432. *See also* Wulfnoð.

Wulred, *333*. *See* Wulfred.

Wulsi or Wulsie, *304*, 333, 372, 402.

Wulsiceod, *321*.

Wulsig or Wulsige, 248, 273, *304*, *321*, 333, 397, 402, 405, 457. *See also* Wulfsig.

Wulstan, *164*, 191, 196, 202, 234, 248, 257, 258, 262, 267, 276, 304, 311, 333, 346, 355. *See also* Wulfstan.

Wulward, *304*. *See also* Wulfward.

Wulwi, *248*, *304*, *333*. *See also* Wulfwi.

Wulwig, *304*, 333, 373. *See also* Wulfwig.

Wulwine, 248, 257, 304, 308, 312, *321*, 333, 402. *See also* Wulfwine.

Wunsi, *248*. *See* Wynsi.

Wunsige, 274, 304, 315. *See also* Wynsige.

Wunstan, 164, 175, 202, 239. *See also* Wynstan.

Wurfurd, 333, 156
Wurreb, 333, 402
Wuwerd, 321.
Wydecoc, 333
Wydia, 301 See Widia
Wyllaf, 202 See Wullaf
Wyltsig, 103, 120
Wynberht, 33, 78, 81, 84, 97 See also Uuynbearht and Uynberht
Wynegos, 202 See Winegos
Wynhelm, Wynnehelm, or Wynnelm, 123, 139, 143.
Wynred, 218 See Winred
Wynsi or Wynsic, 218, 301
Wyusig or Wynsige, 164, 175, 191, 196, 202, 214, 218, 274, 285, 287, 301. See also Wihtsige
Wynsige and Wamanea, 304
Wynstan, 164, 175, 202, 239, 218, 285, 333, 446. See also Winstan and Wunstan
Wynwid, 218

þ

Þealda, 304
Þegenwine, 218, 262, 321
Þeodberht, 143
Þeodgar, 164, 170, 191, 202
Þeodgeld or Þeodgyld, 202
Þeodmær, 143, 153
Þeodred, 143, 202, 216, 218, 160, 166
Þeodric, 333, 136
Þeodulf, 123, 139, 143, 151
Þeoræð or Þoreð, 218
Þeiman, 218, 301
Þermod, 123, 110
Þermon, 160, 170
Þinern, 164
Þiðulf, 202
Þor or Þorr, 333, 361, 362, 364, 365, 366, 367, 369, 370 102

Þorald, 202
Þorcetel or Þorctel, 202, 218, 321, 333 See also Þurcetel
Þorcil, 333 See Þorcetel
Þorel, 202 See Þorcetel
Þorctel, 333 See Þorcetel and Þorcil
Þoreð, 218 See Þeoræð
Þorferð or Þorford, 333, 119
Þorgim, 202
Þorr See Þor
Þorsige, 202
Þorstæn or Þorstan, 202, 216, 321, 333, 419 See also Þurstan
Þorulf, 202 See Þurulf
Þreodred or Þreoðred, 333, 378
Þudinci, 304
Þunstan, 218 See Dunstan
Þurcetel or Þurcetl, 202, 236, 218, 304, 333 See also Þorcetel
Þurcil or Þurceil, 218, 321, 333, 411, 412, 413, 460.
Þurcferð, 218 See Þurferð.
Þurcstan, 218 See Þurstan.
Þurferd or Þurferð, 143, 156, 164, 187, 218
Þurfurð or Þuruerð, 333, 419.
Þurgod, 202, 218, 264, 460, 174
Þurgrim, Þurngrim, or Þurim, 218, 269, 304, 310, 321, 333, 362, 393, 420.
Þurim, 218, 269 See also Þurgrim
Þurimod, 172 See Þurmod
Þurlac, 81, 103
Þurmod, 143, 154, 156, 164, 172, 187, 190
Þurngrim, 333 See also Þurgrim
Þurnu or Þurrin, 333, 360
Þurstan or Þurstann, 103, 120, 164, 202, 213, 218, 294, 304, 321, 333, 420, 436, 460, 169 See also Þorstan
Þuruerð, 333, 119.
Þurulf, 143, 154, 156, 158, 202, 218, 294, 304, 333
Þustan, 294 See Þurstan

2 M 2

III.—INDEX OF TYPES.

A.

Ⲁ, 9, 10, 12, 36.

A. Ⲱ. (monogram), 2.

A. Ⲱ., divided by hand of Providence, 192, 203, 204.

Agnus Dei, 207, 208.

Annulet in centre of short cross voided, 305.

Annulet in centre of short cross voided; limbs terminating in three crescents, 336.

Annulet in each angle of long cross voided; limbs terminating in three crescents, 252.

Annulet in each angle of short cross voided, 253, 322.

Annulet, broken, or crescents, in each angle of short cross voided, 253, 322.

B.

BAⴆ in one line, 84.

BAⴆ and moneyer's name in two lines, 37.

Bird with branch, 86.

Building or church, 86, 103.

C.

CANT (monogram), 9.

Christian monogram, 10.

Christian temple, façade of, 27.

Church or building, 27, 86, 103.

Circle in centre of short cross voided, 253, 254, 305, 322, 323.

Circle, segment of, at ends of short cross voided, 337.

Circles, two, and cross voided, dividing moneyer's name, 86.

CNVT on limbs of cross, 36.

Crescent or broken annulet in each angle of short cross voided, 253, 322.

Crescents, two, in angles of long cross voided, 207.

Crescents, four, around pellet, 2.

Crescents, four, enclosing cross pattée, 5.

Cross, on limbs CNVT, 36.

Cross, king's name and trefoil slipped in each angle, 34.

Cross of four ovals, 255, 304, 321.

Cross of pellets, 123.

Cross on which moneyer's name, &c., 12, 21, 22.

Cross over cross pommée, 12.

Cross, sideways, dividing moneyer's name, 37.

Cross, two limbs cross crosslet, two pattés, 12.

Cross, two limbs moline, two pattés, 2, 11, 13.

Cross, five limbs pattés, 4.

Cross, six limbs pattés, 4.

Cross crosslet, 2, 3, 11, 12, 104, 105, 124.

Cross crosslet, pellet in each angle, 27

Cross floriated with leaf in each angle, 22

Cross moline, 12

Cross moline within lozenge, 34

Cross moline over cross pommée, forming rose, 86.

Cross pattée, 3, 4, 5, 35, 36, 37, 84, 85, 86, 103, 104, 123, 124, 143, 156, 157, 165, 166, 167, 192, 202, 203, 206, 208, 248, 250, 322, 334, 337, 338

Cross pattée over cross pattée, 10, 11, 12, 13

Cross pattee over cross pommée, 11

Cross pattée within cross pattée, and three pellets, 167

Cross pattée within four crescents, 5

Cross pattée within four crosses pattées, 167, 203

Cross pattée within four pellets, 103

Cross pattée within lozenge, from each corner of which issues beaded straight line, 34.

Cross pattée, CYNT in angles, 9

Cross pattee, pellet in each angle, 10, 11, 27

Cross pattée, wedge in each angle, 3

Cross pattée, voided, 103

Cross pommée on cross, 12

Cross pommée on cross pattee, 11

Cross pommee over cross moline, forming rose, 86

Cross potent, 2, 3, 4, 5, 11

Cross voided between two circles, dividing moneyer's name, 86

Cross voided, long, CRVX in angles, 206

Cross voided, long, PACX in angles, 305, 335

Cross voided, long, fleur-de-lis in each angle, 306, 324

Cross voided, long, fleurs-de-lis and trefoil in angles, 306

Cross voided, long, trefoil in each angle, 306

Cross voided, long, limbs terminating in one crescent, PACX in angles, 323, 335

Cross voided, long, limbs terminating in three crescents, 205, 206, 249, 251, 336

Cross voided, long, limbs terminating in three crescents, PACX in angles, 252

Cross voided, long, limbs terminating in three crescents, annulet in each angle, 252

Cross voided, long, limbs terminating in three crescents, crescents in two angles, 207

Cross voided, long, limbs terminating in three crescents and bisecting ornamented square, 207, 249.

Cross voided, long, on quatrefoil, limbs terminating in three crescents, 249, 250, 251, 252

Cross voided, short, 337

Cross voided, short, annulet in centre, 305

Cross voided, short, circle in centre, 253, 254, 305, 322, 323

Cross voided, short, pellet in centre 254, 334

Cross voided, short, CRVX in angles, 205, 322

Cross voided, short, PACX in angles, 323, 335

Cross voided, short, annulet in each angle, 253, 322

Cross voided, short, broken annulet or crescent in each angle, 253, 322

Cross voided, short, martlet in each angle, 336, 337

Cross voided, short, pyramid in each angle, 338

Cross voided, short, on which quadri-

Literal ornament, 254, 255, 305, 321, 334, 335

Cross voided, short, limbs expanding, 335

Cross voided, short, limbs expanding, cross pattée in each angle, 336

Cross voided, short, limbs terminating in segment of circle, 337

Cross voided, short, limbs terminating in three crescents, annulet in centre, 336

Cross voided, short, limbs terminating in three crescents, pyramid in each angle, 339

CRVX in angles of long cross voided, 206

CRVX in angles of short cross voided, 205, 322

CVNT in angles of cross pattée, 9

D.

DORIB or DORIBI, 9

DOROB C (monogram), 1, 2

Dove, 207

Dove and olive-branch, 86

E.

EXA (Exanceaster) in pale, 37

F.

Figures, two, seated, 34

Fleurs-de-lis in angles of long cross voided, 306, 324

Fleurs-de-lis and trefoil in angles of long cross voided, 306

Floral ornament surmounting or dividing moneyer's name, 86

Floriate stem with two branches enclosing moneyer's name, 143

Floriated cross, leaf in each angle, 22

Flower and rose-branch above and below moneyer's name, 124

Four crosses pattées around central one, 167, 203

G.

GLEAPA (Gleawaceaster), divided by T, 37

H.

Hand of Providence, 86, 204

Hand of Providence giving benediction, 204

Hand of Providence between A ꞷ, 192, 203, 204

Hand of Providence between ꞷ A, 204

K.

King seated on throne, 337.

King's name and mint (Orsnaforda) in three lines, 36, 37

King's name in four lines, 37, 84

L.

LINCOLLA divided by moneyer's name, 35

Lincoln, monogram of, 35

London, monogram of, 35, between moneyer's name, 35

Long cross voided   See Cross voided, long

Lozenge, within which cross pattée; beaded line issuing from each angle of lozenge, 34

M.

Martlet in each angle of short cross voided, 336, 337

Mint name (BAÐ), in one line, 84

Mint name (BAÐ), and moneyer's name in two lines, 37.

Mint name dividing moneyer's name, 157, 166

Mint names in pale (EXA and PIN), 37

Mint and king's names in three lines, 36, 37.

Moneyer's name across field, 85

Moneyer's name between two lines, 85, 157

Moneyer's name between rose-branch and flower, 124

Moneyer's name between two stars, 85

Moneyer's name divided by cross, sideways, 37

Moneyer's name divided by floriate stem, 113

Moneyer's name divided by ornament, &c, 157

Moneyer's name divided by saltire, 85

Moneyer's name, divided or surmounted by floral ornament, 86

Moneyer's name, &c, in two lines across field, 36, 37, 84, 85, 86, 103, 104, 123, 124, 143, 156, 157, 165, 166

Moneyer's name in two lines across field and divided by mint name, 157, 166

Moneyer's name in three lines across field, 27, 33

Moneyer's name in four lines across field, &c , 27

Moneyer's name on limbs and between angles of cross, 12, 21, 22

Moneyer's name within and without leaves of quatrefoil, &c , 33, 34

Moneyer's name and mint (BAÐ) in two lines, 37

Monograms. A Ꞷ , 2

  ,,   CANT, 9

Monograms, Christian, 10

  ,,   DORIB or DORIBI, 9

  ,,   DOROB C , 1, 2

  ,,   of Lincoln, 35

  ,,   of London, 35

  ,,   of Roiseng, 36

  ,,   Γ A (SAX), 5

  ,,   SAX, 5

  ,   SAXON, 5

  ,,   SAXONV, 10

  ,,   ⋈, 4

O.

OCCIDENTALIVM around SAXONIORVM in three lines, 10

Olive-branch held by Dove, 86

Ornament dividing moneyer's name, 157

ORSNAFORDA in two lines divided by king's name, 36, 37

Ovals four, forming cross, 255, 304, 321

P.

PACX in angles of long cross voided, 305

PACX in angles of long cross voided, limbs terminating in one crescent, 323, 335

PACX in angles of long cross voided, limbs terminating in three crescents, 252

PACX in angles of short cross, voided, 323, 335

PAX across field, 339, 461

Pellet in centre of short cross voided, 251, 331

Pellets, three, and cross pattee around central cross pattee, 167

Providence, hand of, 86, 201

Providence, hand of, giving benediction, 201

Providence, hand of, between A Ꞷ, 192, 203, 201

Providence, hand of, between Ꞷ A, 201

Pyramid in each angle of short cross voided, 338

Pyramid in each angle of short cross voided, limbs terminating in three crescents, 339

Q.

Quadrilateral ornament on short cross voided, 254, 255, 305, 321, 334, 335

Quatrefoil with moneyers name within, 31

Quatrefoil with moneyer's name within and without, 33

Quatrefoil within long cross voided, limbs terminating in three crescents, 249, 250, 251, 252

R.

Roiseng, monogram of, 36

Rose formed of cross pommée over cross moline, 86

Rose-branch and flower above and below moneyer's name, 124

Rosette, 85, 104, 124, 143, 166

S.

ᚱᚨ (SAX), monogram of, 5

St Andrew, coinage of, 7

St Eadmund, coinage of, 36

Saltire dividing moneyer's name, 85

SAX ? (monogram), 5

SAXON (monogram), 5

SAXONIORVM in three lines 5, 10

SAXONIORVM in three lines, around OCCIDENTALIVM 10

SAXONV (monogram), 10

Short cross voided   *See* Cross voided, short

Solidus type on coin of Ælfred, 34.

Sovereign type of Edward Conf , 337

Square, ornamented, bisected by long cross voided, limbs terminating in three crescents, 207, 249

Star, above and below moneyer's name, 85

Star of six points between two pellets, 103

Star of six rays pattés, 11

Star of eight rays pattés, 3

Star of nine rays pattés, 3

T.

T with limbs extended, dividing name of mint, 37

Temple, façade of, 27

Throne, on which king seated, 337

Trefoil in each angle of long cross voided, 306

Trefoil ornament enclosing moneyer's name, 143

Trefoil, slipped, in each angle of cross, 34

Tribrach, limbs fourchée, 3

Tribrach moline, 3

W.

PIN (Winceaster) in pale, 37

ᚷ (monogram), 4

ᚷ (monogram), 10

Ꞷ A divided by hand of Providence, 204

IV.—INDEX OF MINTS *

See General Index for historical notices, &c of Mints

Aylesbury (Æglesburh), Æthelræd II, 208, Cnut, 255, Edward Conf, 339

Bardney (Bardanig), Æthelræd II, 208, Cnut, 255

Bath (Baðan), Ælfred, 38, Eadweard the Elder, 87, Æthelstan, 105, Eadgar, 168, Eadweard II, 192, Æthelræd II, 200, Cnut, 256, Harold I, 307, Edward Conf, 339.

Bedford (Bedanford or Bedeford), Eadwig, 158, Eadgar, 168, Eadweard II, 192, Æthelræd II, 209, Cnut, 256, Harold I, 307, Edward Conf, 311, Harold II, 461.

Bedwin (Bedewine), Edward Conf, 312

Berkeley (Beorclea), Edward Conf, 312

Brewton (Briutune), Cnut, 257

Bristol (Bricgstow), Cnut, 257, Harold I, 307, Edward Conf, 312, Harold II, 461

Buckingham (Buccingaham), Æthelræd II, 210

Cadbury (Cadanburh), Cnut, 258.

Cambridge (Grantebrycge), Æthelræd II, 218, Cnut, 271, Harold I, 310, Edward Conf, 374, Harold II, 465

Canterbury (Cæntwaraburh or Dorobernia), Ecgbeorht, 6, Æthelwulf, 13, Ælfred, 38, Æthelstan, 106,

Eadgar, 168, Eadweard II, 193, Æthelræd II, 210, Cnut, 258, Harold I, 308, Edward Conf, 343, Harold II, 462

Castle Rising (Roiseng), Ælfred, 54

Chester (Leigeceaster), Æthelstan, 108, Eadmund, 124, Eadgar, 171, Æthelræd II, 220, Cnut, 276, Harold I, 312, Edward Conf, 388, Harold II, 467.

Chichester (Cisceeastre or Cicestrie), Æthelræd II, 211, Cnut, 258, Harold I, 308, Edward Conf, 348, Harold II, 462

Colchester (Colenceastre), Æthelræd II, 211, Cnut, 259, Harold I, 308, Edward Conf, 350, Harold II, 462

Crewkerne (Crucern), Cnut, 260

Cricklade (Creegelade or Croegelade), Cnut, 259, Edward Conf, 351.

Derby (Deoraby), Æthelstan, 105, Eadgar, 169, Eadweard II, 193, Æthelræd II, 212, Edward Conf, 352, Harold II, 462

Dereham (Dyrham), Edward Conf, 356

Dorchester (Dorceastre), Cnut, 261, Edward Conf, 355

Dorobernia See Canterbury

Dover (Doferan), Æthelræd II, 212, Cnut, 260, Harold I, 309, Edward Conf, 353 Harold II, 463

Edmundsburh   *See* St Edmundsbury

Eoforwic or Loferwic   *See* York

Exeter (Exancestre, Excecastre, &c), Ælfred, 46, Æthelstan, 106, Eadgar, 169, Æthelred II, 213, Cnut, 264, Harold I, 309, Harthacnut, 325, Edward Conf, 357, Harold II, 164

Geoðaburh   *See* Jedburgh

Gifeleeaster   *See* Ilchester

Gipeswic   *See* Ipswich

Gloucester (Gleaweceaster), Ælfred, 46, Æthelstan, 108, Æthelred II, 217, Cnut, 270, Harthacnut, 325, Edward Conf, 373, Harold II, 465

Grantebrycge   *See* Cambridge

Guildford (Gildeforda or Guldeforda), Harthacnut, 325, Edward Conf, 375, Harold II, 164

Hamtune   *See* Southampton

Hastings (Hestinga or Hestingport), Cnut, 272, Harold I, 311, Edward Conf, 376, Harold II, 466

Hereford, Æthelstan, 108, Æthelred II, 219, Cnut, 273, Harthacnut, 325, Edward Conf, 380, Harold II, 166

Hertford (Heortford), Eadweard II, 194, Æthelred II, 218, Cnut, 273, Edward Conf, 379

Horndon (Horninduna), Edward Conf, 382

Huntingdon (Huntandune), Eadwig, 159, Eadgar, 170, Æthelred II, 219, Cnut, 274, Edward Conf, 382, Harold II, 466

Hythe (Hyða), Cnut, 274, Edward Conf, 383

Ilchester (Gifeleeaster), Æthelred II, 216, Cnut, 269; Edward Conf, 371, Harold II, 164

Ipswich (Gipeswic), Eadweard II, 193, Æthelred II, 217, Cnut, 270; Harold I, 310, Edward Conf, 371, Harold II, 165

Jedburgh (Geoðaburh), Æthelred II, 216

Lancaster (Landcaster), Cnut, 275

Langport (Lancport or Longport), Æthelstan, 112, Cnut, 275, Edward Conf, 386

Leicester (Lehercenster), Cnut, 275, Harold I, 311, Harthacnut, 326, Edward Conf 387, Harold II, 467

Leigececaster.   *See* Chester

Lewes (Læwes), Eadgar, 170, Æthelred II, 208, 219, Cnut, 274, Harold I, 311, Edward Conf, 384, Harold II, 466

Lincoln (Lincolla or Lincolne), Ælfred, 46, Eadweard II, 194, Æthelred II, 221, Cnut, 278, Harold I, 312, Harthacnut, 326, Edward Conf, 391, Harold II, 467

London (Londonia or Lundene), Ælfred, 47, Æthelstan, 111, Eadmund, 125, Eadgar, 172, Eadweard II, 195, Æthelred II, 223, Cnut, 281, Harold I, 313, Harthacnut, 326, Edward Conf, 397, Harold II, 468

Longport   *See* Langport

Luffwick (Luueie), Eadweard II, 195

Lydford (Lydanford), Æthelred II, 230

Lymne (Limene), Eadweard II, 194

Maldon (Mældune), Æthelræd II, 230, Cnut, 287, Edward Conf, 417

Malmesbury (Mealmesburh), Cnut, 288, Edward Conf, 418

Newark (Newe), Eadwig, 160

Newport (Niweporte), Edward Conf, 418

Norwich (Norðwic), Æthelstan, 112, Eadmund, 125, Eadred, 141, Æthelræd II 231, Cnut, 288, Harold I, 315, Edward Conf, 418, Harold II, 469

Nottingham (Snotingaham), Æthelstan, 113, Cnut, 292, Harold I, 316, Harthacnut, 327, Edward Conf, 429, Harold II, 470.

Oxford (Orsnaforda or Oxnaford), Ælfred, 50, Æthelstan, 112, Æthelræd II, 232, Cnut, 288; Harold I, 315, Harthacnut, 327, Edward Conf, 420, Harold II, 469

Richborough (Ricycburh), Cnut, 289, Edward Conf, 422

Rochester (Rofeccastre), Eadgar, 173, Æthelræd II, 232, Cnut, 290, Harold I, 315, Edward Conf, 422, Harold II, 470

Roiseng See Castle Rising

Romney (Rumenea), Æthelræd II, 233, Cnut, 290, Edward Conf, 423, Harold II, 470

St Eadmundsbury (Eadmundsburh), Edward Conf, 356

Salisbury (Sereburh), Cnut, 291, Edward Conf, 428

Sandwich (Sandwic), Æthelræd II, 233, Edward Conf, 424

Shaftesbury (Sceftesburh), Æthelræd II, 233, Cnut, 290, Edward Conf, 425, Harold II, 470

Shrewsbury (Scrobesburh), Æthelstan, 113, Æthelræd II, 233, Cnut, 291, Harold I, 316, Edward Conf, 427

Sidbury (Siðesteburh), Æthelræd II, 231, Cnut, 292

Snotingaham See Nottingham

Southampton (Hamtune), Eadwig, 159, Eadgar, 170, Eadweard II, 194, Æthelræd II, 218, Cnut, 272, Harold I, 311, Edward Conf, 379, Harold II, 465

Southwark (Suðgeweorc), Æthelræd II, 235, Cnut, 291, Harthacnut, 327, Edward Conf, 433, Harold II, 471

Stafford (Stæfforda), Edward Conf, 429

Stamford (Stanford), Eadgar, 173, Eadweard II, 195; Æthelræd II, 231, Cnut, 293, Harold I, 316, Edward Conf, 431, Harold II, 471

Stanwick (Stanwic), Æthelræd II, 233

Steyning (Stænig), Cnut, 292, Harthacnut, 327, Edward Conf, 430, Harold II, 470

Sudbury (Suðburh), Æthelræd II, 235, Edward Conf, 433

Suðgeweorc See Southwark

Tamworth (Tamweorð), Edward Conf, 434

Taunton (Tantune), Cnut, 294, Edward Conf, 435

Tempsford (Temesforda or Temesanford), Eadgar, 173

Thetford (Deotford), Eadgar, 175, Æthelræd II, 210, Cnut, 299, Harold I, 318, Edward Conf, 453, Harold II, 471

Torksey (Turecsuge), Æthelred II, 236

Totness (Totannes), Æthelred II, 236, Cnut, 295

Turecsuge   See Torksey

Wallingford (Wealingaford or Weligaford), Æthelstan, 114, Eadgar, 174, Æthelræd II, 237, Cnut, 296, Harold I, 317, Edward Conf, 436, Harold II, 471

Wareham (Werham), Æthelstan, 114, Æthelred II, 237, Edward Conf, 438, Harold II, 472

Warwick (Wæringwic), Æthelstan, 114, Cnut, 295, Harold I, 316, Edward Conf, 435, Harold II, 471

Watchet (Weccdport), Æthelred II, 236, Cnut, 295, Edward Conf, 438

Welmesford, Cnut, 296

Wilton (Wiltune), Eadgar, 174, Æthelræd II, 237, Cnut, 297, Harold I, 317, Edward Conf, 440, Harold II, 472

Winchcombe (Winccleumb), Cnut, 299

Winchelsea (Wincelsea), Eadgar, 174; Edward Conf, 453

Winchester (Winccastre or Wintonia), Ælfred, 55, Æthelstan, 115, Eadwig, 160; Eadgar, 175, Eadweard II, 196, Æthelræd II, 238; Cnut, 297, Harold I, 317, Harthacnut, 328, Edward Conf, 443, Harold II, 473

Worcester (Wihraccaster or Woriceaster), Æthelræd II, 240; Cnut, 296, Edward Conf., 439

York (Eboracum or Eoferwic), Æthelstan, 106, Eadwig, 158, Eadgar, 169, Eadweard II., 193, Æthelræd II, 214, Cnut, 262, Harold I, 309; Edward Conf, 359; Harold II, 463

Þeotford.   See Thetford

TABLES.

TABLE

OF

THE RELATIVE WEIGHTS OF ENGLISH GRAINS AND FRENCH GRAMMES.

Grains.	Grammes.	Grains.	Grammes.	Grains.	Grammes.	Grains.	Grammes.
1	·064	41	2·656	81	5·248	121	7·840
2	·129	42	2·720	82	5·312	122	7·905
3	·194	43	2·785	83	5·378	123	7·970
4	·259	44	2·850	84	5·442	124	8·035
5	·324	45	2·915	85	5·508	125	8·100
6	·388	46	2·980	86	5·572	126	8·164
7	·453	47	3·045	87	5·637	127	8·229
8	·518	48	3·110	88	5·702	128	8·294
9	·583	49	3·175	89	5·767	129	8·359
10	·648	50	3·240	90	5·832	130	8·424
11	·712	51	3·304	91	5·896	131	8·488
12	·777	52	3·368	92	5·961	132	8·553
13	·842	53	3·434	93	6·026	133	8·618
14	·907	54	3·498	94	6·091	134	8·682
15	·972	55	3·564	95	6·156	135	8·747
16	1·036	56	3·628	96	6·220	136	8·812
17	1·101	57	3·693	97	6·285	137	8·877
18	1·166	58	3·758	98	6·350	138	8·942
19	1·231	59	3·823	99	6·415	139	9·007
20	1·296	60	3·888	100	6·480	140	9·072
21	1·360	61	3·952	101	6·544	141	9·136
22	1·425	62	4·017	102	6·609	142	9·200
23	1·490	63	4·082	103	6·674	143	9·265
24	1·555	64	4·146	104	6·739	144	9·330
25	1·620	65	4·211	105	6·804	145	9·395
26	1·684	66	4·276	106	6·868	146	9·460
27	1·749	67	4·341	107	6·933	147	9·525
28	1·814	68	4·406	108	6·998	148	9·590
29	1·879	69	4·471	109	7·063	149	9·655
30	1·944	70	4·536	110	7·128	150	9·720
31	2·008	71	4·600	111	7·192	151	9·784
32	2·073	72	4·665	112	7·257	152	9·848
33	2·138	73	4·729	113	7·322	153	9·914
34	2·202	74	4·794	114	7·387	154	9·978
35	2·267	75	4·859	115	7·452	155	10·044
36	2·332	76	4·924	116	7·516	156	10·108
37	2·397	77	4·989	117	7·581	157	10·173
38	2·462	78	5·054	118	7·646	158	10·238
39	2·527	79	5·119	119	7·711	159	10·303
40	2·592	80	5·184	120	7·776	160	10·368

TABLE

OF

THE RELATIVE WEIGHTS OF ENGLISH GRAINS AND FRENCH GRAMMES.

Grains.	Grammes.	Grains.	Grammes.	Grains.	Grammes.	Grains.	Grammes.
161	10·432	201	13·024	241	15·616	290	18·79
162	10·497	202	13·089	242	15·680	300	19·44
163	10·562	203	13·154	243	15·745	310	20·08
164	10·626	204	13·219	244	15·810	320	20·73
165	10·691	205	13·284	245	15·875	330	21·38
166	10·756	206	13·348	246	15·940	340	22·02
167	10·821	207	13·413	247	16·005	350	22·67
168	10·886	208	13·478	248	16·070	360	23·32
169	10·951	209	13·543	249	16·135	370	23·97
170	11·016	210	13·608	250	16·200	380	24·62
171	11·080	211	13·672	251	16·264	390	25·27
172	11·145	212	13·737	252	16·328	400	25·92
173	11·209	213	13·802	253	16·394	410	26·56
174	11·274	214	13·867	254	16·458	420	27·20
175	11·339	215	13·932	255	16·524	430	27·85
176	11·404	216	13·996	256	16·588	440	28·50
177	11·469	217	14·061	257	16·653	450	29·15
178	11·534	218	14·126	258	16·718	460	29·80
179	11·599	219	14·191	259	16·783	470	30·45
180	11·664	220	14·256	260	16·848	480	31·10
181	11·728	221	14·320	261	16·912	490	31·75
182	11·792	222	14·385	262	16·977	500	32·40
183	11·858	223	14·450	263	17·042	510	33·04
184	11·922	224	14·515	264	17·106	520	33·68
185	11·988	225	14·580	265	17·171	530	34·34
186	12·052	226	14·644	266	17·236	540	34·98
187	12·117	227	14·709	267	17·301	550	35·64
188	12·182	228	14·774	268	17·366	560	36·28
189	12·247	229	14·839	269	17·431	570	36·93
190	12·312	230	14·904	270	17·496	580	37·58
191	12·376	231	14·968	271	17·560	590	38·23
192	12·441	232	15·033	272	17·625	600	38·88
193	12·506	233	15·098	273	17·689	700	45·36
194	12·571	234	15·162	274	17·754	800	51·84
195	12·636	235	15·227	275	17·819	900	58·32
196	12·700	236	15·292	276	17·884	1000	64·80
197	12·765	237	15·357	277	17·949	2000	129·60
198	12·830	238	15·422	278	18·014	3000	194·40
199	12·895	239	15·487	279	18·079	4000	259·20
200	12·960	240	15·552	280	18·144	5000	324·00

TABLE

FOR

CONVERTING ENGLISH INCHES INTO MILLIMÈTRES AND THE MEASURES OF MIONNET'S SCALE.

ENGLISH INCHES

MIONNET'S SCALE

FRENCH MILLIMETRES

LONDON: PRINTED BY WILLIAM CLOWES AND SONS, LIMITED, STAMFORD STREET AND CHARING CROSS.

AETHELBEARHT

AETHELRED I.

AELFRED.

AELFRED.

ALFRED

,

EADWEARD THE ELDER.

EADWEARD the ELDER

,

AETHELSTAN

'

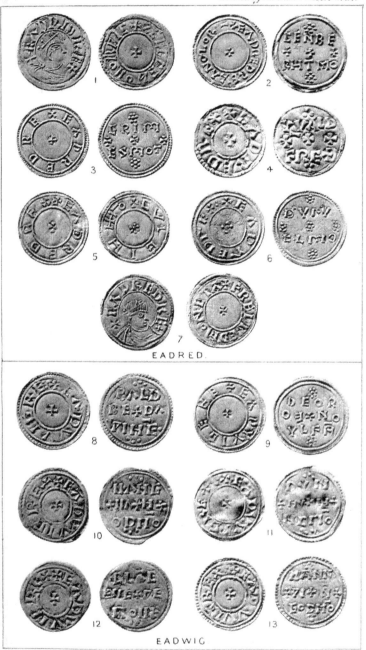

EADRED.

EADWIG

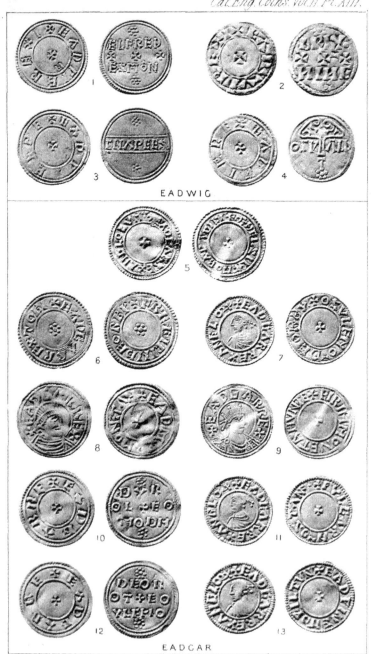

EADWIG

EADGAR

EADGAR

EADWEARD II.

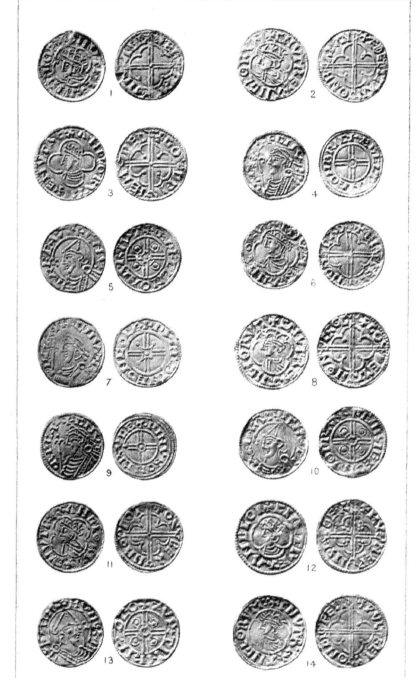

CNUT

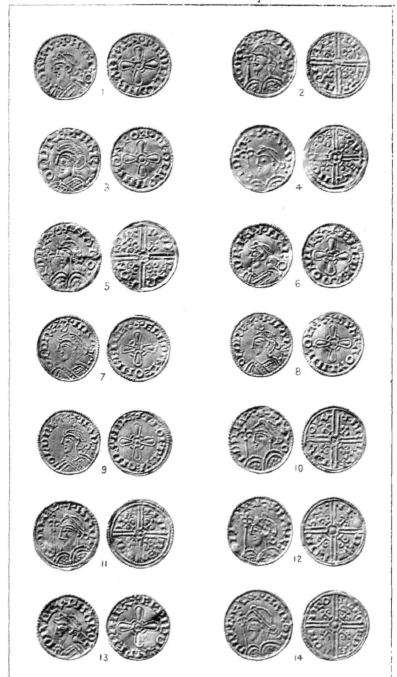

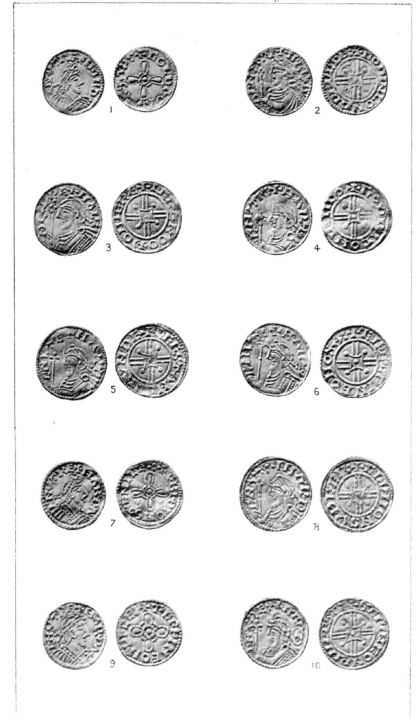

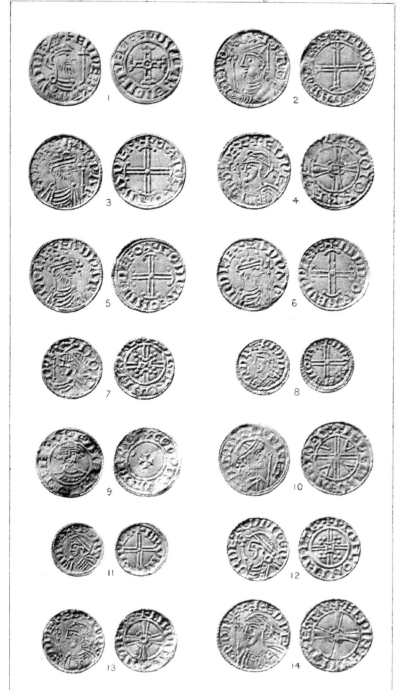

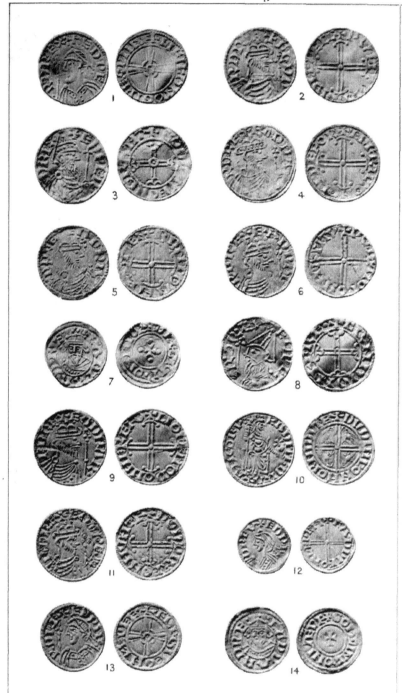

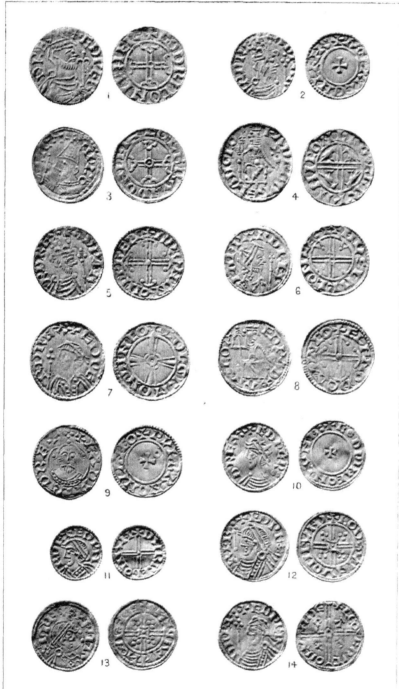

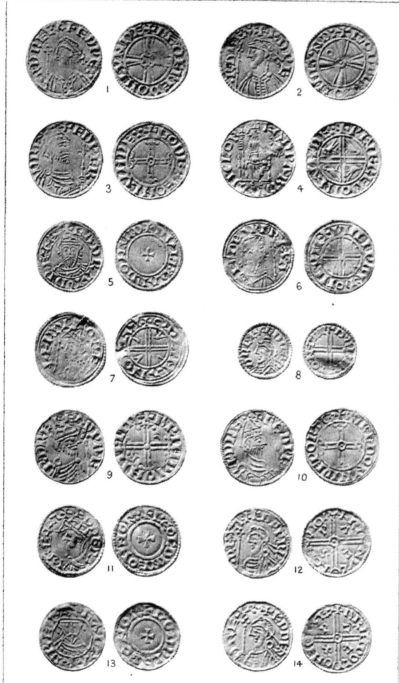

book is DUE on the last date stamped below

date		

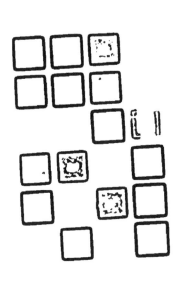